Dan W. French
TEXAS CHRISTIAN UNIVERSITY

Security and Portfolio Analysis

Concepts and Management

Merrill Publishing Company
A Bell & Howell Information Company
Columbus Toronto London Melbourne

To my grandparents
Irene and Burton French
Beatrice and C. B. Wright

Published by Merrill Publishing Company
A Bell & Howell Information Company
Columbus, Ohio 43216

This book was set in Garamond Light

Administrative Editor: John D. Stout
Developmental Editor: Dwayne Martin
Production Coordinator: Linda Hillis Bayma
Art Coordinator: Ruth Kimpel
Cover Design Coordination: Brian Deep

Library of Congress Catalog Card Number: 88-63823
International Standard Book Number: 0-675-20810-6
Printed in the United States of America
1 2 3 4 5 6 7 8 9—92 91 90 89

PREFACE

The objective of this book is to provide a broad overview of investments in marketable securities and to delve into many of the details, both theoretical and practical, of the valuation and analysis of the various types of securities. I have attempted to integrate theory and practice in the presentations. The book uses many practical tools and techniques of investment analysis to illustrate, support, and expand upon theoretical models. Although the principal viewpoint of the book is that of an individual investor or, where appropriate, a professional investor managing a client's portfolio, the institutional side of investment is also presented. This textbook should therefore be useful for students who wish to learn about investment management for their own personal portfolios and for those who desire a foundation to enter the professional investment field.

Dramatic changes in security markets have taken place over the past couple of decades, and the rate of change shows no apparent indication of slowing. The theory and applications presented in the text are as up to date as possible. Many supporting illustrations from empirical research are drawn from recent publications, and examples in the text use data that were the most current available. Some of the most recent investment analysis techniques have been specifically included because of their relevance to the current investment environment.

Some of the most significant developments in security markets in recent years have occurred in the futures and options markets. The expansion in the number of instruments offered and in the total volume of trading has been phenomenal. Although the chapters on both the futures and options topics contain material not usually covered in a first-semester investments course, the emerging importance of these areas merits increased attention in the classroom.

This book contains seven major sections. Part 1 introduces the types of securities the text will cover, describes fundamental concepts of risk and return, and presents a description of security markets and their operating environment. Part 2 presents chapters on risk, diversification, capital market theory, and market efficiency. Part 3 gives a framework and essential tools for accomplishing fundamental analysis of securities. The following three parts address specific types of securities. Part 4 covers bonds, Part 5 deals with common stocks, and Part 6 covers contingent claim securities and futures. Each of these parts begins with descriptive material on the security and its markets, follows with theoretical models, and ends with a presentation of specific analytical methods and trading strategy. Finally, Part 7 is concerned with portfolio management strategies and with the evaluation of investment performance.

The cooperative effort of many people has made this book possible. My family deserves a major portion of the credit. My wife Carmen's patience, understanding, and tolerance of the long and late hours needed to complete the manuscript was an essential ingredient. My son Dan and daughter Niki have contributed in their own special way. Following is a list, as inclusive as possible, of the individuals who have contributed to the effort along the way: Steve Caples, Pam Davies, Ron Fuqua, Micha Heyman, Deryl Martin, Linda Martin, Keith Pomykal, and Patricia Wolf.

Of special mention are the staff at Merrill Publishing Company and the reviewers: Stanley Atkinson, University of Central Florida; Randall Billingsley, Virginia Polytechnic Institute and State University; Gerald A. Blum, University of Nevada; Robert A. Brown, University of Colorado; Paul G. Fellows, University of Iowa; Tim Gallagher, Colorado State University; Lawrence R. Glosten, Norwestern University; Robert W. Greenleaf, Indiana University; Sheri Kole, College of Financial Planning, Denver, Colorado; Joan Lenowitz, San Diego State University; David C. Leonard, Miami University of Ohio; Linda J. Martin, Arizona State University; Paul A. Mueller, Bowling Green State University; William B. Riley, Jr., West Virginia University; R. Stephen Sears, University of Illinois at Urbana-Champaign; Donald E. Sorenson, University of Wisconsin, Whitewater; James M. Tipton, Baylor University; Allan J. Twark, Kent State University; Mark F. Uchida, Butler University; and David E. Upton, Texas Tech University.

CONTENTS

PART SIX Contingent Claim Securities, Futures Markets, and Other Securities

PART SEVEN Portfolio Management and Performance Evaluation

PART ONE

Securities and Their Markets

CHAPTER 1

Overview of Investments

Decision making is a fact of life. We all must make choices every day of our lives. This book is about making choices in the field of investment finance. It is fair to say that investment finance involves decision making under conditions of uncertainty, with limited information, and within a limited time. These constraints are the practical aspects of investment decision making.

Specifically, this book addresses investing in marketable, publicly traded securities. A *security* is a financial instrument that evidences ownership or debt. The security is *marketable* if there exists a market through which the investor can transfer ownership of the security to another investor quickly and inexpensively.

Investing in securities provides millions of investors with opportunities for producing income and accumulating wealth. Investors in securities include individual investors and institutional investors such as investment banking firms, pension funds, and mutual funds. The stakes in the investment game can be very high, with millions of dollars riding on one investment decision. Some well-known families have built fortunes in the stock market. The Morgans, Kennedys, and Vanderbilts owe a great amount of credit for their wealth to the market. More recently, famous investors such as T. Boone Pickens and the Bass family (see Exhibit 1–1) of Fort Worth, Texas, have had outstandingly successful ventures in the market.

Although the total investments of a small individual investor may not add up to such amounts, the accumulation and maintenance of a degree of personal independence with several tens of thousands of dollars of security investments can be relatively just as important to the individual as millions are to a large institution. With such a high level of importance attached to the game of investments, the study of securities and their markets assumes an important role in financial education.

EXHIBIT 1–1

The Texaco Greenmail

Because corporate takeovers are not always friendly affairs, the management of a company that is the target of a takeover attempt often takes measures to avert the takeover. A target of an unfriendly takeover has several alternatives available to try to avoid merger with the acquiring firm. These techniques include seeking another friendly partner for the merger, fighting the takeover attempt, and buying off the acquiring party. This last method usually involves purchasing the shares owned by an investor, a group of investors, or a company that has accumulated a sizable block of stock. The price paid for the block of stock is often greater than the current market price for the stock, which probably explains why the term *greenmail* has been used to describe the process.

During the final months of 1982, the Bass family of Fort Worth, Texas, began quietly accumulating shares of stock in Texaco, Inc. To engineer their security investment strategies, the family had hired astute professional investment managers from prestigious Wall Street firms. They continued to purchase stock throughout 1983 until they had purchased shares representing more than five percent of the outstanding stock in Texaco. The five percent level is important because at that point the stockholder must report the holding to the Securities and Exchange Commission, which then releases the information to the public. In mid-January 1984 the Bass interests disclosed that they owned 7.2 percent of the stock of Texaco. Soon after, on January 20, they exercised call options to buy another 286,700 shares at $35 per share.

As is common in the securities markets, rumors quickly began to make the circuits. Speculators began anticipating a move by the Bass family to attempt to acquire a controlling interest in Texaco, and trading volume increased. A rumor even began circulating that the Bass interests had already increased their stake to 17 percent. A flurry of trading in Texaco followed, and Texaco stock rose to close at a price of 44⅝ on March 5. Throughout the entire period, however, the Bass family steadfastly maintained that they had no interest in acquiring Texaco.

The presence of a block of stock large enough to threaten a potential takeover move was enough to awaken the management of Texaco. On March 6, 1984, the management of Texaco announced that the company had reached an agreement to buy out the Bass stock at prices substantially above the current market value. Texaco stock closed that day at 38¾, down 5⅞ for the day.

The deal gave the Bass family, who had ultimately acquired 9.9 percent of the stock in Texaco (25.6 million shares), $50 per share in cash for about half of their holdings plus a new preferred stock valued at $50 per share. Texaco retained the right to buy back the preferred stock from the Basses for $52 per share before they could sell to other parties. The total value of the transaction was about $1.28 billion. Observers estimated the Bass profits to be about $400 million. Texaco's management remained unwilling to discuss the affair.

INVESTMENTS VS. SECURITIES

To a financial economist *investment,* loosely described, involves foregoing current consumption in exchange for future consumption opportunities; it therefore should compensate the investor for the time value of money, loss of purchasing power (inflation), and any risks associated with owning the asset. Investment is therefore a far-reaching economic term to describe the allocation of resources in a capital market. The allocation price—paying a "fair" price indicative of its value—is a good indicator of the efficiency of the investment market to the economist.

Although a security is always an investment, an investment is not always a security. The basic test for establishing if an investment is a security is whether the individual invests money in a common enterprise and is led to expect profits from the managerial efforts of the promoter or a third party. If so, then the paper product (evidence of ownership) is usually a security.

WHY STUDY INVESTMENTS?

Managing Your Own Investments

Because investing is a necessary ingredient for the accumulation of a person's wealth, it is important that individuals be familiar with the various aspects of investment strategy. Certainly, anyone who manages his or her own investments would want to know as much as possible about investing profitably. In addition, people who do not manage their own investments but pay an investment manager to make investments for them should be well informed about the investments being made in their name. Investing in securities has provided a path to fortune for many people, but the common characteristic of success in investing is knowledge. It is this knowledge about securities, the companies they represent, and the markets in which they trade that gives investors the advantage needed to receive superior performance from their investments.

Investments as a Career

In addition to managing one's own investments, entering the investment field as a professional can lead to an exciting career. The investment profession provides a wide variety of challenges, and the monetary rewards to those in the investment field can be substantial.

Account Executive

Probably the type of investment professional that most people know best is the *account executive,* who is often called a *stockbroker*. Account executives provide advice and counsel to their investing clients and execute buy and sell orders for their clients' securities. Their compensation is usually a commission based on the volume of trades that they execute for their clients. To qualify for a job as an account executive, most securities brokerage firms want applicants to have a bachelor's degree in finance or marketing Sales experience and aptitude can also be important.

Securities Analyst

Another challenging career in the investments field is that of *securities analyst.* Securities analysts specializing in stocks prepare company reports that summarize and interpret financial data about the company. These analysts often concentrate their reports on companies within one or several industries. Other analysts specialize in bonds and fixed-income instruments. Their reports make recommendations based on the credit-worthiness of a bond issuer.

Securities analysts can work for either the "buy side" or the "sell side." Buy side analysts are employed by investors and institutions who manage investments and are searching for the best securities to buy. Sell side analysts work for brokerage firms, who are in the business of selling securities. They use their analysts' recommendations as the basis to counsel clients to make security transactions.

At the entry level, employers of security analysts usually require a bachelor's degree in finance, accounting, or economics. A master's degree in business administration (MBA) is often helpful. For higher level analysis positions, firms usually require several years experience and an MBA degree.

Chartered Financial Analysts. Most firms also ask experienced analysts to work for professional certification by participating in the *Chartered Financial Analyst (CFA)* program. In order to qualify for the CFA study and testing program, a candidate must have a bachelor's degree from an accredited college or university, have at least three years' experience related to investment decision making, and agree to abide by the Institute of Chartered Financial Analysts' code of ethics and standards of professional conduct. To receive the CFA designation, a candidate must study for and successfully pass a sequence of three examinations. The exams are given one year apart, and each lasts about six hours. Each of the exams has questions in the areas of professional ethics, financial accounting, economics, fixed-income security analysis, equity security analysis, and portfolio management.

Portfolio Analyst

Portfolio analysts and portfolio managers perform administrative functions over investment portfolios. Portfolio analysts have usually spent several years as security analysts before being promoted to portfolio analysts. They typically possess the CFA and an MBA degree. Portfolio analysts perform such tasks as reviewing reports prepared by securities and industry analysts, deciding which securities to add to or sell from the portfolio, monitoring the performance of the investment portfolio, and preparing portfolio reports for management and clients.

Financial Planner

The financial planning industry is an emerging area. In general, financial planners provide financial planning services to individuals and businesses. The term *financial planner* represents a broadly defined profession of those who work in the financial-planning service industry. Those who call themselves financial planners include investment counselors; real estate brokers and property managers; stockbrokers; banking employees in the savings area; life insurance salespersons; and people involved in selling annuities, retirement plans, and mutual funds.

Investor Relations Executive

While all of these careers approach investments from the perspective of the investor, the field of investor relations represents the corporate side. Investor relations is a hybrid of two traditional functions in large corporations: public relations and financial analysis. Investor relations executives in a corporation have the responsibility of disseminating financial information about the company to stockholders, news media, securities analysts, and other prospective investors. Investor relations professionals can play an important role in molding and maintaining a favorable corporate image.

WHY MARKETABLE SECURITIES?

Investors may choose among many investment opportunities. For example, in addition to publicly traded securities, investments may include real estate, antiques, rare stamps and coins, art, and precious metals. With such a wide range of investment alternatives, why should this text concentrate on marketable, publicly traded securities? Marketable securities provide some advantages that make them suitable to the majority of individuals. Advantages of marketable securities over other types of investments include the following:

1. Their high degree of marketability and liquidity.
2. The fact that they usually represent some real, income-producing assets.
3. The wide availability of investment information on securities.
4. The relatively low expense of investing in securities.

We will consider each of these in turn.

Marketability and Liquidity

Liquidity, the ability to convert quickly an asset into cash, is usually an important and desirable characteristic of an investment. Liquidity typically accompanies *marketability,* although marketability does not always accompany liquidity. For example, a bank savings account is quite liquid but not marketable.

An acquaintance who dabbles in collectibles provides a good example of the desirability of marketability and liquidity in an investment. After finding a number of old baseball cards, he became interested in determining the value of a 1958 card with Mickey Mantle and Yogi Berra. At a baseball card collectors' show where dealers buy and sell cards, he found several dealers offering the card for sale for $10 to $12. Upon offering his card to the dealers, he found none willing even to make a bid to purchase. Had he needed to unload the card and been willing to accept a very low, distress price, he probably could have sold it. The fact that there were no willing buyers at any price even close to the "market" price shows how little marketability and liquidity often accompany such types of investment items. (See Exhibit 1–2.)

Real, Income-Producing Assets

Typically, a security represents ownership in some entity that uses real assets to produce an income stream. For example, the money from the sale of bonds may build a factory that produces income to pay interest on the bonds. A new issue of common stock can provide funds to purchase new cost-saving machinery, allowing a company to increase its dividend. The new municipal auditorium financed by a city bond issue could increase the tax base, and the city would be able easily to meet its interest obligations.

EXHIBIT 1–2

Diamonds: The Liquid Investment?

Salespeople peddling collectibles and other "things" as investments often recommend the purchase of diamonds because they claim diamonds are small, easy to transport, and hold their value. However, the investor who is forced to sell diamonds may find that their highly touted advantages are counteracted by disappointing liquidity. The following case reveals the plight of one seller of diamonds.

Stanley M. Rifkin, a thirty-two-year-old computer consultant for Security Pacific National Bank of Los Angeles, discovered a way to become an instant millionaire. In 1978, he learned the bank's secret codes for transferring funds to other banks and set up a plan to transfer money to a New York bank account he had opened under an alias. His problem was to convert the money into a liquid asset before the bank caught him. Obviously he could not withdraw cash, since a large withdrawal would quickly draw suspicion from bank officials.

He hit upon the ingenious idea of buying diamonds. For a large purchase he could buy at the best wholesale prices, and he contacted a reputable diamond broker who agreed to arrange for the purchase of $8 million in high quality, perfectly cut, round brilliant diamonds from the Soviet Union.

On October 25, 1978, Rifkin transferred $10.2 million to his New York account and then to the Russian account in Switzerland. Using a fake passport, he flew to Switzerland, got the diamonds (which weighed less than five pounds), and easily smuggled them back to the United States. Back at home, he began contacting dealers, none of whom wanted to buy any diamonds. Meanwhile, Security Pacific had found the discrepancy, and the FBI was investigating. On November 8, they arrested Rifkin after receiving a tip from an informant.

Bank officials were quite happy that the thief had the foresight to invest the money in such a prudent investment as diamonds. Diamond investment had been booming and prices increased, while "experts" were calling diamonds "the ideal investment." Appraisers for the bank estimated the worth of the diamonds at $13 million.

The bank, anticipating a nice profit on the diamonds, placed the lot up for auction with a minimum bid of $7.5 million. By the bidding deadline, the bank had received only one bid, and it was for several million less than the minimum. Confused, the bank began seeking other buyers. It offered to sell the diamonds back to the Russians at the original price. The Russians refused to buy them back at any price.

The bank finally found that it had no choice but to leave the diamonds with a diamond broker to sell on consignment. The terms of the agreement, which left Security Pacific unable to receive funds from the sale for eighteen months, were hardly favorable to the bank. The diamonds—a tangible asset investment, popularly considered wise and conservative, and purchased at wholesale price—could find virtually no buyers in the market at the time the seller wanted to sell. This is the type of investment an investor needing *any* liquidity should avoid.

In contrast, the gains from items such as precious metals or rare coins result from the sale of the item at a profit. During the holding period, the asset produces no income. Securities, on the other hand, often pay dividends or interest.

In addition, an economic benefit is associated with securities. The accumulation of capital to finance business and industry is necessary in a free enterprise economy. It takes capital to promote business growth, new jobs, a better standard of living, and a vital national economy. Without new capital, financing for such goals is limited. Securities provide the vehicle for this capital formation, while investments such as gold and art provide little, if any, of such economic benefit.

Availability of Investment Information

Information about investments and the markets in which they trade is important to investors. A large amount of information about publicly traded securities is widely available at reasonable cost to the investing public. Federal law states that all corporations whose securities trade in the public markets must make available information about their financial status. The *Securities and Exchange Commission* is the government agency that regulates the dissemination of such information and, to some extent, requires that financial reports be prepared according to certain standardized guidelines.

Compare the availability of information on securities to other investments. In varying degrees, information about other investments is usually either expensive or not easily obtained. For example, an investor purchasing a plot of land might need to know the geological structures underlying the surface to determine the suitability of the land for a specific purpose. Geologists can provide such studies, but usually at considerable expense.

Low Investment Expense

Generally, expenses associated with investing in securities are lower than those of other types of investments. Expenses can be classified as follows: (1) search expense, (2) transaction costs, (3) holding costs, and (4) expenses of management and administration.

Search expenses can be minor or considerable for any investment, depending on the amount of resources an investor wants to commit to searching for desirable investments. However, transaction costs are usually significantly less for securities. A typical sale of $20,000 worth of stock would probably result in a commission of about $200 (about 1 percent of the price) at a discount brokerage, but selling a $20,000 plot of land would generate a commission of about $1,200 (6 percent), while a stamp collector would pay an auctioneer $4,000 (20 percent) to sell an equivalent amount of stamps. Holding costs for securities are minor, especially when compared to, for example, investing in gold. The gold investor needs insurance, a safe location, and space to store the gold, all of which can be a considerable expense. Expenses of management and administration for securities can vary also, but usually are lower with securities than with other investments.

BRIEF RECORD OF INVESTMENT PERFORMANCE FOR SECURITIES

The potential for wealth accumulation by investing in marketable securities is substantial. Of course, the actual returns that securities achieve will rise and fall with the economic environment and market conditions, but we can get a good idea of the potential for future aggregate investment performance by examining the record of returns on securities over past time periods.

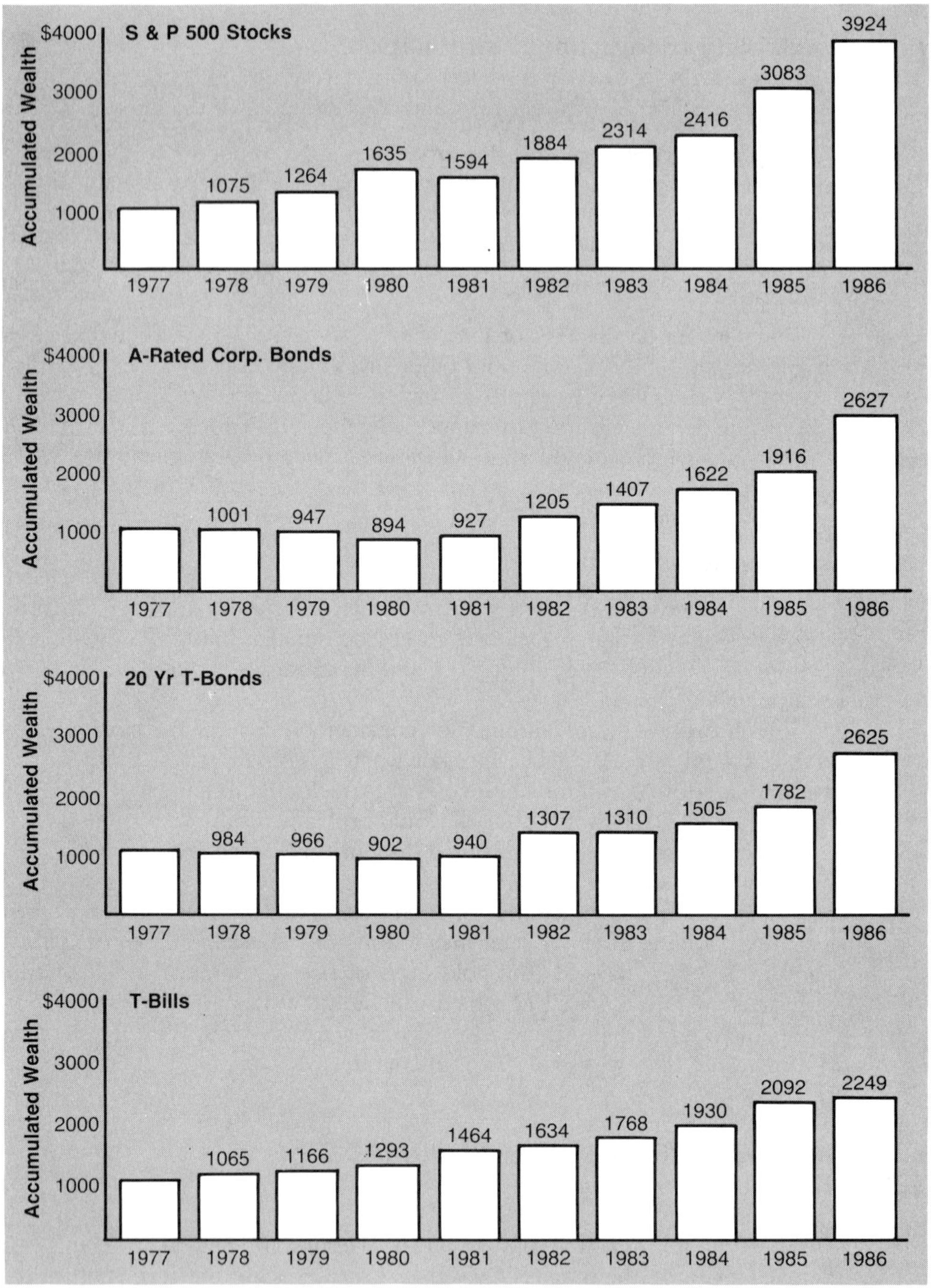

FIGURE 1–1
Result of an initial $1000 investment in various marketable securities

Looking at a recent ten-year period, Figure 1–1 shows the amount to which an initial investment of $1000 would have grown from the end of 1977 to the end of 1986. Investing in U.S. Treasury bills and reinvesting all of the interest would have resulted in a final wealth of $2249. This compares to a sum of $2625 in long-term Treasury bonds, $2627 in corporate bonds, and $3924 in common stocks.

The pattern of investment performance over longer periods is similar. For example, a comprehensive study of long-run investment results for various securities by Ibbotson and Sinquefield[1] shows that a $1000 investment in Treasury bills in 1926 would have grown to $5251 by the end of 1981. Over the same time period, the $1000 placed in Treasury bonds would have yielded $5162; corporate bonds, $7215; and common stocks, $133,616.

These numbers, however, do not show the impact of taxes and inflation. Because income taxes would have to be paid out of each year's gains, the after-tax sum of the $1000 initial investment would be less. Just how much less would depend upon the investor's tax rate. In addition, inflation has the effect of lowering an investment's real return over a period of time. For example, the $1000 investment in 1926 would have yielded the following inflation-adjusted buying-power levels in 1981: Treasury bills, $979; long-term Treasury bonds, $955; long-term corporate bonds, $1337; and common stocks, $25,129. Note that investors in Treasury bills and bonds would have lost ground to inflation. However, common stock investment in general over that time period resulted in a large positive growth in real wealth. For this reason, common stocks are usually considered to be a hedge against inflation over the long run.

This book takes a dual approach to the study of investments. The two aspects, theory and application, are presented in an integrated fashion so that the relationship between the two is apparent. Sections on financial and investment theory present the foundations upon which investment analysis rests. They cover topics such as valuation models, capital market theory, portfolio theory, and efficient markets. Sections discussing applications, which present investing from an applied standpoint, will lead the reader through the numerous types of investment securities available in today's markets. The study of each type of security will include such topics as techniques for analyzing the investment potential of that security, the effects of inflation on the security, alternative strategies for investment in the security, possible effects of changing interest rates, methods of valuation, and strategies for portfolio management. The book also studies the markets themselves and their influence on the investment environment. Throughout the book, the interaction of investment return and risk is important.

SUMMARY

Securities are financial instruments that are evidence of ownership or debt of a business or other entity. Securities are marketable if they may be bought and sold with relative ease. Investment opportunities provided by the securities markets offer investors a wide range of alternative strategies to produce investment income and accumulate wealth.

The field of investments provides several fascinating and rewarding career paths. Account executives for securities brokerage firms offer investment counseling and make securities transactions for their clients. Securities analysts provide the research on securities upon which investors can base their investment decisions. Portfolio analysts monitor and manage investment portfolios, usually basing their decisions on input from securities analysts and other information sources. Financial planners provide investment and financial planning services. Investor relations executives play an important role for corporations by communicating with shareholders and other investors.

Advantages of marketable securities include the liquidity provided by their marketability; the fact that they usually represent some type of real, income-producing asset or business venture; readily available information about the securities; and reasonably low expenses of investing.

Investment finance is a blend of both the theory of choice and its practice. The practice keeps economic theory from degenerating into an uninteresting art form, and the economic theory keeps practice from becoming dull or dangerous. A strong blend of both is necessary in understanding investment finance. The remainder of this book will present such a blend.

IMPORTANT TERMS

account executive
Chartered Financial Analyst (CFA)
liquidity
marketable
Securities and Exchange Commission
security
stockbroker

QUESTIONS AND PROBLEMS

1. Distinguish between an investment and a security.
2. Comment on the degree of marketability and liquidity that you would expect from each of the following investments:
   silver ingots
   common stock of General Motors
   common stock of your brother's local tobacco store
   West German marks
   Polish zloty (unit of currency)
   one acre of prime land on a thoroughfare in your city
3. Explain why an investor relations executive would draw experience from the two disciplines of public relations and financial analysis.
4. Summarize the main advantages that marketable securities offer investors over other types of investments in real assets.

NOTES

1. Roger G. Ibbotson and Rex A. Sinquefield (1982), *Stocks, Bonds, Bills and Inflation: The Past and the Future,* Financial Analysts Research Foundation, Monograph Number 15.

SELECTED REFERENCES

Brooks, John (1969). *Business Adventures.* New York: Bantam.
Brutus (1971). *Confessions of a Stockbroker.* New York: Bantam.
Engel, Louis (1971). *How to Buy Common Stocks.* New York: Bantam.
Galbraith, John Kenneth (1972). *The Great Crash, 1929,* 3rd ed. Boston: Houghton Mifflin.
Malkiel, Burton G. (1982). *Winning Investment Strategies.* New York: W. W. Norton.
Malkiel, Burton G. (1985). *A Random Walk Down Wall Street.* New York: W. W. Norton.

CHAPTER 2

Survey of Markets and Securities

Before advancing to detailed topics in investments, it is worthwhile to give a brief overview of financial markets and a survey of the types of securities available in these markets. This chapter presents such a survey, to give a panoramic view of the range of investment alternatives and to establish some fundamental definitions and terms before we turn to specific investment topics addressed in the following chapters.

In addition, this chapter introduces risk and return. The relationship of risk and return recurs constantly throughout a study of investments, and it is useful to begin with a short introduction to the concepts before continuing with a more in-depth and technical discussion of risk and return in Chapter 6.

MARKETS FOR SECURITIES

Most securities transactions occur in one of the *financial markets.* In a financial market, buyers and sellers meet to establish prices for securities and to buy and sell them. The financial market may be in a location where the buyers and sellers face each other, or it may have another type of organization, where buyers and sellers are brought together by some other means, such as on-line participation in a computerized network of security traders.

Financial markets can be categorized as *primary markets* or *secondary markets.* A primary market transaction occurs when a firm (or government) raises capital by selling its securities to investors. When investors sell securities to other investors, the transactions take place in a secondary market.

Primary Markets

Primary markets allow firms to have a source of capital through the sale of their securities. Money flows from investors to the firm, and the investors receive some type of financial security, such as common stock or bonds, in return. The primary market is therefore the market for *new issues.*

There may be another party involved, who arranges the transaction. Institutions that assist issuers of securities in selling their instruments to investors are *investment bankers.* The investment bankers are an important part of the primary markets and handle most of the transactions occurring there.

For the securities of any one firm, primary market transactions are relatively infrequent; a company sells securities only from time to time when it needs funds. On the other hand, a firm's securities may trade quite often in the secondary markets.

Secondary Markets

Once a security has been issued by a firm in the primary market, it becomes a *seasoned issue.* Upon deciding to sell the security, the investor will offer it for sale to another investor in one of the secondary markets. An investor who wants to buy the security can make a bid for it in the secondary market. In the secondary markets, money flows from one investor to another in exchange for the security.

The third party who arranges for transactions for public investors in the secondary markets is the investment *broker.* Brokerage firms maintain memberships on securities exchanges and other markets where securities are traded. In exchange for their services, brokerage houses receive a commission. Quite often, a brokerage house also acts as an investment banker in the primary markets, and many of the large firms such as E. F. Hutton and Dean Witter participate in both the primary and secondary markets. In fact, the two businesses go well together because all investors, whether they have bought in the secondary or primary markets, are potential clients of both investment bankers and brokerage houses.

Economic Importance of Markets

The existence of both the primary and secondary markets is important and necessary for the growth and development of an economy based on enterprise and private ownership of business. The primary markets are of direct importance because they provide the mechanism through which companies can generate externally provided capital. Companies need this capital to fund their growth and expansion. If all companies have access to capital markets, then the markets provide not only a vehicle for company growth but also for growth of the economy. Economists agree that economic growth is desirable because it is necessary to increase consumption opportunities and economic welfare of the society that the economy serves. The primary markets are therefore beneficial to the economy because they provide a vehicle to fund economic growth. In addition, they provide investors with greater freedom in the number of choices of investments where they can invest their savings. In summary, the primary market allows both for increased investment opportunities and for increases in standards of living.

For a primary market to be successful, however, investors who buy the newly issued securities must have the opportunity to sell them at a later date should they need to raise cash or desire to shift their funds into other investments. All of the well-developed countries with market economies have both a primary market and a secondary market for trading existing issues. To be induced to invest in a security, most investors desire that the security have some degree of liquidity. The secondary markets provide this liquidity.

Even though the corporation does not participate in the secondary market and obtains no funds through it, the market for a corporation's existing securities is quite important to the firm. Should the firm ever need to issue additional securities, conditions prevailing in the secondary markets usually indicate how investors will accept the firm's new issue and at what price.

OVERVIEW OF TYPES OF SECURITIES

This section presents an overview of the main types of securities available to the public. Each description is only an introduction; the remaining chapters of this book present each type of security in more detail, including such topics as legal aspects of the security, established markets that exist for the security, techniques of analyzing the security, and characteristics associated with including the security in a portfolio of other securities. Before covering such topics in detail, however, the investor needs to be aware of and have some familiarity with the different marketable securities that exist in today's market.

Debt Instruments

All *debt instruments* represent a promise to pay a specific amount of money (the *principal* amount) to the holder of the security on a specific date (the *maturity date*). In exchange for investing in the security, the investor, or holder of the security, receives interest. This interest may be paid upon maturity of the security (as with most short-term debt instruments) or in periodic installments (as with most longer-term debt securities).

Money Market Instruments

The market for debt securities of relatively short maturity (generally one year or less) is called the *money market*. The money market gives a considerable amount of liquidity to all participants in the financial market. Companies and government entities that find themselves temporarily short of cash can raise funds quickly by issuing money market instruments. Investors who have cash to invest for short periods of time can invest in money market instruments that will provide them with a return while not committing their funds for long periods.

Several types of money market instruments exist. The first three mentioned in this section (U.S. Treasury bills, negotiable certificates of deposit, and commercial paper) are those that are generally available to all investors in the public markets.

U.S. Treasury Bills. *U.S. Treasury bills* are direct debt obligations of the U.S. government, and the Treasury sells them in *face value* (principal amount) denominations in multiples of $5000 with a minimum of $10,000. T-bills, as they are commonly called, are *pure discount bonds,* meaning that they sell at a discount from their face value, and the government redeems them for face value on maturity. The difference between the amount the investor pays for the bill and the face amount is the interest that the investor receives. Table 2–1 presents interest rates on T-bills and other money market instruments in recent years.

Negotiable Certificates of Deposit. A *certificate of deposit* (CD) is an instrument issued by a bank or other depository institution representing funds placed on deposit at the bank for a certain period of time. Although there are many types of CDs, those in denominations of $100,000 or more (typically $1 million) are considered to be money market instruments because they can be traded among investors after their initial issue. They are called *negotiable certificates of deposit.* Negotiable CDs are generally not redeemable before maturity, but an investor who purchases, for example, a six-month CD may sell it to another investor one month later rather than wait until the CD matures.

TABLE 2–1
Money market rates (3-month maturities)

Year	*T-bills*	*Neg. CDs*	*Comm. paper*
1972	4.07%	—[a]	4.66%
1973	7.04	—	8.20
1974	7.89	10.27%	10.05
1975	5.84	6.43	6.26
1976	4.99	5.15	5.24
1977	5.26	5.52	5.54
1978	7.22	8.22	7.94
1979	10.06	11.22	10.97
1980	11.51	13.07	12.66
1981	14.03	15.91	15.32
1982	10.69	12.27	11.89
1983	8.52	9.07	8.88
1984	9.57	10.37	10.10
1985	7.47	8.05	7.95
1986	5.96	6.52	6.49
1987	5.45	5.87	5.84

Source: Federal Reserve Bulletin, various issues.
[a]Rates on CDs are available only since 1974 because they became popular and generally available during that year.

The interest on CDs is calculated on the face amount of the CD. It is a nondiscount instrument and pays the face amount plus accrued interest at maturity. The rates available to investors in CDs are typically somewhat higher (averaging about 1 percent higher) than those on T-bills of equal maturity (see Table 2–1). This yield differential can be attributed to several factors: (1) the somewhat thinner market for CDs, (2) the tax differential, and (3) the risk factor of the issuing financial institution.

Commercial Paper. *Commercial paper* is the term for the short-term promissory notes issued by large corporations with high credit ratings. The maturity of commercial paper is 270 days or less, which allows the issuer to avoid registration of the issue with the Securities and Exchange Commission. Face amount denominations of commercial paper vary, but the minimum is usually $250,000.

Commercial paper usually carries no stated interest rate and sells at a discount from its face value as do T-bills. As Table 2–1 shows, interest rates available with commercial paper are higher than those on T-bills but have usually been lower than rates on negotiable CDs.

Bankers' Acceptances. *Bankers' acceptances* are time drafts drawn on a commercial bank for which the bank guarantees payment of the face amount upon maturity. They are commonly used to finance international transactions for the short term. For example, a jewelry retailer in the United States might purchase watches from a manufacturer in Switzerland, paying for the goods by sending a time draft (a draft payable at some future date) drawn upon the jeweler's bank. When the bank accepts the draft, it stamps "accepted" on the reverse side of the draft, meaning that the bank guarantees payment of the draft upon maturity. In effect, the bank is guaranteeing the credit of the jeweler. Because the credit behind the draft is now the bank's, the draft can be traded in the money market along with other short-term debt instruments. Although bankers' acceptances are available to individual investors, they are typically most popular with commercial banks and foreign investors.

Eurodollar Deposits. *Eurodollar deposits* are U.S. dollar-denominated deposits that are held in commercial banks outside the United States or in foreign branches of U.S. banks. Investors can participate in this market by investing in Eurodollar CDs of foreign banks. Because these deposits are denominated in U.S. dollars, they are not subject to currency fluctuation risks associated with traditional debt investments in foreign countries.

Federal Funds. *Federal funds* are deposits of commercial banks with one of the Federal Reserve banks or branches. There is an active market among banks borrowing and lending these deposits, usually overnight or for several days for short-term needs.

Fixed Income Capital Market Instruments

The *capital market* supplies longer-term funds to corporations, government entities, and other users of capital. The general type of debt instrument of the capital market is the *bond.* Bonds usually pay interest to the holder once every six months (semiannually) and pay the principal or face amount upon maturity. Although the face amounts of bonds do vary, the typical bond has a face value of $1000. The *market value* of the bond, the price for which it trades in the market, can be greater or less than par depending on interest rates and other market factors.

The three main issuers of bonds that are covered in this book are the U.S. government, municipalities and other political subdivisions with the United States, and corporations. Table 2–2 presents average yields on these securities for recent years.

U.S. Government Issues. Bond issues of the U.S. government originate from both the U.S. Treasury and from other agencies of the federal government that have the authority to issue debt. The Treasury issues are direct obligations of the U.S. government. Agency issues, depending upon the agency and the issue, may or may not be guaranteed as to payment of principal and interest by the federal government. The interest payments of all federal government issues are taxable at the federal level but are exempt from any state or city income taxes.

The long-term bond issues of the Treasury that are available to investors are the *Treasury notes* and the *Treasury bonds.* Treasury notes have original fixed maturities of not less than one and not more than ten years from the date of issue. They are available in denominations as small as $1,000, except that notes of less than four years are usually not issued for less than $5,000. Treasury bonds are like notes in every

TABLE 2–2
Capital market rates (approximately 15-year maturities)

Year	*U.S. T-bonds*	*Municipal bonds*	*Corporate bonds*
1970	6.59%	6.42%	8.51%
1971	5.74	5.62	7.94
1972	5.63	5.04	7.63
1973	6.30	4.99	7.80
1974	6.99	5.89	8.98
1975	6.98	7.05	9.57
1976	6.78	6.64	9.01
1977	7.06	5.68	8.43
1978	7.89	6.03	9.07
1979	8.74	6.52	10.12
1980	10.81	8.59	12.75
1981	12.87	11.33	15.06
1982	12.23	11.66	14.94
1983	10.84	9.51	12.78
1984	11.99	10.10	13.49
1985	10.75	9.11	12.05
1986	7.67	7.32	9.71
1987	8.39	7.64	9.91

Source: Federal Reserve Bulletin, various issues.

respect except that their original maturities are from more than ten years to as long as thirty years.

Municipal Bonds. Municipal bonds, in spite of the word *municipal,* include all bond issues of states, counties, cities, and other political subdivisions of the United States. An important distinguishing feature of municipal bonds is that all interest payments are exempt from U.S. income taxes. They are also usually exempt from any state or city income taxes within the issuing municipality. As shown in Table 2–2, the interest rates available on municipal bonds are somewhat lower than those of other issuers. This rate differential is due mainly to the tax-exempt status of municipal bonds. Actually, municipal yields on an after-tax basis are often greater than yields on other issues, depending upon the investor's tax bracket.

Corporate Bonds. Debt securities of corporations with maturity of longer than one year are corporate bonds. The usual par value of a corporate bond is $1,000, and maturities range from about two to as many as thirty years. In recent years, however, corporate bond issues have been of shorter maturities as inflation and economic uncertainties have caused investors to be less willing to commit their funds for longer periods of time. As Table 2–2 shows, returns available to investors in corporate bonds have historically been higher on average than those of long-term government securities. This yield differential reflects the higher credit risk of the individual corporations issuing the bonds.

An alternate view of corporate bonds is that they represent a fixed ownership in the corporation. For example, each bondholder has a $1,000 interest in the company. The bondholder is guaranteed this $1,000 portion of the company regardless of how badly the company performs (assuming that it does not declare bankruptcy, and even then the bondholders have preferred claims on the company's assets). However, the bondholder gives up any benefits of growth in the company and receives only the fixed annual interest payments and the guaranteed principal upon maturity.

Equity Instruments

Equity securities represent the residual ownership of the firm. Residual ownership means that the debt holders must first be paid off before the company belongs completely to the equity holders. The two types of equity securities are *common stock* and *preferred stock.*

Common Stock

The common stockholders are the risktakers; they own a portion of the firm that is not guaranteed, and they are last in line with claims on the company's assets in the event of a bankruptcy. In return for taking this risk, they share in the growth of the firm because the growth in the value of the company accrues to the common shareholders. The company may make a periodic cash payment called a *cash dividend* to the common stockholders. Cash dividends are commonly paid to shareholders on a quarterly basis, but they may be paid annually, irregularly, or even not at all. The common shareholder has no guarantee of receiving a dividend payment.

Common stockholders usually have *voting rights* that allow them to vote on the corporation's *board of directors*. Since the board of directors hires the top management of the company, the stockholders indirectly determine the company's management.

Preferred Stock

Preferred stock is technically an equity interest in the company, but its characteristics are more like those of bonds. *Preferred* means that this type of stock has a stated *par value* that represents a claim against corporate assets that supersedes the claims of the common stockholders, but is subordinate to the claims of bondholders. Preferred stock also carries a fixed-dollar cash dividend that the corporation must pay before it can pay any cash dividends to the common shareholders. Like debt, preferred stock is often systematically retired through a sinking fund. It also does *not* represent true residual ownership because preferred shareholders usually do not participate in earnings growth by receiving higher dividends, as common shareholders do.

Contingent Claim Securities

Contingent claim securities are securities that give the holder a claim upon another asset, contingent upon the holder's meeting certain contract conditions. Although there are many types of contingent claim securities, the three most popular kinds in investments today are *options, warrants,* and *convertible securities.*

Options

An option is a contract giving its holder the right to buy or sell an asset or security at a fixed price. All options are valid only for a specified time period, after which they expire. A *call option* gives its holder the right to buy the underlying asset and thereby guarantees the purchase price of the asset for the duration of the option. A *put option* carries the right to sell and guarantees the selling price of the underlying security.

For example, an investor might purchase a call option to buy common stock for \$30. Suppose that the investor paid \$2 for the call option, and the stock goes up to \$35. The investor can buy the stock using the option at \$30, sell the stock in the open market for \$35, and make a \$5 profit (\$3 after deducting the initial cost of the option).

Warrants

Warrants are like call options that are issued by the corporation. They give their holders the right to purchase the common stock from the corporation at a fixed price. Warrants usually have longer lives than options, typically five to seven years, although a few perpetual warrants exist. Corporations usually issue warrants in conjunction with another issue of securities and offer a "package deal." For example, the purchase of one share of preferred stock might entitle the investor to receive one warrant to purchase common stock of the company. Companies offer such packages to sweeten the deal and make the other security easier to sell.

Convertible Securities

Convertible securities are securities that may be converted into common stock. A *convertible bond* is a bond that the holder may exchange for common stock of the corporation. The other common type of convertible security is the *convertible preferred stock,* which is simply a preferred stock that the holder can exchange for a certain number of shares of common stock of the corporation.

Futures Contracts

A contract that arranges for delivery and payment of an asset at a future date is a *futures contract.* Futures contracts are traded publicly on the futures exchanges, and these exchanges have developed contracts on a number of assets, such as corn, wheat, soybeans, and frozen pork bellies. These contracts, often called *commodity futures* because of the nature of the underlying asset, allow producers and consumers of the commodities to plan their production and sales in advance as well as allow speculators to enter the market. A second group of futures, on such assets as U.S. Treasury bills, negotiable CDs, and stock market indexes, is called *financial futures.* These futures allow investors in such securities to spread some of the risk to speculators and aid in the investment process. The futures chapter of this text deals primarily with various types of, and markets for, financial futures.

Investment Companies

Investment companies invest their capital in the securities of other companies. Therefore, anyone who purchases stock issued by the investment company is indirectly an investor in the portfolio of securities in which the investment company has invested. The existence of investment companies provides many investors with a vehicle for participating in the market that they would not have otherwise. For example, the minimum purchase of a negotiable CD is $100,000, but an investor with as little as $1,000 or so can purchase shares of an investment company that invests in negotiable CDs and thereby participate in that market.

Investment companies exist with many types of investment goals. The money market funds invest in short-term money market securities; tax-exempt funds purchase municipal bonds; and others purchase common stocks, preferred stocks, or bonds. Investors can usually find a fund that matches or comes very close to their financial goals.

RISK AND RETURN

Every investment decision involves two major considerations: the risk that the investor takes on by making an investment and the return that the investor receives or hopes to receive as a result of the investment.

What Is Return?

Investors invest their funds to make a profit. The *return* on an investment is this profit stated per dollar of funds required to establish and maintain the investment. Return, rather than dollar profit, is the item of interest to investors because return shows how well every dollar invested profits the investor. The goal of investment is to maximize the investor's utility, and maximizing expected return, or profit per dollar invested, is consistent with this goal.

What Is Risk?

Investment risk exists when there is more than one possible future return associated with an investment. To be even more specific, if more than one possible return exists, and the investor has no idea of the probabilities associated with the occurrence of any of the possible future returns, the situation is of complete investment *uncertainty*. Investment *certainty* exists when there is only one possible return; the investor is certain of the investment's return, as in the case of the return on a U.S. Treasury bill or an FDIC-insured savings account at a bank (barring, of course, the possibility of financial failure of the U.S. government).

Between the two extremes of investment certainty and investment uncertainty lies the area of investment *risk*. Under conditions of risk, investors realize that there is a range of possible returns and can associate some probability to each possible return. This dispersion of possible returns represents risk. The greater the dispersion of possible returns on an investment, the greater the risk.

Measuring Return

Return, or profit per dollar invested, is a *flow concept*. That is, profit flows or accrues to the investment over a period of time. Return can be measured as a dollar amount or as a rate of return. To measure the rate of return, an investor needs to know three items:

1. The period of time that the measurement covers.
2. The net profit of the investment over the time period.
3. The dollar amount needed to establish and maintain the investment.

The final component of return, the dollar investment required, is usually the purchase price of the security. It is a *stock concept,* meaning that we measure its value at a particular point in time rather than over a time period.

Holding Period Return

In the typical security investment, an investor purchases and pays for the security at the beginning of the holding period and then sells it at the end of the time period. In such a situation, the holding period return on the investment is:

$$R_t = \frac{P_t - P_{t-1} + Y_t}{P_{t-1}} \tag{2-1}$$

where R = the holding period return on the investment
P_t = the price of the security at time t, the end of the holding period
P_{t-1} = the price of the security at time $t-1$, the beginning of the holding period
Y_t = the income from the investment during the holding period.

Equation 2–1 says that the holding period return is equal to the profit on the security (the sale price less the purchase price plus any intervening cash flows) per dollar invested in the security (the purchase price at the beginning of the holding period).

EXAMPLE 2–1

What is the holding period return for a security purchased for $6800 and sold two months later for $6500?

$$R = \frac{6500 - 6800}{6800}$$

$$R = -.044 \text{ or } -4.4 \text{ percent}$$

The holding period return in Example 2–1 is $-.044$, or -4.4% as investors often say it. Although people commonly use a percentage to describe return, using decimals in computations helps avoid misplacing the decimal point. (This text will normally specify returns in decimals rather than as percentages. Following this convention helps avoid confusion.)

The general formula for holding period return for an investment is

$$R_t = \frac{P_s - P_p + Y_t - C_t}{I} \tag{2-2}$$

where P_s = the sales price of the security
P_p = the purchase price of the security
C_t = the costs and expenses of transacting and holding the security
I = the dollar investment required to establish and maintain the position in the security.

Equation 2–2 is a more generalized formula for computing returns. It is useful in all situations, not just the usual situation described by Equation 2–1. Equation 2–2 recognizes that not all transactions fall into the category of Equation 2–1, for several reasons:

1. Although the normal sequence of transactions is the purchase of a security followed by its sale, sometimes the sale of the security precedes the purchase (see the section on short sales in Chapter 3), and Equation 2–2 takes this into account.

2. There may be expenses associated with making the transaction, such as commission costs and taxes, and with holding the security, such as the cost of money borrowed to finance the purchase of the security.
3. The amount of money that the investor puts up to establish the investment may be different from the cash price of the security. In the case of margin purchases (see Chapter 3), the dollar investment is less than the security's price. A short option position may even require an investment of more than the security's price (see Chapter 17).

EXAMPLE 2–2

Mr. Bill Bond purchased stock for $4000, borrowing $2000 at 12 percent from the bank and putting up the remainder of the cost of the investment from his personal funds. He paid the broker a $35 commission on the purchase. Three months (90 days) later he sold the stock for $4200, again paying a $35 commission. During the holding period, Bill collected cash dividends of $150 on the stock. What is his holding period return?

The expenses of the position are the two commissions ($70) and the interest on the loan ($.12 \times 2000 \times 90/360 = \$60$). (Note that bankers assume a 360-day year.) Bill invested $2035 of his own money (the $2000 portion of the purchase price plus the first $35 commission paid up front).

$$R = \frac{4200 - 4000 + 150 - 130}{2035}$$

$$R = .108$$

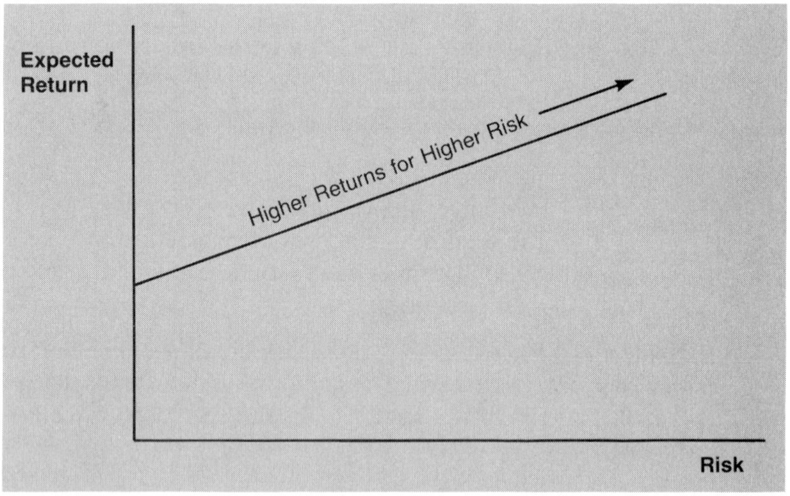

FIGURE 2–1
The general relationship between the expected return on an investment and the expected risk

The General Risk-Return Relationship

Risk and return are probably the two main concerns of all investors, and we might say that they are the two sides of the investment coin. The relationship between the two for an investment is that investors will want more return from investments that have greater risk. Investments with higher risk levels should have higher levels of return. Figure 2–1 shows the relationship graphically. Chapter 8 provides a formal framework, a derivation, and a detailed discussion of this important relationship in investments.

SUMMARY

Transactions for securities occur in either a primary market or a secondary market. The primary market transactions are the initial sales of securities, when the original issuer first sells them to the investing public. When these investors buy and sell the securities among themselves, they do so in the secondary markets.

The main categories of marketable securities are debt instruments, equity securities, contingent claim securities, futures, and investment companies. Debt securities include issues of both the government and corporations. Governments at all levels, including federal, state, and local, issue debt securities to finance many of their projects. Short-term debt (less than one year in maturity) securities are money market instruments and include U.S. Treasury bills, negotiable certificates of deposit, and commercial paper. The capital market provides longer-term funds. Federal government long-term debt includes U.S. Treasury notes, Treasury bonds, and issues of U.S. government agencies. Debt securities of states, localities, and other political subdivisions of the United States are called municipal bonds, and their important distinguishing feature is that the interest from these securities is exempt from all federal income taxes. Corporate bonds are the long-term debt of business firms.

Equity instruments represent the residual ownership of the firm—that part of the firm left after the bondholders and other creditors have been paid. Preferred stock is equity, although it represents a fixed portion of equity ownership. Common stock, on the other hand, provides a variable residual interest. It is variable because as the firm earns more money, these benefits accrue to the common stockholder either as retained earnings or as cash dividends. The dividends paid to the preferred shareholder are usually for a fixed amount.

Contingent claim securities give their holders some type of claim on the ownership of another security and include warrants, options, and convertible securities. Futures contracts are financial contracts agreeing to the delivery in the future of some asset or financial security. Investment companies are companies that invest their funds in a portfolio of securities so that the shareholder in the investment company is indirectly an investor in each of the other securities in the investment company's portfolio.

The rate of return represents the profit per dollar of funds invested in an asset. Holding period return defines return over a specific time period. Risk is the chance that the actual return on an investment will not be equal to the expected return.

Investors generally demand higher returns from investments that have greater levels of risk.

IMPORTANT TERMS

bankers' acceptances
board of directors
bond
broker
call option
capital market
cash dividend
certainty
certificate of deposit
commercial paper
commodity futures
common stock
contingent claim securities
convertible bond
convertible preferred stock
convertible securities
debt instruments
Eurodollar deposits
face value
federal funds
financial futures
financial markets
flow concept
futures contract
investment bankers
investment companies
market value
maturity date
money market
negotiable certificate of deposit
new issues
options
par value
preferred stock
primary markets
principal
pure discount bonds
put option
return
risk
seasoned issue
secondary markets
stock concept
Treasury bonds
Treasury notes
Treasury bills
uncertainty
voting rights
warrants

QUESTIONS AND PROBLEMS

1. What are primary and secondary markets? How do they contribute to the smooth functioning of an enterprise economy?
2. Which of the popular money market instruments are sold on a discount basis?
3. Describe a bankers' acceptance. What are the similarities and differences between certificates of deposit (CDs) and bankers' acceptances?
4. Describe the characteristics of a bond.
5. If a municipal bond has less liquidity and more risk than a corporate bond of equal maturity, why might it have a lower yield?
6. Explain why common stockholders are referred to as the residual owners of the firm while the bondholders are fixed owners.
7. What is a call option? Why might an investor purchase a call option on Texaco rather than purchasing the Texaco stock itself?
8. Describe an investment company, and explain how purchasing shares in an investment company might be useful for a small investor.

9. Distinguish between risk and uncertainty. Do you believe most investors make investment decisions under conditions of risk or uncertainty? Why?
10. An investor purchased stock for $37 per share and sold it one year later for $26. The stock paid a 50-cent dividend during the year.
    a) Ignoring any commissions, what was the investor's return?
    b) If there was a 75-cent per share commission on each transaction, what was the investor's return?
11. Joan Turner purchased a bond for $942. She received a $35 interest payment and sold the bond six months later for $960. Compute Ms. Turner's holding period return (ignoring commissions).
12. What should be the general relationship between expected return and risk? Use the relationship to explain an observation that the yield on a U.S. Treasury note is 10 percent while twenty-year bonds of Black and Decker yield 14 percent on the same date.

SELECTED REFERENCES

Ibbotson, Roger G., and Rex A. Sinquefield (1982). *Stocks, Bonds, Bills and Inflation: The Past and the Future.* Charlottesville, Virginia: The Financial Analysts Research Foundation.

Teweles, Richard J., and Edward S. Bradley (1982). *The Stock Market.* New York: John Wiley and Sons.

CHAPTER 3

Organization and Operation of Securities Markets

This chapter explains and discusses the structure and operation of the primary and secondary security markets. Although a knowledge of the operation of the markets is not essential to understand investment security selection and portfolio management, it is important for investors to be familiar with these topics for several reasons.

1. A knowledge of the operation of markets is helpful when communicating buy and sell orders to brokers. For example, the investor must decide which type of order to place and clearly instruct the broker to place the order.
2. It helps the investor understand the mechanism for selling short.
3. It prepares the student for questions asked on the various examinations required to obtain a license to sell securities, because these exams stress rules and operational aspects of securities markets rather than investment theory and analysis.

PRIMARY MARKETS

When a corporation[1] wants to raise funds from an external source, it may choose to borrow from a financial institution, such as a commercial bank, or to sell securities in the securities markets to institutions, individuals, or other investors. When the corporation elects the second of these alternatives, it creates securities and sells them in the primary market.

In a primary market transaction, money flows from the investor to the corporation. In exchange for supplying capital to the corporation, the investor receives a security such as common stock. Although the corporation may sell the new issue directly to the investor, the company usually deals with an investment banker who handles the details of the new issue and the sale of the securities to the investor. Figure 3–1 shows the flow of funds in the primary market, including the investment banker as intermediary in the transaction.

Public vs. Private Placement

When selling new securities to investors, the corporation has the choice of a *private placement* or a *public placement*. When selling securities in a private placement, the company arranges to sell its securities to one large investor or to a small group of investors. A private placement offers ease of selling, because the securities do not have to be marketed to many different investors. In addition, it is not necessary to register most private placements with federal and state regulatory authorities. In a common type of private placement, an insurance company may purchase an entire bond issue from a company issuing bonds.

In a public placement, the corporation (or its investment banker) offers securities to all investors through a public issue. Public placements have the advantage of offering the corporation a wider base of security holders, and a corporation can usually raise larger sums of capital through a public placement than through a private placement. When offering securities to the public, the company must register the issue with the necessary federal and state offices.

The Investment Banker

The investment banking function is a very important part of the structure and operation of the primary markets. Companies usually do not attempt to sell their securities directly to the public, both because a specialized knowledge of securities laws is necessary to initiate a sale of securities to the public and because the sales expertise of the company does not usually lie in selling securities. A company could develop a department within the firm to carry out this function, but most companies issue new securities so infrequently that they are better served by calling upon an outside investment banker, who specializes in these areas. Investment bankers retain lawyers who are well versed in securities law, they are knowledgeable about market conditions

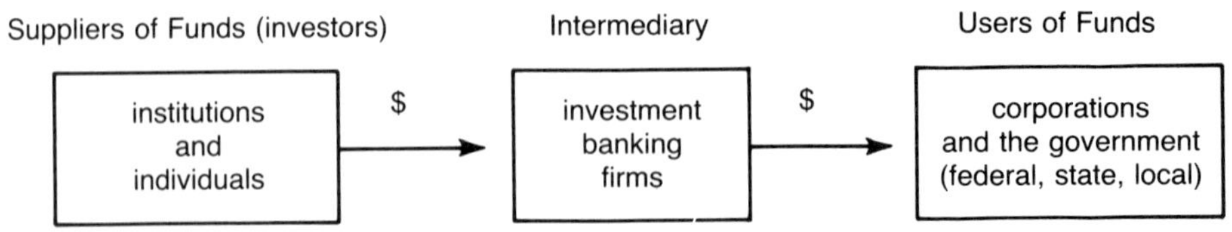

FIGURE 3–1
Flow of funds in the primary markets

regarding timing and pricing of new issues, and they have established clients to whom they regularly sell securities.

Investment bankers can offer a new issue of a security to the public in several ways. The most common of these methods is negotiated *underwriting,* in which the investment banker purchases the issue from the corporation for a guaranteed amount and then sells it to the public for a slightly higher price. The investment banker underwrites the issue and thus takes on some degree of risk if it cannot sell the entire issue at the new issue price. Most corporations prefer this method because it transfers the risk from the corporation to the investment banker.

The Underwriting Sequence

A typical underwriting has several steps:

1. The firm and the investment banker meet and agree to discuss a public offering. Sometimes the company approaches the investment banker, and sometimes the investment banking firm initiates the discussion.
2. The firm and the underwriter then proceed to a pre-underwriting conference during which they discuss the amount of financing needed, the type of security to which the market might be most receptive, and the terms of their contract.
3. The investment banker then forms an *underwriting syndicate,* a temporary association of investment bankers organized by the initial managing underwriter to facilitate the sale of the new security issue and to assume part of the risk. The size of the syndicate will vary; a large offering of new securities may call for a syndicate with dozens of members, while the managing underwriter might handle an entire small issue without inviting others into a syndicate. Syndicate members hope to make a profit on the difference, or *spread,* between what they pay the issuer for the security and the price at which they sell the security to investors. If the issue sells for a price less than the price paid to the issuer, the syndicate takes the loss. Often the managing underwriter will assume a major portion of the risk and limit the risk of the other syndicate members.

   The syndicate's contract with the company is the *underwriting agreement,* which formally specifies the terms of the new issue. At this point, the price for which the new security will sell is still not certain, but the parties have agreed on an *upset price,* which is the price below which the security issuer may cancel the offering.
4. The firm and the underwriters then file the appropriate forms with the Securities and Exchange Commission (SEC) to comply with federal law. This filing includes a *preliminary prospectus.* The new issue's final *prospectus,* which contains any corrections and changes required by the SEC, is the document that the underwriters must make available to investors before selling the new issue. The preliminary prospectus is also called a *red herring* because of the red lettering on the front that distinguishes it

from the final prospectus. The parties also file forms with the appropriate state commissions to comply with the state security laws regulating the new issue of securities within that state.

5. Next, the underwriters form a selling group composed of all members of the syndicate plus any other investment banking firms that might be able to assist in selling the issue. These other members in the selling group receive a commission for selling the security, assume none of the risk, and agree not to sell the new issue below its *pegged price,* or offering price, until the syndicate dissolves. The selling group begins to allow investors to *subscribe to the issue,* which means the investor indicates an interest in purchasing a certain number of shares but has no obligation to do so.
6. Just before the date on which the new issue is scheduled to be brought to the market, the firm and the underwriters hold a *due diligence meeting* during which they check all pertinent details. They agree on the selling price for the issue and arrange to have the final prospectus printed.
7. Finally, the selling group can proceed to sell the issue. If the issue is popular or has been oversubscribed, it will sell out quickly, and the syndicate will dissolve. If not, the securities may remain in inventory for several days, after which the syndicate will break up and the managing underwriter will lower the price to clear the inventory. During the period when the underwriting group is trying to sell the issue at its offering price, the managing underwriter may attempt to stabilize the price by offering to buy the issue in the secondary market at a price not less than the offering price. This is called *price pegging* and is the only form of security price manipulation that is legal because it is considered essential to the smooth offering of new issues in the market.

Buying a New Issue

Most security transactions are secondary market transactions involving investors selling existing issues, so most investors will seldom, if ever, purchase a security as a new issue. However, an astute investor will recognize that situations may arise in which purchase of a new issue is advantageous. There are at least two reasons why purchase of a new issue might be wise.

1. To save on commissions. The investor pays no commission when purchasing a new issue; the corporation pays the "commission" as part of the flotation cost of the issue. If the offering is an additional issue of stock in a company whose existing stock already trades in the market, then the price of the new issue is usually set at or slightly above the price of the existing stock. The price of the new issue will often be less than the price of the existing stock plus commissions.
2. To take advantage of a "hot" new issue. New issues of companies offering their stock to the public for the first time often give investors a chance for a stake in a new company with excellent potential for capital gains. Some

studies of the price performance of new issues have concluded that an investor able to purchase all new issues entering the market and to sell them several months later would make substantial profits.[2] However, as a cautionary note to those who might think that new issues are an easy route to riches, the most desirable new issues are usually oversubscribed, and brokers ration their shares to their largest and best customers. An individual investor buying new issues might receive only the less popular issues.

SECONDARY MARKETS

In the secondary market, the counterpart of the primary market's investment banker is the investment brokerage firm. Because the two businesses are so closely related, an investment banker usually also conducts a brokerage business, although many brokerage firms are not involved in investment banking.

Services Offered by Brokerage Firms

The broker offers investors a wide range of investment-related services. The main functions of the brokerage firm are transaction services, account maintenance services, extension of credit, and investment advisory services.

Transaction Services

Probably the most-utilized service of the brokerage business is that of executing securities transactions for customers. Of course, an investor desiring to sell a security always has the option of finding a buyer without using the services of a broker, but doing so would probably be more costly and troublesome than it is worth. In exchange for the transaction, or brokerage, services, the investment brokerage firm receives compensation in the form of a commission added to the price of the security.

Before May 1, 1975 (referred to as "Mayday" in the brokerage business), the New York Stock Exchange (NYSE) effectively set commission rates by requiring that its member firms adhere to the commission schedule promulgated by the Exchange. After that date, commission rates became subject to negotiation between the individual investor and the brokerage firm. In effect, this has meant that each brokerage firm sets its own rate schedule for its small clients, while high-volume, large investors can negotiate for lower rates.

The advent of these negotiated rates has caused changes in the securities industry. One noticeable change has been the consolidation of the industry. Many of the smaller firms merged into large firms, and many large firms then merged into other conglomerate companies. For example, Dean Witter Reynolds, one of the large brokerage firms, is now a subsidiary of Sears, Roebuck and Co. Another change has been the division of brokerage houses into two types: the *full-service brokerage firm* and the *discount brokerage firm.*

The Full-Service Brokerage Firm. The full-service brokerage firm offers a full line of brokerage and other financial services. Generally, the commission schedule of the full-service broker is quite high, although it is always possible that the individual investor can negotiate a lower commission.

Customers of the full-service firms usually deal with a person assigned to give the account personal attention. This person is the *account executive* or *registered representative,* often referred to as a customer's "broker." (An outdated and somewhat sexist term for the account executive was "customer's man.") Account executives usually receive a portion of the commission as their compensation.

The Discount Brokerage Firm. The discount brokerage firm offers a commission schedule of rates that are a discount, sometimes substantial, from the commission schedules of the full-service firms. Table 3–1 compares representative commissions for full-service and discount brokerage firms. Discount firms usually do not offer all the other services of full-service houses. The area most often omitted is the investment advisory service; most customers of discount firms make their own investment decisions without the aid of the broker. Customers of discount firms usually do not have their own account executive; instead, they place their orders through an order clerk who is generally paid a salary instead of a commission.

Many banks now offer discount brokerage along with their other banking services. Although the Glass-Steagall Act prohibited commercial banks from engaging in investment banking or brokerage (except in the case of certain bond issues), banks have been able to offer the brokerage services either by purchasing a brokerage subsidiary or by contracting with an outside discount broker to offer brokerage services to bank customers.

Full-Service or Discount: Which Way to Go? Since every investor must eventually deal with a brokerage firm, the choice of a full-service or a discount house becomes important. The advantages of full-service firms include the personal service and attention of the account executive, investment research and advice (usually at no additional charge), and a wider variety of services. In addition, sometimes a full-service firm's commission on small trades will be lower than that of a discount firm. The

TABLE 3–1
Sample brokerage commissions[a]

	Average Brokerage Commission for		
Broker	***200 shares at 10***	***300 shares at 25***	***800 shares at 35***
Bank	$44	$63	$148
Discount brokerage firm	40	79	168
Full-service brokerage firm	72	157	434
NYSE fixed commission (pre-1975)	55	134	370

[a]Based on a survey of brokerage firm commissions and on NYSE schedule of commissions valid before May 1, 1975. Additional discounts are usually available for large-volume traders.

main advantage of discount houses is their lower commissions. Investors should shop for a brokerage firm by carefully comparing services and costs. Many investors choose to have two accounts, one at each type of firm, using the account that is most advantageous for each transaction or service.

Account Maintenance Services

Although an investor can deal with a brokerage firm by paying cash for the securities purchased and taking delivery of the security, it is usually much easier and simpler to keep an open account at the brokerage firm. There are two basic types of brokerage firm accounts: the *cash account* and the *margin account*. Investors may deposit cash and securities into each type of account just as they would deposit cash into a bank account. The difference between a cash and a margin account is that securities purchased in the cash account must be paid for in full while the brokerage firm may lend money for a portion of a purchase in a margin account.

Figure 3–2 shows a stock certificate, which gives evidence of ownership of stock in a corporation. The name of the registered owner appears on the face of the certificate.

FIGURE 3–2
Sample stock certificate (Courtesy of the Mead Corporation)

When an investor deposits the stock with the broker to hold in either a cash or margin account for safekeeping, the brokerage firm will transfer the stock registration from the customer's name to that of the brokerage firm. This is called holding the stock in *street name*. It is much easier for an investor to direct a broker to hold stock in street name for at least two reasons. First, the stock is safe because the Securities Investor Protection Corporation (SIPC) insures accounts in member brokerage firms up to $500,000. Second, the customer enjoys the convenience of having the broker collect all dividends, credit them to the investor's account, and send the investor a monthly statement. When the investor wants to sell the stock, there is no need to locate the certificate, endorse it, and deliver it safely to the broker. On the other hand, some investors prefer to keep their stock registered in their own names for several reasons. First, the company represented by the stock will mail its corporate reports only to the registered investor. Second, only the registered owner retains the voting rights of the stock. Finally, many stockholders like to take advantage of automated dividend reinvestment plans offered by many companies. To do this, the stockholder must be a registered shareholder.

Most full-service brokerage firms and a few discount houses have followed the lead of Merrill Lynch, the nation's largest brokerage firm, in offering a type of brokerage account that bundles many financial services into one account. Merrill Lynch calls this a Cash Management Account. For an initial deposit of cash or securities of about $10,000 and an annual fee of $100 or less, these types of accounts give customers such services as unlimited checking, a single consolidated statement, automatic reinvestment of dividends, a money market fund for investment of idle cash balances, a major credit card, and free traveler's checks.

Extension of Credit via Margin Accounts

Another function of security brokerage firms is extending credit to customers through a margin account. Although the commissions generated by transactions are an important source of revenue for brokerage firms, the largest segment of income for most brokerage houses comes from interest income.

Leverage is the term that applies when assets are acquired with borrowed money. Leverage increases the possible return on the investment, but it also increases the risk associated with the investment. When investors borrow funds from the brokerage firm, using securities on deposit in their accounts as collateral, the specific term used in the securities industry is *margin*. Investors may use this credit to purchase additional securities, or they can withdraw cash from the account to use for any other purpose. As Examples 3–1 and 3–2 show, margin even applies to a current purchase, which means that an investor using margin can purchase more of a security than an investor paying the full amount.

The *initial margin requirement* is the percentage of the purchase price of a security that the investor must deposit with the broker to buy the security. The board of governors of the Federal Reserve System, mainly through the authority of Federal Reserve Regulations T and U, determines the initial margin requirement for purchase of stocks and convertible bonds. The security exchanges or individual brokerage firms set initial margin requirements for the purchase of bonds and government securities.

EXAMPLE 3–1

John Taylor opens a margin account at a brokerage firm. If the initial margin requirement is 50 percent, how much cash must Mr. Taylor deposit into the account to purchase 500 shares of Accro-tron at \$15 per share? This transaction requires the purchase of \$7500 of stock with a margin requirement of 50 percent (0.50). Substituting for the values in Equation 3–2 and solving gives

$$.5 = \text{equity}/7500$$
$$\text{equity} = 3750$$

Mr. Taylor must therefore deposit \$3750 in equity (cash) into the margin account.

EXAMPLE 3–2

Suppose Mr. Taylor (see Example 3–1) wanted to purchase the Accro-tron shares by depositing shares of Wizard Corp. instead of cash. If Wizard currently sells for \$10 per share, how many shares would Mr. Taylor have to deposit?

The use of securities to provide equity adds market value to the margin account, so the solution is not just to deposit \$3750 of Wizard. Since the Wizard securities will also now be margined, we use an equity of \$3750 in Equation 3–2 and solve:

$$.5 = 3750/\text{market value}$$
$$\text{market value} = 7500$$

Mr. Taylor would need to place \$7500 (750 shares) of Wizard into his margin account.

The following formulas are useful for computing margin requirements:

$$\text{equity} = \text{market value} - \text{loan} \quad \textbf{(3–1)}$$
$$\text{margin percentage} = \text{equity}/\text{market value} \quad \textbf{(3–2)}$$

Current Federal Reserve rules set an initial margin requirement percentage of 50 percent, although this number has varied from as low as 45 percent to as high as 100 percent. A margin requirement of 100 percent means that a brokerage firm may not extend credit for the purchase of securities. Generally, the Federal Reserve uses the margin requirement on the macro level as a tool to discourage excessive speculation in the securities markets and on the micro level to protect individual investors from over-leveraging their security investments. During periods of high stock prices and speculation, the Federal Reserve will often raise the margin requirement; lower margin requirements follow when the market cools down. Studies show that the regulation of margin credit has been an effective device for the Federal Reserve. One study found that when the Federal Reserve raised the margin requirement, margin loan growth always slowed or decreased.[3] Another determined that there has been a positive relationship between the equity in investors' margin accounts and the margin requirement.[4]

New York Stock Exchange requirements for its member firms also set the following initial margin requirements: 5 percent of the principal amount of U.S. government securities; the lesser of 15 percent of the principal amount or 25 percent of the market value of municipal bonds; and 25 percent of the market value of nonconvertible corporate bonds. In addition, the NYSE requires each margin account at its member brokerage firms to have a minimum equity of $2000.

In addition to the initial margin requirement, investors must always maintain a sufficient amount of equity in their account to satisfy the *maintenance margin requirement.* As Equation 3–2 reveals, any change in the market value of the securities in a margin account causes the margin percentage to change. To recompute the equity and debt in brokerage accounts is to *mark-to-market.* Most firms mark-to-market on a daily basis. When the value of margined securities decreases to the point where the margin is less than the maintenance margin requirement, the investor will receive a *margin call.* Upon receiving a margin call, the investor must provide additional equity in the account (either in cash or in additional securities) to bring the margin above the maintenance requirement. Individual brokerage firms and the exchanges determine maintenance margin requirements. The NYSE currently requires margin accounts of its member firms to maintain a 25 percent margin, although many individual brokerage firms require more than the minimum.

EXAMPLE 3–3

The $7500 of Accro-tron stock purchased by Mr. Taylor on 50 percent margin (see Example 3–1) has declined to $5000. What is the margin that Mr. Taylor now has in his account?

Equation 3–1 shows that Mr. Taylor's loan is for $3750:

$$3750 = 7500 - \text{loan}$$
$$\text{loan} = 3750$$

The amount of the loan is fixed; it is the equity that changes when the securities change in price. Substituting the new market value of Accro-tron into Equation 3–1 gives the current equity in the account:

$$\text{equity} = 5000 - 3750$$
$$\text{equity} = 1250$$

Substituting the current equity into Equation 3–2 gives the current margin:

$$\text{margin} = 1250/5000$$
$$\text{margin} = .25$$

The interest charged on the loan balances in margin accounts is a source of additional revenue for brokerage firms. Brokerage firms can borrow money from banks by putting up as collateral stock that the brokers hold in margin accounts. These loans, termed *call loans* because the banks can call them in for payment at any time, typically carry an interest rate about equal to the prime rate. The brokers charge their margin accounts interest at a rate usually equal to the rate on call money plus about 0.5 percent for large customers, ranging up to 2 percent or more on small accounts.

As mentioned previously, investors use the leverage provided by margin to increase their potential return. However, margin works both ways, and when security prices fall, losses will accrue to the margin trader at a faster rate than to the investor purchasing securities in cash. The effect of this increased variation in the value of the position is to increase the risk of the investment position.

Investment Advisory Services

Security brokerage firms also offer investment advice to clients. Full-service brokerage firms usually make available a wide range of advisory services. For investors who have little knowledge of money management or who do not wish to direct their own investments, account executives at full-service firms will administer a *discretionary account,* in which the account executive has the authority to buy and sell securities for the account. The account executive should make these transactions for the account after careful consideration of the investor's financial position and goals. Although most account executives are reliable, the goal of the investor (maximizing investment income) and the goal of the account executive (maximizing commission income) may conflict. Any investor opening a discretionary account should do so with great care and should regularly monitor the investment decisions of the account executive. An alternative to the discretionary account is to allow the account executive to make recommendations, which the investor may accept or reject.

Most full-service brokers have research departments that analyze investments and make recommendations based on their analysis. The account executives use this research to guide their decisions for discretionary accounts and to make recommendations to other clients. The firms often make copies of these research reports available to their regular customers on request. They also subscribe to investment information and advisory services of many independent research firms. This information also is usually available to the firm's clients.

Full-service firms usually offer their investment advice and assistance at no additional charge to regular customers and prospective clients. They charge for this service indirectly by charging a commission higher than that charged by the discount firms. Some discount firms offer limited investment research services to their accounts, for which they may charge a service fee rather than a higher commission schedule.

Brief History of Securities Markets

After the end of the American Revolution, the corporate form of business ownership began to grow. The first informal association of dealers in financial securities was organized in 1791 in Philadelphia. The following year the New York Brokers for the Purchase and Sale of Public Stock organized, agreeing to give business preference to each other and to charge a minimum rate of commission.

By 1800, there were 295 publicly owned corporations in the country. In 1803 about $130 million worth of securities were publicly held, about two thirds of which were federal government obligations while one third were shares of private issuers. New York began to emerge as the financial center of the nation, and various securities exchanges began to form in New York and around the country.

Functions of a Securities Exchange

To some extent, even these early securities exchanges provided all of the major functions of an exchange. The first important exchange function is to provide a continuous market for the purchase and sale of securities. Second, the exchange provides a mechanism for determining a fair market price for securities. A third function is that of providing reports of all transactions and price quotations of securities traded on the exchange. Fourth, the exchanges impose some degree of standardization regarding the release of financial information by the companies whose securities trade on the exchange. Finally, the exchanges attempt to protect investors who maintain accounts at member brokerage firms. They do this by regulating trading practices and imposing financial standards upon member firms.

Securities Exchanges

The most important stock exchange in the United States since the mid-1800s has been the New York Stock Exchange, often called the "Big Board." The total dollar value of transactions on the NYSE greatly exceeds that of all other U.S. exchanges combined. The second most important exchange is the American Stock Exchange (AMEX), and there are several minor regional exchanges. In addition, some special-purpose exchanges exist, such as the Chicago Board Options Exchange.

The New York Stock Exchange

Brokers of securities began to trade their wares in New York during the late 1700s and early 1800s in the neighborhood of Wall Street. In 1817, they formally organized into the New York Stock and Exchange Board. The members of the exchange began to protect their business by accepting new members, or *seats,* only sparingly. The fortunes of the exchange rose and fell with the changing economic conditions of the nation, but by the late 1800s the exchange was dominant among exchanges located in New York. The New York Stock Exchange adopted its present name in 1863.

In 1869, the exchange combined with the Open Board of Brokers and the Government Bond Department and fixed the total number of seats at 1060. A seat became a valuable piece of property; the only way a new applicant could become a member was to purchase an existing seat from a present member willing to sell. At that time, the NYSE listed 145 stocks and 162 bonds for trading. This number grew steadily through the century, until the total stood at 511 stocks and 1082 bonds in 1914.

As a new prosperity took hold of the nation in the early 1900s, trading in securities—which until then had been mostly the dominion of professional traders, investors, and speculators—began to attract more members of the general public. Speculation increased through the 1920s. Low margin requirements, typically about 10 percent, fueled increases in stock prices. (At that time, the Federal Reserve had no authority to set margin requirements.) The stock market crash of 1929 brought an abrupt halt to this era of securities speculation. Following the crash, the NYSE faced a difficult time in its history. The total market value of NYSE-listed stocks fell from $89.7 billion in 1929 to $15.6 billion in 1932. Government investigations revealed many abuses and unethical business practices such as stock price manipulation, some of which had been perpetuated by NYSE members. These investigations resulted in the enactment of the federal securities laws discussed in the next chapter and in a reorganization of the NYSE.

Although change has come slowly to the NYSE, the institution has maintained its dominance as the main mechanism for the trading of stocks in the United States. By the mid-1980s, more than 2200 different equity issues traded on the NYSE, and the list included practically all of the largest companies in the country. Figure 3–3 shows the growth of the NYSE in volume of shares traded.

The American Stock Exchange

As the NYSE grew to dominance during the early and mid-1800s, a group of brokers began trading securities outdoors in the areas of Hanover and Wall Streets in New York City. At that time in history, informal outdoor markets were not unusual, and this group of traders comprised many brokers excluded from trading on the NYSE by the harsh entrance procedures. This "curb market," as it came to be known, finally took up trading on the sidewalks and street in the area around Broad Street about the turn of the century. The curb market specialized in trading issues that were too small or of insufficient interest to trade on the Big Board, and therefore it did not compete directly for business with the NYSE. For this reason, the NYSE made no

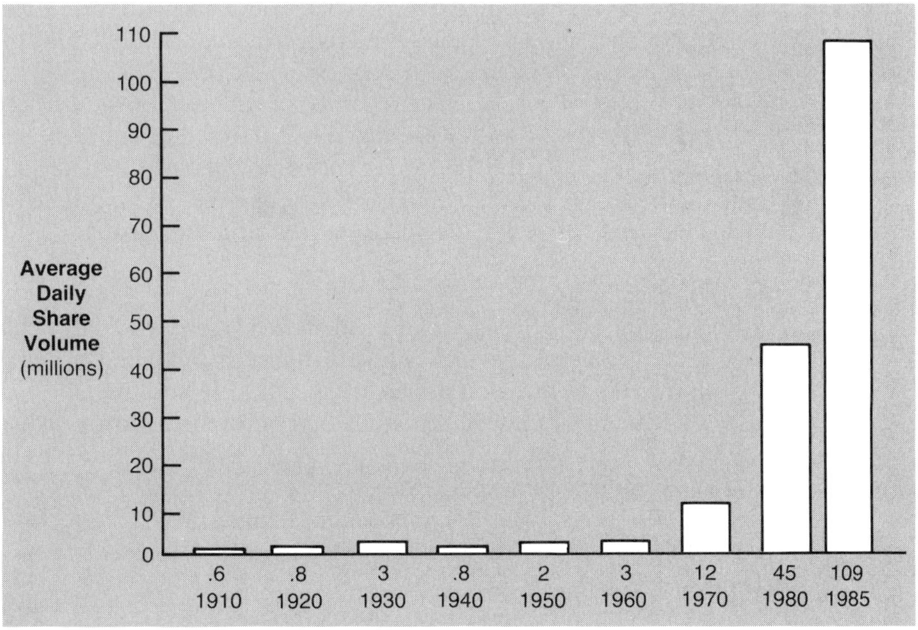

FIGURE 3–3
Growth of NYSE trading volume

attempts to merge with the curb market or to drive it out of business, as it had done with other exchanges located in New York City.

During the early twentieth century, the colorful characteristics and traditions of the curb market developed fully. In 1908 E. E. Mendels organized the New York Curb Market Agency as an association of curb brokers who supported a set of ethical business standards. Several years later the agency formalized itself as an exchange, taking the name of the New York Curb Market. Throughout this period, the members continued to conduct their trading outside. As business increased, the brokers rented offices in the buildings surrounding the trading area on Broad Street. Clerks occupying the offices would take orders for securities over their wire services and transmit the orders to the brokers on the street using a system of shouts and hand signals. The brokers distinguished themselves from others in the crowd by wearing colored hats. Over-excited clerks, leaning a bit too far out the windows, reportedly took the plunge to Broad Street from time to time.

The Curb Market moved indoors in 1921 into its current location on Trinity Place. Brokers of the day maintained that the move indoors was not to escape the elements but rather to promote prestige and respect for the market. Trading boomed throughout the 1920s and had increased thirtyfold by the end of the decade. In 1929, the market's name was changed to the New York Curb Exchange.

As it was for the Big Board, the market crash of 1929 was the beginning of a difficult period for the Curb Exchange. Business did not again flourish for the exchange until the economic prosperity following World War II and the accompanying bull market. In 1953 the exchange voted to change its name to the American Stock Exchange to emphasize its national character and reflect its importance to the American economy.

In 1975, the AMEX began trading in stock options, and the volume of option trading soon became an important source of revenue for the exchange and its members. By the 1980s the AMEX listed about 850 different equity security issues. These AMEX-traded issues generally represent companies that are smaller than those that trade on the NYSE, and the AMEX is often considered to be the exchange where such companies trade until they decide to move to the Big Board.

Regional Exchanges

Regional stock exchanges are the smaller exchanges located throughout the country. They trade smaller issues that attract a regional following but might not generate enough interest to trade on the NYSE or AMEX. In addition, the regional exchanges today trade many issues that also trade on one of the national exchanges. Companies believe that this *dual listing* helps their stock achieve a wider distribution, and the additional trading volume helps the exchange to survive financially. Finally, the regional exchanges, especially the Pacific Stock Exchange, also trade stocks of bankrupt companies that have been removed from listing, or "delisted," by one of the major exchanges.

The number of regional exchanges has dwindled considerably in recent years. While many towns had their own securities exchanges during the early part of the twentieth century, the number had declined to fourteen in 1960, and only six remained by 1985. Table 3–2 summarizes these regional exchanges and their locations.

TABLE 3–2
Regional stock exchanges (registered with the SEC)

Name	*Location*	*Securities Traded*	*1987 Volume (millions of shares)*
Boston Stock Exchange	Boston, MA	Stocks	820
Cincinnati Stock Exchange	Cincinnati, OH	Stocks, bonds	177
Midwest Stock Exchange	Chicago, IL	Stocks	3,429
Pacific Stock Exchange	Los Angeles, CA	Stocks, bonds	
	San Francisco, CA	Stocks, bonds, options	2,034
Philadelphia Stock Exchange	Philadelphia, PA	Stocks, bonds, options	835
Spokane Stock Exchange	Spokane, WA	Stocks	25

Source: *SEC Monthly Statistical Review*, various issues.

Operation of the New York Stock Exchange

Listing Requirements

The NYSE has an interest in providing a market for the shares of publicly held companies. To have its shares traded on the exchange, a company applies for a listing. In considering listing applications, the NYSE gives attention to such qualifications as the extent of national interest in the company, the company's position in its industry, the company's stability, and its prospects for maintaining its growth and relative position. Although there are no strict rules for determining whether a company qualifies for listing, the minimum qualifications presented in Table 3–3 are the guidelines that the exchange usually requires.

TABLE 3–3
NYSE minimum listing requirements

1. Pretax income of $2.5 million in the latest year and $2 million for each of the two preceding years.
2. Net tangible assets of $16 million.
3. Market value of publicly held shares of $16 million.
4. One million shares held by the public.
5. At least 2000 shareholders of 100 or more shares.

Types of Seats

There are 1366 seats on the NYSE, each of which represents ownership in the exchange and may be sold. In addition, the exchange allows some additional members to trade by payment of an annual fee. The members perform different functions depending upon their type of business. The main types of traders on the NYSE are: *commission brokers, floor brokers, specialists,* and *registered competitive market makers.* In addition, there are some members who have only the right to trade bonds. We will consider each of the main types of traders in turn.

Commission Brokers. Most numerous among the NYSE membership are the commission brokers who represent brokerage houses that deal with the public. Approximately one third of the members are commission brokers. Most brokerage firms have a seat on the NYSE, and through these seats they buy and sell securities for the accounts of their customers.

Floor Brokers. Floor brokers are the "broker's brokers" because they deal only with other brokers, mainly commission brokers on the floor of the exchange. They compose somewhat less than one third of the NYSE membership. Floor brokers never deal with the public; rather, they assist commission brokers by making transactions for commission brokers when they have more orders than they can comfortably handle or when they must be absent from the trading floor. Floor brokers receive a fee from commission brokers for this service. Although inflation has long since caused them to raise this fee, the customary charge for many years was two dollars per transaction. For this reason, floor brokers were and still are often called "two-dollar brokers."

Specialists. Slightly less than one third of NYSE members function as specialists. Specialists locate themselves at one of the designated positions called *trading posts* behind one of the horseshoe-shaped counters on the floor of the exchange. Specialists "specialize" in one or more specific stock issues in which they "make a market," taking on the responsibility to maintain and assure a continuous, liquid market in the stock. In doing so, a specialist may function as either a *broker* or a *dealer* in a security transaction.

Acting as a broker, the specialist is simply the agent who matches the buy order with the sell order to execute the transaction. Example 3–4 is a typical transaction in which the specialist has acted as a broker. To keep track of the orders placed by floor brokers or commission brokers, which are not executed immediately, the specialist maintains a book that lists each order to buy and its specific *bid price* along with the sell orders and their *ask prices.* A bid price is the price at which an investor has offered to buy stock, while an ask price represents an investor's sell price. The *current quote* of a stock would be the highest bid price and the lowest ask price that the specialist has on the book. The *spread* is the difference between the bid and the ask prices.

When functioning as dealers, specialists actually buy and sell securities for themselves, acting as principals rather than agents in the deal. In Example 3–4, assuming that there was no better (lower) ask price from another broker, the ask price of 63⅝ could have represented the specialist's own asking price if he or she owned the stock.

The specialist actually owns the stock while acting as a dealer but not when acting as a broker. Exchange rules state, however, that the specialist must first act in the interest of the trading public, and the specialist must always give priority to orders with better or equal prices from the public.

EXAMPLE 3–4

Joan Marker, a floor broker, has an order to buy 100 shares of Ray Tropic Suntan Products, Inc. at its current quote. She approaches the specialist and asks the market for Ray Tropic. "Sixty three to five eighths," the specialist responds, indicating that the current bid is 63 and the ask $63\frac{5}{8}$. (On the NYSE, stocks trade in *points,* or dollars, and eighths of a point.) The $63\frac{5}{8}$ ask quote represents a sell order by an investor; the specialist is holding this order on the book. Ms. Marker then purchases the stock at $63\frac{5}{8}$. The specialist has acted as broker in this transaction.

For services as brokers, specialists receive a commission. When acting as dealers, specialists may make a profit or suffer a loss on a transaction. In fulfilling the charge to maintain an orderly market, specialists may find themselves in the position of having to buy or sell stock as dealers at unfavorable prices to keep the market from rising or falling too rapidly.

It is easy to see that specialists, with this "inside" knowledge of the market and their ability to make transactions for themselves, might use their position to further their personal wealth rather than acting in the public interest. Criticisms of the specialist system generally fall into one of the following categories:

1. The specialist has inside information on buy and sell orders that others do not have and is in a position to take advantage of this information.
2. Specialists have opportunities to manipulate the market.
3. Conflicts of interest between the functions of broker and dealer may encourage specialists to neglect their duties as brokers, even to the extreme of committing fraud or other indiscretions.

To help ensure that specialists act in a responsible manner, rules of the SEC and NYSE govern specialists' activities. For example, specialists may not disclose the contents of their book to anyone except an exchange official. Specialists may not engage in price manipulation or own options on any of their stocks. Specialists may quote from or make transactions for their own accounts (as dealers) only if there are no other orders at equal or better prices; public orders always have precedence over transactions for a specialist's own account. Although irregularities of conduct have occurred in the past, specialists generally conduct their activity honestly, observing professional ethics.

Registered Competitive Market Makers. The final type of exchange participant, the registered competitive market maker (RCMM), is also the least common. Although there are about fifty members registered with the NYSE as RCMMs—about 4 percent of total NYSE membership—only a fraction of these are usually active at any one time. RCMMs, previously called floor traders or registered traders, do not deal as brokers; rather, they buy and sell securities only for their own account, hoping to make money solely from the profit from their transactions, saving on commissions because of their exchange membership. These traders were at one time more common, but restrictions on their activities have made their positions less lucrative. For example, RCMMs may be forced to assist specialists in maintaining an orderly market even if it means an unprofitable trade for the RCMM; in a rapidly changing market, for example, a specialist might require that each RCMM buy (or sell) 100 shares of the specialist's stock to provide a more liquid market.

Operation of the American Stock Exchange

With a few exceptions, operation of the AMEX is quite similar to that of the NYSE. The listing requirements, shown in Table 3–4, are less stringent than those of the NYSE to allow the listing of smaller, growing companies. There are 675 regular members, who divide themselves into the same categories as NYSE members. In addition, there are 200 Option Principal Members who must restrict their trading to options listed on the AMEX. All trading is based on the specialist system, as is the case on the NYSE.

The Over-the-Counter (OTC) Markets

Many securities do not trade on any of the national or regional exchanges. The mechanism for trading these securities lies with the *over-the-counter (OTC) markets.* The OTC markets are a very important part of the secondary markets in the United States, although in other countries most securities trading takes place on an exchange. In the United States, the OTC markets handle almost all of the trading in U.S. and municipal government securities and in money market instruments. In addition, the majority of all corporate bonds and many stock issues trade "over the counter."

The OTC market has no physical location for trading as the exchanges do. Instead, the OTC market is composed of many individual brokerage firms trading OTC securities. These firms conduct their trading by telephone or by other electronic means of communication such as computer networks. The market is composed of participants who act as broker-dealers and those who act only as brokers.

TABLE 3–4
AMEX minimum listing requirements

1. Net income of $400,000 in latest year.
2. Net tangible assets of $4 million.
3. Market value of publicly held shares of $400,000.
4. At least 150,000 shares held by public in 100-share lots or greater.
5. Price of at least $5 per share.

Dealers: The Market Makers

Brokerage firms that act as dealers in OTC trading are the *market makers*. They "make a market," or maintain an active bid and ask for the securities in which they have chosen to deal. The market makers therefore carry an inventory of these securities, increasing the inventory when they buy and cutting the inventory when they sell. The market makers of the OTC markets are similar to specialists on the exchanges.

Every security on the OTC market will have at least one market maker. Thinly traded stocks will probably have only one market maker, while popular issues may have several dozen.

The market maker has two sources of profit. First, the spread is a potential profit source for the market maker, as it is for the specialist. Second, when market makers execute a transaction with an investor, they generally charge a commission on the ask price. When dealing with another broker, market makers generally charge no commission.

The Brokers

If every investor who wanted to buy an OTC stock had to locate and deal with that stock's market maker, the process of OTC investing would indeed be inconvenient and confusing. Fortunately, an investor's usual broker can handle OTC transactions, even if the broker is not a market maker for that particular OTC security. The broker simply contacts the appropriate market maker, buys the OTC stock for the client, and then charges the client an appropriate commission.

The National Association of Securities Dealers (NASD)

The organization that helps bind all of these OTC market participants together and coordinate the operation of the OTC markets is the National Association of Securities Dealers (NASD), which is registered with the SEC as a representative of the OTC market. The NASD has three main functions. First, it provides a voluntary association through which its members cooperate towards such goals as standardizing trade practices and promoting high standards of commerce. Second, by nature of its SEC registration, the NASD is the self-regulatory arm of the OTC market. It adopts, administers, and enforces rules of fair practice and equitable principles of trade for the protection of investors. It also establishes qualifications for and conducts registration of OTC dealers, brokers, and registered representatives. Security sellers who are not affiliated with the NASD must register with the SEC. For this reason, almost all OTC market participants become members of the NASD. Third, the NASD contributes to the smooth functioning of and trading in the OTC markets by providing mechanisms for trading, such as *NASDAQ*.

NASDAQ

The OTC markets took a progressive step in February 1971, when the NASD introduced NASDAQ, the NASD Automated Quotations System. Before that date, when a broker received an order for an OTC stock, the broker had to contact by telephone at least several of that stock's market makers to get the current quote (bid-ask). After deciding upon the best quote for the customer, the broker would contact the chosen market maker again and execute the trade. This process could be long and costly. The introduction of NASDAQ provided for automation of the quotations portion of this process.

The NASDAQ list includes only about 4,000 of the most actively traded OTC issues. The remaining 25,000 or so stock issues—those with mainly local interest and thin markets—still trade in the old way. Although some 30,000 different stocks trade over the counter compared to only about 3000 on the NYSE and AMEX, the total volume and dollar volume on the exchanges are much greater than those of the OTC system because the stocks traded on the exchanges represent the largest corporations with the most active markets.

NASDAQ has three levels of service available to its subscribers, who access the system through computer terminals or special electronic stock quote machines. Level 1 service, available to both members and nonmembers of the NASD, provides subscribers with a representative quote for each security. This quote is the median bid and ask of all market makers for each stock. NASDAQ distributes this level of service through the same organizations that distribute listed stock quotations. Level 2 service, mainly of interest to brokers and active traders, gives current quotes of all market makers in each security. Level 3 service, which is available only to member market makers, provides Level 2 service and, in addition, allows the user to enter and change quotations for which the user is a current market maker.

At the end of each trading day, all market makers report the volume of shares traded for each of their issues. The financial press reports this volume and representative closing quotations for many OTC issues. Keep in mind that these OTC prices represent quotes only; trades did not necessarily take place at these prices.

In April 1982, NASDAQ initiated its National Market System (NMS). Only the most actively traded NASDAQ issues, about 2,500, qualify for the NMS. Because the issues on the NMS are more active, they usually have more market makers than other NASDAQ stocks. The NMS stocks average about seventeen market makers per stock, while the non-NMS NASDAQ stocks average seven to eight. The main difference between the NMS and regular NASDAQ trading is that the market maker must report each NMS trade within ninety seconds of its occurrence, while non-NMS trades are aggregated and reported at the end of each day. The result is that the NASDAQ terminal shows for the NMS issues the daily high, low, and last sales prices and volume in addition to the bid-ask quotes.

Getting quotes on non-NASDAQ OTC stocks is a bit more involved. The National Quotation Bureau, Inc., publishes *The National Daily Quotation Service.* This publication, called the "pink sheets" because it is printed on pink paper, gives quotes and names of market makers with their telephone numbers for thousands of additional OTC securities. To receive current quotes, the broker must call the appropriate market maker.

The Third Market

The *third market* is the term applied to over-the-counter transactions of stocks listed on one of the exchanges. The third market accounted for a higher volume of trading before the advent of negotiated commissions. At that time, OTC brokers dealing in the third market and who were not exchange members offered the only way that investors could trade for a commission less than that posted by the NYSE. Since May Day, however, third market trading has diminished in importance.

The existence of NYSE Rule 390 also has impeded third market trading. Rule 390 forbids NYSE members to trade listed stocks away from the exchange floor. In effect, this gives the NYSE a monopoly over trading in listed issues. In May 1980, the SEC ruled that stocks not listed before 1979 were exempt from Rule 390, but most issues still remain under the rule, and the NYSE steadfastly continues to defend the rule as necessary to the smooth and equitable functioning of the market.

A National Market for Securities

In 1975 Congress mandated the securities industry and the SEC to come up with one integrated system for the trading of securities. This "national market" envisioned by the lawmakers would result in a competitive market of optimum liquidity and efficiency. Although there is still disagreement within the industry and among regulators as to how to structure this national market system, some progress has been made.

One area of progress has been the criticism of NYSE Rule 390. Although the NYSE and others have argued that abolishing Rule 390 would result in an undesirable fragmentation of the securities markets and that all trades should be processed through one exchange, others believe that a system of competing market makers linked electronically can best serve the market system.[5] As mentioned earlier, stocks entering listing since 1979 are exempt from the rule. In May 1982, some of these stocks began trading on an experimental electronic system that allowed OTC brokers and dealers to get quotes and execute trades using a computer terminal.

In March 1976, the *Designated Order Turnaround (DOT) System* began, allowing brokers to transmit orders directly to the trading posts on the NYSE. Originally set up to handle 100-share orders, the system has been expanded to include orders for up to 599 shares. The DOT System executes most orders and confirms them to the originating brokerage firm within two minutes.

The *Intermarket Trading System (ITS)* is an electronic system linking all major exchanges in a nationwide communication and trading network. Through the ITS, brokers can check competing markets for the best prices on different securities.

The INside System is an electronic execution system for executing orders for OTC stocks. In contrast to NASDAQ, which only supplies quotes and trading records, users of INside can place orders and receive confirmations directly on the system. The Midwest Stock Exchange operates the system, and execution prices are based on the current quotes in the NASDAQ system.

To List or Not to List: OTC vs. Exchange Listing

The description of the operation of the OTC market and the exchanges indicates that both appear to provide investors with a ready liquid market for their securities. To be listed on an exchange, companies must pay an annual listing fee. The potential benefits that the exchanges mention when discussing listing are added prestige to the firm and increased marketability of the company's shares. These should result in higher share prices (and lower costs of equity capital) for the firm than it would have without the listing.

One question that has interested market students is: Do the benefits of exchange listing compensate for the additional expense to the company? Several studies have addressed this question.[6] The various studies examined stocks changing from the OTC to the AMEX and NYSE. They typically found that market prices of stocks generally are not higher after listing, their risk levels remain the same after listing, and listing does not affect the stock's liquidity. In general, exchange listing appears to have little or no benefit for the firm and does not lower the firm's cost of capital. As Cooper, Groth, and Avera[7] stated, "The over-the-counter markets appear to offer liquidity that is very competitive with that offered by the New York and American Stock Exchanges, despite the apparent beliefs of some corporate financial officers to the contrary."

In light of these findings, why do companies continue to list their common stocks on the exchanges? The answer to this question is not readily apparent, but many corporate officers must feel that there are psychological and other nonquantifiable benefits that accrue to exchange listing that induce them to pay the costs of listing.

BUYING SECURITIES IN THE SECONDARY MARKET

Specifying Orders for Security Transactions

Orders for security transactions fall into several categories, and investors should be familiar with all of these so that no problems arise in communicating securities orders to the registered representative. Table 3–5 shows the main classifications of orders.

TABLE 3–5
Specifying security orders

I. Type of transaction	IV. Special orders
A. Buy	A. Stop
B. Sell	B. Discretionary
1. Long	C. All or none
2. Short	D. Fill or kill
II. Order size	
A. Round lot	
B. Odd lot	
III. Price	
A. Market	
B. Price limit	
1. Day order	
2. Open or GTC order	
3. Other time limit	

Buy or Sell

The investor must identify each order as either a buy or sell. Orders to purchase are straightforward, but orders to sell fall into two classes: *sell long* and *sell short.* When an investor buys a security outright, the result is a *long position,* and the subsequent sale of that security is selling long. The sale of a security that the investor does *not* own is a *short sale* resulting in a *short position.*

The sale of an asset that one does not own may seem a bit perplexing, but it is not uncommon in the securities markets. Short sales generally account for about 8 percent of the total share volume of trading on the NYSE. Short selling allows the short seller to profit from a fall in the security's price. A Wall Street maxim on how to make profit in the market says, "Buy low and sell high." This is true, and with short selling it does not have to be done in that order. The investor can sell short now at the high price and buy later at the low price, profiting by the difference.

The process of short selling is somewhat more involved than a regular sale. In a short sale, the short seller borrows stock from another investor and then sells it. Table 3–6 gives a simplified example illustrating this process, showing that before the short sale, Ima Landon owned 100 shares of General Shoe Company (GSC). Because she had not planned to sell her GSC shares, Ms. Landon allows Al Shole to borrow her stock to sell short. Lenders of shares may ask for some payment in exchange for the loan of the shares. Table 3–6 also shows the accounts of the parties after Mr. Shole sold the stock to Ann West. Note that although the net number of shares is still 100, both Ms. Landon and Ms. West consider that they own 100 GSC shares. In reality, Ms. West does not even know that the shares she bought were sold short. This lending of stock and "creation" of shares is similar to the way the banking system lends money and increases the money supply. To close out, or *cover,* his short position, Mr. Shole simply buys 100 GSC shares and repays them to Ms. Landon. Although the table shows that he repurchased the shares from Ms. West, any investor's shares of GSC would suffice to repay the loan.

In practice, a broker almost always handles the loan of stock for a shortseller. The brokerage firms lend stock that they hold in street name. If the firm has an insufficient quantity in street accounts of the needed stock, it simply borrows the needed shares from another cooperating brokerage firm. For the investor, then, the process of short selling is little different from selling long because the broker arranges for a loan of stock and handles all of the details.

TABLE 3–6
Illustration of short selling[a]

	Al Shole	*Ima Landon*	*Ann West*
Before short sale		+100 GSC	
After short sale	−100 GSC	+100 GSC	+100 GSC
After covering short		+100 GSC	

[a] + = long position
− = short position

EXHIBIT 3–1

The Short Corner

Allan Ryan, president of the NYSE firm of Allan A. Ryan & Co., was a clever market operator who had gained some notoriety for his success in the technique of squeezing shortsellers. Ryan invested in many areas of the economy, but one of his biggest investments was in the Stutz Motor Car Company of America, Inc., makers of the Stutz Bearcat. Ryan had accumulated a controlling interest and became the company's president in 1916. The company prospered and Ryan predicted a profit of around $5 million for 1920.

Stutz stock began rising in early 1920, from about 100 at the beginning of the year to 134 on February 2. At this point, a group of market operators who thought Stutz stock was too high formed a bear pool and began selling the stock short to force the price down. (There was no uptick rule at that time.) A successful bear raid on the stock would drive the price down to a point so low that the price of the stock would collapse, at which time the shortsellers would buy back the stock and make a considerable profit.

Ryan, however, was a bull operator and quite experienced at countering bear raids. His strategy was to buy all of the Stutz stock offered for sale until he had purchased virtually all of the supply of Stutz stock, even lending stock to the shortsellers and then buying it back from them. At this point he could then squeeze the shortsellers by demanding that they replace their short stock. Since Ryan would control the supply of stock, he could then name his price and the unsuccessful bear raiders would have to pay up.

Initially, the shortsellers drove Stutz down to about 100 by early March, but by the morning of March 24, Stutz had climbed to 245. It closed at 282 that day, and shot up to 391 one week later. By this time, Ryan had purchased virtually all of Stutz stock and owned most of the stock the bear raiders had been selling short. Ryan had successfully maneuvered the bears into a short corner. Normally, the losers in such a game would take their losses and move on to the next challenge. This time, however, Ryan had tackled a bear pool that included some of the exchange's leading members.

On the last day of March, the NYSE's Business Conduct Committee summoned Ryan to explain the recent rise in Stutz stock. Although he knew that the reason was the short corner, Ryan diplomatically attributed the increase to a shortage of supply of the stock. Ryan did acknowledge that some people might have shorted the stock, and said he would be happy to sell them shares to fulfill their short contracts at $750 per share. Because this would mean a significant loss to the bear pool, its members were not pleased. That afternoon the Law Committee joined in and threatened to suspend Stutz stock from trading. Ryan countered that if the exchange did that, his price would rise to $1000 per share. Meanwhile, even though the short-

To prevent short selling from being used excessively to manipulate stock prices downward (see Exhibit 3–1), some restrictions have been placed on short selling. First, the shortseller usually does not have access to the proceeds of the sale. The broker will hold the funds in escrow until the shortseller closes the position. Also, the shortseller has to deposit additional funds with the broker equal to the initial margin requirement times the short sale price. Although often called "margin," these additional funds actually serve as a security deposit for the broker, who charges no margin interest since there is no margin loan. The second restriction is that a short sale must occur on an *up tick (plus tick)* or a *zero-plus tick*. An up tick is the sale of a security at a price higher than the previous price, and a zero-plus tick represents the sale at the same price as a previous trade when the previous trade was an up tick. The sale of stock at a price lower than the previous trade price results in a *down tick (minus tick)*. The SEC instituted the up tick rule in 1938 to discourage the use of short sales to drive the price of a stock down. (Specialists, in their capacity as market makers, are exempt from the up tick rule.)

sellers knew they were cornered, some of them continued to borrow stock from Ryan to sell short. At the close of business that day, the exchange suspended trading in Stutz stock.

Allan Ryan was now in trouble. Even though he had successfully cornered the shorts, he had borrowed large sums of money to finance his purchases. However, he was comforted by the tradition that a short sale is an implied contract between lender and shortseller, and the lender can call the stock back on demand at any time. If the shortseller refuses, the lender has the right to "buy it in"—buy it back on behalf of the shortseller and charge the shortseller for the cost.

Unfortunately, Ryan did not anticipate the exchange's next move. On April 5, the Law Committee announced that it considered Ryan's contracts void. By so doing, the exchange was repudiating the business principles upon which its business was founded. After several days, Ryan countered with a public statement to the press, releasing a list of nine prominent exchange members who were short Stutz stock. He also resigned his seat on the exchange. The exchange, becoming nervous because of negative publicity from the event and the possibility of legislative investigation, recanted its stance on the contracts and formed a mediation committee to settle the matter.

Ryan, who was becoming impatient, announced that if no settlement were reached by April 24, he would buy in all of the outstanding short shares owed him. Because trading had been suspended on the NYSE, Ryan would buy them in on the outdoor Curb Market, the forerunner of the American Stock Exchange. At several minutes before the 10 a.m. deadline on the morning of April 24, Ryan's office announced that a settlement had been reached at $550 per share, representing a profit of at least $1 million for Ryan.

Ryan's victory was not quite as sweet as it may first have seemed. Bank loans financing his purchases were coming due, and his profit from the short corner was not nearly enough to pay them off. Stutz stock, still not trading on the NYSE, was not very marketable. The exchange had not accepted his resignation, and the Governing Committee tried him and found him guilty of conduct inconsistent with equitable principles of trade. As summer came, the banks were continuing to press for repayment of the loans. Other stocks that Allan Ryan owned strangely began to fall in value also.

Ultimately the banks closed in, and in July 1922 Ryan filed for bankruptcy, listing assets of $644,000 against total debts of more than $32 million. Stutz had taken a dive over the past two years and then stood at about $5 per share on the Curb. Ryan's 135,000 shares were sold at public auction the next month for $20 per share. Stutz's new owners were not very adept at running an automobile company, and the company finally went broke in 1938.

Several disadvantages of short selling tend to discourage its use, especially among less sophisticated investors. First, a short position represents limited profit potential but theoretically unlimited loss. A Wall Street saying goes, "Ask not how low your stock can go, it can only go to zero." Because a stock can only fall to zero, the most profit the shortseller can make is equal to the short sale price of the stock. However, since there is no limit on the upside, the price that the shortseller might have to pay to replace the short stock could be two, three, or more times the short sale price. Second, the borrower (shortseller) has to *pay* dividends declared by the company for the stock. Recall that after the short sale in Table 3–6, both Ms. Landon and Ms. West considered that they owned 100 GSC shares. Because Ms. Landon lent the stock to Al Shole, who sold it to Ms. West, Ms. West would be the registered owner and would receive the dividend from the company. The broker would debit Mr. Shole's brokerage account for the dividend and credit it to Ms. Landon. Third, the lender has the right to *call* the stock loan at any time, demanding repayment. Such a situation might force the shortseller to cover the short position at an unfavorable time. In practice, this almost never occurs because the broker can usually locate additional share loans from other investors.

Size of the Order

The order must specify the number of shares, bonds, options, and so forth. All transactions on the exchange are *round lots*, or multiples of 100 shares. Any portion of an order less than 100 shares is an *odd lot,* although bonds and some thinly traded preferred stocks trade in round lots of ten. Because only round lots trade on the exchange floor, odd lots must be handled differently. One way is for the broker to pool the odd lot orders for a security until the quantity reaches a round lot, execute the round lot, and divide the shares among the odd lot customers. A second way is for the specialist (on an exchange) or market maker (OTC) to supply the odd lot. Another method available on NYSE trades is to route the order through the DOT System.

There are two disadvantages of trading odd lots. First is the *odd lot differential.* The price basis for an odd lot trade is the last round lot trade. To this price, the party executing the odd lot may add one eighth of a point (or subtract one eighth on a sale) as the odd lot differential to compensate for the extra paperwork involved. For example, if the last round lot traded for 47¾, the customer buying thirty-eight shares would pay 47⅞. The odd lot differential, once required by the NYSE and AMEX, is now an optional charge. A second disadvantage is that the commission on a per share basis is higher for odd lots than for round lots. The odd lot trader, therefore, pays a higher percentage commission in addition to a higher price for the stock.

Price and Time Limits

It is possible to classify orders by the price and the time allowed for execution.

Market Orders. The *market order* is an order to make the transaction at the "best possible price" as soon as possible. For buyers, the best price will be the lowest quoted price, while the best price for a seller will be the highest quote.

Market orders are the most common type of order. Their advantages are speed and certainty of execution. The disadvantage is that the investor is a price taker, although with the liquidity present in today's securities markets, investors can usually estimate the execution price of a market order within about a quarter of a point.

Limit Orders. In a *limit order* the trader specifies the "worst" price at which the transaction should take place. For example, suppose an investor wants to purchase Tex-matic Corp., which has been fluctuating between $35 and $40, but the investor wishes to pay no more than $38 for the stock. The "worst," or highest (in the case of the buyer), price that the investor is willing to pay is $38, so he places a limit order to buy at $38. If the broker can locate the stock for $38, the purchase will be made. Of course, if the stock is available for less than $38, the transaction will occur at this lower, more favorable price.

The advantage of the limit order is that the investor knows in advance the highest price he will pay (if buying) or the lowest price he will receive (if selling) for the security. The disadvantage is that the transaction may never occur. Even if the price of the security is very close (one eighth of a point away from the limit price), the order will not be executed until the stock reaches the limit.

Because a limit order may not be executed immediately, the investor must specify the length of time the order is to remain active. This may be the remainder of the trading day (a *day order*), the week, or the month. A limit order with no specific expiration date is an *open order,* also called a *good-til-canceled (GTC) order,* although NYSE Rule 123 requires reconfirmation of these orders at a minimum of six-month intervals.

Special Orders

Stop Orders. *Stop orders* are "inactive" market orders, which become active when the stock reaches or passes a prespecified *stop price.* There are two types of stop orders: the *stop-loss order,* a stop order to sell at the market when the stock reaches or passes the stop price, and the *stop-buy order,* which directs the broker to purchase the stock at market when the stock reaches the stop price.

Investors typically use stop-loss orders either to protect an existing profit or to prevent or reduce a loss. For example, suppose you purchased Kiddo Day Care Center stock for $48 and decided that if it fell to $43 you wanted to take your losses and get out. Instead of having to watch the stock market all day, checking on Kiddo's price, you can place a stop-loss order with your broker with a stop at $43. As long as Kiddo's price remains above $43, your stop-loss order will not be executed, but if Kiddo does trade at $43 or below, your stop order immediately becomes a market order to sell. Therefore, the stop order provides no guarantee at what price the transaction will actually occur—at, somewhat below, or even (possible but unlikely) above the stop price.

Investors issue stop-buy orders to take immediate advantage of an upward trend by purchasing the stock when it begins moving upward. Stop-buy orders can also protect profit or reduce losses for short positions.

Stop orders are not the same as limit orders, and there are several differences between them. First, limit orders never become market orders. Even if the stock trades at the limit, the limit order *may not* actually be executed, but if the stop order's stop price is reached, the execution of the stop order *will* follow. Second, the limit order's worst price is certain, while the stop order's is not. Third, for a stop-loss order to sell, the stop price is always *below* the current market price, while for a limit order to sell the limit price is always *above* the current market price. The stop on a stop-buy is always above current market, and a limit buy order's limit price is below market.

An investor who wants to place a stop order but also wants to be certain of the price can issue a *stop-limit order,* which becomes a limit order when the stock reaches the stop price. However, investors rarely use stop-limit orders and should do so with caution because in a rapidly changing market, the market price may pass the limit before the order is executed.

Other Special Orders. There are many other miscellaneous kinds of orders. Those mentioned here are some of the most commonly used. A *discretionary order* gives the account executive a certain amount of discretion in filling the order. For example, if you are going on vacation, you might instruct your broker to sell your Kiddo Day Care Center stock if it looks as though the market for Kiddo is headed downward.

Normally, the broker will fill a portion of a limit order if the entire amount is not available at the limit price. An *all-or-none order* instructs the broker to fill the entire order or none of it. The customer who places a *fill-or-kill order* wants it executed immediately at the limit or canceled.

Execution of an Order

Figure 3–4 traces the path of a typical order for a stock or other security. The investor initiates the process by placing the order with an account executive at a brokerage

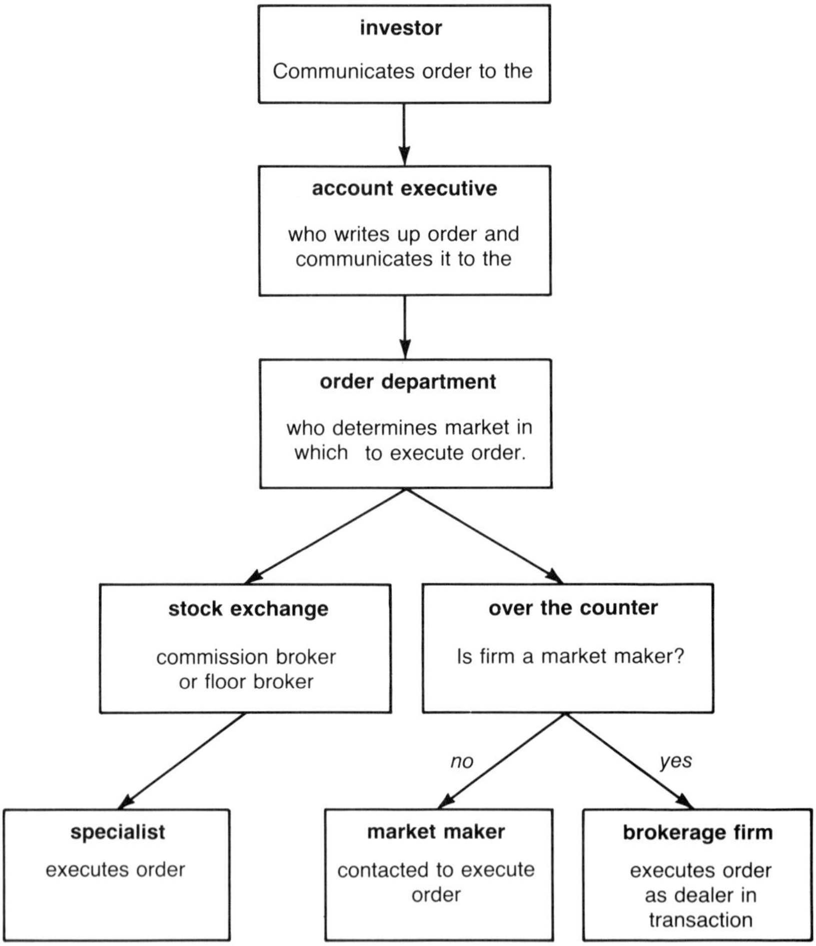

FIGURE 3–4
Execution sequence of a typical stock order

firm. The account executive writes all of the information required to place the order on an order slip, including the *stock symbol.* Stock symbols are letters that identify each issue of common stock; exchange-listed stocks have one to three letters, while OTC stocks have four or five. (These symbols are *not* the same as the abbreviations used in the financial press to report daily stock prices.) Some of these symbols are easy to remember. International Business Machines is IBM, Exxon is XON, but others are not so obvious. For example, Texas Instruments is TXN (not TI). Other companies have adopted symbols describing their business. For example, Anheuser-Busch is BUD; Comdata Network, a money transfer company, uses CASH; and 1 Potato 2, Inc., is SPUD. Account executives use small computer terminals or quote machines to enter these stock symbols to receive news reports and current quotes on the stocks.

The account executive gives the completed order to a clerk, who wires it to the firm's order desk. The order desk then determines whether the security is traded OTC or through an exchange. If it is exchange-traded, the order desk then communicates the order to the exchange floor. The firm's representative either takes the order to the appropriate specialist or finds a floor broker to handle the order. After the specialist executes the order, the confirmation travels back up the system until the investor receives word of the trade. (An order for NYSE stock of 599 or fewer shares may bypass the floor and go directly to the specialist via the DOT System.)

If the order is for an OTC security, the OTC trading department checks to see who the market makers are. If the firm is a market maker for the security, it completes the trade. Otherwise, the OTC trader contacts a market maker to execute the transaction. Again, the confirmation of the order travels up the system.

The investor must pay for all securities purchased and must deliver all securities sold to the broker on or before the *settlement date.* For stocks and bonds, the settlement date is five business days (normally one week unless there is an intervening holiday) after the transaction date. The settlement date for options is the day following the trade. After selling a stock or bond, if the investor has possession of the certificate rather than keeping it in street name in the brokerage account, the properly endorsed security must be delivered to the brokerage firm by the settlement date. This would not apply to the sale of options because all options are normally kept in brokerage firm accounts.

SUMMARY

Investment banking firms are important principals in the primary securities markets where they underwrite and sell to the public new issues of corporate and government securities. Over-the-counter markets and stock exchanges are secondary financial markets where stocks, bonds, and other financial securities continue to trade among investors. Securities brokerage firms, which often are also investment banking firms, provide investors in these secondary markets with services such as securities transactions, account maintenance, margin credit, and investment counsel.

Margin is the practice of borrowing a portion of the purchase price of a security. The effect of margin is to increase both the expected return and the risk of an investment. The Federal Reserve Board sets the initial margin requirement, the minimum amount of money that an investor must deposit with a broker to purchase stock on margin.

Stock exchanges are locations where members trade securities among themselves and for outside clients. The New York Stock Exchange is the largest exchange in the United States, followed by the American Stock Exchange. The NYSE has four types of members, classified according to their function: commission brokers, floor brokers, specialists, and registered competitive market makers. Securities not traded on an exchange trade in the over-the-counter market, where there is no one location for security trading, but rather a system of market makers and brokers who trade using the telephone or computerized trading networks.

Investors may buy and sell securities by placing market orders, which are orders to be executed at the best current price, or limit orders, which specify a certain price limit acceptable to the investor. Normally, these orders are day orders and are valid only for the rest of the trading day. However, an investor may either specify another time period during which the order is valid or may issue a good-till-canceled or open order. Investors can also issue stop-loss orders to sell stock when it falls to a certain price, thereby protecting a profit position or limiting losses.

Short selling is the practice of selling a security that the investor does not own. Shortsellers profit from a fall in the security's price and must always sell short on an up tick.

IMPORTANT TERMS

account executive
all-or-none order
ask price
bid price
call loan
cash account
commission broker
day order
Designated Order Turnaround (DOT) System
discount brokerage firm
discretionary account
discretionary order
down tick (minus tick)
dual listing
due diligence meeting
fill-or-kill order
floor broker
full-service brokerage firm
GTC order
initial margin requirement
Intermarket Trading System (ITS)
leverage
limit order
long position
maintenance margin requirement
margin
margin account
margin call
mark-to-market
market maker
market order
NASDAQ
odd lot
odd lot differential
open order
over-the-counter market
pegged price
point
preliminary prospectus
price pegging
private placement

prospectus
public placement
red herring
registered competitive market maker
registered representative
round lot
seats
settlement date
short position
specialist
spread
stock exchange
stock symbol
stop-buy order
stop-limit order
stop-loss order
stop price
street name
subscribe to an issue
third market
underwriting
underwriting agreement
underwriting syndicate
upset price
up tick (plus tick)
zero-plus tick

QUESTIONS AND PROBLEMS

1. Distinguish between public and private placements. When might a corporation prefer a private placement? When might a public placement be more advantageous?
2. Why might an issuer of a new security choose a negotiated underwriting over some other method (such as a direct sale to the public).
3. Give arguments for and against using a discount brokerage firm as opposed to a full-service firm.
4. Why would a stockholder prefer to leave stock in street name? Why would the brokerage firm also prefer this?
5. What chain of events might result from the Federal Reserve's raising the initial margin requirement? From the NYSE's raising the maintenance requirement?
6. Compare and contrast the market environments fostered by the exchanges and by the OTC markets. How do the functions of the NYSE specialists differ from those of the OTC market makers?
7. Trading in the third market has decreased since the advent of negotiated commissions. Why do you think this has occurred?
8. Explain how short selling works. What are its advantages and disadvantages? Do you think that short selling opportunities contribute to or detract from the smooth functioning of the market?
9. If the initial margin requirement is 50%, how much cash would you need to deposit into a margin account to purchase 200 shares of Macho Spas, Inc., at $24? What would be the equity in the account? The loan balance?
10. Assume the market falls, and Macho Spas, Inc., (see Problem 9) begins to drop in price. If the maintenance margin requirement is 30%, at what price will you receive a margin call?
11. Let the initial margin requirement for stocks equal 60%; for corporate bonds, 30%; for government bonds, 20%; and for convertible bonds, 45%. How much of each security can an investor with $5000 buy on margin?
12. If you deposit 500 shares of Micro Software House Corp. (trading at $8) into a margin account, how much cash could you borrow from your account?
13. The current quote on Martin Harkware Supply, Inc., is 34½ to ⅞. If you place a market order to buy 100 shares, what is the most likely price at which you will receive the stock? Why?

14. Following a trade at 27½, Bullock Dozer Co. trades at (1) 27¼; (2) 27; (3) 27⅛; (4) 27⅛; (5) 27¼; (6) 27⅛. Which trade numbers could have been short sales, based on the up-tick rule? Which could not have been short sales?
15. Identify the types of seats on the New York Stock Exchange. What are the functions of each type?
16. What are the main services provided by the NASD for the OTC markets?

NOTES

1. The term *corporation* as used in this book means any issuer of a security. Other entities, such as government authorities, also issue securities, but because corporations are the largest group of issuers, this book will use the terms *corporation, company,* or *firm* for the sake of brevity.
2. For example, see Roger G. Ibbotson (1975), "Price Performance of Common Stock New Issues," *Journal of Financial Economics,* 2 (September), 235–272.
3. J. I. Bogen and H. E. Kroos (1960), *Security Credit: Its Economic Role and Regulation,* Englewood Cliffs: Prentice-Hall.
4. Dudley G. Luckett (1982), "On the Effectiveness of the Federal Reserve's Margin Requirement," *Journal of Finance,* 37 (June), 783–795.
5. For an example of a study supporting the exchanges' viewpoint, see Kalman J. Cohen, Steven F. Maier, Robert A. Schwartz, and David K. Whitcomb (1982), "An Analysis of the Economic Justification for Consolidation in a Secondary Security Market," *Journal of Banking and Finance,* 6, 117–136. For opposing arguments, see Hans R. Stoll (1982), "Comments: 'An Analysis of the Economic Justification for Consolidation in a Security Market' by Kalman J. Cohen et al.," *Journal of Banking and Finance,* 6, 137–140.
6. For examples of these studies, see the following: H. Kent Baker and James Spitzfaden (1982), "The Impact of Exchange Listing on the Cost of Equity Capital," *Financial Review,* 17 (September), 128–141; Frank J. Fabozzi (1981), "Does Listing on the Amex Increase the Market Value of Equity?," *Financial Management,* 10 (Spring), 43–50; and Donald R. Fraser and John C. Groth (1983), *Listing and the Liquidity of Bank Stocks,* College Station: Texas A & M University.
7. S. Kerry Cooper, John C. Groth, and William E. Avera (1983), *Liquidity, Exchange Listing, and Common Stock Performance,* College Station: Texas A & M University.

SELECTED REFERENCES

Baker, H. Kent, and James Spitzfaden (1982). "The Impact of Exchange Listing on the Cost of Equity Capital." *Financial Review,* 17 (September), 128–141.

Blum, Gerald A., and Wilbur G. Lewellen (1983). "Negotiated Brokerage Commissions and the Individual Investor." *Journal of Financial and Quantitative Analysis,* 18 (September), 331–343.

Bogen, J. I., and H. E. Kroos (1960). *Security Credit: Its Economic Role and Regulation.* Englewood Cliffs: Prentice-Hall.

Bosshardt, Donald I. (1984). "Equity Clienteles, Short-Sale Restrictions, and the Miller Equilibrium." *Financial Review,* 19 (May), 240–250.

Cohen, Kalman J., Steven F. Maier, Robert A. Schwartz, and David K. Whitcomb (1982). "An Analysis of the Economic Justification for Consolidation in a Secondary Security Market." *Journal of Banking and Finance,* 6, 117–136.

Cooper, S. Kerry, John C. Groth, and William E. Avera (1983). *Liquidity, Exchange Listing, and Common Stock Performance.* College Station: Texas A & M University.

Fabozzi, Frank J. (1981). "Does Listing on the Amex Increase the Market Value of Equity?" *Financial Management,* 10 (Spring), 43–50.

Fabozzi, Frank J., and R. A. Hershkoff (1979). "The Effect of the Decision to List on a Stock's Systematic Risk." *Review of Business and Economic Research,* 15 (Spring), 77–82.

Fraser, Donald R., and John C. Groth (1983). *Listing and the Liquidity of Bank Stocks.* College Station: Texas A & M University.

Ibbotson, Roger G. (1975). "Price Performance of Common Stock New Issues." *Journal of Financial Economics,* 2 (September), 235–272.

Lechner, Alan B., and David J. Londoner (1976). "Brokerage Profits under the Pressure of Negotiated Commissions." *Financial Analysts Journal,* 32 (January), 12–17, 31.

Luckett, Dudley G. (1982). "On the Effectiveness of the Federal Reserve's Margin Requirement." *Journal of Finance,* 37 (June), 783–795.

National Association of Securities Dealers (1982). *The Financial Services Industry of Tomorrow.* Washington: Author.

Peterson, David R., and Donald M. Waldman (1984). "A Model of Heterogeneous Expectations as a Determinant of Short Sales." *Journal of Financial Research,* 7 (Spring), 1–16.

Schreiner, J., and K. Smith (1980). "The Impact of Mayday on Diversification Costs." *Journal of Portfolio Management,* 6 (Summer), 28–36.

Stoll, Hans R. (1982). "Comments: 'An Analysis of the Economic Justification for Consolidation in a Secondary Market' by Kalman J. Cohen et al." *Journal of Banking and Finance,* 6, 137–140.

Teweles, Richard J., and Edward S. Bradley (1982). *The Stock Market.* New York: John Wiley & Sons.

Yagil, Joseph (1982). "Margin Trading: A Risk-Return Analysis." *Journal of Business Finance and Accounting,* 9 (Winter), 483–487.

Zarb, Frank J., and Gabriel T. Kerekes (eds.) (1970). *The Stock Market Handbook.* Homewood, IL: Dow Jones-Irwin.

CHAPTER 4

Securities Regulation and Taxation

The government affects the securities markets through two main channels: regulation and taxation. Regulation of the securities markets occurs at both the federal and the state levels, although the authority of the federal government extends further than most state legislation. The effects of federal and state laws have helped shape the structure, operation, and trading activity of both the primary and secondary securities markets. In addition, federal and state taxation has an effect on the securities markets. Rather than affecting the structure of the markets, taxation tends to show its presence by altering after-tax risk and returns on the various types of investments. The result of this is to encourage or discourage different investments for different investors, depending upon their tax brackets. The government can use tax policy to attempt to achieve certain national goals. For example, when the public utilities industry began to have difficulty raising capital and faced high costs of equity capital, Congress included in the tax law a provision allowing investors to reinvest dividends from a public utility company back into the same company and receive a tax break by deferring the tax on the dividend. The purpose of the provision was to encourage investment in the utility industry.

REGULATION OF SECURITIES MARKETS

Before 1933, no significant federal legislation existed that governed the securities markets. Regulation lay in the hands of the various state laws, most of which were nonexistent or weak, and in the self-regulatory rules of trade organizations, chiefly the New York Stock Exchange. Although the self-regulatory rules of the NYSE were well intentioned, they fell short of providing the supervision that the markets needed. Also, as is often the case in self-regulation, conflicts of interest often occurred that resulted in abuses of the system. The stock market crash of 1929 and the Great Depression that followed marked the beginning of a new era of legislation and regulation of the markets.

Following the market crash, investigations revealed to the public some of the shortcomings and abuses of the system. The following are some examples of the types of abuses that occurred during the prelegislation period.

Market operators, often including NYSE members, would form *pools* to manipulate the price of a stock. Their techniques often included driving the price of a stock down by selling short, to the point of complete collapse in the stock's price and financial failure of the company. Or they might buy the stock, causing its price to rise. As the unsuspecting public would jump on the bandwagon and begin buying the stock, the pool would be selling out. Ultimately the speculative bubble would burst, and the stock's price would tumble down, but usually not before the pool had successfully sold out its position. The attitude of most market participants of the time was *laissez faire;* they believed that anything was fair game in the market. Unfortunately, they did not realize that unless the investing public has confidence that it is being treated equitably in the financial markets, the public will eventually forsake the market, resulting in a financial crisis.

Sometimes manipulators would try to *corner the market,* that is, buy up a security until they controlled its price. Or they could try a *short corner,* buying up shares that other investors (or manipulators) were selling short until they had control of the supply of shares. At this point they would put a *short squeeze* on the shortsellers by forcing them to buy back the shorted shares at very high prices.

One tool that stock manipulators often used to create the illusion of heavy trading activity in a stock was the *wash sale,* essentially no sale at all. A wash sale can occur, for example, when one manipulator sells stock to another, who then turns around and sells it back to the first manipulator. If these prices were at an increase from the previous prices of the stock, it would appear that the stock was increasing in price when in reality both manipulators' positions were where they were before, and no independent sale really occurred.

Sometimes stock brokers would churn an account. *Churning* occurs when a broker who has discretion over an account buys and sells too often, generating an excessive amount of commissions. Even if a broker does not have discretion over an account, too many "hot tips" or recommendations to the client to buy or sell can constitute churning.

Another area of abuse was the excessive use of margin for financing security purchases. No governmental agency at that time had the authority to set margin requirements, and individual brokerage firms usually set their margin requirement very low, typically about 10 percent. Both public traders and the securities industry were guilty of overextending their financial resources by borrowing too much money on margin to finance their security purchases. With margin requirements so low, only a slight drop in security prices would mean a margin call. As a result, margin calls generated by the fall in stock prices beginning in late 1929 forced investors to sell, thereby causing more downward pressure on stock prices and more margin calls. The Dow Jones Industrial Average fell 89 percent from its high in 1929 to its low in 1933.

Market and corporate insiders abused their positions of public faith by taking security positions on the basis of their knowledge of inside information. Corporate officers sometimes withheld news from the public until they could establish advantageous positions in the market. At the extreme, there were even cases of fraud and deceit by the issuance of false or misleading statements designed to manipulate security prices.

Federal Legislation

As long as economic prosperity and increasing stock prices continued, complaints about abuses and fraudulent practices in the markets were seldom advanced and fell on deaf ears. Although several members of Congress introduced legislation during the early twentieth century seeking greater financial disclosure requirements for publicly traded companies, none of these proposed acts ever advanced out of committee in either the House or the Senate. The attitude of the government, the markets, and even much of the public seemed to be, "If it works, why try to fix it?"

Following the 1929 market crash and the onset of the 1930s depression came the awareness that something indeed was wrong with the system. The Senate passed a resolution in March 1932 directing the Banking and Currency Committee to investigate the securities industry. Congress began conducting investigations into the securities markets and particularly into the operation of the NYSE during following months. The extent of the potential for conflicts of interest, fraud, and abuse that existed within the exchange became public information. Although most exchange business had been carried out admirably, a significant portion raised a number of questions. The investigation reached even the highest levels, as evidenced by the resignation of Richard Whitney, then head of the NYSE.

One of the congressional investigations addressing the 1920s period reported that

> some 50 billions of new securities were floated in the United States. Fully half or $25,000,000,000 worth of securities during this period have been proved to be worthless.
>
> These cold figures spell tragedy in the lives of thousands of individuals who invested their life savings, accumulated after years of effort, in these worthless securities. The flotation of such a mass of essentially fraudulent securities was made possible because of the complete abandonment by many underwriters and dealers in securities of those standards of fair, honest, and prudent dealing that should be basic to the encouragement of investment in any enterprise.
>
> Alluring promises of easy wealth were freely made with little or no attempt to bring to the investor's attention those facts essential to estimating the worth of any security. High pressure salesmanship rather than careful counsel was the rule in this most dangerous of enterprises.[1]

As a result of these investigations, Congress began a series of legislation in 1933 that initiated a period of stricter federal regulation and supervision of the financial markets.

Glass-Steagall Act of 1933

The banking act of 1933, also called the Glass-Steagall Act after its sponsors Rep. Henry Bascom Steagall and Sen. Carter Glass, prohibited commercial banks from activities in the securities markets. The act specifically forbade the investment banking functions that a number of large banks conducted in addition to their commercial banking activities. Although the act prohibited underwriting corporate stocks and bonds, it did allow banks to continue their activity in the primary market for certain government and municipal bond issues.

Many U.S. banks failed during the Great Depression, and the Glass-Steagall Act's purpose was to remove some of the risk to which commercial banks were exposed. After passage of the act, banks that engaged in both investment banking and commercial banking activities had to choose one or the other or split into two separate, unrelated institutions—as did the House of Morgan, which became the Morgan Guaranty Bank and Trust and the investment banking firm of Morgan-Stanley.

Securities Act of 1933

The Securities Act of 1933, also called the "truth in securities" law, was primarily legislation requiring disclosure of pertinent financial information about new security issues being offered to the public. The main target of the act was the primary markets; the act does not deal with the trading of existing securities in the secondary markets.

The 1933 act provided that companies issuing new securities for public sale must file a registration statement and must furnish investors a prospectus giving the financial details of the company and of the specific new issue. The purpose of the act was not to judge the merits of a security, but rather to ensure that the investing public has adequate and truthful information about the company, upon which to base informed investment decisions. The prospectus also contains the actual offering price of the security.

Certain types of security issues are exempt from registration. Naturally, a private offering of a security to a limited number of people is not a public issue and is therefore exempt. If a company that has shares traded publicly issues additional shares in a private offering, then these unregistered shares cannot be sold in the secondary market. Such stock is called *letter stock* because the buyer signs a letter stating that the stock will not be resold to the public for a certain time period, usually at least two years. The act also exempts issues of federal, state, and municipal government authorities. In addition, an issue offered only to residents of one state may possibly be exempt if certain conditions are met.

Securities Exchange Act of 1934

Because it provided no regulation of the secondary markets, the Securities Act of 1933 fell short of the reforms that Congress had in mind. No specific governmental agency had the power to enforce the provisions of the 1933 act, and the act's limitations quickly became clear. In response, Congress passed the Securities Exchange Act the following year. In general, it contains the authority needed to provide for regulation and supervision of securities trading on all the major exchanges.

Provisions of the Act. The 1934 act contains provisions in six main areas.

1. It created the Securities and Exchange Commission (SEC) to administer and enforce federal securities legislation.
2. The 1934 act requires that all organized securities exchanges doing significant national business register with the SEC. In effect, this includes virtually all of the national and regional exchanges except the smallest exchanges doing mostly a local business. The act requires the exchanges to adopt certain rules for disciplining members who do not obey the letter or spirit of the law, and it requires disclosure from the exchanges to ensure that they carry out these rules. The SEC has broad powers, including intervention into running the exchange, to force compliance with the law.
3. It requires that all companies whose securities trade on the exchanges register with the SEC. This registration requires disclosure similar to but not as detailed as that required in a prospectus by the 1933 act. In addition to initial registration, companies must file periodic reports with the SEC disclosing financial information and other materially important facts. Chapter 5 describes these reports and their contents. Like the 1933 act, the 1934 act does not guarantee the accuracy of the companies' financial reports, but it does give the SEC power to file suit against or suspend the trading in securities of companies that repeatedly fail to make timely and accurate reports.
4. The 1934 act contains provisions designed to protect investors and to provide for a fair securities market. In general, it prohibits security price manipulation and trading by insiders on information not available to the public. To enforce this, the law requires all investors holding more than 5 percent of a company's stock and all corporate officers and directors to report their holdings of that company and any changes in their holdings to the SEC and to the exchanges where the company's stock trades. The company may recover any short-term trading profits or any gains from short sales that these insiders make. Often, however, illegal trading by insiders is difficult to trace. For every case that makes the headlines, there may be many that have never been discovered. (See Exhibit 4–1.)
5. The Securities Exchange Act requires disclosure of other information, in two areas. First, the SEC has the authority to regulate *proxy solicitation* for elections of the board and votes on other corporate matters. Solicitation of a proxy occurs when some party asks stockholders to sign over their right to vote their shares in the corporate election. This is a common strategy used by those trying to maintain or gain control of the corporation. The purpose of the proxy rule is to force the solicitors to give investors enough information to make an informed decision about their vote. The second area deals with disclosure of *tender offers,* offers to purchase the shares of a corporation or to exchange other securities for them. Under

The Texas Gulf Sulphur Case

Although the Securities Exchange Act and rules of the SEC prohibit insiders from benefiting from their inside information on short-term trades, the agency enforced the law only in blatant cases from its inception in 1934 until the early 1960s. Some people even argued that the laxity of the SEC was due to the attitude that insider trading, regardless of how contrary it may be to the concept of fair play, was necessary to the smooth functioning of the market. However, the landmark Texas Gulf Sulphur case signaled a broader interpretation of the law and rules against insider trading and introduced an era of increased SEC surveillance of insider activity.

It began in 1959, when Texas Gulf Sulphur Company identified several promising mining locations in Ontario, Canada. On October 29, an engineer conducted a ground survey of an area known as Kidd-55, some fifteen miles north of the town of Timmins. Satisfied with the survey, he drilled a test hole on November 8, and two days later the test began to reveal a promising find. Of course, more than one good test hole is required to prove the existence of profitable deposits, so Texas Gulf quietly began to acquire the land to drill more test holes.

In the meantime, Texas Gulf employees were busy in the stock market. By the end of November, several employees and officers had purchased several thousand additional shares of the company's stock. In December, an employee in charge of the drilling operation tipped a girlfriend (the "tippee") in Washington, D.C., of the find, and she told two other people (the "sub-tippees"). They subsequently bought several thousand shares and call options on another several thousand shares of Texas Gulf.

By the end of March 1960, Texas Gulf had the land to continue testing. Drilling resumed, and new test holes confirmed that the ore contained generous deposits of copper, zinc, and silver. Texas Gulf stock, which had traded around 17 and 18 the previous November, had risen to about 30. Rumors began to make the rounds that Texas Gulf was on the verge of an important discovery, and on April 11 articles appeared in U.S. newspapers reporting the rumors. Texas Gulf followed the next day with a statement characterizing the rumors as unreliable and saying that additional testing was necessary to prove mineable deposits. The company's stock responded by falling several points, and some of the insiders continued to accumulate Texas Gulf stock and call options.

Rumors continued to filter out, and the company decided to release news of the find at its directors' meeting on April 16. That morning, the market was anticipating the big announcement. Although the meeting ended around 10 a.m., the news inexplicably did not come out over the Dow Jones news wires until 10:54. Between those two times, one of the directors purchased stock, and another recommended it to a friend and also purchased some himself. Texas Gulf closed for the day at 36⅜. Within a couple of weeks, it sold for 58⅜, and by the end of 1966, when the mine was in full production, the stock sold for over 100 per share.

After the release of the news and speculation of insider trading, the SEC investigated and then filed suit. It asked the court to (1) issue an injunction against those who traded the stock based on inside information; (2) order the defendants to make restitution; and (3) enjoin Texas Gulf for making misleading statements to the public. The judge trying the case exonerated those who bought the stock before the final test hole results by ruling that they acted only on supposition and not proof that the reserves actually existed. However, the judge did find guilty those two employees who bought stock shortly before the announcement. He also decided that although Texas Gulf's first press release was incomplete, it was not misleading. Finally, the judge ruled that the two directors who purchased stock before the news came across the Dow Jones wire were not guilty because they presumed that the news had been dispersed because the meeting was over.

The SEC pursued the decisions in the appeals courts, which reversed practically all of the not-guilty decisions of the lower court. The reversal broadened the interpretation of insider trading and strengthened the SEC's position against the use of inside information in stock trading. Essentially, the court said that all of the insiders, including the tippees and sub-tippees, were acting on information not available to other investors. The court also interpreted the company's first press release, which implied that there was no reason for optimism, as misleading to the investing public. Finally, the court's decision against the two directors who traded after the meeting implies that the insider has the responsibility to ascertain that the information is indeed public before acting in the markets.

these rules, the buyer must disclose its principal business, the source of any funds involved in the transaction, the purpose of the transaction, and the amount of stock it will purchase. The purpose of these regulations is to prevent surprise takeovers and to allow all parties involved time to consider the offer.

6. The act authorized the Federal Reserve Board of Governors to control the amount of credit, or margin, used for the initial purchase and maintenance of equity securities. The Fed responded with regulations T and U which direct the Board of Governors to set initial margin requirements and which leave maintenance requirements to the exchanges and individual brokerage firms. Enforcement of this provision remains with the SEC.

The SEC. The ruling board of the SEC is a five-member commission of which no more than three members may belong to the same political party. The president appoints each commissioner for a five-year term, and the terms are staggered so that one expires on June 5 of each year. The headquarters of the SEC is located in Washington, D.C., and there are nine regions with regional and branch offices in major cities. Figure 4–1 shows the SEC regions and their offices.

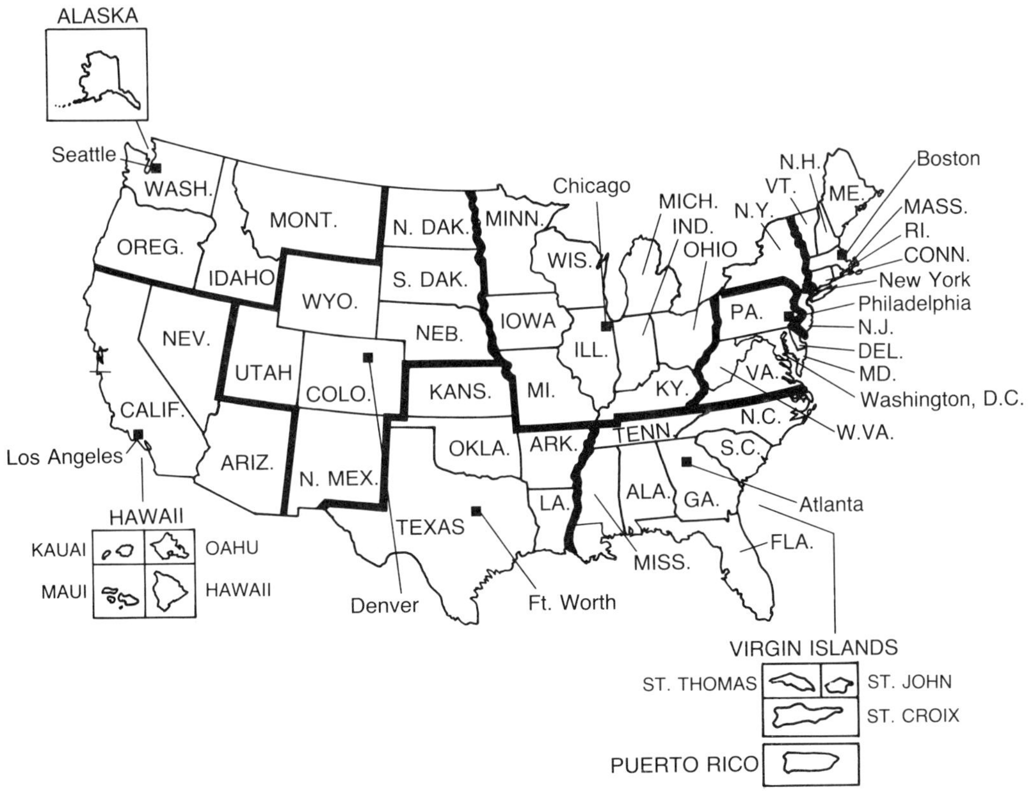

FIGURE 4–1
Regions of the Securities and Exchange Commission

The SEC divides its duties among five divisions. The Division of Corporation Finance establishes disclosure standards required by the various acts of Congress and reviews all the registration statements and periodic reports required by the law. The Division of Market Regulation supervises the registration and reports of the securities exchanges, brokers and dealers, and other registered market organizations (namely, the NASD). The Division of Enforcement directs all investigations and enforcement activities to ensure compliance with the law. The Division of Corporate Regulation administers the Public Utility Holding Company Act of 1935 and serves as advisor to the federal district courts for bankruptcy proceedings. The Division of Investment Management Regulation administers registration and reporting requirements of investment companies and investment advisors.

Public Utility Holding Company Act of 1935

During the early 1900s, systems of utility holding companies emerged, controlling empires composed of large numbers of subsidiaries—unrelated power and gas companies in scattered locations around the country. These holding companies were built by pyramiding subsidiaries into highly leveraged financial structures. The risks associated with these leveraged holding companies prompted Congress to pass the Public Utility Holding Company Act of 1935. The goal of the act was to encourage the formation of utility companies with simplified capital structures that would restrict themselves to operating within some defined geographic region. It empowered the SEC to require registration and periodic statements from utility holding companies, to regulate the type of securities issued by the companies, and to regulate the companies' accounting systems, acquisition and disposition of assets, and intercompany loans and dividend payments.

Maloney Act of 1936

The Maloney Act was the first and most significant of several amendments to the Securities Exchange Act of 1934. Introduced into Congress by Sen. Francis T. Maloney, its purpose was to bring the over-the-counter markets into the regulatory picture along with the exchanges. It provided for the registration of associations of securities dealers that would supervise their membership and establish rules of ethical business practice and standards of financial responsibility and accountability for members.

One association, the National Association of Securities Dealers, is registered under the act. Although the SEC does not have the degree of direct power over the NASD that it has over the exchanges according to the 1934 act, it does have the authority to suspend the NASD's registration. The NASD has responded with a respectable record regarding the amount of self-regulation of its members. It has used such procedures as requiring prospective members to pass a securities test before being admitted to membership, adopting a set of rules forbidding price manipulation, and accepting a uniform code to standardize and expedite security transactions. The NASD also has procedures for disciplining and expelling members who fail to meet NASD rules and standards.

Trust Indenture Act of 1939

The Trust Indenture Act of 1939 requires that public offerings of debt securities (except exempted commercial paper and government bond issues) be issued under a trust *indenture* approved by the SEC. An indenture is a contract between the bond issuer and the trustee representing the interest of the bondholders. The trustee has to be an independent corporation with no conflicts of interest and must have a minimum capitalization of $150,000.

Congress passed this law in response to the number of bond issues with inadequate protection for investors under their indentures. Sometimes corporations would violate the indenture, and the trustee might not file suit because of conflict of interest. For example, if the trustee for the bond issue were the commercial bank where the corporation had on deposit large sums of money, then the bank might be reluctant to take any action that could anger the company's management into withdrawing the funds. Using the information in the registration application, the SEC rules on the suitability of the trustee.

Investment Company Act of 1940

The Investment Company Act of 1940 is Title I of Public Law 768, 76th Congress. Title II is the Investment Advisors Act. Congress passed these acts after a four-year investigation into investment companies and investment advisors that revealed a number of abuses. The Investment Company Act requires that all investment companies register with the SEC, disclose their financial condition and investment policies, and periodically report to the SEC. In addition, the companies must provide semiannual reports to all stockholders.

The act also contains provisions that prohibit the following: association with an investment company by anyone guilty of fraud, transactions between companies and their officers or directors without SEC approval, and pyramids of investment companies and cross-ownership of their securities. It also prohibits investment companies from issuing senior securities (debt or preferred stock) except under certain circumstances.

Investment Advisors Act of 1940

The Investment Advisors Act of 1940 requires the registration of investment advisors with the SEC. Registration of an investment advisor does not mean that the SEC approves of the advisor's ability or even that the advisor knows anything about securities. As with the registration requirements of the other securities acts, registration only means disclosure. Investment advisors must disclose information to the SEC and to their clients about their backgrounds, business affiliations, and the bases for computing their fees.

Securities Investor Protection Act of 1970

Just as the failure of an uninsured bank results in the loss of at least a portion of the depositors' money, the failure of a securities brokerage firm results in the loss of money and securities of the firm's clients holding securities in street name and cash in their accounts. The NYSE had maintained a fund to reimburse clients of failed member firms, but because of several brokerage firm failures, this fund was practically depleted by the late 1960s. To help avoid financial disaster for the investor clients of securities firms, Congress passed the Securities Investor Protection Act of 1970. It created the Securities Investor Protection Corporation (SIPC) as a nonprofit corporation to provide insurance for customers' accounts at securities brokerage firms.

All registered brokerage firms, broker-dealers, and members of security exchanges must become members of the SIPC. To provide for the insurance fund, the SIPC collects fees based on each member's size. The fund provides insurance for accounts at member firms in the amount of $500,000 for each account.

The president appoints five members of the seven-member SIPC board, the secretary of the treasury appoints one, and the Federal Reserve Board appoints one. Two of these directors must not be associated with the securities industry. The SIPC makes annual reports to the SEC, and the SEC retains certain control over the SIPC's rules and bylaws.

SEC Rules

The various securities acts authorize the SEC to adopt rules and regulations to carry out the broad purpose of the SEC. Although they are not legislation passed by Congress, these SEC rules are important legal aspects of the securities business. They cover a number of categories, such as standards of statements of financial condition, record-keeping practices of brokers and investment companies, and *hypothecation* of securities. Hypothecation occurs when an investor pledges stock as collateral for a margin loan. When a broker pledges that stock to a bank as collateral for a loan, it is *rehypothecation.*

Some of the most significant rules affecting the securities industry are the SECO rules. These rules apply to securities dealers and brokers who are not NASD members and therefore are not under NASD jurisdiction. The rules set standards and qualification requirements for such non-NASD firms. The SECO qualification examination is similar to the exams of the other security organizations, and passing the SECO exam will usually also qualify the broker-dealer applicant under the exams of most exchanges, states, and the NASD.

State Legislation

Kansas, in 1911, was the first state to adopt securities legislation. Within the next decade, about half the states passed some form of securities law, and the variety of provisions and requirements in these laws soon made it evident that some kind of standardization would be beneficial. In 1929, the Conference of Commissioners on Uniform State Laws of the American Bar Association approved a Uniform State Securities Act, which it updated in 1956. All states except Delaware have adopted securities legislation, most modeling their law after the Uniform Act.

Blue sky laws is the term applied to state securities legislation. These blue sky laws usually regulate securities in one or more of three areas. First are the antifraud provisions of these laws, covering misrepresentation and misleading statements. Second are the state law provisions dealing with the activities of brokers and dealers. These provisions include registration of brokers, dealers, and sellers; minimum capital requirements of dealers; and *suitability rules,* which require investment advice given to investors to be compatible with the investors' needs and goals. Although some of the state laws are more stringent than the federal law, brokerage firms must always meet federal registration and other requirements in addition to any state requirements. The third area of regulation in blue sky laws is the registration of new security issues. States have no authority to regulate interstate commerce and therefore generally have no control over secondary markets, but most states require some kind of registration of new issues, usually by one of three methods.

1. *Registration by notification* occurs when the registration becomes effective a certain period of time after filing unless denied by the state securities commission.
2. *Registration by coordination* means that state registration becomes effective at the same time as the federal registration.
3. *Registration by qualification,* in which the issue must meet certain qualifications before receiving approval, is required in some states. The law in some states is more than just a disclosure statute, and the state securities administrator may have broad powers to approve or disapprove of the issue of securities according to their suitability as investments. It is this type of provision that produced the name "blue sky laws," because the state can disapprove of a security that has nothing behind it but the "blue sky above."

States may use laws in other areas to exercise additional control over the securities industry. The *law of agency* would apply to registered representatives, requiring them to serve their employer with skill, judgment, and discretion. Most states regulate the types of investments that certain types of investors may make. They accomplish this either by using a *legal list* or by application of the *Prudent Man Rule.*

In legal list states, the state approves a list of investments that it deems appropriate for the regulated institutional investors, which usually fall into one of three groups. The first group, over which the state exercises fairly close control, usually contains life insurance companies, savings institutions, commercial banks, and trust companies. The state exercises partial control over the second group, usually fire and casualty insurance companies, requiring them to invest a portion of their assets in high grade bonds and allowing them to invest the remainder of their funds at their discretion. States usually exercise no control over the final group, which contains investment companies, educational endowments, charitable foundations, and unrestricted trust funds.

In most states, including those with and without legal lists, trustees operate under the Prudent Man Rule. The rule descended from a court decision in Massachusetts in 1830, which stated that a trustee should invest as a "prudent man" would. Although the Prudent Man Rule requires trustees to select investments carefully, it does not state exactly which types of investments qualify. Through various court decisions and practices common among trustees, a set of guidelines has evolved as to what would be an investment of a "prudent man." For example, only common stocks that pay a current cash dividend would normally be considered appropriate under the Prudent Man Rule.

TAXATION

Taxation affects investments both from the standpoint of the investor and from that of the security issuer. The effect of taxes on investors is to alter the return on investment; therefore, the expected return *after taxes* is what really affects an investor's net wealth, and the structure of taxation can have a great influence on investors' decisions regarding their investments. The effect of taxes on security-issuing corporations is to alter their net income. Because companies pay dividends from their after-tax income, and investors value stocks based on the expected dividend flow, corporate taxes indirectly affect security prices and investors' investment decisions.

Taxation may occur at all levels of government, but usually is imposed at the federal and state levels. Because the tax laws of each state are so different, this text makes no attempt to describe the taxes of individual states. Federal taxation is significant, and this text presents the major points of federal tax law regarding investments, but keep in mind that Congress passes a new tax law every year, and the structure and extent of federal taxes can change from year to year.

Taxation of Investors

The Federal Personal Income Tax

Taxation of personal income at the national level of government is probably the most direct and significant tax to investors. The Tax Reform Act of 1986, a massive piece of legislation totaling 952 pages, was probably the most significant tax law revision in forty years. The act simplified and lowered tax rates, broadened the tax base, significantly curtailed allowable deductions, and eliminated preferential treatment of long-term capital gains income.

The taxpayer's *taxable income* and *filing status* determine the amount of tax payable. Taxable income is equal to the investor's *gross income* less any allowable *deductions*. Gross income includes practically all revenue from all sources, including wages and investment income. The main income sources that taxpayers may omit from gross income are social security benefits, interest on municipal securities, and life insurance proceeds. Table 4–1 shows the computation of taxable income for individuals, including most of the common categories of deductions.

After determining taxable income, the taxpayer consults the tax schedule issued by the Internal Revenue Service (IRS) to identify the amount of tax owed. The tax schedule states the tax as a percentage of taxable income; the tax schedule is *progressive* because the percentage of tax on additional income rises as taxable income increases. The 1986 act greatly simplified the tax tables and reduced the number of tax brackets. Table 4–2 shows a sample federal income tax schedule. Note that as an investor's income rises, the effective tax rate also rises, and this leads to a common misconception that a taxpayer can be worse off by making more money. The misconception is that

TABLE 4–1
Computation of taxable income

Description	*Numerical Example*
Gross income	
Salaries	$42,000.00
Rent received	2,000.00
Investment income	5,000.00
Income from a business	1,000.00
Adjusted gross income (AGI)	50,000.00
Itemized deductions	
Mortgage interest expense	9,000.00
Medical expenses over 7.5 percent of AGI	0.00
Charitable contributions	1,000.00
State income taxes	1,000.00
$2000 for each exemption (yourself, spouse, and dependents)	8,000.00
Taxable income	31,000.00

the higher tax rate resulting from a higher tax bracket applies to all of one's income. In fact, it does not. The higher tax rate applies only to the *additional* income. The result is that although investors entering a higher tax bracket pay a higher tax rate on marginal income, their after-tax income will not fall simply because they move up into the higher bracket.

However, one problem of the tax system for many years was that of *bracket creep,* which occurs when inflation pushes taxpayers into higher tax brackets. Although individuals' before-tax income may have been keeping pace with inflation, they saw their after-tax real income falling because of the higher taxes they had to pay on inflated incomes. Current provisions in tax legislation require adjustment of the tax schedules and personal exemptions each year to counteract the impact of inflation.

TABLE 4–2
Federal income tax schedule for individuals, 1988

Filing Status	*Breakpoint Between 15% and 28% Tax Rate*[a]
Married filing jointly	$29,750
Unmarried	17,850
Heads of household	23,900
Married filing separately	14,875

[a]Only two tax rates apply to income in 1988: 15% and 28%. The lower rate applies to income below the breakpoint, and the higher rate applies to all income above the breakpoint. For tax years after 1988, the breakpoints are adjusted to reflect inflation. Note that depending on filing status and taxable income, a taxpayer may be subject to pay an additional 5% tax, making the marginal rate a total of 33%. In no case, however, is the total tax greater than 28%.

Dividends. Investors should declare all cash dividends received from corporations as income. The effective tax rate applicable to dividends is the same as for any ordinary income.

A *stock dividend* occurs when a company pays an additional number of shares to its existing stockholders as a dividend. For example, if a company declared a 5 percent stock dividend, its shareholders would receive one additional share in the company for each twenty shares held. Instead of issuing fractional shares, companies paying stock dividends usually buy the fractional share from the investor for cash or let the investor purchase an additional share fraction to equal a whole share. A *stock split* is similar, occurring when a company divides its existing shares. The most common stock split is a two for one split, in which the company doubles its shares outstanding by issuing one additional share for each existing share. Both stock splits and stock dividends are nontaxable, since the only real objective they accomplish is to divide the corporation into a larger number of smaller pieces. The only difference between stock splits and stock dividends is in the way that accountants reflect the change on the balance sheet.

Capital Gains. Selling an asset for a profit results in income called *capital gain;* selling for a loss is a *capital loss.* Before 1986, tax law qualified the gain on an asset held for more than six months as a *long-term capital gain,* and a lower tax rate applied to these long-term gains. Current law, however, makes no distinction between short-term and long-term capital gains income.

Tax treatment of all capital gains income is the same as for other ordinary income. If capital losses exceed capital gains, up to $3000 of the loss may be used to offset other income. Losses over $3000 in one year are carried forward into the next tax year.

Bonds. The interest on bonds is ordinary interest income and included as part of total income for tax purposes. The exception is tax-exempt municipal securities, whose interest is free from federal income tax.

Investors often acquire bonds at a discount or premium from face value. When the bonds mature, the investor declares the amount of the discount as profit (or the amount of the premium as a loss). Of course, if the investor sells the bond before maturity, the net profit (or loss) becomes capital gain (or loss) at the time of sale. The exceptions are zero-coupon bonds. Investors holding these types of bonds must compute the accrued interest on the instrument based on the amount of the discount from the face value at the time of purchase. This accrued interest must be declared as interest income each year even though there was no receipt of an interest payment. For this reason, usually only tax-exempt investors such as pension funds and charitable endowments purchase zero-coupon bonds.

Tax-Deferring Strategies. Postponing the gain on an investment until the next taxable year may be a beneficial strategy. It can postpone the payment of taxes until the following year, allowing the taxpayer an extra profit equal to the interest income from investing the tax payable for another year. (Since many investors must file quarterly estimated tax payments or face a penalty if they owe much additional tax at year end, this benefit may be substantially lower than it might first appear.) Of course, simply waiting to sell a stock until after December 31 would accomplish this purpose, but in some cases it might be wise to try to take the gain on the investment before the end of the year. For example, if an investor had a nice gain on a stock on December 1 and was afraid that the stock was about to decline in price, the investor would want to take the gain but try to postpone paying the tax for another year.

One way to accomplish this is to go *short against the box,* which involves selling short the stock in which a gain is to be postponed. This locks in the investor's gain at the short sale price because the net position is then perfectly *hedged,* that is, any gain in the long position occurring after the short sale would exactly offset any corresponding loss in the short position, and vice versa.

One word of caution is that investors cannot sell securities at year-end to recognize a loss if they repurchase the same securities within thirty days of the sale. This is the *wash sale rule* of Section 1091 of the Internal Revenue Code, and its purpose is to discourage people from selling securities before the end of the year to take a tax loss and then buying them back at the beginning of the following year. In spite of this rule, it may still be profitable to sell a security to take a tax loss and then buy it back more than thirty days after the sale to avoid the wash sale rule.[2]

Other methods that investors can use to postpone gains into the following taxable year involve hedging strategies using put and call options. These strategies can be complex, and investors who use them should familiarize themselves thoroughly with the tax implications of their actions.

Investment-Related Tax Deductions. The 1986 Tax Act placed limitations on the tax deductibility of investment-related expenses. An investor may deduct interest expense on a margin account only to the extent of investment income. However, an investor may carry margin interest expenses in excess of investment income over into the next tax year. Deduction of other investment-related expenses, such as subscriptions to investment advisory services, is limited. Only the portion of these other investment expenses exceeding 2 percent of the investor's adjusted gross income (AGI) are deductible.

Tax Shelters. A *tax shelter* is an investment that offers taxpayers a potential reduction in their taxable income, thereby reducing taxes. Tax shelters usually defer taxes for periods of time longer than one year, up to as many as fifty years or so, while some actually result in *tax avoidance,* in which the tax is simply reduced.

Before the 1986 Tax Act, investors had a wide range of tax shelters available to them. These tax shelters often produced sizable tax deductions, especially during the early years of the shelter. The 1986 act, however, severely limited the use of tax deductions from passive activity such as tax shelters. In general, the act limits deductions to the total income generated by passive activity. Passive activity is an enterprise in which the investor takes no active part in generating income. An example is the limited partners in a limited partnership, and the law specifies most rental income (including real estate) to be passive.

Contributions to individual or employer-sponsored pension and retirement plans are major forms of tax shelters available to many taxpayers. These plans let the taxpayer reduce taxable income by an amount equal to the contribution, subject to certain maximum contributions. The tax on this deferred income does not become due until the investor withdraws the funds, usually at retirement age. Therefore, an individual of age twenty can defer paying taxes on that income until reaching a maximum age of seventy, a period of fifty years.

Another vehicle for sheltering income from tax is the *limited partnership*. Brokers sell limited partnerships in units of usually $1000 each, with a minimum purchase of five units. Each unit represents a portion of ownership in the business, which takes the form of a limited partnership to take advantage of the flow-through of tax write-offs to the partners while still maintaining the limited liability of the limited partners. Because these units represent partnership ownership rather than a share of stock in a corporation, they are generally not marketable. To offset this disadvantage, many of the sponsoring brokerage firms have some type of agreement to buy the partnership units back from investors at a fair market value should the investor want out.

The partnerships invest their funds in types of business ventures that typically generate large tax write-offs or other tax benefits during the first few years, such as oil drilling, livestock breeding, or property management. These partnerships can offer good after-tax returns, but they have their risks. Any investor considering the purchase of a limited partnership unit should study the prospectus carefully and make the decision based on the overall investment merits of the partnership, not just on the quick tax benefits.

The Federal Estate Tax

When a person dies, the federal government assesses an *estate tax,* based on the deceased's *estate,* or total net value of assets owned at the time of death. In contrast, many state death taxes are *inheritance taxes* in which the state assesses taxes based on who the beneficiaries of the estate are and how much each receives. The federal estate tax, like the income tax, is progressive in nature, and the marginal tax rate increases as the value of the estate increases.

In general, there is no tax levied on the first $600,000 of the estate, and the administrator of the estate may deduct reasonable funeral and administrative expenses and bequests to any charitable or other qualified tax-exempt organization from the taxable estate. In addition, the *marital deduction* allows the taxability of the remainder of the estate to be transferred to a surviving spouse. Table 4–3 shows examples of the estate tax rates. Planning for death taxes can be an important part of an investor's strategy.

The Federal Gift Tax

Federal law also places a tax on gifts that one individual makes to another. There is a one-time tax-free allowance, whereby a person may give up to $10,000 tax-free to each recipient. Above that amount, tax rates equivalent to the estate tax rates apply.

TABLE 4–3
Unified transfer tax schedule, 1988

Base for Tentative Tax		*Tentative Tax*[a]				
Over	*Up to*	*This amount*	*plus*	*This percentage*	*of*	*Excess over*
$	$ 10,000	$ 0		18%		$ 0
10,000	20,000	1,800		20		10,000
20,000	40,000	3,800		22		20,000
40,000	60,000	8,200		24		40,000
60,000	80,000	13,000		26		60,000
80,000	100,000	18,200		28		80,000
100,000	150,000	23,800		30		100,000
150,000	250,000	33.800		32		150,000
250,000	500,000	70,800		34		250,000
500,000	750,000	155,800		37		500,000
750,000	1,000,000	248,300		39		750,000
1,000,000	1,250,000	345,800		41		1,000,000
1,250,000	1,500,000	448,300		43		1,250,000
1,500,000	2,000,000	555,800		45		1,500,000
2,000,000	2,500,000	780,800		49		2,000,000
2,500,000	and up	1,025,800		50		2,500,000

[a]The tentative tax is the tax before any reductions for the unified transfer credit, credit for state death taxes, credit for gift taxes, and certain other credits.

Taxation of Corporations

The major form of corporate taxation at the federal level is the corporate income tax. Generally speaking, the corporation's taxable income is equal to revenues less business expenses and depreciation. The tax schedule applied to corporate taxable income is progressive. Table 4–4 shows this schedule.

Dividends

The payment of a cash dividend is a cash outflow for the corporation. However, the tax law does not allow the deduction of dividends as an expense from corporate

TABLE 4–4
Corporate income tax schedule, 1988

Income Levels	*Marginal Tax Rate*
$0–$50,000	15%
$50,000–$75,000	25%
over $75,000[a]	34%

[a]On income between $100,000 and $355,000, there is an additional 5% tax, making the marginal rate at that point 39%. In no case, however, is the total tax greater than 34% of income.

income. The corporation must pay dividends out of its after-tax net income. When investors receive this dividend, they pay taxes on it again, at their respective individual tax rates. This results in a double taxation of corporate income. There are a number of economists who oppose this double taxation on the grounds that it discourages dividends, thereby discouraging investors to buy common stock, and retarding the growth of the economy through private investment. Proposed solutions to the problem include making dividends tax-deductible for corporations or making dividends tax-exempt for investors.

Often one corporation owns shares of stock in another corporation; this is the case for a corporation's subsidiaries. Triple taxation of intercorporate dividends would occur if the first corporation paid taxes on its income, then the second corporation paid taxes on the dividends from the first corporation, and the investor paid taxes on dividends from the second corporation. To minimize triple taxation, a corporation may exclude from its taxable income 85 percent of the dividends it receives from other corporations. Since the maximum tax rate on corporate income is 34 percent, this makes the maximum effective tax rate on intercorporate dividends equal to 5.19 percent.

SUMMARY

This chapter has summarized the major legislation affecting the securities markets and important aspects of tax law affecting investments. The main purpose of most federal legislation is to require disclosure of important information to the investing public and to provide regulation and supervision of principals in the securities markets. The Securities Act of 1933 required disclosure of financial information of primary market issues. The Securities Exchange Act of 1934 included the secondary market under the purview of federal government regulation and created the Securities and Exchange Commission to carry out and enforce the securities laws. Public utilities, investment companies, and investment advisors are also subject to federal government registration and reporting requirements. States also regulate the sale and issuance of securities within their jurisdiction through the various blue sky laws.

Taxation at the federal level affects investments by taxing both investors and the corporations issuing securities. The federal personal income tax contains many provisions that are important to investors, and investors should include planning for the tax effect of their investments in their overall investment strategy. Any tax planning should also include the other important federal taxes, the estate tax and the gift tax.

IMPORTANT TERMS

blue sky laws
bracket creep
capital gain
churning
corner the market
estate tax

filing status
gross income
hedge
hypothecation
indenture
inheritance tax
law of agency
legal list
letter stock
limited partnership
marital deduction
progressive tax
proxy solicitation
Prudent Man Rule
registration by coordination
registration by notification
registration by qualification
rehypothecation
short against the box
short corner
short squeeze
stock dividend
stock split
suitability rules
taxable income
tax avoidance
tax shelter
tender offer
wash sale
wash sale rule

QUESTIONS AND PROBLEMS

1. What were some of the abuses and violations of common law that occurred before the passage of federal securities legislation?
2. What were the main accomplishments of the Securities Act of 1933? How did it fall short of reaching the objectives of Congress?
3. Outline the main provisions of the Securities Exchange Act of 1934. How did this act remedy the shortcomings of the Securities Act of 1933?
4. What did the Glass-Steagall Act accomplish in the securities market? In view of the deregulation of the banking system, do you think that the time has come to repeal or modify the act? Why?
5. How did the NASD, which is an industry association, achieve the power to regulate the market in a fashion similar to a government agency? What happens to securities dealers who do not join the NASD?
6. What are the main divisions of the Securities and Exchange Commission and their responsibilities?
7. What are blue sky laws, and what are their objectives? In view of the extent of federal securities legislation, why do states bother to pass blue sky laws?
8. Explain the Prudent Man Rule and how it would affect the investment policy of the following types of investors:
   a) bank trust department
   b) individual investor
   c) fire insurance company
9. What are some ways that the federal government uses tax policy to influence investments and to influence national goals and objectives?
10. Explain how there is a double taxation on corporate income. What are some possible changes to the tax laws which would eliminate the double tax?
11. What is letter stock? Why might a corporation prefer to issue letter stock?

NOTES

1. House of Representatives (1933), *Federal Supervision of Traffic in Investment Securities in Interstate Commerce,* H. R. Report No. 85, 73rd Congress, 1st Session.
2. For an example of a trading strategy showing after-tax profits by avoiding the wash sale rule, see John O. Everett and Curtis L. Norton (1981), "Evaluating the Effectiveness of Code Section 1091 as a Deterrent to Wash Sales," *Financial Review,* 16 (Fall), 44–56.

SELECTED REFERENCES

Everett, John O., and Curtis L. Norton (1981). "Evaluating the Effectiveness of Code Section 1091 as a Deterrent to Wash Sales." *Financial Review,* 16 (Fall), 44–56.

Kess, Sidney, and Bertil Weslin (1979). *Estate Planning Guide.* Chicago: Commerce Clearing House.

National Association of Securities Dealers (1971). *NASD Training Guide.* Washington, DC: Author.

National Association of Securities Dealers (1973). *Reprint of the Manual.* Chicago: Commerce Clearing House.

Securities and Exchange Commission (1938). *United States of America before the Securities and Exchange Commission in the Matter of Richard Whitney, et al., Individually and as Partners Doing Business as Richard Whitney and Company.* Washington, DC: U.S. Government Printing Office.

Securities and Exchange Commission (1976). *Securities Act of 1933.* Washington, DC: U.S. Government Printing Office.

Securities and Exchange Commission (1977). *General Rules and Regulations under the Investment Company Act of 1940.* Washington, DC: U.S. Government Printing Office.

Securities and Exchange Commission (1977). *Investment Advisors Act of 1940 and General Rules and Regulations Thereunder.* Washington, DC: U.S. Government Printing Office.

Securities and Exchange Commission (1977). *Investment Company Act of 1940.* Washington, DC: U.S. Government Printing Office.

Securities and Exchange Commission (1977). *Securities Exchange Act of 1934.* Washington, DC: U.S. Government Printing Office.

Securities and Exchange Commission (1978). *The Work of the Securities and Exchange Commission.* Washington, DC: U.S. Government Printing Office.

Skousen, K. Fred (1980). *An Introduction to the SEC.* Cincinnati, OH: South-Western Publishing.

U.S. Treasury Department, Internal Revenue Service (annual). *Your Federal Income Tax.* Washington, DC: U.S. Government Printing Office.

CHAPTER 5

Sources of Market and Security Information

Financial information about the investment environment and potential individual investment vehicles are the building blocks from which analysts construct research analyses. These analyses form the bases for their investment recommendations. While most of the remainder of this book discusses the tools that analysts use to examine investment information, such as theoretical models for the valuation of a security, this chapter summarizes many of the sources of investment information that investors have at their disposal.

The cost of financial information varies from virtually free to quite expensive; subscriptions to selective investment advisory services, for instance, may cost thousands of dollars per year. Fortunately for individual investors, most public libraries carry a wide variety of investment information sources. The selection available in most libraries is generally large enough to satisfy investors who want to perform their own analyses upon which to base their investment decisions.

INFORMATION ON THE ECONOMY

All firms operate within the limits defined by the economic environment. Because the economic environment has a strong influence on the profitability of the firm, and ultimately the profitability of an investment in the firm's securities, awareness of the economy is an important component of an investor's knowledge. The responsibility for compiling economic statistics lies principally with the government, mainly at the federal level and to a lesser degree at the state and local levels. Therefore, a primary resource for much of the available economic information is the publications of the

TABLE 5–1
Sources of economic information from the U.S. government

Publication (frequency)	***Government Agency***	***Content Summary***
Federal Reserve Bulletin (monthly)	Board of Governors, Federal Reserve System	Extensive coverage of economic data, including information on the banking system, monetary data, financial markets, and interest rates
Monthly Bulletin (monthly)	Federal Reserve Banks	Each of the twelve Federal Reserve Banks publishes its own newsletter of special interest to its region.
Survey of Current Business (monthly)	Department of Commerce	General economic and commercial data, national income and product accounts, and employment data
Business Conditions Digest (monthly)	National Bureau of Economic Research	Time series of general economic data, presented in tabular and graphic form
Quarterly Financial Report (quarterly)	Federal Trade Commission	Aggregate financial statistics of U.S. corporations, including income and financial position data and ratios
Economic Report of the President (annual)	U.S. President	President's annual summary of past year's economy and discussion of coming year's major areas of concern

TABLE 5–2
Nongovernmental sources of economic information

Publication (frequency)	***Publisher***	***Content of Summary***
Business Week (weekly magazine)	McGraw-Hill	Current economic statistics and articles on topics of general economic interest
The Economist (weekly magazine)	The Economist Newspaper, Ltd.	British publication containing articles on various economic topics, good in the international area
Various titles[a] (usually monthly)	Various banks (such as Citibank and Chase Manhattan)	Information of national (from major banks) or regional interest
The Outlook (weekly newsletter)	Standard & Poor's	Summaries of general economic statistics with discussions and forecasts

[a]Most large regional and major banks issue their own newsletters, usually at no charge.

various governmental agencies that compile and report economic data. In addition, other services analyze this economic data and use it to make forecasts and representations of the data in other useful ways. Table 5–1 gives a list of major governmental publications and summarizes their contents.

In addition to the federal government, many private consulting firms, commercial banks, and publishing companies gather and analyze economic and financial information. The services that these firms offer range from reasonably inexpensive subscriptions to newsletters or magazines to expensive, detailed private reports and forecasts. Table 5–2 presents a summary of some of the more widely available of these sources of economic information.

MARKET INFORMATION

As following chapters will discuss, there is a definite relationship between the economy and the performance of the securities of companies in the economy. Just as current economic information is helpful and important, so is information about the general securities markets within the economy.

Market Indexes

Probably the most frequently asked question addressed to a stockbroker is, "How is the market doing today?" Most brokers, when answering this question, interpret what the "market" is doing by looking at one of the widely used *market indexes.* Although they typically measure the performance of only a certain sample of securities within a market, these market indexes are important for several reasons:

1. They give an idea of the performance of the market in general.
2. They provide a benchmark against which investors can compare an investment portfolio to evaluate the portfolio's investment performance.
3. They form the basis for a number of options and futures contracts whose value depends on the value of the index.

Figure 5–1 shows a chart of the values of a popular market index, the Dow Jones Industrial Average, from 1929 to 1986. Note that there are periods of extended upward trends and downward trends.

Stock market indexes identify market trends. According to stock market tradition, a rising market is called a *bull market,* while a *bear market* means that stock prices are falling. Market analysts, therefore, often classify themselves as bullish or bearish, depending on whether they believe that the market will rise or fall in the near future. Market tradition notwithstanding, recent research[1] supports the idea that we should define a bull market as one in which the return on common stocks exceeds the return on a riskless security, while any return less than the riskless rate would identify a bear market.

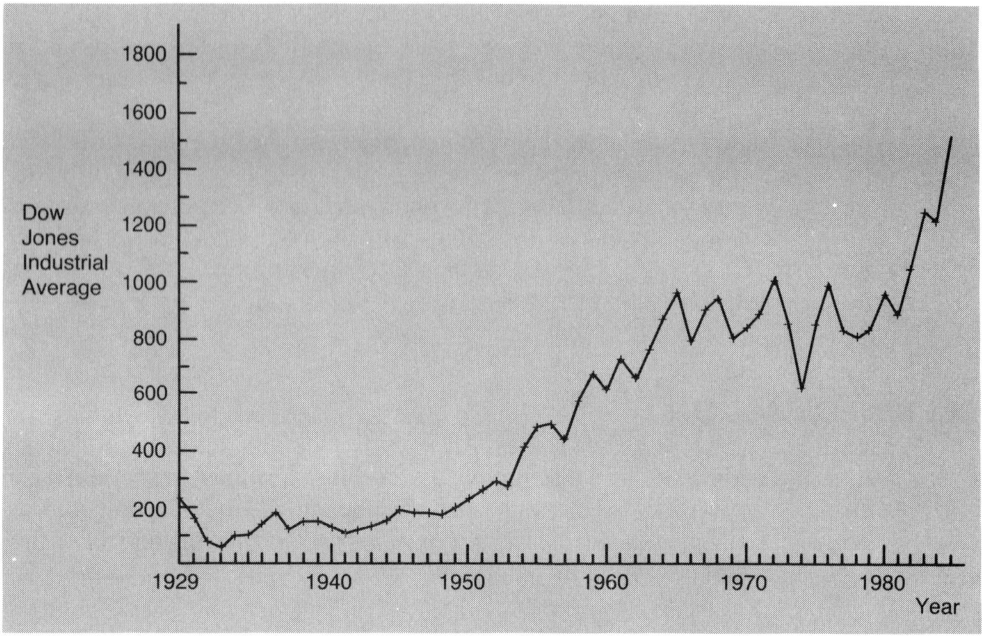

FIGURE 5–1
The Dow Jones Industrial Average, 1929–1986

Different indexes have different methods of construction that can lead to different index performances. For this reason, it is important to know the construction of these indexes so as to correctly interpret the statistics that they yield.

Methods of Index Construction

There are three important aspects of index construction:

1. The sample
2. The weighting scheme used
3. The procedure used to compute the index

The Sample. The sample is the actual securities that the index includes in its computation. The important points of this sample are its size, breadth, and source. The sample size represents the number of different securities that the index includes. As any beginning statistics student knows, the larger the sample size, the better the sample represents the general population it is intended to measure—in this case, the "market." The breadth of a sample is the cross section of the population that the index measures. For example, an index that measures the market in general should include securities of at least several companies from each of the major industries and sectors in the economy. On the other hand, to measure the computer manufacturing industry, an index could be constructed using a sample of firms in that specific industry. Finally, the source of a sample identifies its origin. For market indexes, the source is generally the public quotation of the security in the market where it trades, such as the closing price for stocks traded on the NYSE.

The Weighting Scheme. A *weighting scheme* is a systematic technique for assigning each security's weight, or proportion in a portfolio. There are three generally recognized mechanical weighting schemes for security portfolios:

1. Price weighting
2. Equal weighting
3. Value weighting

Price weighting means that the portfolio contains one unit of each security included. In that way, each security's weight in the portfolio is proportional to its price. Table 5–3 gives a hypothetical, price-weighted index of a portfolio containing one share each of stocks X, Y, and Z priced at 50, 25, and 75 respectively. The index is a simple sum of the prices of the individual securities in the index, giving a total index value of 150. Note that each security has a weight, or importance, in the portfolio proportional to its price. For example, the highest priced stock, Z, selling at 75, represents a weight of .5; it constitutes 50 percent of the total portfolio value.

Assuming changes in stocks X, Y, and Z to 75, 50, and 100, respectively, the table shows the changed value of the index and the return on the index. Given these stock price changes, the index increased by 50 percent.

The main criticism of a price-weighted index is that the relative importance (weight) of each security in the portfolio is determined solely by its price. The price of a security may have no relationship to the company's importance or size and therefore could represent an arbitrary weight. For example, consider two companies, each worth exactly $10,000. If the first company had 10 shares of common stock outstanding, it would be priced at $1000 per share. The second company, with 1000 shares outstanding, would carry a price of $10 per share. Obviously, the first company would carry a much greater weight in a price-weighted portfolio simply because of its higher per share price and not because of any greater economic or financial importance.

TABLE 5–3
Calculation of a price-weighted index

Stock	*Price at End of Year 1*	*Price at End of Year 2*
X	50	75
Y	25	50
Z	75	100
Index value	150	225

Return = (225 − 150)/150 = 0.50

One way of adjusting for this is to give each security in a portfolio the same proportional weight; this is called *equal weighting*. An equally weighted portfolio contains an equal dollar amount invested in each security. To accomplish this, the quantity of each security included in the portfolio is proportional to the reciprocal of the security's price. Table 5–4 shows how to compute an equally weighted index for the stocks X, Y, and Z from Table 5–3.

Computing the return on an equally weighted portfolio is actually easier than the procedure used in Table 5–3. The easy way is to compute the mean return of all the securities in the portfolio. Table 5–4 shows both procedures and confirms a return of 0.61 on the hypothetical, equally weighted index.

There are also criticisms of an equally weighted index. First, like a price-weighted index, it is somewhat arbitrary, considering that it treats all companies, both big and small, on an equal basis. Second, to maintain the equal weighting, the portfolio requires rebalancing at each time period, unless each security in the portfolio experienced the same return for that period. In Table 5–4, you will note that at year 2 the index is no longer equally weighted. For example, the price of 75 for stock X would mean a quantity of 1/75 = 0.013 would have to be in the index to maintain the equal weighting. The rebalancing procedure to accomplish this would indicate selling portions of the holdings in some of the securities and increasing others so that the portfolio once again contains equal quantities of each. Such a process in a real portfolio would be costly and time-consuming.

The final weighting scheme for portfolios that is frequently used for constructing stock indexes is *value weighting*. Securities in a value-weighted portfolio have weights proportional to their *total market value*. Total market value represents the aggregate value of all of the firm's stock outstanding, computed as follows:

$$\text{Total market value} = (\text{stock price}) \times (\text{shares outstanding}) \qquad \textbf{(5–1)}$$

As Equation 5–1 shows, the total market value of a company's stock is equal to the current market value per share times the total shares outstanding. Table 5–5 shows the sample computation of a value-weighted index containing stocks X, Y, and Z.

TABLE 5–4
Calculation of an equally weighted index

Stock	*Price at End of Year 1*	*Quantity*	*Value in Index*	*Price at End of Year 2*	*Value in Index*	*Return on Stock*
X	50	0.020	1.00	75	1.50	0.50
Y	25	0.040	1.00	50	2.00	1.00
Z	75	0.013	1.00	100	1.33	0.33
Index value			3.00		4.83	

$$\text{Return on index} = (4.83 - 3.00)/3.00 = 0.61$$

$$\text{Mean return on stocks} = (0.50 + 1.0 + 0.33)/3 = 0.61$$

TABLE 5–5
Calculation of a value-weighted index

Stock	*Shares Outstanding*	*Price at End of Year 1*	*Market Value*	*Price at End of Year 2*	*Market Value*
X	50	50	2500	75	3750
Y	10	25	250	50	500
Z	25	75	1875	100	2500
Index value			4625		6750

Return on index = (6750 − 4625)/4625 = 0.46

As Tables 5–3, 5–4, and 5–5 show, indexes constructed using the same stocks over the same time periods can show markedly different returns, depending upon the weighting scheme. Although the returns for these example indexes are hypothetical and somewhat exaggerated because of the small sample size, they do demonstrate how important it is that the investor be aware of the technique used to compute an index. This is especially important when an index is being used for investment performance evaluation. A cunning analyst could even go so far as to select the index that would show his investment performance in the best possible light.

Computational Procedures. The computational procedures of an index relate to the formula used to calculate the index and the method of adjusting for stock splits and changes in market capitalization. Although computation of most indexes involves the use of a simple arithmetic average using some divisor, a few indexes are computed using a geometric mean. (A geometric mean is equal to the nth root of the product of n numbers.) This is important to know because, if other factors are equal, over a given time period an arithmetic-average index will usually have a greater return than one computed using a geometric mean. In addition, the index can be set equal to its computed mean, or it can be indexed to a certain time period (for example, 1978 = 100). Consequently, some "indexes" are technically averages, while those indexed to a given time are true indexes.

The method of adjusting for stock splits (or stock dividends) and changes in the number of outstanding shares is also an important feature of computing a stock index. For the value-weighted indexes, a stock split will not change the value of the index because a split should not change a stock's total market value. However, it can be important for the other weighting schemes. (The next section of this chapter explains just one of many possible methods of adjusting for splits, the one used in the calculation of the Dow Jones Averages.) The issuance of new common stock would not change a price-weighted or equally weighted index, but it would affect the value of a value-weighted index because the number of shares outstanding would change. (The section of this chapter about the Standard & Poor's indexes shows how they adjust for these changes.)

It is important to note that market indexes are computed without any regard to cash dividends paid on the stocks in the index. Therefore, when comparing the total return on some investment to the return on some stock market index, an investor should remember to include the dividend return on the index in addition to the percent change in the index when computing the index total return. Over periods of time, omission of dividends from the total return of a market index can be dramatic. For example, Figure 5–2 charts the values that the Dow Jones Industrial Average would have had if the index computation assumed that all cash dividends were reinvested in the index. At the end of 1986, instead of having a value of 1896 as reported, the Dow Jones Industrial Average would have had a value of 7122!

Some Popular Market Indexes

Organizations that compute stock indexes usually fall into one of three categories:

1. Investment research and publishing companies
2. Securities exchanges and industry organizations
3. Government agencies

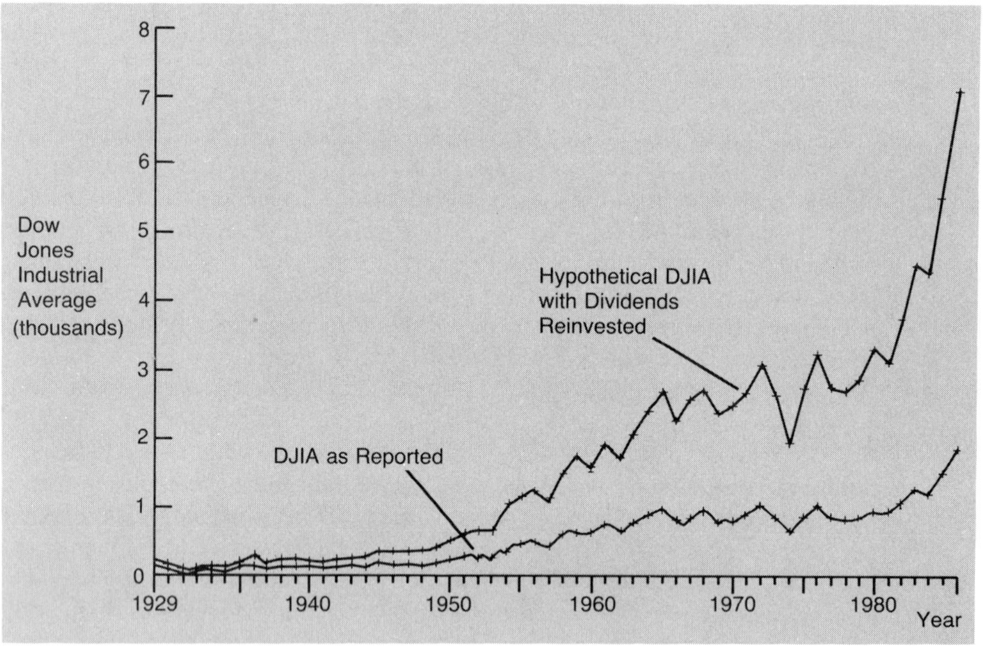

FIGURE 5–2
The Dow Jones Industrial Average, 1929–1986, compared to a hypothetical Dow Jones Industrial Average computed as if dividends had been reinvested

Table 5–6 summarizes some of the most widely quoted U.S. stock indexes, giving their source and some information about their construction. In addition, there are indexes for bonds, options, and futures. There are also market indexes for other major security markets in the world such as Toronto, Tokyo, London, Zurich, and Paris.

The Dow Jones Averages. One of the first published stock indexes, which still survives today, was the Dow Jones Industrial Average. Charles Dow, founder and then-editor of *The Wall Street Journal,* computed and published his first average, the Dow Jones

TABLE 5–6
Some popular stock market indexes

Index	*Sample Size*	*Weighting*
Investment publishing firms:		
Dow Jones		
Industrial	30	price
Transportation	20	price
Utility	15	price
Composite	65	price
Standard & Poor's		
500 Index	500	value
Industrial	400	value
Transportation	20	value
Utilities	40	value
Financials	40	value
Others: individual industries	various	value
Wilshire		
5000 Equity Index	all stocks with daily quotes	value and equal
Total Performance Index	all stocks with daily quotes[a]	value and equal
Exchanges:		
American Stock Exchange		
AMEX	all AMEX stocks	value
New York Stock Exchange		
Composite	all NYSE stocks	value
Various other subindexes	varying	
NASDAQ		
OTC Composite	numerous OTC stocks	value
Various other subindexes	varying	
Government:		
SEC	various exchange-traded stocks	value

[a]Assumes dividend reinvestment.

stock average, in *The Wall Street Journal* on July 3, 1884. It was composed of nine railroad companies, one steamship line, and the Western Union telegraph company. On May 26, 1896, the Dow Jones Industrial Average (DJIA), consisting of a dozen industrial stocks, made its debut. Dow added another average solely for railroad stocks on January 2, 1897, and the Dow Jones Utilities Average appeared several years later. On January 2, 1970, the rail average became the Dow Jones Transportation Average, after airplanes and other means of transportation had become important. Dow Jones also combines the three averages into one Composite Average.

The Dow Jones Averages are price weighted. Dow Jones computes them by summing the prices of the individual stocks in the average and dividing by a "divisor." The original divisor for the DJIA of thirty stocks was equal to thirty. As stock splits and stock dividends occurred, Dow Jones adjusted the divisor. *The Wall Street Journal* publishes the averages and the divisors used to compute them on a daily basis. The Dow Jones Averages adjust for stock splits (and stock dividends greater than 5 percent) by changing the divisor. Dow Jones adjusts its divisors for stock splits as follows:

$$\text{postsplit divisor} = \frac{P_n + P_s(1/SF)}{\text{DJA}} \tag{5–2}$$

where P_n = sum of the presplit prices of all nonsplitting stocks
P_s = presplit price of the splitting stock
SF = split factor (example: 2 for 1 split is $SF = 2$)
DJA = presplit Dow Jones Average

EXAMPLE 5–1

Eastman Kodak declared a 3 for 2 stock split effective on May 20, 1985. The DJIA had closed on the previous trading day (May 17) at 1285.34. The divisor was 1.132. The new divisor to use on May 20 is computed as follows:

$$\text{postsplit divisor} = \frac{1392.75 + 62.25 \times (2/3)}{1285.34}$$

$$= 1.116$$

The divisor reported in *The Wall Street Journal* for use on May 20 was 1.116.

The Dow Jones Industrial Average is probably the most widely quoted stock market barometer. A call to a stockbroker, asking, "How is the market?" will likely invoke a response answered with the day's change in the DJIA. However, there are many critics of the Dow Jones Averages.

The most obvious criticism leveled at the Dow Jones Averages is that the sample size is too small. For example, the DJIA contains only thirty stocks while other industrial indexes have hundreds or thousands. A second criticism of the Dow Jones Averages is that they have only stocks of large, "blue chip" companies and thus ignore a large segment of the market. A third criticism is that the price weighting places too much emphasis on the higher priced shares in the average. Finally, critics charge that the method of adjusting for stock splits does not represent a logical or reasonable portfolio management strategy. In effect, the Dow Jones method of adjusting the divisor is akin to an investor's selling the additional shares received from a stock split and reinvesting the proceeds in additional stock in each of the other issues existing in the portfolio in their existing proportions. In practice, however, the split of a stock does not usually induce an investor to take any action at all to buy or sell.

Standard & Poor's Indexes. The indexes produced by Standard & Poor's Corp. (S&P) are quite popular. Their sample size is greater than the Dow Jones' and the sample includes the larger companies on the major exchanges and the OTC. The indexes are value weighted and indexed to 1941–1943 = 10. In addition to the usual industrial, transportation, utility, and financial groupings, there are also several indexes for individual industries. Figure 5–3 shows the S&P indexes.

As mentioned earlier, a value-weighted index must compensate for any changes in the number of shares outstanding. Standard & Poor's uses the following relationships to compute its value-weighted indexes:

$$\text{index value} = \frac{\text{total current market value}}{\text{total base-period adjusted market value}} \times 10 \qquad \textbf{(5–3)}$$

The beginning value for the total adjusted market value is equal to the sum of the market values of the individual stocks in the index during the base (indexing) period. Thereafter, every time there is a change in capitalization, the new total base period adjusted market value is recalculated as follows:

$$\begin{matrix}\text{new base-period} \\ \text{total adjusted} \\ \text{market value}\end{matrix} = \begin{matrix}\text{old base-period} \\ \text{total adjusted} \\ \text{market value}\end{matrix} \times \frac{\begin{matrix}\text{base-date market value} \\ \text{reflecting capitalization change}\end{matrix}}{\begin{matrix}\text{base-date market value} \\ \text{without capitalization change}\end{matrix}} \qquad \textbf{(5–4)}$$

Relationships between Indexes

What relationship would we expect to see between different stock market indexes? Generally, they should move in unison for two reasons. First, there is usually some degree of overlap between any two indexes. For example, many of the stocks in the NYSE Composite Index are also included in the S&P 500 Index. Second, because markets are related to the economies within which they operate, one would expect to see all stock indexes responding similarly to a given set of economic circumstances. As an example, Figure 5–4 shows how two quite different indexes, the Wilshire 5000 and the Dow Jones Industrial, behaved over the time period 1982–1984.

Studies generally have indicated a high degree of correlation between the different U.S. stock market indexes (see, for example, Lorie and Hamilton[2]). Conducting a correlation analysis on the two stock indexes in Figure 5–4 shows them to have a very high level of correlation during 1982–1984. The correlation coefficient was 0.957 (a coefficient of 1.0 is perfect correlation, while a value of zero indicates no correlation).

Weekly Stock Price Indexes---1941–43 = 10

261

	Close Oct 29	Close Oct 22	Close Oct 15	Close Oct 8	Close Oct 1	1986 Range High	1986 Range Low
†500 **Stocks Combined**	240.94	236.26	238.80	236.68	233.60	253.83	203.49
400 **Industrials**	267.18	262.19	264.74	262.02	258.51	282.24	224.88
20 **Transportation**	205.25	199.64	201.73	199.57	194.81	217.28	176.16
40 **Utilities**	112.10	109.39	110.85	110.83	109.98	123.74	90.33
40 **Financial**	27.72	27.27	27.76	27.49	27.16	31.13	25.19
250 **OTC**	211.37	207.03	206.91	204.09	203.19	240.42	190.49
104 Capital Goods	222.39	218.68	214.40	220.90	221.05	238.78	206.94
179 Consumer Goods	271.38	263.53	265.33	259.87	253.99	305.36	208.14
25 High Grade Common	184.45	187.13	183.28	174.72	177.29	195.99	150.02
20 Low Price Common	576.62	578.53	574.25	558.25	563.02	657.10	505.03
INDUSTRIALS							
10 Aerospace/Defense	320.95	314.13	320.95	320.75	319.25	361.45	290.63
4 Aluminum	154.95	155.22	157.06	157.80	158.64	180.03	141.32
4 Automobile	131.60	127.94	127.41	128.42	126.59	151.15	110.95
Excl General Motors	80.22	77.28	77.55	78.37	75.87	87.31	54.77
4 Auto Parts—After Mkt	32.48	31.94	31.81	31.37	30.50	33.77	27.00
5 Auto Parts—Orig Equip	36.89	35.92	35.23	35.11	34.90	39.15	32.21
4 Auto Trucks & Parts	62.89	63.19	65.13	64.28	63.48	78.39	62.89
3 Beverages Brewers	172.04	165.76	173.69	169.09	159.85	187.13	133.36
4 Distillers	495.00	478.90	480.25	482.58	474.14	495.65	362.24
3 Soft Drinks	324.38	324.94	323.85	306.86	300.25	392.53	240.82
6 Broadcast Media	2290.84	2219.13	2231.28	2221.86	2165.81	2446.35	1782.76
9 Building Materials	171.86	163.08	169.74	164.50	162.89	186.43	125.15
8 Chemicals	121.50	116.55	118.38	117.21	111.68	125.76	87.43
6 Chemicals(Diversified)	31.63	29.68	29.75	29.20	28.71	31.63	23.55
4 Coal	351.36	337.01	354.74	348.23	344.52	364.23	299.71
6 Communication Equip Mfrs	27.66	27.21	27.24	26.82	26.28	29.93	25.06
14 Computer & Business Equipment	193.75	190.99	193.15	197.17	203.06	229.43	190.99
Excl I.B.M.	385.81	373.43	370.33	367.14	368.00	407.37	320.41
3 Computer Services	67.58	66.79	65.92	62.40	59.54	69.23	55.38
7 Conglomerates	46.87	45.71	45.79	45.92	44.79	48.16	38.38
4 Containers:Metal & Glass	148.50	144.00	148.78	144.28	143.44	155.58	103.18
3 Paper	709.61	674.14	672.80	656.00	680.64	709.61	470.00
3 Copper	50.51	52.12	52.60	52.41	51.06	55.02	38.07
6 Cosmetics	80.26	77.18	78.84	76.12	74.26	90.03	65.69
12 Drugs	515.14	505.39	504.21	493.09	483.84	573.09	386.28
4 Electrical Equipment	652.14	651.34	649.66	648.32	640.51	716.16	623.89
4 Electronic Defense	110.00	108.01	110.02	110.39	110.64	121.22	94.26
2 Electronic Major Cos	273.46	273.82	273.82	265.28	260.96	299.29	237.48
4 Electronics:Instrumentation	70.58	67.91	68.87	68.57	69.38	81.29	65.29
6 Semiconductors/Components	41.92	40.60	41.72	41.33	42.82	55.80	39.88
4 Entertainment	594.67	576.26	588.83	569.02	549.21	723.80	486.43
16 Foods	332.26	315.80	320.96	309.27	301.76	348.91	235.29
6 Forest Products	30.42	30.02	30.06	28.87	28.33	30.42	22.89
*4 Gaming Cos.	19.88	19.76	19.81	19.11	19.37	25.33	17.79
4 Gold Mining	118.09	121.57	121.62	129.83	118.88	139.62	92.52
3 Hardware & Tools	15.26	15.46	15.37	15.41	15.60	18.26	14.25
5 Homebuilding	53.99	54.80	55.38	54.03	53.74	62.47	41.29
4 Hospital Management	51.89	50.47	51.96	51.59	53.37	62.08	49.27
5 Hospital Supplies	116.45	115.77	114.95	112.41	110.63	130.19	86.20
5 Hotel-Motel	178.05	175.28	177.34	173.46	172.84	198.18	142.42
7 Household Furnish & Appliances	425.02	423.98	427.57	399.70	383.49	513.07	331.92
5 Leisure Time	180.28	171.87	172.60	165.35	167.13	218.39	145.61
5 Machine Tools	126.37	128.75	131.38	127.61	128.38	169.57	123.61
12 Machinery:Diversified	151.99	149.95	150.95	150.81	151.74	195.07	149.95
3 Manufactured Housing	117.62	116.04	121.12	122.13	125.58	178.76	113.27
9 Manufacturing Diversified Ind'l	166.61	160.37	161.93	159.14	159.13	166.61	130.49
3 Metals-Miscellaneous	92.88	92.62	98.55	99.85	99.22	105.50	83.06
3 Offshore Drilling	27.67	30.49	30.86	31.51	31.08	63.63	27.67
Oil:Composite	403.47	414.63	418.34	427.44	419.94	427.44	327.69
9 Domestic Integrated	412.94	423.92	432.14	440.92	427.69	440.92	362.41
5 Int'l Integrated	190.94	196.34	197.02	201.45	199.26	202.52	144.72
7 Oil Wells Equip. & Service	960.92	966.30	999.74	1013.23	987.20	1105.14	864.17
4 Canadian Oil & Gas Exploration	17.68	17.76	17.95	18.15	18.05	22.16	15.18
9 Paper	549.22	537.74	549.18	529.17	527.88	560.14	429.28
4 Pollution Control	156.13	153.50	150.95	146.67	138.41	156.13	103.49
6 Publishing	1337.01	1316.97	1323.20	1314.60	1297.71	1525.21	1078.18
6 Publishing (Newspapers)	108.66	106.28	108.17	105.91	101.23	122.50	84.47
5 Restaurants	133.13	126.30	128.73	127.25	122.32	161.32	111.53
Retail Stores Composite	259.80	251.79	253.94	248.92	242.71	283.30	196.71
8 Department Stores	602.26	590.47	582.74	579.78	564.32	616.55	460.86
4 Retail Stores (Drug)	85.11	84.91	86.47	84.01	83.40	98.19	69.25
8 Food Chains	179.75	174.49	177.04	174.48	171.34	185.98	133.60
5 Gen. Merchandise Chains	20.73	19.93	20.31	19.71	19.38	23.30	15.15
7 Retail (Specialty)	417.34	403.12	402.42	396.62	373.64	494.05	330.58
4 Shoes	169.38	161.47	162.92	159.35	154.81	189.87	140.11
4 Soaps	361.95	355.09	359.22	353.72	342.18	388.14	292.82
6 Steel	32.49	33.37	34.01	35.09	32.64	38.08	24.13
Excl. U.S. Steel	20.96	21.11	22.11	21.59	23.06	38.18	20.89
5 Textiles Apparel Mfrs	178.37	169.04	172.23	165.79	163.35	186.56	122.27
5 Textile Products	156.67	155.41	155.86	155.66	151.55	172.84	134.36
3 Tires and Rubber Goods	336.14	300.77	273.10	269.73	254.54	336.14	225.14
3 Tobacco	335.61	319.03	324.99	318.02	308.10	345.95	206.60
4 Toys	27.25	26.90	30.99	31.61	32.60	37.39	25.39
PUBLIC UTILITIES							
21 Electric Companies	59.75	57.83	57.45	57.12	57.17	65.24	48.21
11 Natural Gas Pipelines(& Dstr)	324.16	320.23	327.77	329.90	329.00	342.61	298.71
8 Telephone(New)	185.24	181.75	187.15	187.82	184.86	210.12	144.23
TRANSPORTATION							
3 Air Freight	57.32	54.06	54.84	55.01	54.48	62.87	45.56
5 Airlines(Formerly Air Transport)	226.06	220.44	228.27	222.17	217.67	228.27	178.21
6 Railroads	139.63	136.48	135.66	134.85	130.94	158.76	123.84
4 Truckers	304.29	302.85	312.11	307.45	304.86	319.79	229.94
FINANCIAL							
6 New York City Banks	110.79	108.84	111.30	112.56	111.08	129.51	95.06
11 Banks Outside N.Y.C.	113.40	109.08	109.90	110.79	107.41	126.88	99.20
4 Life Insurance	765.36	756.37	762.28	730.64	714.10	822.70	689.69
6 Multi-Line Insurance	45.07	44.80	45.51	45.15	44.78	53.78	43.92
5 Property-Casualty Insurance	308.38	302.27	307.88	300.06	295.94	355.17	284.89
3 Savings & Loan Holding Cos.	48.69	47.53	50.22	51.87	52.86	62.21	42.39
2 Personal Loans	237.11	240.15	241.92	236.98	236.61	241.92	171.12
*5 Brokerage Firms	71.61	67.36	67.20	63.10	61.62	72.86	58.17
*5 Real Estate Investment Trusts	5.07	4.97	4.98	4.96	4.93	5.12	4.02
*4 Investment Cos. (Closed-End)	81.54	79.55	79.79	79.43	79.99	84.34	71.38
*5 Investment Cos. (Bond Funds)	10.88	10.99	10.84	10.81	10.84	11.26	9.83

† Includes total of 37 miscellaneous cos.

*Not included in Composite indexes.

FIGURE 5–3
Standard and Poor's stock indexes (Reprinted with permission from *Standard and Poor's Stock Guide,* November 1986, © 1986, Standard & Poor's Corp.)

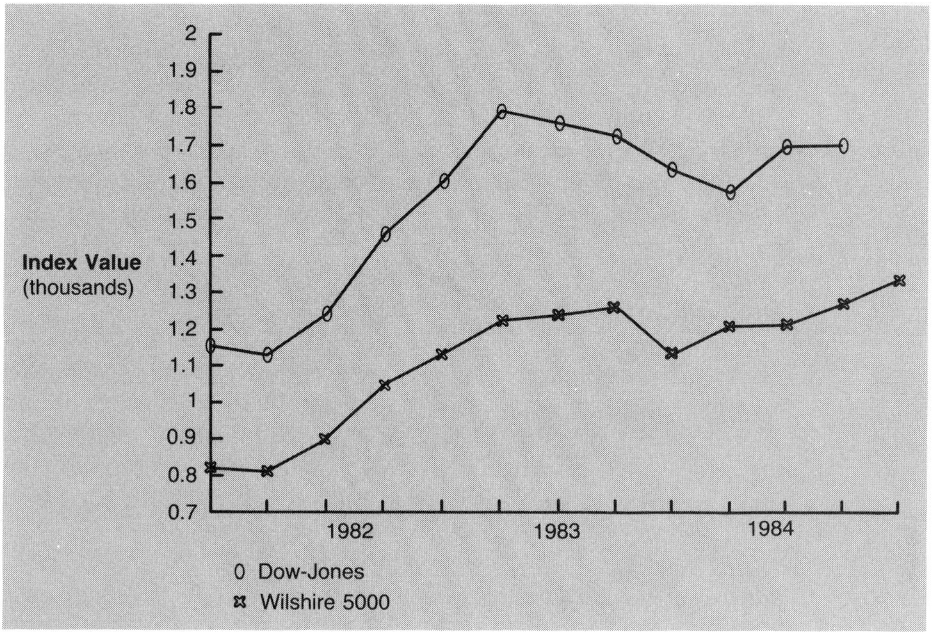

FIGURE 5–4
The Dow Jones Industrial Average and the Wilshire 5000 Value-Weighted Equity Index, 1982–1984

Table 5–7 gives this correlation coefficient and also coefficients between other indexes. As we would expect, the correlations between the larger indexes are even higher than those with the Dow Jones.

Even the various indexes of major worldwide exchanges show some coherence.[3] There seems to be even more dependence between two geographically or culturally close countries. For example, the New York and Toronto exchanges are more closely related than the New York and Tokyo exchanges.

TABLE 5–7
Correlations between pairs of major stock market indicators, 1982–1984

Index Pair		*Correlation Coefficient*
Wilshire 5000	S&P 500	0.990
Wilshire 5000	Dow Jones Industrial	0.957
Wilshire 5000	NYSE Industrial	0.987
S&P 500	Dow Jones Industrial	0.960
S&P 500	NYSE Industrial	0.987
Dow Jones Industrial	NYSE Industrial	0.948

General Market Publications

Many publications provide general securities market information. While some of these dedicate a significant portion of their space to the market, others devote themselves entirely to security investment. Table 5–8 lists some of the more widely used sources of market information.

Many smaller investment research and publishing companies also provide market information and forecasts. The advertisements appearing in *Barron's* provide a good sample of those available.

The Wall Street Journal

One of the most widely read daily newspapers in the United States is *The Wall Street Journal.* The front page contains summaries of major news items in the areas of both general worldwide news and business and financial news. Page one also contains a special reports column and articles of general business interest. Inside the *Journal* are articles and news items covering subjects from general economic data to news announcements of individual companies to editorials. The final section contains the

TABLE 5–8
Sources of market information

Publication (frequency)	***Content Summary***
Investment publishing firms:	
Barron's National Business and Financial Weekly (weekly)	Articles of market interest, detailed security price data, economic and market statistics
The Wall Street Journal (daily)	News of general and market interest, security prices, and market data
Forbes (biweekly)	Articles of general market interest, items on specific companies
Securities industry organizations:	
American Stock Exchange Annual Report (annual)	Facts on membership, trading activity, new listings
NASD Annual Report to Members (annual)	Activities on NASD and OTC trading information
New York Stock Exchange Fact Book (annual)	Security trading activity on the NYSE
Government:	
SEC Monthly Statistical Review (monthly)	Detailed securities trading data and new issue registrations

NEW YORK STOCK EXCHANGE COMPOSITE TRANSACTIONS

Monday, September 12, 1988

Quotations include trades on the Midwest, Pacific, Philadelphia, Boston and Cincinnati stock exchanges and reported by the National Association of Securities Dealers and Instinet

52 Weeks High	52 Weeks Low	Stock	Div.	Yld %	P-E Ratio	Sales 100s	High	Low	Close	Net Chg.
24¼	6¾	Amre	.12	.5	24	117	23¾	23¼	23½	– ¼
30¼	20½	AmSth	1.24	5.1	9	x101	24½	24⅜	24⅜	...
11½	3¾	Anacmp		...	10	893	8¼	8⅛	8¼	+ ¼
33	19¼	Anadrk	.30	1.2	66	718	25	24⅜	24⅜	– ⅝
20¼	8⅜	Analog		...	17	133	12	11¾	11⅞	+ ⅛
29¾	11¼	AnchGl	.08	.7	13	376	11⅝	11¼	11¼	– ½
31¾	18½	Angelic	.72	3.3	12	412	22	21⅜	22	+ ¼
13	9⅝	AngelRl	1.52e	14.7	61	71	10⅜	10⅛	10⅜	+ ¼
39	25¾	Anheus	.72	2.3	14	4103	31½	31	31⅜	...
17⅜	6¾	Anthem		...	14	227	11⅜	11¼	11¼	– ⅛
17⅛	7¾	Anthony	.44b	2.7	9	64	16⅜	16	16¼	+ ⅜
28⅞	20½	Aon cp	1.28	4.6	10	115	27⅞	27⅝	27⅝	– ¼
11½	6⅝	Apache	.28	4.1	...	526	7	6⅞	6⅞	...
7	2¼	ApcP un	.25	10.5	...	1157	2½	2⅜	2⅜	...
83	66	ApPw pf	7.40	9.8	...	z230	75½	75½	75½	...
36	17¼	ApplBk		...	7	1	32⅝	32⅝	32⅝	– ⅛
20⅞	8½	ApplM s		...	10	419	14¼	13¾	13¾	...
27⅜	17½	ArchDn	.10b	.5	9	1609	19	18⅞	18⅞	– ¼
38¾	17	ArcoCh	.80	2.5	...	295	31⅞	31½	31⅝	...
39	16¾	Aristec	.92	3.0	5	458	30¾	29⅞	30¼	+ ⅜
23⅞	15⅝	Arkla	1.08	5.7	16	1403	19⅛	18¾	19	...
51½	34½	Arkla pf	3.00	7.4	...	17	40½	40½	40½	– ¼
14¾	7⅛	Armco		...	21	1771	10¼	9⅞	10⅛	...
25½	18¼	Armc pf	2.10	8.8	...	12	24	23¾	23⅞	+ ⅛
46	37¾	Armc pf	4.50	10.8	...	4	41⅝	41½	41⅝	+ ⅜
44¾	22½	ArmWl	1.00	2.9	10	354	34¾	34¼	34½	...
51	43½	ArmW pf	3.75	7.5	...	z100	50	50	50	+ ½
47	13	Armtek	.48	1.1	15	4577	45⅝	45⅝	45⅝	– ⅝
12⅛	4⅞	ArowE		...	191	291	7¾	7⅜	7⅝	– ⅛
21½	12	ArowE pf	1.94	11.9	...	16	16¼	16⅛	16¼	...
41¾	11	Artra		...	...	27	23⅝	23⅜	23⅜	– ¼
32¾	14¾	Arvin	.68	3.0	27	193	23	22⅝	22¾	– ⅛
38¼	14⅝	ChiPac s		...	14	53	34½	34⅛	34⅛	– ⅛
11	5⅜	ChkFull	.31t	3.3	28	83	9⅝	9⅜	9½	– ¼
28	10¾	ChrisCr	.53t	2.5	25	59	21½	21⅛	21⅜	– ⅛
45	19⅝	Chryslr	1.00	4.4	5	2486	23	22¾	22⅞	...
69⅝	50⅞	Chubb	2.16	3.7	7	728	58⅝	57⅝	57⅝	– ⅞
10⅛	5	Churchs	.20	2.7	37	3400	7⅝	7¼	7⅜	...
7½	3⅝	Chyron	.14b	3.4	34	36	4¼	4	4⅛	+ ⅛
36	29	Cilcorp	2.40	7.5	14	40	32⅛	31⅞	32⅛	+ ⅜
32¾	19⅜	CinnBel	1.12	3.5	13	172	32	31¾	32	+ ½
29	23⅛	CinGE	2.24	8.4	12	121	26¾	26⅜	26⅝	– ⅛
97	85⅛	CinG pf	9.52	10.6	...	z30	90	90	90	–1
32⅞	14	CinMil	.72	3.2	...	233	22½	22	22⅜	...
15⅜	7¾	CineOd		...	11	1451	11¼	10¾	11⅛	+ ⅜
16⅜	7	CircleK	.28	2.1	14	1907	13⅝	13¼	13⅜	...
38¾	17	CirCty	.12	.3	16	1633	38⅜	38	38	+ ⅜
34¾	17½	Circus s		...	15	192	30¾	30⅝	30⅝	...
30	15⅞	Citicrp s	1.48	6.1	4	11316	25⅛	24¼	24¼	– ¼
80½	62½	Citcp pf	6.00e	9.4	...	10	64	63¾	64	...
5	1	Clabir	.04j	...	...	5	1½	1½	1½	+ ⅛
8½	2⅝	ClairSt	.10	2.4	...	421	4¼	4	4¼	+ ⅛
35⅞	17¼	ClarkE		...	137	266	29¼	28¾	28¾	– ½
13⅛	7	ClayHm		...	10	73	11⅛	11	11⅛	+ ⅛
9	4⅜	ClemGlb		...	...	202	7⅛	7	7	...
26	7¾	ClvClf		...	7	69	25½	25⅛	25⅛	...
76	67	ClvEl pf	7.56	11.2	...	z220	67¾	67¾	67¾	...
84½	74¾	ClvEl pf	8.73e	11.7	...	1	74½d	74½	74½	– ¼
33¾	23½	Clorox	1.04	3.3	13	1013	31⅜	30⅞	31⅜	+ ⅛
23⅝	9	ClubMd	.20	1.3	17	5	15¼	15⅛	15⅛	– ⅛
13⅝	6⅝	Coachm	.40	3.6	36	37	11½	11¼	11¼	– ¼
8⅜	3⅝	Cstam		...	11	106	6⅝	6½	6⅝	+ ⅛
22	12¾	CoastSL.	.40	2.6	4	26	15⅝	15⅜	15⅜	– ⅜
38½	21	Coastal	.40	1.2	15	288	33⅛	32½	32½	– ¾

AMERICAN STOCK EXCHANGE COMPOSITE TRANSACTIONS

Monday, September 12, 1988

Quotations include trades on the Midwest, Pacific, Philadelphia, Boston and Cincinnati stock exchanges and reported by the National Association of Securities Dealers and Instinet

52 Weeks High	52 Weeks Low	Stock	Div.	Yld %	P-E Ratio	Sales 100s	High	Low	Close	Net Chg.
13¾	5⅜	Diag B		...	10	15	7¼	7¼	7¼	...
3 7/16	1 1/16	Diasonc		...	15	180	2 11/16	2 9/16	2⅝	– ⅛
11	4¼	DckMA g	.15e	...	...	18	4¼	4¼	4¼	– ⅛
52	24	Dillard	.16	.4	14	395	42⅛	41⅝	41⅞	+ ⅜
4⅝	1⅜	Diodes		...	19	18	3	2⅞	2⅞	– ¼
4¼	1⅞	DirActn		...	21	10	3	3	3	...
12⅜	5¾	DiviHtl	.25e	2.9	11	32	8⅝	8⅜	8⅝	...
12¼	5½	DixnTi s		...	13	44	12⅜u	11⅞	12	– ⅛
13¾	10¾	Donely	.28	2.4	11	8	11½	11⅜	11½	+ ⅛
6½	2⅛	Ducom	.05j	...	...	20	2⅛	2⅛	2⅛	...
23½	13¾	Duplex	.68	3.8	12	24	18¼	18⅛	18⅛	+ ⅛
		–E–E–E–								
16⅝	5½	EECO s	.12j	...	19	1	6⅜	6⅜	6⅜	– ⅛
22⅜	6⅞	ENSR		...	39	230	10⅞	10¼	10¼	– ⅛
7¼	3	ESI	.29t	8.9	6	25	3¼	3¼	3¼	...
2	½	EaglCl		...	...	38	1	15/16	15/16	– 1/16
11¼	7⅜	EaglFn	.40	4.3	...	8	9⅜	9⅜	9⅜	...
20¼	12⅛	EAL pf	2.84	19.1	...	22	14⅞	14¾	14⅞	...
17¼	6½	EAL pf	2.72	32.5	...	6	8⅜	8⅛	8⅜	+ ¼
19	8⅛	EAL pf	3.24	37.6	...	175	8⅞	8⅝	8⅝	– ¼
18⅜	7¼	EAL pf	3.12	35.7	...	5	8¾	8¾	8¾	+ ¼
12⅛	3	LoriCp		...	...	4	6⅝	6⅝	6⅝	– ⅛
17⅛	6⅝	LorTel		...	14	411	13⅞	13⅝	13¾	+ ⅛
15⅞	8	Lumex	.08	.7	...	2	12	12	12	...
21¾	12⅞	Lydal		...	13	20	15⅜	15	15⅜	+ ½
		–M–M–M–								
17¾	7¾	MCO Hd		...	4	36	13¾	13⅝	13¾	– ⅛
10¼	7¼	MSA	1.00e	10.7	14	11	9⅜	9¼	9⅜	...
1⅛	3/16	MSA wt		...	...	75	½	½	½	+ 1/16
19⅛	8	MSI Dt s		...	17	2385	17⅝	17¼	17⅝	+ ¼
3	1¼	MSR		...	...	71	1½	1⅜	1½	+ ⅛
9⅛	1½	MacGrg		...	...	40	1¾	1⅝	1⅝	...
20¾	9⅞	MacNSc	.28	2.7	14	92	10⅜	10¼	10⅜	+ ⅛
37¼	23	MePS	2.60	7.2	7	6	35⅞	35½	35⅞	+ ½
11	6	Malart g	.20	...	...	14	6⅜	6⅜	6⅜	...
17½	6½	ManfHo		...	...	6	12	11⅞	12	...
2⅝	⅛	vjMrthO		...	...	2	⅛	⅛	⅛	...
2¼	½	Marlton		...	...	52	13/16	¾	13/16	+ 1/16
6⅞	2½	MarsG		...	8	4	3⅛	3⅛	3⅛	...
9½	2¾	MatRsh		...	...	56	5½	5⅛	5½	– ⅛
24½	10¾	MatSci		...	12	11	14⅜	14¼	14⅜	...
10	3⅞	Matrix		...	68	27	9⅝	9½	9½	...

FIGURE 5–5

Sample NYSE and AMEX price quotations (Reprinted by permission of *The Wall Street Journal,* © Dow Jones & Company, Inc. 1988. All Rights Reserved.)

statistical coverage, which includes daily stock, bond, option, futures, and mutual fund prices; dividends; interest rates; and other market statistics. The daily column appearing in this section, "Heard on the Street," provides insight and analysis concerning news of individual stocks, industry groups, and overall market trends.

The quotations for common stocks in the *Journal* begin with the prices of NYSE stocks in the final section, followed by prices from the OTC and AMEX markets. Figure 5–5 shows how the *Journal* reports these stocks' prices. The first two columns give a stock's high and low prices over the latest fifty-two weeks. The next column contains the name of the company, abbreviated if necessary. (Remember, this abbreviation is *not* the *stock symbol*—the one to five letters used by the exchanges and the NASD for reporting stock transactions over the wire. The abbreviations used in *The Wall Street Journal,* and on the financial pages of other newspapers, are abbreviations of the companies' names, and they may or may not resemble the stock symbol.) The next two columns give the stock's dividend for the last twelve months and the *dividend yield,* the dividend divided by that day's closing stock price. The next column has the

NASDAQ NATIONAL MARKET ISSUES

4:00 p.m. Eastern Time Prices

Monday, September 12, 1988

365-day High	365-day Low	Stock	Div	Yld	P-E	Sales (hds)	High	Low	Last	Net Chg.
20¾	11	Concurrent C		..	16	32	19½	19¼	19¼	– ¼
6⅛	4½	ConferTech I		..	..	178	5	4½	5	+1-16
27⅜	12	Connght Bios		..	..	150	22¼	21⅞	21⅞	– ⅜
10⅛	7⅛	ConnerPerph		..	..	3874	8⅜	7⅞	8¼	+ ½
7½	2¾	CONMED Cp		..	12	28	5¼	5¼	5¼	– ¼
23	17¾	CnnWtrS	1.52	7.8	9	6	19½	19½	19½	...
10	5	ConsCpl	2.60b	45.	..	122	5⅞	5⅝	5¾	+ ⅛
4¼	2⅜	CnCpRI	.85d	72.	..	49	2½	2½	2½	...
8	4	CnCpSTr	4.26a	90.	..	115	4¾	4½	4¾	+ ⅛
8⅜	5	Consol Fibres		..	5	10	7½	7½	7½	+ ⅛
43½	23⅜	ConsPapr sl		..	13	701	39½	38¾	39	...
7¾	3	ConslProd	.12	1.7	8	36	7⅛	7	7⅛	...
36¼	20½	ConstlBcp	1.08	3.8	9	4	28¼	28¼	28¼	– ½
1⅞	¾	Consul Restrt		..	..	76	1⅜	1 5-16	1 5-16	–1-16
20	15½	ConstnBcp NE		..	..	2	17	17	17	– ⅜
20	15	Consum W	.96	5.2	13	28	19	18¼	18½	...
19½	14⅛	ContelCel A		..	..	170	16⅝	16⅝	16⅝	+ ⅛
8⅜	2½	ContlHlth Affil		..	10	35	6¾	6½	6¾	– ¼
15¼	7	Cont'l MdSys		..	27	40	8	7⅞	7⅞	– ⅛
29¾	9½	Continuum		..	23	95	13¼	12¾	13	– ¼
18¾	3⅛	ContrlRes In		..	..	1815	6⅞	6½	6⅝	+ ⅛
19¼	5¼	ConvFdM 10k		..	6	11	5½	5½	5½	– ½
7¾	2¾	Convergnt Inc		..	..	3262	6 3-16	6⅛	6⅛	–1-16
3¾	5-16	Conversion In		..	..	72	1	15-16	1	...
15⅜	6¼	Convex Cmpt		..	27	315	7⅜	7⅛	7¼	...
15½	6	Cooper Dev		..	..	181	10⅞	10¾	10¾	...
21¼	5	CooperLife Sci		..	..	102	10⅛	10	10	...
15¾	8½	Co-Op Bcp	.60	5.3	6	78	11¼	11	11¼	+ ⅛
25	16¼	CoorsCo B	.50	2.5	16	393	20¼	19⅞	19⅞	– ¼
16¾	3⅜	Copytele Inc		..	..	240	10⅛	9⅞	10	– ⅛
6	2¾	Corcom Inc		..	22	3	3⅛	3⅛	3⅛	...
21½	8⅝	Cordis Corprn		..	..	427	17⅜	16⅞	17¼	+ ⅜
41⅞	29⅛	CoreStFin	1.50	3.8	10	246	39½	39¼	39½	+ ⅛
14	7	CornrstnF	.36	3.7	3	15	9⅞	9¾	9¾	– ¼
15	5	Corp Softw		..	..	30	10	9¾	9¾	...
7¾	3	Correct Corp		..	..	25	5⅞	5⅝	5⅞	...
7⅜	1 15-16	CorpData Sci		..	..	91	7⅛	7	7	– ¼
21	9	CostarCorp s		..	23	27	20½	20	20	+1½

365-day High	365-day Low	Stock	Div	Yld	P-E	Sales (hds)	High	Low	Last	Net Chg.
36⅞	10⅞	Environdyn In		..	11	455	26½	26	26½	+ ¼
22½	9⅞	Envirosafe Sv		..	13	149	13⅜	13	13⅛	– ⅛
10	2 7-16	Enzon Inc		..	..	10	5⅛	4⅞	5⅛	...
16	3	Enzon Inc wt		..	..	95	6	5¼	5½	– ½
14¾	(L)	Epsilon Data		..	26	10	8¼	8¼	8¼	– ¼
9	4	Equion Corp		..	13	33	8¾	8⅝	8⅝	– ⅛
25	16	EquitlBc	.92g	4.2	8	32	22¼	21¾	21¾	– ½
26¾	15	Equtbl IB	1	4.6	8	3	21¾	21¾	21¾	...
⅜	⅛	Equitex Inc		..	..	2687	9-32	¼	9-32	+1-32
6¼	3⅜	EquityOil	.05b	1.1	64	46	4⅝	4½	4½	– ¼
43⅝	25¼	Ericsson	1.73d	4.0	20	115	43⅝	43⅝	43⅝	+ ⅛
152	109	Erie lackawn		..	21	11	151	150	151	–1
12¾	5¾	Escalade Inc		..	7	1	9¼	9¼	9¼	...
20	8½	Essef Corp		..	8	25	9¾	9½	9¾	...
29½	14⅛	Evans Suthrld		..	11	21	18	17½	17½	– ½
14¼	5	Everex Systm		..	..	631	6	5⅝	5⅝	– ⅜
23¼	15	EvrGrn B	.72	3.2	8	10	22¾	22¼	22¼	...
11¼	4¼	Exar Corp		..	..	80	5¾	5¾	5¾	– ⅜
18½	7	Excelan Inc		..	23	1490	12	11	11½	+ ¼
16⅜	10⅛	ExchBc	.15f	.9	14	21	16⅜	16⅛	16⅜	+ ⅛
5⅝	2¼	EXECUTON		..	..	196	3½	3¼	3¼	...
13¼	8½	ExcelBncp	.60	5.5	..	425	10⅞	10⅝	10⅞	+ ¼
14¼	2⅞	Exovir Inc		..	..	135	8¾	8¼	8½	+ ⅛
19¼	11⅝	Expeditrs Intl		..	16	21	17	16¾	16¾	– ¼
16¾	8½	E-Z-EM Inc		..	15	5	13	13	13	– ⅜
		--F F--								
10⅞	6	FabricInd	.16	1.7	11	38	9⅜	9⅜	9⅜	...
7	4½	Fair Isaac		..	..	293	7	6½	7	...
3¾	2¼	Falcon OilGas		..	12	13	3⅜	3⅜	3⅜	...
12¼	6¾	Family Bancp		..	..	314	10	9⅞	9⅞	...
7⅝	2¼	FamlyStk Hs		..	17	24	2⅝	2½	2½	...
3½	1⅜	Famous Rest		..	14	251	1½	1⅜	1⅜	–1-16
18	13	F&M Natl	.50	3.8	10	23	13⅞	13¼	13¼	– ¼
3¾	1¼	Faradyne Elc		..	6	2	2⅝	2⅝	2⅝	...
22¼	11	Farm & Hm	1	5.3	7	41	19	18⅞	19	...
18¾	8½	Farm Fresh		..	..	489	12⅝	12½	12½	...
4⅝	1¼	FarmHsFd 5k		..	..	2	1 15-16	1¾	1 15-16	+3-16
(H)	37¾	FrmrsGp	1.44	2.0	17	2417	70⅝	70¾	70⅝	+ ¼

FIGURE 5–6

Sample OTC stock price quotations (Reprinted by permission of *The Wall Street Journal,* © Dow Jones & Company, Inc. 1988. All Rights Reserved.)

stock's price-earnings ratio, or *P/E ratio,* which is equal to the stock's closing price divided by the last twelve months' earnings per share. The volume of shares traded (in hundreds of shares) appears in the next column. The next three columns present the stock's high price for the day, the low price for the day, and the price of the last reported trade. The final item gives the price change from the previous day's closing price. As is the custom for all stock trading in the United States, all prices are given in points (dollars) and eighths of a point. For example, in Figure 5–5, the closing price for Arkla Gas on the NYSE was 19, unchanged from the previous day. The day's trading volume was 1403 round lots (140,300 shares).

Similarly detailed price reporting appears also for the over-the-counter NASDAQ National Market. For the less actively traded OTC issues, quotations contain only the bid and ask of the issue. Figure 5–6 gives some examples of OTC price reporting.

Trading of corporate bonds is also at one-eighth intervals. Quotes for bonds are per $100 of principal amount, even though most bonds have a total principal amount of $1000. Figure 5–7 shows examples of corporate bond price quotes. Consult the

NASDAQ BID AND ASKED QUOTATIONS

Stock & Div	Sales 100s	Bid	Asked	Net Chg.
Acclaim E	125	2¾	2⅞	−1-16
AcclmEnA wt	3	2½	2 11-16	...
AdelphiaCm A	16	19	19½	...
Advatex Assc	2	2⅞	3 1-16	− ⅛
AFN Inc	4	⅞	1	...
Airsensors	25	1 1-32	1 1-16	+1-32
AJRossLog ut	10	2⅞	3⅛	...
All Amer Tel	10	2⅞	3⅛	...
Am Biodynm	142	1¾	2	− ⅛
AmAircrft s	178	1 15-32	1½	+1-32
ACityB pf1.50	7	15¼	15¾	− ¼
Am ConsltgCp	35	2¾	3½	− ½
Amerihost P	300	1-16	3-32	...
ARecreatn .13	2	7⅞	8½	...
Am W Air deb	z16	56	58½	...
Andrews Grp	401	5⅜	5⅝	+ ⅜
APCO Argent	z90	5½	6	...

Stock & Div	Sales 100s	Bid	Asked	Net Chg.
FstFnMg deb	6	93	93¾	...
FirstNatl Cp	40	2⅜	2⅝	...
FstWorld ut	4	31¾	32½	+ 2¼
Fisons PLC	425	16	16⅛	+ ¼
FNB Corp .24	5	15½	17	...
GAC Liqd 1b	3	2¼	2 7-16	...
Galagraph ut	3	3½	4	...
Genl Kinetic	30	2¼	2¾	...
GenesseC 1.20	2	45	46½	...
GNI Group	104	3½	3¾	− ⅛
GoldCoAm ut	19	6¼	7	...
Goldenbell Res	2	1⅜	1¾	...
Golden Knight	30	8⅜	8¾	− ⅞
Golden Triang	75	11-32	13-32	...
Green C .25d	15	11	11¼	...
GrfflhCn .10b	22	5¼	6	− ¼
GrueneInc s	4	8¾	9½	...

Stock & Div	Sales 100s	Bid	Asked	Net Chg.
PetHlcoptr .08	6	9¾	10¼	...
Picktt ut LP	7	9¼	9¾	...
Piezo Elec Pr	16	1-16	⅛	...
PionFd pf1.88	18	23	25	...
PolicyMS db	2	77	78½	− ½
Prec Std Inc	189	3 5-16	3 7-16	...
Prima Energy	5	3⅝	3⅞	...
Profit Techn	11	5¼	5½	...
Provdnt Bcrp	10	41½	43½	+ ½
RadaElec bd	170	1 3-16	1¼	...
Rainbw Tech	z50	6¼	6¾	...
RCM TchB ut	5	5 9-16	5⅞	+1-16
RealAmer Corp	5	4¼	4¾	...
Realistl .20	12	11½	11⅞	...
RgnlFdB .20d	5	10½	10¾	...
Retiremt 1.08b	12	16	17	...
RF&P Corp	3	31	31½	...

ADDITIONAL NASDAQ QUOTES

	Bid	Asked
Acclaim E	2¾	2⅞
ACS Enterprise	1⅛	1¼
Action Staffing	1¼	1 7-16
AdvDisplay Tec	11-32	⅜
AdvPrdctsTc A	27-32	⅞
AdvPrdctsTc C	1 3-32	1 5-32
AdvMedical Pr	1-32	1-16
AdvnNMR Syst	4⅜	4⅝
AdvNMRSys wt	4⅛	4½
Advanced Pr	3 5-32	3 7-32
AdvisorsCp Tc	2¼	2¾
Aerosonic Corp	1½	1⅝
AFP Imaging	1 7-16	1 9-16
Agouron Pharm	13	13½
AirshipIntl Ltd	9-16	⅝
AJ Ross Logist	1 7-16	1½
Alaska Apollo	9-16	21-32
Alcide Corp	4⅜	4½
Alfa Interntl	3	3⅜
Alpha Solarco	7-16	15-32
Alternatv Hlth	11-16	13-16
Amer Bionetics	1⅜	1½

	Bid	Asked
Crown Resourc	2 3-16	2 5-16
Cryodynamics	1	1⅛
Cucos Inc	2⅜	2 11-16
Cumo Resource	1-32	1-16
Cusac Industr	1 1-32	1⅛
Cyanotech Cp	1 1-32	1 3-32
Cybermedic Inc	3-16	¼
CytRx Bio wt	11-16	¾
CytRx Biopool	1 7-16	1 9-16
CytRx Corp ut	15¼	16
Dallas OilMin	¼	9-32
Daltex Medical	1 1-16	1 3-16
Daltex Med wt	⅜	7-16
DASA Corp	3-32	5-32
Dart Drug St	2⅛	2⅜
Datamag Inc	7⅛	7¼
DataMd Clinic	⅝	11-16
Delta DataS	5-32	7-32
DenningMobil R	1 9-16	1⅝
Denpac Corp	1-16	⅛
Dense-Pac Mic	1	1¼
Diagnostic Sci	¼	5-16

	Bid	Asked
Intl Electronic	3⅛	3⅝
Intl Microcmp	5-32	3-16
Intl Micro wt	3-32	⅛
qInterst CellT	⅛	5-32
Investors Htg	26	28
Invest Tech	1-16	3-32
Investors Trst	1 3-16	1½
IPM Inc	5-16	11-32
Irvine Sensors	3-16	¼
Isramco Inc	1 3-16	1¼
IstecInd Tech	3⅜	3⅞
JackCarl 312Fut	9-32	⅜
JAM Inc	9-16	⅞
Jean Philippe	1 3-16	1¼
Judicate Inc	2 1-16	2⅛
KCR Technolgy	2 3-16	2⅜
Kentucky Med	10½	11½
Keystone Med	1 15-16	2
KrischAm Inn	2	2 1-16
Knowledg Data	11-16	13-16
Kyle Technolg	¾	15-16

	Bid	Asked
Psychemedics	⅝	13-16
Quadrax Corp	3¾	4
Quality Systm	1	1⅛
Qubix Grphc	3-32	⅛
Radiation Disp	7⅜	7½
Radon Testing	7-32	¼
Rapitech Syst	2	2⅛
Raycomm Tran	2 1-16	2⅛
RCM Technolg	3 15-16	4 1-16
RCM TchB ut	5 9-16	5⅞
Red Eagle Res	1 3-16	1 5-16
Renaissn GRX	2	2⅛
Renaissance wt	¼	11-32
Rent Rite Inc	1½	1⅝
Repco Inc	½	⅞
Research Frnt	5¾	6¼
Rexcom System	1-32	1-16
Rise Technolgy	1¼	1 9-32
Ritzy's GD	¼	⅜
Roadmaster Inc		

FIGURE 5–6
(continued)

NEW YORK EXCHANGE BONDS

Friday, September 9, 1988

Total Volume $33,730,000

SALES SINCE JANUARY 1

1988	1987	1986
$5,283,445,000	$6,821,855,000	$7,441,916,000

	Domestic Fri.	Domestic Thu.	All Issues Fri.	All Issues Thu.
Issues traded	633	603	638	607
Advances	313	269	315	270
Declines	183	219	184	221
Unchanged	137	115	139	116
New highs	11	11	11	11
New lows	6	7	6	7

Dow Jones Bond Averages

-1986- High	-1986- Low	-1987- High	-1987- Low	-1988- High	-1988- Low		---Friday--- -1988-		-1987-		-1986-	
93.65	83.73	95.51	81.26	91.25	86.92	20 Bonds	88.78	+0.07	85.07	-0.15	91.34	+0.04
95.79	81.85	98.23	79.51	91.88	86.05	10 Utilities	88.15	+0.01	84.69	-0.37	92.63	-0.02
91.64	84.82	93.10	83.00	90.64	86.96	10 Industrial	89.41	+0.12	85.44	+0.06	90.04	+0.09

Bonds	Cur Yld	Vol	Close	Net Chg.
Mobil 7⅝91	7.9	50	96⅝	- ⅝
Mobil 13.76s04	13.1	2	105⅛	...
Mobil 8¼92	8.4	221	98⅜	+ ½
Mobil 8⅝94	8.8	54	98⅛	+ ⅜
Mobil 8.7s91	8.7	10	99¾	+ 1
MonyM 7s90	cv	10	96	...
Moran 8¾08f	cv	75	70½	+ ½
Morgn 4¾98	cv	11	190	+ 4⅜
MtSTI 7⅜11	9.6	5	77⅛	- ⅜
MtSTI 7¾13	9.5	20	81½	+ ⅞
MtSTI 9⅝15	9.8	8	98	+ ⅝
MtSTI 7⅞16	9.5	1	82½	+ 2¼
MtStTI 9¼14	9.8	1	94	...
NBI 8¼07	cv	11	42	...
NCNB 8⅜99	9.3	5	90	+ 1¾
NConv 9s08	cv	1	83	+ 1½
NtGyp zr04	...	36	69½	- ¼
NInd 10s99	10.9	1	92	- ⅛
NMed 9s06	cv	112	103¾	- ¼
NMed 8s08	cv	39	89¼	- ½
NMed 12¾99A	12.4	4	103	...
NMed 12½00	12.1	9	103	- 2
NMed zr04	...	3	29½	...
NRUt A9¾09	10.0	15	97⅜	- 1⅛
NStl 8⅜06	11.0	7	76⅜	+ 1
Navstr 6¼98	8.2	5	76⅝	+ 1⅜
Navstr 8⅝95	9.3	8	92½	+ 1
Navstr 9s04	10.3	3	87⅛	- 1
NavFin 8⅝91	9.0	5	96¼	- ⅛
NavFin 7⅝93	8.5	5	89¼	...
NJBTI 7¾13	9.7	30	80¼	- ¾
NJBTI 8s16	9.7	3	82⅜	- ⅝
NJBTI 8¾18	9.5	25	91⅞	+ ⅞
NYEG 7⅝01	9.2	1	83	+ 1¾
Newhal 6¾11	6.2	25	108½	+ 3¼
NiMP 8.35s07	9.9	7	84⅜	+ 1⅞
NoNG 8s91	8.3	10	95⅞	...
NwnBl 7⅞11	9.5	56	83¼	+ ½
NwnBl 7½05	9.2	5	81¾	+ ⅛
NwnBl 9½16	9.9	65	96¼	...
Oakwd 6½12	cv	25	58	...
OccP dc9.65s94	9.9	357	97⅜	...
OcciP d8.95s94	9.4	131	94¾	+ ⅛
OcciP 10s91	9.9	17	101⅛	+ ⅛
OcciP 10½93	10.3	20	101⅝	+ ⅛
OcciP 10⅞96	10.6	110	103	- ¼
OhBIT 7⅞13	9.5	5	82½	...

Bonds	Cur Yld	Vol	Close	Net Chg.
TennGas 8⅞03	9.7	15	91⅛	+ ⅛
TennGas dc6s11	9.7	209	62	- ⅝
TennGas 12⅝88	12.6	4	99 29/32	- 11/32
TennGas 9⅜17	10.4	5	90	- ¾
TVA 7s97	8.1	85	86	+ ⅛
TV 7.35s97B	8.4	10	88	+ ⅛
Tesor dc12¾01	14.3	5	89	...
Texco 13⅝94	12.4	92	109¾	+ ¾
Texco 13s91	12.7	124	102½	- ⅜
Texco 10¾00t	10.8	4	99⅝	...
Texco 5¾97	7.8	62	73⅜	+ ⅜
Texco 7¾01	9.6	114	80⅜	+ ⅛
Texco 8⅞05	10.4	95	85	- ¼
Texco 8½06	10.3	65	82½	+ ¾
TxABnc 15½92	41.8	45	37⅛	- ⅞
TexEst 12s09	cv	30	107¼	+ ⅜
TxInd 9s08	cv	5	104	- 1
TxOG 16⅝91	16.2	29	102½	- ½
Textrn 9¼16	10.5	10	88⅛	- ⅜
Thermo 5¾12	cv	1	82½	...

Bonds	Cur Yld	Vol	Close	Net Chg.
WUTI 16s91f	...	24	91½	+ 1½
WstC 7.6s97	8.1	1	94	+ 5
WisBl 8s14	9.7	5	82⅛	- 1¾
Witco 5½12	cv	1	81	...
Woolw 9s99	9.4	10	95⅞	+ ⅜
Xerox 6s95	cv	22	88	- 1
Zapt 10⅞01f	...	88	90⅛	- ⅜
Zapt 10¼97f	...	85	88	- ½
Zayre 7¼10	cv	73	81½	- ¼
Zenith 6¼11	cv	10	84	...

FOREIGN BONDS
Volume, $170,000

Bonds	Cur Yld	Vol	Close	Net Chg.
EurCS 9s96	9.1	4	98⅝	...
EurIn 9¼98	9.7	5	95⅛	- 1
EurIn 10.15s99	10.0	100	101¼	+ ½
EurIn 14⅝91	12.7	10	115	...
Mexco 8⅛97	10.9	2	74¾	+ ¼

Bonds	Cur Yld	Vol	Close	Net Chg.
JohnAm 9¾95f	cv	25	24	- 1
Koor 12s96	15.0	3	80	...
LeisT 13⅝96	16.1	100	84½	- 1
MCO 13½00	15.3	24	88½	...
Matrx 7½11	cv	44	67¼	- ¼
Maxam 13⅝92	14.9	1	91½	+ ½
Mediq 7¼06	cv	10	63	...
Moog 9⅞06	cv	23	93	+ 1
Multm 16s05B f	...	36	83	- ½
NV Ry 10s02	cv	68	77¼	- ¾
Nich 15s00	16.3	3	92	- ⅛
Nich 14⅞99	15.7	71	94½	+ ½
Oakwd 7½01	cv	20	64½	- 1
Openh 12¾03	13.6	115	93¾	- ½
PopeEv 13½02f	...	1	42	- ½
Pulte 8½08	cv	20	69	+ ¼
ResrtInt 16⅝04	16.3	10	102¼	- ¼
ResrtInt 10s99	14.2	20	70½	+ ¼
ResrtInt 10s98	13.8	16	72½	- 1
ResrtInt 11⅜13	15.6	18	73	...

FIGURE 5–7
Sample corporate bond price quotations (Reprinted by permission of *The Wall Street Journal*, © Dow Jones & Company, Inc. 1988. All Rights Reserved.)

NYSE-traded bond issued by Navistar labeled "9s04." This means that the bond has a coupon of 9 percent and matures in the year 2004. Its closing price of 87⅛ (87.125) indicates that the purchaser would have to pay 871.25 for the bond (plus any accrued interest since the last interest payment date).

Figure 5–8 shows a sample price listing of U.S. Treasury bonds, notes, and bills. Prices for government bonds are in dollars and thirty-seconds of a dollar. Consult the Treasury note maturing in October 1990 with a coupon of 11.5 percent. The bid of 105-20 for the note means 105 20/32 (105.625), or $1056.25 per $1000 principal amount of the note.

Barron's National Business and Financial Weekly

While *The Wall Street Journal* provides much general interest and general business news in addition to market news, *Barron's* devotes itself almost exclusively to news relating to securities markets and investments. It typically contains about a half dozen feature articles and a statistical section providing weekly security price data and detailed financial and market trading data.

TREASURY BONDS, NOTES & BILLS

Friday, September 9, 1988

Representative Over-the-Counter quotations based on transactions of $1 million or more as of 4 p.m. Eastern time.

Hyphens in bid-and-asked and bid changes represent 32nds; 101-01 means 101 1/32. a-Plus 1/64. b-Yield to call date. d-Minus 1/64. k-Nonresident aliens exempt from withholding taxes. n-Treasury notes. p-Treasury note; nonresident aliens exempt from withholding taxes.

Source: Bloomberg Financial Markets

U.S. TREASURY BONDS AND NOTES

Rate	Mat.	Date	Bid	Asked	Bid Chg.	Yld.
6⅜	1988	Sep p	99-28	99-31	+ 01	6.82
11⅜	1988	Sep p	100-04	100-07	.....	6.58
15⅜	1988	Oct n	100-17	100-20	− 02	7.90
6⅜	1988	Oct p	99-23	99-26	.....	7.62
6¼	1988	Nov p	99-19	99-22	+ 01	7.59
8¾	1988	Nov n	100-02	100-05	.....	7.62
8⅝	1988	Nov p	100-01	100-04	− 01	7.68
11¾	1988	Nov n	100-18	100-21	− 01	7.63
10⅝	1988	Dec p	100-19	100-23	− 01	7.99
6¼	1988	Dec p	99-12	99-16	+ 01	7.86
6⅛	1989	Jan p	99-08	99-12	+ 01	7.75
14⅝	1989	Jan n	102-03	102-07	− 02	7.74
8	1989	Feb p	99-30	100-02	+ 01	7.80
6¼	1989	Feb p	99-05	99-09	.....	7.83
11⅜	1989	Feb n	101-09	101-13	− 01	7.88
11¼	1989	Mar p	101-20	101-24	.....	7.91
6⅜	1989	Mar p	99-03	99-07	+ 01	7.85
7⅛	1989	Apr p	99-10	99-14	.....	8.03
14⅜	1989	Apr n	103-16	103-20	− 02	7.93
6⅞	1989	May p	99-04	99-08	+ 01	8.02
9¼	1989	May n	100-22	100-28	+ 02	7.86
8	1989	May p	99-25	99-29	.....	8.11
11¾	1989	May n	102-06	102-10	− 01	8.11
7⅜	1989	Jun p	99-10	99-14	+ 01	8.09
9⅝	1989	Jun p	101	101-04	+ 01	8.11
7⅝	1989	Jul p	99-14	99-18	+ 01	8.13
14½	1989	Jul n	104-31	105-03	− 01	8.07
7¾	1989	Aug p	99-16	99-20	+ 01	8.16
6⅝	1989	Aug p	98-17	98-21	.....	8.15
13⅞	1989	Aug n	104-29	105-01	.....	8.09
8½	1989	Sep k	100-05	100-09	+ 01	8.21
9⅜	1989	Sep p	100-31	101-03	− 01	8.26
11⅞	1989	Oct n	103-18	103-22	− 01	8.25
7⅞	1989	Oct p	99-15	99-19	.....	8.24
6⅜	1989	Nov p	97-27	97-31	+ 01	8.21
10¾	1989	Nov n	102-18	102-22	− 01	8.28
12¾	1989	Nov p	104-30	105-02	.....	8.12
7¾	1989	Nov p	99-10	99-14	+ 02	8.23
7⅞	1989	Dec p	99-10	99-14	.....	8.32
8⅜	1989	Dec p	99-30	100-02	.....	8.31
7⅜	1990	Jan k	98-23	98-27	+ 02	8.27
10½	1990	Jan n	102-18	102-22	.....	8.32
3½	1990	Feb	94-18	95-04	+ 01	7.16
6½	1990	Feb k	97-16	97-20	.....	8.30
7⅛	1990	Feb k	98-09	98-13	+ 02	8.30
11	1990	Feb p	103-12	103-16	+ 01	8.33
7¼	1990	Mar p	98-12	98-16	+ 03	8.30
7⅜	1990	Mar p	98-18	98-22	+ 02	8.29
10½	1990	Apr n	103	103-04	+ 02	8.35
7⅝	1990	Apr p	98-25	98-29	+ 01	8.35
7⅞	1990	May k	99-04	99-08	+ 02	8.35
8¼	1990	May	99-24	100-02	.....	8.20
8⅛	1990	May p	99-16	99-20	+ 01	8.35
11⅜	1990	May p	104-14	104-18	.....	8.38
7¼	1990	Jun p	97-31	98-03	+ 01	8.40
8	1990	Jun p	99-07	99-11	+ 01	8.39
10¾	1990	Jul n	103-25	103-29	+ 01	8.40
8⅜	1990	Jul p	99-27	99-31	+ 01	8.38
7⅞	1990	Aug k	99	99-04	+ 03	8.37
9⅞	1990	Aug p	102-15	102-19	+ 03	8.38
10¾	1990	Aug n	103-30	104-02	+ 01	8.41
8⅝	1990	Aug	100-11	100-15	+ 02	8.36
6¾	1990	Sep p	96-26	96-30	+ 02	8.40
11½	1990	Oct n	105-20	105-24	.....	8.43
8	1990	Nov p	99-01	99-05	+ 01	8.42
9⅝	1990	Nov k	102-07	102-11	+ 04	8.41
13	1990	Nov n	108-25	108-29	+ 02	8.42
6⅝	1990	Dec p	96-05	96-09	+ 03	8.43
11¾	1991	Jan n	106-24	106-28	+ 03	8.44
7⅜	1991	Feb p	97-19	97-23	+ 03	8.43
9⅛	1991	Feb k	101-10	101-14	+ 03	8.45
6¾	1991	Mar p	96	96-04	+ 04	8.47
12⅜	1991	Apr n	108-25	108-29	+ 04	8.47
8⅛	1991	May p	99-04	99-08	+ 05	8.44
14½	1991	May n	114-17	114-21	+ 04	8.26

U.S. Treas. Bills

Mat. date	Bid (Discount)	Asked (Discount)	Yield
-1988-			
9-15	4.51	3.49	3.54
9-22	7.82	7.78	7.91
9-29	7.21	7.09	7.21
10- 6	6.96	6.89	7.02
10-13	7.16	7.12	7.26
10-20	7.11	7.07	7.22
10-27	7.39	7.35	7.52
11- 3	7.27	7.23	7.41
11-10	7.29	7.22	7.41
11-17	7.27	7.20	7.40
11-25	7.38	7.34	7.56
12- 1	7.32	7.28	7.50
12- 8	7.30	7.26	7.49
12-15	7.27	7.21	7.45
12-22	7.32	7.28	7.54
12-29	7.18	7.12	7.38
-1989-			
1- 5	7.29	7.23	7.50

U.S. Treas. Bills

Mat. date	Bid (Discount)	Asked (Discount)	Yield
1-12	7.34	7.28	7.57
1-19	7.38	7.32	7.62
1-26	7.40	7.34	7.65
2- 2	7.40	7.34	7.67
2- 9	7.41	7.35	7.69
2-16	7.45	7.39	7.74
2-23	7.42	7.36	7.72
3- 2	7.44	7.40	7.78
3- 9	7.43	7.39	7.78
3-16	7.45	7.41	7.81
4-13	7.48	7.42	7.82
4-20	7.57	7.51	7.93
5-11	7.56	7.50	7.93
6- 8	7.51	7.45	7.90
7- 6	7.58	7.52	8.01
8- 3	7.57	7.51	8.03
8-31	7.53	7.49	8.04

GOVERNMENT AGENCY ISSUES

Friday, September 9, 1988

Mid-afternoon Over-the-Counter quotations usually based on large transactions, sometimes $1 million or more.

Hyphens in bid-and-asked represent 32nds; 101-01 means 101 1/32. a-Plus 1/64. b-Yield to call date. d-Minus 1/64.

Source: Bloomberg Financial Markets

Fed. Home Loan Bank

Rate	Mat	Bid	Asked	Yld
8.00	9-88	99-29	100-01	6.94
6.35	10-88	99-20	99-26	7.75
8.90	10-88	99-31	100-02	8.10
11.40	10-88	100-08	100-12	7.89
9.55	10-88	100-01	100-05	7.94
8.90	11-88	100-02	100-05	7.91
14.20	11-88	101-01	101-09	7.47
7.50	11-88	99-24	99-27	8.10
10.70	12-88	100-19	100-23	8.00
7.80	12-88	99-24	99-27	8.22
7.40	1-89	99-18	99-21	8.28
11.38	1-89	101	101-04	8.12
6.50	2-89	99-01	99-05	8.39
6.95	2-89	99-08	99-11	8.41
8.30	2-89	99-29	100-01	8.20
10.80	2-89	101	101-04	8.22
15.10	2-89	102-19	103-04	7.98
6.90	3-89	99-04	99-07	8.39
7.45	3-89	99-10	99-15	8.46
6.90	4-89	98-26	99-04	8.36
7.35	4-89	99-09	99-12	8.38

FNMA Issues

Rate	Mat	Bid	Asked	Yld
8.55	9-88	99-31	100-02	1.01
13.20	9-88	100-01	100-04	1.83
9.50	10-88	100-01	100-04	7.58
12.75	10-88	100-07	100-13	7.11
8.95	11-88	99-31	100-03	8.11
11.00	11-88	100-12	100-15	7.76
11.70	11-88	100-15	100-19	7.67
11.25	12-88	100-20	100-24	7.97
11.75	12-88	100-24	100-28	7.95
11.10	1-89	100-27	100-30	8.01
11.60	2-89	101-08	101-12	8.06
12.10	3-89	101-21	101-29	8.09
7.55	4-89	99-10	99-16	8.44
9.30	6-89	100-17	100-21	8.35
9.50	6-89	100-22	100-25	8.37
8.00	7-89	99-12	99-22	8.38
10.05	8-89	101-02	101-12	8.43
13.13	8-89	103-30	104-04	8.31
12.10	10-89	103-17	103-23	8.40
12.75	10-89	104-07	104-13	8.37
9.85	11-89	101-10	101-16	8.45

FIGURE 5–8
Sample U.S. government bond price quotations (Reprinted by permission of *The Wall Street Journal,* © Dow Jones & Company, Inc. 1988. All Rights Reserved.)

INDUSTRY INFORMATION

Wall Street firms often assign their security analysts to follow complete industries. These "industry analysts" conduct research on such areas as future growth of the industry's product, competition from substitute goods and other industries, competition and market share of firms within the industry, and analyses of the industry's companies. Chapter 7 of this text introduces some of the methods that analysts use to study industry groups. Table 5–9 summarizes some popular publications used as sources for industry data.

COMPANY INFORMATION

Sources of information about individual companies are the most numerous, covering the thousands of public companies in the United States and other countries. There are two primary sources of this information: the company and the investment information publishers.

Investment Information from Companies

Most investment information, even that published in other sources, originates with a company. For example, a company's quarterly earnings originally carried in its quar-

TABLE 5–9
Sources of industry information

Publication (publisher)	***Frequency***	***Content Summary***
Key Business Ratios (Dun and Bradstreet)	annual	Financial ratios by industry group
RMA Annual Statement Studies (Robert Morris & Associates)	annual	Financial ratios by industry group
Analysts Handbook (Standard & Poor's)	quarterly	Per share income and selected financial ratios by industry
Industry Surveys (Standard & Poor's)	weekly	Forecasts and an update on one or more industries per issue, with ratios and data of individual companies
Almanac of Business and Industrial Financial Ratios (Leo Troy)	annual	Financial ratios by industry group
The Value Line Investment Survey, Part III (Value Line, Inc.)	weekly	Updates on several industries in each issue, accompanied by detailed data on companies in the industry

terly report may be quoted in the financial press and other investment advisory services as current information and for many quarters to come as historical data. A company provides information to investors through two main channels:

1. Its own reports to shareholders and news releases
2. Reports required to be filed with the SEC

Reports to Shareholders

A company makes two major reports to its stockholders. These are the quarterly and annual reports giving income and financial position data (income statements and balance sheets) for the latest reporting period. The annual reports are generally much more detailed than their abbreviated quarterly counterparts. They traditionally contain a statement by the chief executive officer, discussion of the latest financial results, news of possibilities or plans for the future, and financial statements. When using an annual report, investors must remember that a company's annual report is its yearly chance to "market itself" to investors on slick paper in full color. Firms' annual reports usually try to cast the company in the most favorable light possible, and investors should be cautious when utilizing information from annual or quarterly reports, especially from the discussion sections.

Reports to the SEC

As mentioned in Chapter 4, the federal securities statutes are generally disclosure laws. They require that companies selling their securities to the public make available certain items of information about their position and operations. The SEC has developed a complete series of reports that companies must periodically file to comply with the disclosure requirements of the law.

The best-known of these statements is the *Form 10-K.* The 10-K is the company's annual report to the SEC, covering detailed financial and operating data. Figure 5–9 summarizes the categories of information that companies provide in their 10-K and other SEC filings. The *Form 10-Q* is the quarterly counterpart of the 10-K, containing the same basic information in less detail.

In addition to the Forms 10-K and 10-Q, the filings of most interest to investors are the *Form 8-K, proxy,* and prospectus. The company must file a Form 8-K to report unscheduled material events or corporate changes. Items that should trigger an 8-K filing are events such as changes in control of the company, acquisition or disposition of assets, bankruptcy or receivership, changes in the company's certifying accountants, resignation of directors, amended financial statements, and other "materially important events." To announce its annual meeting for stockholders and the agenda, the company must file its proxy statement. The proxy contains the date, time, and location of the scheduled annual meeting and lists important matters that are scheduled to come up for a vote at the meeting. A final statement of interest, the prospectus, accompanies a new issue of securities. The prospectus is particularly important to investors considering a company going public for the first time, because no previous public financial history of such a company exists.

REPORT CONTENTS	10-K	19-K 20-F	10-Q	8-K	10-C	6-K	Proxy Statement	Prospectus	Registration Statements '34 Act F-10	Registration Statements '34 Act 8-A 8-B	Registration Statements '33 Act "S" Type	ARS	Listing Application	N-1R	N-1Q
Auditor															
☐ Name	A	A	■				■	A	A		A	A	■	A	
☐ Opinion	A	A	■						A			A		A	
☐ Changes				A			■								
Compensation Plans															
☐ Equity	■		■				F	F	A		F		■	■	
☐ Monetary	■		■					F	A		F		■		
Company Information															
☐ Nature of Business	A	A				F		A	A		A	■	■		
☐ History	F	A						A			A	■	■		
☐ Organization and Change	F	F		A	■	F	■	A		F	A	■			
Debt Structure	A					F	■	A	A		A	A		A	
Depreciation & Other Schedules	A	A				F		A	A		A				
Dilution Factors	A	A		F		F		A	A		A	A			
Directors, Officers, Insiders															
☐ Identification	F	A				F	A	A	A		A	F			
☐ Background	■	A				F	F	A	■		A	■			
☐ Holdings	■	A		■			A	A	A		A				
☐ Compensation	■	A		■			A	A	A		A				
Earnings Per Share	A	A	A			F			A			A		A	
Financial Information															
☐ Annual Audited	A	A							A			A		A	
☐ Interim Audited		A					■	■			■				
☐ Interim Unaudited	■		A	■		F		F			F	F			
Foreign Operations	A						■	A	A		A	■	F		
Labor Contracts		■		■			■		F		F				
Legal Agreements	F	■		■					F		F				
Legal Counsel				■				A			A		■		
Loan Agreements	F		F	■			■		F		F			■	
Plants and Properties	A	F		■				F	A		F	■			
Portfolio Operations															
☐ Content (Listing of Securities)															A
☐ Management														A	
Product-Line Breakout	A							A			A	■			
Securities Structure	A	A			■			A	A		A				
Subsidiaries	A	A					■	A	A		A	■	■		
Underwriting				■				A	A		A				
Unregistered Securities	■			■			■	F			F				
Block Movements	■			F			■		A				■		

TENDER OFFER/ACQUISITION REPORTS	13D	13 G	14D-1	14D-9	13E-3	13E-4
Name of Issuer (Subject Company)	A	A	A	A	A	A
Filing Person (or Company)	A	A	A	A	A	A
Amount of Shares Owned	A	A				
Percent of Class Outstanding	A	A				
Financial Statements of Bidders			F		F	F
Purpose of Tender Offer			A	A	A	A
Source and Amount of Funds	A		A		A	
Identity and Background Information			A	A	A	
Persons Retained, Employed or to be Compensated			A	A	A	A
Exhibits	F		F	F	F	F

A-always included – included – if occurred or significant **F**-frequently included ■ special circumstances only

FIGURE 5–9

Quick reference chart to contents of SEC filings (Reprinted with permission from *A Guide to SEC Corporate Filings,* © 1985, Disclosure Information Group.)

Other Sources of Company Information

Many independent sources provide information to the investment community about individual companies and their prospects for investment. These range from small newsletters with a few dozen subscribers to major publishers with multiple publications; from small computer investment software marketers to mainframe online investment database services; and from regional brokerage firms giving advice on a few issues to national firms providing complete investment counseling and management services. The sample discussed here includes some of the services available to most individuals for a reasonable fee or that would likely be found at a university or public library.

Standard & Poor's Corporation

Standard & Poor's Corporation is one of the largest suppliers of investment information and advice. Some of its publications provide only information and financial data, while others go further, making projections and recommendations. Table 5–10 summarizes some of Standard & Poor's most widely used publications, and Figures 5–10, 5–11, and 5–12 show samples from some of these publications.

Moody's Investor Services

Moody's Investor Services has a family of investment publications that cover areas similar to Standard & Poor's. Moody's has a series of *Moody's Manuals* that is comparable to S&P's *Corporation Records.* These manuals are bound volumes, issued annually, with the following titles: *Moody's Industrial Manual, Moody's OTC Industrial*

TABLE 5–10
Company information sources of Standard & Poor's

Publication	*Frequency*	*Content Summary*
Bond Guide	monthly	Major corporate and foreign bond price, financial and ratings data; municipal bond ratings
Corporation Records	updated periodically	Basic corporate information in binders, arranged alphabetically
Earnings Forecaster	weekly	Earnings forecasts made by brokerage firms and security analysts
Stock Guide	monthly	Brief financial and price data on NYSE, AMEX, and major OTC stocks
Stock Reports	quarterly for each company	Looseleaf updates containing basic company position, recent earnings and financial position history, prospects for future
Stock Market Encyclopedia	quarterly	Bound edition of *Stock Reports*

120 Pot-Pru STANDARD & POOR'S CORPORATION

Title-Industry Code & Co. Finances (In Italics) / Individual Issue Statistics, Exchange	Ind. Code / Interest Dates	Chgs. 1983 / S&P Quality rating	Eligible	Times Earn. 1984 / Bond Form	1985 / Legality M a	Legality N H	Yr. End / Legality N Y	Cash & Eqv / Redemption Provisions: Refund Earliest/Other	Current Assets / Call Price: For S.F.	Liabs Date (Million $) / Call Price: Regular	L. Term Debt (Mil $) / Out-st'd'g (Mil $)	Debt % Prop / Underwriter Firm	Underwriter Year	Price Range 1972-84 High	1972-84 Low	1985 High	1985 Low	1986 High	1986 Low	Mo. End Price Sale(s) or Bid	Curr Yield	Yield to Mat.
Potom El Pwr 1st 3⅜s '91	Jd	AA	X	CR	✓	✓	✓	....	....	±100.55	10.0	H1	'56	64½	40	76	63½	84½	75¼	83½	4.32	8.04
• 1st 14¼s '92	fA15	AA	X	R	✓	✓	✓	[1]106.11	....	±106.11	11.6	M4	'82	112	100	113¾	106	115¼	108	108½	13.09	12.03
1st 4½s '93	jD	AA	X	CR	✓	✓	✓	....	....	±101.05	25.0	K1	'58	70¼	40	72½	59⅝	80¼	71	79½	5.79	8.54
1st 5¼s '94	jD	AA	X	CR	✓	✓	✓	....	....	±101.59	15.0	D3	'59	76½	41½	73½	60½	81¼	72½	80¾	6.50	8.66
1st 5s '95	jD15	AA	X	CR	✓	✓	✓	....	....	±101.38	40.0	D3	'60	73¼	38½	69½	56¾	77½	68½	77½	6.46	8.68
1st 4½s '98	Fa15	AA	X	CR	✓	✓	✓	....	....	±102.04	50.0	D3	'63	65½	32½	61½	48¾	69½	60	69	6.34	8.80
1st 4½s '99	Mn15	AA	X	CR	✓	✓	✓	....	....	±101.84	45.0	K1	'64	66½	31½	60¼	47½	68½	58¾	67½	6.63	8.81
1st 5½s 2001	Ao	AA	X	R	✓	✓	✓	....	....	±102.62	15.0	K1	'66	72½	34	62¼	49¼	70½	60¾	70	7.32	8.87
1st 5⅞s 2002	Mn	AA	X	R	✓	✓	✓	....	....	±103.42	35.0	K1	'67	81½	37¾	67	53¼	75½	65½	75	7.83	8.89
1st 6⅝s 2003	Fa15	AA	X	R	✓	✓	✓	....	....	±103.95	40.0	K1	'68	90½	41¾	72¼	58	81¼	70½	80½	8.22	8.91
1st 7¾s 2004	Ms15	AA	X	R	✓	✓	✓	....	....	±103.57	45.0	D3	'69	102½	48	81	65¼	90½	79	89½	8.65	8.94
1st 8.85s 2005	Fa15	AA	X	R	✓	✓	✓	....	....	±104.69	35.0	D3	'70	109½	54½	89¾	72¾	100	87½	99½	8.93	8.94
• 1st 9½s 2005	fA15	AA	X	R	✓	✓	✓	....	....	±105.03	70.0	D3	'70	119	57½	95½	76	105	91½	s102½	9.23	9.17
• 1st 7¾s 2007	aO	AA	X	R	✓	✓	✓	....	....	±104.71	50.0	F2	'72	103¾	48	79½	63⅝	93¾	76½	88½	8.77	8.99
• 1st 8⅜s 2009	Jj15	AA	X	R	✓	✓	✓	....	....	104.49	100		'74	101½	52	85	66¾	98½	82½	s98	8.55	8.57
• 1st 11¼s 2015	mN	AA	X	R	-	✓	-	[2]108.06	....	±110.21	6.71	S1	'85	....	....	99½	99½	105½	104½	118	9.53	9.42
• 1st 9¼s 2016	Ms	AA	X	R	-	✓	-	[3]107.40	....	±109¼	75.0	M4	'86	....	....	....	....	106½	100	110½	8.37	8.28
• 1st 8¾s 2016	mN15	AA	X	R	-	✓	-	[4]105¼	....	±107	75.0	D7	'86	....	....	....	....	100½	96½	98½	8.89	8.90
PPG Industries[5]	*29*	*6.74*		*8.71*	*7.85*		*Dc*	*N/A*	*1498*	*841 9-86*	*979*	*37.7*										
• SF Deb 9s '95	Jd15	A+	X	R	✓	✓	-	....	100	±101.70	73.5	F2	'70	115	63¼	96	83¼	105	93¾	102½	8.77	8.55
• SF Deb 8½s 2000	Fa15	A+	X	R	✓	✓	-	....	100	±103½	66.1	F2	'75	106	56¾	87	76½	100	88½	s100	8.50	8.50
• Nts 9½s '91	Jd	A+	X	R	-	✓	-	....	....	[6]100	100	S1	'85	....	....	101¾	99½	106¾	103¼	109¼	8.70	7.02
• Nts 10½s '95	jD	A+	X	R	-	✓	-	....	....	[7]100	75.0	S1	'85	....	....	102½	99½	109½	103	109½	9.26	8.59
Price Communications	*8*	*0.54*		*0.89*	*0.28*		*Dc*	*212*	*243*	*22.1 9-86*	*423*	*643*										
Sub Nts 11¾s '95	Fa15	B-	Y	R	-	-	-	[8]100	....	100	[9]80.0	M8	'85	....	....	92½	82	97¼	88	92¾	12.67	13.23
• SubNts 13s '96	jJ15	B-	Y	R	-	-	-	....	....	[10]105	150	M8	'86	....	....	....	....	100½	99	100	13.00	13.00
Private Export Funding	*26*	*Gtd by Export-Import Bk U.S.*																				
Sec Nts L 11¾s '87	aO30	AAA	X	R	✓	✓	-	....	....	NC	100	D3	'80	104	80½	105½	100¾	105½	103½	104½	11.24	6.10
Sec Nts N 16.20s '89	mS30	AAA	X	R	✓	✓	-	....	[9]100	NC	12.0	S1	'81	118	99	117	105½	110½	101½	102½	15.82	15.10
Sec Nts P 14½s '91	Jd	AAA	X	R	✓	✓	-	....	[9]100	NC	53.4	M4	'82	110	94½	111½	106½	110½	104½	109½	12.94	11.43
Sec Nts Q 12.35s '90	mN	AAA	X	R	✓	✓	-	....	[9]100	NC	39.7	D3	'82	104½	91½	110	100	110	103½	105½	11.75	10.68
Sec Nts R 10¾s '89	mN	AAA	X	R	✓	✓	-	....	[9]100	NC	81.5	S1	'82	101	87¼	104¾	96½	105½	102	103½	10.39	9.31
Sec Nts S 11¼s '92	Fa31	AAA	X	R	✓	✓	-	....	[9,11]100	NC	122	M4	'83	102	87½	106½	94½	109½	102½	108½	10.33	9.05
Sec Nts T 11¼s '95	aO31	AAA	X	R	✓	✓	-	....	[9]100	NC	114	D3	'83	102	83½	109½	95¾	115½	103¼	106¾	10.54	10.07
Sec Nts U 12½s '94	aO	AAA	X	R	-	✓	-	....	[9]100	NC	95.0	S1	'84	104½	100	113½	102¾	118½	105½	109½	11.74	10.99
Sec Nts V 9.10s '91	Jj31	AAA	X	R	-	✓	-	....	....	NC	100	M4	'86	....	....	....	....	106¾	100	105½	8.62	7.47
Sec Nts W 7.30s '92	Jj31	AAA	X	R	-	✓	-	....	....	NC	100	D3	'86	....	....	....	....	100	100	100	7.30	7.30
Sec Nts X 7.70s '97	Jj31	AAA	X	R	-	✓	-	....	....	NC	200	S1	'86	....	....	....	....	100	99½	99½	7.71	7.71
Procter & Gamble Co.	*64*	*14.80*		*10.51*	*5.01*		*Je*	*644*	*4864*	*3601 9-86*	*2473*	*38.5*										
• SF Deb 7s 2002	Mn15	AAA	X	R	✓	✓	-	....	100	±102.64	30.0	G2	'72	102½	48½	78½	62½	92	75½	89¼	7.84	8.24
• SF Deb 8¼s 2005	Ms	AAA	X	R	✓	✓	-	....	100	±104.13	178	G2	'75	108	55	89¾	71	100	85¼	97½	8.45	8.50
SF Deb 10⅝s 2015	mN15	AAA	X	R	-	✓	-	[12]105.312	[13]100	±110.094	300	G2	'85	....	....	105½	100	112¼	103½	111	9.57	9.50
SF Deb 8⅝s 2016	Ao	AAA	X	R	-	✓	-	[14]104	[15]100	±108	298	G2	'86	....	....	....	....	103¼	96½	99¾	8.65	8.64
Prudential Rlty Secur	*26*	*N/A*		*N/A*	*N/A*		*Dc*	*7.41*		*9-86*	*136*											
• Zero Cpn Mtg-Bk s '87	[16]	AAA	X	R	-	✓	-	z100	....	NC	[9]25.8	P5	'83	76½	66½	87½	79¼	97.312	92	99	...	4.04
• Zero Cpn Mtg-Bk s '88	[16]	AAA	X	R	-	✓	-	z100	....	NC	[9]26.0	P5	'83	62	58½	82	69¼	91½	80½	s91½	...	6.90
• Zero Cpn Mtg-Bk s '89	[16]	AAA	X	R	-	✓	-	z100	....	NC	[9]26.0	P5	'83	59½	52	71¾	62¼	84	72	82¾	...	8.60
• Zero Cpn Mtg-Bk s '90	[16]	AAA	X	R	-	✓	-	z100	....	NC	[9]26.0	P5	'83	50¼	46¼	63½	54	77¼	65	77½	...	8.15
• Zero Cpn Mtg-Bk s '91	[16]	AAA	X	R	-	✓	-	z100	....	NC	[9]25.0	P5	'83	49	33	57	46	72	56½	69½	...	8.70

Uniform Footnote Explanations—See Page 1. Other: [1]Red rest'n(14.39%)to 8-15-87. [2]Red rest'n(11.36%)to 11-1-90. [3]Red rest'n(9.32%)to 3-1-91. [4]Red rest'n(8.9921%)to 11-15-91. [5]See Pittsburgh Plate Glass. [6]Fr 6-1-90. [7]Fr 12-1-92. [8]Red rest'n(14 3/4%)to 2-15-90. [9]Incl disc. [10]Fr 7-15-91. [11]Fr 8-31-87. [12]Red rest'n (10 5/8%) to 11-15-95. [13]Fr 11-15-96. [14]Red rest'n(8.684%)to 4-1-96. [15]Fr 4-1-97. [16]Due Apr 1.

FIGURE 5–10

Example from *Standard & Poor's Guide* (Copyright © 1987 by Standard & Poor's Corp. Reprinted by permission.)

Manual, Moody's Bank and Finance Manual, Moody's Public Utility Manual, Moody's Transportation Manual, and *Moody's Municipal Government Manual.*

Moody's *Dividend Record* contains dividend payment dates and their amounts. The *Handbook of Common Stocks* is a quarterly publication containing a one-page synopsis of each of 1500 companies with widely held common stock.

The Value Line

The Value Line Investment Survey consists of weekly updates of each of three sections:

1. "Summary and Index" indexes and gives summary statistics of all 1700 stocks followed by *Value Line.*
2. "Selection and Opinion" offers forecasts of future economic conditions and gives special reports on an industry and one or two interesting stocks.
3. "Ratings and Reports" contains full-page reports of each stock covered (see Figure 5–13). This section is broken into ninety-two industry groups, and an industry report precedes the stocks in its section. All ninety-two groups are covered over a thirteen-week period.

The Wall Street Transcript

The Wall Street Transcript is a weekly newspaper publication that presents investment information in two formats. The first is the weekly "Round Table," the transcript of a panel discussion of leading security analysts in which they give their views, opinions, and forecasts of the economy, industries, and individual securities. The second reproduces reports issued by security analysts and brokerage firms around the country. Although these reports are available from the original analysts, *The Wall Street Transcript* is a handy one-stop source for much of this material. Each issue contains a cumulative index, making it easy to locate a report on a particular company printed within the last six months.

Brokerage Firms

Many brokerage firms have their own research departments that issue reports and give opinions and recommendations about securities. Although some of these are available only to institutional clients of the brokerage firms, many are available to individual investors. Sometimes they are available on a subscription basis, but brokerage firms often provide them at no additional charge to their commission-paying customers. *The Wall Street Transcript* reproduces many of these reports.

Computer-Accessible Sources

Computerized databases have become very popular sources of investment data. They are available on a subscription basis, with charges ranging from several dollars per minute of online computer time to thousands of dollars for the purchase of a complete database. While many large institutional investors purchase complete databases, individual and smaller investors also have access to the data through time-sharing services. They can access the service through a remote terminal or microcomputer equipped with telecommunication capability. In addition, many abbreviated databases

128 Ker-Kni

Standard & Poor's Corporation

Index (¶S&P 500 •Options)	Ticker Symbol	Name of Issue (Call Price of Pfd. Stocks)	Market	Com. Rank. & Pfd. Rating	Par Val.	Inst. Hold Cos	Inst. Hold Shs. (000)	Principal Business	Price Range 1971-84 High	1971-84 Low	1985 High	1985 Low	1986 High	1986 Low	Dec. Sales in 100s	December, 1986 Last Sale Or Bid High	Low	Last	% Div. Yield	P-E Ratio
1	KER	Kerr-Addison Mines	To	B	No	14	1224	Canada gold mine: invests	25	5⅝	18	14	18½	14⅛	311	16⅝	14⅞	15⅝	3.9	..
2	KGM	Kerr Glass Mfg	NY,M	B–	50¢	15	1172	Glass containers: closures	22	8½	13⅞	9⅜	17½	11	1216	14¼	12½	12⅞	3.4	d
3	Pr D	$1.70 cm CvB Pfd SerD([51]20.51)	NY	↓B–	50¢	3	120	packaging products	30⅝	13¼	21¾	17½	25½	19⅞	151	22½	21	21⅛	8.0	..
¶4•[1]	KMG	Kerr-McGee	NY,B,C,M,P,Ph,To	B+	1	248	26969	Petroleum, chem,nuclear,coal	47¹⁵⁄₁₆	15¹³⁄₁₆	36	26¼	33⅞	23½	22288	30¼	28	28⅛	3.9	d
5	KCH	Ketchum & Co	AS	B–	1	3	70	Drug distributor & mfr	18⅝	1⅛	22⅜	13½	25⅜	15	390	23⅞	21	22⅜	s...	d
6	KEVX	Kevex Corp	OTC	↓C	1¢	16	1679	Analytical instruments	28¼	4½	8½	5¼	8¾	3⅞	1236	4⅜	3⅞	3⅞B	...	d
7	KVLM	Kevlin Microwave	OTC	B+	10¢	5	160	Mfr devices for radar sys	8¼	¹⁄₁₆	7¾	3⅞	5¾	2⅜	782	3½	2⅜	2⅜B	...	59
8	KEQU	Kewaunee Scientific	OTC	B+	2½	10	343	Furniture & eqp for labs	11¾	1¼	15¾	11¾	13¾	10⅛	402	11½	10⅛	10⅛B	4.3	d
9	KC.B	Key Co Cl'B	AS	B	1	2	51	Builds single-family homes,	6¾	³⁄₁₆	4¾	2⅞	9½	3¼	261	5⅞	4⅝	4¾	5.3	12
10	KC.A	Class'A'(1/10 vtg)	AS	B	1	2	48	townhouses & patio homes	....	....	4	2⅛	8¼	3	445	4⅞	3⅝	3⅝	6.9	9
11	KTCC	Key Tronic Corp	OTC	NR	No	28	3242	Mfrs computer keyboards	24¾	7½	11	6¾	17¼	6¼	5356	7¼	6⅝	6⅞B	...	d
12	KEY	KeyCorp	NY,M	A	5	67	5031	Multi bank hldg:central NY	15½	4¼	26	15⅛	30⅝	21	10469	24¼	21	22⅛	4.5	8
13	KYC	Keystone Camera Prod	AS	C	40¢	15	743	U.S.mfr point/shoot camera	345	5	7⅞	2¼	6½	3⅛	4998	6	5¼	5¾	...	d
14	WS.A	Wrrt(Pur 1 com at $8.25)([52]75¢)	AS	...	....	3	255	mfrs videocassettes	....	....	2½	¼	1¾	½	499	1⅛	⅞	1	...	..
15	WS.B	Wrrt(Pur 1 com at$7.50)([52]75¢)	AS	...	....	...	....		....	....	....	....	1¾	1	418	1½	1¼	1½	...	..
16	KES	Keystone Consol Ind	NY,M	NR	1	3	74	Mfr steel & wire products	6¾	2½	5	2½	9¾	3⅛	299	7⅜	6¾	7⅛	...	d
17	KII	Keystone Int'l	NY,M	B+	1	72	8423	Mfrs flow control prod & sys	18½	½	15¼	12⅛	19⅛	11⅜	9786	15	13¾	14⅜	3.3	21
18	KDE	Kidde Inc	NY,B,M,P,Ph	A–	1¼	110	20004	Aircraft access:fire prev eq	37	4⅛	37½	28½	38½	28⅜	10225	34¼	29¾	31¼	3.8	28
19	WS	Wrrt(Purch 1 Com at $40)	AS	...	....	5	256	security sys:electronics	8⅞	2¼	4⅞	2½	5¾	1½	2816	2⅞	1½	1⅝	...	..
20	Pr B	$4.00 cm Cv B Pref(90)vtg	NY	BBB	1	7	30	mobile hydraulic cranes	85	32	85¾	65	88	70	13	79	72½	71½B	5.6	..
21	Pr C	$4.00 cm Cv C Pref(100)vtg	NY	BBB	1	11	219	consumer & recreational	85	40	86	66	87	69	26	79	70	70¼	5.7	..
22	Pr D	$1.64 cm Cv D Pref(25)vtg	NY	BBB	1	2	44	products	57¼	20	57¾	44	58	44½	33	53	47	47	3.5	..
23	KPI	Killearn Properties	AS,Ph	NR	10¢	1	9	Develop communities:Florida	23½	¹⁄₁₆	4½	3½	8⅝	4¼	190	6⅝	5½	5½	...	12
24	KBALB	Kimball Int'l Cl B	OTC	A–	62½¢	26	2113	Furniture,pianos,organs	29½	4⅞	35½	26¾	32	24½	1603	32	29½	30B	2.1	12
25	KIMB	Kimbark Oil & Gas	OTC	C	10¢	...	....	Oil & gas,expl & prod'n	13	4½	7	1¾	2⅛	⅞	978	1¼	⅞	1⅛B	...	d
¶26	KMB	Kimberly-Clark	NY,B,C,M,P,Ph	A+	5	386	26641	Consumer paper pr: newsprint	49½	9⁵⁄₁₆	70	45	92⅝	63⅜	16465	89¾	79¾	79⅞	3.1	13
27	KIN	Kinark Corp	AS,P	C	10¢	6	345	Chemical packag g/dstr:mfg	6⅞	½	4⅜	3⅛	5	2⅜	869	3⅛	2⅜	2⅞	...	d
28	KNCD	Kincaid Furniture	OTC	NR	1⅓	30	1748	Mfrs bedroom,din'g furniture	16¼	5¾	9¾	6	16½	8	4311	11¾	10	10¾B	...	14
29•[2]	KNDR	Kinder-Care Learn'g	OTC	↑A–	50¢	140	18121	Operates day care centers	13⅝	⅛	16⅛	10⅞	17¾	11⅝	45413	15⅝	13⅝	13⅞B	0.4	17
30	KWP	King World Prod'ns	NY	NR	1¢	53	7626	Dstr/synd'n of TV programs	2½	1¾	10¼	2⅛	19¼	10⅛	19274	15⅜	12⅞	14	...	22
31	KREN	Kings Road Entmt	OTC	NR	1¢	16	1555	Produces motion pictures	....	....	10½	6½	8⅜	2¾	6367	4½	2¾	3B	...	d
32	KEX	Kirby Exploration	AS,M	C	10¢	24	4148	Transp'n sv,insur,oil & gas	45¾	⅞	4	2¼	3¼	1¾	6658	2½	2⅛	2½	...	d
33	KIT	Kit Mfg	AS	B–	No	4	48	Mobile hms:recr'l vehicles	23⅝	1	6	4⅛	12¼	4⅞	445	7½	5¼	7½	...	9
34	KLAC	KLA Instruments	OTC	B	.1¢	81	7578	Electro-optical test sys	20⅝	2⅜	24½	15½	26¼	11	16000	15¾	12¾	13⅝B	...	24
35	KVU	Kleer-Vu Indus	AS	B–	10¢	7	408	Plastic transparent items	5	⅛	3⅝	2	2½	1⅛	1752	1⅞	1⅛	1¼	...	62
36	KBA	Kleinwort Benson Aus	NY	NR	.001	...	....	Closed-end investment co	....	....	....	....	10¼	9¾	2219	10¼	9¾	10⅛	...	..
37	KLLM	KLLM Transport Sy	OTC	NR	1	6	196	Temperature ctr transport	....	....	....	....	18	12¾	3826	18⁷⁄	15¼	17¼B	...	18
38	KLM	KLM Royal Dutch Air	NY,B,M,P,Ph	NR	ƒ100	49	5567	Worldwide air transport	16⅝	2½	20⅜	12¾	23⅞	17½	16678	21⅛	17½	18⅛	3.8	8
39	KLOFY	Kloof Gold Mining[61]	OTC	NR	R.25	16	5881	South Africa gold mining	14⅜	¹³⁄₁₆	10¹⁵⁄₁₆	5	9	4⅝	10041	8	7⅛	7⅝B	5.9	8
40	KLOS	Kloss Video	OTC	NR	20¢	2	29	Mfr projection TV systems	14¾	2⅞	8⅜	2½	4⅛	1⅞	666	3¼	2¼	2¼B	...	d
¶41•[3]	KM	K mart	NY,B,C,M,P,Ph	B+	1	600	102073	Discount: variety stores	51⅛	15⅛	41½	30⅝	57⅜	33⅝	136874	51¼	43¼	43⅞	3.4	11
42	KMSI	KMS Indus	OTC	NR	1¢	9	678	Scientific research:optical	19	⅛	1⅞	⅞	2⅛	1⅛	4696	1¼	1⅛	1⅛B	...	37
43	KMWS	KMW Systems	OTC	NR	10¢	9	432	Mfrs electronic sys & equip	9⅞	5¾	9⅜	5⅜	10⅛	7⅛	1718	9¼	8	8B	...	20
44	KNAP	Knape & Vogt Mfg	OTC	B+	2	18	1586	Mfr specialty hardware	14⅞	2⅜	14⅛	10⅛	19¾	12⅞	1201	18	15⅛	17B	†3.1	14
45	KNE	KN Energy[62]	NY,M	NR	5	46	3903	Nat'l gas,mineral resources	56	10	40⅜	13½	24¼	15⅜	3331	21⅞	19⅜	20¾	7.1	26
¶46•[4]	KRI	Knight-Ridder Inc	NY,M,P	A+	2¹⁄₁₂¢	257	32921	Newspapers:business info svs	31	3⅜	41⅜	28	57⅞	37½	28793	49⅜	46½	46⅞	2.1	18

Uniform Footnote Explanations—See Page 1. Other: [1]CBOE:Cycle 1. [2]P:Cycle 1 Pilot Program. [3]CBOE:Cycle 3. [4]Ph:Cycle 1. [51]△$0.26,'82. [52]To 8-31-87,scale to $20 in'89. [53]□$2.41,'83. [54]Fr 3-20-87. [55]Restr to 5-6-88(com equals 140% exercise price). [56]Stk dstr of Keycon Indus Inc. [57]□$0.17,'82. [58]p$0.84,'85. [59]®$3.18,'85. [60]△$0.31,'82. [61]ADR shrs. [62]Approx. [63]®$0.48,'86 [64]Mesa Ltd Partnership prop acq,$24.

FIGURE 5–11

Example from *Standard & Poor's Stock Guide* (Copyright © 1987 by Standard & Poor's Corp. Reprinted by permission.)

Splits ◆ Index	Cash Divs. Ea. Yr. Since	Dividends: Latest Payment Per$	Date	Ex. Div.	Total $ So Far 1986	Ind. Rate	Paid 1985	Financial Position Mil-$ Cash& Equiv.	Curr. Assets	Curr. Liab.	Balance Sheet Date	Capitalization Lg Trm Debt Mil-$	Shs. 000 Pfd.	Com.	Earnings $ Per Shr. Years End	1982	1983	1984	1985	1986	Last 12 Mos.	Interim Earnings Period	$ Per Shr. 1985	1986	Index
1	1940	gQ0.15	12-10-86	11-4	g0.60	0.60	g0.60	40.2	58.8	11.8	ⁿ12-31-85	5.00	...	17299	Dc	Δ[11]0.63	0.99	1.04	0.14	....	p0.05	9 Mo Sep	0.22	0.13	1
2	1975	Q0.11	12-17-86	11-26	0.44	0.44	0.44	2.55	70.4	36.9	9-30-86	49.7	487	3635	Dc	1.03	d6.27	d1.04	d1.65	....	d0.86	9 Mo Sep	d0.11	0.68	2
3	1979	Q0.42½	12-31-86	12-11	1.70	1.70	1.70	Cv into 1.4545 com,$13.75				....	487	...	Dc	b1.32	bd1.04	bd0.59	b0.16	....	....				3
4	1941	Q0.27½	1-2-87	12-1	1.10	1.10	1.10	134.	642.	602.	9-30-86	636.	...	48358	Dc	3.98	2.24	1.22	2.62	Ed6.10	d5.63	9 Mo Sep	2.07	■d6.18	4
5◆	.....	4% Stk	11-10-86	10-20	4% Stk	Stk	4% Stk	0.31	52.5	50.0	7-31-86	1.74	...	1220	Ap	d1.25	□[12]0.20	•0.71	•0.53	•0.16	d0.87	6 Mo Oct	•0.19	d0.84	5
6	.....	None Since Public			....	Nil	....	3.74	20.1	4.87	7-31-86	0.31	...	5125	Jl	0.50	0.01	0.41	0.03	d0.50	d0.49	3 Mo Oct	Nil	•0.01	6
7◆	.....	None Since Public			....	Nil	....	2.76	5.29	0.61	8-31-86	0.05	...	2492	My	0.16	0.24	0.31	0.38	0.25	0.04	6 Mo Nov	0.19	d0.02	7
8◆	1943	Q0.11	1-2-87	12-4	0.44	0.44	0.44	4.37	30.1	13.3	7-31-86	8.86	...	2560	Ap	0.98	■0.69	1.22	1.28	d0.31	d1.18	6 Mo Oct	0.28	d0.59	8
9◆	1978	0.15	10-31-86	9-29	0.25	0.25	0.20	2.02	19.9	13.7	7-31-86	....	...	±2257	Oc	0.16	0.34	1.01	0.58	P0.39	0.39				9
10	1985	0.15	10-31-86	9-29	0.25	0.25	0.15	...	...	...		....	...	1129	Oc	0.16	0.35	1.01	0.58	P0.39	0.39				10
11	.....	None Since Public			....	Nil	....	22.2	50.8	13.9	9-20-86	4.02	...	8898	Je	0.61	0.05	1.26	0.32	0.06	d0.15	3 Mo Sep	d0.04	d0.25	11
12◆	1841	Q0.25	1-15-87	12-24	0.966	1.00	0.833	Book Value $17.44			3-31-86	p193.	1000	p26638	Dc	▲1.55	▲1.87	▲2.20	▲2.61	....	2.84	9 Mo Sep	1.92	2.15	12
13◆	.....	None Since Public			....	Nil	....	3.05	32.7	21.5	9-30-86	15.1	47	4857	Dc	d11.80	Δd6.40	0.75	d0.58	....	d0.99	9 Mo Sep	d0.15	d0.56	13
14	.....	Terms&trad. basis should be checked in detail						Cv into ⅛ com shr at expir'n				....	...	848	Red rstr to Mar 20'87							Wrrts expire 3-20-90			14
15	.....	Terms&trad. basis should be checked in detail						Cv into ¾ shr com				....	...	1150	Dc	....	....	....	....	....	....	Wrrts expire 5-7-91			15
16	.....	h[66]...	3-2-84	3-5	....	Nil	....	...	61.7	45.5	9-30-86	7.37	...	1874	Je	Δd8.60	■d10.29	Δpd3.80	□d4.82	d4.71	d3.62	3 Mo Sep	d0.69	•0.40	16
17◆	1972	Q0.12	2-26-87	2-2	s0.477	0.48	0.434	24.9	194.	62.6	9-30-86	*112.	...	25371	Dc	[17]□0.76	Δ0.60	0.76	[18]0.80	....	0.70	9 Mo Sep	0.59	0.49	17
18	1972	Q0.30	12-31-86	12-16	1.20	1.20	1.20	25.2	1119	495.	9-30-86	*534.	674	21333	Dc	4.02	■d6.30	3.75	[18]3.31	....	1.12	9 Mo Sep	2.67	0.48	18
19	.....	Terms&trad. basis should be checked in detail						Warrants expire Nov 15, 1987				....	...	3000	Dc	....	....	....	....	....	....				19
20	1969	S2.00	1-15-87	12-26	4.00	4.00	4.00	Conv into 2.326 shrs common				....	129	...	Dc	b1.93	b2.39	b2.36	b1.93	....	....				20
21	1976	S2.00	1-15-87	12-26	4.00	4.00	4.00	Conv into 2.326 shrs common				....	305	...	Dc	b1.93	b2.39	b2.36	b1.93	....	....				21
22	1977	Q0.41	1-15-87	12-26	1.64	1.64	1.64	Cv into 1.574 shrs common				....	278	...	Dc	b1.93	b2.39	b2.36	b1.93	....	....	Mand red 7-15-92,$25			22
23	.....	None Paid			....	Nil	....	Equity per shr $7.08			4-30-86	p18.0	...	p1274	Ap	•0.43	Δ0.54	0.32	0.12	0.24	0.46	6 Mo Oct	0.17	0.39	23
24◆	1954	Q0.16	1-15-87	12-18	0.60	0.64	0.54	n/a	153.	57.2	9-30-86	16.2	...	±10683	Je	1.40	■1.50	2.03	Δ2.68	2.44	2.55	3 Mo Sep	0.63	0.74	24
25	.....	None Since Public			....	Nil	....	0.52	1.88	3.31	9-30-86	7.87	...	7195	Dc	0.26	0.18	0.08	d2.88	....	d3.37	9 Mo Sep	d0.05	d0.54	25
26◆	1935	Q0.62	1-2-87	12-1	2.44	2.48	2.29	52.5	1057	801.	9-30-86	504.	...	45933	Dc	[26]Δ4.10	4.19	Δ4.77	5.84	E6.00	5.64	9 Mo Sep	4.67	4.47	26
27	.....	0.06¼	10-12-55	11-9	....	Nil	....	n/a	6.89	5.10	9-30-86	12.6	...	3482	Dc	Δd0.13	0.36	0.21	d0.64	....	d0.50	9 Mo Sep	d0.11	0.03	27
28	.....	None Since Public			....	Nil	....	0.02	22.0	7.11	8-2-86	9.57	...	*3425	Ja	0.83	1.05	0.68	0.48	....	0.78	9 Mo Oct	0.29	0.59	28
29◆	1977	Q0.01½	2-4-87	1-8	0.05¼	0.06	0.04½	92.7	119.	20.8	6-6-86	391.	...	44727	Au	0.25	□0.34	0.47	0.63	P0.75	0.81	12 Wk Nov	0.21	0.27	29
30◆	.....	None Since Public			....	Nil	....	23.8	74.7	46.7	5-31-86	....	...	30746	Au	0.01	0.02	0.12	0.34	P0.65	0.65				30
31	.....	None Since Public			....	Nil	....	1.30	6.74	0.86	7-31-86	8.70	...	4714	Ap	d0.01	0.09	0.11	0.53	d1.18	d1.39	6 Mo Oct	d0.45	d0.66	31
32	.....	None Paid			....	Nil	....	n/a	22.7	22.3	9-30-86	45.7	...	24004	Dc	d0.44	d0.73	□d0.43	0.11	....	d0.34	9 Mo Sep	0.10	d0.35	32
33	.....	None Paid			....	Nil	....	0.44	8.45	4.24	7-31-86	0.11	...	1472	Oc	0.03	d0.51	•0.20	0.40	P0.82	0.82				33
34◆	.....	None Since Public			....	Nil	....	26.5	79.1	23.7	9-30-86	....	...	17127	Je	0.11	0.20	0.35	0.50	0.56	0.56	3 Mo Sep	0.14	0.14	34
35◆	1986	0.03	1-6-86	12-16	0.03	Nil	....	1.04	16.5	11.3	6-30-86	5.28	...	7135	Dc	0.22	0.18	d0.19	0.10	....	0.02	6 Mo Jun	0.05	d0.03	35
36	.....	Plan qtly divd			....	Nil	....	Net Asset Val $9.50			12-26-86	....	...	*5500	Dc	....	....	....	....	....	....				36
37	.....	None Paid			....	Nil	....	0.40	7.89	5.34	10-1-86	8.00	...	2563	Dc	0.53	0.59	0.61	0.46	....	0.96	9 Mo Sep	0.42	0.92	37
38◆	1985	†0.688	9-5-86	8-15	†0.688	0.69	†0.514	1244	3365	2065	ⁱ3-31-86	3009	2000	50849	Mr	0.83	0.92	2.15	2.35	....	2.14	3 Mo Jun	0.85	0.64	38
39◆	1970	[62]0.214	2-27-87	12-18	0.423	0.43	0.407	308.	330.	274.	ⁱ6-30-86	....	...	±120960	Je	0.87	1.21	1.04	0.93	0.94	0.94	No interim reporting			39
40	.....	None Since Public			....	Nil	....	0.01	7.98	7.60	9-30-86	0.57	...	1752	Dc	0.39	0.58	d0.43	d1.71	....	d2.38	9 Mo Sep	d1.22	d1.89	40
41	1913	Q0.37	12-8-86	11-14	1.46	1.48	1.36	666.	7098	4534	10-29-86	p2929	...	p133329	Ja	∫2.06	∫3.80	3.84	1.73	E4.10↓	2.33	9 Mo Oct	1.64	2.24	41
42	.....	None Paid			....	Nil	....	3.07	5.83	1.63	9-30-86	0.25	...	15745	Dc	□•0.02	•0.02	•0.03	•0.03	....	0.03	9 Mo Sep	•0.03	•0.03	42
43◆	.....	None Since Public			....	Nil	....	1.03	7.93	2.31	9-30-86	2.03	...	2205	Je	0.17	0.27	0.38	0.38	[63]0.51	0.41	3 Mo Sep	0.18	0.08	43
44◆	1934	Q0.12½	12-5-86	11-17	†0.508	0.53	†0.491	n/a	26.2	5.51	9-30-86	....	...	3888	Je	0.45	0.73	1.21	1.34	1.24	1.24	3 Mo Sep	0.33	0.33	44
45◆	1937	Q0.37	12-31-86	12-9	1.48	1.48	h1.48	3.39	75.1	151.	9-30-86	102.	278	9061	Dc	2.85	2.37	□2.22	Δ0.93	E0.80	0.22	12 Mo Sep	Δ1.70	0.22	45
46◆	1941	Q0.25	1-9-87	12-22	0.88	1.00	0.76	80.7	389.	305.	9-30-86	349.	...	57005	Dc	1.57	1.80	2.15	2.19	E2.60	2.36	9 Mo Sep	1.49	1.66	46

◆ **Stock Splits & Divs By Line Reference Index** [5]Adj to 4%,'86. [7]2-for-1,'82:3-for-2,'82. [8]3-for-2,'84,'85. [9]2-for-1,'83:2-for-1 in Cl'A,'85. [12]3-for-2,'84,'86. [13]1-for-20 REVERSE,'84. [17]5-for-4,'82,'85:Adj to 5%,'86. [24]2-for-1,'83. [26]2-for-1,'84. [29]5-for-4,'82:3-for-2,'84:4-for-3,'83,'86. [30]2-for-1,'85:3-for-1,'86. [34]2-for-1 twice,'83:3-for-2,'84. [35]2-for-1&3-for-2,'83:5-for-4,'82,'84:10%,'82;10% twice,Dec'84. [38]5-for-1,'84. [39]4-for-1,'85. [43]3-for-2,'86. [44]3-for-1,'86. [45]10%,'82:No adj for '85 spinoff. [46]2-for-1,'83.

FIGURE 5–11
(continued)

Kerr-McGee 1295

NYSE Symbol KMG Options on CBOE (Jan-Apr-Jul-Oct) In S&P 500

Price	Range	P-E Ratio	Dividend	Yield	S&P Ranking	Beta
May 12'86	1986					
$30\frac{5}{8}$	$33\frac{7}{8}$-25	12	1.10	3.6%	B+	1.01

Summary

KMG's basic business is finding and producing oil/gas, but it has diversified into a wide array of energy-related activities. While the current depressed oil price environment is expected to take its toll on earnings, KMG appears to have the financial flexibility to pursue its goal of adding reserves (slanted heavily toward natural gas and toward acquisitions). To help it along, KMG is trimming its exploration spending and stretching out its share-repurchase program.

Current Outlook

Earnings for 1986 are projected to decline to about $1.35 a share from 1985's $2.62.

Even so, dividends are expected to continue at $0.27½ quarterly.

Revenues and profits for 1986 are targeted down on much lower average oil prices, lower natural gas prices, a deeply depressed offshore contract rig market, and the negative impact on uranium net results from a KMG plant shut-down. As a partial offset, gasoline profits should be good this summer and full-year chemical profits higher.

Sales & Services (Million $)

Quarter:	1986	1985	1984	1983
Mar.	719	809	899	851
Jun.	---	846	905	836
Sep.	---	790	837	898
Dec.	---	900	896	923
	---	3,345	3,537	3,508

Revenues for the 1986 first quarter declined 11%, year to year. Net income was off 22%.

Common Share Earnings ($)

Quarter:	1986	1985	1984	1983
Mar.	0.45	0.54	0.76	0.45
Jun.	E0.30	0.77	0.72	0.71
Sep.	E0.30	0.76	0.41	0.75
Dec.	E0.30	0.55	d0.67	0.33
	E1.35	2.62	1.22	2.24

Important Developments

Apr. '86—KMG said that it would reduce the rate of its common stock repurchase program that commenced May, 1985 and was expanded in November, 1985. Under the program, KMG had been authorized to repurchase up to 20% of its shares

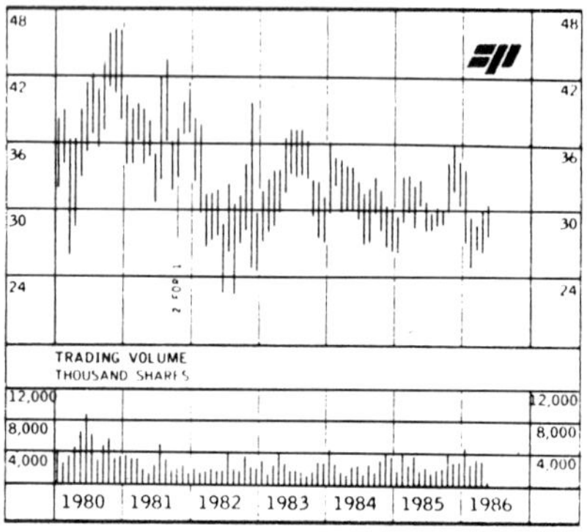

outstanding May 7, 1985 or approximately 10.6 million shares. At the end of March, 1986 4,105,800 shares had been repurchased.

Oct. '85—Kerr-McGee completed the acquisition of DeltaUS Corp.'s oil and gas properties and interests in two gas processing plants. The $140 million purchase included producing oil and gas properties in east Texas, northern Louisiana, and the Permian and Appalachian basins. Also included were mineral and royalty interests onshore along the Gulf Coast of Texas and Louisiana. Undeveloped leases acquired in the purchase totaled approximately 138,000 net acres. KMG estimated the reserves, including those from infill drilling, acquired from DeltaUS to be 5.7 million barrels of oil and gas condensate and 157.9 billion cubic feet of natural gas.

Next earnings report due in late July.

Per Share Data ($)

Yr. End Dec. 31	1985	1984	1983	1982	1981	1980	1979	1978	1977	1976
Book Value	34.65	32.97	32.83	31.69	28.95	25.91	23.37	21.06	19.40	17.66
Earnings	2.62	1.22	2.24	3.98	4.07	3.51	•3.09	2.29	2.31	2.60
Dividends	1.10	1.10	1.10	1.10	1.02½	0.90	0.77½	0.62½	0.62½	0.59½
Payout Ratio	40%	90%	49%	28%	25%	26%	25%	27%	27%	23%
Prices—High	36	$36\frac{3}{8}$	$37\frac{1}{2}$	$39\frac{7}{8}$	$43\frac{3}{4}$	$46\frac{1}{2}$	$34\frac{1}{4}$	$26\frac{5}{8}$	$37\frac{3}{8}$	$41\frac{1}{2}$
Low	$26\frac{1}{4}$	$26\frac{3}{8}$	$27\frac{1}{8}$	$22\frac{1}{2}$	$30\frac{3}{4}$	26	23	$19\frac{7}{8}$	$22\frac{5}{8}$	$30\frac{3}{8}$
P/E Ratio—	14-10	30-22	17-12	10-6	11-8	13-7	11-7	12-9	16-10	16-12

Data as orig. reptd. Adj. for stk. div(s). of 100% Nov. 1981. d-Deficit. E-Estimated

Standard NYSE Stock Reports
Vol. 53/No. 96/Sec. 11

May 19, 1986

Standard & Poor's Corp.
25 Broadway, NY, NY 10004

FIGURE 5–12

Example from *Standard & Poor's Stock Reports* (Copyright © 1986 by Standard & Poor's Corp. Reprinted by permission.)

1295

Kerr-McGee Corporation

Income Data (Million $)

Year Ended Dec. 31	Revs.	Oper. Inc.	% Oper. Inc. of Revs.	Cap. Exp.	Depr.	Int. Exp.	Net Bef. Taxes	Eff. Tax Rate	Net Inc.	% Net Inc. of Revs.
1985	**3,345**	**684**	**20.4%**	**384**	**336**	**119**	**[2]272**	**49.6%**	**137**	**4.1%**
1984	3,537	697	19.7%	349	339	142	[2]109	40.4%	65	1.8%
1983	3,508	549	15.6%	422	304	143	[2]199	40.4%	118	3.4%
1982	3,777	670	17.8%	547	262	164	[2]341	38.5%	210	5.6%
1981	3,826	627	16.4%	606	188	149	[2]378	44.1%	211	5.5%
1980	3,478	524	15.1%	527	160	[1]86	[2]332	45.2%	182	5.2%
1979	2,683	441	16.4%	389	130	58	[2]288	43.1%	[1]160	6.0%
1978	2,072	311	15.0%	270	98	40	[2]214	43.3%	118	5.7%
1977	2,165	322	14.9%	269	96	29	[2]211	41.8%	119	5.5%
1976	1,955	319	16.3%	338	82	23	[2]221	36.9%	134	6.9%

Balance Sheet Data (Million $)

Dec. 31	Cash	Current Assets	Current Liab.	Current Ratio	Total Assets	Ret. on Assets	Long Term Debt	Common Equity	Total Cap.	% LT Debt of Cap.	Ret. on Equity
1985	**212**	**797**	**686**	**1.2**	**3,702**	**3.8%**	**666**	**1,722**	**2,845**	**23.4%**	**8.2%**
1984	283	1,011	779	1.3	3,771	1.7%	665	1,740	2,833	23.5%	3.7%
1983	230	929	713	1.3	3,807	3.1%	816	1,733	3,009	27.1%	7.0%
1982	190	1,011	695	1.5	3,763	5.8%	895	1,672	3,009	29.7%	13.1%
1981	218	926	556	1.7	3,415	6.8%	927	1,501	2,804	33.1%	14.8%
1980	170	727	519	1.4	2,807	7.1%	521	1,342	2,158	24.1%	14.3%
1979	116	627	378	1.7	2,339	7.3%	375	1,209	1,833	20.4%	13.9%
1978	107	561	368	1.5	2,022	6.1%	255	1,089	1,533	16.6%	11.3%
1977	104	562	316	1.8	1,833	6.9%	299	1,003	1,433	20.9%	12.4%
1976	80	547	278	2.0	1,626	8.9%	321	913	1,325	24.2%	15.6%

Data as orig. reptd. **1.** Reflects accounting change. **2.** Incl. equity in earns. of nonconsol. subs.

Business Summary

Kerr-McGee is an integrated unit in the domestic oil industry and is a major factor in contract offshore drilling. It also mines coal, manufactures chemicals, processes uranium, and owns timberland.

Profits (million $)	1985	1984
Petr. expl. & prod.	$47	$90
Petr. ref. & mkt.	$25	$14
Contract drilling	$4	-$2
Coal	$51	$57
Chemicals	$12	$25
Uranium	$4	$44
Other	$2	$3

In 1985 net crude oil and condensate production averaged 47,500 b/d, natural gas liquids production 8,200 b/d, natural gas sales 183 million cubic feet a day, crude refinery runs 121,800 b/d, and petroleum product sales 160,400 b/d. Net proved reserves at the 1985 year-end stood at 120,500,000 barrels of crude oil and condensate (37% U.S. and 63% foreign) and 826.4 billion cubic feet of natural gas (81% U.S. and 19% foreign).

Coal shipped during 1985 totaled 15,500,000 tons; proved and probable coal reserves at the 1985 year-end stood at 758,000,000 tons.

Dividend Data

Dividends have been paid since 1941. A dividend reinvestment plan is available.

Amt. of Divd. $	Date Decl.	Ex-divd. Date	Stock of Record	Payment Date
0.27½	Jul. 9	Aug. 30	Sep. 6	Oct. 1'85
0.27½	Nov. 12	Dec. 2	Dec. 6	Jan. 2'86
0.27½	Mar. 4	Mar. 11	Mar. 17	Apr. 1'86
0.27½	May 6	Jun. 2	Jun. 6	Jul. 1'86

Next dividend meeting: early Jul. '86.

Capitalization

Long Term Debt: $666,000,000 (12/31/85).

Minority Interest: $84,000,000.

Common Stock: 48,674,000 shs. ($1 par). Institutions hold approximately 60%. Shareholders of record: 15,000.

Office—Kerr-McGee Center (P.O. Box 25861), Oklahoma City, Okla. 73125. **Tel**—(405) 270-1313. **Chrmn & CEO**—F. A. McPherson. **Pres**—J. W. McKenny. **VP-Secy**—W. E. Heimann. **VP-Treas**—T. B. Stephens. **Investor Contact**—R. W. Bird. **Dirs**—M. K. Hambrick, R. D. Harrison, E. L. Kennedy, R. S. Kerr, Jr., G. T. McBride, Jr., D. A. McGee, N. McKay, J. W. McKenny, F. A. McPherson, W. C. Morris. **Transfer Agents & Registrars**—Manufacturers Hanover Trust, NYC; Liberty National Bank & Trust Co., Oklahoma City. **Incorporated** in Delaware in 1932.

 Earl L. Lester, CFA

FIGURE 5–12
(continued)

GEN'L. DYNAMICS NYSE-GD

RECENT PRICE	P/E RATIO		RELATIVE P/E RATIO	DIV'D YLD	VALUE LINE
74	7.5	(Trailing: 8.6 / Median: 8.0)	0.54	1.6 %	561

	1971	1972	1973	1974	1975	1976	1977	1978	1979	1980	1981	1982	1983	1984	1985	1986
High	6.4	7.0	5.7	5.8	11.3	13.0	12.3	18.7	30.5	44.9	43.0	36.6	61.8	69.8	84.0	89.3
Low	3.6	4.5	3.1	2.7	3.8	7.5	8.9	7.4	13.6	25.2	21.0	18.8	30.6	42.0	62.0	64.3

Insider Decisions 1985

	M	A	M	J	J	A	S	O	N	D	J	F	M	A	M
to Buy	4	3	2	1	1	0	1	2	3	1	0	3	2	1	3
to Sell	3	3	3	3	3	5	5	0	0	3	1	2	2	8	3

Institutional Decisions

	2Q'85	3Q'85	4Q'85	1Q'86	2Q'86
to Buy	69	68	70	91	66
to Sell	74	49	61	72	77
Hldg's(000)	13761	14062	14097	15917	15187

1988	1989	1990	1991

October 17, 1986 Value Line

TIMELINESS (Relative Price Performance Next 12 Mos.) **3** Average
SAFETY (Scale: 1 Highest to 5 Lowest) **3** Average
BETA 1.30 (1.00 = Market)

1989-91 PROJECTIONS

	Price	Gain	Ann'l Total Return
High	145	(+95%)	19%
Low	95	(+ 30%)	9%

1970	1971	1972	1973	1974	1975	1976	1977	1978	1979	1980	1981	1982	1983	1984	1985	1986	1987	© VALUE LINE, INC.	89-91E
42.20	35.47	29.19	31.38	37.69	39.93	47.02	54.55	60.70	76.30	88.00	94.44	112.95	135.55	181.43	192.30	**217.65**	**248.80**	Sales per sh	**312.00**
.86	1.34	1.45	1.71	1.95	2.60	3.33	3.72	.91	5.32	5.76	4.56	6.26	8.65	13.22	14.02	**15.30**	**17.25**	"Cash Flow" per sh	**22.75**
d.12	.39	.49	.77	.99	1.52	1.82	1.90	d.90	3.43	3.58	2.25	3.74	5.30	8.08	8.80	**9.20**	**10.45**	Earnings per sh (A)	**14.25**
.10	--	--	--	--	--	--	--	--	.60	.63	.72	.72	.93	1.00	1.00	**1.00**	**1.20**	Div'ds Decl'd per sh (B)	**1.80**
.94	1.15	1.19	1.02	2.07	3.10	2.70	1.94	2.99	4.17	4.02	2.73	2.45	4.08	5.83	9.74	**10.00**	**8.25**	Cap'l Spending per sh	**9.40**
6.01	6.43	6.89	7.70	8.65	10.07	11.86	13.78	12.76	15.53	18.54	19.99	21.56	23.91	24.58	31.46	**40.00**	**49.15**	Book Value per sh (C)	**85.50**
52.69	52.69	52.73	52.32	52.23	54.09	54.31	53.19	52.80	53.21	53.90	53.61	54.49	52.72	43.21	42.45	**42.50**	**42.50**	Common Shs Outst'g (D)	**42.50**
--	12.7	11.1	5.5	4.3	5.2	5.7	5.7	--	5.5	9.9	13.1	7.7	9.4	6.9	8.3	Bold figures are Value Line estimates		Avg Ann'l P/E Ratio	**8.5**
--	.81	.76	.54	.60	.69	.73	.75	--	.80	1.31	1.59	.85	.79	.64	.67			Relative P/E Ratio	**.70**
2.4%	--	--	--	--	--	--	--	--	3.2%	1.8%	2.4%	2.5%	1.9%	1.8%	1.4%			Avg Ann'l Div'd Yield	**1.5%**
						2553.5	2901.2	3205.2	4059.6	4742.7	5063.4	6154.5	7146.3	7839.0	8163.8	**9200**	**10150**	Sales ($mill)	**13250**
						9.8%	9.9%	NMF	9.8%	7.9%	5.9%	7.9%	9.4%	10.9%	10.9%	**10.5%**	**10.5%**	Operating Margin	**10.0%**
						81.2	94.4	95.9	100.1	117.8	122.5	137.5	171.8	189.4	222.6	**360**	**290**	Depreciation ($mill)	**365**
						99.6	103.4	d48.1	185.2	195.0	124.1	205.8	286.6	381.7	372.5	**390**	**445**	Net Profit ($mill)	**600**
						32.9%	42.0%	--	35.4%	24.0%	36.8%	41.7%	43.8%	44.2%	43.1%	**42.5%**	**40.0%**	Income Tax Rate	**34.0%**
						3.9%	3.6%	NMF	4.6%	4.1%	2.5%	3.3%	4.0%	4.9%	4.6%	**4.2%**	**4.4%**	Net Profit Margin	**4.6%**
						325.5	415.8	232.2	319.1	464.9	487.8	326.3	526.4	595.2	310.4	**775**	**800**	Working Cap'l ($mill)	**1150**
						77.3	52.4	70.6	66.8	58.9	26.9	23.7	21.3	17.6	28.2	**450**	**400**	Long-Term Debt ($mill)	**360**
						644.2	732.9	703.5	856.0	1028.2	1098.6	1202.0	1260.6	1062.1	1335.8	**1700**	**2090**	Net Worth ($mill)	**3600**
						14.3%	13.5%	NMF	20.4%	18.2%	11.2%	16.9%	22.4%	35.4%	27.4%	**19.0%**	**18.5%**	% Earned Total Cap'l	**16.0%**
						15.5%	14.1%	NMF	21.6%	19.0%	11.3%	17.1%	22.7%	35.9%	27.9%	**23.0%**	**21.0%**	% Earned Net Worth	**16.5%**
						15.5%	14.1%	NMF	18.2%	15.9%	7.7%	14.1%	18.6%	31.4%	24.7%	**20.5%**	**19.0%**	% Retained to Comm Eq	**14.5%**
						--	--	--	19%	19%	33%	20%	18%	13%	11%	**11%**	**11%**	% All Div'ds to Net Prof	**13%**

CAPITAL STRUCTURE as of 6/29/86
Total Debt $658.8 mill. **Due in 5 Yrs** $638.0 mill.
LT Debt $24.9 mill. **LT Interest** $2.5 mill.
(2% of Cap'l)

Leases, Uncapitalized Annual rentals $50.8 mill.

Pension Liability None in '85 vs. None in '84

Pfd Stock None

Common Stock 42,453,850 shs. (98% of Cap'l)

CURRENT POSITION ($MILL.)	1984	1985	6/29/86
Cash Assets	186.7	13.4	18.7
Receivables	316.9	407.2	486.1
Inventory(Avg Cst)	1038.2	1711.8	2069.9
Other	26.7	45.2	91.5
Current Assets	1568.5	2177.6	2666.2
Accts Payable	436.7	590.5	*625.0*
Debt Due	6.0	412.5	633.9
Other	530.6	864.2	*1189.2*
Current Liab.	973.3	1867.2	2448.1

ANNUAL RATES of change (per sh)	Past 10 Yrs	Past 5 Yrs	Est'd '83-'85 to '89-'91
Sales	16.5%	17.5%	*10.5%*
"Cash Flow"	19.0%	24.5%	*11.5%*
Earnings	21.0%	29.5%	*11.5%*
Dividends	—	9.5%	*10.5%*
Book Value	11.5%	11.5%	*21.0%*

Cal-endar	QUARTERLY SALES ($ mill.) Mar. 31	June 30	Sept. 30	Dec. 31	Full Year
1983	1827	1775	1735	1809	7146.3
1984	1860	1903	2005	2071	7839.0
1985	1914	1963	2024	2263	8163.8
1986	2066	2332	**2350**	**2452**	**9200**
1987	**2350**	**2450**	**2600**	**2750**	**10150**

Cal-endar	EARNINGS PER SHARE (A) Mar. 31	June 30	Sept. 30	Dec. 31	Full Year
1983	1.03	1.32	1.43	1.52	5.30
1984	1.52	1.97	2.22	2.37	8.08
1985	1.98	2.31	2.38	2.13	8.80
1986	1.64	2.43	**2.50**	**2.63**	**9.20**
1987	**2.35**	**2.65**	**2.70**	**2.75**	**10.45**

Cal-endar	QUARTERLY DIVIDENDS PAID (B) Mar. 31	June 30	Sept. 30	Dec. 31	Full Year
1982	.18	.18	.18	.18	.72
1983	.18	.25	.25	.25	.93
1984	.25	.25	.25	.25	1.00
1985	.25	.25	.25	.25	1.00
1986	.25	.25	.25		

BUSINESS: General Dynamics Corp. is a leading U.S. defense contractor. Aerospace prods. include military aircraft (F-111 parts, F-16), Atlas and Centaur boosters, Tomahawk cruise missiles and tactical missiles. Marine div. produces LNG tankers, naval vessels and submarines (SSN-688, Trident). Also makes data output devices. Acquired Chrysler Tank bus. (now GD Land Sys.) in '82; Cessna Aircraft in '85. Gov't. business, 90% of sales; R&D, 2.8%. '85 deprec. rate: 9.1%. Est. plant age: 6 years. Has 103,300 empls., 31,040 stkhldrs. Insiders control 25% of stock. Chairman & C.E.O.: S.C. Pace. President: O.C. Boileau. Inc.: DE. Address: Pierre Laclede Ctr., St. Louis, MO 63105. Tel.: 314-889-8200.

Strong backlogs in the aerospace and submarine divisions should support good earnings gains through decade's end. . . Growth opportunities abound within the F-16 program as the enormously successful aircraft gains popularity outside of the U.S. Additional exports aside, shipments will continue to accelerate in coming years; deliveries seem likely to peak in 1989 at 300 aircraft a year (price range: $15-$20 million each). GD's array of missiles and gun systems offer substantial growth potential as well. And despite competition for the Navy's submarine production, the company has a strong backlog of Los Angeles class fast-attack subs. Moreover, GD will probably garner the largest share of upcoming awards for Trident and SSN-21 sub production.

. . .although defense-related margins are likely to shrink a bit. An increasingly cost-concious Pentagon is bolstering rivalries among defense contractors. With profit margins likely to be somewhat tighter in coming years, the risk of cost overruns on fixed price contracts will increase. And bidding expenses will almost certainly rise, partly as a result of higher contractor investment in the manufacture of prototypes (a significant factor in the upcoming competition for the ATF award).

Meanwhile, the Cessna division remains in the doldrums. First-half operating losses amounted to nearly 70¢ a share; even the stoppage of all single-piston engine aircraft production for nearly a year won't boost results to breakeven until 1987, by our analysis. Although at current depressed levels only a modest boost in demand would translate into sharply improved results, we see little cause for optimism.

Tax reform has mixed implications for GD. Earnings will get a modest boost in 1987 and beyond, but cash flow will be restricted due to a sharp increase in the payment of cash taxes. We look for earnings of $9.20 a share this year and $10.45 a share in 1987. The stock should about keep pace with the year-ahead market and through decade's end. *Daniel C. Polinak/Morton L. Siegel*

Restated Sales (and Pretax Margins) by Business Line

	1983	1984	1985	1986
Aerospace	3546.4(10.0%)	3919.4(10.3%)	4307.8(10.5%)	*4700(10.5%)*
Submarines	1423.9(6.2%)	1527.7(9.5%)	1644.7(9.9%)	*1725(10.0%)*
Tanks	1292.3(3.2%)	1112.0(3.9%)	1136.6(4.0%)	*1175(4.0%)*
Gen'l Aviation	--(--)	--(--)	162.3(12.1%)	*450(d5.0%)*
Other	717.7(2.2%)	936.7(2.4%)	912.4(d1.4%)	*1150(Nil)*
Company Total	6980.3(7.2%)	7495.8(8.2%)	8163.8(8.2%)	*9200(7.5%)*

(A) Based on average shares outstanding. Excl. extraordinary earnings: '71, 3¢; '72, d4¢; '73, 2¢; '74, 3¢; Discont. ops.: '82, d51¢; '85, 25¢; nonrecurring loss: '82, 84¢. Next earnings report due early Nov. Est'd current cost egs./sh.: '85, $7.90. (B) Next dividend meeting about Jan. 11. Goes ex about Jan. 14. Aproximate dividend payment dates: Feb. 15, May 15, Aug. 15, Nov. 15. (C) Incl. intangibles. In '85; $429.5 mill., $10.12/sh. (D) In millions, adjusted for stock splits and dividends.

Company's Financial Strength	A+
Stock's Price Stability	50
Price Growth Persistence	90
Earnings Predictability	65

FIGURE 5–13
Example of stock report from *The Value Line Investment Survey*
(Copyright © 1986 by Value Line, Inc. Reprinted by permission.)

TABLE 5–11
Computerized sources of investment information

Database	*Content Summary*
Center for Research in Security Prices (CRSP)	Daily prices for common stocks
Standard & Poor's Compustat Services	Quarterly and annual financial statements for many companies, daily price data; also available for microcomputers
Value Line	Financial statement data; also available for microcomputers
Disclosure II	Online database of financial statement data; also available for microcomputers

are available on floppy diskettes or other microcomputer storage media. Table 5–11 summarizes some of the computerized databases and systems available to investors.

Others

In addition to the above sources, there are dozens of other companies that print newsletters providing information and recommendations to investors. These publications have subscriber lists numbering from the dozens to the thousands. Among the more popular of these are *Dow Theory Forecasts* and several letters published by Zweig Securities Advisory Service. Consult advertisements in any issue of *Barron's* to find names of these types of services.

SUMMARY

This chapter outlines sources for economic, market, industry, and company information for investors. Government publications provide important economic information. Market indexes provide measures of the level of security prices in general. These indexes, such as the Dow Jones Industrial Average and the Standard & Poor's Composite Index, gauge overall market performance. To understand how a particular index represents the market, an investor should be familiar with the construction of the index. Information about individual companies comes from the companies' reports and from private services offering financial data or recommendations about the company.

IMPORTANT TERMS

bear market
bull market
dividend yield
equal weighting
market index
P/E ratio
price weighting
total market value
value weighting
weighting scheme

QUESTIONS AND PROBLEMS

1. Identify and summarize the contents of some of the economic publications issued by U.S. government agencies.
2. Visit a library and locate some nongovernmental sources for current economic information. List and briefly describe these sources.
3. Given the following information:

Stock	*Number of Shares Outstanding*	*Market Price per Share*
A	1,200,000	$24.00
B	840,000	18.50
C	430,000	68.00

   a) Compute the total market value of each stock.
   b) If Company A used its extra cash to purchase 100,000 shares of its stock, what do you think would happen to the price per share? What would happen to the total market value?
4. Using the stocks in Problem 2, construct a price-weighted index. Assuming the prices of stocks A, B, and C change to 20, 18, and 50, respectively, compute the new value for your index and the return on the index.
5. Repeat Problem 4 with a value-weighted index.
6. Repeat Problem 4 with an equally weighted index.
7. Locate a company's annual report and 10-K report for the same year. Compare and contrast the presentation of the company in the two reports.
8. You are seeking information about the items listed below. For each item, list one or more possible sources where you would likely find the information.
   a) the annual earnings for Exxon for the last three years
   b) the interest yield on Treasury bills for the past 10 years, annually
   c) the interest yield on a Treasury bill yesterday
   d) aggregate earnings for the petroleum-refining industry for recent years
   e) an opinion about the investment merits of IBM common stock
   f) the significant accounting procedures used by Mobil.

NOTES

1. Mary Lindahl-Stevens (1980), "Redefining Bull and Bear Markets," *Financial Analysts Journal,* (November–December), 76–77.
2. James H. Lorie and Mary T. Hamilton (1971), "Stock Market Indexes," in James Lorie and Richard Brealey (1976), *Modern Developments in Investment Management,* New York: Praeger, 68–83.
3. Jimmy E. Hilliard (1979), "The Relationship between Equity Indices on World Exchanges," *Journal of Finance,* 34 (March), 103–114.

SELECTED REFERENCES

Bauman, W. Scott (1982). *Guidelines for Communications to Professional Investors.* Charlottesville, VA: The Financial Analysts Research Foundation.

Disclosure Information Group (1985). *A Guide to SEC Corporate Filings.* Bethesda, Md.: Author.

Foster, Taylor W., III, D. Randall Jenkins, and Don W. Vickrey (1983). "Additional Evidence on the Incremental Information Content of the 10-K." *Journal of Business Finance and Accounting,* 10 (Spring), 57–66.

Greenleaf, James, Ruth Foster, and Robert Prinsky (1983). *Understanding Financial Data in The Wall Street Journal.* New York: Dow Jones & Company, Inc.

Hilliard, Jimmy E. (1979). "The Relationship between Equity Indices on World Exchanges." *Journal of Finance,* 34 (March), 103–114.

Knight, R. F., and J. F. Affleck-Graves (1986). "The Impact of Disclosure Requirements on the Systematic Risk of South African Companies." *Journal of Business Finance and Accounting,* 13 (Spring), 87–94.

Lindahl-Stevens, Mary (1980). "Redefining Bull and Bear Markets." *Financial Analysts Journal,* (November–December), 76–77.

Walker, Martin (1985). "Forecast Disclosure: An Information Economics Perspective." *Journal of Business Finance and Accounting,* 12 (Autumn), 355–371.

PART TWO

Risk, Diversification, and Capital Market Theory

CHAPTER 6

Concepts of Risk and Return

Chapter 2 identified the fundamental concepts of risk and return. A thorough understanding of risk and return is an essential foundation to the formal development (see Chapters 7 and 8) of the association between risk and return. This chapter provides more detailed descriptions of risk and return, beginning with a discussion of different ways to classify risk. Following that, the chapter presents various measures of return and of risk.

In addition to understanding the concepts of risk and return, one also needs to understand the attitudes investors have about risk and return. These attitudes, such as risk aversion and utility maximization, are also covered in this chapter and are very important to the derivation of the theoretical models associating risk and return developed in Chapter 8.

Finally, Appendix 6A presents the concepts and mathematics of the time value of money. Many of the theoretical developments and valuation models used in investments utilize the idea of time value. The discussion of time value includes the present value of a single payment, the future value of a single payment, the present value of an annuity, and the future value of an annuity.

RISK CLASSIFIED BY NATURE

Investors can classify risk by either its source or its nature. Risk classified by source breaks down the different causes of risk, while classification by nature identifies risk based on whether the risk is affected by actions specific to the individual investment or by broader, macro-economic factors.

Systematic Risk

Changes in broad economic, social, or political factors can influence the return on an investment. The fluctuation in an investment's return attributable to changes in these broad factors is *systematic risk*. The systematic risk of a security causes its return to be affected by such variables as interest rates, consumer demand, currency exchange rates, government monetary and fiscal policy, and other aspects of the economic and political system. Systematic risk is common to all securities (except risk-free securities), although some securities are more sensitive to systematic factors than others. Because systematic risk is always present in a security or a diversified portfolio of many different securities, investors often call systematic risk *undiversifiable risk*.

Unsystematic Risk

Unsystematic risk is the variation in returns due to factors related to the individual firm or security. For example, a firm's labor contract, its sources of raw materials, and its exposure to weather conditions might all be specific sources of unsystematic risk of the firm. All risky securities have some degree of unsystematic risk, but, as the study of portfolio theory later in this text shows, combining securities into diversified portfolios reduces and can virtually eliminate unsystematic risk from the portfolio. For this reason, unsystematic risk is often also referred to as *diversifiable risk* because it can be "diversified away."

Total Risk

As mentioned above, all risky securities have varying degrees of both systematic and unsystematic risk. The *total risk* of a security is the sum of its systematic and unsystematic risks as the following relation shows:

$$\text{Total risk} = \text{systematic risk} + \text{unsystematic risk}$$

The total fluctuation in return on an investment is the total risk of the investment.

RISK CLASSIFIED BY SOURCE

In addition to classifying risk by its nature, investors often identify risk by its general source. Each source of risk affects to some degree the total risk of a security. The effect may be principally systematic in nature, or it may be unsystematic. It is often possible, however, to partition total risk into both systematic and unsystematic natures.

Business Risk

Business risk is identifiable as the variation in a firm's earnings due to the company's business or product line. The principal determinants of a firm's business risk are the variability of sales and the firm's *operating leverage*. Operating leverage represents the firm's ability to translate increased sales into increased profit.

Several factors influence the variability of a company's sales or revenue. Among these are systematic factors, such as aggregate consumer demand and interest rates for financing sales, as well as unsystematic factors, such as the company's expenditures on advertising, the customer profile, actions of competitors, and the availability of substitutes for the company's product.

A mathematical definition of a firm's operating leverage is the percent change in operating profit that the firm can achieve from a given percent change in sales. The main variable affecting a firm's operating leverage is the relationship of fixed costs to variable costs. If variable costs make up a large portion of total costs, then a given change in sales will be followed by a similar change in costs, and percentage profits will change relatively little. This would describe a firm with a low degree of operating leverage. On the other hand, a company in which a high portion of total costs are fixed costs would have a high degree of operating leverage.

Financial Risk

The uncertainty of a firm's earnings attributable to the firm's method of financing investment produces *financial risk*. Financial risk, therefore, is a function of the company's capital structure, or *financial leverage*. Financial leverage is the percent change in net earnings for a given percent change in operating earnings, and it results from the use of debt financing in the capital structure of a firm. If a firm uses a large amount of debt, then it has contracted to pay a relatively large fixed amount for its sources of capital. When operating profits fall, the company still must pay large interest payments (unless it defaults), and the net percentage profits will fall even more. This would be an example of high financial leverage. In contrast, the firm that finances its investments mostly by selling common stock would have little or no contractual interest payments and would have low financial leverage.

Purchasing Power Risk

The *purchasing power risk* of a security is the variation of real returns on the security caused by inflation. As prices rise, the purchasing power of the dollar falls, and the real (inflation-adjusted) return on an investment may fall even though the nominal return in current dollars rises. For example, if an investment increased in value last year by 12 percent while prices rose 12 percent, the investor had no net gain in real wealth. (After taxes, this investor would even be behind because taxes are computed on profits without adjusting for inflation.) Table 6–1 shows the return on common stocks, inflation as measured by the Consumer Price Index (CPI), and the inflation-adjusted return on common stocks for recent years.

Interest Rate Risk

The prices of debt securities and all other securities with fixed payout (such as preferred stocks) are dependent upon the level of market interest rates. When interest rates rise, bond values will generally fall. (This relationship is explored in detail in

TABLE 6–1
Returns on common stocks, inflation, and inflation-adjusted returns

Year	*Return on Common Stocks*	*Consumer Price Index*	*Cumulative Wealth of Initial $10,000*	*Inflation-Adjusted Cumulative Wealth*
1971	.177	1.033	$11,768	$11,392
1972	.180	1.069	13,884	12,988
1973	−.185	1.163	11,313	9,727
1974	−.284	1.305	8,102	6,208
1975	.385	1.396	11,218	8,036
1976	.266	1.463	14,201	9,707
1977	−.026	1.563	13,827	8,846
1978	.093	1.703	15,109	8,872
1979	.256	1.930	18,971	9,829
1980	.337	2.170	25,359	11,686
1981	−.038	2.363	24,408	10,329
1982	.187	2.455	28,975	11,802
1983	.042	2.534	30,180	11,910
1984	.221	2.642	36,864	13,953

Chapter 12, on bond pricing.) Returns on other types of securities also depend upon interest rates. The earnings of many companies, and hence the performance of their common stocks, are sensitive to interest rate changes. Potential variability of investment returns due to interest rate fluctuations is *interest rate risk*.

The degree of sensitivity to interest rate changes will naturally differ from firm to firm. For example, one would expect companies in industries that depend heavily on the availability of credit to be more affected by interest rates. Savings and loan institutions, residential construction companies, and automobile manufacturers are companies that would likely fall into the classification of firms with high levels of interest rate risk.

Management Risk

The quality of a company's management has an important impact upon the value of the company's securities. The portion of the firm's risk arising from the strengths and weaknesses of the company's management is *management risk*.

Market Risk

One observation that most people are quick to note about the security markets is that returns on securities tend to move together. That is, on a good day, the fact that some stocks in the market are rising seems to fuel enthusiasm, and other stocks tend to rise also. In contrast, when some stocks begin to fall, others will tend to fall also as a mood of pessimism pervades the market. This market psychology is the explanation of the existence of *market risk,* which is the volatility of a security's return attributable to changes in the level of market returns.

In studying the direction of the market, investors usually break the market cycle into the periods of rising prices (positive returns) and periods of falling prices (negative returns). As noted earlier, market tradition labels the rising markets as bull markets and the falling markets as bear markets. (Some writers have called a sideways market, one that has no definite upward or downward trend, a chicken market.)

Some securities are quite sensitive to changes in the market and have a high degree of market risk, while others fluctuate very little as the market changes. When a relatively small increase in the market usually accompanies a relatively larger increase in the price of a stock, the stock has a high degree of market risk.

Since we can think of the market as a proxy representing the economy or economic system, then market risk is identifiable as systematic in nature. Because of this, the term *market risk* is often used synonymously with *systematic risk,* and measures of market risk are useful as measures of a security's systematic risk.

Liquidity Risk

Liquidity risk arises from the inability to convert an investment quickly into cash. Liquidity risk is also present when there is a *price of immediacy.* The price of immediacy is the price an investor pays to convert an investment quickly into cash. When the price of immediacy is relatively high, the investor pays dearly even though the investment can be quickly converted to cash.

In security markets, liquidity risk is a function of the marketability of the security. For example, one might have stocks of two almost identical companies, with the only difference being that one stock is actively traded and very marketable, while the other is closely held and rarely trades. Assume that the true worth of both companies is $50 per share, and the stock of the actively traded company sells for $50. The value of the inactive stock is also $50, but an investor who wants to sell shares quickly might find an immediate bid of only $48 for the stock. The lower marketability of this stock has given it a degree of liquidity risk that makes the price of the stock a bit more uncertain.

MEASURES OF RETURN

Chapter 2 introduced return in the form of holding period return, the profit per dollar invested over a particular period of time. There are other definitions of return that are useful for particular applications.

Annualized Return

When comparing the returns on two different investments, the holding periods for the investments must be of equal length for the comparison to be meaningful. The most commonly used holding period for reporting and comparing returns is annual returns. For example, banks always quote the annual interest rate paid on saving certificates even though the maturity of the certificate may be more or less than one calendar year. Therefore, it is often desirable to convert holding period returns to their annual equivalents.

Annualizing returns is not as simple as dividing the holding period return by the portion of a year represented by the holding period. For example, a 12 percent return over six months is not a 24 percent annualized return. This is explained by the compounding of returns; that is, if one invested at 12 percent for six months and then invested at 12 percent for another six months, during the second six months one would earn returns on the 12 percent return earned during the first six months in addition to the return on the original investment. For example, \$100 invested for six months at a 12 percent holding period return would be \$112 at the end of six months. For another six months, the interest on the \$112 balance would be \$13.44 (.12 × 112), giving a total balance of \$125.44 at year's end. The annual return would actually be 25.44 percent! To annualize holding period returns, use the following formula:

$$R_a = [1 + R]^{(365/T)} - 1 \tag{6–1}$$

where R_a = the annualized return on investment
T = the time (in days) of the holding period return, R

Example 6–1 shows how to use Equation 6–1.

EXAMPLE 6–1

What is the annualized return of an investment that yields a holding period yield of 10.8 percent over ninety days?

$$R_a = [1 + .108]^{(365/90)} - 1$$
$$= (1.08)^{4.056} - 1$$
$$= .516$$

Holding period return and its annualized equivalent are *simple rates of return.* A rate is simple interest if it represents the amount that one dollar will grow to at the end of the period.

Continuously Compounded Return

The preceding section showed that one could not simply double the 12 percent return to get its annual equivalent because of the effects of compounding. Because of compounding, simple interest rates are not additive over time. One method that financial analysts sometimes use to get around this problem is to quote a *continuously compounded rate of return* rather than quoting returns on a simple nominal interest basis.

An example will help to explain the concept of continuously compounded returns. If you invested \$100 at the beginning of the year and six months later had a total of \$112, your holding period return is .12 simple (and, remember, .2544 percent annual, compounded semiannually). There was no compounding during the six-month period—but what if there had been? What interest rate, compounded infinitely, would have given \$112 at the end of six months? The answer lies in the use of natural logarithms. The following formula converts a simple interest rate to its continuously compounded equivalent:

$$R_c = ln(1 + R) \qquad \textbf{(6–2)}$$

It is easy to conceive of semiannual compounding, or even compounding ten or a hundred times a year, but the concept of compounding a value continuously may be difficult to grasp. Continuous compounding represents the mathematical limit of compounding interest an infinite number of infinitely small compounding periods. (For a more complete explanation of continuous compounding and the economic interpretation of the natural logarithm, refer to Chiang[1].) The base of the natural log, $e = 2.7183$, represents the total amount to which \$1 would grow in one year if invested at 100 percent compounded continuously.

Returning to the example, the .12 simple rate is equivalent to a .113 rate compounded continuously [$ln(1.12) = .1133$]. The convenient characteristic of continuously compounded returns is that they are additive over time. This makes annualizing continuously compounded rates easy; one simply multiplies the holding period continuously compounded return by the number of holding periods in a year. Therefore, the annualized .1133 six-month rate is .2266 (2 × .1133) because there are two six-month periods in a year.

The general continuous compounding function is:

$$V_t = V_{t-1} \times e^{[R_{ca} \times (T/365)]} \qquad \textbf{(6–3)}$$

where
V_t = the dollar value of an investment at time t
V_{t-1} = the dollar value of the investment at time $t-1$
e = the base of the natural log, = 2.7183
R_{ca} = the annual continuously compounded return
T = the number of days from t to $t-1$

Example 6–2 shows how to use continuously compounded returns to compute the ending value of an investment. Note that to use Equation 6–3, if the simple interest rate is given, it must first be converted to its continuously compounded equivalent. Also, if the holding period return given is for other than an annual period, the return must be annualized.

EXAMPLE 6–2

The six-month holding period return on an investment is 12 percent simple interest. Use continuously compounded returns to find the value of an initial investment of \$100 at the end of two holding periods (one year).

The first step in this problem is to find the continuously compounded equivalent of 12 percent simple interest.

$$ln(1 + .12) = .1133$$

The second step is to annualize the continuously compounded six-month return by multiplying the six-month return by two (because there are two six-month periods in a year).

$$2 \times .1133 = .2266$$

The third step is to use Equation 6–3 to find the ending amount of the investment as follows:

$$V_t = 100 \times e^{[.2266 \times (365/365)]}$$
$$= 100 \times 1.2544$$
$$= 125.44$$

Expected Return

Under conditions of risk, investors realize that an investment can actually yield a number of different returns, and they are able to associate or estimate each possible return with its respective probability of occurring. These probabilities may have been determined using precise mathematical methods and past data or by using subjective, judgmental assessments. For example, Figure 6–1 shows a probability distribution of annual returns on a security.

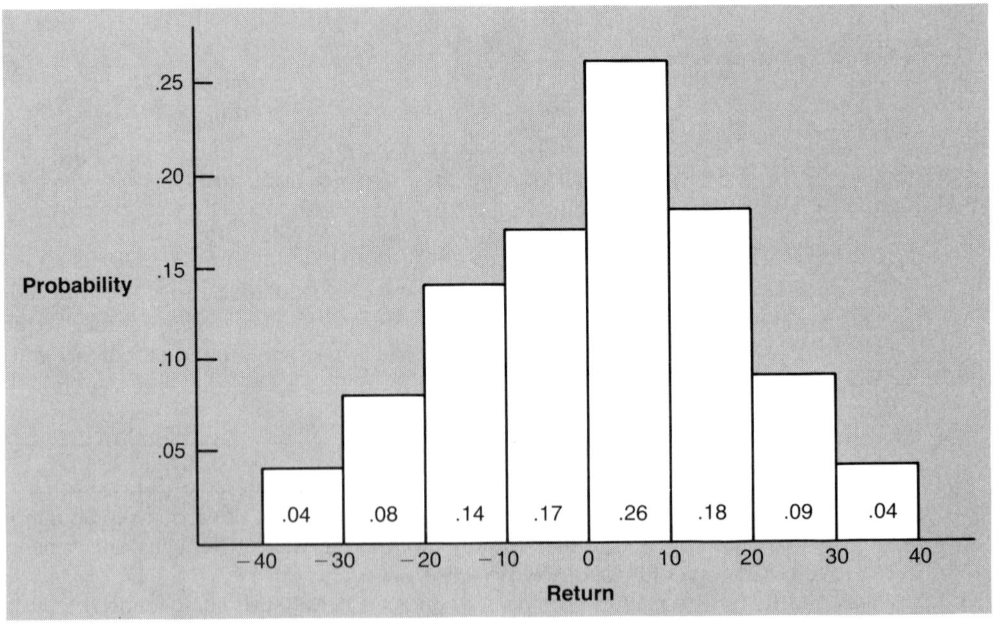

FIGURE 6–1
Example probability distribution of returns on a security

Probability distributions of returns represent the total risk of the investment. The larger and more spread out the distribution, the greater the risk of the investment. Investments with lower levels of risk correspond to narrower distributions of possible returns.

Any time there is uncertainty about the return on an investment, the concept of *expected return* becomes useful. An easy definition of expected return would be the average return that one expects to receive on an investment over the long run. A more rigorous and mathematically sound definition is that expected return represents the weighted average holding period return on the asset, where the possible returns are weighted by the various probabilities of their occurrence. The following formula computes the mean or expected return:

$$E(R) = \sum_{i=1}^{n} R_i p_i \tag{6–4}$$

where $E(R)$ = the expected return on an investment
n = the number of possible returns
R_i = the ith possible return
p_i = the probability of the ith return R_i

Equation 6–4 shows that the expected return is equal to the sum of each possible return times its probability of occurrence. If there is an equal probability of each return occurring, then Equation 6–4 simplifies to:

$$E(R) = \frac{\sum_{i=1}^{n} R_i}{n} \tag{6–5}$$

Example 6–3 shows how to compute the expected return given a probability distribution of returns.

EXAMPLE 6–3

Using the probability distribution in Figure 6–1, compute the expected return on the security.

Let each possible return be equal to the midpoint of each classification. For example, the lowest classification has a midpoint of −.35.

Return	×	*Probability*	=	
−.35		.04		−.014
−.25		.08		−.020
−.15		.14		−.021
−.05		.17		−.008
.05		.26		.013
.15		.18		.027
.25		.09		.023
.35		.04		.014
		Expected value	=	.014

MEASURING RISK

In addition to measuring return, investors need to be able to quantify and measure risk. As mentioned earlier in this chapter, the probability distribution of the possible returns on the investment represents an investment's total risk. Therefore, measures describing the distribution of returns are appropriate measures of risk.

Unfortunately, there is no one "best" measure that details a probability distribution. Depending upon the shape of the distribution, different measures may be better descriptors of the distribution's risk characteristics. The measures presented here represent those that have some degree of statistical validity that the investment profession generally accepts and uses.

Total Risk

Measures to account for total risk consider the dispersion of the distribution of total returns.

Range

The simplest measure of the dispersion of a distribution is the *range of returns.* The range is equal to the highest value that the variable can be less the lowest possible value. Table 6–2 shows the monthly returns for Digital Equipment Corporation for 1982. The highest return over that period was .241 and the lowest return was −.109. The range, therefore, was .35. The higher the range of returns, the riskier the security.

TABLE 6–2
Monthly holding period returns (continuously compounded) for Digital Equipment Corp.

Month	*Return*
1-82	.026
2	−.050
3	−.109
4	.053
5	−.058
6	−.076
7	−.057
8	.241
9	−.063
10	.125
11	.161
12	−.053

Expected value = .012
Range = .35
Variance = .011
Standard deviation = .106

The advantage of the range as a measure of risk lies in its simplicity. To calculate the range, an investor needs only two numbers, the high and the low return. *The Wall Street Journal* gives the high and low prices for stocks over the last fifty-two-week trading period, so the information for calculating quickly and easily a range based on historical data for those stocks is readily available.

Unfortunately, there are drawbacks to using the range to measure risk. Its main disadvantage is that the range tells us only the difference between two extreme values and nothing about the values in the middle or their probability of occurring. It is quite possible to have two different securities with the same range of returns but with different distributions. One distribution may have more values in the extreme returns, while the other distribution might show most of its returns gathered closely in the middle of the range of returns. The distribution with more returns occurring in the tails (extreme values) is the one that investors would consider riskier. What is needed is a return measure that accounts for probabilities of returns occurring along the complete range of possible returns.

Variance

Better measures than the range take into account the deviations of all possible returns from their mean or expected value. The statistical measure that accomplishes this purpose is the *variance of returns*. The formula for the variance is as follows:

$$\sigma^2 = \sum_{i=1}^{n} [R_i - E(R)]^2 \times p_i \tag{6–6}$$

Equation 6–6 defines the variance as the weighted average of the squared deviations of the returns from their mean. If there is an equal probability of each return occurring (for example, when using all the returns over some time period without grouping them into probability groups), Equation 6–6 becomes:

$$\sigma^2 = \frac{\sum_{i=1}^{n} [R_i - E(R)]^2}{n} \tag{6–7}$$

Table 6–2 shows the variance computed for Digital Equipment Corp. using Equation 6–6. The greater the variance of a security, the higher the security's total risk level.

Standard Deviation

Computation of the variance of returns makes use of the squared deviations of returns from the mean, and therefore the resulting variance is stated in squared terms. Since it is usually easier to work with two measures stated in the same units (for example, comparing inches to inches is easier than inches to feet), investment professionals prefer the *standard deviation of returns* as risk measure as opposed to the variance. The standard deviation is equal to the square root of the variance:

$$\sigma = \sqrt{\sigma^2} \tag{6–8}$$

The standard deviation also has statistical properties that are useful for computing probabilities. For example, empirical studies of the distribution of stock returns (on a continuously compounded basis) show that the distributions are close to being symmetric and normal.[2] If we knew or could estimate the standard deviation of the expected future return distribution, we could then estimate the probability of any particular level of return occurring. This could be quite useful for investment purposes, such as limiting the portfolio to securities with a given probability of losing a certain amount of money.

The main advantage of the variance is that it is approximately proportional to time, while the standard deviation is not. For example, if the variance of monthly returns is .01, the expected variance over one-year (twelve-month) periods would be .12. Another important use of the variance is for computing the risk of a portfolio.

Systematic Risk

As mentioned earlier, if the securities market represents the economy or economic system, then systematic risk is market risk. The systematic risk of a security would be the degree of variability in the security's returns caused by variability of the economy (market). Therefore, variations in an individual security's returns related to variations in general market returns should be a measure of systematic risk. The measures of systematic risk attempt to capture this "comovement" of returns on individual securities with market returns.

What Represents "the Market"?

If the key to measuring systematic risk lies with identifying changes in security return related to changes in market return, the first step is to identify how to measure market return. Theoretically, this market return would be a portfolio representing the entire economy. It should therefore contain a little of every investment in the economy—every stock, bond, option, mortgage security, CD, and so forth in proportion to its importance in the economy. Obviously, no such portfolio actually exists, and the job of constructing a hypothetical one would be tremendous if not impossible.

Since we cannot measure this theoretical market portfolio exactly, a proxy will have to suffice. Market practitioners and theoreticians use one of the stock market indexes, such as the Dow Jones Industrial Average or the Standard & Poor's Composite Index, to represent the market portfolio. They recognize that such an index is not a perfect measure of the market, but it is one that should have in practice a very close relationship to the market and economy. Chapter 5 explained the construction of these indexes and discussed the pros and cons of using the various indexes as proxies for the market portfolio.

Covariance

A measure of systematic risk should pair the individual security's return and the market's return for a given time period. To bring risk into the picture, the measure should incorporate the deviations of these returns from their respective means. A statistical measure that accomplishes this is the *covariance,* defined mathematically as:

$$\text{cov}_{j,m} = \frac{\sum_{i=1}^{n} [R_{j,t} - E(R_j)] \times [R_{m,t} - E(R_m)]}{n} \tag{6–9}$$

where $\text{cov}_{j,m}$ = the covariance of the returns on security j with the returns on the market,
$R_{j,t}$ = the return on security j for time period t
$E(R_j)$ = the expected return on security j
$R_{m,t}$ = the return on the market for time period t
$E(R_m)$ = the expected market return
n = the number of time periods

Equation 6–9 shows that the covariance is equal to the average of the products of the deviations of security and market returns. The covariance is directly associated with systematic risk; the greater the covariance, the greater the systematic risk of a security.

If the individual variances of the security and the market are already known, another equation for the covariance may be simpler. This alternate formula, which also aids in the interpretation of the meaning of the covariance, is as follows:

$$\text{cov}_{j,m} = \sigma_j \times \sigma_m \times r_{j,m} \tag{6–10}$$

where $r_{j,m}$ = the correlation coefficient of returns on the security with returns on the market.

Equation 6–10 defines covariance as the product of the standard deviations of the security and the market and of the *correlation coefficient* of security returns with market returns.

The correlation coefficient measures the degree of association of one variable with another. In this case, the correlation coefficient shows how well the variation of the market explains variation in the individual security returns. The correlation coefficient can take on values from −1 to +1. As the value of the correlation coefficient approaches a value of +1 or −1, the degree of linear association between the returns on the security and the market becomes closer. When the correlation coefficient is positive, then a greater return on the security is generally associated with a greater return on the market. When the coefficient is negative, then greater security returns are usually associated with smaller market returns. If there is no relationship at all between the security and market returns, the correlation coefficient is 0. Most securities have some degree of positive correlation with the market, which would give them correlation coefficients between 0 and 1.

Table 6–3 shows the returns on the Wilshire 5000 Index for 1982. Its standard deviation for that period was .053. The computed correlation coefficient of the Wilshire 5000 with Digital Equipment Corp. (Table 6–2) is .825.[3] Example 6–4 uses the data from Table 6–2 and Table 6–3 to compute the covariance of Digital Equipment Corp. returns with market returns.

TABLE 6–3
Monthly holding period returns (continuously compounded) for the Wilshire 5000 Index

Month	*Return*
1-82	−.029
2	−.057
3	−.010
4	.042
5	−.029
6	−.025
7	−.021
8	.113
9	.016
10	.111
11	.048
12	.014

Expected value = .014
Standard deviation = .053
Correlation of Wilshire 5000 returns with Digital Equipment Corp. returns = .825

EXAMPLE 6–4

What is the covariance of Digital Equipment's returns with the market using data from Tables 6–2 and 6–3?

Using Equation 6–10:

$$\text{cov} = .106 \times .053 \times .825$$
$$= .0046$$

Beta

The disadvantage of using the covariance as a systematic risk measure is that, viewed alone, the covariance tells little about the relative riskiness of the security. It would be convenient to define a systematic risk measure that measures the systematic risk of a security relative to the systematic risk of an "average" or "typical" security. If we let the riskiness of an "average" security be equal to the riskiness of the market, then such a measure could be stated as follows:

$$\beta_j = \frac{\text{cov}_{j,m}}{\sigma_m^2} \qquad \textbf{(6–11)}$$

where β_j = the beta coefficient of security j

Equation 6–11 defines *beta,* the measure of relative systematic risk. It is the security's risk ($\text{cov}_{j,m}$) relative to the risk of the market (σ_m^2). A security with a beta of

1.0 has a level of systematic risk equivalent to that of the market, or "average" security. A beta of less than 1.0 means the security's level of systematic risk is less than that of the market. Likewise, a beta greater than 1.0 signifies that the security has higher than average systematic risk.

The Characteristic Line

A security's *characteristic line* gives an alternate definition of beta. The characteristic line shows the linear relationship between the return on a security and the return on the market. An example can best describe the characteristic line. Figure 6–2 shows a plot of the returns on Digital Equipment Corp. with the returns on the Wilshire 5000 Index. The line through the points is a regression line that best fits the points.[4] This line is the security's characteristic line. Its slope is equal to the security's beta. The slope of Digital's characteristic line in Figure 6–2 is 1.66. (This differs from the previously computed beta of 1.64 because of rounding.)

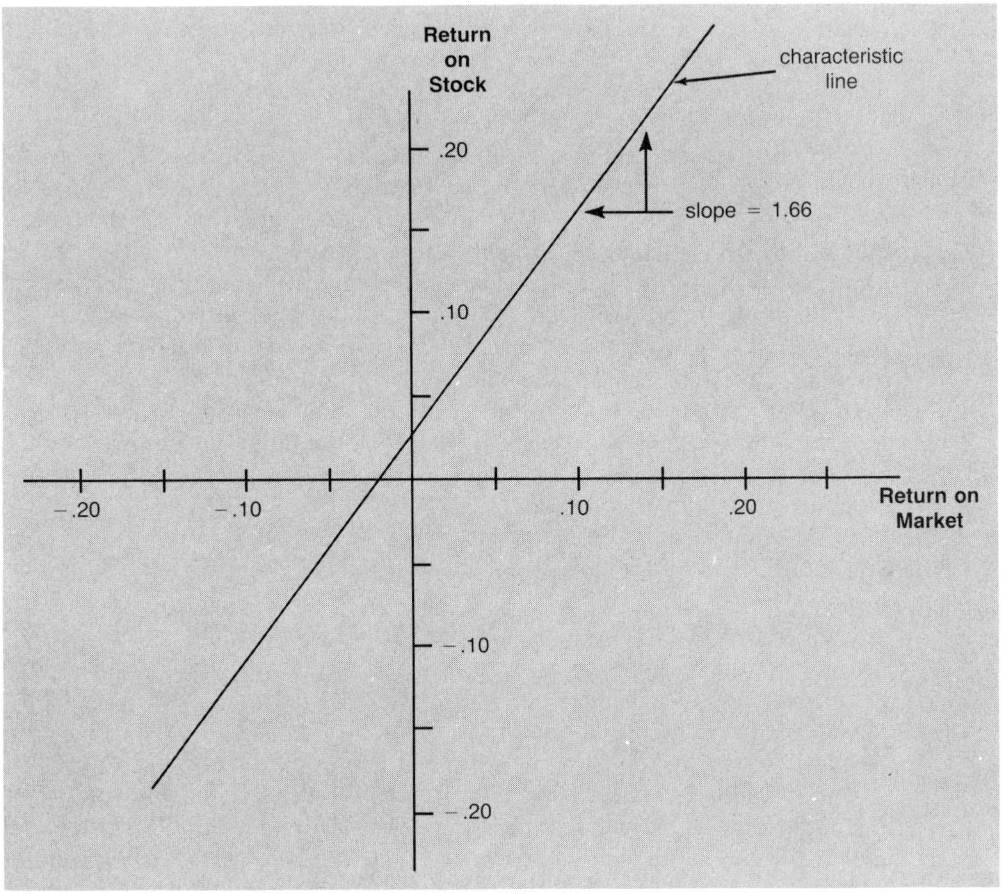

FIGURE 6–2
Characteristic line of Digital Equipment Corp.

This presentation shows why a common interpretation of beta is "the expected return on the security for a 1 percent return on the market." For example, the expected return for Digital if the market were up 3 percent would be 4.98 percent (3×1.66). Chapter 7, "Portfolio Theory and Diversification," develops the concept and uses of beta in more detail.

UTILITY MAXIMIZATION

An important notion is that investors will make investment decisions designed to maximize their *expected utility*. The expected utility of an investment is the total benefit that an investor expects to receive from the investment. We assume that investors will attempt to make decisions that will maximize this expected utility. That is, they will aim to receive the most benefit possible from their investments.

However, utility maximization is not necessarily the same as wealth maximization. A measurement of the success of an investment is the return on that investment, and wealth is simply a result of positive returns. However, the expected utility of an investment is not the same as its expected wealth. The reason for this is that even though an investor receives positive utility from wealth, there is a negative utility associated with risk. If the negative utility of a risky investment overwhelms the positive utility from the expected return on that investment, then expected utility does not equate to expected wealth. Therefore, we cannot say that investors will attempt to maximize their wealth. They will attempt to maximize their utility, which means that they will try to maximize their wealth within the constraints dictated by the negative aspects of risk. For example, consider an investor choosing between two different investments: a utility stock with very low risk and an expected return of .12, and a high technology stock with very high risk and an expected return of .20. If the investor were strictly a wealth maximizer, the preferred investment would be the high tech stock. However, if worries about the riskiness of a high risk stock would keep the investor from getting a good night's sleep, then the utility stock might be the utility-maximizing choice.

RISK PREFERENCES

The first step in developing a formal asset valuation model for investments is to identify investor preferences for accepting risk. We assume that investors seek to maximize expected utility. To maximize utility from one's investments, one must find the combination of risk and expected return that yields the most satisfaction, or highest level of utility.

An *indifference map* in risk-return space is useful for studying risk preferences. Indifference maps show combinations of two factors, resulting in various levels of utility. The curve represented on the map is an *indifference curve*. Each indifference curve shows the varying quantities of the two factors that result in the investor's being indifferent, or yield the same amount of utility. A series of indifference curves forms the indifference map, with higher indifference curves representing higher levels of utility. Figure 6–3 shows a sample indifference map for an investor. The map contains three indifference curves: U_1, U_2, and U_3. Curve U_1 shows the various combinations of risk and return that give this investor a utility level of U_1. This investor would be equally satisfied with any investment whose risk-return lies on curve U_1. However, the investor would prefer any investment on U_2 over any investment on U_1 because investments on U_2 represent higher utility levels. U_3 represents the highest level of utility on this map.

Risk Preference Possibilities

Investors could regard the risk-return trade-off in three distinct ways:

1. Investors could be risk seeking.
2. Investors could be risk indifferent.
3. Investors could be risk averse.

Risk-Seeking Investors

If risk preferences of investors show them to be *risk-seeking investors,* then these investors like to accept risk. This means that they are willing to purchase investments of increasingly higher risk for the promise of increasingly smaller increments of return. Extreme risk seekers would be willing to purchase investments of higher risk for less return. Naturally, such extreme risk seekers would by most definitions have a distorted view of personal satisfaction.

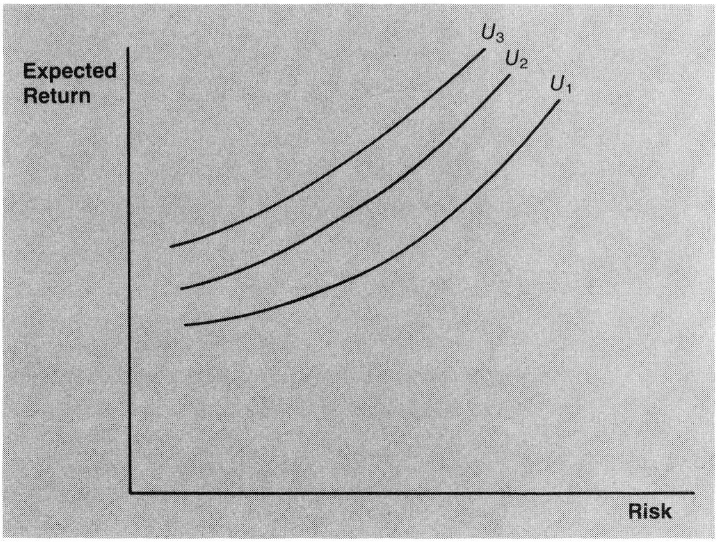

FIGURE 6–3
Example of an indifference map with indifference curves

Figure 6–4 depicts an example utility function for a risk-seeking investor. The utility that a risk seeker receives from each additional increment of wealth becomes increasingly greater. This person is willing to accept higher and higher risk as long as it results in higher expected return and higher wealth. Such a person is happier as the variability of returns increases—however, the logic behind such an attitude is the opposite of most individuals' normal thought.

Risk-Indifferent Investors

A *risk-indifferent investor* receives the same incremental utility for each increase in wealth. As illustrated in Figure 6–5, a risk-indifferent individual has an upward-sloping linear utility function. Risk-indifferent investors would be willing to continue accepting investments of higher risk by receiving the same increase in return. This situation does not seem logical either, because at some point, a reasonable person would likely say, "Stop, I don't want a riskier investment, no matter how much extra money it brings me."

Risk-Averse Investors

When investors require successively greater increments of return to compensate them for each additional unit increase in risk, they are *risk-averse investors.* Figure 6–6 shows a utility function for a risk-averse investor. Risk-averse investors receive smaller increments of utility for each additional increment of wealth. They will accept additional risk, but only if they are adequately compensated for doing so, and adequate compensation for a risk averter means being paid more and more for accepting higher risk.

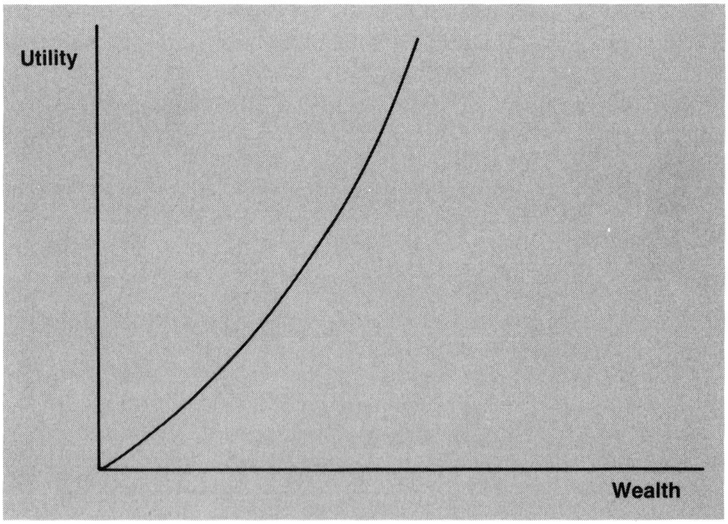

FIGURE 6–4
Example utility function for a risk-seeking investor

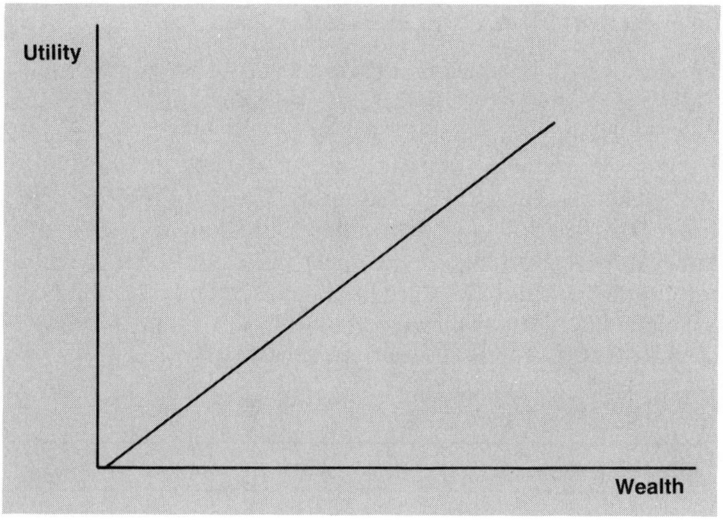

FIGURE 6–5
Example utility function for a risk-indifferent investor

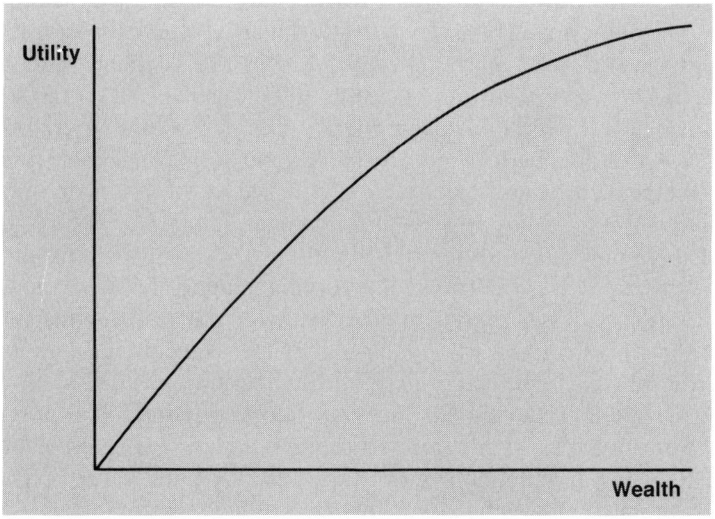

FIGURE 6–6
Example utility function for a risk-averse investor

Risk Aversion: The Logical Alternative

It should already be obvious that the logical investor will fall into the risk-averse category. The concept of *diminishing marginal utility of wealth* provides a formal reason explaining why rational investors will be risk-averse. Diminishing marginal utility is an economic concept that states that each additional unit of a good or service provides diminishing increases in utility. Consider the example of a child offered a lollipop. The first lollipop makes the child shout with glee. After finishing the first lollipop, the second lollipop also makes the child cry out with joy, but not quite as loudly as the first time. The third lollipop also makes the child happy, but not as much so as the first two. The child welcomes each succeeding lollipop, but with less interest than the previous lollipop received. This is the principle of diminishing marginal utility.

EXAMPLE 6–5

Compute the beta of Digital Equipment Corp. using information from Example 6–4 and Tables 6–2 and 6–3.

$$\beta = .0046/.0028$$
$$= 1.64$$

The principle also applies to wealth. Each succeeding $1000 an investor accumulates results in a higher level of utility, but the marginal increase decreases with every increment in wealth. Another way to state the principle is: To generate the same increases in the level of utility, an investor has to increase wealth by larger and larger succeeding amounts. The utility curve for the risk-averse investor in Figure 6–6 would result from such a situation. In terms of utility in risk-return space, only succeedingly larger returns for given unit increases in risk can result in the same level of utility. The principle of diminishing marginal utility of wealth therefore leads to the assumption that all investors must be risk-averse. Risk-averse investors have indifference curves that are positively sloped and concave to the risk axis, such as the curves in Figure 6–3.

It is important to remember that the relationship is between *expected risk* and *expected return*. It is not true that accepting a higher level of risk assures the investor of a correspondingly higher rate of return. It only means that investors will *expect* greater return from investments of higher risk. After the fact, an investor with a risky security may find that the unexpected happened and the stock went down. By the same reasoning, reducing risk does not necessarily reduce *ex post* (realized) returns. However, investors in general will require greater expected returns to compensate them for accepting higher levels of expected risk. Only the belief that they will receive adequate payment for the risk taken can induce investors to invest their money. The actual realized return that an investor receives may be less than the expected return, but that is one of the consequences of risk.

To illustrate, assume that Mrs. Smith has two investment alternatives. One is certain to return 10 percent; the other has equal probabilities of returning 20 percent or zero. Thus the expected return for each alternative is 10 percent, but the expected risk (variability) is much greater for the second. Which one is Mrs. Smith more likely to choose? If she behaves like most investors, she will prefer the less risky alternative. But what if the riskier venture projected an expected return of 12 percent? How about 14 percent? 16 percent? At some point Mrs. Smith will be indifferent between the two options; the additional expected return exactly compensates her for assuming additional uncertainty. The rate of return on an investment that exactly compensates the investor for the risk taken is the *required rate of return* on the investment.

Capital market theory, developed in Chapter 8, is based on the assumption that investors are risk-averse. We have shown that this makes sense intuitively. In addition, considerable research supports this assumption. As one example, consider the yield differential among various grades of corporate bonds. The promised yield of the safest bonds, rated AAA, is lower than that of the next safest, AA, which in turn is lower than that of the next class, and so on. Thus purchasers of bonds require a higher expected return to compensate them for holding bonds carrying greater perceived risk.

The only exceptions we might observe are instances in which other factors besides the monetary return contribute to the total utility of an investment. For example, gamblers wager at race tracks and casinos although the expected returns are known to be negative, which implies that the participants are willing to pay for the excitement of the risks involved. The utility curves of such individuals may be risk-seeking where small amounts of money are involved, and risk-averse for larger amounts. The assumption of risk aversion does not mean that all investors abhor risk. It does mean that investors as a whole (and most individuals) must be rewarded with increasingly greater amounts to compensate them for assuming greater risk.

A RISK-FREE RETURN

Before describing the relationship between risk and return, we need to consider the possibility of an investment that has no risk. An investor who invested solely in such an asset would represent the extreme of risk aversion. Because a risk-free investment represents the absolute minimum level of risk of an investment, it should also represent the minimum level of expected returns.

Strictly speaking, a risk-free asset is a concept for which there is no counterpart in reality because there exists some catastrophic event, improbable though it may be, which could inject risk into any security. However, for practical purposes, there are several types of highly liquid, extremely safe investments that we might use to represent a risk-free asset. The security that most researchers use as a surrogate for a risk-free asset is U.S. Treasury bills because the probability of default by the U.S. government is considered to be nil.

SUMMARY

The rate of return represents the profit per dollar of funds invested in an asset. Risk is the chance that the actual return on an investment will not be equal to the expected return.

Classifying risk by its nature breaks it down into systematic risk and unsystematic risk. Changes in a company's earnings due to broad economic factors are causes of systematic risk, while changes in the firm's earnings caused by factors relating specifically to the firm determine the unsystematic risk. Total risk is the sum of the two parts: systematic risk and unsystematic risk. Risk can be placed into categories dealing with the source of the risk as follows: business risk, financial risk, purchasing power risk, interest rate risk, management risk, market risk, and liquidity risk.

Holding period return defines return over a specific time period, and annualized return states return on an annual basis. A continuously compounded return represents an investment's return as if the profit had been received continuously over the holding period. An investment's expected return is the amount that investors believe they will receive. It is equal to each possible return weighted by its respective probability.

Measures of total risk include the range, variance, and standard deviation, while covariance and beta measure systematic risk.

Investors seek to maximize their total utility. A set of indifference curves forms a utility map, which is useful for studying investors' risk preferences. Higher indifference curves represent higher levels of utility. We assume that investors are risk-averse, meaning that they will take on additional risk only if promised correspondingly higher levels of return. The principle of diminishing marginal utility of wealth leads to the conclusion that all investors with such utility functions must be risk-averse.

IMPORTANT TERMS

beta
business risk
characteristic line
continuously compounded rate of return
correlation coefficient
covariance
diminishing marginal utility of wealth
diversifiable risk
expected return
financial leverage
financial risk
indifference curve
indifference map
interest rate risk
liquidity risk
management risk
market risk
operating leverage
price of immediacy
purchasing power risk
range of returns
required rate of return
risk-averse investor
risk-indifferent investor
risk-seeking investor
simple rate of return
standard deviation of returns
systematic risk
total risk
undiversifiable risk
unsystematic risk
variance of returns

QUESTIONS AND PROBLEMS

1. Define systematic risk, unsystematic risk, and total risk.
2. Why is systematic risk often called undiversifiable risk, while unsystematic risk is called diversifiable risk?
3. Summarize the different sources of risk.
4. Mr. Freed purchased a bond for $892. He received a $35 interest payment and sold the bond six months later for $910.
   a) Compute the holding period return (ignoring commissions).
   b) Compute the annualized return.
   c) Compute the continuously compounded equivalent of the annual return.
5. The common stock of Heartbeat Pacemakers Co. has the following probability distribution:

Stock Return	*Probability*
−.06	.05
−.02	.15
.05	.25
.07	.25
.10	.20
.14	.05
.20	.05

   a) Compute the expected return on Heartbeat.
   b) Compute the range of returns.
   c) Compute the variance of returns.
   d) Compute the standard deviation of returns.
   e) Assuming that the variance of market returns is .01, and Heartbeat has a correlation coefficient of .4 with market returns, compute the beta.
6. How would you assess the riskiness of a stock with a beta of less than 1.0? Greater than 1.0?
7. Distinguish between risk-seeking, risk-indifferent, and risk-averse investors. Explain why risk aversion is the rational alternative. What are the characteristics of indifference curves for risk-averse investors?
8. Define an indifference curve. Illustrate your definition with a graph showing indifference curves.
9. Explain the principle of wealth maximization.

NOTES

1. Alpha C. Chiang (1979), *Fundamental Methods of Mathematical Economics,* 2nd ed., New York: McGraw-Hill.
2. See, for example, M. F. M. Osborne (1964), "Brownian Motion in the Stock Market," in Paul Costner (Ed.), *The Random Character of Stock Prices,* Cambridge, MA: MIT Press.
3. The computation of the correlation coefficient is somewhat involved. The most direct way of computing the correlation coefficient is to use a calculator with a correlation function or a computerized statistical package. This book assumes that readers have these tools at their disposal.

4. The technique for defining the line is the method of least squares, which minimizes the sums of the squared deviation of the observed returns from the line to determine the line with the best fit. Consult any statistics or econometrics text for a discussion of regression.

SELECTED REFERENCES

Bernard, Victor L., and Thomas J. Frecka (1983). "Evidence on the Existence of Common Stock Inflation Hedges." *Journal of Financial Research,* 6 (Winter), 301–311.

Bernstein, Peter L. (1982). "The Gibson Paradox Revisited." *Financial Review,* 17 (September), 153–164.

Brealey, Richard A. (1983). *An Introduction to Risk and Return from Common Stocks.* Cambridge: MIT Press.

Chu, Chen-Chin, and David T. Whitford (1982). "Stock Market Returns and Inflationary Expectations: Additional Evidence for 1975–1979." *Journal of Financial Research,* 5 (Fall), 261–271.

Ibbotson, Roger G., and Rex A. Sinquefield (1982). *Stocks, Bonds, Bills and Inflation: The Past and the Future.* Charlottesville, VA: The Financial Analysts Research Foundation.

Kosmicke, Ralph (1986). "The Limited Relevance of Volatility to Risk." *Journal of Portfolio Management,* 13, No. 1 (Fall), 18–20.

APPENDIX 6A

The Time Value of Money

COMPOUND INTEREST

The compound interest formulas necessitate raising numbers to powers higher than one. Because raising numbers to higher powers requires lengthy calculations when computed by hand, the traditional approach to compound interest formulas uses tables of factors to avoid the tedious calculation. However, many pocket calculators available today have built-in functions for raising numbers to powers, finding roots, and solving present and future value problems. The need to use tables is therefore less today than in years past. This appendix will present the computing formulas and the table value approach to compound interest. Readers of this text who use a calculator with compound interest functions should consult their calculator's manual for correct operation, but these users should also be familiar with the principles underlying present and future value computations.

FUTURE VALUE

An amount of money invested at a particular rate of return today will grow as time passes and the return accumulates. Since rates are typically stated on a simple, per period (usually annual) basis, computing the future value of money involves consideration of the accumulating return and subsequent returns paid on the accumulated return. This is the phenomenon of compound interest, often called the compound sum or future value of an investment. The first case presented is the future value of a single payment; we will then examine the future value of a series of payments (annuity).

Future Value of a Single Amount

The formula for the compound sum of a single amount is as follows:

$$FV = P(1 + r)^n \qquad \textbf{(6A–1)}$$

where FV = the future, compound value of a single payment
P = the initial payment amount

r = the per period rate of interest or return
n = the number of time periods

The $(1 + r)^n$ portion of Equation 6A–1 represents the compounding factor, and it is these values that appear in the future value tables. When using a table the future value becomes:

$$FV = P \times FVF_{r,n} \qquad \textbf{(6A–2)}$$

where $FVF_{r,n}$ = the future value of a dollar factor

Example 6A–1 shows a sample future value application.

EXAMPLE 6A–1

If \$1000 is placed in an account paying 12 percent interest compounded annually, how much is in the account at the end of ten years?

Using the future value of a dollar table (Appendix 1 at the end of the book), we find a factor of 3.1058.

$$FV = 1000 \times 3.1058$$
$$= 3105.80$$

If the account paid interest at an annual rate of 12 percent compounded quarterly, how much would the account contain after ten years?

The annual interest rate is the same as previously, but it is compounded four times per year (quarterly) instead of only once. If the annual rate is 12 percent, then the quarterly rate is 12/4, or 3 percent. Over the ten-year time period, there are forty quarters. The problem therefore is to find the future value of \$1000 invested for forty time periods at 3 percent per period. The future value factor from Appendix 1 is 3.2620.

$$FV = 1000 \times 3.2620$$
$$= 3262$$

The accumulated sum is greater with quarterly compounding because interest is being paid on the accumulated interest more often.

Future Value of an Annuity

If there is a payment during each compounding period, then we have a compound sum of an annuity. In this text, we deal with ordinary annuities, in which the payment occurs at the end of each time period. The following formula gives the future value of an annuity:

$$FVA = P \times \sum_{t=1}^{n} (1 + r)^{n-t} \qquad \textbf{(6A–3)}$$
$$= P \times \frac{(1 + r)^r - 1}{n}$$

where FVA = the future value of an annuity
P = the periodic payment of the annuity
r = the periodic rate of return or interest
n = the number of payments or time periods

For use with a future value of an annuity table, Equation 6A–3 becomes:

$$FVA = P \times FVAF_{r,n} \tag{6A–4}$$

where $FVAF_{r,n}$ = the future value of an annuity factor.

Example 6A–2 shows how to compute the future value of an annuity.

EXAMPLE 6A–2

If an investor deposits $10 at the end of every year for twenty-five years, how much will the account contain at the end, with interest paid at the rate of 14 percent?

The future value of an annuity factor for 14 percent, twenty-five time periods is 181.87 from Appendix 3.

$$FVA = 10 \times 181.87$$
$$= 1818.70$$

PRESENT VALUE

Present value yields the current worth of funds to be received at some time in the future. First we look at the present value of a single payment in the future, followed by the present value of a series of payments.

Present Value of a Single Amount

The present worth of a single payment is as follows:

$$PV = P \times \frac{1}{(1+r)^n} \tag{6A–5}$$

where PV = the present value of a single payment
P = the single payment to be received in the future
r = the periodic rate
n = the number of time periods

Using symbols representing the tables, Equation 6A–5 becomes:

$$PV = P \times PVF_{r,n} \tag{6A–6}$$

where $PVF_{r,n}$ = the present value of the dollar factor

Example 6A–3 presents a sample computation of present value.

EXAMPLE 6A–3

Ann West is considering the purchase of a rare inverted airmail stamp. She believes that she will be able to sell the stamp at the end of five years for $50,000. If Ms. West's required rate of return on her stamp investments is 15 percent, what is the greatest price she should offer for the stamp?

The stamp has a maximum value to Ms. West equal to the present value of $50,000 five years hence at 15 percent. The present value factor from Appendix 2 is .4972.

$$PV = 50{,}000 \times .4972$$
$$= 24{,}860$$

Present Value of an Annuity

The present value of an annuity represents the current worth of a series of payments, with each payment being received at the end of each period. The formula for the present value of an annuity is as follows:

$$PVA = P \times \sum_{t=1}^{n} \frac{1}{(1+r)^t} \qquad \textbf{(6A–7)}$$
$$= P \times \left[\frac{1}{r} - \frac{1}{r(1+r)^n}\right]$$

where PVA = the present value of an annuity
P = the period annuity payment
r = the rate per period
n = the number of payments of the annuity

Using the factors from the present value of an annuity table, Equation 6A–7 becomes:

$$PVA = P \times PVAF_{r,n} \qquad \textbf{(6A–8)}$$

where $PVAF_{r,n}$ = the present value of an annuity factor

Example 6A–4 presents the computation of the present value of an annuity.

EXAMPLE 6A–4

What is the value of an investment that pays $3000 per year for eight years with a rate of 8 percent?

From Appendix 4, the present value of an annuity factor at 8 percent for eight years is 5.7466.

$$PVA = 3000 \times 5.7466$$
$$= 17{,}239.80$$

QUESTIONS AND PROBLEMS

A-1. Compute the future value of an initial investment of the following:

	Initial Investment	*Years in Future*	*Annual Rate*	*Compounded*
a)	3000	4	.11	annually
b)	20000	8	.10	semiannually
c)	12000	10	.08	semiannually
d)	6000	5	.12	quarterly
e)	7500	2	.12	monthly

A-2. Ann West places $10,000 in a three-year savings certificate that pays interest at a rate of 8 percent compounded quarterly. How much will the account contain at maturity?

A-3. Arnold Cash plans to place $4000 at the end of each year for twelve years into a retirement account. How much will he have at the end of the fifteenth year if the interest rate is 13 percent compounded annually?

A-4. Compute the present value of the following:

	Future Payment	*Years in Future*	*Annual Rate*	*Compounded*
a)	5000	8	.11	annually
b)	12000	2	.14	annually
c)	8000	14	.08	semiannually
d)	2500	4	.16	quarterly
e)	20000	12	.10	annually

A-5. Mrs. Cohen is considering the purchase of a rare gold coin. She believes that she will be able to sell the coin after ten years for $75,000. At a rate of 14 percent, what is the value of the gold coin today?

A-6. Albert Lopez is considering the purchase of a ten-year annuity that pays $2500 per year. Albert figures that his required rate is 9 percent. What is the value of the annuity today?

A-7. Mary O'Hara plans to retire at the end of fifteen years. She plans to deposit $8000 per year into a retirement policy that pays 10 percent annually. Upon retirement, her policy will give her an annual income for twenty years. How much will that annual income be?

CHAPTER 7

Portfolio Theory and Diversification

When examining a portfolio of securities, the risk and return of these securities are treated as a group rather than individually. Chapter 6 introduced some basic concepts of risk and return. Up to this point we have applied these concepts to individual securities. This chapter expands upon those principles, applying them to security portfolios.

The overall goal of investors is to maximize their utility. This goal applies not just to individual securities or segments of an investor's portfolio, but is rather a general statement that pertains to an investor's entire portfolio. The process of adding securities to one's investment holdings to build a portfolio and reduce risk is *diversification.*

Diversification is probably the most important element in the process of managing investment risk. This chapter shows that diversification is a desirable objective for investors because it can lower the risk of the portfolio. Because of this, portfolio management has become an important part of the study of investments. Institutional investors, such as pension funds, bank trust departments, and mutual funds, maintain specialized professional staffs whose responsibility is management of the investment portfolio. Chapter 21 deals with portfolio management and strategy.

The purpose of this chapter is to introduce portfolio theory. Portfolio theory defines the effects of diversification on the risk and return of investment portfolios. The chapter explains both simple diversification and methodically structured diversification. Because diversification alters the risk of portfolios, this chapter also presents the concepts of risk measurement for portfolios.

PORTFOLIO RETURN

The expected return on a portfolio of securities is simply a weighted average of the expected returns on each security in the portfolio. The weight of each security is equal to the proportion of portfolio funds invested in the security. Stated as a formula, the expected return on a portfolio of securities is:

$$E(R_p) = \sum_{i=1}^{n} w_i \times E(R_i) \qquad \textbf{(7–1)}$$

where $E(R_p)$ = the expected return on the portfolio
n = the number of different securities comprising the portfolio
w_i = the weight of the *i*th security in the portfolio
$E(R_i)$ = the expected return on the *i*th security

Equation 7–1 shows that the expected return on a portfolio is the sum of the weighted returns on the component securities. The weight for each security, w_i in Equation 7–1, can be computed with the following formula:

$$w_i = \frac{V_i}{V_p} \qquad \textbf{(7–2)}$$

where V_i = the dollar value of security *i* in the portfolio
V_p = the total dollar value of the portfolio

Example 7–1 shows the use of Equations 7–1 and 7–2 in computing expected portfolio returns.

EXAMPLE 7–1

Mr. Albert Lopez has a portfolio of five stocks. The expected return and amount invested in each stock is as follows:

Stock	*Expected return*	*Amount invested*
A	.14	$ 200
B	.08	100
C	.15	300
D	.09	250
E	.12	150
Portfolio value =		1000

Compute the expected return on Mr. Lopez's portfolio.

$$E(R_p) = (200/1000).14 + (100/1000).08 + (300/1000).15 + (250/1000).09 + (150/1000).12$$

$$= .028 + .008 + .045 + .0225 + .018$$

$$= .1215$$

Equation 7–1 also applies on an *ex post* basis. The realized return on a portfolio is equal to the weighted average return on the individual component securities in the portfolio.

RANDOM DIVERSIFICATION

The simplest way of diversifying one's portfolio is to buy different securities. Buying more securities and adding them to the portfolio without any regard to the securities' risk or the effects they will have on the portfolio is *random diversification,* or *naive diversification.* Is it possible to lower the risk of a portfolio in this manner? The answer is yes. Although they did not fully understand why, early market analysts and investors knew that random diversification reduced risk. They observed that even when an individual security added to the portfolio had a relatively high risk, the risk of the entire portfolio could fall.

Figure 7–1 shows graphically the effects of random diversification. The figure presents the relationship between the total risk of a portfolio and the number of securities in the portfolio. Note that the total risk declines sharply as the first few securities enter the portfolio. As more securities are added to the portfolio, the rate of decline in total risk becomes less, finally leveling out. When the portfolio contains a large number of different securities, adding more securities will generally cause the portfolio risk to fall only a very small amount. At this point, the risk-reduction benefits of additional diversification are minimal.

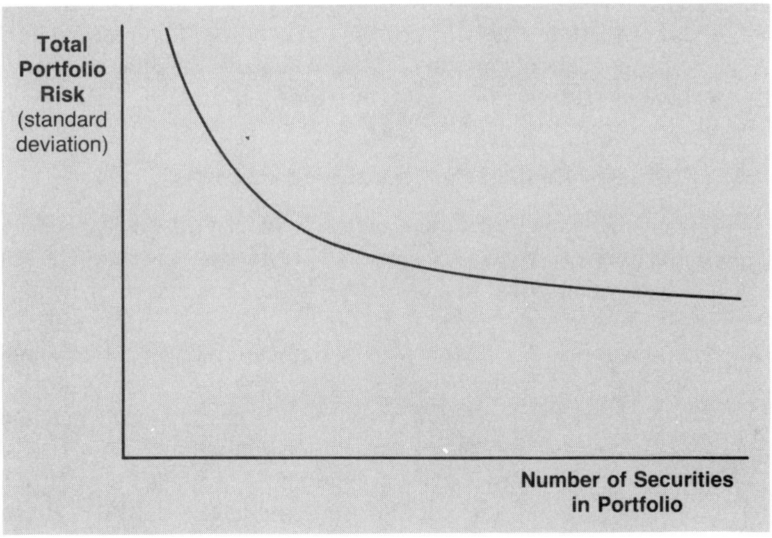

FIGURE 7–1
Effects of random diversification on the risk level of a typical portfolio

It may be surprising that most of the benefits of diversifying are achieved with the first twenty or so securities. By the time a portfolio has about twenty different securities, it will have received around 95 percent of the total risk reduction that is attainable by diversification. Thus, even small investors with relatively few securities can diversify their holdings effectively.

PORTFOLIO RISK

Although the expected return for a portfolio is an average of the individual securities' returns, a portfolio's risk can be less than the average of the risk of its component securities. This fact yields the risk-reducing benefits of diversifying.

The key to the amount of risk reduction that diversification can achieve is the degree of correlation between the returns on the security and the returns on the existing portfolio. As discussed in Chapter 6, correlation is the strength of the relationship between two variables; it is positive when the two variables move together a majority of the time and negative when they move primarily in opposite directions. For example, we would expect the returns on automobile stocks to be highly positively correlated with the returns on steel stocks because of the dependence of steel sales upon automobile sales. On the other hand, sales of sugar and artificial sweeteners are probably negatively correlated since consumers usually substitute one for the other. If the action of one variable is completely independent of the other variable, then the two variables have no correlation.

The measure of the degree of correlation is the *correlation coefficient,* which will always take on a value between −1 and +1. A correlation coefficient of 0 indicates no correlation. When the correlation coefficient is greater than 0, correlation is positive, while coefficients less than 0 show negative correlation. The following examples will demonstrate the effects of correlation on diversification.

Perfectly Positively Correlated Returns

The first example is the case of perfectly positively correlated returns. When the returns of two stocks are perfectly positively correlated, they always move in the same direction and their relationship is linear. Positive returns on one stock are associated with positive returns on the other.

Figure 7–2 presents a hypothetical example of two stocks whose returns are perfectly positively correlated. Whenever the low risk stock has a +.04 return, the high risk stock matches it with a +.12 return, three times that of the low risk stock. When the low risk stock has a −.04 return, the high risk stock has triple that, or −.12. The series of returns in Figure 7–2 gives the low risk stock a total risk (standard deviation) of .04 and the high risk stock a standard deviation of .12.

Figure 7–2 also shows the return on a portfolio having half of its funds invested in the high risk stock and half in the low risk stock. The return on the portfolio is the average of the return on the two stocks. This results in a series of portfolio returns that give the portfolio a risk (standard deviation) equal to .08. (A later section of this

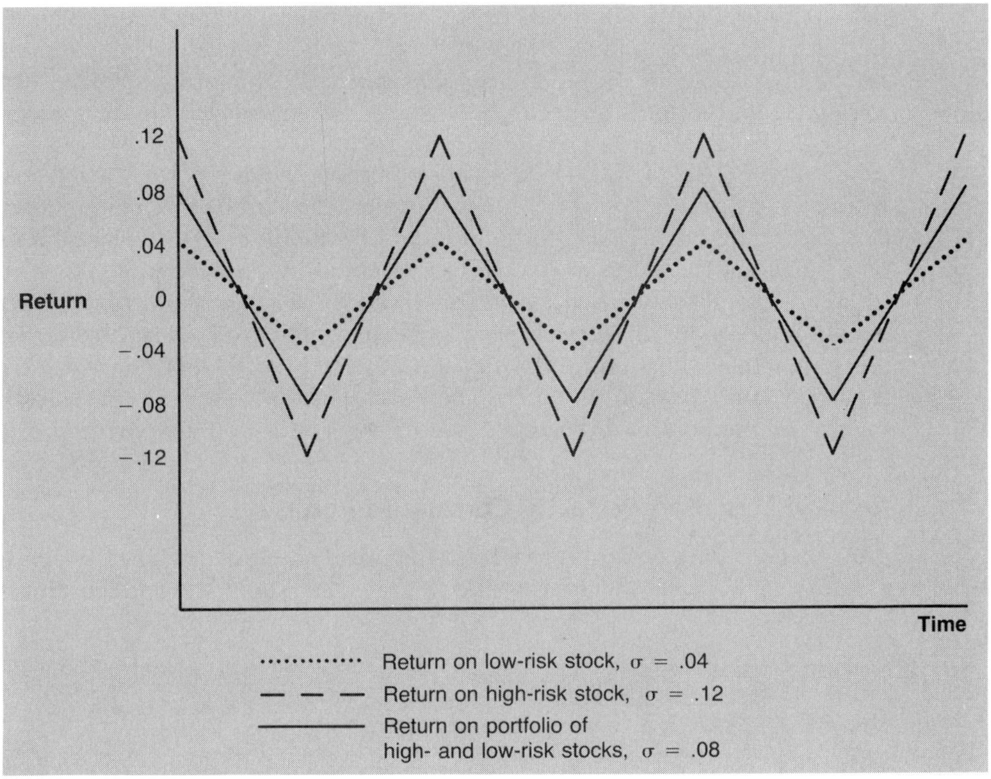

FIGURE 7–2
Diversification with perfectly positively correlated returns (correlation coefficient = +1.0)

chapter will show how to compute portfolio standard deviation.) However, this is just an average of the standard deviations of the two individual stocks.

In this case, there was absolutely no reduction in risk beyond the average through diversification. The reason is that these two stocks were perfectly positively correlated. In reality, though, it is doubtful that two different stocks would ever be perfectly positively correlated. This example represents the theoretical extreme in which diversification does not reduce risk. However, any time the returns on two securities are less than perfectly positively correlated, some risk reduction will occur when the securities are combined to form a portfolio.

Perfectly Negatively Correlated Returns

Going to the other extreme, perfectly negatively correlated returns result when the return on one security is always associated with an opposite return on the other security. Again, this is a hypothetical position that probably never exists in reality with different stocks. (It can, however, exist with short sales.) Figure 7–3 gives an example in which the return on the low risk stock of +.04 is associated with a return of −.12 on the high risk stock. These returns yield standard deviations of .04 and .12 for the low and high risk stocks respectively. Note that these risk levels are the same as those of the stocks in Figure 7–2.

Combining the two stocks in equal proportions yields a portfolio with a risk that is much less than the average of the two components. In the example in Figure 7–3, the standard deviation of the portfolio is only .04. In this case, diversification resulted in a significant reduction in risk. In fact, it would be possible to combine the two negatively correlated stocks in a combination such that the portfolio standard deviation would reduce to 0. An alternative way to get a portfolio with a standard deviation of 0 is to combine equal proportions of two negatively correlated stocks that have the same standard deviation. In this manner, each positive return on one stock will be exactly canceled out by a corresponding negative return on the other.

Reality: Less than Perfectly Correlated Returns

The two preceding examples represent the two theoretical extremes, which seldom exist in reality (except in the case of hedges involving short sales). In most investment

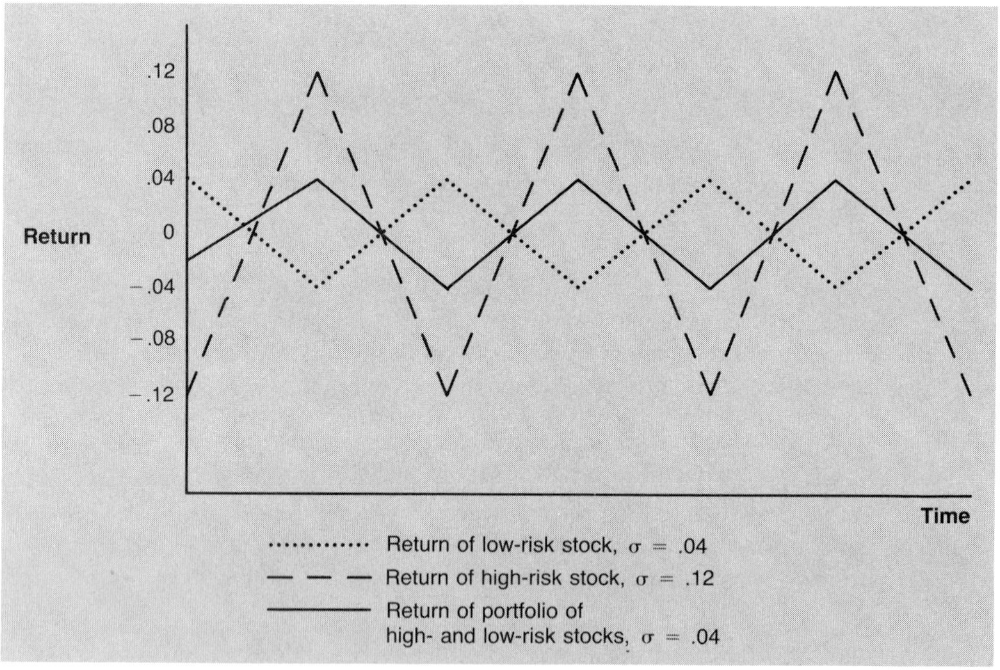

FIGURE 7–3
Diversification with perfectly negatively correlated returns (correlation coefficient = −1.0)

environments and with most securities, returns will be somewhat positively correlated. A typical correlation coefficient between two securities might be +.4. As an example, Figure 7–4 shows the returns on two securities whose correlation coefficient is +.33.

Once again, the risks of the high and low risk stocks are .12 and .04 respectively. Combining them in equal proportions results in an equally weighted portfolio. The variation of the line representing the portfolio of the two stocks is somewhat more than the portfolio in Figure 7–3, but it is less than the portfolio in Figure 7–2. The standard deviation of this portfolio is about .075; there was some risk reduction resulting from diversification. For additional risk reduction, more securities could be added to the portfolio.

MARKOWITZ DIVERSIFICATION

The examples in the preceding section show that the risk reduction from diversification is greater when the securities added to the portfolio have returns with lower correlations to the portfolio returns. Harry Markowitz[1] first demonstrated this principle in 1952. Since then, the term *Markowitz diversification* has been applied to the process

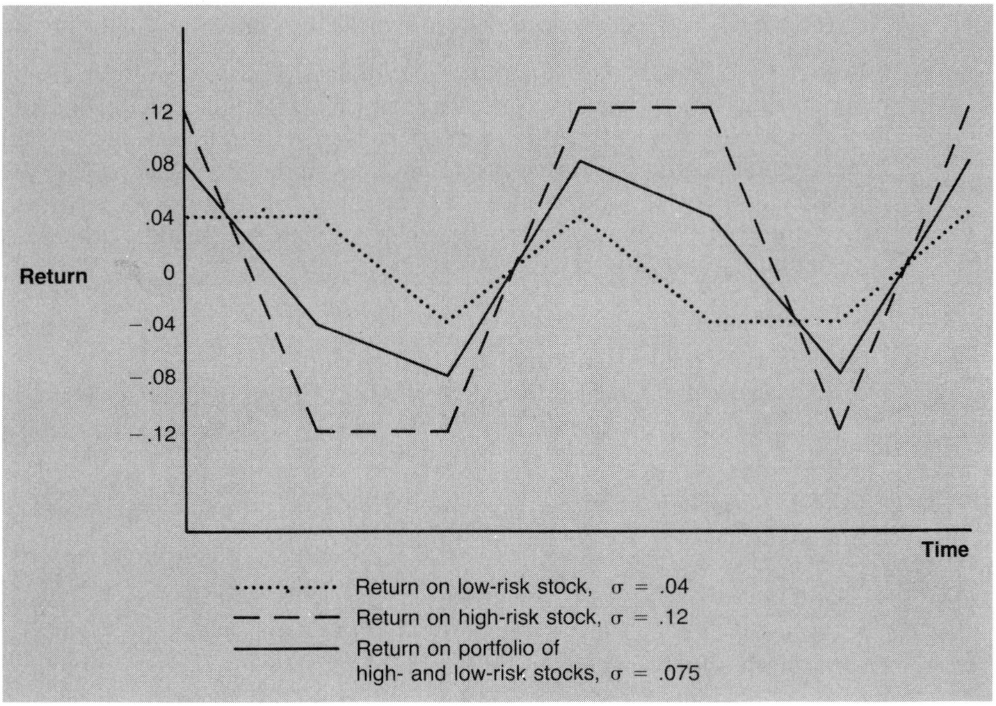

FIGURE 7–4
Diversification with less than perfectly correlated returns (correlation coefficient = +.33)

of selecting securities for a portfolio based on their correlations. To achieve the maximum risk reduction from diversifying, an investor applying Markowitz diversification would construct a portfolio containing securities with the lowest possible correlations to each other. The reason for this becomes clear after examining the formula for portfolio standard deviation.

Portfolio Standard Deviation as a Measure of Risk

Markowitz identified the procedure for computing the standard deviation for a portfolio, given the portfolio securities' standard deviations and correlations with each other. Of course, since the variance is equal to the standard deviation squared, we can cast the Markowitz formulas in terms of the variance also. This formula for the variance of a portfolio is as follows:

$$\sigma_p^2 = \sum_{i=1}^{n} \sum_{j=1}^{n} w_i \times w_j \times \text{cov}_{i,j} \qquad \textbf{(7–3)}$$

where w_i = the proportion of funds invested in the *i*th security
w_j = the proportion of funds invested in the *j*th security
n = the number of securities in the portfolio
$\text{cov}_{i,j}$ = the covariance of security i with security j

Equation 7–3 shows that the variance of a portfolio is equal to a weighted sum of the covariances of all combinations of security pairs in the portfolio. Chapter 6 introduced the covariance and stated that it is a measure of systematic risk. Now, Equation 7–3 demonstrates that the covariance is relevant to computing portfolio risk. Recall from Chapter 6 that one of the methods for computing the covariance of two securities defines the covariance as equal to the product of their standard deviations and their correlation. Equation 7–4 restates this relationship:

$$\text{cov}_{i,j} = \sigma_i \times \sigma_j \times r_{i,j} \qquad \textbf{(7–4)}$$

where σ_i = the standard deviation of the returns on security i
σ_j = the standard deviation of the returns on security j
$r_{i,j}$ = the correlation coefficient of the returns on security i with security j

Equation 7–3 gives the variance of the portfolio. To get the standard deviation of the portfolio, take the square root of the variance as follows:

$$\sigma_p = \sqrt{\sigma_p^2} \qquad \textbf{(7–5)}$$

Equations 7–3, 7–4, and 7–5 can be used to compute the standard deviation of returns of a portfolio containing any number of securities. An analyst wanting to know the effects of adding a few more securities to a portfolio can predict the results using these formulas if the inputs are known.

For an example, let us expand Equation 7–3 to the simple case of a portfolio of two securities (security 1 and security 2).

$$\sigma_p^2 = \sum_{i=1}^{2} \sum_{j=1}^{2} w_i \times w_j \times \text{cov}_{i,j}$$

$$= w_1 w_1 \text{cov}_{1,1} + w_1 w_2 \text{cov}_{1,2} + w_2 w_1 \text{cov}_{2,1} + w_2 w_2 \text{cov}_{2,2}$$

Because the covariance of security 1 with security 2 is the same as the covariance of security 2 with security 1, simplifying, we have

$$= w_1^2 \text{cov}_{1,1} + 2 w_1 w_2 \text{cov}_{1,2} + w_2^2 \text{cov}_{2,2}$$

Substituting Equation 7–4 for the covariance, noting that the correlation of any variable with itself is 1, and taking the square root gives

$$\sigma_p = \sqrt{w_1^2 \sigma_1^2 + 2 w_1 w_2 \sigma_1 \sigma_2 r_{1,2} + w_2^2 \sigma_2^2} \tag{7–6}$$

Equation 7–6 is the portfolio standard deviation that should result when combining securities 1 and 2 into a portfolio. Using Markowitz diversification and these formulas, an investor could find the combination of securities that would yield the lowest risk portfolio. This would be fairly straightforward when constructing two-security portfolios from a small universe of securities. Example 7–2 shows a sample computation of the portfolio standard deviation for a two-stock portfolio.

EXAMPLE 7–2

Mr. Nat Bunker holds a two-stock portfolio. Stock A has a standard deviation of returns of .6, and stock B has a standard deviation of .4. The correlation coefficient of the two stocks' returns is .25. Mr. Bunker holds equal dollar amounts of each stock.

$$\begin{aligned}\sigma_p &= \sqrt{.5^2 \times .6^2 + 2 \times .5 \times .5 \times .6 \times .4 \times .25 + .5^2 \times .4^2} \\ &= \sqrt{.09 + .03 + .04} \\ &= \sqrt{.16} \\ &= .4\end{aligned}$$

However, as the number of securities in the universe increases and the number of securities to include in the portfolio also increases, the number of calculations increases geometrically. For example, suppose that we had narrowed down the number of stocks in which we wanted to invest to 100. We want to construct a minimum-risk portfolio of 20 stocks from these 100. First, we would need to compute the correlation coefficient of each of the 100 stocks with every other of the 100 stocks (i.e., 1 with 2, 1 with 3, . . . 2 with 3, 2 with 4 . . .). This would require computing 4950 correlation coefficients. Then, we would have to expand Equation 7–3 for portfolios of 20 stocks. This would give a formula with 400 terms. Finally, we would need to compute Equation 7–3 for every different combination of 20 stocks from the universe of 100. This would involve solving the equation over 500 quintillion times (5 followed by 20 zeros), quite a task even for today's sophisticated computers. Software packages are available to compute portfolio risk using Markowitz techniques for moderately sized portfolios.

Use of Markowitz diversification techniques to minimize portfolio risk is therefore limited to selecting relatively small portfolios from a small universe of securities. However, Equation 7–6 shows the important point that covariance is the relevant risk when constructing diversified portfolios. Therefore, since covariance is a measure of systematic risk, systematic risk must be the important risk to holders of diversified portfolios of securities. This conclusion is one of the important contributions of Markowitz's work to modern portfolio theory.

Beta as a Measure of Portfolio Risk

Since the Markowitz techniques are limited to very small portfolios, another tool is needed to measure portfolio risk. There are two keys to this other tool. First is the observation that because diversification can lower risk *without* lowering return, all rational utility-maximizing investors should seek diversification. Second, since all investors will want to hold portfolios, and systematic risk is the only risk that matters to holders of portfolios, then systematic risk is the *only* risk that investors need be concerned with. Unsystematic risk of any individual security does not matter because the unsystematic risk disappears (almost) when considering the securities as a portfolio.

The second measure of systematic risk introduced in Chapter 6 was beta, a measure of systematic risk of a security relative to market risk. Beta was identified as the covariance of the security returns with market returns divided by the variance of market returns, restated here for convenience as follows:

$$\beta_j = \frac{\text{COV}_{j,m}}{\sigma_m^2} \qquad \textbf{(7–7)}$$

where β_j = the beta of security j
σ_m^2 = the variance of the returns on the market portfolio

One of the advantages of beta mentioned in Chapter 6 was that beta is a relative measure of systematic risk. It gauges securities' systematic risk relative to the market portfolio, where a security with a beta of 1.0 has systematic risk equal to that of the market. Stocks with betas with absolute values less than 1.0 are conservative and less volatile, while stocks with betas that have absolute values greater than 1.0 are more aggressive.

Another advantage of beta is that it is additive. That is, the beta of a portfolio is equal to the weighted average of the betas of the individual stocks in the portfolio, as follows:

$$\beta_p = \sum_{i=1}^{n} w_i \times \beta_i \qquad \textbf{(7–8)}$$

where β_p = the beta of the portfolio
n = the number of securities in the portfolio
w_i = the weight, or portion of funds invested in security i
β_i = the beta of security i in the portfolio

Equation 7–8 is much more manageable than Equation 7–3 for computing the risk of a portfolio. Example 7–3 shows the computation of a portfolio beta.

EXAMPLE 7–3

Mrs. Doris Markwell owns a portfolio containing four stocks. Her broker gave her the estimates of each stock's beta. Compute the portfolio beta using the following data:

Stock	*Beta*	*Amount*
W	.73	$ 200
X	1.86	400
Y	1.45	100
Z	1.15	300
Portfolio value =		$1000

$$\beta_p = (200/1000).73 + (400/1000)1.86 + (100/1000)1.45 + (300/1000)1.15$$

$$= .146 + .744 + .145 + .345$$

$$= 1.38$$

Chapter 5 introduced the concept of portfolio weighting by discussing several mechanical weighting schemes: price, equal, and value weighting. Equal weighting is a convenient strategy for computing betas because for an equally weighted portfolio, Equation 7–8 simplifies to:

$$\beta_p = \frac{\sum_{i=1}^{n} \beta_i}{n} \qquad \textbf{(7–9)}$$

Equation 7–9 is a shortcut to computing portfolio beta when an equal amount of money is invested in each security in the portfolio.

The Effects of Diversification on Unsystematic and Systematic Risk

It is now evident why even random diversification reduces risk: it is highly unlikely that any two securities are perfectly positively correlated. Therefore, blindly selecting securities for a portfolio will include securities that are sufficiently uncorrelated to reduce the risk of the portfolio.

Since systematic risk is the meaningful risk to a portfolio, and unsystematic risk is not, then the risk that diversification reduces from the portfolio must be the unsystematic risk. As securities are added to a portfolio, it is the unsystematic risk of the portfolio that falls. Of course, since a portfolio's total risk is equal to its systematic risk plus its unsystematic risk, the total risk also falls. Figure 7–5 shows the effects of random diversification on the total, unsystematic, and systematic risks of a portfolio.

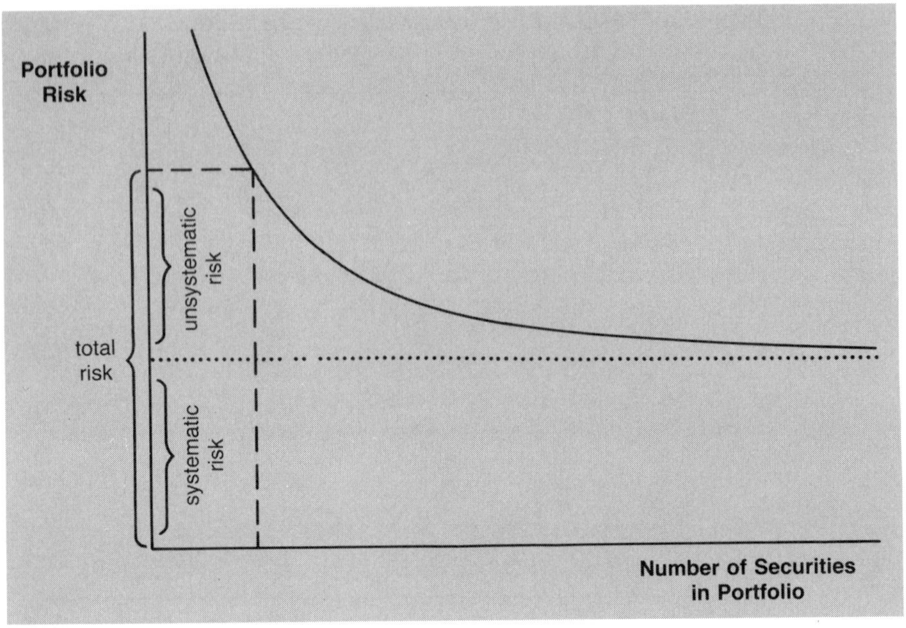

FIGURE 7–5
Effects of random diversification on total, systematic, and unsystematic risk in a portfolio

Fisher and Lorie[2], in a study of the risk and returns on common stock portfolios, computed figures that verify the concept displayed in Figure 7–5. They identified a universe of 510 common stocks and computed their returns over the forty-year period from 1925 to 1965. From this universe, they then randomly generated portfolios containing 1, 2, 8, 16, 32, and 128 stocks and computed the portfolio returns and standard deviations. Table 7–1 presents a summary of these statistics. The average standard deviation of the 1-stock portfolios was .554. As the portfolio size increased, the standard deviation fell. The standard deviation of the portfolio of all stocks (the market portfolio) was .315.

Since the .315 standard deviation of the market represents systematic risk, the .554 risk of the 1-stock portfolios is 43 percent unsystematic and 57 percent systematic risk. As the number of securities in the portfolios increases, the standard deviations fall, and the portion of risk attributable to unsystematic variation in returns falls to the point where, in the 128-stock portfolios, only 1 percent of the risk left is unsystematic.

Chapter 2 introduced a fundamental concept of the relationship between risk and return: investors expect higher return from investments with higher levels of risk. This linear relationship, called the Security Market Line, will be developed in the next chapter. In this chapter, though, we need to use the Security Market Line model to

TABLE 7–1
Annualized risk and return on portfolios of varying sizes

Portfolio Size	*Mean Return*	*Systematic Risk (Standard Deviation)*	*Unsystematic Risk as Percentage of Total Risk*	*Systematic Risk as Percentage of Total Risk*
1	.148	.554	43%	57%
2	.148	.451	30	70
8	.148	.354	11	89
16	.148	.335	6	94
32	.148	.325	3	97
128	.148	.318	1	99
all	.148	.315	0	100

Source: Lawrence Fisher and James H. Lorie (1970), "Some Studies of Variability of Returns on Investment in Common Stocks," *Journal of Business*, 43 (April), 99–134.

define the expected return on an investment. Stated in terms of a portfolio, the relationship is:

$$E(R_p) = R_f + \beta_p[E(R_m) - R_f] \qquad \textbf{(7–10)}$$

where $E(R_p)$ = the expected return on a portfolio
R_f = the riskless interest rate
β_p = the beta of the portfolio
$E(R_m)$ = the expected return on the market portfolio

Equation 7–10 describes the expected return on a portfolio as a function of the portfolio's beta and the expected market return and riskless rate.

The use of this relationship to estimate the expected rate of return on an individual stock is subject to quite a bit of error. In addition to any error caused by misestimation of the expected market return, unsystematic deviation in a stock's price can result in the *ex post* realized return on a stock being much different from the *ex ante* expected return. Recall that unsystematic deviation is fluctuation in a stock's price *not* associated with market fluctuations. Because the unsystematic risk can be a large portion of an individual stock's total risk, there is a relatively high error in estimating security returns with Equation 7–10 for individual stocks.

The estimation of portfolio expected return with the relationship in Equation 7–10 is more reliable. Because the greater number of securities in a portfolio diversifies away unsystematic risk, the unsystematic deviation in a portfolio will be relatively small. For a well-diversified portfolio, unsystematic risk becomes insignificant. The absence of unsystematic variation in a diversified portfolio results in less error and more reliable expected return estimates when using Equation 7–10.

Because the unsystematic risk of a portfolio becomes smaller and smaller as the number of securities in the portfolio increases, many students of the market refer to unsystematic risk as *diversifiable risk*. It can be reduced and ultimately virtually eliminated by diversification. The systematic risk of the portfolio is unaffected by diversification, leading it to be called *undiversifiable risk*.

However, the term *undiversifiable risk* applied to systematic risk may be misleading. It means only that random diversification does not reduce systematic risk. An investor may, however, lower the overall systematic risk of a portfolio by including in the portfolio more securities with low betas, thereby lowering the portfolio's beta (systematic risk). In addition, an investor can achieve the benefits of diversification more rapidly than happens with random diversification. This would be accomplished by using Markowitz techniques, selecting securities with low or negative correlations for inclusion into the portfolio. A portfolio selected in such a manner would fall in risk more rapidly than one being diversified randomly, as shown in Figure 7–6.

The Limits of Diversification

Even with Markowitz diversification, the total risk of a portfolio will never fall below the portfolio's systematic risk level. The limit of risk reduction through diversification is the systematic risk level of the portfolio.

Note in Table 7–1 that with portfolios of 32 stocks, only 3 percent of the standard deviation in the returns was left to be diversified away. At this point, the marginal

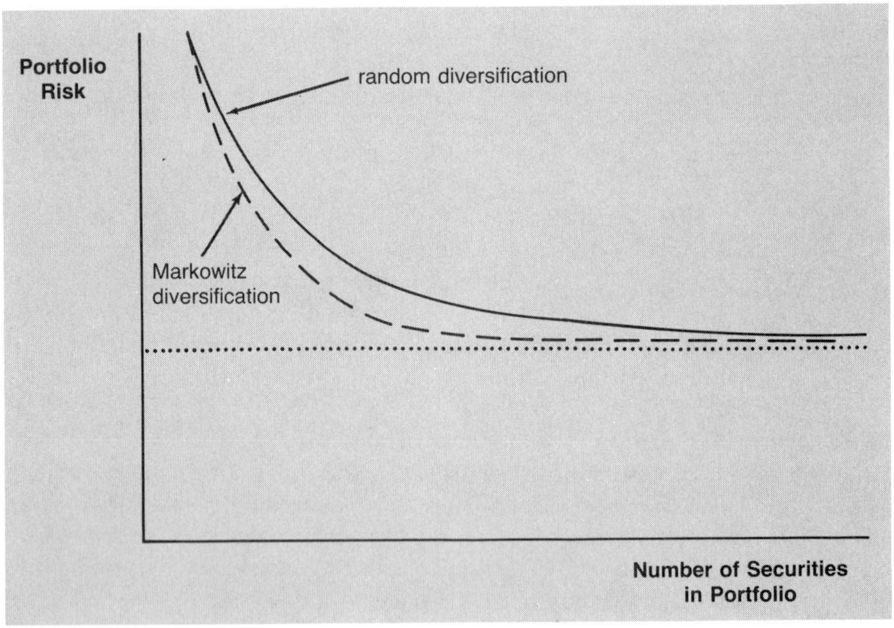

FIGURE 7–6
Effects of Markowitz diversification on portfolio risk

benefit of adding securities to the portfolio is very small. To eliminate another 2 percent of the variation, the size of the portfolio would have to be increased to 128 stocks. At that point only 1 percent of the total portfolio risk is left to be diversified away, and it would take many securities to accomplish this. There is some point beyond which the costs of additional diversification overcome the benefits. Diversification beyond that point is *superfluous diversification*. Diversification beyond the point of superfluous diversification is unnecessary and would lower investors' net wealth in the long run.

The point at which diversification becomes superfluous varies with the costs of managing the portfolio, but it probably occurs somewhere between 25 and 50 different securities. Examples of costs associated with diversification that influence the point of superfluous diversification are costs of searching for new investments, expenses of managing the portfolio, and transaction costs.

INTERNATIONAL DIVERSIFICATION

The discussion of diversification so far has assumed only diversification into domestic securities. When the possibility of investing in securities of several countries exists, the prospect of international diversification arises. The potential of international diversification is interesting.

Investing in foreign securities holds additional risks. Over and above the usual risks of investing in securities, investing in securities of other countries involves exchange rate risk and political risk. However, the prospect of making additional returns can often compensate an investor for taking on these additional risks.

Another aspect of international diversification is the potential for risk reduction past the point possible with portfolios of only domestic securities. Figure 7–7 illustrates an example of potential risk reduction with international diversification. Note how the risk of the international portfolio falls below the risk of the domestic portfolio. Empirical studies examining international diversification have found evidence to support the hypothesis that international diversification provides the potential for risk reduction beyond the point offered by domestic portfolios.[3]

The purchase of foreign securities poses additional problems. Transaction costs may be more for purchasing foreign securities, and the exchange of currency may add expense. In addition, some countries restrict the purchase of their securities by foreigners, or they restrict or tax the cash dividends that companies may remit to foreign investors.

One method that has been proposed for avoiding the problems of buying foreign stocks on overseas exchanges has been to purchase the shares of corporations headquartered domestically but that have multinational operations. However, a study by Jacquillat and Solnik[4] examined the returns of multinational stocks and found that their behavior was too similar to their domestic counterparts to provide any significant international diversification benefits.

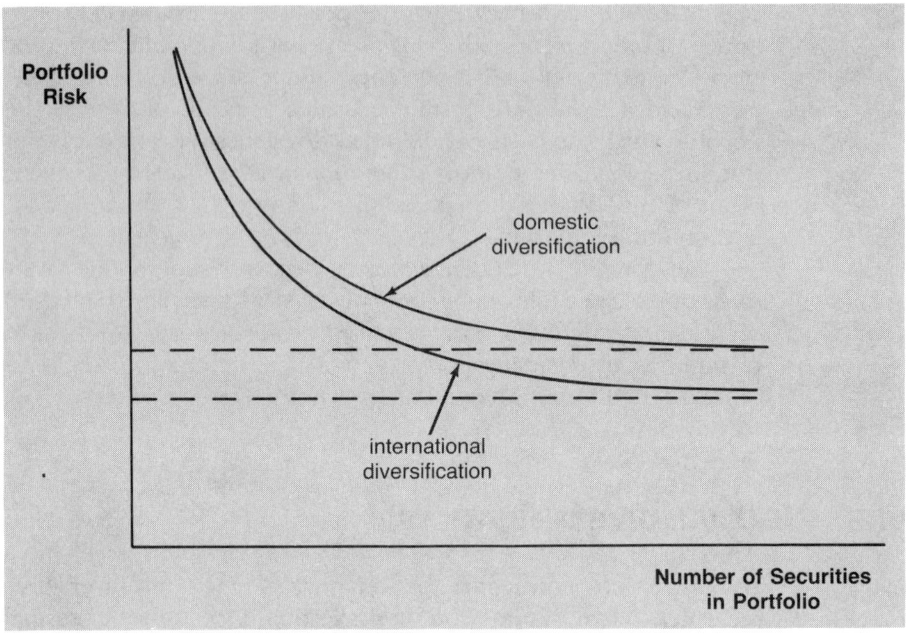

FIGURE 7–7
Effects of international diversification on portfolio risk

SUMMARY

Diversification is the process of adding securities together to form a portfolio. Diversification results in a portfolio whose expected return is equal to the weighted average of the expected returns on the individual securities in the portfolio. On the other hand, diversification lowers the risk of a portfolio to a level that is lower than the average risk of the securities in the portfolio. This is true even for random diversification, the addition of securities to a portfolio without regard to their risk characteristics.

Selecting securities for a portfolio by considering their risk characteristics is Markowitz diversification. Markowitz diversification techniques are based on the fact that the correlation of returns among securities affects the risk reduction benefits of diversification. If securities' returns were perfectly positively correlated, diversification would not lower the risk level of a portfolio. However, when securities are less than perfectly positively correlated, diversification does reduce risk to a level lower than the average risk of the securities in the portfolio. The lower the correlation, the greater the risk reduction will be.

A portfolio's risk (variance) is a weighted sum of the individual securities' covariances, showing that systematic risk is the important risk to holders of diversified portfolios. Further, since all investors should seek to lower risk by diversifying, systematic risk is the only risk that is relevant to investors. Unsystematic risk is the risk that diversification reduces and ultimately eliminates from a portfolio.

Since systematic risk is the relevant risk, beta, the measure of systematic risk, can be used to represent adequately the risk of a portfolio. Computing the beta of a portfolio is much simpler than computing the standard deviation or variance. A portfolio's beta is a weighted average of the component securities' betas.

International diversification has the potential to increase the return on a portfolio and lower the risk beyond what is possible with only domestic stocks. However, diversification into foreign securities brings risks that are not associated with domestic companies.

IMPORTANT TERMS

diversification
Markowitz diversification
naive diversification
random diversification
superfluous diversification

QUESTIONS AND PROBLEMS

1.

Stock	*Price*	*Expected Return*
A	$40	.15
B	22	.12
C	86	.09
D	53	.17

a) Compute the expected return on a portfolio containing $100 worth of each of the above stocks.

b) Compute the expected return on a portfolio containing 100 shares of each of the above stocks.

2. Explain why random or naive diversification lowers the risk of a portfolio as the number of securities in the portfolio increases.
3. Two stocks, each with a standard deviation of returns of .1, have returns that are perfectly negatively correlated. What is the standard deviation of an equally weighted portfolio of the two stocks?
4. What would be the portfolio standard deviation in Question 3 if the two stocks were perfectly positively correlated?
5. Define and explain the differences between random diversification and Markowitz diversification.

6.

Stock	*Expected Return*	*Standard Deviation*	*Correlation of Returns with Stock*		
			A	*B*	*C*
A	.12	.30	1.0	.6	.7
B	.10	.20	.6	1.0	.8
C	.16	.40	.7	.8	1.0

a) Compute the expected return and standard deviation of an equally weighted portfolio containing stocks A and B above.
b) Compute the expected return and standard deviation of an equally weighted portfolio containing stocks A and C above.
c) Compute the expected return and standard deviation of an equally weighted portfolio containing stocks A, B, and C above.
d) Discuss how and why the expected returns and standard deviations computed above differ among the portfolios.

7. The expected standard deviation of the market is .12 and you have the following information:

Stock	*Price*	*Expected Return*	*Standard Deviation*	*Correlation with Market Returns*
A	15	.130	.20	.8
B	60	.150	.40	.5
C	63	.100	.25	.4
D	24	.095	.15	.6
E	36	.090	.20	.4

a) Compute the expected return and beta of a portfolio containing an equal dollar amount of each of the above stocks, A to E.
b) Compute the expected return and beta of a portfolio containing 100 shares of each of the above stocks.
c) Would you like to have to compute (using a calculator) the expected standard deviation of these portfolios? Why?
d) How well do you think that the above portfolios have diversified away unsystematic risk? Explain.

8. Explain why systematic risk is often called undiversifiable risk and unsystematic risk is often called diversifiable.
9. Explain superfluous diversification. Under what conditions might a portfolio have to contain superfluous diversification?
10. What are some of the potential rewards and risks of international investing and diversification?

NOTES

1. Harry Markowitz (1952), "Portfolio Selection," *Journal of Finance,* 7 (March), 77–91.
2. Lawrence Fisher and James H. Lorie (1970), "Some Studies of Variability of Returns on Investment in Common Stocks," *Journal of Business,* 43 (April), 99–134.
3. See, for example, Bruno Solnik (1974), "Why Not Diversify Internationally Rather Than Domestically?," *Financial Analysts Journal,* (July–August), 48–54.

4. Bertrand Jacquillat and Bruno Solnik (1978), "Multinationals Are Poor Tools for Diversification," in Peter L. Bernstein (ed.), *Security Selection and Active Portfolio Management,* New York: Institutional Investor, 262–272.

SELECTED REFERENCES

Adler, Michael and David Simon (1986). "Exchange Risk Surprises in International Portfolios." *Journal of Portfolio Management,* 12 (Winter), 44–53.

Beaver, W., and J. Manegold (1975). "The Association between Market-Determined and Accounting-Determined Measures of Systematic Risk: Some Further Evidence." *Journal of Financial and Quantitative Analysis,* 10 (June), 231–284.

Brealey, Richard (1983). *An Introduction to Risk and Return from Common Stocks.* 2nd ed., Cambridge: MIT Press.

Fisher, Lawrence, and James H. Lorie (1970). "Some Studies of Variability of Returns on Investments in Common Stocks." *Journal of Business,* 43 (April), 99–134.

Jacquillat, Bertrand, and Bruno Solnik (1978). "Multinationals Are Poor Tools for Diversification." In Bernstein, Peter L. (ed.). *Security Selection and Active Portfolio Management.* New York: Institutional Investor, 262–272.

Lorie, James H. (1977). "Diversification: Old and New." In Bernstein, Peter L. (ed.). *Portfolio Management and Efficient Markets.* New York: Institutional Investor, 102–112.

Markowitz, Harry (1952). "Portfolio Selection." *Journal of Finance,* 7 (March), 77–91.

Markowitz, Harry (1984). "The 'Two-Beta' Trap." *Journal of Portfolio Management,* 11 (Fall), 12–20.

McEnally, Richard W. (1985). "Time Diversification: The Surest Route to Lower Risk?" *Journal of Portfolio Management,* 11 (Summer), 24–26.

Olsen, Robert (1983). "Sample Size and Markowitz Diversification." *Journal of Portfolio Management,* 10 (Fall), 18–22.

Rosenberg, Barr, and James Guy (1976). "Prediction of Beta from Investment Fundamentals: Part One, Prediction Criteria." *Financial Analysts Journal,* 32 (May–June), 60–72.

Rosenberg, Barr, and James Guy (1976). "Prediction of Beta from Investment Fundamentals: Part Two, Alternative Prediction Methods." *Financial Analysts Journal,* 32 (July–August), 62–70.

Shaked, Israel (1985). "International Equity Markets and the Investment Horizon." *Journal of Portfolio Management,* 11 (Winter), 80–84.

Sharpe, William F. (1963). "A Simplified Model for Portfolio Analysis." *Management Science,* 9 (January), 277–293.

Solnik, B. (1974). "Why Not Diversify Internationally Rather Than Domestically?" *Financial Analysts Journal,* (July–August), 48–54.

Tole, Thomas M. (1982). "You Can't Diversify without Diversifying." *Journal of Portfolio Management,* 8 (Winter), 5–11.

Vora, Ashok, and Gabriel A. Hawawini (1983). "Is Adjusting Beta Estimates an Illusion?" *Journal of Portfolio Management,* 10 (Fall), 23–26.

Wagner, W., and S. Lau (1971). "The Effect of Diversification on Risk." *Financial Analysts Journal,* 26 (November–December), 50.

CHAPTER 8

Capital Market Theory

Chapter 6, "Concepts of Risk and Return," identified the basic relationship between the expected return on an investment and its risk. The idea that an investor should expect and require more return from an investment with greater risk is fundamental to the study of investments. Although this relationship between expected return and risk is logical and needs no theoretical development to explain, there is a benefit from developing a formal model defining the risk-return relationship. A formal model allows us to be more precise in the definition of the risk-return relationship. It also provides a framework upon which we can develop quantitative and analytical tools for investment analysis and evaluation. This chapter outlines the development of formal models explaining the relationship between risk and expected return.

The concepts of investor risk preferences from Chapter 6 allow us to develop criteria for choosing among risky alternative investments. These concepts lead to the derivation of the *Capital Asset Pricing Model (CAPM).* The Capital Asset Pricing Model is a formal presentation of the relationship between expected return and risk. Although we cannot attribute the model to one person, the pioneers of its development were William F. Sharpe,[1] John Lintner,[2] and Jan Mossin.[3]

This chapter also discusses a number of uses of the CAPM. Since its initial development, the Capital Asset Pricing Model has generated much discussion and controversy, and this chapter also presents the criticisms leveled at the model and its use. Finally, some alternatives to the CAPM are presented.

CAPITAL MARKET ASSUMPTIONS

Capital market theory is normative rather than descriptive. In other words, the theory attempts to describe how investors' behavior should affect security prices rather than explaining what investors actually observe in the market. In creating a model to represent the workings of something so complex as the market for invested capital, some simplifying assumptions are necessary. The Capital Asset Pricing Model rests on nine assumptions:

1. *The investor's objective is to maximize the utility of terminal wealth.* This is not the same thing as maximizing wealth itself. Instead, it means that investors seek to attain some point on the highest possible utility curve. They maximize wealth within their risk constraints.
2. *Investors make choices solely on the basis of risk and return.* Investors consider only risk and return as the relevant criteria for investment decisions. The mean (expected value) of portfolio returns measures return and the variance (or standard deviation) of returns measures risk.
3. *Investors have homogeneous expectations.* All investors estimate similar probability distributions for future rates of return for a given investment alternative. Without a consensus of expectations (and thus of the relative value of each investment), it would be impossible to derive a single pricing model—there would instead be many investor-specific models. Similarly, an implication of this assumption is that there is no inflation or change in interest rates other than those which investors already fully anticipate.
4. *Investors have identical one-period time horizons.* Although it does not perfectly match reality, this assumption is necessary to construct a single-period model. Single-period models are much more straightforward to develop. The single-period model can be extended to multi-period or continuous cases (see, for example, Merton[4]), but these are more complex to understand and use.
5. *Information is freely available.* Market efficiency also depends upon this assumption, which is necessary if one is to presume homogeneous expectations. Without a set of known information and common forecasts, an asset pricing model could not identify a single set of desirable investments.
6. *There is a risk-free asset, and investors can borrow and lend any amount of money at the risk-free rate.* This may be the most crucial assumption behind CAPM. If the risk-free asset is to be some liquid short-term U.S. government-backed security, such as ninety-day Treasury bills, then it is always possible for investors to lend sufficiently large amounts at this rate. It will not always be possible for investors to borrow at the risk-free rate, but in fact imposing a higher borrowing rate does not alter the results very much.
7. *There are no taxes, transaction costs, or other market imperfections.* This essentially allows equal treatment of all investors, permitting none an advantage over others attributable to taxes, commissions, barriers to market entry, or other market imperfections. This is the *frictionless market* assumption.
8. *Total asset quantity is fixed, and all assets are marketable and divisible.* This assumption removes liquidity as a factor in risk analysis. It also allows us to depict investment activity as continuous curves.

9. *Capital markets are in equilibrium.* Initially, all assets are efficiently priced in terms of their associated risk.

It may seem that some of these assumptions do not represent reality. If so, what does this imply about the validity of the model based upon them? There are two important points to be made. First, we can relax many of these assumptions with only minor impact on the model; the basic conclusions and major implications remain intact. Second, the value of any model lies in how well it helps to explain and predict results in the real world. If the theory works well in spite of unrealistic assumptions, then the factors removed from the model must not be vitally important. Put simply, the most important test of a model is how well it works.

DERIVING THE EFFICIENT FRONTIER OF RISKY ASSETS

The next step in deriving the asset pricing model is to define a set of criteria for identifying preferred investments. Probably the most straightforward method, and one that is consistent with the assumptions, is the *mean-variance criteria*. The mean-variance criteria utilize only the mean and variance (or standard deviation, which is the square root of the variance) of expected returns to identify the investments that *dominate*. An investment A dominates investment B if investors always prefer A to B.

The mean-variance criteria assume that continuously compounded returns (log returns) on investments are normally distributed, as in Figure 8–1. The expected value of this distribution is the mean, and the measure of dispersion of values around the mean is the standard deviation. These two statistical measures, the mean and the standard deviation, can describe any normal distribution of returns.

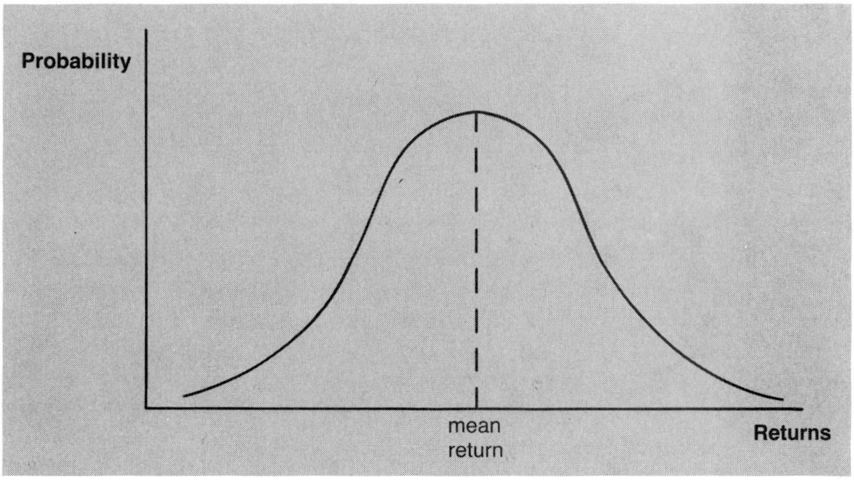

FIGURE 8–1
Normally distributed returns

Using the mean as the measure of expected return and the standard deviation as the measure of risk, we can represent any investment in risk-return space as a single point. Figure 8–2 shows an example of investment *A* with expected return $E(R)_A$ and standard deviation σ_A.

Suppose there are two investment alternatives, *A* and *B,* with identical expected mean values. The standard deviation of investment *B,* however, is greater than the standard deviation of *A.* The distribution of returns might be as shown in Figure 8–3.

Figure 8–3 also shows the plot of the expected return and risk of investment *B.* Given a choice, risk-averse investors would always prefer *A* to *B.* Because it offers the same expected return at lower risk, *A* dominates *B* by the mean-variance criteria.

By the mean-variance criteria, an investment *A* dominates investment *B* if the expected return on *A* is greater than the expected return on *B,* and the standard deviation of *A* is less than or equal to the standard deviation of *B.* Essentially, one investment or portfolio dominates another if it offers a more favorable risk-reward relationship—either higher return for the same risk or lower risk for the same return.

Figure 8–4 graphically illustrates dominance of several alternative investments. Investment *A* dominates *B* because *A*'s risk is less than *B*'s while the return is at least as high. Investment *A* also dominates investment *C.* Investment *A*'s risk is the same as *C*'s, but *A*'s return is higher.

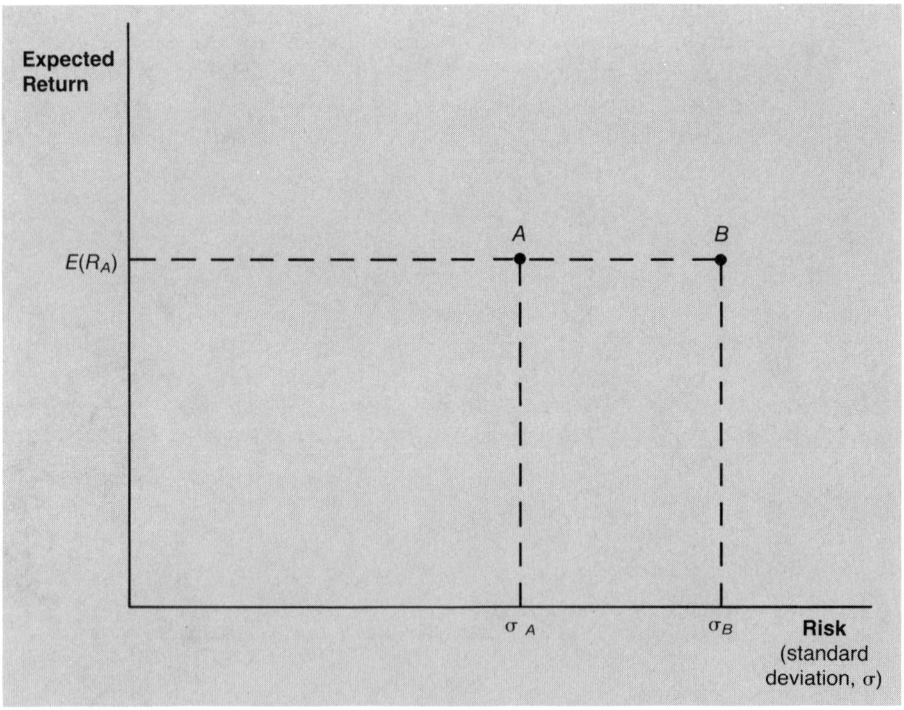

FIGURE 8–2
Investments *A* and *B* in risk-return space

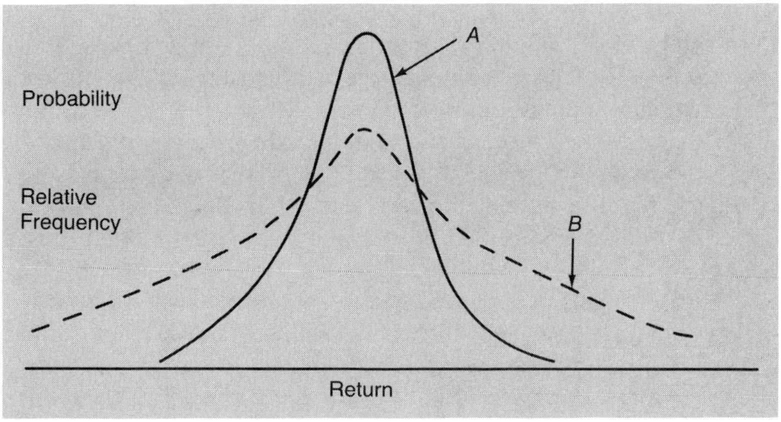

FIGURE 8–3
Distributions of returns on investments *A* and *B*

With the mean-variance criteria, the situation often arises in which no dominance exists. In Figure 8–4, this relationship occurs between investments *B* and *C*. Investment *B*'s expected return is greater, but so is its risk, so we cannot unequivocally state that a risk-averse investor will prefer *B* over *C*. It is likely that a given investor will have a preference regarding *B* or *C*, but we cannot know which one with the information available at this point.

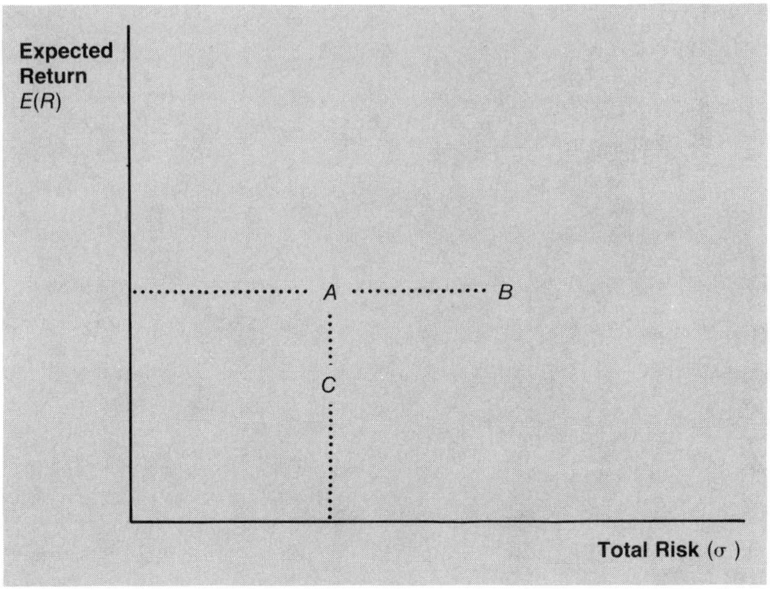

FIGURE 8–4
Map of dominant investments using mean-variance criteria

Given the capital market assumptions, if these were the only investments available, all investors would prefer to hold investment *A* because it exhibits the most efficient trade-off between risk and return. In reality, of course, choices of investments are virtually unlimited considering that each security can be combined with other securities to form portfolios. Each portfolio offers its combination of risk and reward. The universe of all potential assets or portfolios of assets is called the *feasible set.* Within the feasible set are all assets and all possible combinations of assets (all possible portfolios). Figure 8–5 illustrates a feasible set plotted in risk-return space.

Certain assets and portfolios in the feasible set will dominate others in the set. Investments lying upward and to the left dominate those lying below and to the right. Ultimately, a subset will exist whose members are not dominated by any others. This is the *mean-variance efficient set.* The efficient set contains every portfolio that offers the maximum expected return for every level of risk and the minimum risk for every level of expected return. Figure 8–5 shows a plot of the efficient set, often called the *efficient frontier of portfolios of risky assets.* Every portfolio not lying on the efficient frontier is dominated by at least one alternative, and no portfolio from the efficient set is dominated by any other.

The efficient frontier contains only portfolios, not individual securities. The risk-reducing principle of diversification explains this observation. Recall that we can combine two securities into a portfolio and reduce the risk while not reducing the

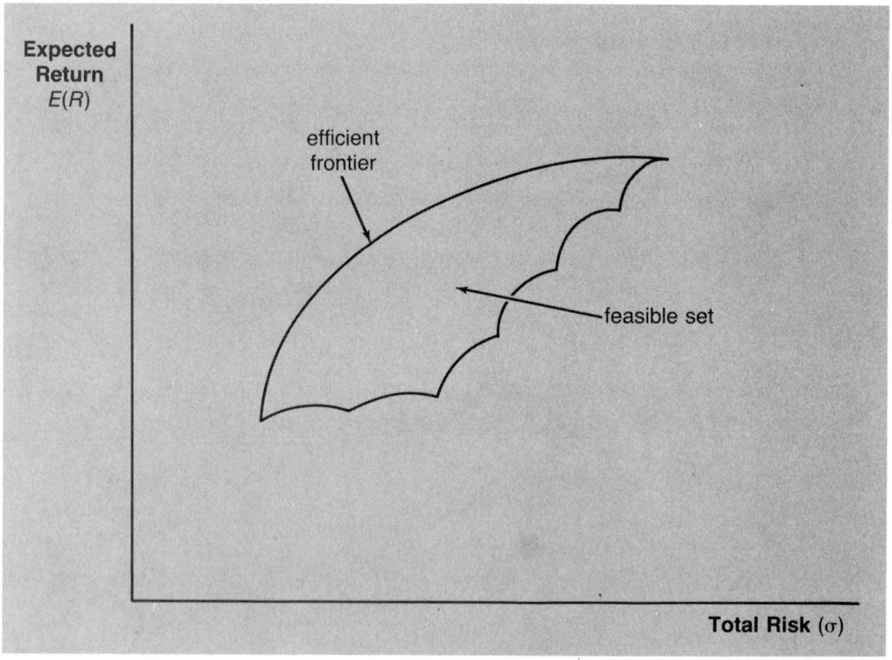

FIGURE 8–5
The feasible set of investments and the efficient frontier

return (as long as the returns on the securities are not perfectly correlated). By definition, therefore, the portfolio dominates the individual securities. Any individual security or asset in the feasible set can be combined with some other asset (or combination of assets) to form a portfolio that will dominate the individual asset. Therefore, as the set of investments that maximize return for a given risk level, the efficient frontier must contain only portfolios.

Because of the second CAPM assumption, a rational investor will eliminate all inefficient portfolios from consideration. The only portfolios an investor should be interested in purchasing are within the efficient set. What now determines which portfolio is the most desirable choice? Notice that, moving up along the efficient set, each point offers additional return and some incremental risk. Referring to Figure 8–6, an investor might hold portfolio *J* on the efficient frontier. Would this investor prefer to move to portfolio *K*? Maybe, because *K* offers a higher expected return. However, it also offers a higher level of risk. Knowledge of this investor's risk preferences is necessary before we can make any statements about the investor's preferred portfolio.

Because indifference curves represent investors' risk preferences, let us include in our analysis indifference curves that might represent this investor's risk preferences. Figure 8–7 contains the indifference curves superimposed over the efficient frontier. (For simplicity, we henceforth will drop the remainder of the feasible set from view

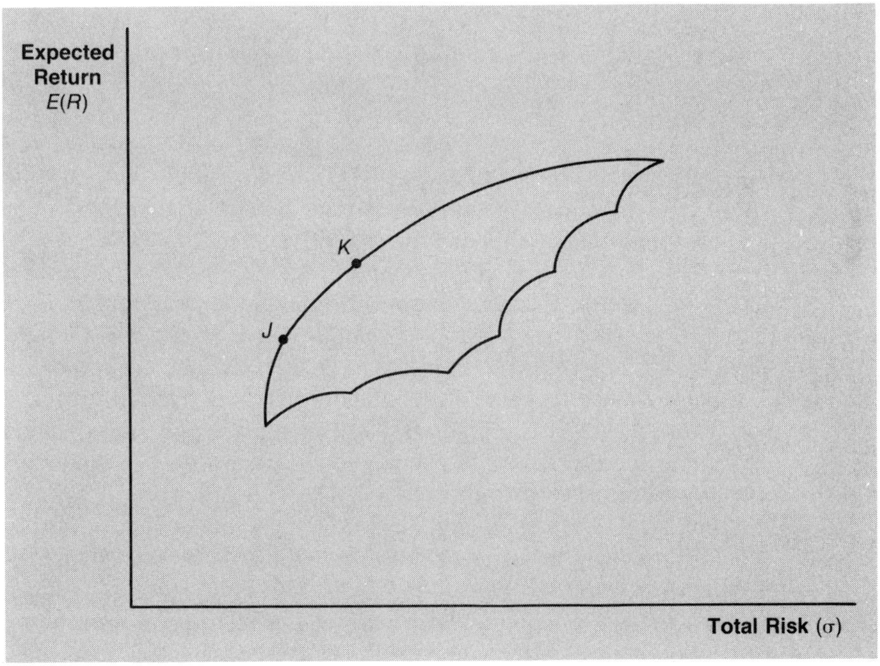

FIGURE 8–6
Possible portfolio choices on the efficient frontier

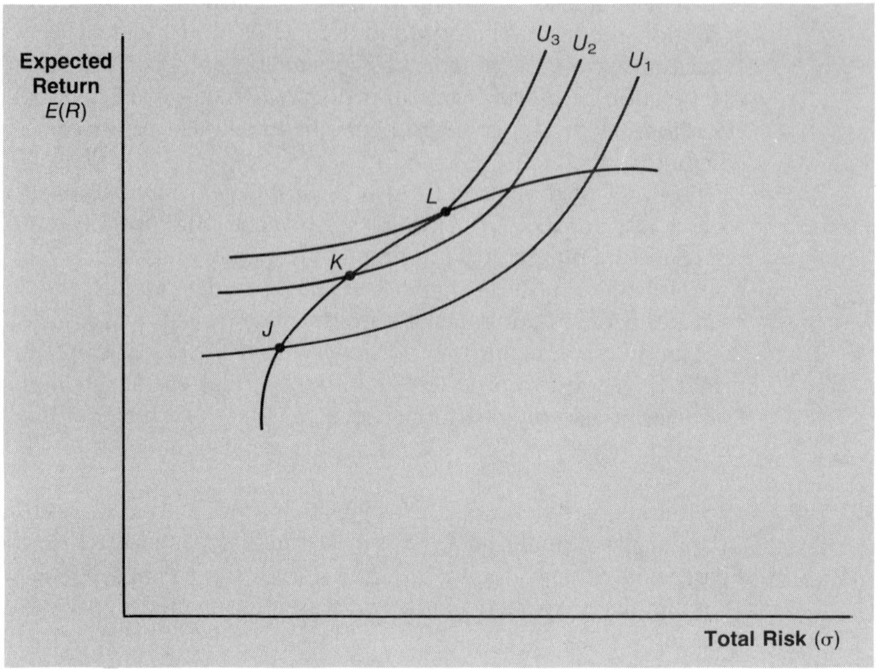

FIGURE 8–7
Indifference curves and the efficient frontier, making possible identification of the preferred portfolio

in the plots.) With the inclusion of this investor's utility map, composed of indifference curves U_1, U_2, and U_3, we can now reach some conclusions regarding which of the efficient portfolios the investor would prefer. Indeed, this investor would prefer portfolio *K* over portfolio *J* because *K* lies on indifference curve U_2, which lies above curve U_1. Curve U_2 represents a higher utility than curve U_1.

To find the best portfolio for an investor, we need to identify the portfolio lying on the highest possible indifference curve. Graphically, this indifference curve will be the one just tangent to the efficient frontier. The point of tangency identifies the *preferred portfolio.* In Figure 8–7, this would be portfolio *L* on indifference curve U_3. For this investor, portfolio *L* would be the investment alternative that maximizes expected return within the investor's risk constraints and yields the highest possible utility. While investors probably do not go through this type of formal analysis to determine their desired levels of risk and return, it is likely that they combine subjective judgments with formal analysis to make some rational decision. In doing so, investors may act *as if* they had gone through the formal indifference curve analysis procedure.

Notice that the efficient set is determined by what is available in the market at any given time—the expected risk-return trade-off of every possible investment or combination of investments. The frontier may change over time, but the feasible set of investment opportunities at any moment is always the same for every investor.

Utility preferences, however, are investor-specific. This is the reason why investors will choose to array themselves along the length of the efficient frontier. Of course, two individuals with identical risk profiles may select identical portfolios of assets, but it is a basic tenet of capital market theory that the optimal portfolio is a function of both individual risk-return preference and available asset combinations.

DEVELOPMENT OF THE CAPITAL MARKET LINE

The previous section showed the identification of the efficient set and the preferred portfolio within the efficient set. However, the portfolios within the feasible set all contain only risky securities. This section explores the effects of the introduction of a riskless asset on the opportunity set of investment alternatives.

Combining the Risk-free Asset with Risky Portfolios

If the definition of risk is the variability of returns, then a risk-free asset is one that offers absolutely certain returns. If such an asset exists, it can be used in combination with other assets. Since a risk-free return cannot be perfectly correlated with the returns on risky assets, the inclusion of a riskless asset in a risky portfolio has some additional risk-reducing benefits for the portfolio. The positive return with zero risk improves the overall risk-adjusted performance of a portfolio. Just how does this occur?

The expected return on a portfolio of two assets is simply the weighted average of the two returns:

$$E(R_p) = w_i \times E(R_i) + (1 - w_i) \times E(R_j) \qquad \textbf{(8–1)}$$

where $E(R_p)$ = the expected return on the portfolio of i and j
w_i = the proportion of the portfolio invested in asset i
$1 - w_i$ = the proportion of the portfolio invested in asset j
$E(R_i)$ = the expected return on asset i
$E(R_j)$ = the expected return on asset j

The expected risk of a two-asset portfolio is not a simple weighted average, because this computation must also take into account the correlation of returns between the two assets. As discussed in Chapter 7, the expected variance is generally expressed by the following formula:

$$\sigma_p^2 = w_i^2\sigma_i^2 + (1 - w_i)^2\sigma_j^2 + 2w_i(1 - w_i)r_{ij}\,\sigma_i\sigma_j \qquad \textbf{(8–2)}$$

where σ_p^2 = the variance of the portfolio
σ_i = the standard deviation of returns on asset i
σ_j = the standard deviation of returns on asset j
r_{ij} = the correlation of the returns on asset i with asset j

If the two assets are the risk-free asset R_f and risky portfolio j, Equation 8–2 becomes:

$$\sigma_p^2 = w_{Rf}^2\sigma_{Rf}^2 + (1 - w_{Rf})^2\sigma_j^2 + 2w_{Rf}(1 - w_{Rf})r_{Rf,j}\sigma_{Rf}\sigma_j \qquad \textbf{(8–3)}$$

where w_{Rf} = the portion of the portfolio invested in the risk-free security
σ_{Rf} = the standard deviation of the risk-free security
$r_{Rf,j}$ = the correlation of the returns on the risk-free security with the returns on portfolio j

By definition, the variance of a riskless asset must be zero (i.e., $\sigma_{Rf}^{2\,2} = 0$). Therefore the standard deviation (the square root of the variance) must also be zero (i.e., $\sigma_{Rf} = 0$). Any product that includes either of these factors must be zero, so the formula for the variance of a portfolio containing the risk-free asset reduces to:

$$\sigma_{pr}^2 = (1 - w_{R_f})^2\sigma_j^2 \tag{8–4}$$

where σ_{pr}^2 = the variance of returns on a portfolio containing the riskless asset.

The standard deviation is the square root:

$$\begin{aligned}\sigma_{pr} &= \sqrt{(1 - w_{Rf})^2\sigma_i^2} \\ &= (1 - w_{Rf})\sigma_i\end{aligned} \tag{8–5}$$

This is a linear function. The standard deviation of a portfolio that combines risky assets with a risk-free component increases linearly with the proportion of the risky assets in the combined portfolio.

Since the expected return for such a combined portfolio is also a linear function, the potential risk-return combinations are represented by a straight line between the portfolio alone and the riskless asset alone. Figure 8–8 shows this relationship. It reveals the combinations of risk and return available by investing various proportions of available funds in the risk-free asset and portfolio J.

The Capital Market Line: An Optimal Set

It is possible to attain any point along line $R_f J$ by investing part of the portfolio in the risky assets included in J and the rest in the risk-free asset R_f. Doing this is obviously beneficial. Every portfolio along a segment of the efficient frontier of portfolios of risky assets (below J) is dominated by some point along line $R_f J$. For each point on the efficient frontier to the left of J, there is some point on line $R_f J$ directly above with equal variance but higher expected return.

Even the line $R_f J$ does not contain the best attainable risk-return combinations. Combinations of the riskless asset and portfolio K would yield a line that dominates line $R_f J$. Figure 8–9 illustrates how points on $R_f J$ are dominated by points on $R_f K$. For every point on $R_f J$, there is a point on $R_f K$ where a mean-variance rational investor would prefer to be. The same applies to portfolios K, L, and M.

Ultimately the single best line is the one just tangent to the efficient set, intersecting at point M. This choice creates a "portfolio possibility line" that dominates every other point along the efficient frontier. The line in Figure 8–9 beginning at R_f and tangent to the efficient frontier at portfolio M is the highest line possible that still touches the frontier. It represents the combinations of the risk-free asset and portfolio M that yield the highest attainable return for each level of risk. All rational investors will seek to position themselves along this line.

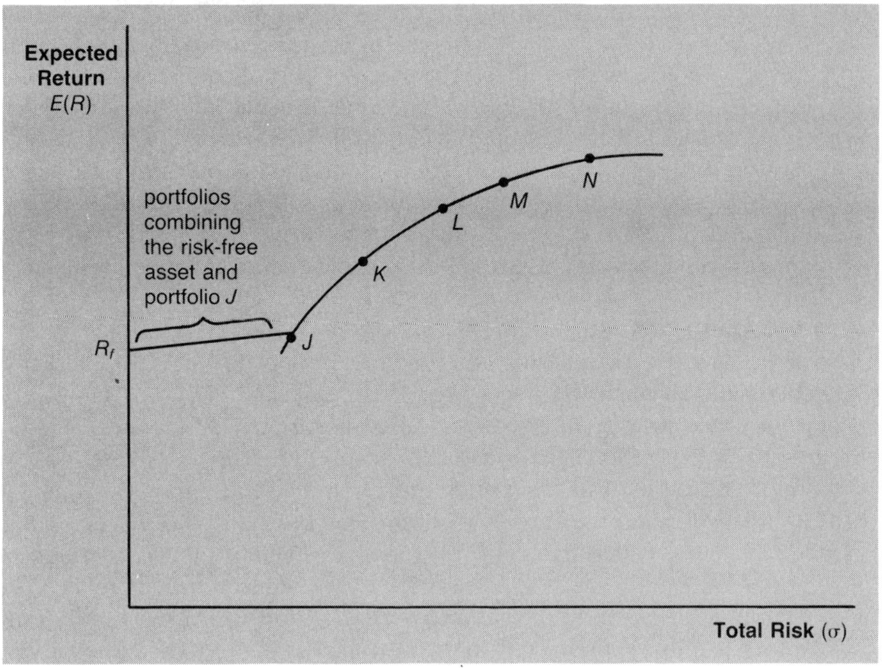

FIGURE 8–8
Risk-return combinations possible by investing in the risk-free asset and in portfolio *J*

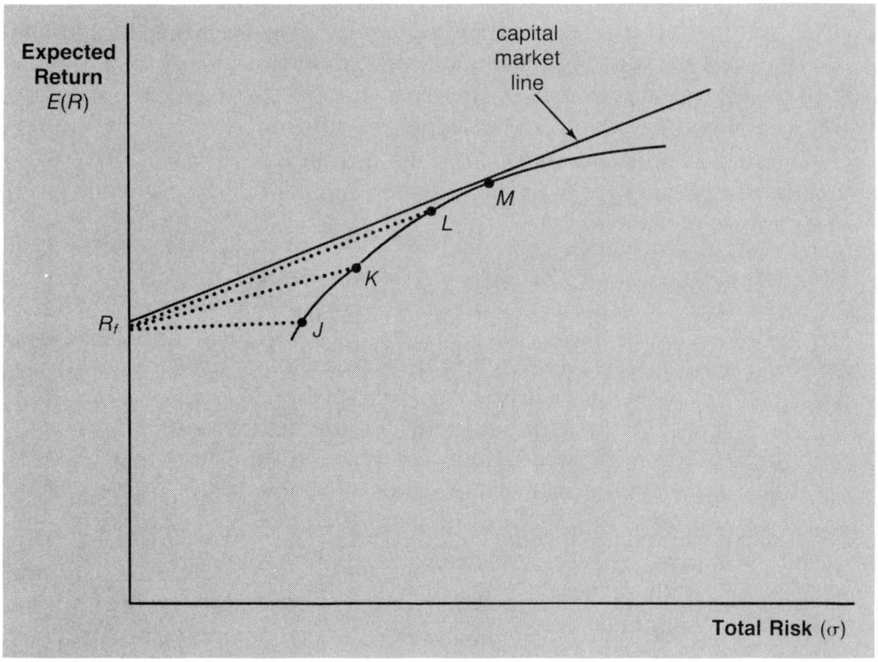

FIGURE 8–9
Risk-return combinations possible by investing in the risk-free asset and either portfolio *J, K, L,* or *M*

Every point along the efficient frontier of portfolios of risky assets is dominated by some point on line $R_f M$ except for point M itself. This line therefore effectively becomes the new efficient frontier. We can call this line an *efficient frontier of portfolios of risk-free and risky assets.* This line represents the equilibrium relationship between expected return and total risk of an investment. It is the *Capital Market Line (CML).* The *Capital Asset Pricing Model* provides a formal framework for the value of investments (capital assets) in a world with characteristics that meet its nine assumptions.

The Market Portfolio

Portfolio M must include all risky assets in proportion to their market value. This encompasses all classes of assets: securities, real estate, art, gold, stamps, and anything of value. The portfolio must contain all assets because all investors will want to own part of this portfolio. For an asset to be excluded, it must have no demand and therefore no value. If an asset were represented in too great or too little proportion to its relative value, the forces of supply and demand would act to adjust its price until its value equaled its proportionate share. This is all a consequence of the assumption of equilibrium: the price of every asset must correctly reflect its true value.

Portfolio M is called the *market portfolio.* In a CAPM world, the only portfolio investors would be interested in is portfolio M. If the total value of all IBM stock represented .53 percent of the value of all capital assets in the economy, .53 percent of portfolio M's value would be in IBM stock. Because portfolio M contains all of the risky assets in the economy, it is completely diversified. The unique risk of any one asset is perfectly offset by the risk or variability of the rest of the portfolio. Thus only systematic risk remains—the macroeconomic factors that affect the value of all assets. Even with perfect diversification, this element of risk remains. It can be measured by the standard deviation of returns from the market portfolio. The level of systematic risk can change over time as the macroeconomic factors affecting asset values change, but it is always present to some degree.

Having identified portfolio M as the market portfolio, we can define the mathematical specification of the CAPM relationship. Since the CML is linear, the formula is as follows:

$$E(R_j) = R_f + \left[\frac{E(R_m) - R_f}{\sigma_m}\right]\sigma_j \qquad \textbf{(8–6)}$$

where
$E(R_j)$ = the expected return on portfolio j
R_f = the riskfree rate
$E(R_m)$ = the expected return on the market portfolio
σ_m = the standard deviation of returns on the market
σ_j = the standard deviation of returns on portfolio j

Equation 8–6 states that the expected return on a portfolio j is equal to the riskless rate plus an expression representing the premium for risk. This premium for risk is equal to the product of the *market price of risk* (the expression within brackets) and the risk of the portfolio. The market price of risk is the extra return on a risky portfolio, over the riskless rate, per unit of risk of the risky portfolio. The intercept of the CML is at the riskless rate, and the slope is the market price of risk.

Example 8–1 provides a sample use of the CML to estimate the expected return on a portfolio. Although it is possible to use the CML to estimate the return on a portfolio, the difficulty of computing a portfolio's standard deviation points to one of the difficulties in applying the CML. For example, as Chapter 7 mentioned, it is impractical to try to compute the standard deviation of a portfolio containing more than just a few securities.

EXAMPLE 8–1

Mr. Charles Meade owns a diversified portfolio of securities, which he estimates to have a standard deviation of .37. The return on short-term T-bills is .09, and Mr. Meade estimates the expected market return to be .14 and the market standard deviation to be .28. What is the expected return on Mr. Meade's portfolio according to the CML?

$$E(R_p) = .09 + (.14 - .09)\frac{.37}{.28}$$

$$= .09 + .066$$

$$= .156$$

Indifference Curves: The Preferred Portfolio Mix

Suppose an investor's initial optimal location along the old efficient frontier was point L. This combination of return and variance resulted in the greatest measure of satisfaction, or the greatest utility. If this individual could obtain higher returns without increasing risk, he would certainly do so. With the introduction of the risk-free asset as an alternative investment, the investor could construct portfolio B on line $R_f M$, which would offer superior utility compared to portfolio L.

As in the case of the efficient frontier of portfolios of risky securities, investor risk preferences dictate the ultimate desired combination of risk and return. Using indifference curves to represent risk preferences, Figure 8–10 locates the *preferred portfolio mix,* which shows the desired risk-return combination for the investor. To achieve this combination, the investor would place a portion of the available funds in portfolio M and the remainder in the riskless asset.

Borrowing and Lending Portfolios

Note that to achieve portfolio B, the investor buys portfolio M and purchases the risk-free security. The investor's purchase of the risk-free security is a loan to the risk-free borrower at the riskless rate. Because of this, portfolio B is a *lending portfolio.* Figure 8–11 defines the region of lending portfolios in the CAPM.

What about less risk-averse investors? What if an investor's optimal portfolio had been at point X, beyond point M? Obviously no combination of investment in R_f and M will dominate this alternative. But remember one of the assumptions behind capital market theory: investors can borrow or lend at the risk-free rate. Thus it is possible to add *leverage* to a portfolio by borrowing at the risk-free rate and investing the proceeds in the assets represented by M. Since the expected returns of M exceed the risk-free rate, this will generate positive net returns. The relationship between risk

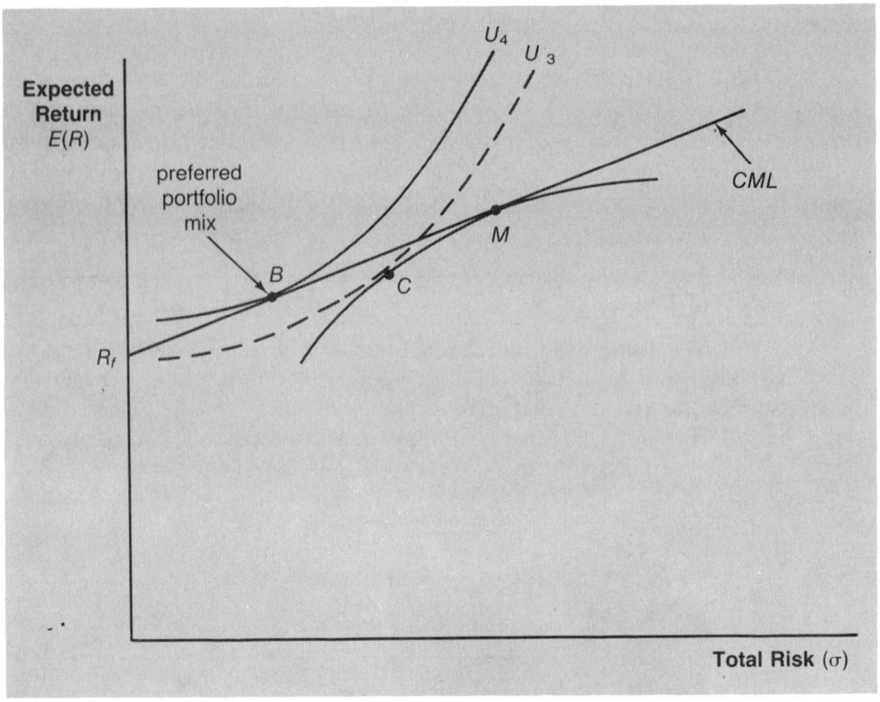

FIGURE 8–10
The Capital Market Line with the preferred portfolio mix identified with indifference curves

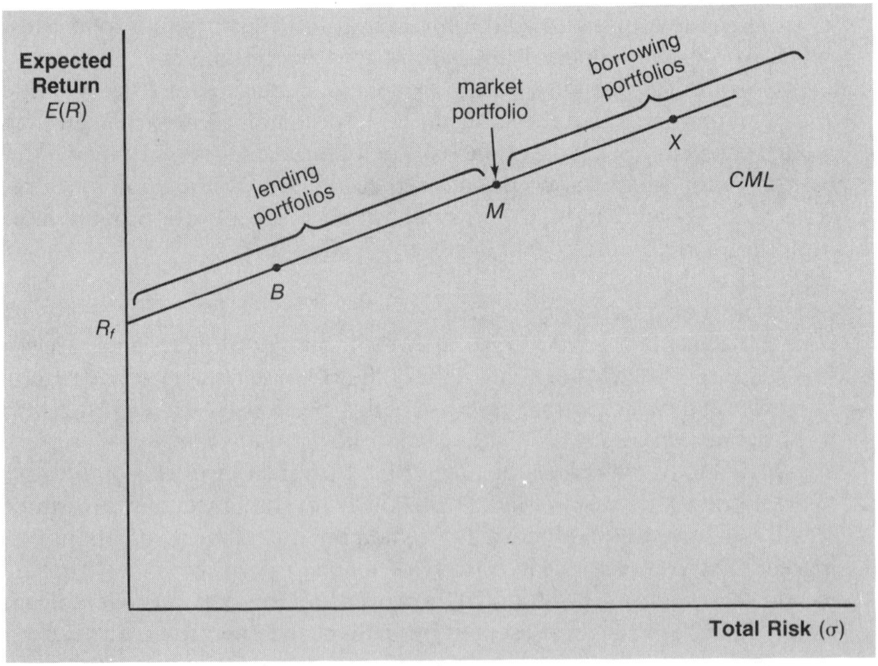

FIGURE 8–11
Borrowing and lending portfolios

and return remains linear, so the marginal returns from additional risk are constant rather than diminishing. The use of leverage enables an investor to increase returns above those that would ordinarily be expected (at a given level of risk) without the presence of a riskless asset. Therefore, we can refer to such a portfolio as a *borrowing portfolio.* As Figure 8–11 shows, the borrowing portfolios lie to the right of the market portfolio.

THE SECURITY MARKET LINE

The Capital Market Line depicts the equilibrium relationship between expected return and total risk. However, it is valid only for efficiently diversified portfolios. Its use in practice is limited to efficient portfolios. Although most investors hold diversified portfolios, it is likely that they are not efficient portfolios in the strict sense. In addition, the CML provides no information about the relationship between expected return and risk for an individual security. If the concept of the CAPM is to be useful for security selection or other applications to individual securities, we must find an avenue to bring individual securities into the framework.

Recall that Chapter 7 demonstrated that the relevant risk for portfolios and for individual investments is systematic risk. This risk is relevant for a portfolio even if the portfolio is not perfectly diversified. Since an individual security is definitely not diversified, systematic risk is also the appropriate representation of risk for individual securities. We can now show how the CAPM can be recast into the relationship between the expected return on a portfolio or individual security and its systematic risk.

The measure of systematic risk of a security is its covariance with the other securities in the portfolio to which the security is being added. In CAPM theory, the benchmark portfolio against which we measure other portfolios is the market portfolio. To continue this treatment, the relevant systematic risk measure for an individual security is its covariance with the market portfolio.

To express the relationship in terms of systematic risk, we can substitute the covariance of a security of portfolio j for σ_j in Equation 8–6, giving:

$$E(R_j) = R_f + \left[\frac{E(R_m) - R_f}{\sigma_m^2}\right] \text{cov}_{j,m} \qquad \textbf{(8–7)}$$

where $\text{cov}_{j,m}$ = the covariance of the returns on security j with the market portfolio

Note that because the risk of the security or portfolio j in Equation 8–7 is a covariance, the risk of the market portfolio must also be stated in terms of a variance.

At this point, it is useful to break down the covariance into its components, as we did in Chapter 7:

$$\text{cov}_{j,m} = \sigma_j \, \sigma_m \, r_{j,m} \qquad \textbf{(8–8)}$$

where $r_{j,m}$ = the correlation of returns on security j with the market

Substituting Equation 8–8 into Equation 8–7 and rearranging gives:

$$E(R_j) = R_f + \frac{\text{cov}_{j,m}}{\sigma^2_m}[E(R_m) - R_f] \quad \textbf{(8–9)}$$

$$E(R_j) = R_f + \frac{\sigma_j r_{j,m}}{\sigma_m}[E(R_m) - R_f] \quad \textbf{(8–10)}$$

To see that this development is consistent with the CML, note that when j is a perfectly diversified portfolio, its correlation with the market will be 1.0, and Equation 8–10 reduces to the CML of Equation 8–6.

Equation 8–10 presents the expected return on a security as the risk-free rate plus a premium for risk. The premium for risk is equal to the product of the excess expected return on the market and the systematic risk of the security (covariance) relative to the market risk (variance of the market). Chapter 6 introduced this measure of relative systematic risk as beta:

$$\beta_j = \frac{\text{cov}_{j,m}}{\sigma^2_m} \quad \textbf{(8–11)}$$

where β_j = the beta coefficient of security (or portfolio) j

Equation 8–11 again shows beta is equal to the covariance of security returns with market returns divided by the variance of market returns. Substituting Equation 8–11 into Equation 8–10 yields:

$$E(R_j) = R_f + \beta_j[E(R_m) - R_f] \quad \textbf{(8–12)}$$

Equation 8–12 gives the equilibrium relationship between the expected return on a security or portfolio of securities and its systematic risk measured by beta. This relationship is the *Security Market Line (SML).* The graphical representation of the SML is shown in Figure 8–12.

The principal advantages of the SML (Equation 8–12) over the CML (Equation 8–6) are twofold. First, the SML is valid for individual securities and small portfolios as well as for perfectly diversified, efficient portfolios. Second, the SML uses beta to measure the risk of the security, and we have already seen in Chapter 7 that beta is a desirable measure of risk. It is easier to interpret and, for portfolios, easier to calculate than the standard deviation of returns.

Example 8–2 provides an example of the use of the SML (Equation 8–12) to estimate the expected return on a security. In market equilibrium, the expected return on a security is equal to the required rate of return on the security. The SML therefore provides a theoretical framework for estimating the required rate of return. If we know (or can estimate) the variables in the model, then the SML is also useful to estimate expected and required returns in practice. Chapter 15, "Stock Valuation: Techniques of Fundamental Analysis," will use the SML in this context to estimate required rates for common stock.

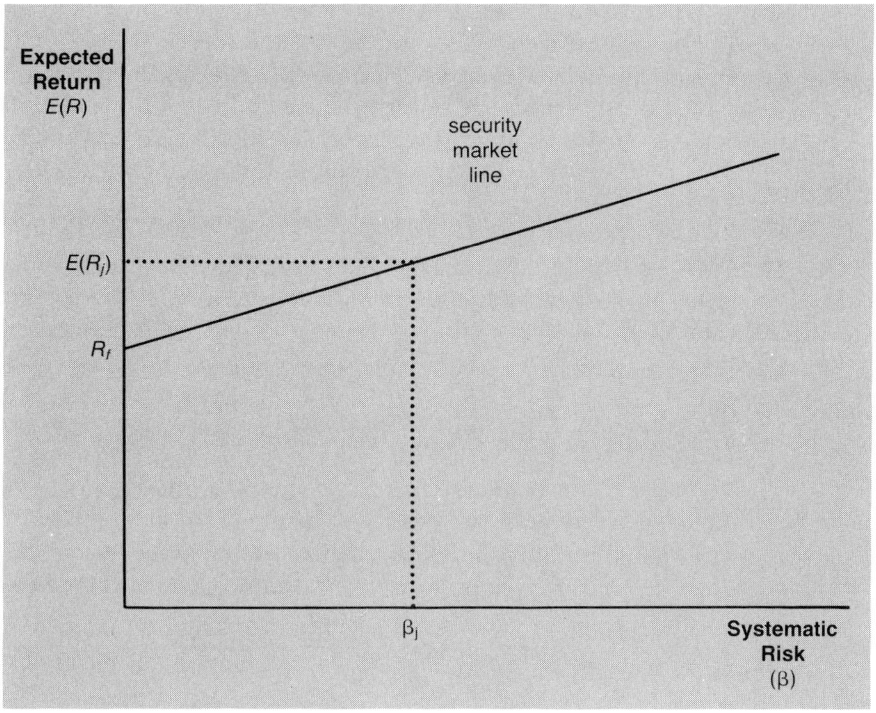

FIGURE 8–12
The Security Market Line

EXAMPLE 8–2

Ms. Pamela Stark is considering the purchase of a stock that has a beta coefficient of .75. She estimates the expected market return to be .12 while T-bills yield .08. What rate should she expect and require on this stock, according to the SML?

$$E(R) = .08 + .75(.12 - .08)$$
$$= .11$$

The SML also provides a framework for fundamental analysis and the selection of individual securities. Fundamental analysts use all the tools at their disposal to seek out and identify securities that are *undervalued,* meaning those which sell for a price that is less than their true value. Using their estimates of a security's true fundamental value, an analyst can estimate its expected rate of return. The analyst would recommend buying an undervalued security because, as the market realizes the true value of the security and bids the price up, the security will realize returns above the level of required returns for that security. In other words, when a security is undervalued, its expected return is greater than its required return. Wait a moment! you might say. We just stated that the expected return on a security is equal to its required rate of return. This is only true *in equilibrium*. But if undervalued securities exist in the market, then they do not sell for their equilibrium price, and the market is not in equilibrium. We can show this graphically using the SML, as in Figure 8–13. Securities *A, B,* and *C* are undervalued because their expected return is greater (lies above the SML) than their required return.

Securities that sell for their equilibrium price would lie directly on the SML. Securities *D* and *E* in Figure 8–13 are examples. Overvalued securities sell for prices greater than their real values and fall under the SML. The securities represented by *F* and *G* in Figure 8–13 are overvalued. An analyst might recommend selling them short.

The Separation Theorem

The CAPM and SML give rise to a very important concept in investments. The CAPM implies that every investor will seek some position along the CML. Obviously the points and portfolios along the graph are purely theoretical representations. No one investor could ever hope to own a portion of all assets, much less in their exact

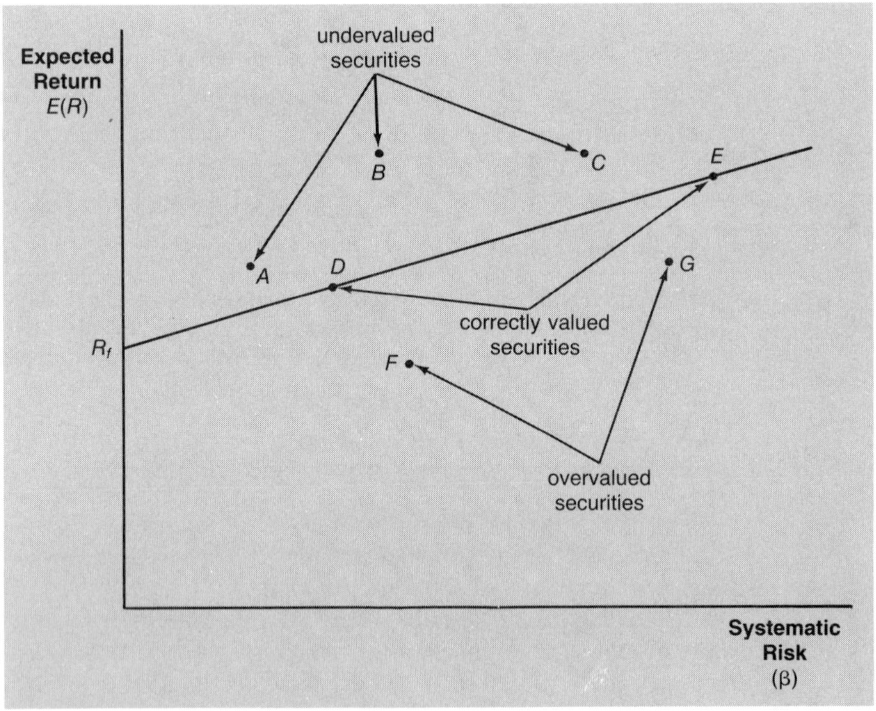

FIGURE 8–13
Overvalued and undervalued securities and the SML

proportions. But the collective behavior of all investors should move toward this state. The aggregate of all risky assets is the market portfolio, and the Capital Market Line represents the best attainable return for every level of risk.

In the context of the CAPM, when a risk-free asset exists, investor risk preferences do not affect the determination of the optimal portfolio of risky assets. Given the existence of the CML, every investor should seek to hold the same portfolio, the market portfolio *M*. Individual investors' risk preferences enter the picture only to determine the amount lent or borrowed at the risk-free rate. Therefore, investors' utility preferences are independent of or *separate from* the choice of an optimal portfolio of risky assets. Very risk-averse investors may prefer to lend some major portion of their assets at the risk-free rate, while those who are willing to take more risk will choose to borrow funds at that rate and invest everything in the market portfolio. This concept is the *separation theorem*.

The important consequence of this idea is that the security selection process can be completely separate from the portfolio management process. Investors cannot in practice purchase the market portfolio, but the SML shows the return that an investor can expect from any security or portfolio. An investor can select securities for a portfolio *without regard to the risk of those securities*. This is the *security selection decision*. Investors can use whatever criteria they believe valid for making their selection. The criteria could be based on fundamental analysis, technical analysis, or efficient markets (random selection).

The investor can then estimate the risk of the portfolio using beta. Having independently identified the desired risk (desired beta) of the portfolio, the investor can take up the task of weighting the portfolio with the risk-free security so that the risk of the combined portfolio of risky and risk-free securities becomes equal to the desired beta. This is the *portfolio management decision*. The separation theorem allows investors to separate the security selection decision from the portfolio management decision by permitting them to take a portfolio of any given risk level and transform it into a portfolio of any other risk level by mixing in the appropriate quantity of risk-free asset.

If an investor knows the beta of the portfolio of risky securities and the desired combined portfolio beta, identifying the portions of funds to invest in the risky securities and the risk-free security is straightforward. The formulas are as follows:

$$w_j = \frac{\beta_d}{\beta_j} \tag{8–13}$$

$$w_{Rf} = 1 - w_j \tag{8–14}$$

where w_j = the portion of funds to invest in risky portfolio j
β_d = the desired beta level of the combined portfolio
β_j = the beta of the portfolio of risky assets
w_{Rf} = the portion of fund to invest in the risk-free asset

If w_j is equal to 1.0, then there is no need to purchase any risk-free security. If w_j is less than 1.0, then the investor buys the risk-free asset and has a lending portfolio.

A w_j greater than 1.0 means that the investor should construct a borrowing portfolio by borrowing an amount equal to w_{Rf} and investing it in the risky portfolio. Example 8–3 illustrates the situation of an investor needing to modify the risk of a portfolio with Equations 8–13 and 8–14.

EXAMPLE 8–3

Mr. Charles Meade has $10,000 to invest. He is a fairly conservative person, so he sets a target beta for his portfolio of 0.8. He then proceeds to analyze stocks and select them based on his analysis. After careful analysis, he arrives at a group of eighteen stocks with mean beta of 1.6. Determine how he can weight his portfolio to reach his risk target.

$$w_j = \frac{.8}{1.6}$$
$$= .5$$

Mr. Meade should invest half of his money, $5000, in the portfolio of stocks. He should invest the other half in T-bills or some other appropriately low-risk security such as a money market fund.

The concepts introduced and developed in the CAPM, the SML, and the separation theorem are often grouped into the term *modern portfolio theory (MPT)*. Adherents to MPT espouse the use of beta to measure risk and to construct portfolios. They often go to great lengths and consume large amounts of computer time to estimate betas scientifically and to apply the principles of the CAPM and diversification to the management of portfolios.

A major consequence of the separation theorem has been to elevate the position of portfolio managers. At one time, portfolio managers may have been thought of as "financial interior decorators" whose job was to match investments to investors' risk preferences. For example, the only investments considered appropriate for conservative investors were highly rated bonds and very conservative stocks. However, with MPT, it is possible to transform a portfolio of very risky securities into a conservative portfolio by adding the risk-free security. This gives portfolio managers a much freer hand to use a wide variety of securities in balancing the portfolio to achieve a desired level of risk.

RELAXING THE CAPM ASSUMPTIONS

It should be obvious that a number of the assumptions upon which the CAPM rests do not strictly represent what we observe in the real world. This section will examine the effects on the CAPM of relaxing some of these assumptions.

The Existence of a Risk-Free Asset

Although we typically use the rate of return on a very short-term, highly liquid, safe security such as U.S. T-bills to represent the risk-free rate, in reality there may be no perfect riskless asset. Even if we assume that there is absolutely no default risk or marketability risk with T-bills, they are still subject to purchasing power risk or interest rate changes.

One alternative to requiring the existence of a risk-free asset has been proposed by Fisher Black.[5] Black stated that there are no truly risk-free assets, only *minimum-risk assets*. Although these minimum-risk assets may have a very small degree of risk, they are still not completely risk-free. Black proposed that the CAPM could still be valid by using the rate on a *zero-beta portfolio* instead of a risk-free asset. The zero-beta portfolio would have no systematic risk and no correlation with the market. Zero-beta portfolios are possible when we include short selling in the portfolio. For example, a common strategy using stock options is to establish a zero-beta option position by buying stock and selling short a call option. (Appendix 17–A provides an explanation of this technique.) The Capital Market Line resulting from Black's zero-beta return substituted for a risk-free asset would have a slope somewhat less than the slope of the standard CML.

The Ability to Borrow and Lend at the Risk-Free Rate

If we accept the existence of a risk-free asset, then it is difficult to dispute the assumption that investors can lend at the risk-free rate. Lending at the risk-free rate is a simple matter of buying the risk-free asset. However, borrowing at the risk-free rate is probably not possible except for very few—if any—investors. Most investors may find it possible to borrow at a rate slightly above the risk-free rate. For example, the prime lending rate is usually a point or so above the T-bill rate, and the rate on margin loans at brokerage houses is a point or so above prime.

Assumptions of different borrowing and lending rates affect the slope, intercept, and linearity of the CML. As an example, assume that all investors can lend at one rate and borrow at another rate that is above the lending rate. This situation would lead to a situation like the CML represented in Figure 8–14.

The CML in Figure 8–14 begins at the riskless lending rate and extends to a point tangent to the efficient frontier. The borrowing portion of the CML begins at a point tangent to the line extending from the borrowing rate and extends on out. However, a segment of the efficient frontier lies between the two points of tangency. This results in a curved portion of the CML. It also implies that there is not one unique market portfolio, but an unlimited number of efficiently diversified portfolios along this segment.

The Assumption of No Transactions Costs, Taxes, or Other Market Imperfections

Regarding the assumption of no taxes, if differential tax rates exist for capital gains and dividend income, then different securities may appeal to investors in different tax brackets (although current U.S. income tax law makes no provision for different tax rates on capital gain and other income). Brennan[6] has shown that differential tax rates still lead to a linear CML, but with a slightly different slope and intercept than the standard CML.

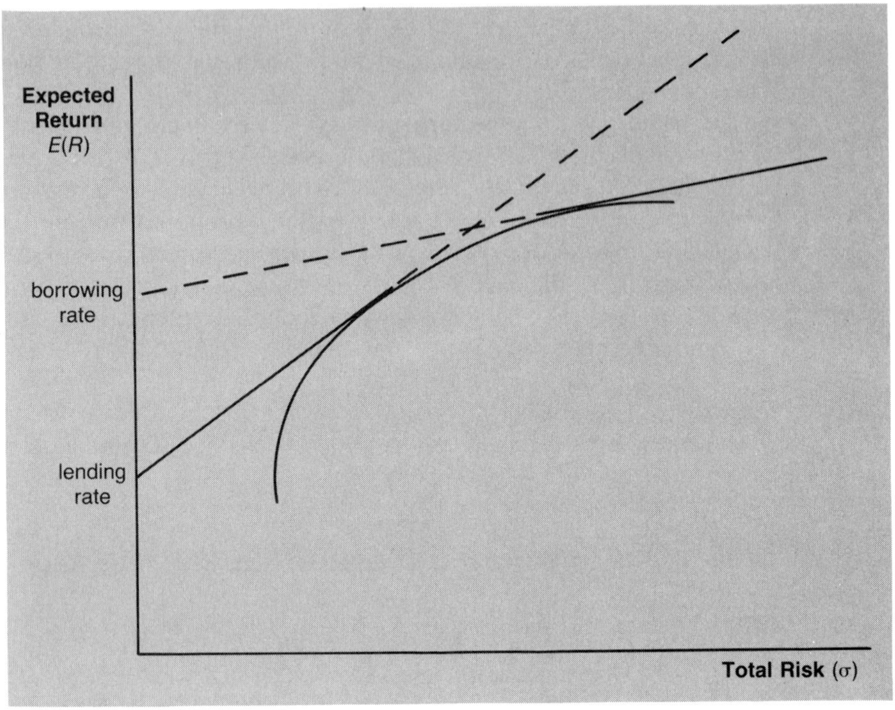

FIGURE 8–14
A Capital Market Line with different borrowing and lending rates

TESTS OF THE CAPM AND SML

In view of the restrictive nature of some of the assumptions behind the CAPM, and considering that investors may not act according to the behavioral assumptions, the question of the validity of the model becomes important. We cannot observe the model in an ideal, experimental state that meets the assumptions. We therefore can address the merit of the model only by empirical methods using real-world data.

This empirical procedure allows consideration of two important general questions.

1. Is the Capital Asset Pricing Model a good description of the observed relationship between risk and return in the financial markets?
2. Is the CAPM a useful tool for predicting the return on an investment given its level of risk?

Many empirical studies have addressed these two questions and the many additional questions that each encourages. This section will briefly summarize a few of these studies. The controversy over the empirical validity of the CAPM has continued since the introduction of the model. Although the debate is yet unresolved, it is possible to draw some general conclusions about the model.

Tests of the Slope and Intercept

Since investors should consider systematic risk rather than total risk in forming portfolios, empirical tests of the CAPM usually utilize the SML relationship. This first group of studies attempts to estimate empirically the SML relationship to see whether the slope and intercept are as theory would have us expect.

Although the SML (Equation 8–12) is an *ex ante* model, if the model is valid, then investors' expectations about the future should, on average and in the long run, be realized. Therefore, the model should be useful for examining the *ex post* relationship between historical returns and observed risk. Stated on an *ex post* basis, the SML becomes:

$$\bar{R}_j = \hat{\alpha}_j + \hat{\beta}_j(\bar{R}_m - \bar{R}_f) \qquad \textbf{(8–15)}$$

where $\bar{R}_j$ = the mean realized return on a security or portfolio j

$\bar{R}_f$ = the mean risk-free rate

$\bar{R}_m$ = the mean realized market return

$\hat{\alpha}_j$ = the estimated intercept of the SML

$\hat{\beta}_j$ = the estimated historical risk of security or portfolio j

Regression can be used to estimate the coefficients of Equation 8–15 for each security or portfolio in a sample. The average of these estimates then forms the general observed SML relationship. Different researchers use variations of this procedure, but they all use some process for using historical data to estimate the SML (CAPM) relationship over a particular time period.

Early studies conducted by Douglas[7] and by Miller and Scholes[8] began to raise concerns about the CAPM. Douglas's study examined the risk-return relationship on a sample of more than 600 individual stocks for various periods between 1926 and 1960. His results showed that the intercept and the actual riskless rate over the period of the study were not equal. Miller and Scholes reexamined Douglas's and other studies. Although they concluded that measurement errors and statistical problems relating to the use of individual stock returns could have caused Douglas's results, they still could find little concrete evidence to support the CAPM.

To minimize the problems caused by using individual stocks, Black, Jensen, and Scholes[9] used returns on diversified portfolios of NYSE stocks for the 1931–1965 time period. They found that the relationship between returns and risk for the portfolios in the study conformed to a linear relationship as in the CAPM. The intercept, however, was significantly greater than the average risk-free rate for the period, implying that the CAPM did not completely define the risk-return relation for the time period of the study. This return greater than the riskless rate for the no-systematic-risk level led Black to develop the zero-beta CAPM.

Other studies have followed these early studies. The generalized conclusions tend to agree with Black, Jensen, and Scholes that the SML zero-risk return tends to be greater than the rate on T-bills (in contradiction to the CAPM) and that the relationship between risk and return seems to be linear (as predicted by the CAPM).

Beta as a Measure of Risk

The SML implies that beta is the only relevant measure of risk, whether for individual securities or for portfolios. Empirical tests of the model tend to confirm this. Beta appears to be the best measure of risk for explaining average returns. This tends to support the CAPM.

While beta appears to be the best *single* measure of risk, there are other measures of risk that do seem to impart additional information to investors about the riskiness of a security. These measures are the *skewness* and *kurtosis* of the distribution of returns. Skewness is the tendency of a distribution to have more than normal observations in the left (or right) side, and kurtosis is the tendency to have more observations in the middle (or tails) of the distribution. Since using only the standard deviation assumes a normal distribution, its use as a risk measure would not capture the same information available in the skewness or kurtosis.

CAPM Tests: A General Consensus?

Unfortunately, no general consensus exists regarding the status of the CAPM as an acceptable model for asset pricing and the risk-return relationship. The empirical tests of the model do find many similarities between the relationship predicted by the model and observed risk and returns. On the other hand, there are a number of important conflicts that at least lead one to question the model.

APPLICATIONS OF THE CAPM

There do appear to be a sufficient number of researchers and practitioners who believe in the model to have developed a body of applications for it. One of the main uses of the CAPM is to estimate the required rate of return on a security. If we know the riskless rate, an expected market return, and the appropriate systematic risk (beta) of a security, a straightforward application of the SML is to compute the expected rate of return. In terms of required return, an investor should require a return at least as great as the equilibrium expected return. Therefore, the expected rate of return is the required rate of return.

In a similar fashion, the SML can provide required rates of return for capital budgeting problems in corporate financial management. The only change is that the appropriate beta must represent the systematic risk of the capital investment project under consideration.

There are several applications in the area of the evaluation of investment performance. Chapter 22, "Evaluation of Investment Performance," deals with this topic.

CRITICISMS OF THE CAPM AND MODERN PORTFOLIO THEORY

As with any model whose validity cannot be confirmed to a high level of satisfaction, several criticisms have been made of the Capital Asset Pricing Model and the beta-based modern portfolio theory that has evolved from it. One group of criticisms centers upon the assumptions underlying the model. These critics contend that since the real world does not match the set of ideal assumptions, the CAPM cannot describe capital markets in the real world.

A second criticism relates to the stability of betas. Even if betas are good measures of systematic risk, if they change through time and are unstable, the validity of their actual *use* as historical risk measures is questionable. Perhaps more important, if betas are unstable, then the use of betas to predict future systematic risk, and hence to predict future required rates of return, is even more questionable. Empirical research shows the betas of individual securities to be quite unstable over time, while the betas of portfolios become more stable as the portfolios become larger. Some studies even show beta to change in a predictable fashion, such as regressing towards a value of 1.0 over time (for example, Blume[10]). Based on this, researchers have proposed various methods to adjust betas so that they will provide better estimates of the future systematic risk of the security (or portfolio).[11]

A third criticism also relates to beta. Although tests of the CAPM tend to show that beta is not a perfect measure of systematic risk, beta usually does a decent job of explaining returns, on average, over a longer period of time. For short-term returns—over a few weeks or months, or even a year—beta is usually not a reliable estimator of systematic risk.

A fourth group of criticisms comes from the work of Richard Roll.[12] The main thrust of Roll's criticisms of the CAPM and the tests of the model is that it is not possible to observe the market return. In theory, the market portfolio is composed of a proportional share of all of the assets in the economy. In addition to stocks and bonds, this includes investments in assets such as real estate, rare stamps, diamonds, and gold—in short, every possible investment. Since it is not possible to construct such a market portfolio, CAPM tests and applications typically use the return on some broadly based index of stock returns, such as the S&P 500. Roll contends that such proxies for the market portfolio are not good enough and produce imperfect estimates of the risk-return relationship observed in the market. To illustrate his point, Roll shows that if someone estimates the SML relationship twice, each time using a different market index, the results will yield two different SMLs.

ALTERNATIVES TO THE CAPM

In spite of the problems inherent in the CAPM and the criticisms leveled against it, the CAPM is probably the most generally accepted and applied model of asset pricing. However, there are alternatives to the standard CAPM. This section presents two ways to approach the association between risk and return in a market.

Stochastic Dominance

The first is not an asset pricing model, but it provides an alternative technique for determining dominance. Recall that the basis for dominance in the development of the CAPM is the mean-variance criteria. The main restriction of the mean-variance criteria is that they require that asset returns be normally distributed so that the variance is a complete representation of an asset's risk. (These criteria also require that individual utility functions be quadratic with negative second derivative—in other words, a specific form of diminishing marginal utility of wealth.)

Another set of rules for discriminating between risky alternative investments is the *stochastic dominance criteria*. These have the advantage that they rely upon neither a particular mathematical form of utility function nor a particular distributional form of returns. These rules consider *every point* on assets' distributions to determine dominance, not just the mean and variance. There are fairly convincing arguments that hold that stochastic dominance rules offer superior criteria on which to base investment decisions.

There are three levels of stochastic dominance; each is based upon a progressively stronger assumption about investors' utility functions.

1. *First order stochastic dominance* assumes investors prefer more to less.
2. *Second order stochastic dominance* assumes investors prefer more to less and that they are risk-averse.
3. *Third order stochastic dominance* assumes investors prefer more to less, that they are risk-averse, and that they have decreasing absolute risk aversion.

As an example, consider first order stochastic dominance. Figure 8–15 shows hypothetical distributions of returns for several securities. Note that although the

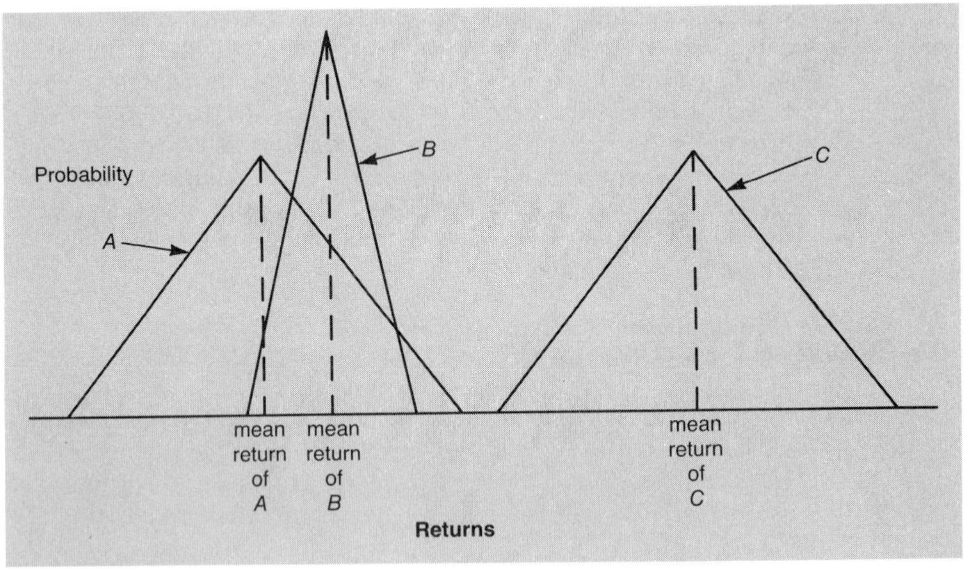

FIGURE 8–15
Example distributions of returns for determining first order stochastic dominance

distributions are similar to normal distributions, they are not normal. Comparing distribution *A* to distribution *B* using mean-variance criteria would result in *B* dominating *A* because *B* has an obviously higher mean and lower variance. However, application of first order stochastic dominance criteria would yield no dominance. Note that there are points in the right tail of *A* in which the investor would have higher return than on any point on *B*. Because first order stochastic dominance assumes only that investors always prefer more to less, under some circumstances *A* is better, and under others *B* is better. Therefore, no dominance exists. On the other hand, on all points on distribution *C*, the investor is better off than anywhere on distributions *A* or *B*. *C* therefore dominates *A* and *B* according to the first order criteria. To apply first order stochastic dominance criteria in practice, it is necessary to compare two investments' cumulative probability functions, not their probability distribution functions as in Figure 8–15. The formal statement of the first order stochastic dominance criteria is: if the cumulative probability of *A* is never greater than the cumulative probability of *B* (and *A* is strictly less than *B* on at least one point), then *A* dominates *B*. The rules become more complex for higher order stochastic dominance.

Although stochastic dominance may be theoretically superior to mean-variance selection criteria, it has several drawbacks. For example, there is no accepted procedure for forming portfolios of securities using stochastic dominance. Another serious problem is that the sampling characteristics of stochastic dominance can lead to errors.

Arbitrage Pricing Theory (APT)

Stephen Ross[13] has proposed an alternative model, which is challenging the CAPM as the prime asset pricing model in financial theory. Ross's model, called *arbitrage pricing theory (APT),* is based on the *law of one price,* which states that two assets that are the same or are perfect substitutes for one another must sell for the same price.

APT is a more general model than the CAPM because it does not rely on a mean-variance assumption; instead, it replaces the mean-variance assumption with an assumption regarding the process that generates investment returns. APT states that asset returns are linearly related to a set of indexes. Each index represents a factor that influences the return on an asset or security. These factors could be any number of things, such as government fiscal policy, interest rates, the price of oil, or foreign exchange rates. In addition, a particular factor might influence all securities, some securities, a small group of securities, or even just one security. APT does not specify what these factors are, only that they exist.

The set of factors that linearly generates individual security returns yields an APT model as follows:

$$R_i = \alpha + \sum_{j=1}^{k} \beta_{ij} \times I_j \qquad \textbf{(8–16)}$$

where R_i = the return for security i
α = the expected return on security i if all indexes are zero
k = the number of factors that drive the arbitrage pricing process

β_{ij} = the sensitivity of security i's returns to index j

I_j = the value of index j, which influences the return on security i

Equation 8–16 gives the return on a security as a function of the index of k different factors. Ross also argues that market participants develop expectations about the values of each β_j. They will buy and sell securities in the market so that, according to the law of one price, securities affected equally by the same factors will have equal expected returns. This buying and selling is the arbitrage process, which determines the prices of securities. Since this depends upon expectations, Equation 8–16 can also be stated in terms of expected returns.

In essence, the CAPM is a special case of APT. It is the case that would result if the single common factor affecting all security returns were the return on the market portfolio. With only one factor, Equation 8–16 reduces to the SML, where α is the riskless rate.

APT has several theoretical advantages over the CAPM. First, APT requires no assumptions about the distribution of security returns or investors' utility functions. The CAPM assumes that returns are normally distributed and investors have a specific form of risk-averse utility function. The second advantage is that APT does not require investors to have homogeneous expectations as does the CAPM. Third, APT does not require the existence of a mean-variance efficient market portfolio.

The principal disadvantage of APT is that it identifies neither the number nor the definition of the factors that influence security returns. These questions have been relegated to empirical work. There is ample room for empirical work that addresses the identification of the APT factors and which tests the validity of APT. The studies that have been reported generally find that there are at least several factors influencing security returns and that APT is a valid pricing model.

SUMMARY

All investors seek to maximize their total utility. A set of indifference curves forms a utility map, which is useful for studying investors' risk preferences. Higher indifference curves represent higher levels of utility. We assume that investors are risk-averse, meaning that they will take on additional risk only if promised correspondingly higher levels of return. The principle of diminishing marginal utility of wealth leads to the conclusion that all investors with such utility functions must be risk-averse.

According to the mean-variance criteria, investment A dominates investment B if A has higher expected return and a level of risk that is no greater than B. By plotting the dominant investments in risk-return space, we can identify the set of investments that are not dominated by any other investment. This is the mean-variance efficient set or efficient frontier of portfolios of risky assets. The point of tangency between the efficient frontier and the highest possible indifference curve of an investor will identify the investor's preferred portfolio.

Introduction of a risk-free asset with borrowing and lending at the risk-free rate leads to the Capital Market Line. The CML is a linear relationship between expected return and total risk. It becomes the new efficient frontier. The point of tangency between the CML and the old efficient frontier of risky assets identifies the market portfolio. The market portfolio is a perfectly diversified mean-variance efficient portfolio containing every investment in quantities proportional to their total market value. The tangency point between the highest indifference curve and the CML reveals the investor's preferred portfolio mix.

The investor's preferred mix will be composed of the market portfolio and either borrowing or lending at the risk-free rate. Lending portfolios buy the risk-free asset, while borrowing portfolios are leveraged, borrowing at the risk-free rate and using the proceeds to purchase the market portfolio.

Casting the CML in terms of systematic risk yields the Security Market Line. The SML is the equilibrium relationship between expected return and the systematic risk of an investment.

The separation theorem is a result of the CAPM. It states that the choice of securities to include in a portfolio can be independent of the risk level of those securities. In essence, it separates the security selection decision from the portfolio management decision.

Although the assumptions underlying the CAPM might seem to restrict its validity, many of these assumptions can be relaxed with little effect. The validity of the model has been tested many times at the empirical level. The tests generally show that the CAPM is a fairly good representation of the market. However, there seem to be significant deviations of empirical results from the theory, and the conclusions of many studies are often inconclusive or conflicting. These deviations have resulted in several criticisms of the model.

There are several alternatives to the CAPM approach to asset pricing. Stochastic dominance criteria provide alternative rules to the mean-variance criteria for identifying dominant investments. Arbitrage pricing theory provides a model for pricing assets that relies upon assumptions that are not as strict as those of the CAPM.

IMPORTANT TERMS

arbitrage pricing theory (APT)
borrowing portfolio
Capital Asset Pricing Model (CAPM)
Capital Market Line (CML)
dominate
efficient frontier of portfolios of risk-free and risky assets
efficient frontier of portfolios of risky assets
feasible set
frictionless market
kurtosis (of returns)
law of one price
lending portfolio
leverage
market portfolio
market price of risk
mean-variance criteria
mean-variance efficient set
minimum-risk assets
modern portfolio theory (MPT)
portfolio management decision
preferred portfolio
preferred portfolio mix
Security Market Line (SML)
security selection decision
separation theorem
skewness (of returns)
stochastic dominance criteria
zero-beta portfolio

QUESTIONS AND PROBLEMS

1. Summarize the assumptions underlying the Capital Asset Pricing Model.
2. What are the mean-variance criteria? List their advantages and drawbacks.
3.

Stock	*Expected return*	*Standard deviation*
A	.15	.24
B	.16	.28
C	.12	.20
D	.16	.30
E	.15	.29
F	.14	.25

   Graph the above stocks in risk-return space. Identify the efficient set, assuming that these are the only investments available.
4. Describe and show how the mean-variance criteria lead to an efficient frontier. What is necessary to identify a preferred portfolio for a particular investor along the efficient frontier?
5. Describe and show how the addition of the risk-free asset leads to the Capital Market Line. Explain how indifference curves identify the preferred portfolio.
6. Why does the CML identify one portfolio as the efficient portfolio all investors should be interested in? Describe this portfolio.
7. If all investors are interested in this one risky portfolio, how can investors achieve portfolios of different risk levels? Explain borrowing and lending portfolios.
8. Describe and show the derivation of the Security Market Line from the CAPM.
9. Explain the separation theorem and its importance in modern portfolio management.
10. Summarize how we can relax some of the assumptions underlying the CAPM. What is the effect of relaxing these assumptions?
11. Summarize the conclusions of tests examining the validity of the CAPM.
12. What are the criticisms leveled at the CAPM?
13. Explain first order stochastic dominance. Why would stochastic dominance criteria be superior to mean-variance criteria for determining dominance? What are the drawbacks associated with stochastic dominance?
14. What is arbitrage pricing theory? What advantages might it offer over the CAPM? How does the CAPM relate to APT?

NOTES

1. William F. Sharpe (1964), "Capital Asset Prices: A Theory of Market Equilibrium under Conditions of Risk," *Journal of Finance,* 19 (September), 425–442.
2. John Lintner (1965), "The Valuation of Risky Assets: The Selection of Risky Investments in Stock Portfolios and Capital Budgets," *Review of Economics and Statistics,* 47 (February), 13–37; and John Lintner (1965), "Security Prices, Risk, and the Maximal Gains from Diversification," *Journal of Finance,* 20 (December), 587–615.
3. Jan Mossin (1966), "Equilibrium in a Capital Assets Market," *Econometrika,* 35 (October), 768–783.
4. Robert C. Merton (1973), "An Intertemporal Capital Asset Pricing Model," *Econometrika,* 41 (September), 867–887.

5. Fisher Black (1972), "Capital Market Equilibrium with Restricted Borrowing," *Journal of Business,* 45 (July), 444–455.
6. Michael J. Brennan (1971), "Capital Market Equilibrium with Divergent Borrowing and Lending Rates," *Journal of Financial and Quantitative Analysis,* 6 (December), 1197–1205.
7. George Douglas (1969), "Risk in the Equity Markets: An Empirical Appraisal of Market Efficiency," *Yale Economic Essays,* 9 (Spring), 3–45.
8. Merton Miller and Myron Scholes (1972), "Rate of Return in Relation to Risk: A Reexamination of Some Recent Findings," in *Studies in the Theory of Capital Markets,* Michael Jensen (Ed.), New York: Praeger, 47–78.
9. Fisher Black, Michael Jensen, and Myron Scholes (1972), "The Capital Asset Pricing Model: Some Empirical Tests," in *Studies in the Theory of Capital Markets,* Michael Jensen (Ed.), New York: Praeger, 79–121.
10. Marshall Blume (1971), "On the Assessment of Risk," *Journal of Finance,* 26 (March), 1–10; and (1975) "Betas and Their Regression Tendencies," *Journal of Finance,* 30 (June), 785–796.
11. See, for example, Dan W. French, John C. Groth, and James W. Kolari (1983), "Investor Expectations and Better Betas," *Journal of Portfolio Management,* 9 (Fall), 12–17; and Joe Lavely, Gordon Wakefield, and Bob Barrett (1980), "Toward Enhancing Beta Estimates," *Journal of Portfolio Management,* 6 (Summer), 43–46.
12. Richard Roll (1977), "A Critique of the Asset Pricing Theory's Tests; Part 1: On Past and Potential Testability of the Theory," *Journal of Financial Economics,* 4 (March), 129–176.
13. Stephen A. Ross (1976), "The Arbitrage Theory of Capital Asset Pricing," *Journal of Economic Theory,* 3 (December), 341–360.

SELECTED REFERENCES

Bawa, Vijay S., James N. Bodurtha, M. R. Rao, and Hira L. Suri (1985). "On the Determination of Stochastic Dominance Optimal Sets." *Journal of Finance,* 40 (June), 417–431.

Bey, Roger P., Richard C. Burgess, and Richard B. Kearns (1984). "Moving Stochastic Dominance: An Alternative Method for Testing Market Efficiency." *Journal of Financial Research,* 7 (Fall), 185–196.

Black, Fisher B. (1972). "Capital Market Equilibrium with Restricted Borrowing." *Journal of Business,* 45 (July), 444–455.

Brennan, Michael J. (1971). "Capital Market Equilibrium with Divergent Borrowing and Lending Rates." *Journal of Financial and Quantitative Analysis,* 6 (December), 1197–1205.

Casabona, Patrick A., and Ashok Vora (1982). "The Bias of Conventional Risk Premiums in Empirical Tests of the Capital Asset Pricing Model." *Financial Management,* 11 (Summer), 90–95.

Chen, Nai-Fu (1983). "Some Empirical Tests of the Theory of Arbitrage Pricing." *Journal of Finance,* 38 (December), 1393–1414.

Cho, D. Chinyung, Cheol S. Eun, and Lemma W. Senbet (1986). "International Arbitrage Pricing Theory: An Empirical Investigation." *Journal of Finance,* 51 (June), 313–329.

Dybvig, Philip H., and Stephen A. Ross (1985). "Yes, the APT is Testable." *Journal of Finance,* 40 (September), 1173–1188.

Fama, Eugene F., and James D. Macbeth (1974). "Tests of the Multiperiod Two Parameter Model." *Journal of Financial Economics,* 1, 43–66.

French, Dan W., John C. Groth, and James W. Kolari (1983). "Current Investor Expectations and Better Betas." *Journal of Portfolio Management,* 9 (Fall), 12–17.

Hadar, Josef, and William R. Russell (1971). "Stochastic Dominance and Diversification." *Journal of Economic Theory,* 3 (September), 288–305.

Hawawini, Gabriel, and Vora Ashok (1983). "Is Adjusting Beta Estimates an Illusion?" *Journal of Portfolio Management,* 9 (Fall), 23–26.

Ingersoll, Jonathan E., Jr. (1984). "Some Results in the Theory of Arbitrage Pricing." *Journal of Finance,* 39 (September), 1021–1039.

Jean, William H. (1984). "The Harmonic Mean and Other Necessary Conditions for Stochastic Dominance." *Journal of Finance,* 39 (June), 527–534.

Lintner, J. (1965). "The Valuation of Risky Assets: The Selection of Risky Investments in Stock Portfolios and Capital Budgets." *Review of Economics and Statistics,* 47 (February), 13–37.

Merton, Robert C. (1973). "An Intertemporal Capital Asset Pricing Model." *Econometrika,* 41 (September), 867–887.

Pari, Robert A., and Son-Nan Chen (1984). "An Empirical Test of the Arbitrage Pricing Theory." *Journal of Financial Research,* 7 (Summer), 121–130.

Stein, William E., Roger C. Pfaffenberger, and Dan W. French (1987). "Sampling Error in First Order Stochastic Dominance." *Journal of Financial Research,* 10 (Spring), 259–268.

Trzcinka, Charles (1986). "On the Number of Factors in the Arbitrage Pricing Model." *Journal of Finance,* 41 (June), 347–368.

Wei, K. C. John (1988). "An Asset Pricing Theory Unifying the CAPM and APT." *The Journal of Finance,* 43 (September), 881–892.

CHAPTER 9

Market Efficiency

The concept of an *efficient securities market* has generated controversy over the past couple of decades. Whether a market is efficient or not has implications for several areas in investing. The controversy surrounding the acceptance of the efficient markets hypothesis raises such questions as:

1. Should an investor keep track of past stock prices to predict future prices?
2. Is it worthwhile to pore over financial statements and other financial data to improve investment performance?
3. How profitable is "inside information"?
4. Can investors really "beat the market"?

This chapter presents the various theories of market efficiency, examines the evidence or lack thereof for the existence of efficient markets, and identifies strategies that investors should consider when investing in markets that tend toward efficiency.

EFFICIENT MARKETS

In an efficient market, the prices of all assets traded always reflect all the information available about those assets. This means that in an efficient securities market, the price of a company's stock reflects the information contained in sources such as the following: the firm's financial statements, statements that the news media make about the company, past performance of the company's stock, how the current economic situation will affect the company, and all other possible information that investors might find useful in assessing the investment merits of the stock. The price to which participants in an efficient market will bid the company's stock will be a *fair value.* If a stock is worth \$25, then its price in an efficient market will be \$25. Since, in an efficient market, the market value is equal to the intrinsic value, investors cannot expect to be able to use any of the information available to them to make any above-normal or excess profits on a risk-adjusted basis in that market. Therefore, in an efficient securities market, prices of securities reflect all currently available information, and investors cannot use the information to consistently beat the market.

Why then would prices fluctuate in an efficient market? The answer is that new information constantly becomes available to market participants. Throughout the course of a day, many new bits of information may be released that in some way affect the prospects of a company. This information could have an obvious, direct connection to the future of the company, such as the latest quarterly earnings report or the announcement of a strike settlement. The information could also be something that has an indirect influence on the company's prospects. For example, if the company imports raw materials from western Africa, news of political instability or inclement weather conditions in that region that might eventually affect the supply of the raw materials would probably have some impact upon the market price of the company's securities. Fluctuations of security prices could also be caused by the reevaluation of existing information.

Rationale for an Efficient Market

What would cause a market to become efficient? Assuming that all investors seek to maximize the utility of their wealth, competition will develop among investors wanting to maximize their profits in the market. The most important advantage that one investor can have in the quest for market profits is the possession of information that no one else has about an investment. This causes a race among investors in the market to obtain this information before others obtain it. They will pay close attention to all news releases, dig into the financial condition of the company and analyze all of the information obtained, interview corporate officials and interpret what they hear, and, in short, do everything they can to seek out clues to help them reach an estimate of the "true" value of the firm that the rest of the market does not recognize. When these investors find that the market value of a security approximates its estimated "true" value, they will take no action. However, should the market price deviate from the estimated value, investors who have this knowledge will try to capitalize on it by buying or selling the security in the market.

For example, suppose a company called Macho Manufacturing sells in the market for \$36 per share. A certain group of investors has just completed a study of the company that convinces them the firm's stock is worth at least \$45. They also believe that, sooner or later, other participants in the market will recognize this and the stock will sell for its "true" value. They therefore direct their brokers to purchase Macho for them. As a result of this new demand for Macho's stock, the price quickly begins to rise, and interest in Macho's stock increases among other investors. They immediately begin doing the same types of analyses the original group was doing. At the same time, one of the members of the group tells his brother-in-law about this money-making opportunity. The brother-in-law buys some stock and passes the same information along to several friends who respond accordingly. As this information continues to leak out and as other investors find out the same information, they buy Macho as long as its market price remains below the fundamental value of $45. This demand will drive the price of Macho up until it reaches its equilibrium price of $45—assuming of course that no other new information reaches the marketplace in the meantime.

This is the process that drives security prices toward their "true" values. As investors see this process at work, they realize that to make the most profits, they have to be among those in the first group to recognize that the security is underpriced in the market. This creates a race to be the first to obtain new information and to analyze completely and thoroughly all information at the disposal of investors. The faster people race for new information and react to new information, the faster security prices will begin reflecting the information. As the process speeds up, prices of securities in the market change very rapidly as new information comes available. At the extreme, prices of securities react immediately upon the knowledge of any new information. Such a market would be a *perfectly efficient market;* security prices would immediately and always reflect all available information.

In a perfectly efficient market, therefore, investors would not be able to use available information to make above-normal profits because as soon as any information became known, it would immediately be impounded into the price of the security. Any transaction by the investor would take place at the security's "fair" market value, which reflects all that is known about the security's prospects.

An interesting paradox about the efficient markets hypothesis is that for the market to remain efficient, a significant number of investors must believe that the market is *not* efficient. Their belief that the market is not efficient drives them to seek the information and conduct the analyses that ultimately push security prices to their "true" values and make the market efficient.

Sufficient Conditions for an Efficient Market

For a market to be perfectly efficient, there must be no time lag. That is, no interval of time can elapse between the arrival of new information in the market and the adjustment of prices to reflect that information. Such an interval would allow investors to react to the information and exchange securities before the securities reached their new equilibrium value. For the market to be perfectly efficient, four ideal conditions are sufficient.

1. All investors are *utility maximizers;* they are rational and make investment decisions that will maximize their utility.
2. Investors have *homogeneous expectations* resulting from the availability of information to all individuals at the same time at no cost.
3. Markets are *frictionless,* meaning that there are no taxes, transaction costs, or other barriers to trading.

4. Investors are *price takers;* that is, no individual trader in the market is large enough to affect the price of a security.

Obviously, conditions in modern security markets do not meet all four of the conditions for an efficient market. Note, however, that these are *sufficient* conditions for an efficient market; they are not *necessary*. This means that the market will be efficient if they are met, but they do not have to be met in order for the market to be efficient.

Even though these conditions do not have to exist for a market to be efficient, how close do actual security market conditions come to meeting the hypothetical efficient market conditions? Let us consider each of the four conditions in order.

First, all individuals may not always be expected utility maximizers. This would explain why some people are willing to purchase for $5 a lottery ticket with an expected payoff value of only $3. Such behavior can be termed rational, though, when one considers that the lottery ticket purchaser may receive some utility from the thrill of waiting for the announcement of the winning numbers and checking for the winning number. However, it is probably safe to assume that the vast majority of all investment decisions are expected to result in maximizing investors' utility.

Second, information does come at a cost. Magazines and newspapers charge for their subscriptions, access to the news service databases is for a fee, and other sources of information have either an explicit cost for purchase or an implicit cost associated with collection. Even though this information does cost something, consider the vast amount of information that an investor can receive for a modest price. In fact, an investor who does not want to spend any out-of-pocket dollars can probably find more information than she can possibly analyze at the local public library. Therefore, although information does cost something, its cost is generally not prohibitive. What about all information being available to everyone at the same time? Of course, there are cases in which a member of the board of directors of a company may give inside information to a friend who can profit from it, but the great majority of information is available very quickly, given the current state of electronics and communication. News of an important event can spread over the entire world in a matter of minutes.

Third, we know that there are taxes, commissions, and other market realities that may serve as barriers to trade. For example, an investor may postpone selling at the end of the tax year to shift the tax on the gain into the next taxable year. In this example, taxes are an artificial inducement not to trade. In addition, securities laws restrict trading in certain ways. All of these barriers to free trading could contribute to market inefficiencies. However, if taxes are equitable across groups of investors, and transaction costs are relatively low (as they are in securities markets), then even this condition comes close to being met.

Finally, from time to time we see evidence that some large investor violates the assumption that no individual or institution is large enough to influence the price of a security one way or the other. Sometimes even the rumor that a particular investor who is experienced in takeovers or market maneuvers is accumulating some stock in a company is enough to spark a sudden price change of several points. However, large trades take place every day, even block trades of tens of thousands of shares, with little or no effect on the price of the stock. The ability of the market to absorb these trades with barely a quiver indicates that the system approaches meeting even the fourth condition.

Market Reality: An Economically Efficient Market?

Even without consulting any studies examining the existence of efficient markets, it is difficult after considering the above assumptions to imagine that capital markets are perfectly efficient. On the other hand, it is logical to assume that investors want to maximize profits and will begin a race for information that will lead them to those profits. This brings us to the concept of an *economically efficient market.*

In an economically efficient market, some securities may sell for slightly less than their "real" value while others sell for slightly more. There may be some lag between the time that information reaches the market and the moment that the market prices of securities reflect that information. However, these differences are not large enough for investors to exploit them for above-normal profits, after considering the impact of commissions, taxes, and other costs of investing. In an economically efficient market, no investor can consistently reap excess return in the *long run* after the real costs of investing.

The Long Run and the Short Run

When discussing market efficiency and the possibility of making above-normal profits in the market, it is necessary to emphasize that investors can make excess profits, even in a perfectly efficient market, in the *short run* by chance alone. Such a situation would be similar to the first-time visitor to the horse races hitting it lucky with a few big wins. Obviously this person is no expert horse handicapper, but judged on the performance during one afternoon at the races, it certainly appears that the person knows a lot about horses and racing.

For an example using efficient market notions, consider the following scenario. The SIR (Strike It Rich) Oil Company is drilling its latest oil well. If SIR successfully brings in the well, its stock will be worth $40 per share. Should the effort produce a dry hole, SIR's stock will have a value of $20. Assume that the true probability of the well producing oil is 0.5 and that the market, being efficient, knows this and values the stock at its expected value of $30 per share [.5(20) + .5(40) = 30].[1] Believing that the company will strike oil, Mr. Ed Marquette decides to buy 100 shares of SIR at the $30 market price. Two weeks later, SIR strikes oil, and the market price of its stock promptly rises to $40, giving Mr. Marquette a quick $10 profit.

Is Mr. Marquette a superior investor, achieving excess returns by beating the market? No, he was just lucky. There was an equal chance that he would have been wrong and would have lost $10 per share. Naturally, had the loss occurred, we would not consider him to be an inferior investor; he was just unlucky. Over the long run, Mr. Marquette, investing in other situations with similar probabilities, would win some and lose some, earning profits that would be normal and equitable considering the risks he took.

Suppose that Mr. Marquette was a trained geologist who knew something about the geological formations surrounding the SIR well, and that he had made his investment because he was able to associate a 0.8 probability to the well's success. His estimate of SIR's value would be \$36 [.2(20) + .8(40) = 36]. This information, if correct, would allow Mr. Marquette to invest in SIR with a high degree of confidence that he would profit. Of course, this would not be a perfectly efficient market if Mr. Marquette had and used information unavailable to the rest of the market.

ALTERNATIVE HYPOTHESES OF MARKET EFFICIENCY

We have defined an efficient market as one in which the prices of securities reflect available information. By identifying the available information set that we expect a security's price to reflect, we define the degree of expected efficiency in the market. Market theorists traditionally classify the degree of efficiency in a market into one of three categories. Each category relies on a successively larger set of information that determines security prices. Figure 9–1 represents the universe of total information and the subsets of information that separate the various degrees of market efficiency.

The forms of the efficient markets hypothesis that represent these three levels of efficiency are the *weak form,* the *semi-strong form,* and the *strong form.* As Figure 9–1 indicates, each form, beginning with the weak form, reflects a larger portion of

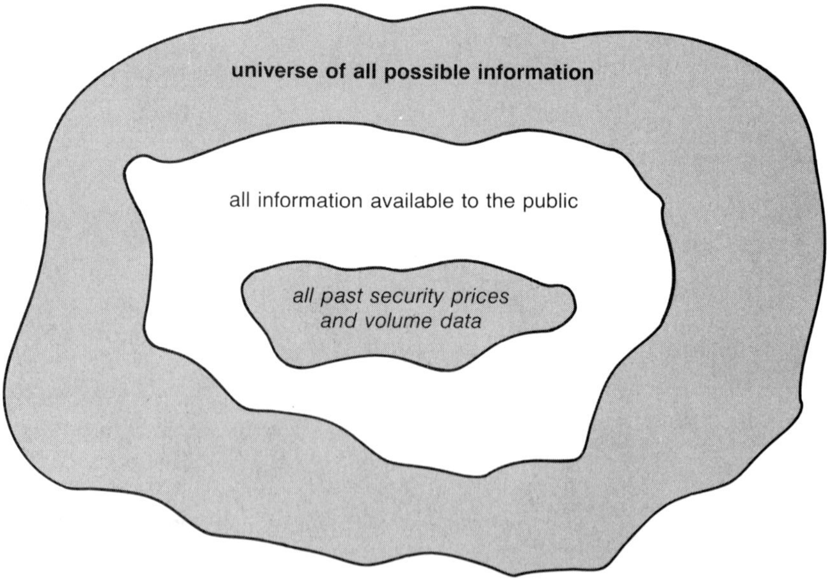

FIGURE 9–1
Sets of information for efficient markets hypotheses

all available information. Each successive form is cumulative—that is, existence of a semi-strong efficient market implies existence of a weak-form market, whose information set is a subset of the semi-strong form's set.

The Weak Form Efficient Markets Hypothesis

The weak form of the efficient markets hypothesis states that the information set that prices of securities in the market reflect is composed of all data regarding the historical market prices and trading volume of securities. Table 9–1 gives examples of the types of information that the weak form represents. It says that all information conveyed in past patterns of a stock's price and volume of trading is currently impounded into the price of the stock. The implication of the weak form is that it is fruitless for an investor to study a chart of the past price patterns of a stock in hopes of determining when to buy and sell the stock.

Existence of a weak form efficient market means that there could be no patterns in security prices (or volume) that repeat themselves over time. Since no patterns or regularities that would allow investors to predict future stock prices from past prices (or volume) could exist, then each price change that occurs in the market would be independent of the previous price change. There could be no dependencies (patterns) that could exist from price change to price change. If successive price changes are independent of each other, then they behave randomly. Because of this, students of market behavior often call the weak form of the efficient markets hypothesis the *random walk theory,* borrowing a term from the physical sciences that describes the motion of a particle moving randomly through its environment.

The Semi-Strong Form Efficient Markets Hypothesis

For the semi-strong form of the efficient markets hypothesis, the information set expands to encompass *all public information.* This information includes both the original raw information about the economy or an individual security and any publicly available analyses or projections made using the raw data. The semi-strong form theorizes that each security's price fully reflects all information contained in the company's financial statements, potential analysis of that information, news releases, economic data, and so forth. Table 9–1 shows some examples of this kind of information.

The existence of an efficient market at the semi-strong level means that investors would have no generally available source of information that could lead them to beat the market. Of course, they could expect to make profits in the market, but these profits would be only a normal amount considering the riskiness of the investments. However, such activities as analyzing financial statements, forecasting company earnings, and following the advice of a popular investment newsletter would not contribute to increased investment profits, and might even lower returns by increasing costs while not adding to profits.

TABLE 9–1
Examples of information reflected in security prices according to the efficient markets hypothesis

Hypothesis	*Example of Information*
Weak form	Yesterday the price of Exxon fell by 1 point. Last month the Dow Jones Industrial Average increased 6%. Volume on the NYSE last quarter reached a record high. General Cigar's price has been trending upward.
Semi-strong form	Last quarter's earnings for Revlon were up 12%. The financial structure of GAF appeared weak. ASARCO's current ratio is 2.1. GNP showed strong growth for the latest quarter. New York analyst forecasts inflation to fall. Auto industry expects strike soon. E. F. Hutton predicts market to rise.
Strong form	Fed chair sees money supply up on day before announcement of money supply change. Company director knows earnings will unexpectedly rise. Field geologist for oil firm finds unexpected prospects.

The Strong Form Efficient Markets Hypothesis

The set of information reflected in security prices in a strong form efficient market is *all* information; this includes everything that is known, whether it is public or private. This form says that the market reflects all inside information in addition to all public information. It also reflects everything that is knowable, anything that a host of investment analysts could possibly uncover using all of their talents and all of the tools at their disposal. Table 9–1 also gives some examples of this type of information.

Under such circumstances, it would be impossible to ferret out any information that is not already discounted in the market price of a security. No investor could achieve consistent above-normal returns in a strong form efficient market over the long run, nor would it be advantageous for anyone to pay for professional investment advice or analysis. Consistently superior performance would be impossible.

EVIDENCE OF MARKET EFFICIENCY

It is readily apparent that it is important to know to what degree our security markets are efficient in actuality. Indeed, the degree of market efficiency should logically influence the direction of study in an investments course as well as the investment strategy implemented by an investor. This section summarizes the important and widely known studies that have addressed the issue of market efficiency.

The question of market efficiency has no easy answer. In fact, as some studies show, much of the evidence is contradictory. Although it would be possible to present only tests supporting market efficiency or those refuting it to prove either side, this section provides an objective cross section of rigorous studies that appear to contain no bias toward either side of the issue. This will allow us to reach some general conclusions about market efficiency, will assist readers in reaching more specific conclusions on their own, and will give those who have an interest in exploring the issue further a knowledgeable beginning.

Research on market efficiency usually approaches the problem by defining a subset of information lying within the set identifying the degree of market efficiency under study. The researcher then usually applies one of the following approaches:

1. Examination of the movement of security prices following the release of the information to see how quickly prices react.
2. Examination of returns to investors who would have had the information to see if they could have made *excess returns*.

Excess returns are those over and above the level that one would normally expect from an investment. Two methods are generally used to test for excess returns. The first is to compare the sample returns to a simple *buy-and-hold strategy*. A buy-and-hold strategy entails purchasing stocks but not trading them, just holding them until the end of the holding period. The second method of testing for excess returns involves adjusting the returns for the investment's risk level (*risk-adjusted returns*) to see if they are significantly positive. If the prices react slowly to the release of information, or if investors who had the information could have reaped excess returns, then the researcher concludes that market efficiency is rejected. Otherwise, the research supports the notion of market efficiency with respect to the information under study.

Weak Form Tests

Tests of the weak form usually fall into one of two categories. The first reflects the "random walk" nature of the weak form by examining time series of security returns for evidence of randomness and the lack of identifiable patterns. The second category tests various trading rules utilizing weak form information to see if investors could have made excess returns using such rules.

Tests of Randomness

Although as early as 1900 a French mathematician named Bachelier suggested that security returns could be random, extensive research on the subject did not become available until the period of the 1960s. Roberts[2] suggested that patterns that investors often claim to see in stock price changes could be duplicated using some mechanical chance device such as a roulette wheel or table of random numbers. Using a random number table, Roberts did just that, producing the simulated market changes shown in the top frame of Figure 9–2. The bottom frame of the exhibit shows actual example price changes of the Dow Jones Industrial Average. Note the similarity between the randomly generated time series and the real one. Using a statistical test called a *runs test,* which explores the likelihood of a given price change being followed by another price change in the same direction (a trend) or in the other direction (a reversal), Roberts found that the number of reversals in price was just about what one would expect to see by chance alone. There appeared to be no significant patterns or trends in the DJIA.

Fama[3] broke the Dow Jones Industrial Average into its thirty components and computed returns and their serial correlation coefficients for each of the thirty stocks for the period from 1957 to 1962. Figure 9–3 shows these correlation coefficients for differencing intervals of one, four, nine, and sixteen days. The starred numbers represent correlations that were statistically different from zero. Since there is only a

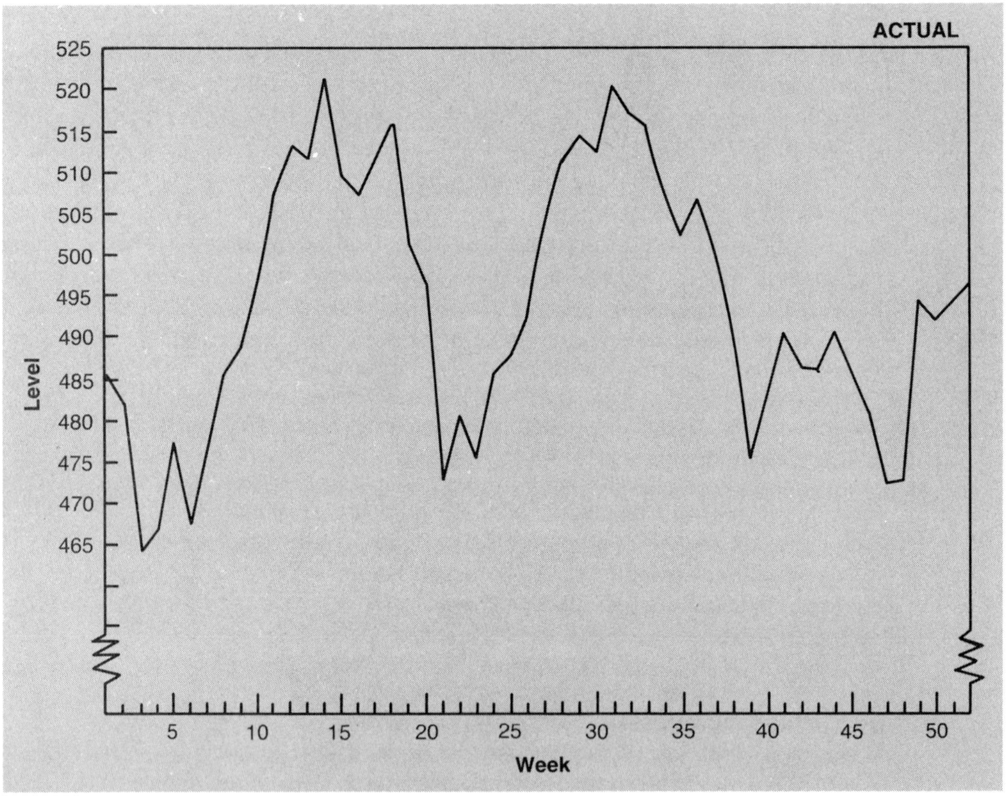

FIGURE 9–2
Simulated and actual market changes for 52 weeks (*Source:* Harry V. Roberts (1959), "Stock Market 'Patterns' and Financial Analysis: Methodological Suggestions," *Journal of Finance,* 14 (March), 5–6. Reprinted by permission.)

scattering of these starred numbers, the number of significant correlation coefficients is not greater than what we would expect from chance alone. For example, the .118 coefficient for Alcoa means that more often than not, a rise followed a rise in the price of Alcoa (and a fall followed a fall) from day to day. It might appear that an investor who knew this would be able to profit by buying Alcoa on a rising day, knowing that it would probably rise again the next day. However, with the daily trading that would result from using the one-day correlations, commissions costs would probably consume any extra profits that might occur. (Of course, the broker would be quite happy.) Note also that for the longer differencing intervals, which would generate fewer trades and less trading costs, the number of starred correlation coefficients declines.

Researchers have conducted numerous other tests to detect randomness in stock prices. Armed with the powerful computers and plentiful security price databases available today, it is possible to produce reams of statistical analyses in relatively little

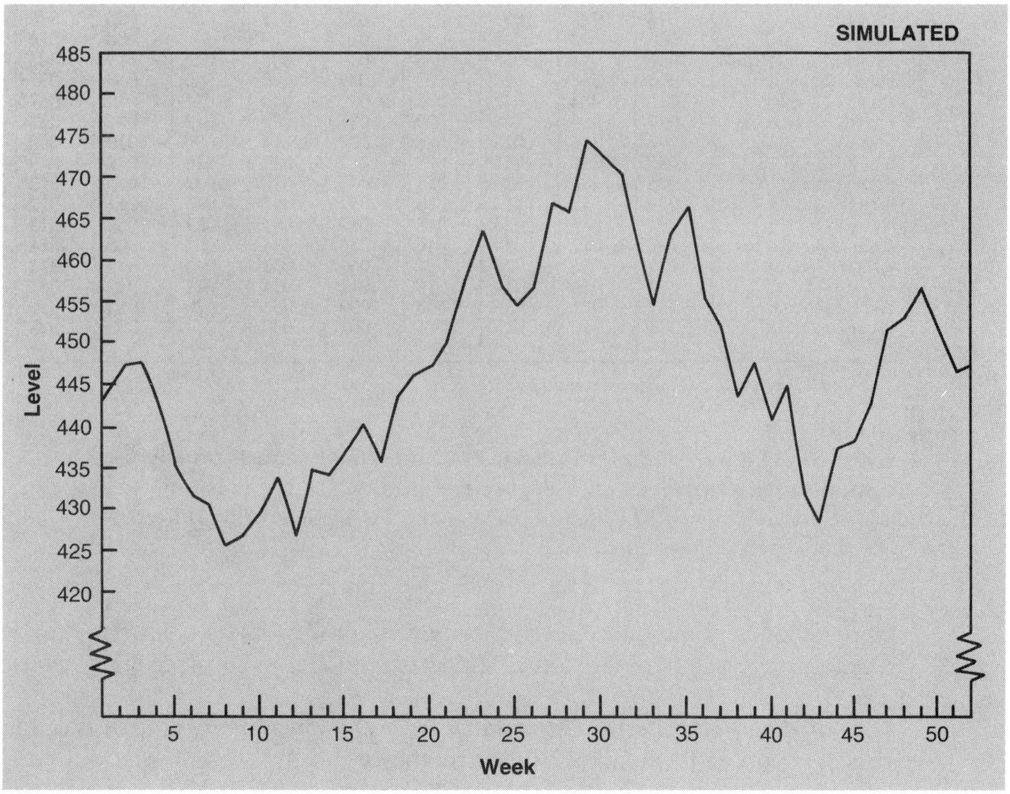

FIGURE 9–2
(continued)

TABLE 10

DAILY SERIAL CORRELATION COEFFICIENTS FOR LAG $\tau = 1, 2, \ldots, 10$

STOCK	LAG									
	1	2	3	4	5	6	7	8	9	10
Allied Chemical	.017	−.042	.007	−.001	.027	.004	−.017	−.026	−.017	−.007
Alcoa	.118*	.038	−.014	.022	−.022	.009	.017	.007	−.001	−.033
American Can	−.087*	−.024	.034	−.065*	−.017	−.006	.015	.025	−.047	−.040
A.T.&T	−.039	−.097*	.000	.026	.005	−.005	.002	.027	−.014	.007
American Tobacco	.111*	−.109*	−.060*	−.065*	.007	−.010	.011	.046	.039	.041
Anaconda	.067*	−.061*	−.047	−.002	.000	−.038	.009	.016	−.014	−.056
Bethlemen Steel	.013	−.065*	.009	.021	−.053	−.098*	−.010	.004	−.002	−.021
Chrysler	.012	−.066*	−.016	−.007	−.015	.009	.037	.056*	−.044	.021
Du Pont	.013	−.033	.060*	.027	−.002	−.047	.020	.011	−.034	.001
Eastman Kodak	.025	.014	−.031	.005	−.022	.012	.007	.006	.008	.002
General Electric	.011	−.038	−.021	.031	−.001	.000	−.008	.014	−.002	.010
General Foods	.061*	−.003	.045	.002	−.015	−.052	−.006	−.014	−.024	−.017
General Motors	−.004	−.056*	−.037	−.008	−.038	−.006	.019	.006	−.016	.009
Goodyear	−.123*	.017	−.044	.043	−.002	−.003	.035	.014	−.015	.007
International Harvester	−.017	−.029	−.031	.037	−.052	−.021	−.001	.003	−.046	−.016
International Nickel	.096*	−.033	−.019	.020	.027	.059*	−.038	−.008	−.016	.034
International Paper	.046	−.011	−.058*	.053*	.049	−.003	−.025	−.019	−.003	−.021
Johns Manville	.006	−.038	−.027	−.023	−.029	−.080*	.040	.018	−.037	.029
Owens Illinois	−.021	−.084*	−.047	.068*	.086*	−.040	.011	−.040	.067*	−.043
Procter & Gamble	.099*	−.009	−.008	.009	−.015	.022	.012	−.012	−.022	−.021
Sears	.097*	.026	.028	.025	.005	−.054	−.006	−.010	−.008	−.009
Standard Oil (Calif.)	.025	−.030	−.051*	−.025	−.047	−.034	−.010	.072*	−.049*	−.035
Standard Oil (N.J.)	.008	−.116*	.016	.014	−.047	−.018	−.022	−.026	−.073*	.081*
Swift & Co.	−.004	−.015	−.010	.012	.057*	.012	−.043	.014	.012	.001
Texaco	.094*	−.049	−.024	−.018	−.017	−.009	.031	.032	−.013	.008
Union Carbide	.107*	−.012	.040	.046	−.036	−.034	.003	−.008	−.054	−.037
United Aircraft	.014	−.033	−.022	−.047	−.067*	−.053	.046	.037	.015	−.019
U.S. Steel	.040	−.074*	.014	.011	−.012	−.021	.041	.037	−.021	−.044
Westinghouse	−.027	−.022	−.036	−.003	.000	−.054*	−.020	.013	−.014	.008
Woolworth	.028	−.016	.015	.014	.007	−.039	−.013	.003	−.088*	−.008

* Coefficient is twice its computed standard error.

FIGURE 9–3
Serial correlation coefficients for 1, 4, 9, and 16-day continuously compounded returns (*Source:* Eugene F. Fama (1965), "The Behavior of Stock-Market Prices," *Journal of Business* 38 (January), 72. © 1965 by the University of Chicago. Reprinted by permission.)

time. Although some of the tests document slight deviations from randomness, the general consensus of these studies supports randomness in security price changes.

Tests of Trading Strategies Using Stock Price Data. Although the tests of randomness do support the random walk hypothesis and the weak form of the efficient markets hypothesis, it is still possible that certain patterns could exist in stock prices that tests of serial correlation and randomness would not detect. The way to test for such patterns would be to identify them and then see if a trading strategy using those patterns would yield the investor excess returns. The use of charts and patterns in past stock prices in an attempt to forecast future stock prices forms the set of stock trading strategies called *technical analysis*. Therefore, any test of technical analysis of stock prices is also a test for weak form market efficiency. Chapter 16 of this text discusses technical strategies in more detail.

Tests of Filter Rules. We can generalize *filter trading rules* as follows:

1. Determine a percentage to serve as a "filter."
2. When the security's price increases by the filter percentage over its previous low point, buy the security.
3. When the price falls by the filter percentage from a high point, sell the security (or sell it short).

For example, suppose we set a 10 percent filter as our decision point. If a stock that we follow rises 10 percent from its previous low price, say from 20 to 22, our rule would indicate a buy signal. If our stock rose to a high of 30 and then began falling, a sell signal would arise when the stock fell by 10 percent from the high of 30, to 27. Filter rules generate easily identifiable buy and sell signals and therefore provide good tests of a security trading strategy based on price patterns.

Fama and Blume[4] computed returns to various filter percentage trading rules. Figure 9–4, summarizing their results, shows that most of the filters produced disappointing returns, especially after considering commissions. These results lead to a conclusion of a weak form efficient market. Even the apparent existence of several filters (.12 to .25) with positive returns does not refute a weak form efficient market for at least two reasons. First, the annualized returns were small, less than rates available on savings accounts during the time period. Second, as Jensen and Bennington[5] mention, "patterns" seem to exist even in series of random numbers, and given enough computer time, a person could find a trading rule that "works" on a table of random numbers if allowed to test the rule on the same table of random numbers. The implication is that any trading rule that appeared to work on past price data should also be tested using future data when they come available.

Tests of Stock Seasonality. If stock prices showed seasonal patterns, then such information might suggest that the market is not efficient according to the weak form. For example, if the stock of H & R Block showed annual price increases around April 15 (tax time), we could consistently profit by purchasing the stock at the beginning of the income tax season and selling it by the end of April. Because of seasonal revenue patterns, many companies' earnings exhibit repeating seasonal earnings patterns. Do their stock prices show the same patterns? A study of seasonal stock price patterns by Hadaway and Rochester[6] indicates the existence of only minor seasonality in common stock prices and thus provides support for the weak form of market efficiency.

Semi-Strong Form Tests

Since the semi-strong form of market efficiency hypothesizes that security prices reflect all public information, tests of that form single out certain subsets of public information

TABLE 2

NOMINAL ANNUAL RATES OF RETURN BY COMPANY: AVERAGED OVER ALL FILTERS

Security	Average Returns Adj. for Divds.		Breakdown of Col. (1)		Average Returns	Buy and Hold Returns not Adj. for Comm.		Profitable Filters/ Total Filters: Adj. for Divds.	
	Not Adj. for Comm. (1)	Adj. for Comm. (2)	Long (3)	Short (4)	Not Adj. for Divds. or Comm. (5)	Adj. for Divds. (6)	Not Adj. for Divds. (7)	Not Adj. for Comm. (8)	Adj. for Comm. (9)
Allied Chemical	−.0079	−.2371	.0486	−.1453	−.0221	.0712	.0384	9/23	4/23
Alcoa	.0664	−.1388	.0744	.0627	.0643	−.0064	−.0224	13/24	4/24
American Can	−.0489	−.3022	.0052	−.1347	−.0639	.0507	.0061	9/22	6/22
Amer Tel. & Tel.	.1410	.0581	.2156	−.0727	.1221	.1824	.1484	21/21	17/21
Amer. Tobacco	.1095	−.0491	.1706	−.0724	.0814	.1704	.1307	18/23	12/23
Anaconda	−.0170	−.3091	.0398	−.1069	−.0255	.0540	.0125	8/23	4/23
Beth. Steel	−.0459	−.3214	−.0100	−.1282	−.0733	.0283	−.0266	7/23	3/23
Chrysler	−.0609	−.3695	−.0598	−.0643	−.0645	.0017	−.0311	8/23	2/23
Dupont	.0512	−.0164	.1135	−.0605	.0431	.0889	.0348	20/22	12/22
Eastman Kodak	.0757	−.0649	.1786	−.1761	.0653	.1756	.1555	21/22	12/22
General Elec.	−.0125	−.1963	.0394	−.1079	−.0237	.0576	.0285	9/23	1/23
General Foods	.1740	.0103	.2780	−.0621	.1607	.2509	.2283	23/23	12/23
General Motors	−.0581	−.3420	.0337	−.1868	−.0708	.0956	.0500	7/21	1/21
Goodyear	−.0538	−.3501	.0179	−.1942	−.0731	.0843	.0467	10/23	2/23
Int. Harvester	−.0274	−.3474	.1020	−.2624	−.0410	.1677	.1192	7/21	6/21
Int. Nickel	.0776	−.0843	.1517	−.0895	.0632	.1395	.1104	20/22	7/22
Int. Paper	.0167	−.1654	.0346	−.0178	.0026	.0193	−.0238	13/23	2/23
Johns Manville	−.0576	−.3577	.0157	−.2302	−.0707	.0878	.0497	7/23	5/23
Owens-Illinois	.0056	−.1584	.0763	−.1401	−.0010	.0958	.0679	12/22	10/22
Procter & Gamble	.1847	.0480	.2736	−.0459	.1720	.2193	.1966	23/23	15/23
Sears	.1903	.0069	.2772	−.2014	.1735	.2396	.2154	22/22	16/22
Std. Oil (Calif.)	−.0756	−.3405	.0018	−.1911	−.0915	.0748	.0302	3/22	0/22
Std Oil (N.J.)	−.0818	−.3020	−.0314	−.1670	−.0963	.0432	−.0033	2/22	0/22
Swift & Co.	−.0542	−.3793	−.0028	−.2098	−.0623	.0553	.0095	4/22	1/22
Texaco	.0605	−.1516	.1828	−.3054	.0410	.1710	.1349	16/20	4/20
Union Carbide	.0649	−.0335	.0909	−.0031	.0533	.0421	.0133	18/23	9/23
United Aircraft	−.1117	−.4478	−.0459	−.1500	−.1166	.0578	.0066	1/24	0/24
U.S. Steel	.0264	−.1622	.0467	−.0433	.0135	.0303	−.0087	18/24	7/24
Westinghouse	−.0186	−.2804	.0177	−.1164	−.0305	.0610	.0338	9/24	7/24
Woolworth	.0414	−.1491	.1296	−.2158	.0267	.1472	.1080	16/22	10/22
Average	.0185	−.1978	.0822	−.1279	.0032	.0986	.0620	12.5/22.5	6.4/22.5

FIGURE 9–4

Trading profits from filter trading rules (*Source:* Eugene F. Fama and Marshall Blume (1966), "Filter Rules and Stock-Market Trading," *Journal of Business,* 39 (January), 234. © 1966 by the University of Chicago. Reprinted by permission.)

and examine how quickly security prices adjust to account for that information. If prices adjust slowly enough for informed traders to reap above-normal profits, then the market is not efficient regarding that information; otherwise, the market appears efficient.

Practically an infinite number of subsets representing semi-strong form information exist. Because of this, the number of studies questioning this form of market efficiency has become quite large. We will consider several representative groups of these tests. The first contains a set of studies asking how the market responds to information in corporations' announcements of their earnings. The second group is a sampling of tests utilizing other subsets of semi-strong information.

Tests Using Earnings Announcements

One of the most useful areas of information to security analysts is earnings. The release of a firm's earnings report usually receives adequate attention in the financial press, and investors and financial analysts seem to immediately begin to interpret and act upon the implications of each release of new earnings. Therefore, several tests of the semi-strong form of the efficient markets hypothesis examine earnings announcements and their impact on stock prices. Table 9–2 summarizes a sample of these studies.

The studies of earnings have generally, with a few exceptions, tended to reject the notion of a semi-strong efficient market. They usually show that there appears to be some time lag between the announcement of a company's earnings and the time that the market price of the company's stock fully reflects those earnings, especially when the announced earnings show an unexpectedly large change. Some of the studies indicate that investors using information from reported earnings could have achieved some degree of excess returns.

The results of these studies have generated much controversy. Some researchers have criticized the studies on the basis of a contaminated sample or inadequate statistical methods, thus questioning their conclusions. The earlier studies have been especially subject to such critical comment. However, similar results rejecting market efficiency have persisted in more recent studies that attempt to rectify the shortcomings of the earlier studies. Although opinions vary, there do appear to be some obvious exceptions to an efficient market with respect to the information available from earnings.

Tests Using Other Semi-Strong Form Information

In addition to earnings announcements many other types of information are implied in semi-strong efficient markets. Table 9–3 identifies some of these areas and summarizes the results of the studies. As the table shows, some studies provide support for the semi-strong form while others do not. These conflicting conclusions provide more fuel to the controversy over the existence of efficient markets.

As an example of conflicting results and controversy, consider several studies regarding information from the announcement of stock splits. A stock split occurs when a company awards additional shares to its current shareholders. For example, a company announcing a two-for-one stock split will give each stockholder one additional share for each share currently owned, so that each investor has two shares for each previous share. Since this is a financial event only and has nothing to do with the production efficiency and earnings of the firm, some analysts claim that a stock split should have no impact on shareholders' returns. On the other hand, others hypothesize that the announcement of a split imparts information to investors that

TABLE 9–2
Summary of studies using earnings announcements to test for a semi-strong form efficient stock market

Authors of Study[a]	*Set of Information Examined*	*Summary of Findings*	*Support for the Semi-Strong Form*
Basu	Annual earnings reports of 753 companies, 1956–1969	Ranking stocks by their price-to-earnings ratio into quintiles resulted in the low quintiles yielding positive risk-adjusted excess returns.	Does not support
Brown	Price changes of 158 stocks following large quarterly earnings changes, 1968–1971	Significant price trends lasting up to 45 days follow large earnings changes; the market appeared to digest the new information slowly rather than adjust quickly.	Does not support
Jones, Rendleman, and Latane	Standardized unexpected (unforecasted) quarterly earnings announcements of 1503 companies, 1971–1980	Although the market seems to anticipate unexpected earnings changes somewhat, a substantial adjustment in the stock's price also occurs over time after the earnings announcement.	Tends not to support
Jones and Litzenberger	Quarterly earnings announcements that would tend to identify stocks that would be big gainers or big losers	Buying stocks that announced relatively large earnings gains would have yielded high profits.	Does not support
Joy, Litzenberger, and McEnally	Return performance of 96 stocks around their quarterly earnings announcement dates	Stocks with highly favorable earnings announcements generated large post-announcement rates of return.	Does not support
Litzenberger, Joy, and Jones	Quarterly earnings announcements of 261 stocks, 1962–1969	Sorting the stocks by the earnings-to-price ratio identified stocks that yielded higher returns.	Does not support
Patell and Wolfson	Price reactions of actively traded stocks to earnings and dividend announcements	Stock prices tended to adjust about completely to announcements within five to ten minutes after the announcement.	Support
Watts	Forecasted and actual quarterly earnings per share for 73 firms	There were significantly positive excess returns continuing up to 39 weeks after a favorable earnings announcement.	Does not support

[a]Complete citations for these studies are included in the selected references at the end of the chapter.

TABLE 9–3
Summary of various studies testing for a semi-strong efficient stock market

Authors of Study	*Set of Information Examined*	*Summary of Findings*	*Support for the Semi-Strong Form of Efficient Markets*
Ang, Chua, and Desai	Set of inflation forecasts from 1960–1975	The stock market appeared to adjust fully for expected inflation.	Supports
Bidwell and Kolb	Sell recommendations for NYSE listed stocks by a brokerage firm, 1974–1978	Trading on the recommendations would not have yielded excess returns after commissions.	Supports
Bjerring, Lakonishok, and Vermaelen	Stocks recommended by a brokerage house in its newsletter, 1977–1981	Investors who bought recommended stocks achieved positive abnormal returns even after commissions costs.	Does not support
Brauer	Returns to closed-end investment companies announcing changes to open-ended	Funds announcing open-ending showed excess returns, but these were almost completed by the announcement date.	Supports
Lease and Lewellen	Realized returns by individual investors from NYSE, AMEX, and OTC stocks	Stocks traded on the AMEX and OTC seemed to deviate from their equilibrium prices more often than those on the NYSE.	Does not support (for stocks traded at locations other than the NYSE)
Rosenberg, Reid, and Lanstein	Book value to stock price ratios for 1400 stocks, 1974–1984	Buying stocks with high book-to-price ratios provided average monthly excess returns of .4% (5% annual rate).	Does not support
Smirlock and Yawitz	Changes in the Federal Reserve discount rate, 1975–1982	The stock market's adjustment to discount rate changes occurred by the end of the day of the announcement.	Supports
Stickel	Common stock rating changes by the Value Line Investment Survey for 1172 companies, 1976–1980	The stock prices responded to ratings changes over a multi-day period.	Tends not to support

the company's management expects continued favorable financial performance, and it may increase stock ownership and liquidity because of the lower postsplit per share stock price. Regardless of which position one takes, the announcement of a stock split does represent the release of new information and therefore may be used to test the semi-strong form of market efficiency.

An early study examining stock splits by Fama, Fisher, Jensen, and Roll[7] found that the implications of a stock split appear to be reflected in the price of a stock immediately after the split announcement. They noted that announcements of dividend increases often followed splits, but that the postsplit price of a stock adequately reflected this probability. Trading profits from buying stocks announcing stock splits would therefore be nonexistent, and the study supports the idea of an efficient market. Reilly and Drzycimski[8] tested a strategy of buying stocks announcing splits and found a small degree of profit potential, but they noted that investors following such a strategy would likely be disappointed. Their results were consistent with a semi-strong form efficient market. On the other hand, Grinblatt, Masulis, and Titman[9] extensively examined a sample of stock splits, controlled for any dividend announcement and other effects, to find stock price reactions to splits announcements. Their observation that these reactions extended to the actual effective date of the split is contrary to a semi-strong form efficient market.

In short, there appear to be areas in which stock prices do adequately reflect available information and other areas in which prices seem to be less than efficient. These areas of inefficient stock prices could be "pockets of inefficiency" that astute security analysts could exploit to reap extra profits.

Strong Form Tests

The strong form of market efficiency is probably the most difficult to analyze because it implies that the market discounts all information. However, if the market discounts information that is not public, how can we identify that information to test the existence of the strong form? Since we cannot identify nonpublic information, we test this form of market efficiency by examining the investment success of groups of investors who may have access to this type of information. Three groups who might have access to information not available to others are professional portfolio managers, professional security analysts, and corporate insiders.

Tests of Portfolio Managers

Professional portfolio managers—those who run large mutual funds, pension funds, and trust funds—might be able to obtain information before the rest of the market. Tests examining this issue, though, generally cannot demonstrate that these groups show excess returns over any extended period of time. An early study, by Michael Jensen,[10] examined risk-adjusted returns to 115 mutual funds over a twenty-year period. He found that the funds, on average, were not able to beat a buy-and-hold strategy. He also concluded that there was little evidence that any individual fund was able to do better. Findings of more recent reports tend to support these results. For example, Shawky studied the performance of mutual funds throughout the 1970s and found their return was generally only commensurate with their risk levels. Veit and Cheney found that mutual funds were unsuccessful at trying to predict bull or bear markets.[11]

These results tend to support market efficiency at the strong form level if we believe that portfolio managers have access to information that other market participants do not. On the other hand, if they actually do not have such information, then these are tests supporting the semi-strong form.

Tests of Security Analysts

Another group who might have restricted-access information or early information would be professional security analysts. Through their company contacts and in-depth analysis, they might be able to search out information before others. Results of tests examining security analysts' recommendations are mixed. Some show them to be of value while others indicate that investors would have done at least as well by not following the advice of security analysts. However, the existence of some analysts with successful recommendations does tend not to support market efficiency at the strong form level.

Tests of Corporate Insiders

One final group of investors who might have access to information not available to others is corporate executives and other insiders. For example, Nunn, Madden, and Gombola[12] found that corporate insiders generally make transactions in their securities that have profitable results. They attribute this success to the insiders' access to nonpublic information. In another study, Keown and Pinkerton[13] identified profitable trading by insiders before the announcement of mergers. Generally, these studies contest existence of a strong form efficient market with respect to groups with insider information.

IMPLICATIONS OF EFFICIENT MARKETS

The possibility of the existence of efficient markets and the results and conclusions of the empirical studies addressing the issue have important implications for investment analysts and investors. Obviously, if markets are perfectly efficient at the strong form level, security analysis with the goal of increasing investment profits offers no benefit. For most investors, the same would apply if the semi-strong form exists. As the empirical studies indicate, however, it appears that there are significant inefficiencies at the strong form level and pockets of inefficiency from time to time at the semi-strong form level.

Therefore, it is a challenge to the investor, security analyst, and portfolio manager to locate and exploit these inefficiencies. The framework and tools for accomplishing such a task form the fundamental analysis techniques and security selection strategies discussed in Chapters 10 to 16.

There is some evidence that institutional investors show the ability to forecast price performance. One study by Ambachtsheer[14] surveyed their predictions over a two-year period. The results indicated that the managers showed a consistent ability to identify stocks that would perform in the top groups. The study also showed that portfolios constructed using these forecasts in an optimum manner would have outperformed the market. Unfortunately, many managers fail to act upon their forecasts with the decisiveness of the hypothetical portfolios and only show average performance even though they have the ability to perform well.

To take advantage of periodic inefficiencies that might exist, gain positive long-run returns, and not subject the portfolio to significant possibility of negative returns in any one year, an investor needs a portfolio with as many inefficiently priced securities as possible. How many does this mean? Given that any forecast has a high probability of error, Ambachtsheer[15] suggests that the portfolio should include at least 100 "good" stocks.

INVESTMENT STRATEGIES IN AN EFFICIENT MARKET

Even if security markets are efficient, the study of investments is not useless. Although the existence of perfectly efficient markets would preclude long-run investment returns of an abnormally positive amount, it would still be important for investors to be able to manage the risk of their portfolios for a commensurate level of return. An investment strategy consistent with the existence of efficient markets has several important aspects. Table 9–4 presents an outline summary of the elements of such a strategy. The remaining chapters of this text discuss the individual elements in Table 9–4 and their implementation in an overall investment strategy.

TABLE 9–4
Elements of investment strategy consistent with efficient markets

1. Security and market analysis
   a. Do not try to select securities on the basis of their expected relative performance.
   b. Do not try to outguess the market by timing your investment decisions to coincide with market tops or bottoms.
2. Risk
   a. Diversify to reduce total risk.
   b. Control the market risk of the equity portion of the portfolio.
   c. Control the interest rate risk portion of the fixed-income portion of the portfolio.
3. Other considerations
   a. Purchase securities with adequate marketability.
   b. Take taxes into account when planning security transactions.

SUMMARY

This chapter has presented the concepts of market efficiency and some of the current state of evidence regarding the existence of efficient markets. An efficient market contains security prices that reflect the relevant information available about the securities. To further define efficient markets, we classify them into three levels.

At the weak form level, a security's price reflects any information from its past price patterns. This implies that investors cannot study charts of stock prices and patterns and expect to reap excess profits. A semi-strong form efficient market impounds all public information into security prices. It would mean that security analysts could not use such publicly available information as financial statements, news data, and earnings forecasts to "beat the market." Finally, the strong form of the efficient markets hypothesis implies that security prices reflect all possible information, both public and private. If the strong form exists, then investors who have inside information or advance access to information cannot trade in the market to make excess returns.

Examining the accumulated evidence on market efficiency leads us to conclude that the evidence on the weak form overwhelmingly supports its existence. Evidence for the semi-strong form, however, is conflicting. It appears that the market has semi-strong form efficiency with respect to some subsets of information, but is inefficient with respect to others. Evidence on the strong form generally shows that insiders can beat the market and therefore does not support the existence of a strong form efficient market.

IMPORTANT TERMS

buy-and-hold strategy
economically efficient market
efficient securities market
excess returns
filter trading rules
frictionless markets
homogeneous expectations
perfectly efficient market
price takers
random walk theory
risk-adjusted returns
semi-strong form of market efficiency
strong form of market efficiency
utility maximizer
weak form of market efficiency

QUESTIONS AND PROBLEMS

1. Outline the rationale for the existence of efficient capital markets.
2. What conditions contribute to the existence of an efficient market? How closely does each condition describe reality?
3. Explain why the presence of excess returns for a trading strategy would tend to refute the efficient markets hypothesis.
4. What are the implications of a semi-strong form efficient market for security analysts who try to select superior stocks?

5. Based on the evidence from tests of market efficiency, what sources of information would you access to try to select superior stocks?
6. A friend tells you that he has the market figured out and has a system that identifies stock patterns and tells when to buy. As evidence of the method's success, he shows you that his returns were twice the market average for last month. What is your opinion about the chances for success of this system?
7. "The Random Walk Theory cannot be true because stock prices do respond to fundamental economic information in a manner that is not random." Comment on the validity of this statement.
8. Explain how each of the three levels of market efficiency builds upon each previous level.
9. "If the stock market were efficient, then stock prices would be at equilibrium and would not fluctuate as they do." Comment.
10. List several bits of information that you could use to test the semi-strong form efficient markets hypothesis. Include several items that are not included in the examples in the chapter.

NOTES

1. In reality, because of risk, the stock would most likely sell for a price of less than $30.
2. Harry Roberts (1959), "Stock Market 'Patterns' and Financial Analysis: Methodological Suggestions," *Journal of Finance,* 14 (March), 1–10.
3. Eugene F. Fama (1965), "The Behavior of Stock-Market Prices," *Journal of Business,* 38, 34–105.
4. Eugene Fama and Marshall Blue (1966), "Filter Rules and Stock Market Trading," *Journal of Business,* 39 (January), 226–241.
5. Michael C. Jensen and George A. Bennington (1970), "Random Walks and Technical Theories: Some Additional Evidence," *Journal of Finance,* 25 (May), 469–482.
6. Samuel C. Hadaway and David P. Rochester (1982), "Seasonality in Individual Common Stocks: Alternative Test Techniques and Implications for Market Efficiency," *Journal of Economics and Business,* 33 (Fall), 49–55.
7. Eugene F. Fama, Lawrence Fisher, Michael C. Jensen, and Richard Roll (1969), "The Adjustment of Stock Prices to New Information," *International Economic Review,* 10 (February), 1–21.
8. Frank K. Reilly and Eugene F. Drzycimski (1981), "Short-Run Profits from Stock Splits," *Financial Management,* 10(3) (Summer), 64–74.
9. Mark S. Grinblatt, Ronald W. Masulis, and Sheridan Titman (1984), "The Valuation Effects of Stock Splits and Stock Dividends," *Journal of Financial Economics,* 13 (December), 461–490.
10. Michael C. Jensen (1968), "The Performance of Mutual Funds in the Period 1945–64," *Journal of Finance,* 23 (May), 389–416.
11. Hany A. Shawky (1982), "An Update on Mutual Funds: Better Grades," *Journal of Portfolio Management,* 8(2) (Winter), 29–34. Theodore Veit and John M. Cheney (1982), "Are Mutual Funds Market Timers?," *Journal of Portfolio Management,* 8, no. 2 (Winter), 35–42.
12. K. P. Nunn, G. P. Madden, and Michael J. Gombola (1983), "Are Some Insiders More 'Inside' than Others?," *Journal of Portfolio Management,* 9 (Spring), 18–22.
13. Arthur J. Keown and John M. Pinkerton (1981), "Merger Announcements and Insider Trading Activity: An Empirical Investigation," *Journal of Finance,* 36 (September), 855–869.

14. Keith Ambachtsheer (1977), "Profit Potential in an 'Almost Efficient' Market," in Peter L. Bernstein (Ed.), *Portfolio Management and Efficient Markets,* New York: Institutional Investor, 90–99.
15. Ambachtsheer, *ibid.*

SELECTED REFERENCES

Ambachtsheer, Keith P. (1977). "Can Selectivity Pay in an Efficient Market?" In Peter L. Bernstein (Ed.), *Portfolio Management and Efficient Markets.* Institutional Investor: New York, 309–317.

——— (1977). "Profit Potential in an 'Almost Efficient' Market." In Peter L. Bernstein (Ed.), *Portfolio Management and Efficient Markets.* Institutional Investor: New York, 90–99.

Ang, James S., Jess H. Chua, and Anand S. Desai (1979). "Evidence That the Common Stock Market Adjusts Fully for Expected Inflation." *Journal of Financial Research,* 2 (Fall), 97–109.

Basu, S. (1977). "Investment Performance of Common Stocks in Relation to Their Price-Earnings Ratios: A Test of the Efficient Markets Hypothesis." *Journal of Finance,* 32 (June), 663–681.

Bidwell, Clinton M., III, and Robert W. Kolb (1980). "The Impact and Value of Broker's Sell Recommendations." *The Financial Review,* 15 (Fall), 58–67.

Bjerring, James H., Josef Lakonishok, and Theo Vermaelen (1983). "Stock Prices and Financial Analysts' Recommendations." *Journal of Finance,* 38 (March), 187–204.

Boldt, Bob L., and Hal L. Arbit (1984). "Efficient Markets and the Professional Investor." *Financial Analysts Journal,* 40 (July–August), 22–34.

Brauer, Greggory A. (1984). " 'Open-ending' Closed-end Funds." *Journal of Financial Economics,* 13 (December), 491–507.

Brown, S. (1978). "Earnings Changes, Stock Prices and Market Efficiency." *Journal of Finance,* 34 (March), 17–28.

Fama, Eugene F., Lawrence Fisher, Michael C. Jensen, and Richard Roll (1969). "The Adjustment of Stock Prices to New Information." *International Economic Review,* 10 (February), 1–21.

Grinblatt, Mark S., Ronald W. Masulis, and Sheridan Titman (1984). "The Valuation Effects of Stock Splits and Stock Dividends." *Journal of Financial Economics,* 13 (December), 461–490.

Jensen, Michael C. (1968). "The Performance of Mutual Funds in the Period 1945–64." *Journal of Finance,* 23 (May), 389–416.

Jones, Charles P., and Robert Litzenberger (1970). "Quarterly Earnings Reports and Intermediate Stock Price Trends." *Journal of Finance,* 26 (March), 143–148.

———, Richard J. Rendleman, Jr., and Henry A. Latane (1985). "Earnings Announcements: Pre- and Post-Responses." *Journal of Portfolio Management,* 11(3) (Spring), 28–32.

Joy, O. Maurice, Robert Litzenberger, and Richard McEnelly (1977). "The Adjustment of Stock Prices to Announcements of Unanticipated Changes in Quarterly Earnings." *Journal of Accounting Research,* 15 (Autumn), 207–225.

Keown, Arthur J., and John M. Pinkerton (1981). "Merger Announcements and Insider Trading Activity: An Empirical Investigation." *Journal of Finance,* 36 (September), 855–869.

Lease, Ronald C., and Wilbur G. Lewellen (1982). "Market Efficiency across Securities Exchanges." *Journal of Economics and Business,* 34, 101–109.

Litzenberger, Robert, O. Maurice Joy, and Charles P. Jones (1971). "Ordinal Predictions and the Selection of Common Stocks." *Journal of Financial and Quantitative Analysis,* 6 (September), 1059–1068.

Nunn, K. P., G. P. Madden, and Michael J. Gombola (1983). "Are Some Insiders More 'Inside' than Others?" *Journal of Portfolio Management,* 9 (Spring), 18–22.

Patell, James M., and Mark Wolfson (1984). "The Intraday Speed of Adjustment of Stock Prices to Earnings and Dividend Announcements." *Journal of Financial Economics,* 13 (June), 223–252.

Reilly, Frank K., and Eugene F. Drzycimski (1981). "Short-Run Profits from Stock Splits." *Financial Management,* 10(3) (Summer), 64–74.

Rosenberg, Barr, Kenneth Reid, and Ronald Lanstein (1985). "Persuasive Evidence of Market Inefficiency." *Journal of Portfolio Management,* 11(3) (Spring), 9–16.

Shawky, Hany A. (1982). "An Update on Mutual Funds: Better Grades." *Journal of Portfolio Management,* 8(2) (Winter), 29–34.

Smirlock, Michael, and Jess Yawitz (1985). "Asset Returns, Discount Rate Changes, and Market Efficiency." *Journal of Finance,* 40 (September), 1141–1158.

Stickel, Scott E. "The Effect of Value Line Investment Survey Rank Changes on Common Stock Prices." *Journal of Financial Economics,* 14 (March), 121–143.

Veit, E. Theodore, and John M. Cheney (1982). "Are Mutual Funds Market Timers?" *Journal of Portfolio Management,* 8(2) (Winter), 35–42.

Watts, Ross L. (1978). "Systematic 'Abnormal' Returns after Quarterly Earnings Announcements." *Journal of Financial Economics,* 6 (June), 127–150.

PART THREE

Security Analysis Concepts

CHAPTER 10

Fundamental Analysis: Economic and Industry Considerations

Fundamental analysis, the search for the intrinsic value of the firm, is conducted on three levels: (1) the economy, (2) the industry, and (3) the firm. In some instances one level or another may have negligible effects on a change in value of the firm, but the analysis is still carried out to confirm the fact. Briefly, the three levels represent a systematic way of analyzing factors over which the firm has no control (economic and industry considerations) and those over which the firm has some degree of control (conditions existing within the firm). Effects in each of the three levels are analyzed based on the change in value due to strength, duration, and frequency of the event.

Analysis of the economy is a macro-analysis, usually dealing with variables over which the firm's management has no control. For events we cannot control, we are relegated to the task of forecasting, or of using an existing forecast. Material events must be identified and evaluated concerning the firm's outlook if they change any one of the following:

1. The economic environment, such as a change in the growth rate of the money supply
2. The political structure, such as a change in the taxation policy of a political party
3. International relationships, such as a change in available supplies of raw materials.

In general, most events that affect the business cycle will affect the long-run strategic value of the firm.

Analysis of the industry is a pseudo-macro-analysis. It involves the classical study of the relationship of the industry to the business cycle and the market. Today, however, the analysis usually deals with relationships to the economic analysis that the firm can control to some degree in the intermediate term. This is different from the type of industry analysis done only twenty years ago. It is not at all clear that industry effects are as strong as in past markets, or even that they exist, for the top 500 companies. The diversification of product lines, especially large firms, causes most industry effects on the firm's cash flows to be smoothed and thus very difficult to establish. In a single-product line of business, industry analysis is still useful. The value added in the analysis is usually, but not always, related to the firm's size and amount of product diversification. In general, the smaller the company's size and the less diversified its product line, the more payoff for the analytic effort.

Many of today's "due diligence" studies by brokerage houses concentrate more on regional analysis than on industry analysis. Primarily, analysts are looking for intermediate-term changes in the environment that could cause large swings in product demand, or changes in the industry's costs curves (average and marginal) about which the firm's management must make a tactical decision.

Analysis of a firm is a micro-analysis. It focuses on those decisions over which the firm's management has control: marketing/product, operational, and accounting/financing decisions. A change in management, or in management's ability to accomplish the efficient operation in any of these areas, will either increase or decrease the risks associated with the firm's cash flow. Study of a firm's financial statements for trends, "creative accounting," and potential cash drains are basic to fundamental analysis. All the assets over which the management team has control are revalued in market terms, along with the dollar income stream, to determine the "true" performance and risk to which the investor has been, is, and will be exposed. Management's ability to meet future changes, both anticipated and unanticipated, must be determined in order to assess the magnitude of the risk. The stronger the management assessment, the lower the risk of the cash flow to the investor, if all other factors are equal. A strong management team—one with market sophistication, experience, and depth—implies less fluctuation in the after-tax, inflation-adjusted return to the investor. Finally, the realism of the marketing plan determines the revenues the firm can expect. If the plan is unrealistic, more than likely, the forecasted sales will not occur.

Lest an investor become too involved with the process of analysis, rather than its results, a word of warning is necessary. The more confidence the analyst has in the valuation process, usually the lower the discount rate he applies to the cash flow. This sometimes creates errors in the mind, for the "true" worth of the company is not created in the analysis—it already exists. All the analyst can do is try to discover and expose it.

TOP-DOWN OR BOTTOM-UP ANALYSIS?

Some analysts prefer to start on the macro-level (the economy) and work their analysis down to the micro-level (the firm). This approach is *top-down analysis.* Analysis begins with study of the economy and attempts to answer the question, "What investments, such as stocks, bonds, or money market instruments, are appropriate for today's economic environment?" Having addressed the broad economic question, the analyst can then move the analysis to the industry level, which asks, "Given the economic situation, which industries are best positioned to be successful and profitable?" Finally, the analyst will analyze individual firms and their securities to pinpoint the answer to the question, "Which firm in the industry will maximize my investment return?"

Other analysts prefer a *bottom-up analysis,* beginning at the micro-level, expanding the analysis to the company's industry or sector, and terminating with analysis of the market environment.

Most analysts seem to prefer the top-down approach. Its greatest advantage is efficiency. If the macro-analysis identifies industries that are more likely to perform well, then the remainder of the analytical effort can address the process of selecting the best companies within those industries. There are times, however, when micro-conditions dominate, and the bottom-up approach might select companies that would be missed in a top-down analysis. Both approaches are valid and are not mutually exclusive. An astute analyst should be flexible enough to recognize situations when one or the other is preferable. In addition, an analyst can use one approach as a cross check on the other.

In either the top-down or bottom-up approach, analysts usually spend most of their time and effort at the company level. Because of this emphasis on company-related research, we will dedicate most of our study in this book to micro-level analysis. The following reasons explain the concentration of investment analysis at the company level:

1. *Large selection of companies.* For every market or industry analysis, an analyst has many possible companies to scrutinize. The analyst has much more discretion in dealing with decisions related to investment in individual companies. While there are only several dozen industry groups, there are thousands of publicly traded stocks from which an investor can choose. Even when the market is falling, some stocks are usually making new highs. Opportunities seem to exist for the astute analyst who can identify such situations.
2. *Company-related factors mainly determine stock price.* The variation in a stock's price due to firm-specific, or unsystematic, factors is quite large. The actual amount of the *firm effect* differs according to different studies,[1] but it probably accounts for around half of the variation in price of the typical firm's stock. However, it can be quite high—as much as 90 percent or more. In addition, evidence indicates that the importance of the general market factor and the industry factor has been decreasing over time, which means that the importance of the individual firm effect, and hence the analysis of the firm, is becoming more important.
3. *Market prediction is difficult.* Predicting the stock market in general using economic information is quite difficult, if not almost impossible, as the next section shows. And you have to be right in a large majority of cases

to make profits by predicting the market. Studies generally show that a market predictor would have to be correct at least two thirds of the time to beat a strategy of just buying stocks and holding them.[2]

4. *The industry factor is relatively small.* Most studies show that although an industry factor is present, it is the least dominant of the three factors, and its effect is relatively small in relation to the micro-level effect on a stock's price.

This chapter outlines procedures for market and industry or sector analysis. Chapters 11 through 16 deal on a comprehensive level with individual firms and the analysis of their debt and equity securities.

ANALYZING THE ECONOMY AND THE MARKET

The economic environment has great influence over the performance of the individual groups and units that compose the economic system. The earnings of some industries and firms tend to be quite sensitive to the economic cycle, while others seem to be somewhat insulated from economic fluctuations. Since our theory tells us that the earnings potential of a firm is a fundamental determinant of its value, the economy's influence over a firm's earnings power must be an important analytical question.

On a broader basis, not only is an individual firm affected by the economy, but all firms, and hence the aggregate market. Therefore, it should be important to know the relationship between changes in aggregate economic activity and changes in returns in the security markets.

The logical relationship between stock prices and economic activity should be direct: the increased earnings associated with economic prosperity should result in higher values for common stocks. However, investors are more concerned with *earnings potential,* and the evidence indicates that stock price changes tend to precede changes in economic activity. The stock market seems to anticipate changes in the economy and reach turning points before the actual change in the economy becomes evident.

This relationship has been observed since the early years of market activity. In his early treatise on the market, written in 1884, William Samson[3] wrote the following eloquent passage on the relationship between the market and the economy:

> The statement that "coming events cast their shadows before," seems to be particularly applicable to Wall Street, in its relation to the financial and commercial state of the country at large. At a time when the wave of general prosperity is running mountain high, and a reaction is totally undreamed of by the public at large, the share market becomes feverish and unsettled; a period of dullness—that unmistakable precursor of a decline in values—obtains, and when men "cry peace, peace, then sudden destruction cometh," first in Wall Street, and afterward throughout the length and breadth of the land.

This may seem the reverse of the way that the relationship should be ordered. After all, the causal relationship theoretically seems to be that stock values are a function of the economy. Why, then, do stock prices tend to *lead* the economy? There are two reasons that explain this. First, investors base their valuations of securities on *expected* earnings. Expected earnings are a function of investors' expectations about the prevailing economic situation in the *future,* not the present. Second, the stock market does react to the release of important economic information, but much of this information itself tends to lead the economy.

Economic Indicators

Economic indicators are the measures that economists use to track the course of the economy. Economists group these indicators into three categories: *leading indicators, coincident indicators,* and *lagging indicators.*

Leading indicators are those whose turning points tend to precede turning points in general economic activity (Gross National Product). For example, one might expect that an index measuring the amount of new building permits issued would be a leading indicator since the building permits should be followed by construction spending and employment. Indeed, building permits are a leading indicator. The National Bureau of Economic Research (NBER) has identified twelve important leading indicators and reports them monthly in *Business Conditions Digest.* Table 10–1 shows the indicators used by the NBER. Combining the twelve leading indicators into one index yields the composite index of leading economic indicators. Figure 10–1 presents graphs of the composite indicators, showing the number of months that the indicator preceded (−) or followed (+) a turn in business activity. For the time period covered

TABLE 10–1
Composition of the composite indicators

Leading Indicators	
Index of new business formations	Net change in inventory
Index of stock prices: 500 common stocks	Net change in sensitive prices
Index of new building permits	Vendor performance
Layoff rate—manufacturing	Money balance
New orders—consumer goods	Percent change in total liquid assets
Contracts and orders for plant and equipment	Average work week of production worker
Coincident Indicators	
Number of employees, nonagricultural payrolls	Personal income, less transfers
Index of industrial production	Manufacturing and trade sales
Lagging Indicators	
Manufacturing and trade inventories	Ratio of consumer installment debt to personal income
Labor cost per unit output, manufacturing	Average prime rate charged by banks
Commercial and industrial loans outstanding	Average duration of employment

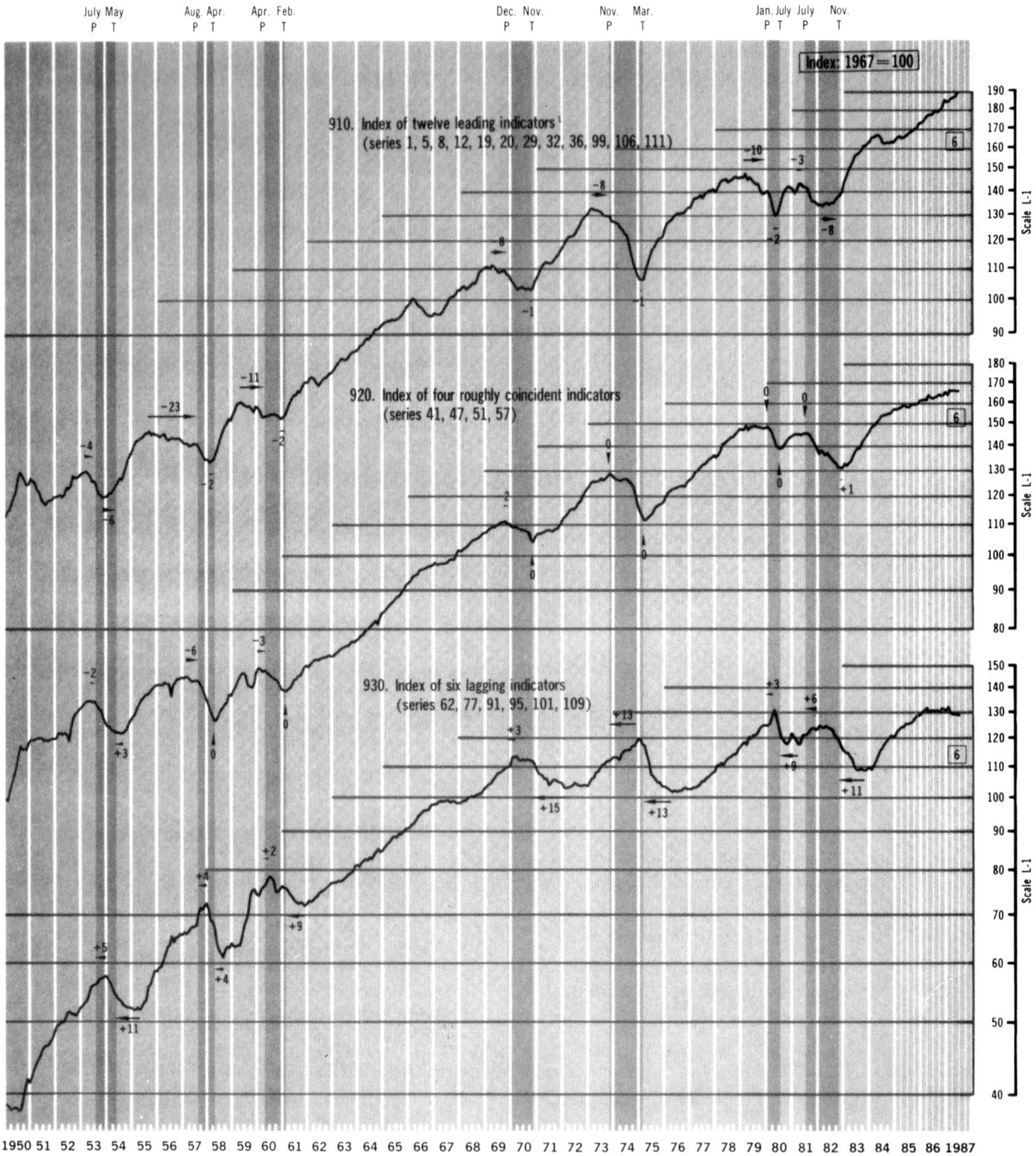

FIGURE 10–1
Composite indicators *(Source: Business Conditions Digest* [July 1987])

in Figure 10–1, the change in the composite indicator preceded changes in the economy by an average of about six weeks.

Coincident indicators tend to reach turning points at the same time as general economic activity, while turning points in lagging indicators generally arrive after changes in the economy. The composite lagging indicator followed general economic trends by an average of about seven and one half months in Figure 10–1.

If an analyst is trying to use economic indicators to predict the market, then indicators that precede the market must be found. However, as we have previously noted, the market itself is a leading indicator. Just how good a leading indicator is the market? One study, by Zarnowitz and Boschan,[4] of the effectiveness of economic indicators gave the index of stock prices a score of 80 out of a possible 100, higher than scores of any of the other eleven indicators that make up the composite leading indicator. Figure 10–2 shows a graph of the index of stock prices. With the dark areas representing periods of economic recession, note how the index generally begins rising before the end of the recession.

If the market itself is the best leading economic indicator, then applying leading indicators to forecasting the stock market would likely be of questionable value. One test, by Heathcotte and Apilado,[5] of the use of leading economic indicators set up an investment strategy that would indicate when investors should buy stocks and when they should sell. The returns generated by the strategy were mixed, indicating that investors on average could not consistently beat the market by studying only leading economic indicators.

Monetary Policy

The government's *monetary policy,* its control over the supply of money in the economy, has traditionally had an impact upon stock prices. Friedman and Schwartz,[6]

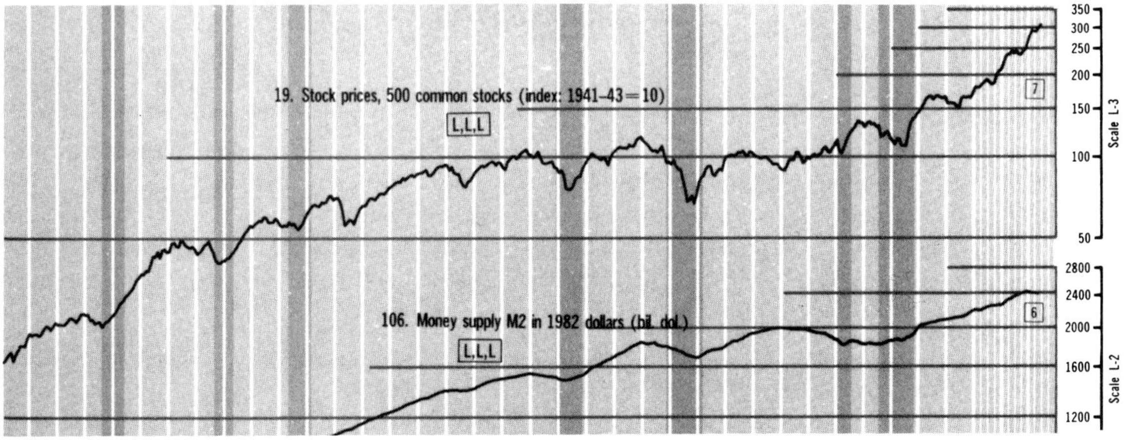

FIGURE 10–2
Index of 500 common stock prices *(Source: Business Conditions Digest* [July 1987])

in a classic study, have shown evidence of a relationship between the money supply and the economy over an extended period of time (1867 to 1960). They showed that periods of expansion in the money supply were usually followed by increased economic activity.

A brief synopsis of the chain of economic events that explains this relationship begins with an expansive monetary policy. When the supply of money increases, assuming the demand for money remains constant, the price of money (interest rates) will fall. Businesses will take advantage of lower interest rates to borrow and expand their business. The resulting increase in production and employment then becomes evidence of the increased economic activity.

If an increase in the economy follows an increase in the money supply, then the relationship between stock prices and the economy tells us that stock prices should also increase when the money supply increases. The main question of interest here is whether the changes in the money supply precede stock price changes. Should money supply changes precede stock price changes, on average, then observing changes in the money supply would be a useful tool for forecasting aggregate stock price movements. On the other hand, if the two change concurrently, then knowledge of money supply changes would prove of little value in predicting stock price.

Most empirical studies examining the relationship between the money supply and stock prices agree that there is an identifiable relationship between the two.[7] However, when analyzing in detail changes in stock prices following money supply changes, the conclusion is generally that stock price changes slightly *precede* changes in the money supply. In other words, the stock market *anticipates* money supply changes by reflecting whether these expected money changes would result in higher or lower economic growth.[8] Recalling our arguments about efficient markets, this finding is consistent with the idea of a semi-strong efficient market. Otherwise, investors using public information about the money supply could outguess the market.

This observation for the leading relationship of stock prices to the money supply seems to hold for short-run money supply changes also. When studying the weekly announcements of changes in the money supply, Pearce and Roley[9] found that stock prices reacted only when money supply changes were out of line with forecasted money supply changes. That is, the stock market reacted only to unanticipated changes in the money supply. In addition, the reactions generally were complete by early in the trading day following the announcement. These quick market reactions to new information also support the semi-strong form efficient markets hypothesis. It is interesting to note that the stock market reactions were the opposite of what we might expect. When money supply changes were unexpectedly *high,* the market usually *fell,* and vice versa. The explanation for this is that unexpectedly high money growth rates would aggravate inflation, which could cause stock prices to fall.

Forecasting the Market Using Risk Premiums

A *risk premium* is the extra return on an investment to compensate for additional risk. For example, we would expect that the long-run return on stocks would be more than the return on bonds because of the additional risk associated with the equity securities. One method analysts use to anticipate the future direction of stock prices is analysis of risk premiums.

When stocks are generally expensive relative to other types of securities, the return on stocks and hence their risk premiums are relatively low. This would be a time when stocks might be reaching their highs, and analysts would conclude that the market is due a downturn. The converse would be the case when stocks are relatively low-priced and risk premiums are relatively high—the market should turn upward.

Researchers have developed several market risk premium measures to determine when risk premiums are high or low. Renshaw[10] is responsible for two of these techniques, and his methods have had some success. Renshaw's first measure is based on the earnings yield on stocks relative to yields on high-grade bonds. To compute the risk premium measure, subtract the yield on Moody's high-grade corporate bond index from the earnings yield on the S&P 500 Index. (The earnings yield is simply a stock's annual earnings per share divided by the stock price.) Renshaw found that this risk premium measure tends to average about .35 percent, and when risk premiums are less than .35 percent at year-end, the market tends to fall. Years with risk premiums greater than .35 percent usually preceded bull markets.

Renshaw's other risk premium measure is based on dividends. To compute this risk premium measure, add the dividend yield of the S&P Public Utility Index to the growth rate in the dividends on the index over the past ten years and subtract the yield on three-month Treasury bills. Again, Renshaw found that years with bull markets tended to follow year-end high risk premiums, and bear markets tended to follow low risk premiums.

Market Forecasting in Perspective

In summary, the evidence indicates that it is quite difficult to predict future movement of stock prices with fundamental economic information. The observation that no reported techniques successfully predict the market over long time periods is consistent with our notions of an economically efficient market.

If the analyst believes that stock prices are due to rise, then the portfolio should be heavily weighted with stocks. Of course, even when the market falls, some stocks will rise, and many analysts continue their pursuit of company analysis in hopes of identifying such stocks. If the analyst is uncertain or believes that stock prices will fall, consideration should be directed toward concentrating more of the portfolio in bonds, money market securities, or other types of investments. The decision for bonds rests heavily on expectations of interest rate changes, as discussed in Chapter 12.

INDUSTRY ANALYSIS

Analysis of an industry is the second step in the three-step sequence of investment analysis. Analysis of industry groups is an important part of most professional analysts' jobs. Most analysts prefer to concentrate on one or a few industries, becoming an expert on the industry and the various companies within that industry.

The Value of Industry Analysis

The value of industry analysis relates to the following three questions:

1. Do different industries perform very differently over the same time period?
2. Does industry performance tend to be consistent over time?
3. Do all the firms in a given industry tend to perform similarly during a given time period?

Studies addressing the first question have generally concluded that investment returns to different industry groups can vary considerably over any particular time period.[11] Some industries show excellent performance as a group, while others may perform dismally over the same time period. Because industries do seem to perform quite differently, foretelling which industries will perform better will give an analyst the advantage toward outperforming the market. Armed with such knowledge, an analyst could then concentrate the individual company analyses on stocks in industries predicted to perform better.

Unfortunately, identifying the industries that should perform better appears to be more difficult than simply looking at those that did well in the past. Milford Tysseland,[12] in a study aimed at answering the second question, found that there seems to be little consistency in industry performance. During a given year, some industries may fare well while others do poorly, but superior performance in that year is not necessarily followed by similar performance in the following year. Picking an industry that will yield good returns in the future is not simply a matter of choosing an industry that did well in the past. This underscores the need for industry analysis to be thorough and to anticipate changes in the industry. To pick a successful industry for future high returns requires superior forecasts of the prospects and performance of the industry.

Finally, within a particular industry, there is quite a bit of dispersion of returns to the individual companies. A company within an industry experiencing rapid growth and high returns may also be doing well, but there are so many variables involved, that there is also a definite chance that the company could be faltering. Some of the financial factors of a company are strongly influenced by the firm's industry, which is the reason why ratio analysis (see Chapter 11) compares a company's data to an average of the industry. These variables themselves have quite a bit of variation. This is one of the reasons why, even with a high degree of commonality of several financial variables, the returns to stockholders of firms within a given industry can vary considerably. However, an analyst selecting a company from an industry that will show good performance does have a better chance of seeing the company do well also.

Does this mean that industry analysis is useless? Even with the dispersion of returns to individual firms and inconsistency of industries over time mentioned above, industry analysis can still be a useful tool in the overall concept of security analysis. Study of an industry gives the analyst a much better understanding of the prospects of individual companies within an industry. Analysis of the industry is essential to the analysis of the competitive environment within which any particular company operates. Much of the securities industry must believe that there is benefit in industry analysis because many professional investment analysts devote a large portion of their time to following a single industry or group of industries.

Methods of Industry and Sector Analysis

Table 10–2 presents a suggested outline for use in conducting analysis of an industry. The analysis usually begins with identification of the product or service offered by the industry and mention of any other industries that might offer competing or complementary products. The influence of the government is also an important consideration.

TABLE 10–2
Suggested outline for industry analysis

- I. Definition of industry
  - A. Nature of product or service
  - B. Competing and complementary industries
  - C. Influence of government
- II. Industry growth
  - A. Product life cycle
    - 1. Typical pattern
      - a. Capital expenditures
      - b. Profit margins
    - 2. Industry's position in cycle
    - 3. Interruptions in the cycle
  - B. Sales growth potential
    - 1. Demand for product
      - a. Saturation of existing market demand
      - b. Competing goods
      - c. Long-run demand growth
    - 2. Supply of inputs for product
      - a. Capital
      - b. Labor
      - c. Raw materials
  - C. Impact of economic environment
    - 1. Interest rates
    - 2. Impact of inflation
- III. Competition within the industry
  - A. Domestic competition
    - 1. Top firms in industry
    - 2. Potential for new competition
  - B. Foreign competition
    - 1. Competition from foreign companies
    - 2. Effects of foreign governments

The growth prospects for an industry are probably the most important portion of any industry analysis. A useful method for examining industry growth is to use the product life cycle approach. Figure 10–3 shows a chart that might represent the sales pattern of a typical product over its life cycle. The growth of an industry usually follows the product life cycle of its major product. During the first phase of a product's life, the industry is concerned with developing the product and getting it to market. As uses for the product become accepted, sales begin to increase. The next phase is one of rapid expansion and growth. Sales increase as more units of the product are demanded. New producers often enter into the market, prices fall, and quantities demanded increase even more. Ultimately, sales growth begins to slow down as the market becomes saturated with the product. The maturity phase of a product is characterized by slow growth, if any. Most sales are replacement sales, and growth can arise only from additional stimulus from sources such as population growth or new uses for the product. Finally, the product may become obsolete or be replaced by a new and better product. In that case, the product and its industry will enter a decline phase.

An industry analysis should forecast long-run sales growth potential for the product and industry. The sales growth depends upon both the demand for the product and the industry's ability to supply it. Analysis of product demand includes such areas as the current saturation of product demand, competition for other goods, and potential for long-run growth in demand for the product. Analysis of product supply should examine the availability of the three basic categories of inputs into a product: capital, labor, and raw materials.

The economic environment is also an important determinant of industry growth. Although economic growth is certainly an important economic factor to consider, an industry analysis should also include the impact of individual economic variables such as interest rates and inflation on the industry.

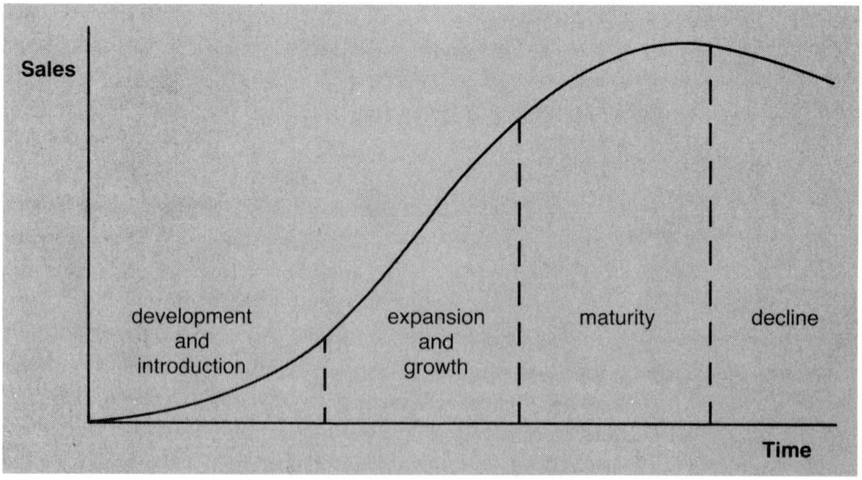

FIGURE 10–3
The product life cycle

Finally, an industry analysis should consider the conditions within the industry. This involves identifying the top firms in the industry and potential for new entrants. Foreign competition in addition to domestic firms should be included in this analysis.

An industry analysis can provide an analyst or investor with an important foundation for identifying superior companies within an industry. Investors should be aware of the shortcomings of industry analysis. They should realize that industry analysis can help identify potentially favorable situations for companies but that only a thorough analysis of an individual company can indicate whether or not the firm is positioned to take advantage of the situation.

SUMMARY

The traditional investment analysis is a three-step process beginning with an analysis of the economic and market environment, followed by an analysis of an industry group, and ending with the analysis of one or more companies within the industry. Some analysts prefer to organize their analysis the opposite way, beginning with a company and terminating with the economy.

The positive relationship between stock prices and economic activity has been consistent through the years. Evidence shows that changes in stock prices tend to precede changes in the economy, making it one of the most reliable leading indicators of economic activity. Stock prices are also related to the money supply. As in the case of the economy, stock prices also seem to anticipate changes in the money supply. Therefore, using economic forecasts or the money supply to predict stock prices would be of questionable value.

IMPORTANT TERMS

bottom-up analysis
coincident indicators
earnings potential
economic indicators
lagging indicators
leading indicators
monetary policy
risk premium
top-down analysis

QUESTIONS AND PROBLEMS

1. "It is well known that increases in stock prices occur about three to six months before an upturn in the economy. Forecasting the stock market is therefore a simple matter of forecasting what the economy will be doing six months and more in the future." Comment on this statement and the difficulties that an investor would have in following its advice.
2. You are an analyst studying the cosmetics industry. You need to construct a model for forecasting industry revenues. Identify the various factors that you expect would influence revenues in that industry.

3. Consult a copy of Standard & Poor's *Industry Surveys.* Choose an industry and identify the top five companies in the industry based on their revenues. What percentage of industry sales does each company have? Are industry sales concentrated in relatively few or many companies? Why?
4. "Industry analysis is of no value because it is the individual company that determines investment performance." Comment on this statement.
5. Define and give examples of leading indicators, coincident indicators, and lagging indicators.
6. A friend says to you, "I will never buy common stocks. They have fallen 30 percent in value over the last two years, and the economy is still weak." Would you agree with your friend? Why?
7. Would you prefer the top-down approach to investment analysis or the bottom-up approach? Why?

NOTES

1. See, for example, Benjamin F. King (1966), "Market and Industry Factors in Stock Price Behavior," *Journal of Business,* 39 (January), 139–190, and Stephen L. Myers (1973) "A Re-Examination of Market and Industry Factors in Stock Price Behavior," *Journal of Finance,* 28 (June), 695–705.
2. See William F. Sharpe (1975), "Likely Gains from Market Timing," *Financial Analysts Journal,* 31 (March-April), 60–69; and Robert J. Jeffrey (1985), "Putting Market Timing to the Test: Is It Worth the Risk?," *AAII Journal,* 7 (September), 10–15.
3. William E. Samson (1884) *The Mysteries of Wall Street: A Complete Guide to the Speculation in Stocks.* Schenectedy: Chas. Burrows, Printer, 32–33.
4. Victor Zarnowitz and Charlotte Boschan (1975), "Cyclical Indicators: An Evaluation and New Leading Index," *Business Conditions Digest,* (November), v–xxiv.
5. Bryan Heathcotte and Vincent P. Apilado (1974), "The Predictive Content of Some Leading Economic Indicators for Future Stock Prices," *Journal of Financial and Quantitative Analysis,* 9, 247–258.
6. Milton Friedman and Anna J. Schwartz (1963), "Money and Business Cycles," *Review of Economics and Statistics,* 45, 32–78.
7. See, for example, Kenneth E. Homa and Dwight M. Jaffee (1971), "The Study of Money and Common Stock Prices," *Journal of Finance,* 26 (December), 1045–1066, and James E. Pesando (1974), "The Supply of Money and Common Stock Prices," *Journal of Finance,* 29, 909–921.
8. See studies by Richard V. L. Cooper (1974), "Efficient Capital Markets and the Quantity Theory of Money," *Journal of Finance,* 29, 887–908, and Michael S. Rozeff (1975), "The Money Supply and the Stock Market," *Financial Analysts Journal,* 31 (September-October), 18–26.
9. Douglas K. Pearce and V. Vance Roley (1983), "The Reaction of Stock Prices to Unanticipated Changes in Money: A Note," *Journal of Finance,* 38 (September), 1323–1332.
10. Edward F. Renshaw (1985), "A Risk Premium Model for Market Timing," *Journal of Portfolio Management,* 11 (Summer), 33–35.
11. See, for example Frank K. Reilly and Eugene Drzycimski (1974), "Alternative Industry Performance and Risk," *Journal of Financial and Quantitative Analysis,* 9 (June), 423–446.
12. Milford S. Tysseland (1971), "Further Tests of the Validity of the Industry Approach to Investment Analysis," *Journal of Financial and Quantitative Analysis,* 6 (March), 835–847.

SELECTED REFERENCES

Day, Theodore E. (1984). "Real Stock Returns and Inflation." *Journal of Finance,* 39 (June), 493–502.

Grossman, S. J., and Robert J. Shiller (1981). "The Determinants of the Variability of Stock Market Prices." *American Economic Review,* 71 (June) 222–227.

Jeffrey, Robert H. (1985). "Putting Market Timing to the Test: Is It Worth the Risk?" *AAII Journal,* 7 (September), 10–15.

Martin, Linda J., and Glenn V. Henderson Jr. (1984). "Industry Influence on Financial Structure: A Matter of Interpretation." *Review of Business and Economic Research,* 19 (Spring), 57–66.

McWilliams, James D. (1984). "Watchman, Tell Us of the Night." *Journal of Portfolio Management,* 10 (Spring), 75–80.

Modigliani, Franco, and Richard A. Cohn (1979). "Inflation, Rational Valuation and the Market." *Financial Analysts Journal,* 35 (March-April), 24–44.

Pearce, Douglas K., and V. Vance Roley (1983). "The Reaction of Stock Prices to Unanticipated Changes in Money: A Note." *Journal of Finance,* 38 (September), 1323–1332.

Reilly, Frank K., Frank T. Griggs and Wenchi Wong (1983). "Determinants of the Aggregate Stock Market Earnings Multiple." *Journal of Portfolio Management,* 10 (Fall), 36–45.

——— and Eugène Drzycimski (1974). "Alternative Industry Performance and Risk." *Journal of Financial and Quantitative Analysis,* 9 (June), 423–446.

Renshaw, Edward F. (1983). "The Anatomy of Stock Market Cycles." *Journal of Portfolio Management,* 10 (Fall), 53–57.

——— (1985). "A Risk Premium Model for Market Timing." *Journal of Portfolio Management,* 11 (Summer), 33–35.

Riley, William B. and William A. Luksetich (1980). "The Market Prefers Republicans: Myth or Reality?" *Journal of Financial and Quantitative Analysis,* 15 (September), 541–559.

Sharpe, William F. (1975). "Likely Gains from Market Timing." *Financial Analysts Journal,* 31 (March-April), 60–69.

Shiller, Robert J. (1984). "Theories of Aggregate Stock Price Movements." *Journal of Portfolio Management,* 10 (Winter), 28–37.

Tysseland, Milford S. (1971). "Further Tests of the Validity of the Industry Approach to Investment Analysis." *Journal of Financial and Quantitative Analysis,* 6 (March), 835–853.

Umstead, David (1977). "Forecasting Stock Market Prices." *Journal of Finance,* 32 (May), 427–441.

CHAPTER 11

Financial Statement Analysis and Forecasting

Before addressing the issues of security valuation and analysis in Parts 4 and 5, we must familiarize ourselves with some of the tools that analysts use. These tools include the analysis of financial statements using financial ratios and the forecasting of key items that allow the analyst to estimate a security's future value.

Fundamental security valuation makes use of many of the company's variables that the financial statements report. It is important to be able to read, interpret, and analyze the financial statements. They give clues regarding the firm's credit worthiness, ability to generate earnings, growth, consistency, and general financial condition.

Chapter 10 showed how today's security prices depend upon expectations about the future. Because of this, fundamental security valuation must use more than just analysis of historical items from the financial statements. It must utilize projections of the financial condition of the firm in the future. For example, a thorough security analysis may contain forecasts of the firm's sales, expenses, taxes, earnings, and need for additional external financing. Using these forecasts, an analyst can even project values for the financial statements in future time periods.

MAJOR FINANCIAL STATEMENTS

Several different types of financial statements exist, and different firms may use different types of statements. However, there are four major financial statements that almost all firms will present in their annual reports. These statements are the *balance sheet, income statement, statement of changes in financial position,* and the *statement of retained earnings.*

Balance Sheet

The balance sheet is a statement of a firm's assets, liabilities, and ownership at a particular point in time. Sometimes accountants call this statement the *statement of financial position.* The annual balance sheet will contain a firm's book values for its assets, liabilities, and equity accounts at the close of business on the last day of the company's *fiscal year.* A company's fiscal year represents twelve months of operations and may or may not coincide with the calendar year that begins on January 1 and ends on December 31. The values that a company reports on its balance sheet are not necessarily *market values* of the firm's assets and liabilities, but rather they are the values carried on the books of the company. (The next section of this chapter discusses differences between book and market values.) Table 11–1 shows an example balance sheet for General Foods Corporation. In the annual report, a company will give the balance sheet for the end of the year and for the end of at least one prior year. The purpose of the prior year's results is to allow the investor to compare this year's position to last year's without having to find last year's report.

TABLE 11–1
Balance sheet for General Foods Corporation

(In millions)	*F1985*	*F1984*
Assets		
Cash and temporary investments	$ 288.4	$ 276.8
Receivables, net	948.6	906.4
Inventories	1,074.5	1,097.1
Other	66.4	66.0
Current assets	**2,377.9**	**2,346.3**
Land, buildings, equipment, net	1,751.5	1,614.6
Other assets	424.3	470.9
Total	**$4,553.7**	**$4,431.8**
Liabilities and stockholders' equity		
Notes payable and current portion of long-term debt	$ 394.7	$ 213.3
Accounts and drafts payable and accrued liabilities	869.4	874.3
Accrued income taxes	138.5	156.9
Current liabilities	**1,402.6**	**1,244.5**
Long-term debt	725.1	750.0
Other non-current liabilities	217.6	180.4
Deferred income taxes	268.2	216.7
Stockholders' equity	1,940.2	2,040.2
Total	**$4,533.7**	**$4,431.8**

Source: Disclosure Inc., Bethesda, MD, General Foods Corporation, 10–K for March 30, 1985.

Income Statement

The income statement measures the company's profits or losses over the reporting period. In contrast to the balance sheet, which is a statement at one point in time, the income statement represents profits generated over a length of time. Another name for the income statement is the *statement of earnings.* In their annual reports, publicly traded companies must report income for the latest fiscal year and for the previous two years. Table 11–2 gives an example income statement for General Foods.

TABLE 11–2
Income statement for General Foods Corporation

(In millions, except per share amounts)	*F1985*	*F1984*
Revenues		
Net sales	$9,022.4	$8,599.8
Other income	68.5	86.3
	9,090.9	**8,686.1**
Costs and expenses		
Cost of sales	5,508.2	5,263.2
Marketing, general and administrative expenses	2,888.8	2,704.5
Interest expense	150.1	145.1
	8,547.1	**8,112.8**
Special items	77.3	—
Earnings from continuing operations before income taxes and change in application of accounting principle	621.1	573.3
Income taxes	**279.2**	**256.2**
Earnings from continuing operations before change in application of accounting principle	341.9	317.1
Special items, net of tax	(17.0)	—
Net earnings	**$ 324.9**	**$ 317.1**
Earnings per share		
Earnings from continuing operations before change in application of accounting principle	$ 6.96	$ 6.10
Cumulative effect of change in application of accounting principle	(.35)	—
Provision for loss on discontinued operations	—	—
Net earnings	**$ 6.61**	**$ 6.10**
Dividends per share	**$ 2.50**	**$ 2.40**

Source: Disclosure Inc., Bethesda, MD, General Foods Corporation, 10–K for March 30, 1985.

Statement of Retained Earnings

The statement of retained earnings shows how the earnings (net income) reported in the income statement and the payment of dividends by the company changed the retained earnings account reported in the balance sheet. Table 11–3 is General Food's statement of retained earnings.

Statement of Changes in Financial Position

The statement of changes in financial position, also called the *statement of sources and uses of funds,* shows how certain changes in the balance sheet occurred, or rather how the firm financed these changes. Table 11–4 gives General Food's statement of changes in financial position. For example, a look at the balance sheet shows that the total of cash and temporary (short-term) investments increased by $11,650,000 from the end of 1984 to 1985. The statement of changes in financial position shows that this difference resulted from cash available from operations ($495.3 million), cash used for investment purposes ($444.2 million), cash used to pay dividends and interest to investors ($204.1 million), and funds provided by external financing ($164.6 million).

Difficulties with Using Reported Financial Statement Numbers

The main problem that analysts face when using financial statements is the fact that values reported in the statements do not always represent the "true" value of the item. In practice, the "true" and reported values are seldom exactly the same.

Investors should realize that *reported earnings* do not necessarily measure the *economic earnings* that are of interest to fundamental analysts. Reported earnings, or *accounting earnings,* are profits reported in the firm's statements using "generally accepted accounting principles." *Economic earnings* is a concept that represents the amount of real consumption opportunities that the firm's owners can withdraw from

TABLE 11–3
Statement of retained earnings for General Foods Corporation

(In millions, except per share amounts)	*F1985*	*F1984*
Net earnings	**$ 324,907**	**$ 317,105**
Retained earnings—beginning of period	1,919,703	1,727,439
	2,244,610	2,044,544
Cash dividends	123,017	124,841
Retained earnings—end of period	$2,121,593	$1,919,703
Weighted average number of shares outstanding (thousands)	49,166	52,003

Source: Disclosure Inc., Bethesda, MD, General Foods Corporation, 10–K for March 30, 1985.

TABLE 11–4
Statement of changes in financial position for General Foods Corporation

(In millions)	*F1985*	*F1984*
Operating cash generated	**$644.3**	**$621.6**
Changes in foreign currency exchange rates affecting working capital	(26.9)	(15.4)
Net (increase) decrease in operating working capital	(122.1)	22.4
Cash available from operations	**495.3**	**628.6**
Purchase price of businesses acquired, net of cash received	(60.1)	(43.7)
Capital additions	(302.9)	(266.7)
Proceeds from sale of businesses	140.0	—
Acquisition of treasury stock	(269.2)	—
Other items, net	48.0	22.1
Cash used for investment activities	**(444.2)**	**(288.3)**
Dividends	(123.0)	(124.8)
Interest, net of tax	(81.1)	(78.5)
Cash used for payments to investors	**(204.1)**	**(203.3)**
Proceeds from issuance of common stock	—	—
Proceeds from long-term debt	31.1	49.5
Net addition (reduction) in short-term notes payable	160.4	(71.4)
Repayment of long-term debt	(26.9)	(123.5)
Cash provided from (used for) financing activities	**164.6**	**(145.4)**
Increase (decrease) in cash and temporary investments	11.6	(8.4)
Cash and temporary investments beginning of year	276.8	285.2
Cash and temporary investments end of year	**$288.4**	**$276.8**

Source: Disclosure Inc., Bethesda, MD, General Foods Corporation, 10–K for March 30, 1985.

the firm during the accounting period without lowering consumption opportunities for the future. The firm could pay dividends to its owners in the amount of the economic earnings each year, and the firm's size would remain the same in perpetuity. However, reported earnings may be more or less than economic earnings, and therefore would not represent the amount of dividends that the firm could pay without growing. It is the amount of economic earnings that is important for security valuation. Security analysts, therefore, must be able to make adjustments in reported earnings so that they more realistically represent economic earnings.

Analysts should also be aware that reported asset and liability values are not necessarily equal to market values. There are several reasons for this:

1. Rates of depreciation on the firm's books do not usually represent the fall in an asset's market value.
2. Fixed assets that may rise in value usually must be carried on the books at their cost.
3. Different methods exist for valuing inventories.

Security analysts need to be familiar with accounting practice, especially regarding those areas in which alternative methods of accounting exist that can result in a difference in reported earnings. Unfortunately, these different accounting methods often result in financial statements that do not reflect the true economic condition of the firm. The accounting profession is aware that problems exist and has tried to improve the meaningfulness of publicly reported financial statements by standardizing some accounting procedures. The Financial Accounting Standards Board (FASB) issues statements addressing areas of major concern and attempting to find standard solutions that will be widely accepted.

The accounting method that would result in higher reported earnings is not always the best alternative for a firm to choose, for a couple of reasons. First, reporting higher earnings through accounting gimmickry usually does not fool security analysts and investors, who try to analyze not only the numbers but also the reasons behind the numbers. Second, reporting higher earnings can lead to unnecessarily higher tax payments, which could reduce the firm's consumption possibilities in the future and actually lower economic earnings.

There are times when analysts need to adjust financial statements to remove or minimize the impact of the different accounting-generated earnings discrepancies. This is especially important when performing analyses to compare different firms using different accounting rules.

Some of the major areas that can result in variation of reported earnings are as follows: valuation of inventories, depreciation, taxes, recognition of sales, and expensing of pension benefits.

Inventory Valuation

Reported earnings can vary depending upon the method that the firm uses for valuing its inventory. During periods of rising prices, the FIFO (first in first out) method will generally result in higher reported earnings than will other inventory valuation methods, such as LIFO (last in first out) or average unit cost.

To illustrate differences in reported earnings, Table 11–5 gives income statements for two hypothetical, identical firms that differ only in their chosen accounting methods. The first firm (Conservative Company) chooses the methods that result in lower reported profits while the second (Aggressive Company) prefers the alternatives that yield higher earnings. Conservative Company uses the LIFO inventory valuation method while Aggressive Company uses the FIFO technique. The higher-priced inventory remaining on the books of Aggressive Company results in a lower reported cost of goods sold and higher reported profit.

TABLE 11–5
Comparison of income statements for identical firms using different accounting techniques

	Conservative	*Aggressive*
Net sales	15,000	17,000
Cost of goods sold:		
Beginning inventory	3,000	3,000
Purchases	10,000	10,000
Less: ending inventory	−3,000	−4,000
Total	10,000	9,000
Gross margin	5,000	8,000
Expenses:		
Depreciation	2,000	1,000
Pensions	1,000	800
Other	2,000	2,000
Total	5,000	3,800
Net earnings	0	4,200

Because inventory valuation methods can yield different reported earnings, security analysts and investors should be familiar with the method in use by the company being analyzed. The footnotes to the financial statements reveal details about inventory valuation.

Depreciation

Methods of accelerated depreciation cause reported expenses to be higher and earnings to be lower in the early years of an asset's life. The several methods of accounting for depreciation allowed by the SEC and the IRS can each result in different earnings. In Table 11–5, Conservative Company uses an accelerated depreciation computation while Aggressive uses the straight-line technique.

Information about depreciation methods is included in the notes section of a company's financial statements. This also includes other meaningful data, such as the remaining useful lives of property, plant, and equipment.

Taxes

Not only do the various profit-changing accounting techniques result in different taxes payable, but also similar firms often seem to be taxed at different rates, even though the standard marginal tax rate for large corporations is 38 percent of income. Several reasons help explain this situation:

1. Tax rates for certain types of income are taxed at lower rates.
2. In some instances, earnings reported to the IRS for tax purposes are different from the amount given in the report to shareholders.
3. Loss carry-back or carry-forward can affect a firm's taxes for a period of several years.

Recognition of Sales

In Table 11–5, Aggressive Company recognizes both its cash sales and all sales made on installment contracts at the time of sale. Conservative Company recognizes only cash sales at sale time and waits to record its installment contracts until final payment is received. Both methods are acceptable, but the alternative chosen by Aggressive Company more truly reflects the economic earnings of the firm, especially if the firm maintains a reserve for bad installment sales.

Pensions

Most companies offer their employees some type of pension plan for retirement. They do have some discretion regarding the amount that they can expense each year for these benefits. Basically, the maximum amount that the company can charge off is based on the concept that pension payments are owed to individual employees. On the other hand, the minimum amount is based on the idea that contributions to the pension go into a fund that will pay benefits to all employees. The difference is that the maximum considers the expected life span of each individual while the minimum looks at the entire group of employees from now until some indefinite time in the future. Pension costs can also vary depending upon the amount of interest that the pension fund manager estimates will be earned on invested funds over the employee's lives. If a higher rate of return is assumed, current pension expenses would be lowered. In Table 11–5, Conservative Company takes the maximum approach, and Aggressive Company chooses the minimum.

Calculation of Earnings per Share

Investors are usually more concerned with earnings per share (EPS) of common stock rather than total earnings of the company. Calculation of EPS is usually not as straightforward as just dividing earnings by the number of shares outstanding. The two main problems in computing EPS occur in the determination of the number of shares outstanding and the effects of dilution.

Number of Shares Outstanding. A firm reports its earnings for a period representing a *span of time,* while a given number of shares are outstanding at *one point in time.* If the number of shares outstanding during the accounting period does not remain fixed, then a weighted average number of shares must be computed using the following guidelines:

1. Treat new shares resulting from stock splits or stock dividends during the accounting period as if they had been outstanding as long as the original shares.
2. Assume that new shares issued as a result of a merger under a pooling of interest were outstanding at the beginning of the accounting period.
3. Record new shares issued for cash, repurchased for cash, or issued in a merger treated as a purchase as outstanding from the date of issue.

Reported EPS figures use the above guidelines, so any projections by the analyst need to take into account changes in shares outstanding by calculating the weighted average number of shares outstanding for the time period. In addition to shares that are outstanding, there are potential shares that may be issued as a result of conversion of convertible securities. These new shares could dilute EPS and therefore are of concern to the investor.

Effects of Dilution. If the company has any securities outstanding that may be converted into common stock, the firm may have to report two EPS figures: *primary earnings per share* and *fully diluted earnings per share.* Convertible securities that might qualify are convertible bonds, convertible preferred stocks, warrants, and executive stock options (options issued by the company to its management to purchase the firm's common stock). To distinguish between primary EPS and fully diluted EPS, accountants classify convertible securities of the firm into three categories:

1. *Common stock equivalents*
2. *Dilutive convertible securities*
3. *Anti-dilutive convertible securities*

The accounting profession has a set of rules that determine whether to consider a convertible security to be a common stock equivalent. These rules are fairly complex, but as a general definition, common stock equivalents (CSEs) are convertible securities that are still outstanding but would be converted today if the company were to say to holders, "Convert now or lose your conversion rights." CSEs are always considered to be common stock shares in the computation of both primary and fully diluted EPS. However, primary earnings per share include only CSEs. Fully diluted earnings per share also consider all other dilutive convertible securities. A convertible is dilutive when computed EPS would be lower if the convertibles were considered as outstanding common stock. When the treatment of a convertible security as common stock results in EPS greater than without it, the convertibles are anti-dilutive. Anti-dilutive convertible securities are never used to compute EPS figures.

The exact formulas accountants use to compute earnings per share can be complex and subject to interpretation depending upon the provisions of the convertible securities outstanding. As a general relationship, the following formula represents the computation of primary EPS:

$$\text{Primary EPS} = \frac{\text{Net income} + \text{CSE income adjustments}}{\text{Weighted shares outstanding} + \text{CSE share adjustments}} \quad \textbf{(11–1)}$$

The numerator of Equation 11–1 says that, to compute primary EPS, earnings must be adjusted for CSEs. This adjustment represents the effect on earnings of the preferred dividends or interest expense attributable to the CSEs. This adjustment is necessary because if the CSEs were converted to common stock, the company would no longer pay their dividends or interest. The denominator is equal to the weighted number of shares outstanding plus the adjustment for CSE shares. This adjustment assumes that the company uses the funds received from conversion to repurchase the firm's common stock at market price.

Fully diluted EPS would result from conversion of *all* CSEs and dilutive securities. A general relationship for fully diluted EPS is as follows:

$$\text{Fully diluted EPS} = \frac{\text{Net income} + \text{CSE and dilutive income adjustments}}{\text{Weighted shares outstanding} + \text{CSE and dilutive share adjustments}} \tag{11–2}$$

RATIO ANALYSIS

The most common technique for analyzing financial statement data is through *financial ratios*. An analyst computes a financial ratio by dividing one financial statement item by another. Because ratios place what they measure on a relative basis, ratio analysis allows comparison of companies of different sizes.

Some Uses of Ratio Analysis

Financial ratios, by their nature, present information based solely on historical results. Do such historical data provide information that is useful to analysts in predicting future results? Most researchers agree that financial ratio analysis does have some value in foreseeing at least some of the financial results of a company. For example, Peterson[1] identifies nine different ratio groups that tend to predict superior long-run stock market performance, nine groups that appear useful in forecasting short-run results, and nine that are valuable in estimating high levels of market risk.

Analysts also use ratio analysis for more specific purposes. For example, ratio analysis appears to be useful in predicting corporate bankruptcy.[2] In addition, there is a high degree of correlation between certain ratios and the risk of insolvency in the banking industry.[3] However, ratio analysis does have its limits. For example, attempts to identify financial ratios that can pinpoint takeover targets find no ratios able to predict whether a firm is a good takeover candidate.[4]

How Analysts Use Ratios

Ratios are very useful screening devices. For example, an investor may want to consider only companies that have liquid cash positions. To do this, the investor can screen out companies whose liquidity ratios do not meet a particular standard. Ratios can indicate financial strength or weakness. By itself, however, a financial ratio is not very useful to a security analyst. It is the comparison of the ratio to other ratios that makes ratios an important tool to investment analysts. For example, one popular measure of a firm's profitability is its return on stockholder's equity. This ratio is equal to the company's net income divided by its average stockholder's equity. General Foods' *return on equity (ROE)* for 1985 was 16.3 percent. Is this good or bad? To reach a conclusion, we need to be able to compare this ratio to others. There are three types of comparisons that analysts find particularly valuable:

1. Comparison to the industry average
2. Analysis of the ratio's trend
3. Comparison of the ratio's trend to the industry's trend

Comparison to the Industry Average

To address the question of whether General Foods' ROE of 16.3 percent is favorable or unfavorable, we can begin by comparing it to other firms. We must take care that we compare our firm to other firms in the same industry. Available evidence from McDonald and Morris[5] indicates that comparing ratios to firms of other industries is not empirically valid. We could compare General Foods to the industry as a whole by computing the ROE for other leading firms in the food industry. However, this would mean that we would have to compare General Foods' ROE to every other ROE in order to conclude whether General Foods' was favorable or unfavorable.

The easiest way to make the comparison is via the industry average ratio. It is simple and direct, and the analyst has to make only one comparison to conclude whether the company is in a favorable position with regard to the industry as far as this ratio is concerned. These averages for standard industrial groups are available from various published sources such as *The Value Line Investment Survey,* Standard & Poor's *Industry Surveys,* RMA (Robert Morris Associates) *Annual Statement Studies,* Troy's *Almanac of Business and Industrial Financial Ratios,* and Dun and Bradstreet's *Key Business Ratios.*

The Value Line reports a food industry average ROE of 15.0 percent for 1985. General Foods ROE of 16.3 percent for the same time period compares slightly favorably, although it is not an area in which General Foods Corp. excels against the industry. Some of the sources of industry ratios provide information on the range of the ratio in addition to the average. For example, some give the first and third quartile. Armed with such data, analysts can even determine whether the company is in the top quarter.

If these quartiles are quite far apart, however, comparison of a ratio to the industry average may not be justified. A study by Martin and Henderson[6] found that a few industries have ratios that vary widely within the industry. They concluded that in such cases, simple comparison of a company ratio to the industry norm is of questionable value.

One problem with using industry averages is determining into which industry a particular company fits. General Foods is easy; it fits nicely into *Value Line's* "food processing" classification. Many companies are more horizontally diversified and may offer products or services from several widely different industries. One solution to this problem is to identify the main industries in which the company operates. After determining the percentage of revenue that each segment contributes to the firm's total revenue, you can compute a weighted average of the component industry averages.

Analysis of the Ratio's Trend

A second technique in ratio analysis is to examine the trend of the ratio over several recent reporting periods. Often, the most dramatic way to present the trend analysis is with a graph. Figure 11–1 provides an example using the ROE for General Foods.

Examination of this graph shows that the trend is generally sideways. Usually, a sideways trend is favorable because it denotes stability. With the exception of a slight drop in 1982, General Foods' ROE over the time period was relatively stable. Of

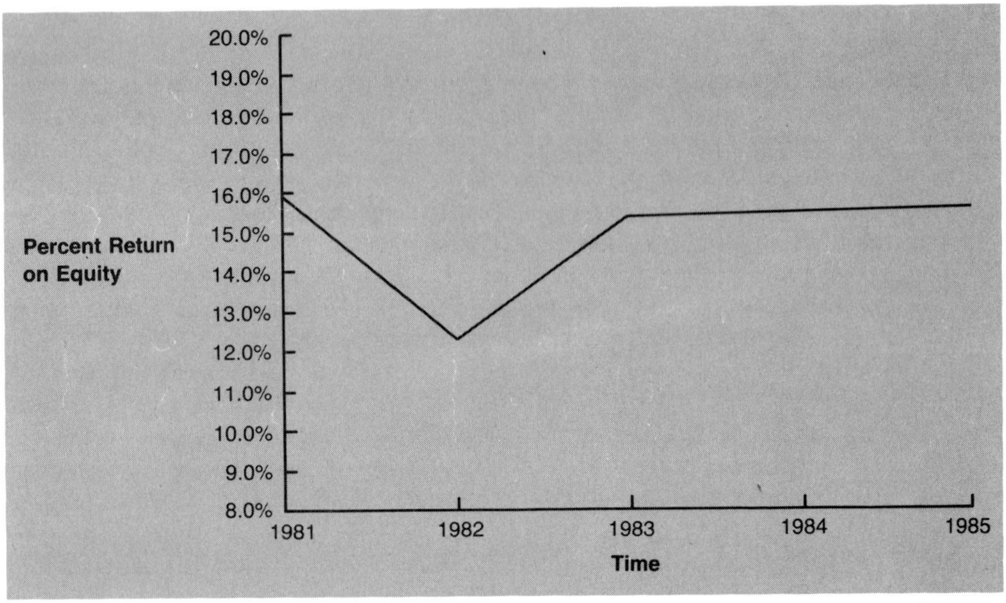

FIGURE 11–1
Trend of return on equity for General Foods Corporation

course, we often would like to see an upward trend in a ratio and would view it as a favorable sign of continuing improvement. However, an upward trend usually cannot continue for very long; it eventually must level out, or even fall. For example, it would be ridiculous to think that any firm could continue to increase its ROE year after year indefinitely. Naturally, a downward trend or an unstable ratio over time would generally be unfavorable.

Ratio Trend vs. Industry Trend

A third ratio analysis tool combines the first two. It involves comparing the trend in the company's ratio to the trend in the industry ratio. Figure 11–2 shows a graph comparing General Foods' ROE to the food industry average. It shows General Foods' ROE to have increased in a generally stable manner as the industry average increased (with the exception of one year, 1982). Most analysts would likely view this as a slightly favorable situation.

Another way to examine the company's ratio trend to the industry norm trend is to compute a *ratio of the ratios.* To do this, divide the firm's ratio by the industry average ratio. If this composite ratio is equal to 1.0, then the firm is the same as the industry. A result greater than 1.0 means the firm's ratio is greater. If the composite ratio is in an upward trend, we would conclude that the firm's ratio is increasing at a faster rate than the industry (a generally favorable sign). However, as in the case of the simple trend analysis, the composite ratio trend cannot continue upward or downward indefinitely.

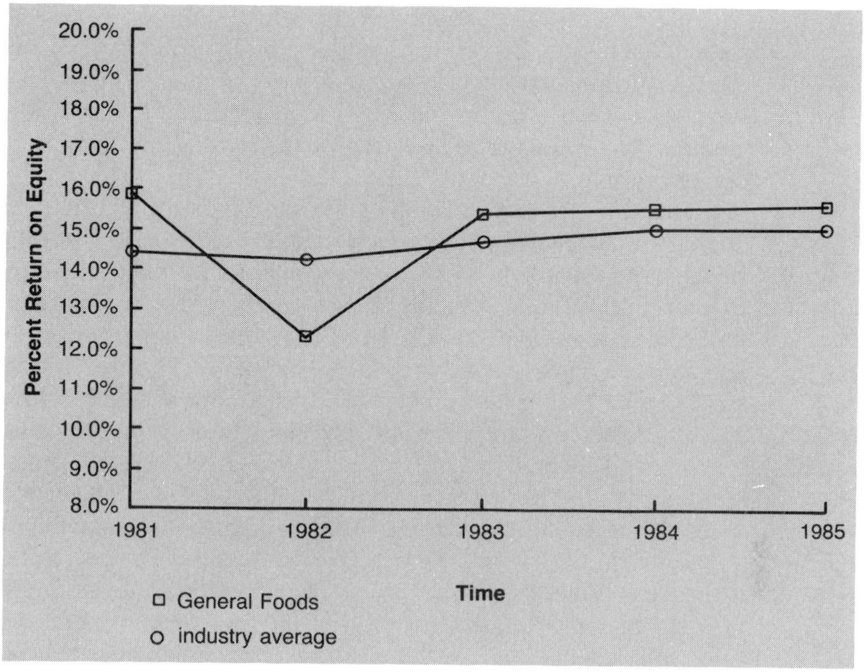

FIGURE 11–2
Trend of return on equity for General Foods Corporation compared to the return on equity trend for the food industry

Key Ratios

Although there are hundreds of possible financial ratios, probably about fifty different ratios are in popular use. Every ratio provides information about a particular financial area of the firm, and most analysts group their ratios according to this area. While there are several of these classification groups for financial ratios, this text presents ratios grouped into five major areas:

1. Liquidity ratios
2. Performance ratios
3. Capital structure ratios
4. Market ratios
5. Others

Within each group are ratios that "overlap" each other. That is, two or more ratios may be very similar in definition, measuring almost the same items. These ratios will be very highly correlated. In such instances, an analyst normally presents only one of these ratios. This allows us to narrow down significantly the set of important ratios. This book presents twenty commonly used ratios that represent the entire spectrum of financial ratio analysis.

Generally speaking, the higher the values of the ratios presented here, the more favorable they are. However, sometimes the interpretation of a ratio's meaning may depend on the analysis of other ratios. For example, many people view low debt levels as a positive factor, but if a firm at the same time has low return on equity, then this may imply that the company is not making adequate use of its debt-financing opportunities.

One note on the calculation of ratios is important. As we have already mentioned, the income statement gives financial results over a period of time, while the balance sheet shows the financial position at one point in time. Therefore, a problem arises when a financial ratio contains at least one item from both statements. It is possible for balance sheet items to be temporarily large or small at the time of the statement. Sometimes a company will even make temporary changes in its financial position at statement time to make its financial position appear better. For example, a company could make its inventory turnover ratio look better by selling off some inventory just before statement time and then replacing it later. Analysts call such maneuvers *financial window dressing*. In an effort to reduce the effects of fluctuations in balance sheet items and to see through a one-time attempt at financial window dressing, analysts should use an average balance sheet figure to compute ratios that mix income statement and balance sheet items. The easiest average to compute is simply to add the current period balance sheet account value to its prior period value and divide by two. A more involved method would be to compute a weighted average over the accounting period, if the data are available. Of course, if only the latest balance sheet account is available, then one must settle for using it and not the average figure.

Liquidity Ratios

The *liquidity ratios* measure the ability of the firm to meet its short-term needs for cash. The *current ratio* measures the number of times the firm could pay off its current liabilities with its investment in current assets.

$$\text{Current ratio} = \frac{\text{Current assets}}{\text{Current liabilities}} \qquad \textbf{(11–3)}$$

Analysts usually view a higher current ratio as more favorable. If the current ratio becomes too high, however, it may indicate that the firm has too much of its capital invested in low yielding short-term assets.

The *quick ratio,* also called the *acid test ratio,* is a more rigorous test of the firm's solvency than the current ratio. Because the company's inventories are probably its least liquid current assets, the quick ratio excludes them:

$$\text{Quick ratio} = \frac{\text{Current assets} - \text{inventories}}{\text{Current liabilities}} \qquad \textbf{(11–4)}$$

Performance Ratios

Performance ratios indicate the firm's ability to use its assets to produce profits. Producing profits, financially, is a two-step process:

1. The firm utilizes its assets to generate sales.
2. It turns those sales into profits.

Ratios measuring the first step are *activity ratios,* while *profitability ratios* are indicative of the firm's success during the second step.

Activity Ratios. Sometimes analysts refer to activity ratios as *turnover ratios* because they are the number of times a particular asset group "turns into" sales during a year. The first of these is *receivables turnover.*

$$\text{Receivables turnover} = \frac{\text{Sales}}{\text{Average accounts receivable}} \qquad \textbf{(11–5)}$$

Receivables turnover is a good indication of the firm's success in collecting its accounts receivable. Slow collections will result in a low receivables turnover, while a company with customers who regularly pay on time will have a higher ratio. Sometimes analysts multiply the reciprocal of the receivables turnover by 365 days to compute *average collection period.* The two ratios are essentially the same thing. The analyst should view the receivables turnover in light of the company's credit policy. For example, a company with a net sixty-day credit policy would have a receivables turnover of 6 if all customers pay exactly on time (assuming all sales are on credit). An analyst would probably view this favorably as a successful collection department. Compare this to another company with credit terms of thirty days. If it collects its accounts in sixty days, it too would have a receivables turnover of 6, but it should be viewed unfavorably compared to the firm's credit policy.

$$\text{Inventory turnover} = \frac{\text{Cost of goods sold}}{\text{Average inventory}} \qquad \textbf{(11–6)}$$

Inventory turnover is a measure of the company's inventory management efficiency and the ability to sell its inventory. It is also a measure of how liquid the firm's inventory is. Usually a high inventory turnover is a favorable sign. If it is too high, however, it could be a sign that inventories are kept too low, possibly resulting in stockouts and lost sales.

$$\text{Fixed asset turnover} = \frac{\text{Sales}}{\text{Average fixed assets}} \qquad \textbf{(11–7)}$$

Fixed asset turnover gauges a company's ability to use its permanent assets (property, plant, equipment) to generate sales. For an industrial firm, it is an indication of management's ability to utilize plant capacity efficiently.

$$\text{Total asset turnover} = \frac{\text{Sales}}{\text{Average total assets}} \qquad \textbf{(11–8)}$$

Total asset turnover is similar to fixed asset turnover, but it includes all of the firm's assets.

Profitability Ratios. Investors often call profitability ratios *efficiency ratios.* The first three of these are the *profit margin ratios.*

$$\text{Gross profit margin} = \frac{\text{Gross profit}}{\text{Sales}} \tag{11–9}$$

Gross profit margin measures management's efficiency in generating gross profit from sales. It indicates how well costs of goods sold are kept under control.

$$\text{Operating profit margin} = \frac{\text{Operating profit}}{\text{Sales}} \tag{11–10}$$

Operating profit margin takes over where the gross profit margin leaves off and measures management's ability to control its general and administrative expenses while generating profits.

$$\text{Net profit margin} = \frac{\text{Net profit}}{\text{Sales}} \tag{11–11}$$

Net profit margin measures profitability after all expenses and taxes. An analyst should use the three profit margin ratios in conjunction. For example, a relatively strong operating profit margin coupled with a low net profit margin may indicate that the company pays too much interest or pays taxes at a higher rate than its competitors.

$$\text{Return on investment} = \frac{\text{Net income}}{\text{Average total assets}} \tag{11–12}$$

Return on investment measures the overall efficiency of the firm's management and its ability to use the total resource of the company to yield profits.

$$\text{Return on equity} = \frac{\text{Net income}}{\text{Average equity}} \tag{11–13}$$

Probably the most important ratio measuring the overall success of management and its ability to operate profitably within an optimum capital structure is the *return on equity.* Although the ratio shown here is the one most commonly presented in the financial literature, many analysts prefer to use *return on common equity,* which is equal to net income less preferred dividends divided by common stockholders' equity.

$$\text{Return on common equity} = \frac{\text{Net income} - \text{preferred dividends}}{\text{Average common equity}} \tag{11–14}$$

Capital Structure

The *capital structure ratios* measure the amount of debt (financial leverage) within the firm's capital and the firm's ability to service that debt. We can divide the capital structure ratios into *debt utilization ratios* and *coverage ratios.*

Debt Utilization Ratios. The debt utilization ratios gauge the extent of the firm's use of debt financing. The *total debt ratio* measures use of total debt (liabilities) relative to stockholder financing, and the *long-term debt ratio* examines the long-term portion of debt in relation to equity.

$$\text{Total debt ratio} = \frac{\text{Total liabilities}}{\text{Total equity}} \qquad \textbf{(11–15)}$$

$$\text{Long-term debt ratio} = \frac{\text{Long-term debt}}{\text{Total equity}} \qquad \textbf{(11–16)}$$

Coverage Ratios. A company must be able to earn sufficient profits from its funds generated by debt financing to benefit from financial leverage. The coverage ratios measure the firm's ability to earn these profits. The first of these is the *interest coverage ratio.*

$$\text{Interest coverage} = \frac{\text{Operating profit}}{\text{Interest expense}} \qquad \textbf{(11–17)}$$

This ratio, also called *times interest earned,* shows how many times a company could pay its current interest charges with its current profits. The higher this ratio, the better credit risk analysts consider the firm to be. This is probably the most important ratio for analyzing bonds.

$$\text{Total fixed charge coverage} = \frac{\text{Operating profit} + \text{lease payments}}{\text{Int. exp.} + \text{lease pmts.} + (\text{Pfd. div.} + \text{Sinking fund pmts.})\,(1 - \text{tax rate})} \qquad \textbf{(11–18)}$$

In addition to interest expense, there are certain payments that the firm has contractually obligated itself to pay (lease payments and payments to a sinking fund to retire debt) and payments that investors expect the firm to pay as long as it is profitable (preferred dividends). The *total fixed charge coverage* ratio shows how many times the firm earns enough to cover these fixed charges. Note that we must multiply the preferred dividends by (1 − tax rate). This gives us the before-tax earnings necessary to make the preferred payment because dividends are not expense items for tax purposes.

Market Ratios

The *market ratios* received their name because some market-determined value influences their computation. First of these is the *dividend yield.*

$$\text{Dividend yield} = \frac{\text{Dividend per share}}{\text{Stock price}} \qquad \textbf{(11–19)}$$

The dividend yield measures the current return from dividend income of the stock. Interpretation of this ratio often depends on the investment goals of the investor. For example, an investor requiring a high level of current cash flow from investments would probably desire stocks with higher dividend yields.

$$\text{Price to earnings ratio} = \frac{\text{Stock price}}{\text{Earnings per share}} \qquad \textbf{(11–20)}$$

The *price to earnings (PE) ratio,* also called the *earnings multiple,* is the number of times investors value earnings in the stock price. It represents investors' expectations about the stock's growth potential and risk. Chapter 14 will deal at more length with the PE ratio.

$$\text{Institutional ownership} = \frac{\text{Number of shares owned by institutions}}{\text{Total number of shares outstanding}} \qquad \textbf{(11–21)}$$

Institutional ownership is the percentage of shares owned by investing institutions such as pension funds, insurance companies, and mutual funds. Some investors prefer stocks with low institutional ownership. They believe that stocks with a large institutional following will be priced more efficiently and that therefore the chance of their being undervalued is slim.

Other Ratios

Two other ratios are important but do not fit easily into any of the previously mentioned categories. The first of these is the *tax rate.*

$$\text{Tax rate} = \frac{\text{Income taxes}}{\text{Earnings before taxes}} \qquad \textbf{(11–22)}$$

Although to a great extent external agencies (the taxing authorities) determine a firm's tax rate, effective tax rates among firms may show quite a bit of variation. A lower rate can be a measure of a company's success in sheltering some of its income from taxes. It can also result from carrying forward losses from prior years, so analysts should closely examine the reasons behind a tax rate that is significantly different from the industry's average.

$$\text{Payout ratio} = \frac{\text{Common stock dividends}}{\text{Net income available to common}} \qquad \textbf{(11–23)}$$

The *payout ratio* is the percentage of earnings that the firm pays out as cash dividends. Note that the denominator is net income available to pay dividends to common stock. This is net income less any dividends to preferred shareholders. Payout ratios can vary widely between industries. For example, the electric utility industry typically pays a high portion of its earnings to its stockholders, while a newer, growing industry may retain most of its earnings to help fund growth. Chapter 14 discusses payout ratios in more depth.

Common Size Statements

Common size financial statements allow comparison of entire balance sheets and income statements of firms of different sizes by comparing each statement item to a common denominator. For the *common size income statement,* the common denominator is net sales. A *common size balance sheet* presents assets and liabilities as a percentage of total assets. Common size statement analysis takes the same approach as analysis using other ratios: comparison to industry averages and analysis of trend.

TABLE 11–6
Common size income statement for General Foods Corporation

Income Statement (In millions)	*1985*	*Common Size*
Net sales	$9,022	100.00%
Cost of goods sold	5,508	61.05
Gross profit	3,514	38.95
Expenses	2,906	32.21
Operating profit	608	6.74
Other income, net	146	1.62
Total profit	754	8.36%
Interest expense	150	
Income before taxes	604	
Income taxes	279	
Net income	$ 325	
Dividends paid	123	
Preferred dividends	0	
Increase in retained earnings	$ 202	
Avg. shares outstanding	49	
Earnings per share	$ 6.61	
Dividends per share	2.50	
Book value	$39.46	

Tables 11–6 and 11–7 give examples of the common size income statement and common size balance sheet for General Foods.

FORECASTING

Financial forecasting—predicting future financial results of a company—is a difficult and often inexact undertaking. An analyst can spend many hours of tedious work to forecast only one financial variable of a firm. The inexactness of the forecast might then become evident several days later if some unexpected event occurs such as a strike.

In financial forecasting, there are many different variables to consider and many different techniques that provide useful computations. For example, consider a forecast of next year's sales of large home appliances such as washing machines. Future sales of home appliances would likely depend on many different factors, including but not limited to the following: consumer disposable income, new home construction, prices of home appliances, prices of substitute goods and services, interest rates, and ap-

TABLE 11–7
Common size balance sheet for General Foods Corporation

Balance Sheet	*1985*	*Common Size*
Assets:		
Current assets:		
Cash and equivalents	$ 288	6.33%
Accounts receivable	949	20.83
Inventories	1,075	23.60
Other	66	1.46
Total current assets	2,378	52.22
Fixed assets:		
Property, plant, equipment	1,917	42.09
Accumulated depreciation	165	3.63
Property, net	1,752	38.46
Other fixed assets	424	9.32
Total fixed assets	2,176	47.78
Total assets	$4,554	100.00%
Liabilities:		
Current liabilities:		
Short-term debt	$ 395	8.67%
Payables	1,008	22.13
Total current liabilities	1,403	30.80
Long-term liabilities:		
Long-term debt	725	15.92
Other long-term liabilities	486	10.67
Total long-term liabilities	1,211	26.59
Total liabilities	$2,614	57.39
Stockholders' equity:		
Common stock	323	7.09
Retained earnings	1,944	42.69
Treasury stock	(327)	−7.18
Total equity	$1,940	42.61%

pliance industry advertising campaigns. To provide the most accurate sales forecast possible, any forecast of home appliance sales should consider all of these factors. In turn, each of these factors may be influenced by other economic or industry circumstances that the analyst would need to study.

After determining all the relevant factors and gathering all the data to use in the forecast, the analyst must choose a forecasting model or technique. These techniques include such tools as linear trend, exponential smoothing, trend-adjusting exponential smoothing, sinusoidal models, Box-Jenkins analysis, and econometric methods. Because the study of just a few of these methods is well beyond the scope of this text, we present here only one of the simplest techniques for forecasting, that of simple linear trend. Even though this technique is simple, it can often provide very good financial forecasts. One study, by Richards, Benjamin, and Strawser,[7] found that earnings forecasts using trend methods averaged about 29 percent error from the actual reported earnings. This compares fairly favorably with forecasts of professional analysts whose errors averaged about 21 percent. Although the professionals did better (as we would expect), naive extrapolation of past trend did a fairly good job.

Forecasting Using Simple Trends

If we assume that past growth patterns of a variable are good predictors of future growth, then simple linear trend provides us with relatively accurate forecasts of the future. It simply takes the past growth pattern and extrapolates it into the future.

When forecasting economic variables such as sales, expenses, or earnings, we normally expect them to grow at a consistent *rate* rather than a consistent *dollar amount*. For example, it is more reasonable to expect a company to expand its sales at a rate of 8 percent per year than by a fixed dollar sum per year. If a company grew by a fixed dollar amount each year, its actual growth rate in percent would be declining. It is for this reason that we use logarithms when projecting most company data using trend. We present here two methods for accomplishing this.

The first of these methods is *graphical trend analysis*. It is the simplest to use unless you have access to good trend-forecasting software and a computer. Figure 11–3 presents a graphical analysis of a forecast of General Foods' sales. To avoid the mathematical complexity of taking logarithms of the sales numbers, we use a special graph paper with a vertical log scale. Then we graph the sales on the paper and visually fit a line through the points. The solid line represents the "fit" through the past sales and the broken line represents the forecast. The projected sales for 1986 are approximately $9,900 million and for 1987 about $10,500 million. This method has a large degree of subjectivity to it because the slope of the visual line through the past data can be altered easily to change the forecasts.

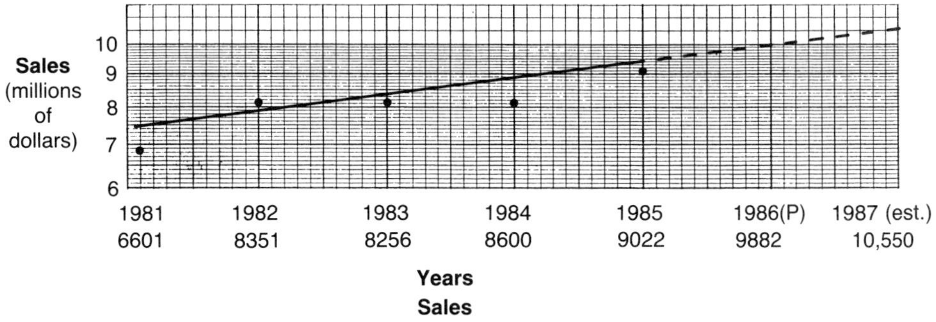

FIGURE 11–3
Graphical trend forecast of General Foods Corporation sales

TABLE 11–8
Pro forma operating income statement for General Foods Corporation

	1985	*1986 (Projected) (In millions)*
Net sales	100.00%	$9,882
Cost of goods sold	61.05	6,033
Gross profit	38.95	3,849
Expenses	32.21	3,183
Operating profit	6.74	666
Other income, net	1.62	160
Total profit	8.36%	$ 826

A second method, *linear regression,* computes this line mathematically and avoids the problem of subjectivity. Linear regression is a statistical procedure that finds a line of "best fit" through past data points, and we defer any discussion of the technique to a statistics book. However, today there are many microcomputer software packages and calculators available that allow the analyst to input the past data points. The program then performs the regression and outputs the formula for the line and the future forecasts. Inputing General Foods' sales for 1981 through 1985 into a trend-forecasting program yields a forecast of $9,882 million for 1985 and $10,550 million for 1986.

Pro Forma Financial Statements

Pro forma financial statements are forecasts of a company's entire financial statement. Pro forma statements are based upon a set of assumptions and forecasts regarding future revenues, expenses, asset levels, and sources of financing. For example, using a forecast of total revenues and assumptions about the relationship of expenses to revenues, we can construct a pro forma income statement and forecast earnings. Table 11–8 presents a 1986 pro forma operating income statement for General Foods. Construction of this pro forma statement was based upon the sales forecast from the previous section and the assumption that the ratios of cost of goods sold, expenses, and other income to sales would remain constant from the common size income statement of 1985 (from Table 11–6).

SUMMARY

The major financial statements are the income statement, balance sheet, statement of changes in financial position, and statement of retained earnings. Although analysts rely heavily upon the financial statements to help them analyze the financial condition and future prospects of a company, some problems may be associated with the numbers reported in the statements. The central problem is the difference between reported earnings and economic earnings. Some financial statement account categories that may be sources of these differences include inventories, depreciation, taxes, sales, and pensions.

Analysts use ratio analysis as their main tool to examine a company's financial condition. Methods of using ratios include comparison to industry averages and analysis of the trend. The major groups of ratios are those measuring liquidity, performance, and capital structure. Other ratios measure market factors and various useful items. Common size income statements present each account in the entire income statement as a percentage of revenue. The common size balance sheet gives its accounts relative to total assets.

Financial forecasting can be a complicated and involved process, but extrapolation of a trend does give analysts a simple and useful tool for forecasting. Pro forma financial statements give analysts' projections of a company's future financial statements.

IMPORTANT TERMS

activity ratios
average collection period
balance sheet
capital structure ratios
common size statement
coverage ratios
current ratio
debt utilization ratios
dividend yield
earnings multiple
economic earnings
efficiency ratios
financial ratios
financial window dressing
fiscal year
fixed asset turnover
graphical trend analysis
income statement
institutional ownership
interest coverage ratio
inventory turnover
linear regression
liquidity ratios
long-term debt ratio
market ratios
market value
net profit margin
operating profit margin
payout ratio
performance ratios
price to earnings (PE) ratio
profit margin ratios
profitability ratios
pro forma statement
quick ratio
ratio of the ratios
receivables turnover
reported earnings
return on equity (ROE)
return on investment
statement of changes in financial position
statement of earnings
statement of financial position
statement of retained earnings
tax rate
times interest earned
total asset turnover
total debt ratio
total fixed charge coverage
turnover ratios

QUESTIONS AND PROBLEMS

1. The Davis Corporation had 750,000 shares outstanding at the beginning of the year. On April 1, it sold 200,000 additional shares to investors at $40 per share.
   a) What was the average number of shares outstanding for the year?
   b) If Davis had a two-for-one stock split on July 1 of the following year, how many shares would be outstanding at the end of that year? What would be the weighted average number of shares outstanding?
2. Greene Mills had net earnings of $6.5 million and 2 million common shares outstanding. It also has $2 million in 8 percent bonds outstanding convertible into 400,000 common shares. These are considered to be common stock equivalents. Greene's marginal tax rate is 34 percent. Compute Greene's primary earnings per share.
3. Orange Mills earned $4 million and had 2 million common shares outstanding. It has $1 million in 12 percent bonds convertible into 100,000 shares. Since investors would not desire to convert these bonds now, they are not common stock equivalents. Compute both primary and fully diluted earnings per share, assuming the firm's marginal tax rate is 34 percent.
4. What would be the impact upon companies' reported earnings if a new tax bill allowed capital assets to be depreciated at a faster rate? What would be the impact upon companies' cash flows? What would happen to the government's revenues from income taxes?
5. Why do analysts use financial ratios instead of the more direct approach of comparing two companies' balance sheets and income statements?
6. Alaska Air's return on equity was .185, .201, and .244 for 1982, 1983, and 1984 respectively. The airline industry's ROE was .105, .120, and .152.
   a) Present this information in a format that you might use to make a presentation to a group of investors.
   b) Discuss Alaska Air's performance regarding this ratio.
   c) During the same time period, Alaska Air's total asset turnover was 1.20, 1.14, and 1.11, while the industry's was 1.30, 1.30, and 1.39. Analyze and interpret this information. Does this help explain Alaska Air's ROE trend relative to the industry ROE trend? Why?
7. You have the following financial statements for Myers Sock Co.:

Income Statement		*Balance Sheet*	
Sales	$56,000	Cash	$ 2,000
Cost of goods sold	39,000	Accounts receivable	7,000
General expenses	8,000	Inventory	6,000
Interest expense	4,000	Fixed assets	30,000
Net income	$ 3,000	Total assets	$45,000
		Current liabilities	8,000
		Long-term liabilities	30,000
		Equity	7,000
		Total liabilities and equity	$45,000

   Compute the following ratios:
   a) current ratio
   b) quick ratio
   c) gross profit margin
   d) net profit margin

e) long-term debt to equity
f) inventory turnover
g) receivables turnover
h) total asset turnover
i) interest coverage

8. Without knowing any of the industry averages for the Myers Sock Company in Problem 7, identify the strong areas of this company and any possible problem areas.
9. Construct a common size income statement and common size balance sheet for Myers Sock Company (Problem 7).
10. Assume that Myers Sock Company (Problem 7) pays all its earnings out as dividends; that income statement accounts will retain the same percentages as in the common size statement of Problem 9 (except interest, which will remain at $4000), and that forecasted sales are $61,000.
    a) Construct a pro forma income statement.
    b) What would happen to earnings if sales fell to $52,000?
11. The Amalgamated Grains Cereal Company had the following sales and earnings per share for the past seven years:

	Year 1	*Year 2*	*Year 3*	*Year 4*	*Year 5*	*Year 6*	*Year 7*
Sales per share	$24.83	$29.77	$33.93	$34.59	$32.75	$41.29	$43.65
Earnings per share	1.00	1.14	1.25	1.30	1.46	1.63	1.88

    a) Using the graphical method, forecast the next two years' sales per share and earnings per share for Amalgamated Grains Cereal. What growth rate in each do you forecast?
    b) If you have forecasting software available, use it to forecast sales per share and earnings per share for two years. What growth rates do these forecasts represent? Compare these forecasts to those you developed in part a.
12. You have just begun reading a financial analysis and report of The Juan Diego Corporation. Over the past three years, the company had consistently and successfully cut costs and had a total operating expense to revenue ratio of .43, .41 and .39 for those years. During that time, the industry average for that ratio had remained constant at .42. The analyst for the report used a straight line forecast to project pro forma income statements for Juan Diego for the next five years. The resulting forecasts were .37, .35, .33, .31, and .29. In your opinion, was the analyst justified in making such a forecast? Explain your reasons.

NOTES

1. Donald M. Peterson (1970), *Financial Ratios and Investment Results,* Lexington, MA: Lexington Books.
2. Peter S. Rose and Gary Giroux (1984), "Predicting Corporate Bankruptcy: An Analytical and Empirical Evaluation," *Review of Business and Economic Research,* 19 (Spring), 1–12.
3. Alan Marcus and Israel Shaked (1984), "The Relationship between Accounting Measures and Prospective Probabilities of Insolvency: An Application to the Banking Industry," *The Financial Review,* 19 (March), 67–83.
4. Udayan P. Rege (1984), "Accounting Ratios to Locate Take-Over Targets," *Journal of Business Finance and Accounting,* 11 (Autumn), 301–311.

5. Bill McDonald and Michael H. Morris (1984), "The Statistical Validity of the Ratio Method in Financial Analysis: An Empirical Examination," *Journal of Business Finance and Accounting,* 11 (Spring), 89–97.
6. Linda J. Martin and Glenn V. Henderson, Jr. (1984), "Industry Influence on Financial Structure: A Matter of Interpretation," *Review of Business and Economics Research,* 19 (Spring), 57–67.
7. R. Malcolm Richards, James Benjamin and Robert H. Strawser (1977), "An Examination of the Accuracy of Earnings Forecasts," *Financial Management,* 6 (Fall), 78–86.

SELECTED REFERENCES

Barnes, P. (1982). "Methodological Implications of Nonnormally Distributed Financial Ratios." *Journal of Business Finance and Accounting,* 9 (Spring), 51–62.

Brown, Lawrence D. (1983). "Accounting Changes and the Accuracy of Analysts' Earnings Forecasts." *Journal of Accounting Research,* 21 (Autumn), 432–443.

Chen, Kung H. and Thomas A. Shimerda (1981). "An Empirical Analysis of Useful Financial Ratios." *Financial Management,* 10 (Spring), 51–60.

Comiskey, Eugene E., Charles W. Mulford and Thomas L. Porter (1986). "Forecast Error, Earnings Variability, and Systematic Risk: Additional Evidence." *Journal of Business Finance and Accounting,* 13 (Summer), 257–266.

Deschamps, Benoit, and Dileep Mehta (1980). "Predictive Ability and Descriptive Validity of Earnings Forecasting Models." *Journal of Finance,* 35 (September), 933–949.

Eckel, Norm (1982). "An EPS Forecasting Model Utilizing Macroeconomic Performance Expectations." *Financial Analysts Journal,* 38 (May-June), 68–77.

Gahlon, J. M., and J. A. Gentry (1982). "On the Relationship between Systematic Risk and the Degrees of Operating and Financial Leverage." *Financial Management,* 11 (Summer), 15–23.

Gallinger, George W., and A. James Ifflander (1986). "The Interest Coverage Ratio: Does It Explain What We Think It Does?" *Akron Business and Economic Review,* 17 (Summer), 22–26.

Givoly, Dan (1985). "The Formation of Earnings Expectations." *Accounting Review,* 60 (July), 372–386.

Lev, B. I., and S. Sunder (1979). "Methodological Issues in the Use of Financial Ratios." *Journal of Accounting and Economics,* 1 (December), 187–210.

Martin, Linda J. and Glenn V. Henderson, Jr. (1984). "Industry Influence on Financial Structure: A Matter of Interpretation." *Review of Business and Economic Research,* 19 (Spring), 57–67.

McDonald, Bill, and Michael H. Morris (1984). "The Statistical Validity of the Ratio Method in Financial Analysis: An Empirical Examination." *Journal of Business Finance and Accounting,* 11 (Spring), 89–97.

McLeay, Stuart (1986). "Student's t and the Distribution of Financial Ratios." *Journal of Business Finance and Accounting,* 13 (Summer), 209–222.

Peasnell, K. V. (1982). "Some Formal Connections between Economic Values and Yields and Accounting Numbers." *Journal of Business Finance and Accounting,* 9 (Autumn), 361–381.

Peterson, Donald M. (1978). "Are Financial Ratios Worth the Effort?" In Peter L. Bernstein (Ed.), *Security Selection and Active Portfolio Management.* New York: Institutional Investor, 134–143.

Rege, Udayan P. (1984). "Accounting Ratios to Locate Takeover Targets." *Journal of Business Finance and Accounting,* 11 (Autumn), 301–311.

Rose, Peter S., and Gary A. Giroux (1984). "Predicting Corporate Bankruptcy: An Analytical and Empirical Evaluation." *Review of Business and Economic Research,* 19 (Spring), 1–12.

Ruland, Williams (1980). "On the Choice of Simple Extrapolative Model Forecasts of Annual Earnings." *Financial Management,* 9 (Summer), 30–37.

Steele, Anthony (1986). "A Note on Estimating the Internal Rate of Return from Published Financial Statements." *Journal of Business Finance and Accounting,* 13 (Spring), 1–14.

Welch, Paul R. (1984). "A Generalized Distributed Lag Model for Predicting Quarterly Earnings." *Journal of Accounting Research,* 22 (Autumn), 744–757.

PART FOUR

Debt Securities

CHAPTER 12

Bond Valuation

Bonds, as introduced in Chapter 2 of this text, give their owners a fixed claim on the assets of the issuer. The amount of this fixed claim is the principal amount of the bond, for which the bond's owner receives periodic interest payments until the principal is repaid.

Why might an investor prefer bonds over other types of investments? Although there are many varied and specific responses to that question, bonds have several general features that might cause an investor to favor them. First, bonds offer a stream of cash income, which is usually less risky and more consistent than offered by stocks. Second, bonds offer an investor the opportunity to take advantage of and profit from general changes in interest rates. Third, bonds offer a specified time horizon during which the investor receives cash flows from the investment. This contrasts with common and preferred stocks, which have unspecified lives.

Investors have traditionally considered bonds to be relatively safe investments because of the priority of bonds' lien position and the relative certainty of interest cash flows. The return of the principal has usually been a sure bet; even when a company goes bankrupt, the bondholders often receive at least a portion of their principal. Receipt of interest payments is also usually a very high probability for the bond investor, although there is always some possibility of default. In case of default, the bond investor will most likely have to forego the interest payments or, in the best case, have them delayed.

In spite of these traditional ideas about bond safety, many recent developments have caused investors to reconsider their notions about the riskiness of bonds as an investment. Fluctuations in interest rates throughout the 1970s and 1980s have caused the prices of bonds to vary widely. During some periods within that time span, bond prices fluctuated more than stock prices. Another factor that has given bonds a more risky label is the increased number of *junk bonds*. Junk bonds are bonds that fall into the more risky classes.

Because of these factors, the bond market is not as docile as it once was. The notion that the bond market is appropriate for "widows and orphans" has passed. In place of a staid bond market, today's bond markets are fast-moving, offering many different types of debt instruments with a wide range of risk-return characteristics. The analysis of the fixed-income portion of an investment portfolio is quite important and deserves a significant portion of an investment analyst's or portfolio manager's time.

BOND CHARACTERISTICS

There are many characteristics of bonds that the investor should know. Table 12–1 summarizes many of the important features that a bond may have. An investor researching a prospective investment in a bond should know these characteristics as

TABLE 12–1
Selected characteristics of bonds

Issuers	Government
	Foreign government
	Federal government
	Federal government agencies
	Political subdivisions (municipals)
	Corporations
	Foreign
	Domestic
Security	Unsecured
	Debentures
	General obligation
	Secured
	Revenue
	Mortgage
	Collateral trust
	Equipment trust
Repayment	Call provision
	Sinking fund
	Serial bond
	Conversion
Interest	Fixed coupon rate
	Variable coupon rate
	Zero coupon

they relate to the bond and should examine the bond's indenture provisions, especially regarding the bond's collateral and repayment.

All bonds issued in the United States must now be in *registered* form. A *registered bond* bears the owner's name on the face of the security and is registered in the name of the owner on the records of the issuer. Ownership of a registered bond can only be transferred by consent of the registered owner. Checks for the interest payments of registered bonds are usually mailed directly to the owner on each interest payment date. Some previously issued bonds that still exist were issued in the form of *bearer bonds*. Such instruments are payable to the bearer and carry coupons representing the interest on the bond. To receive the bond's interest, the holder clips each coupon as its payment date arrives and presents it for payment. For this reason, the annual interest on bonds is called the *coupon amount*. Equation 12–1 says the the *coupon rate* or *coupon yield* is the coupon amount stated as a percentage of the face value of the bond, as follows:

$$Y_{\text{coupon}} = \frac{I}{F} \tag{12–1}$$

where Y_{coupon} = the coupon yield of a bond
I = the annual interest payment or coupon amount
F = the face value or principal of the bond

Since coupon bonds are payable to the bearer, they should be safeguarded and treated as cash. Because of problems with stolen bonds and nonreporting of interest on bearer bonds for tax purposes, federal law now requires that all new bond issues be in registered form.

Bonds that make no payment of interest to their holders before maturity are *zero-coupon bonds*. Zero-coupon bonds sell at a discount from their face value. Upon maturity, the bond's owner receives the entire face amount of the bond. The interest received is equal to the face value of the bond less the bond's purchase price.

Bond Issuers

The three main issuers of bonds covered here are the U.S. government, municipalities and other political subdivisions within the U.S., and corporations. Bonds issued by foreign governments and corporations are also available to investors. Analysis of foreign bonds includes the principles of analysis for domestic bonds plus the added analysis of the currency, economy, and political risk of the foreign country.

U. S. Government Issues

Bond issues of the U.S. government originate from both the U.S. Treasury and from other agencies of the federal government that have the authority to issue debt. The Treasury issues are direct obligations of the U.S. government. Agency issues, depending upon the agency and the issue, may or may not be guaranteed as to payment of principal and interest by the federal government. The interest payments of all federal government issues are taxable at the federal level but are exempt from any state or city income taxes.

Treasury Issues. The short-term debt-management tool of the federal government is the Treasury bill. T-bills are short-term, zero-coupon money market instruments. The U.S. Treasury sells T-bills in a sealed bid auction through the twelve Federal Reserve Banks. An auction for thirteen-week and twenty-six-week bills occurs every Monday, while fifty-two-week bills are offered every fourth Wednesday. Investors may purchase their bills either directly from the government by bidding in the auction, or they may buy them through commercial banks or brokers and pay a small commission. Investors who seek to purchase T-bills directly from the government may submit either a competitive or a noncompetitive bid.

Those who submit a competitive bid specify the face amount of bills they want and the price they are willing to pay on the basis of 100. Competitive bidders should be skilled in making proper bids; if the bid price is too low, the bidder may not receive any securities, and if the bid price is too high, the bidder will receive securities, but the yield on them will be lower than the average, meaning that the investor will forego a portion of the potential interest.

Bidders with less experience and those with smaller amounts to invest are probably better off submitting a noncompetitive bid. Noncompetitive bidders specify only the amount they want to purchase. The Treasury fills all of the noncompetitive bids first and then begins accepting the competitive bids, starting with the highest priced bid and continuing until the issue is fully subscribed. All of the noncompetitive bids are awarded at the average of the competitive bids. Therefore, the two advantages of the noncompetitive bid for the smaller investor are protection against the risk of paying a price that is higher than the average and the assurance of receiving the entire amount bid up to the maximum noncompetitive bid amount of $500,000.

Since the quotes for T-bills in the financial press are on an annualized discount basis, an investor must convert the discount, taking into account the maturity of the bill, to find its actual price. The price of a T-bill is as follows:

$$P_{\text{T-bill}} = F \times [1 - D \times (\frac{T}{360})] \tag{12–2}$$

where $P_{\text{T-bill}}$ = price of a Treasury bill
F = face amount
D = discount rate
T = time to maturity in days

The Wall Street Journal publishes bid and ask discount quotes on T-bills quoted by major government bond dealers. Example 12–1 shows the computation of the price of a T-bill.

Once issued and in the hands of the public, T-bills are a very liquid investment because of the active market for trading existing bills. Government bond dealers maintain active quotes and trade millions of dollars' worth of bills every day.

EXAMPLE 12–1

Compute the price of a $10,000 thirteen-week T-bill sold at a discount of 9.52.

$$P_{\text{T-bill}} = 10{,}000 \times [1 - .0952(91/360)]$$
$$= 9759.36$$

The interest on this T-bill, which the investor would collect at maturity, is the difference between the face and the price:

$$\text{Interest} = 10{,}000 - 9759.36 = 240.64$$

The long-term bond issues of the Treasury that are available to investors are Treasury notes and Treasury bonds. The Treasury auctions these issues as needed in a procedure similar to that for T-bills, except that investors submit their bids on a yield basis instead of a price basis, and the maximim noncompetitive bid is $1 million.

Treasury notes have original fixed maturities of not less than one and not more than ten years from the date of issue. They are available in denominations as small as $1000, except that notes of less than four years are usually not issued for less than $5000. The Treasury sells notes in a sealed-bid auction as financing needs require.

Treasury bonds are like notes in every respect except that their original maturities are from more than ten years to as long as thirty years.

U.S. Government Agency Issues. U.S. government agencies can usually be classified into one or two groups: federal agencies and federally sponsored agencies. The federal agencies are owned by or are actually a part of the U.S. government, and their debt issues usually carry the guarantee of the federal government as to repayment of principal and interest. Examples of federal agencies are the Government National Mortgage Association, the U.S. Postal Service, and the Tennessee Valley Authority. The federally sponsored agencies are not directly owned by the U.S. government, and since they do not receive any direct government funding, their debt issues are generally not guaranteed by the government. Because these agencies are sponsored by the government, however, investors perceive them to have an implicit federal guarantee and believe that the U.S. government would not allow any agency to default on its debt issues. Some of the federally sponsored agencies are the Federal Home Loan Banks, the Federal Land Banks, and the Federal National Mortgage Association.

Municipal Bonds

Municipal bonds include virtually all of the debt issues of political subdivisions within the United States. This includes states, counties, cities, and other special districts or governmental authorities. Examples of these other authorities are public universities, industrial development districts, and toll road authorities.

The main attraction of these issues to investors is that their interest is exempt from U.S. income tax. To compare the yield on municipal issues to that of taxable bonds, an investor should compute the taxable yield equivalent of the municipal issue as follows:

$$TYE = Y_m/(1 - t) \quad \textbf{(12–3)}$$

where TYE = taxable yield equivalent
Y_m = yield on a municipal security
t = the investor's marginal tax rate

Corporate Bonds

Corporate bonds, the long-term debt instruments issued by corporations, provide a significant amount of long-term capital to firms. A bond is a debt contract between the issuing corporation and *trustee* who represents the bondholders. The document between the issuer and the trustee is the bond *indenture.* The indenture specifies all of the terms and provisions of the issue.

Collateral

The collateral, or security, behind a bond is one of the prime considerations should the issuer fall into default or bankruptcy. There is a difference between the security backing municipal bonds and that backing corporate bonds.

Government and municipal bonds almost never have any assets pledged as collateral. Most fall into one of two categories:

1. General obligation bonds
2. Revenue bonds

A general obligation bond is backed by the "full faith and credit" of its issuer. That is, it is nothing more than a promise to repay, and investors judge the reliability of that promise by examining such factors as past interest payment consistency, growth in the tax base, and economic strength of the geographic region. Should the government entity default on the bond, however, the bondholders have no claim on any of the government's assets. Bondholders whose money financed new garbage collection trucks cannot take possession of those trucks should the bond fall into default. Their only legal recourse is to sue for repayment. Revenue bonds only pledge to pay their interest as long as there is sufficient revenue. For example, a county may finance a new bridge with revenue bonds, charging a toll to the users of the bridge. The county could pay interest only out of revenue from the tolls. On the other hand, if the bond had been a general obligation issue, the county would have had to make up the revenue shortfall from other sources to pay the bond's interest or face loss of its good credit rating by defaulting on the bond.

Corporate bonds fall into one of two classes regarding their security:

1. Unsecured
2. Secured

A *debenture* is an unsecured bond. Investors base their judgments about the safety of debentures on factors such as the credit history of the company, the company's earnings, and the amount and quality of the company's unpledged assets. Although debentures are unsecured in that they do not represent claims on specific assets, they do represent a general claim on assets that the company has not otherwise pledged. Within the ranks of debentures, there are *senior issues* and *junior issues.* A company's first debenture issue is usually its senior issue. The senior issue protects its bondholders by stating that they have first, or senior, claims on unpledged assets. Later issues are junior issues that are subordinated in their claims on unpledged assets, giving priority to the senior issues should the need arise to claim corporate assets.

Other corporate bonds do carry specific assets as collateral. In general, the assets that corporations pledge as collateral are those types of assets whose ownership can be registered. The collateral behind *mortgage bonds* is some type of real estate such as land, buildings, or fixed plant. *Collateral trust certificates* pledge securities of other issuers that the corporation owns. *Equipment trust certificates* pledge large equipment or machinery.

Early Repayment

There are three ways that a corporation can repay bonds before their maturity. The first way is to repurchase them in the market and retire them on the company's books. However, this method of repayment has two potential disadvantages. One is that the bond may not be available on the market. A second and more serious disadvantage is that the market price of the bond may be greater than the bond's face value, in which case the firm's earnings would drop by repurchasing them in the open market.

A second way to repay a bond before its maturity is to *call* it. Most corporate bonds have a *call provision* in the indenture, allowing the issuer to call the bond. When an issuer calls a bond, the bondholder must sell the bond back to the issuer. The indenture must set the *call price,* which is the price the company pays to the bondholder upon calling the issue. The call price is usually slightly above the face value, giving the bond a *call premium.* Although some bonds are *freely callable,* most have a *deferred call,* which sets a *call date* several years after the original issue date of the bond. The company may then call the bond any time after the call date.

If a bond issue is convertible into common stock of the corporation, the company may take advantage of a third method of early repayment. In this repayment method, which applies only to convertible issues, the corporation forces investors to convert their bonds before maturity by calling the issue. Chapter 18 discusses convertible bonds in more detail.

There are two features of a bond that relate to early repayment. Investors usually prefer a bond issue with a systematic early repayment plan. If the company pays off some of the bonds early, then the burden of repaying the entire issue at maturity is less. Early repayment helps minimize the possibility that the company will not be able to make its final principal payment.

The first method of approaching planned early repayment is to give the different bonds within a bond issue several different maturities. Some of the bonds will come due in several years while others will have longer maturities. These are *serial bonds*. For example, on September 1, 1985, the State of Mississippi issued serial bonds with maturities ranging from 1986 through 1998 and interest rates from 5¼ percent on the near maturity to 8.9 percent on the longer-term serials. Concurrently, the state also sold a series of "Serial Capital Appreciation Bonds," which are zero-coupon issues.

A second method of systematic retirement of debt is through a *sinking fund*. The bond issuer makes regular contributions into the sinking fund. The trustee then periodically uses amounts accumulated in the sinking fund to retire debt . Sometimes the bond indenture will allow the bond issuer to use sinking fund commitments to increase capital assets. Retirement of debt through a sinking fund is accomplished either by open market purchases or by calling random bonds from the issue (if it is callable). The trustee usually invests sinking fund payments in government securities to earn interest on the sinking fund until the money is used to retire bonds.

Accrued Interest

The prices quoted for bonds in the market are for the sales price of the bond. The purchaser of a bond pays the sales price plus any accrued interest since the last interest payment date. Likewise, an investor who sells a bond receives the interest on the bond since the last interest payment. In this way, there is no "penalty" for selling a bond before its interest payment date because the seller will receive the accrued interest from the buyer. Example 12–2 shows how to compute the accrued interest on a bond traded between payment dates.

EXAMPLE 12–2

On August 23, Theresa Newman purchases a bond through her broker at a quoted price of $837.50. The bond's annual interest payment is $80, paid semiannually on January 1 and July 1 of each year. How much will the broker bill Ms. Newman (ignoring commissions)?

Fifty-three days have passed since the last interest payment occurred.

$$80(53/365) = 11.62$$

The brokerage firm will bill Miss Newman $837.50 for the bond plus $11.62 accrued interest, for a total of $849.12.

The only exception to this practice is bonds that are in default of interest and/or principal payment. In such cases, the bonds trade flat, meaning that they sell for their net quoted price. Because the bond is in default, there is often little chance of it ever paying off. They therefore trade without any accrued interest being billed.

BOND VALUATION

Determining the fundamental value of a bond is similar to estimating a value for any asset. The asset's value should reflect the cash that it will provide the investor in the future. Since the future is seldom known with certainty, the asset's *expected future cash flows* determine the asset's worth. To value the *current* worth of those future cash flows, we should discount them to a present value at some discount rate that reflects the future certainty, or risk, of those cash flows.

Two basic problems arise in evaluating investments using these principles:

1. Estimating the expected future cash flows
2. Estimating the best discount rate

The Present Value Bond Valuation Model

Fortunately for bond valuation, the future cash flows of bonds with fixed interest payments are known in advance. These cash flows are the interest payments and the face value of the bond. As John Burr Williams[1] wrote in an early treatise on valuation, "let us define the investment value of a bond as the present worth of its future coupons and principal." Using this notion, we can express the value of a bond as follows:

$$V_B = \sum_{t=1}^{n} \frac{I_t}{(1+k)^t} + \frac{F}{(1+k)^n} \qquad \textbf{(12–4)}$$

where V_B = the fundamental value of the bond
I_t = the interest payment in time period t
F = the face amount, or principal, of the bond
k = the bond's required rate of return (discount rate)
n = the number of time periods until maturity

Equation 12–4 says that the present fundamental value of a bond is equal to the present value of the bond's interest payments and the present value of its principal. The first expression on the right side represents the present value of the interest payments, and the second expression is the present value of the principal. The appropriate discount rate is the bond's required rate of return, which incorporates the investor's assessment of the bond's risk and the certainty of its interest and principal payments.

One important assumption underlying Equation 12–4 is that the bond's interest payments can be reinvested at the same required rate of return, *k,* used to determine the bond's value. This assumption is necessary because of the implied compounding of interest in both the present value of the interest payments and the present value of the principal.

Solving Equation 12–4 by hand for a longer-term bond would be quite a task. When all of a bond's interest payments are equal, as usually is the case, the present value and annuity tables provide a shortcut to computing a bond's value. To compute a bond's value using the present value and annuity tables, we can express the bond's value in the following form:

$$V_B = I \times PVAF_{k,n} + F \times PVF_{k,n} \qquad \textbf{(12–5)}$$

where $PVAF_{k,n}$ = the present value of an annuity factor for k percent and n time periods
$PVF_{k,n}$ = the present value of one dollar factor for k percent for the nth time period

EXAMPLE 12–3

What is the fundamental value of a 12 percent, eight-year bond that pays interest twice per year while investors require a 10 percent return on bonds of similar risk?

The appropriate present value factors are for 5 percent, sixteen periods to maturity.

$$V_B = 60(10.8378) + 1000(.4581)$$
$$= 1108.37$$

Bond Returns

There are three main sources of return from fixed-income investments:

1. Interest payments
2. Capital gains (or losses)
3. Reinvestment returns

The first two sources are the typical income and capital sources common to all investments. When analyzing bonds, however, one must also consider the effect of *reinvestment returns*—the returns that the investor can get by reinvesting any cash flows before the maturity of the bond (usually the periodic interest payments).

Current Yield

The bond's return derived from its interest payments is it *current yield.* Current yield is simply annual interest income as a portion of the bond's current market price.

$$Y_{\text{current}} = \frac{I}{P_B} \qquad (12\text{–}6)$$

where Y_{current} = the current yield of a bond
P_B = the market price of the bond

The current yield should not be confused with the coupon yield. A bond's current yield will be equal to its coupon yield only if its market price is equal to the face amount. Typically, this is true only at the time of the original issue. Afterward, the normal fluctuation in a bond's price resulting from changing market and company conditions means that a bond's current yield will seldom equal its coupon yield, and then usually by chance.

EXAMPLE 12–4

Melvin's Electronics has $1000 face amount ten-year bonds outstanding that pay $80 per year in interest (semiannually). The current market price of the bond is $770. What are the current yield and coupon yield?

$$Y_{\text{current}} = 80/770$$
$$= .104$$

$$Y_{\text{coupon}} = 80/1000$$
$$= .08$$

Yield to Maturity

The return on a bond that takes into account current yield and capital changes is the *yield to maturity*. Investors say that a bond sells at a *discount (discount bond)* when its market price is less than its face value. It sells at a *premium (premium bond)* if its market price is greater than par. However, at maturity, bondholders will receive the face value. The discount or premium is amortized over the remaining life of the bond. The yield to maturity calculation accounts for this amortization and increases the yield (over the bond's current yield) with the capital gain provided by a discount. Similarly, amortization of a premium results in a yield to maturity that is lower than the current yield. Because of this, identifying whether a bond sells at a premium or a discount allows us to state the relative values of coupon yield, current yield, and yield to maturity. Table 12–2 summarizes these interrelationships. For example, if a bond's yield to maturity is greater than its current yield, we know that it must be a discount bond.

To state a formula for a bond's yield to maturity, we must also make some assumptions about the reinvestment rate. The simplest assumption is that the investor can reinvest the bond's interest payments at the bond's yield to maturity. Although this assumption is valid only if interest rates do not change over the life of the bond, it allows a straightforward computation of the yield to maturity using the present value bond valuation model (Equation 12–5). Using the model, a bond's yield to maturity will be equal to the rate that equates the present value of the bond's cash flows (interest payments plus the final face value) to its current market value. In other words, a bond's yield to maturity is equal to the required rate of return in equilibrium. Placed in terms of Equation 12–5, we have

$$P_B = \sum_{t=1}^{n} \frac{I_t}{(1 + Y_m)^t} + \frac{F}{(1 + Y_m)^n} \qquad \textbf{(12–7)}$$

where P_B = the market price of the bond
I_t = the interest payment in time period t
F = the face amount, or principal, of the bond
Y_m = the bond's yield to maturity
n = the number of time periods until maturity

Unfortunately, the exponents in Equation 12–7 prevent a direct solution for the yield to maturity. The method of solving the yield to maturity is iterative. Begin by picking a reasonable starting yield and solving for P_B. If the computed P_B is too high,

TABLE 12–2
Interrelationships of bond yields

Discount Bond	*Premium Bond*
Bond price < face value	Bond price > face value
Current yield > coupon yield	Current yield < coupon yield
Yield to maturity > current yield	Yield to maturity < current yield

pick a higher yield and solve again. Repeat this process until the computed P_B equals the market P_B.

It is evident that this procedure can be time-consuming. Any process requiring an iterative solution is ideal for a computer. Fortunately, many reasonably-priced small calculators now have the ability to perform these present value calculations.

The first expression in Equation 12–7 represents the present value of the interest payments, and the second expression is the present value of the principal payment. When solving for the yield to maturity without using a computer program or financial calculator, one must use present value tables. We can rewrite Equation 12–7 as follows:

$$P_B = I \times PVAF_{Ym,n} + F \times PVF_{Ym,n} \qquad \textbf{(12–8)}$$

where $PVAF_{Ym,n}$ = the present value of an annuity factor for the yield to maturity percent, n time periods

$PVF_{Ym,n}$ = the present value of one dollar factor for the yield to maturity percent for the nth time period

The solution method is to scan the present value tables (Appendices 1–4 at the end of the book) and iteratively solve for combinations of PVAF and PVF at the same rate and number of periods that will solve Equation 12–8 for a P_B that is equal to or very close to the market P_B.

When computing bond yields to maturity, it is important to consider that most bonds pay interest semiannually (twice per year). To take this into account, determine the interest amount and rate per six-month time period and the number of six-month periods until maturity. For example, a 10 percent bond with eight years remaining to maturity would be a bond that pays 5 percent ($50) interest per period and has sixteen periods to maturity. The resulting yield to maturity is per six-month period. To annualize this rate, multiply it by two. (This is only a close approximation because it ignores a portion of the compounding effect. However, it is standard in the investments business.) Example 12–5 shows a sample computation of a bond's yield to maturity.

EXAMPLE 12–5

Find the yield to maturity of the Melvin's Electronics bond in Example 12–4.

We know that the bond sells for a discount. Therefore, the yield to maturity must be greater than the current yield. The current yield is .104, so try .12 as the first attempt at getting Y_m. Because the bond pays semiannual interest, there are twenty time periods (of six months each). Each time period has a $40 interest payment. Using the present value of a dollar factor from Appendix 2 and the present value of an annuity factor from Appendix 4, at 6 percent per period, twenty periods:

$$\begin{aligned} P_B &= 40(11.4699) + 1000(.3118) \\ &= 770.60 \end{aligned}$$

This is sufficiently close to the bond's market price of $770. The yield to maturity is 6% semiannually, or 12 percent per annum.

Determinants of Bond Yields

What are the factors that influence bond yields? We could pose this question alternatively: What are the factors that influence bond required rates of return? Recall from Chapter 6 that there are two main components of investors' required rates of returns:

1. The riskless rate of return
2. A premium for the risk of the investment

Applying these determinants of required rates of return to bonds, we can identify the main items influencing bond yields:

1. Interest rates in general
2. The riskiness of the individual bond (Factors such as the credit risk of the issuing corporation, bond collateral, callability, taxability, convertibility, and sinking fund provisions affect the risk of an individual bond issue.)

Using the fundamental model for bond values (Equation 12–5), we can identify the effects that changes in the above factors can have on the prices of bonds. Interest rates have fluctuated widely during recent years, underscoring their role in the pricing of bonds. Burton Malkiel[2] summarized the changes in bond prices caused by interest rate changes. He classified them into five bond price theorems. It is useful for bond investors to be familiar with Malkiel's bond price theorems.

Bond Price Theorems

1. *Bond prices and interest rates are inversely related.* If interest rates rise, bond prices will fall. Conversely, bond prices rise when interest rates fall. Table 12–3 illustrates the bond pricing theorems. Illustrating Theorems 1–3, there are three different 8 percent bonds, each with a different maturity. Note that when interest rates (yields to maturity) *rise* from 8 percent to 10 percent, the bond prices *fall.*
2. *Bond price changes will be greater the longer the maturity of the bond.* For a given change in interest rates, a long-term bond will change in value more than a short-term bond. Compare the ten-year and twenty-year bonds in Table 12–3. The percent change in price of the twenty-year bond was greater than the change in the ten-year bond.
3. *Bond price changes associated with longer maturities increase at a decreasing rate.* As bond maturities increase, their price sensitivities increase (Theorem 2), but at a decreasing rate. Note the ten-year, twenty-year, and thirty-year, 8 percent bonds in Table 12–3. When rates rise to 10 percent, the ten-year bond falls in price 12.3 percent, and the twenty-year bond falls by 17.0 percent. The twenty-year bond fell in price by 4.7 percentage points more than the ten-year bond. Now compare the 18.9 percent fall in the thirty-year bond to the twenty-year bond. Its price fell by only 1.9

TABLE 12–3
Illustration of bond price theorems

Theorem	*Bond Description*	*Interest Rate Change*	*Bond Price*	*Percent Change in Bond Price*
1, 2, 3	8%, 10-year	from 8% to 10%	1000 877	−12.3%
	8%, 20-year	from 8% to 10%	1000 830	−17.0%
	8%, 30-year	from 8% to 10%	1000 811	−18.9%
4	12%, 20-year	from 9% to 11%	1274 1080	−15.2%
	8%, 20-year	from 9% to 11%	909 761	−16.3%
5	10%, 10-year	from 10% to 8%	1000 1134	+13.4%
		from 10% to 12%	1000 887	−11.3%

percentage points more than the twenty-year bond. Even though the differences in the maturities of these bonds are the same, their price sensitivities increase at a decreasing rate as maturities increase.

4. *Bond price changes will be greater the smaller the coupon yield of the bond.* When interest rates change, the price of a 6 percent bond will change more than a 9 percent bond, other factors equal. The portion of Table 12–3 illustrating Theorem 4 shows the price changes in an 8 percent and a 12 percent, twenty-year bond, when yields go from 9 percent to 11 percent. The higher coupon (12 percent) bond falls by 15.2 percent while the lower coupon (8 percent) bond falls by 16.3 percent.
5. *The magnitude of the price changes resulting from a decrease in rates of a given percent will be greater than the magnitude of a price change caused by an increase in interest rates of the same percent.* Prices change more when rates decrease than when they increase by the same amount. Check the 10 percent, ten-year bond in Table 12–3. When yields fall by two percentage points from 10 percent to 8 percent, the bond rises by 13.4 percent. When yields rise by the same amount from 10 percent to 12 percent, the bond falls by 11.3 percent.

These five bond price theorems make it clear that an investor's total return from a bond will be highly dependent upon the movement of interest rates. By the same reasoning, an investor can use these principles to benefit from a change in interest rates. Suppose that you have forecasted a fall in interest rates over the next few months and want to profit from your forecast. The first bond price theorem tells us that we should purchase bonds. The second and fourth theorems identify long-term, low-coupon bonds to be the bonds that will allow us to profit most from the fall in rates. Although these theorems do not always unambiguously identify the bond that will be most sensitive to yield changes, they are helpful. The next chapter presents a more exact technique for identifying bond price sensitivities and discusses bond trading strategies in more detail.

INTEREST RATES

The risk-free interest rate is an indication of interest rates in general, but it is a very short-term rate. When considering bonds, which are instruments with fixed maturities, the interest rate influencing the price of the bond is the rate applicable to the bond's time to maturity. This rate may be more or less than the risk-free rate, depending upon the current *term structure of interest rates.* The term structure of interest rates is the relationship of bond yields of given risk level to time to maturity.

Note that the term structure holds constant the risk variable. Therefore, when analysts want to specify the term structure of interest rates, they will look at yields of bonds that are identical (or very similar) in every respect except maturity. An example of identical bonds would be U.S. Treasury notes. Table 12–4 presents the term structure for T-notes for one-year to seven-year maturities at the end of September 1985.

It is appropriate to note that the term structure shown in Table 12–4 is not the *exact* term structure because of the different coupon rates of the different T-note issues. It is, however, a commonly used proxy, since T-notes with equal coupons do not usually exist for all maturities.

Yield Curves

A graphical presentation of the term structure of interest rates is a *yield curve.* Yield curves provide analysts with a picture of the market's assessments of required yields

TABLE 12–4
The term structure of interest on Treasury notes, September 1985

Years to Maturity	*Yield to Maturity*
1	8.0%
2	8.7
3	9.2
4	9.6
5	9.8
6	10.1

Source: *Barron's,* September 30, 1985.

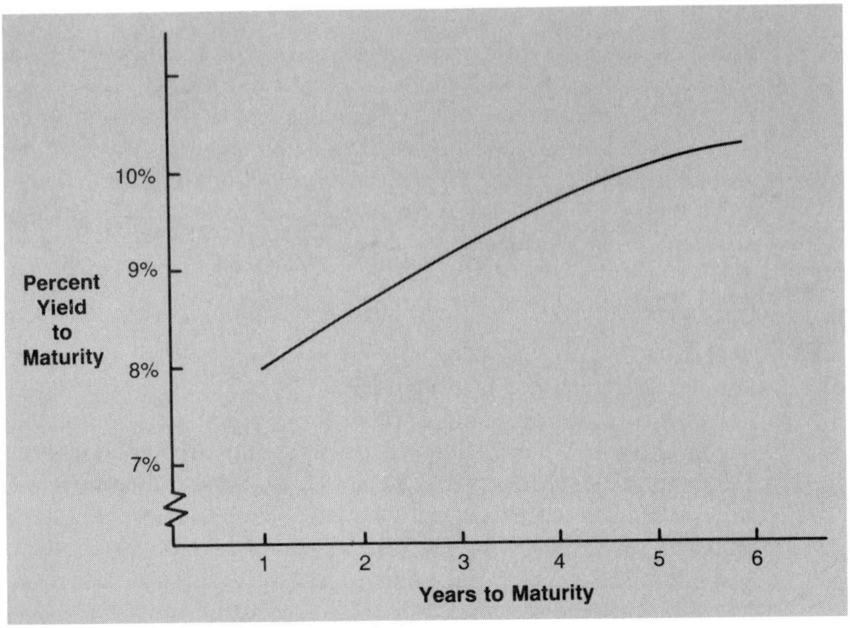

FIGURE 12–1
Yield curve for Treasury notes, September 1985, using data from Table 12–4

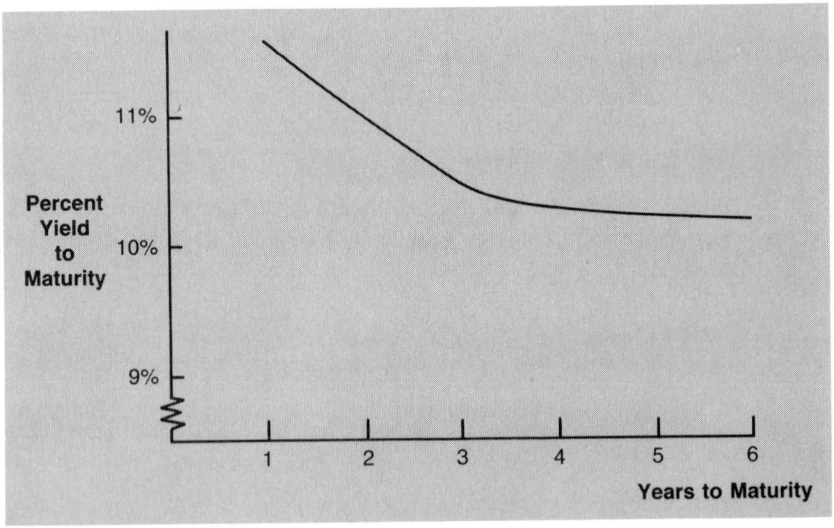

FIGURE 12–2
Yield curve for Treasury notes, December 1979 *(Source: Wall Street Journal,* December 3, 1979.)

for varying maturities. Figure 12–1 is the yield curve that corresponds to the data points for the term structure in Table 12–4.

Although the yield curve in Figure 12–1 is an upward sloping yield curve, yield curves may take on almost any shape. Figure 12–2 shows an example of a time when the yield curve for T-notes was downward sloping. Changing economic environments, expectations, inflation, and other factors contribute to a changing yield curve over time.

Theories Explaining the Yield Curve

Financial theorists have devoted much time to discussing the term structure of interest rates. From this, three major theories have emerged that help explain why the yield curve takes on a particular shape at a given time.

Liquidity Preference Theory

The basic idea behind the *liquidity preference theory* is that, other factors equal, investors prefer less risk over more risk. They view securities with shorter maturities as being less risky than those with longer maturities. (Recall that the second bond price theorem stated that longer-term bonds vary more in price than short-term bonds.) Investors will therefore have a preference for the shorter-term bonds. The only way that investors can be induced to buy long-term bonds is if the yield on the long-term bonds is greater than the short-term bond yield. Thus, in the absence of other factors, this theory results in a yield curve that is upward sloping.

Because the shorter-term bonds will mature earlier, they have a higher degree of liquidity, giving this theory its name.

Expectations Hypothesis

The *expectations hypothesis* theorizes that today's interest rates are determined by investors' expectations about future rates. If investors believe that rates will rise in the future, then the yield curve will be upward sloping. A downward sloping yield curve would be an indication that investors expect interest rates to fall.

To be more specific, the expectations hypothesis means that the long-term interest rate is a geometric mean of current and future shorter-term rates. For example, the rate on a ten-year bond would be the geometric average of the expected rates on one-year bonds over the intervening ten years. A geometric mean is the nth root of the product of n numbers. For returns, the geometric mean return is the same as the mean continuously compounded return. Recall that we compute continuously compounded returns by using natural logarithms. Example 12–6 shows how to compute the interest rate implied in the future by using the yield curve and the expectations hypothesis.

The expectations hypothesis allows explanation of any shape of yield curve, depending upon expectations for future rates. The resulting yield curve can be upward sloping, downward sloping, or even have "humps" or "valleys."

EXAMPLE 12–6

Assume that the current rate on a one-year Treasury bond is 7 percent. You believe that the yield on a one-year T-bond will be 9 percent one year from now and 10 percent two years from now. According to the expectations hypothesis, what should the yield be on a three-year T-bond?

Find the geometric mean by averaging the continuously compounded rates:

$[\ln(1.07) + \ln(1.09) + \ln(1.10)]/3$
$(.06766 + .08618 + .09531)/3$
$.24915/3$
$.08305$

Then convert to nominal rate.

$\exp(.08305) - 1$
$.0866$

Your expectations imply that the current rate on a three-year T-bond should be 8.66 percent.

Segmented Markets Theory

The two previously discussed theories ignore an important factor that determines interest rates: the supply of and demand for loanable funds. The major participants in the supply side of the market are mainly financial institutions: banks, pension funds, and insurance companies. Each participant in the market has its own preferred habitat regarding the maturities that it prefers.

The *segmented markets theory* states that interest rates for short-term maturities are determined by participants whose preferred habitat lies within the shorter maturities. Similarly, the participants for long-term funds determine the rates for longer maturities. For example, commercial banks, which generally prefer to borrow and lend in the short-term market, will be major factors in the determination of rates for maturities of three years and less. This theory explains changing shapes of yield curves as the result of the major participants in the market changing their demand for and supplies of different maturity funds.

These three major yield curve theories are not necessarily mutually exclusive. A description of reality may be a combination of these theories. For example, expectations may be for falling interest rates, but combined with liquidity preferences, an upward sloping yield curve may still result. Introduction of different habitats by institutions in the market may then cause some irregular shapes to appear. Knowledge of these theories can result in some useful applications for yield curves.

Uses of Yield Curves

Analysts use yield curves for a variety of purposes. This section presents several of the major uses that are relevant for investors in bonds.

Forecasting Interest Rates

If we accept that the expectations hypothesis is at least a partial explanation for the shape of the yield curve, then the curve can be useful in predicting future short-term rates given current long-term rates. Looking at Example 12–6, if the yield curve showed the current rate of 7 percent for one-year T-bonds, and we expected an 8 percent one-year rate a year from now, we could forecast the one-year rate two years from now by solving for the rate that would give the present three-year rate of 8.66 percent.

Of course, there are other methods of forecasting future interest rate movements. Economists find, however, that accurately forecasting interest rates is a very difficult task. For example, one popular method of forecasting is to use an econometric model that takes into account several of the different variables that influence interest rates. The use of such models alone, though, generally produces forecasts that have not proved to be very accurate.[3]

Pricing New Issues

Investors can also use the yield curve to price new bond issues for which a market does not yet exist. Suppose that Electro Utilities was issuing a new eight-year bond. What would be a fair market yield on such a bond? This would be fairly easy to determine if Electro had other bonds of similar risk outstanding with maturities surrounding the eight-year maturity of the new issue. Figure 12–3 shows how finding

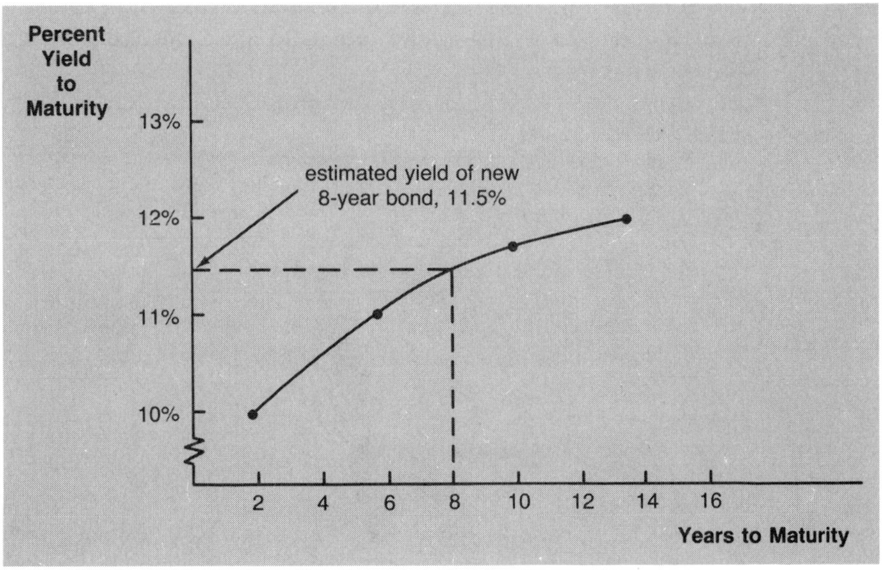

FIGURE 12–3
Estimating the yield on a new issue of Electro Utilities' eight-year bonds using yield curve for outstanding Electro bonds on date of new issue

an estimated location for the new issue on Electro's yield curve could help an investor estimate the yield on the new issue.

Riding the Yield Curve

An upward sloping yield curve has an interesting effect: assuming no change in interest rates, it implies that the price of a bond will rise as it approaches maturity. The reason for this is that required yields fall as maturity nears, causing the price of the bond to rise. The practice of taking advantage of this knowledge to increase bond yields is *riding the yield curve.*

A strategy of riding the yield curve involves purchasing a bond with maturity greater than the intended holding period for the bond. When the investor's holding period is over, if the term structure of interest rates has not changed, then the investor can sell the bond for a higher price. This increases the actual holding period yield on the bond to an amount greater than what the yield curve initially implied. However, note that the important assumption is that *interest rates do not change.* Should rates in general rise, then the investor's yield would naturally suffer because of a fall in the price of the bond. On the other hand, a drop in rates would improve the return.

Assume that investors' expectations imply a flat yield curve (no change in future interest rates), but that because of liquidity preferences the yield curve is actually slightly upward sloping. Figure 12–4 shows a yield curve for T-bonds for such a situation. To ride the yield curve, an investor could purchase a two-year bond (point A) and sell it one year later for a price determined by point B. The investor's one-year return would then be more than if he had originally purchased a one-year bond, assuming, of course, that interest rates did not change. Example 12–7 shows how to compute the return.

EXAMPLE 12–7

Using the yield curve in Figure 12–4 and assuming no change in interest rates, compute the return for a bond investor who wants to ride the yield curve with a two-year, $1000, zero-coupon bond and a one-year holding period.

Current price of the two-year bond at $k = .11$:

$$V_B = 1000(.8116) = 811.60$$

Price of the bond one year later at $k = .10$:

$$V_B = 1000(.9091) = 909.10$$

Bondholder's return:

$$(909.10 - 811.60)/811.60 = .12$$

The "curve rider's" one-year return would have been 12 percent compared to a 10 percent return on the one-year bond.

The critical assumption is that the term structure of interest rates does not change. The chance of its changing is the risk that the investor takes who tries to ride the yield curve.

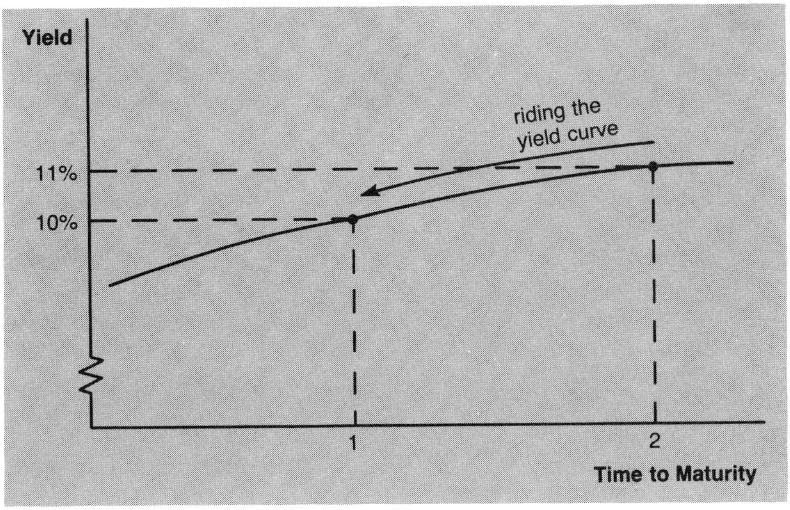

FIGURE 12–4
Riding the yield curve

SUMMARY

Although investors have traditionally treated bonds as conservative investments, patterns of inflation and interest rate changes of the past twenty years have altered that attitude. The value of a bond is the present value of all the interest payments plus the present value of the principal payment. Since an important determinant of the bond's required rate of return (the discount rate for a bond's present value) is market interest rates, changes in interest rates can cause significant changes in bond prices.

The realized return that an investor receives from a bond contains three components: the interest payments, the capital gain or loss, and the reinvestment of interest payments. The yield to maturity of a bond measures the return from both the interest payments and the capital change of the bond, assuming that reinvestment returns are equal to the bond's yield to maturity.

The response of the price of a bond to a change in interest rates depends upon the bond's coupon and its time to maturity. Bond price changes are greater when maturities are greater and coupon amounts are smaller.

The term structure of interest rates is the relationship of yield to maturity and time to maturity of a given risk class of bond. Presented graphically it is the yield curve. The three major theories that explain the yield curve and its shape are the liquidity preference theory, the expectations hypothesis, and the segmented markets theory.

IMPORTANT TERMS

bearer bond
call
call date
call premium
call price
call provision
collateral trust certificate
coupon amount
coupon rate
coupon yield
current yield
debenture
deferred call
discount bond
equipment trust certificate
expectations hypothesis
freely callable bond
general obligation bond
indenture
junior issue
junk bond
liquidity preference theory
mortgage bond
premium bond
registered bond
reinvestment returns
revenue bond
riding the yield curve
segmented markets theory
senior issue
serial bond
sinking fund
term structure of interest rates
trustee
yield curve
yield to maturity
zero-coupon bond

QUESTIONS AND PROBLEMS

1. Might junk bonds be more sensitive to interest rate changes than U.S. Treasury bonds? Why?
2. If a company has both junior and senior bond issues outstanding, why might an investor prefer to purchase the senior issue? Why might the investor favor the junior issue?
3. Identify and define the main types of secured bonds.
4. What is the difference between a registered and a bearer bond? What are the advantages of holding a bond in registered form as opposed to bearer form?
5. Summarize the auction process that the Treasury uses to sell T-bills. What are the advantages and disadvantages of placing competitive bids as opposed to noncompetitive bids?
6. Compute the price and the dollar amount of interest earned (when held to maturity) of the following T-bills:
   a) $100,000, 30-day bill selling at a discount of 8.62 percent
   b) $10,000, 1-year bill selling at a discount of 10.48 percent
   c) $50,000, 112-day bill selling at a discount of 7.03 percent
7. A cash manager needs to invest approximately $1 million for a period of fourteen days. He buys a $1 million face amount ninety-one-day bill at the Treasury's auction for a discount of 8.73 percent. Fourteen days later he sells the T-bill for a quoted discount of 8.69 percent. How much interest did the investment earn over the fourteen days?
8. What are the three sources of return from bonds? How would a fall in interest rates affect each?
9. Burlington Northern has a bond outstanding that pays $85 per year in interest, paid semiannually. If the bond sells for $810 in the market:
   a) Compute the current yield.
   b) Compute the coupon yield.

10. Compute the value of the following $1000 bonds that pay semiannual interest. Assume that the next interest payment is in six months.

	Coupon Yield	*Years to Maturity*	*Required Rate of Return*
a)	10%	7	12%
b)	18%	12	14%
c)	8%	6	10%
d)	12%	6	10%

11. Compute the current yield and the yield to maturity for the following bonds that pay semiannual interest payments. Assume that the next interest payment is six months in the future.

	Coupon Yield	*Years to Maturity*	*Market Price*
a)	14%	12	$1125
b)	6%	20	$ 467
c)	8%	8	$ 892

12. Let today be April 17. A 12 percent bond that pays interest on Janury 1 and July 1 of each year trades in the market for $950. If you buy the bond for its market price, how much will you owe the broker, not including commissions?
13. A bond was originally issued at par with a yield to maturity of 14 percent. The yield to maturity is now 12 percent. Does the bond sell for a discount or a premium?
14. What is the term structure of interest rates? How is the term structure usually presented, and what are some of its uses?
15. Briefly explain the three major theories of the term structure of interest rates.
16. Using a recent issue of *The Wall Street Journal,* construct a yield curve for U. S. Treasury bonds with maturities from one to twenty years. What does this yield curve indicate to you if the expectations hypothesis explains the term structure of interest rates?

NOTES

1. John Burr Williams, (1938) *The Theory of Investment Value,* Cambridge, MA: Harvard University Press.
2. Burton G. Malkiel, (1962), "Expectation, Bond Prices, and the Term Structure of Interest Rates," *Quarterly Journal of Economics,* (May), 197–218.
3. See, for example, Walter J. Elliot and Jerome R. Baier, (1979), "Econometric Models and Current Interest Rates: How Well Do They Predict Future Rates?" *Journal of Finance,* 34 (September), 975–986.

SELECTED REFERENCES

Boardman, Calvin M., Frederick H. Dark, and Ronald C. Lease, (1986). "On the Listing of Corporate Debt: A Note." *Journal of Financial and Quantitative Analysis,* 21 (March), 107–114.

Chatfield, Robert E., and R. Charles Moyer (1986). "'Putting' Away Bond Risk: An Empirical Examination of the Value of the Put Option on Bonds." *Financial Management,* 15 (Summer), 26-33.

Cornell, Bradford (1986). "Inflation Measurement, Inflation Risk, and the Pricing of Treasury Bills." *Journal of Financial Research,* 9 (Fall), 193–202.

Ederington, Louis H. (1986). "Why Split Ratings Occur." *Financial Management,* 15 (Spring), 37–47.

Ferri, Michael G. (1978). "Systematic Return Risk and the Call Risk of Corporate Debt Instruments." *Journal of Financial Research,* 1 (Winter), 1–13.

Ho, Thomas, and Ronald F. Singer (1984). "The Value of Corporate Debt with a Sinking-Fund Provision." *Journal of Business,* 57 (July), 315–336.

Kidwell, David S. and Michael D. Joehnk. "The Impact of Market Uncertainty of Municipal Bond Underwriter Spread." *Financial Management,* 13 (Spring), 37–44.

———, M. Wayne Marr, and G. Rodney Thompson (1985). "Eurodollar Bonds: Alternative Financing for U. S. Companies." *Financial Management,* 14 (Winter), 18–27.

Peavy, John (1984). "Forecasting Industrial Bond Rating Changes: A Multivariate Model." *Review of Business and Economic Research,* 19 (Spring), 46–56.

Robbins, Edward Henry, and John D. Schatzberg (1986). "Callable Bonds: A Risk-Reducing Signalling Mechanism." *Journal of Finance,* 41 (September), 935–949.

Roden, Peyton Foster, and Robert L. Bland (1986). "Issuer Sophistication and Underpricing in the Negotiated Municipal Bond Market." *Journal of Financial Research,* 9 (Summer), 163–170.

Taylor, Richard W. (1988). "The Valuation of Semiannual Bonds between Interest Payment Dates." *The Financial Review,* 23 (August), 365–368.

Wansley, James W., and Terrence Clauretie (1985). "The Impact of CreditWatch Placement on Equity Returns and Bond Prices." *Journal of Financial Research,* 8 (Spring), 31–42.

Weinstein, Mark (1985). "The Equity Component of Corporate Bonds." *Journal of Portfolio Management,* 11 (Spring), 37–41.

CHAPTER 13

Bond Strategy

Chapter 12 introduced bonds and the factors that affect their prices. This chapter begins by examining the risks to which bonds are subject. The following sections discuss three approaches to managing bond portfolios: passive strategies, semi-active strategies, and active strategies.

CONTROLLING BOND RISKS

To control the risk of investing in bonds, it is useful to identify the sources of risk to which bonds are most susceptible. There are four major categories of bond risk: (1) default risk, (2) price risk, (3) call risk, and (4) reinvestment rate risk.

The financial condition of the bond issuer is the most important determinant of default risk, while changes in interest rates are the most important source of the other three bond risks.

Default Risk

The risk associated with the failure to pay a bond's scheduled interest or principal payment when due is *default risk*. Default causes the bondholder's actual rate of return to be less than the bond's expected rate of return. In the best case, when the bond issuer resumes interest payments and completes repayment of the bond, the delay in receiving the defaulted interest payments lowers the return. In the worst case, when the issuer falls into bankruptcy, the consequences can be disastrous, with as much as a complete loss of unpaid interest and principal.

However, most of the losses that bondholders suffer because of default risk do not arise from either actual default or bankruptcy. They result from decreases in bond prices that follow the deteriorating financial position of the company. As a company's financial position weakens, investors realize the additional risk of investing in the company's securities and demand a higher rate of return. As the basic bond valuation model shows, higher required rates cause bond prices to fall.

How can investors monitor a company's financial position and its probability of default relative to other companies? One way is to conduct a thorough analysis of the company's financial statements and future earnings prospects. However, a complete financial analysis is not necessary to get a good idea regarding the safety of most bonds' interest and principal payments. There are a number of credit rating services that perform these analyses and make their findings available to investors.

Bond Quality Ratings

There are two major bond rating services among the various companies that specialize in providing credit ratings for publicly traded bonds. These are Moody's Investor Services and Standard & Poor's Corporation. Each company has its set of *bond quality ratings.* Based on a thorough analysis of the relevant financial factors, these companies will assign one of their ratings to each bond issue that they rate.

Table 13–1 lists and defines the various rating categories. In addition to the major rating classifications listed in the table, minor ratings are also possible. For example, if the rating agency felt a bond was better than A but slightly less than AA, it could assign the bond a rating of AA−. Bond ratings primarily measure expected default risk. The basis for default risk is the probability of a bond going into default relative to the probabilities of other bonds. Therefore, a bond issue rated AA by S&P should have a much lower default risk (probability of default) than a bond rated BBB.

How well have the bond ratings measured the probability of companies that have defaulted in the past? The evidence indicates that they have done a fairly good job. W. B. Hickman,[1] in a classic study, examined bond ratings and default experience over a twenty-year time span. He found that a higher percentage of the low rated bonds ultimately fell in default, while the higher the bond ratings, the lower was the actual default experience.

Global Marine, Inc., an offshore drilling contractor that defaulted on its bonds in August 1985, provides an example. Table 13–2 traces the fall of the ratings of one of the company's bond issues from the beginning of 1985 through the time of default. Global's financial position deteriorated throughout 1985, and as investors perceived it to be more risky, the yields on its bond rose. After Global omitted the dividend on its common stock in May 1985, S&P lowered the rating from B− to CC. Note that during the month before default, the bond was selling for a yield of 33.6 percent! At this point, the market must have been anticipating default in the near future.

Since bond ratings measure the probability of default, and default risk is one of the most important of bond risks, the ratings should have a distinct relationship to bond yields. Because lower ratings represent higher risk, we would expect the lower

TABLE 13–1
Bond ratings

Rating		
S&P	***Moody's***	***Description***
AAA	Aaa	Highest rating. Capacity to pay interest and principal extremely strong.
AA	Aa	Very strong capacity to pay debt service. Only slightly different from highest rating.
A	A	Strong capacity to pay interest and principal. Somewhat more susceptible to adverse conditions than higher ratings.
BBB	Baa	Adequate capacity to repay debt service. Adverse conditions more likely to lead to weakened capacity to pay.
BB	Ba	Somewhat speculative. Only moderate protection of principal and interest payments.
B	B	Speculative. May not provide interest and principal payments, even under good economic conditions.
CCC	Caa	Very speculative. Large uncertainties exist about the ability to continue debt service.
CC	Ca	Highly speculative. May be very close to default or in default. Ability to pay interest and principal questionable.
D		In default.

Source: Standard & Poor's *Credit Overview*

TABLE 13–2
S&P ratings for Global Marine, Inc., 16 percent senior subordinated debenture due 2001, January 1985 to August 1985

Month	***S&P Rating***	***Bond Yield to Maturity***
Jan.	B−	17.9%
Feb.	B−	19.2
Mar.	B−	18.9
Apr.	B−	19.1
May	B−	21.6
Jun.	CC	30.8
Jul.	CC	33.6
Aug.	D	—

Source: Standard & Poor's *Bond Guide,* January to August 1985 ratings to be associated with higher yields. Figure 13–1 gives average yields on Standard & Poor's Bond Yield Index broken down into AAA to BBB rated issues of corporate industrial companies. As the exhibit shows, AAA rated bonds consistently have the lowest yields, and the yields on the lower rated issues are higher.

Because a higher bond rating should allow a bond issuer to pay a lower interest rate on its bond, issuers often try to obtain the best rating possible before a new bond issue. For example, when a city plans a new bond issue, its financial officer may travel to the offices of the bond rating service with complete financial statements and projections. Another potential way to lower the cost of borrowing in the markets is for the bond issuer to purchaser default insurance. Companies such as American Municipal Bond Assurance Corp. (a subsidiary of MGIC Investment) collect premiums and insure bond issues against default. In effect, the insurer transfers its credit rating to the bond issuer for a fee. By paying a premium of .65 to 1 percent of its total *debt service* (interest payments plus principal), an issuer can save .25 to .4 percent off the yield on a bond. Over the life of a thirty-year bond, the saving can be substantial.

Determinants of Bond Ratings. Although the bond rating services do not make public their exact procedures for analyzing bond issuers and assigning a rating to an issue, they do identify the broad areas that they consider when rating a bond. In addition, several empirical studies have identified key factors related to a bond's rating. Table 13–3 shows S&P's broadly defined areas of evaluation for corporate bond ratings

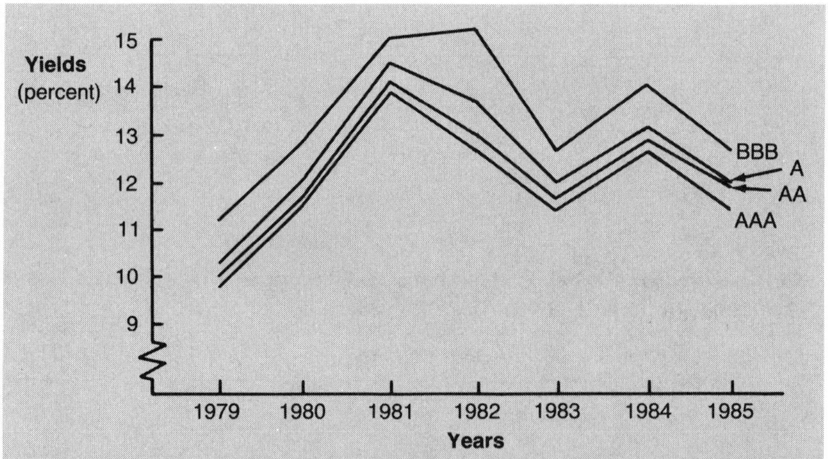

	1979	1980	1981	1982	1983	1984	1985
AAA	9.8%	11.5%	13.9%	12.7%	11.4%	12.5%	11.4%
AA	10.0	11.7	14.1	13.0	11.7	12.9	11.9
A	10.3	12.1	14.5	13.7	12.0	13.2	12.0
BBB	11.2	12.9	15.0	15.2	12.7	14.0	12.7

FIGURE 13–1
S&P Industrial Corporate Bond Yield Index, 1979–1985. (*Source:* Standard & Poor's *Bond Guide,* June 1985)

TABLE 13–3
Broad criteria categories for Standard & Poor's bond ratings

Type of Company	*Bond Rating Criteria*
Industrials	Industry risk
	Issuer's industry position—market position
	Issuer's industry position—operating efficiency
	Management evaluation
	Accounting quality
	Earnings protection
	Leverage and asset protection
	Cash flow adequacy
	Financial flexibility
Utilities	Nonfinancial Criteria
	Market or service territory
	Fuel/power supply
	Operating efficiency
	Regulatory treatment
	Management
	Competition/monopoly balance
	Financial Criteria
	Construction/asset concentration risks
	Earnings protection
	Debt leverage
	Cash flow adequacy
	Accounting quality

Source: Standard & Poor's *Credit Overview: Corporate and International Ratings*

in the industrial and utility categories. There are slightly different criteria for transportation, financial, and other types of firms.

Several key ratios are used in the analysis of bond issues. Probably the two most important ratios for bond analysis are the interest coverage ratio and the total debt ratio. Interest coverage (operating profit divided by interest) measures the firm's ability to generate enough profits to cover its current interest payments. Danger signals appear when a company's interest coverage ratio approaches 1. Generally speaking, from the bondholder's standpoint, the higher the interest coverage, the better. The total debt ratio (total liabilities divided by equity) measures the use of debt in the firm's capital structure. In general, the higher the ratio, the more of the firm's risk is borne by creditors and the less by stockholders. It is a good indicator of the company's capacity to pay off its debt. Bondholders usually prefer a lower total debt ratio.

Other ratios are also relevant. Profit margins and return on capital give interest payment ability in addition to the interest coverage ratio. A firm's commitments to its pension fund are also important. In addition to earnings, a company must have sufficient cash flow to meet its interest payments. In addition to the total debt ratio as a measure of principal repayment ability, such items as the nature and quality of assets, working capital management, and amounts of preferred stock are important.

Effects of Ratings on Security Prices. If higher rated bonds have lower yields to maturity (higher prices) than the lower rated bonds, then does a change in a bond's rating cause a change in its price? The answer to this question lies in the amount of information that bond prices reflect. If bond rating services use publicly available information to determine their bond ratings, and investors and other analysts are as good at analyzing this data as the rating services, then a change in rating would not convey any new information to the market. If the bond market is efficient, then it should already reflect the information. On the other hand, should the ratings imply new information about the possibility of default, the bond's price (and yield) should respond accordingly.

Several studies have examined corporate bond rating changes and their corresponding price changes.[2] For the most part, the studies found that most of the price adjustment of corporate bonds occurs within the few months *before* the rating change announcement. That is, the market generally anticipates a bond rating change. This was especially true for upgrades in bond ratings. However, for ratings downgrades, there was some evidence that a portion of the bond's drop in price occurs soon after the rating change.

Even if corporate bond prices anticipate changes in bond ratings, municipal bonds may not respond to a ratings change until the actual announcement. The reason is that much of the information relevant to a municipal issue is not as available to investors as is the information on publicly traded corporations. The rating service does receive this information as part of its rating agreement with the bond issuer. One study of municipal bond ratings changes, by Ingram, Brooks, and Copeland,[3] looked at bond issues of thirty-three different municipalities that had had ratings changes for their debt issues. The study found that the bonds' price reactions occurred when the ratings changed, not during the time period leading to the change. There was no evidence that the municipal bond yields anticipated the ratings changes. The conclusion of this finding is that bond ratings for municipal issues do convey some information not otherwise available in the market.

Price Risk

The fluctuation in bond prices caused by changes in interest rates is *price risk.* Because it is the major bond risk that is associated with a change in interest rates, price risk is sometimes referred to as *interest rate risk,* even though price risk and the bond risks discussed in the next two sections are all influenced by a change in interest rates.

An investor wanting to minimize price risk would seek to purchase bonds that are least sensitive to interest rate changes. The bond theorems outlined in Chapter 12 identify short-term, high coupon bonds as falling in that category. Zero-coupon and longer-term deep discount bonds fall into the group that would have the most price risk. The concept of duration, introduced in the next section of this chapter, is a useful tool for assessing the interest rate sensitivity of a bond and for controlling price risk.

Call Risk

The possibility that a bond will be called before its maturity, thereby not delivering its promised yield to maturity, is *call risk.* If a bond sells in the market for more than its face value plus one year's interest, then it is likely that the market treats the price of the bond as if it will be called when the call date arrives. In such circumstances, it is appropriate to compute the *yield to call* instead of yield to maturity. Using the time to call instead of the time to maturity in the bond valuation formula will give the yield to call. Because falling interest rates cause bond prices to rise, the probability of call increases as interest rates fall.

Bond investors can control call risk by using one or a combination of several strategies. Because it is only profitable for the issuer to call bonds that are priced at a premium, buying discount bonds will minimize the probability of a call. Even if a discount bond becomes in danger of being called because its price has risen (as a result of a fall in interest rates), the investor who purchased the bond at a discount would have realized a nice capital gain. A second way to minimize call risk is to purchase only those bonds whose yield to call date satisfies the required rate of return. A third strategy is to purchase zero-coupon bonds. Zero-coupon bonds are not usually callable. Even an investor who needs current income could purchase "zeros" at the beginning of the year, sell a portion of them at the end of the year, and use the proceeds as spendable cash. However, an investor attempting such a strategy should realize that it is most successful when interest rates are stable. The price risk of zero-coupon bonds could sabotage this strategy's success during a period of interest rate volatility.

Reinvestment Rate Risk

Not only do changing interest rates affect a bond's price, they also affect the investment income that a bondholder receives from investing the proceeds of the interest payments. When interest rates rise, an investor's reinvestment income will also rise because of the increased interest on reinvesting the bond's payments. To some degree, the higher income from reinvesting the payments will offset the capital loss due to the fall in the bond's price. Variation in return caused by this phenomenon is *reinvestment rate risk.*

The only way to avoid reinvestment rate risk completely is to purchase a bond with no cash flows to reinvest—that is, a zero-coupon bond. On the other hand, zero-coupon bonds have the highest levels of price risk. *Reinvestment rate risk and price risk are therefore inversely related.* Bonds with relatively high price risk have relatively low reinvestment rate risk while those with low price risk have higher reinvestment rate risk.

Just as investors can use duration to help control price risk, they can also use it to control reinvestment rate risk. The section of this chapter on semi-active bond management strategy shows that by considering duration and carefully managing coupon rates and time to maturity in the bond portfolio, an investor can minimize exposure to reinvestment rate risk.

PASSIVE BOND PORTFOLIO MANAGEMENT

Passive bond management and investing involves a buy-and-hold strategy. This means that the bond investor buys bonds and holds them until their maturities, collecting the interest, and usually reinvesting the uncommitted cash from interest payments into similar bonds. The advantages of a passive strategy are its simplicity and lower costs. The passive bond investor will have very low costs of searching for appropriate bonds and costs of transaction. The disadvantage is that changing inflation and interest rates can affect the investor's total return significantly. Passive bond management has fallen in popularity during recent years as portfolio managers have developed more active management strategies.

The passive strategy is most popular with investors whose main investment objective is to maximize coupon income over a given time horizon. Some institutional investors such as endowment funds and insurance companies use passive management for at least a portion of their bond portfolios. The main risk that passive managers should be concerned with is default risk. They can address this by choosing bonds of the appropriate rating category and diversifying by purchasing several different issues. For individual investors who desire a passive bond portfolio, there are a number of investment companies (see the discussion of unit investment trusts in Chapter 20) that should fit the investor's objectives.

SEMI-ACTIVE BOND PORTFOLIO MANAGEMENT

The *semi-active bond management* strategies recognize that changing interest rates and other factors can affect investors' ultimate returns from bonds. These strategies attempt to minimize the fluctuation in bond returns caused by these factors.

Immunization

Immunization is a hybrid bond management strategy involving both active and passive techniques. The goal of immunization is to remove or minimize the risks associated with changes in interest rates—price risk, reinvestment rate risk, and to a lesser degree call risk. Because price risk and reinvestment risk are inversely related, immunization strategies attempt to minimize total bond risk by balancing price and reinvestment risks. By doing so, the bond investor can "immunize" the portfolio against changes in interest rates.

Proponents of immunization strategy are usually accumulation-maximizing investors who desire a high degree of assurance that they will achieve their desired total return over a particular holding period. By accepting a more modest return than an income-maximizing investor, they achieve greater probability of actually receiving their desired total return. This is another example of the traditional trade-off between risk and return. Institutional followers of immunization strategies include life insurance companies, pension funds, and commercial banks. Techniques for immunization include the use of interest rate futures (Chapter 19) and duration.

Duration

Duration is a useful tool for immunization of a bond portfolio. Macaulay[4] introduced the concept of duration in 1938. Duration is defined as the average length of time required to receive the present value of all the future cash payments from the bond. Macaulay originally expressed the equation for duration as follows:

$$D = \frac{\sum_{t=1}^{n} \frac{tI}{(1+Y_m)^t} + \frac{nF}{(1+Y_m)^n}}{\sum_{t=1}^{n} \frac{I}{(1+Y_m)^t} + \frac{F}{(1+Y_m)^n}} \tag{13–1}$$

where D = the bond's duration
n = the number of time periods to maturity
t = time period t
I = interest payment
Y_m = the bond's yield to maturity
F = the bond's face value

Fortunately for those who do not carry around a pocket computer, there is a simpler formula for computing duration.[5]

$$D = n - \frac{I[n - (1 + Y_m)PVAF_{Y_m,n}]}{V_B \times Y_m} \tag{13–2}$$

where $PVAF_{Y_m,n}$ = the present value of an annuity factor for Y_m percent and n periods
V_B = the value (or market price) of the bond

Any security with a specific maturity will have a duration, and if any of the cash flows arrive before maturity, then the security's duration will be less than its maturity. The duration of any coupon bond is therefore less than its maturity, and the duration of any zero-coupon bond is equal to its maturity. This is evident by inspection of the second expression in Equation 13–2. The expression is 0 for a zero-coupon bond (because $I = 0$) and positive for any coupon bond.

Example 13–1 shows how to compute the duration of a bond. The bond's duration is about four years. This does not mean that at the end of four years Mr. Grant will have received the present value of his bond. At that time the largest payment, the face value, will not have been received. However, averaging the first four interest payments received before maturity with the payments received at maturity gives a result of four years.

EXAMPLE 13–1

Mr. Bill Grant is considering buying a 13 percent, five-year bond that pays interest once per year. The bond sells for $1,036, which represents a 12 percent yield to maturity. What is the bond's duration?

$$D = 5 - \frac{130[5 - (1 + .12)3.6]}{1036(.12)}$$

$$= 3.99$$

Using Duration for Immunization

Duration is useful for immunizing a bond against a *one-time* change in interest rates. To use duration in an immunization strategy, the bond investor or portfolio manager takes three steps:

1. Identify the desired time horizon for bond investment.
2. Select the desired rate of return to be assured over that time horizon, taking into account achievable returns for the desired default risk level.
3. Choose a bond whose duration equals the desired time horizon and whose yield to maturity equals the desired rate of return.

If the bond investor follows these steps, then the bond will yield its promised yield to maturity on the duration date even if interest rates have changed once during the holding period. Buying a bond whose duration equals the desired holding period balances a price change with a corresponding reinvestment rate income change due to an interest rate change. Table 13–4 shows how this occurs when interest rates rise, using the bond from Example 13–1. The table shows what happens to the bond's return when yields rise from 12 percent to 14 percent during the second year of the five years in the bond's life. In the second year, the price of the bond falls to $977 because of the rise in rates. At the same time interest begins accumulating on the previously received coupons, and it accumulates at a rate higher than originally expected when the yield was 12 percent. However, during the second year, the effect of the fall in price is much greater than the few extra dollars from the higher reinvestment rate, so the total return at the end of the second year is only 10.06 percent, less than the originally promised 12 percent. By the third year, the extra income from reinvestment at higher rates raises total return to 11.36 percent. At the end of the bond's duration, four years, the total return is equal to 12.01 percent, approximately the bond's original yield to maturity, even though interest rates changed before maturity.

Should interest rates decrease, we can also use duration to immunize the bond's return. Table 13–5 shows an example of the effects of a fall in yields from 12 percent to 8 percent occurring in the second year of the five-year bond. As in the case of rising rates, the total return on the bond at the end of its duration, the fourth year, is about equal to its original yield to maturity of 12 percent.

TABLE 13–4
Duration as an immunization strategy when interest rates rise[a]

	Sources of Bond Return				
Year	***Bond Yield and Reinvestment Rate***	***Market Price of Bond***	***Total of Coupons Received***	***Total of Interest on Reinvested Coupons***	***Total Return from All Return Sources***[b]
1	12%	$1030	$130	$ 0	12.0%
2	14	977	260	18	10.1
3	14	984	390	57	11.4
4	14	991	520	120	12.0
5	14	1000	650	209	12.4

[a]*Bond characteristics:*
Number of years to maturity: 5
Coupon rate of bond: 13%
Yield to maturity: 12%; changes to 14% after one year
Market price of bond: $1036
Bond duration: 3.99
Interest paid once per year at the end of the year
[b]The total return is the return from the change in the bond price, the receipt of coupon payments, and the return on the reinvested coupon payments.

TABLE 13–5
Duration as an immunization strategy when interest rates fall[a]

	Sources of Bond Return				
Year	***Bond Yield and Reinvestment Rate***	***Market Price of Bond***	***Total of Coupons Received***	***Total of Interest on Reinvested Coupons***	***Total Return from All Return Sources***[b]
1	12%	$1030	$130	$ 0	12.0%
2	8	1129	260	10	16.2
3	8	1089	390	32	13.4
4	8	1046	520	66	12.0
5	8	1000	650	113	11.2

[a]*Bond characteristics:*
Number of years to maturity: 5
Coupon rate of bond: 13%
Yield to maturity: 12%; changes to 8% after one year
Market price of bond: $1036
Bond duration: 3.99
Interest paid once per year at the end of the year
[b]The total return is the return from the change in the bond price, the receipt of coupon payments, and the return on the reinvested coupon payments.

Portfolio Strategy Using Duration

Because most bond portfolios will be diversified and contain bonds of a number of different issuers, it is important to be able to apply the duration concept to a portfolio to immunize the entire portfolio from interest rate changes. Accomplishing this is fairly straightforward because the duration of a bond portfolio is simply the weighted average of the durations of the individual bonds in the portfolio, where the weights are equal to the proportion of the portfolio's funds invested in the particular bond. We can formulate as follows:

$$D_p = \sum_{j=1}^{n} w_j \times D_j \qquad \textbf{(13–3)}$$

where D_p = the duration of a bond portfolio
D_j = the duration of the *j*th bond in the portfolio
w_j = the portion of funds of the bond portfolio invested in the *j*th bond, based on market prices of the bonds (not face values)

Example 13–2 shows the computation of a two-bond portfolio's duration. Since the duration of the example portfolio is 6.11, the return on the portfolio should be about equal to its promised yield at that time. Although the yield on one bond will be less than the promised yield, a higher yield on the other bond will offset it to give the desired yield for the portfolio at the duration time. This will be the case for bond portfolios containing any number of bonds.

EXAMPLE 13–2

In addition to the bond in Example 13–1 (price = $1,036, duration = 3.99), Mr. Bill Grant plans to purchase a bond whose price is $873 and whose duration is 8.62. What is the duration of a portfolio of one of each of these bonds?

Compute the total value of the portfolio:

$$= 1036 + 873$$
$$= 1909$$

Compute the duration:

$$D_p = 3.99(1036/1909) + 8.62(873/1909)$$
$$= 2.17 + 3.94$$
$$= 6.11$$

As we have noted, duration immunizes the portfolio against a one-time interest rate change. If interest rates rise one year, rise again the following year, and fall the year after, then on the duration date, the actual yield of a bond portfolio may be different from its originally promised yield to maturity. Any observer of interest rates knows that interest rates change continuously. What we need, then, is a strategy to account for continuously changing rates, not just a one-shot change.

The procedure to accomplish this is *portfolio revision*. Suppose that after analysis of the economic environment, we decide that interest rates will likely change significantly approximately every six months. We then construct a bond portfolio whose duration equals our desired time horizon. After six months, we recompute the duration of our portfolio. If changes in interest rates have caused the duration of our portfolio to change significantly from our target desired horizon, then we revise the portfolio so that its duration will once again equal the desired duration. This revision process may involve either the purchase of additional bonds or the sale of existing bonds in the portfolio. Although this process may not completely immunize the portfolio from changes in interest rates, it will minimize the portfolio's interest rate risk.

Cash Flow Matching

In addition to immunization, a second semi-active bond management strategy is *cash flow matching*. Investors who use cash flow matching are usually institutions that can identify cash flow needs at particular times. They then purchase bonds whose cash payments will coincide with those cash needs. As the cash needs change, the bond investor can revise the portfolio to meet the newly identified cash flow needs. For example, a pension fund can estimate its needs for cash flows to make planned pension payments based on life expectancies. It can then purchase a bond portfolio expected to provide such a cash flow. Although cash flow matching seems to be a fairly simple procedure, planning cash flow needs for funds with thousands of liabilities investing in hundreds of bonds can be a great task. Linear programming is a mathematical technique that can be used to aid in the procedure of cash flow matching. However, bond portfolio managers usually consider immunization to be a superior management strategy when compared to cash flow matching.

ACTIVE BOND PORTFOLIO MANAGEMENT

Active bond management involves continuous management of the bond portfolio to maximize total return. The time horizon for return maximization may be the next period or a number of time periods. The investor's objective is to maximize return, whether it comes from income, capital appreciation, or a combination of the two. Increased volatility of interest rates has stimulated the use of active management strategies. Bond swaps and bond speculation are two popular active strategies.

Bond Swaps

A *bond swap* involves "swapping" one bond in the portfolio for another bond. Actually, the bond manager sells the position in one bond and replaces it with another bond purchased in the market. Swaps can have any of several goals, such as to increase current yield, improve portfolio quality, or change taxes on the portfolio.

There are situations in which an investor might be inclined to enter into a swap rather than moving funds into other securities. For example, a pension fund might be constrained to keep a minimum percentage of its portfolio in bonds. In such a case, the fund could use swaps to exploit anticipated changes in bond market conditions while still maintaining the required percentage concentration in bonds. The following sections describe four popular bond swaps.

Quality Swaps

Quality swaps involve selling bonds of one quality rating group and purchasing bonds from another rating group. For example, if the bond portfolio manager foresees a downturn in the economy and a corresponding increase in corporate bond defaults, then a quality swap involving the sale of lower quality bonds and purchase of higher quality bonds may be appropriate. Should the economic recession occur, then the higher-quality bond portfolio will likely suffer fewer defaults and have a higher total return than if the lower quality bonds had been retained.

Tax Swaps

The objective of a *tax swap* is to minimize the effect of taxes on total return. For example, suppose that to increase the bond portfolio's quality the portfolio manager had sold a group of bonds for which the portfolio had a $50,000 capital gain. To delay paying taxes on that gain, the portfolio manager could offset the gain by also selling a group of bonds in which there was a $50,000 loss and replacing them with similar bonds. Note that the replacement bonds must be similar. If they are identical, the tax authorities may disallow the tax write-off on the grounds that the sale was a wash sale. An investor anticipating the use of a tax swap should carefully consider all tax laws and rulings that address the issue.

Rate Anticipation Swaps

The *rate anticipation swap* or *substitution swap* takes advantage of the inverse relationship between bond prices and interest rates. An investor using this approach would rearrange the bond portfolio mix based upon interest rate projections. If the investor thinks that interest rates will fall, then the rate anticipation swap strategy would indicate selling bonds that are less sensitive to interest rate changes and replacing them with bonds that should rise in price faster when interest rates fall.

Yield Pickup Swaps

A *yield pickup swap* involves switching bonds in the portfolio with relatively lower current yields to bonds with higher current yields. Unless there are circumstances that would indicate otherwise, yield pickup swaps should involve bonds of the same quality and maturity. The swap simply substitutes a high-coupon for a low-coupon bond.

Bond Speculation

Another active bond strategy is based solely on speculating on a change in bond prices resulting from a change in interest rates. It is similar to the rate anticipation swap, but this strategy does not require replacing one bond with another bond. Instead, any type of security may be involved. For example, if a bond speculator believes interest rates will fall, then she may shift funds from stocks or any other security into bonds. Following the rate change, the investor might then sell the bonds and purchase stocks, money market instruments, or any other investment.

To take the greatest advantage of a change in interest rates, the bond speculator should trade those bonds that are the most sensitive to interest rate changes (or the least sensitive, depending on interest rate projections and strategy). For this discussion, let us assume that we have projected interest rates to fall. We therefore want to purchase bonds, and the bonds that we want to purchase are those that are most interest rate sensitive and will give us the greatest capital gain when rates fall.

The bond price theorems of the last chapter are useful guidelines. For example, we know that low-coupon, long-maturity bonds will be most sensitive. However, this does not always unambiguously identify the best choice of bond. For example, suppose we must choose between a 9 percent twenty-three year bond and a ten percent twenty-six year bond. The first bond has a lower coupon but does not have a longer maturity. To identify which of these bonds is most sensitive to interest rates, we need to know more than the guidelines given by the bond price theorems. The tool for determining interest rate sensitivity is duration.

Determining the *interest rate elasticity,* or interest rate sensitivity, of a bond is the second important use of duration (in addition to its use in immunization). The measure of a bond's interest rate elasticity states the percent change in the bond's price for a given percent change in the required rate of return.

$$el = \frac{\text{percent change in bond price}}{\text{percent change in yield}} \qquad \textbf{(13–4)}$$

where el = the elasticity coefficient of a bond

Since bond prices always move inversely with yields, the elasticity coefficient (el) will always be a negative number. Using the bond's duration, we can express the elasticity as follows:

$$el = -\frac{D \times Y_m}{1 + Y_m} \qquad \textbf{(13–5)}$$

Equation 13–5 shows that duration is an important determinant of elasticity. The longer a bond's duration, the more interest rate sensitive will be its price. It is easy to identify zero-coupon bonds as having the most price risk, other factors equal. Example 13–3 shows how to compute the elasticity.

EXAMPLE 13–3

What is the elasticity of a ten-year zero-coupon bond priced to yield 10 percent?

Because it is a zero-coupon bond, its duration is equal to its maturity.

$$el = -\frac{10(.10)}{(1 + .10)}$$

$$= -.9091$$

The elasticity of the example bond is .9091. This means that for a 1 percent rise in interest rates (*not* a rise of one percentage point), the price of the bond should fall by .9091 percent. The following formula is useful for estimating the price of a bond after a change in interest rates:

$$P_1 = P_0[el(\frac{Y_{m1}}{Y_{m0}} - 1) + 1] \qquad \textbf{(13–6)}$$

where P_1 = the price of the bond after an interest rate change
P_0 = the bond's price before a change in interest rates
Y_{m1} = the bond yield after the interest rate change
Y_{m0} = the bond yield before the interest rate change

Equation 13–6 is also appropriate for estimating the change in the value of a bond portfolio following a change in interest rates. Example 13–4 shows the use of this formula by computing the post change price of the bond from Example 13–3. Note that the post change price using the bond valuation model is slightly different from the estimate using the elasticity concept. The reason for this is that elasticity changes as the rate changes. Therefore, its use to predict bond prices after an interest rate change is accurate only for small interest rate changes.

EXAMPLE 13–4

Compute the price of the bond in Example 13–3 before and after a fall in interest rates from 10 percent to 9 percent, using the standard bond valuation formula. Compute the after change price using the bond's prechange price and elasticity.

Prechange price:

$$P_B = 1000(.3855)$$
$$= 385.50$$

Postchange price using bond valuation:

$$P_B = 1000(.4224)$$
$$= 422.40$$

Postchange price using elasticity:

$$P_1 = 385.50[-.9091(.09/.10 - 1) + 1]$$
$$= 420.55$$

A bond investor should use elasticity to estimate bond prices only if interest rates change by only about two percentage points or less. It may seem easier to be accurate and simply forecast the price of a bond after an interest rate change using the bond valuation formula. This would be simple enough for one or a portfolio of several bonds, but for a portfolio of dozens of bonds, the elasticity concept is easier to apply.

Therefore, for an investor speculating on a change in interest rates, a bond or bond portfolio with as high an elasticity as possible will give the investor the greatest capital gain. As Equation 13–5 implies, this usually means the bond with the greatest duration.

COMBINATION STRATEGIES

The basic bond portfolio strategies we have just reviewed are not necessarily mutually exclusive. Under different economic conditions, particular strategies may be appropriate, but often a mix of two or more strategies can provide the optimum alternative. There are two popular *combination bond strategies.* The first of these is an *active/passive strategy,* in which the portfolio contains a portion dedicated to passive management with the remainder under some type of active management. The portfolio manager usually designs the passive component of the portfolio to provide some minimum level of current return. The manager is then free to manage the active component with the goal of maximizing total return.

A second combination is an *active/immunization strategy.* A portfolio constructed for such a strategy has two components: the active portion and the immunized portion. The portfolio manager would immunize the appropriate portion of the portfolio, revising and re-immunizing it as conditions and changing interest rates required. The manager would then be able to use the active portion to take advantage of interest rate changes.

The success of any bond portfolio management strategy clearly depends upon the pattern of interest rates over the holding period. Support for the use of combination strategies comes from a study by Barnes, Johnson, and Shannon[6] of investment results using different management strategies. The study compared returns of passive and semi-active strategies with those of several different publicly traded, actively managed bond funds. It concluded that passive strategies are at least as promising as active strategies.

BOND PORTFOLIO CONSTRAINTS

When choosing an appropriate bond management strategy or combination of strategies, the portfolio manager should always select portfolio risk and return within certain constraints determined by the investor's needs. These constraints usually fall into one of the following five categories:

1. Liquidity needs
2. Tax consideration
3. Investment time horizon
4. Regulatory environment and legal aspects
5. Other requirements unique to the individual investor

For example, the need for liquidity in a fixed-income portfolio is often important, should the cash needs requirements exceed their projections. For example, suppose a bond portfolio provides $100,000 per month to an insurance company to pay expected claims. If a disaster occurs, resulting in twice as many claims as normal, the company must sell some of the portfolio to meet its cash needs. In such a case, it is handy to have at least a portion of the portfolio in bonds that are among the most marketable and liquid.

SUMMARY

There are four main categories of risk associated with fixed-income securities: default risk, price risk, call risk, and reinvestment rate risk. Bond quality ratings are common tools for identifying and controlling default risk. To control call risk, an investor can select bonds with low probabilities of being called. Using duration can control price risk and reinvestment rate risk, which are caused by interest rate changes.

There are passive, semi-active, and active bond portfolio management strategies. A passive strategy consists of buying bonds and holding them until they mature. Semi-active strategies include immunization and cash flow matching. Bond swaps—such as quality, tax, rate anticipation, and yield pickup swaps—are active strategies. Bond speculation using anticipated interest rate changes is also an active management strategy.

Duration is a concept that is useful for immunizing the return on a bond against a one-time change in interest rates and for identifying bonds whose prices are most sensitive to interest rates.

IMPORTANT TERMS

active bond management
active/immunization strategy
active/passive strategy
bond quality ratings
bond swap
call risk
cash flow matching
combination bond strategy
debt service
default risk
duration
immunization
interest rate elasticity
interest rate risk
passive bond management
portfolio revision
price risk
quality swap
rate anticipation swap
reinvestment rate risk
semi-active bond management
tax swap
yield pickup swap
yield to call

QUESTIONS AND PROBLEMS

1. Explain the four categories of bond risk and their relationships to one another.
2. What should happen to the yield of a bond rated A− if Standard & Poor's suddenly and unexpectedly changes the rating to BBB? What would happen to the bond's price?

3. You are given the following statements for two companies:

	Company A	*Company B*
Income Statement:		
Operating income	$ 5,000	$ 8,000
Interest expense	1,000	3,000
Net income	4,000	5,000
Balance Sheet:		
Assets	$40,000	$60,000
Bonds	10,000	30,000
Equity	30,000	30,000

Both companies' bonds are 10 percent, fifteen-year noncallable bonds. The yield to maturity of one of the bonds is 12 percent and the yield of the other is 13 percent. Which one belongs to Company A and which to company B? Support your answer with as many reasons as you can find.

4. You must select between two different bonds while minimizing call risk. The two bonds have the following characteristics:
   Bond X: 14%, 10-year bond callable in 2 years
   Bond Y: 7%, 10-year bond callable in 2 years
   Which bond would you choose? Why?
5. What advantages would a passive bond management strategy have over semi-active and active strategies? If interest rates cannot be accurately forecasted but will not be very volatile, which strategy would probably be optimal?
6. Compute the duration, in years, of the following bonds, assuming annual interest payments:
   a) 12%, 8-year bond selling at par
   b) 12-year, zero-coupon bond selling for $257 to yield 12%
   c) 16-year, 8% bond, selling for $844 to yield 10%
7. Compute the duration, in years, of the following bonds, assuming semiannual interest payments:
   a) 12%, 8-year bond selling at par
   b) 16%, 10-year bond selling at a promised yield to maturity of 14%
   c) 4%, 12-year bond selling at a promised yield to maturity of 10%
8. Compute the elasticity for the following bonds:
   a) yield to maturity of 12% with duration of 14 years
   b) yield to maturity of 10% with duration of 8 years
   c) yield to maturity of 15% with duration of 6 years
9. Denrow Corp. has a twelve-year bond outstanding that makes annual interest payments of $140. The bond sells for a promised yield to maturity of 12 percent.
   a) What is the price of the bond?
   b) What is the bond's duration?
   c) Use the elasticity concept to estimate the price of the bond should its required yield fall to 11 percent.
   d) Using elasticity, what would be the effect of a rise in the bond's yield to 13 percent?
10. Given a choice between the following two bonds (X and Y), select the one that you would purchase if you expect interest rates to fall. Provide evidence to support your choice. (Assume annual interest payments.)
    Bond X: 12%, 18-year bond selling for $1,164, a yield to maturity of 10%
    Bond Y: 11%, 17-year bond selling for $1,080, a yield to maturity of 10%

11. You purchase a portfolio containing one each of the following bonds:

Bond	*Yield to Maturity*	*Duration*	*Price*
A	10%	8 yrs.	$963
B	12	16	892
C	13	20	824

a) What is the value of the portfolio?
b) What is the weighted average yield of the portfolio?
c) What is the portfolio's duration?
d) If the required return on the portfolio rises to 13 percent, what will be the value of the portfolio?

NOTES

1. W. B. Hickman (1958), *Corporate Bond Quality and Investor Experience,* Washington, DC: National Bureau of Economic Research.
2. See, for example, G. Hettenhouse and William Sartoris (1976), "An Analysis of the Informational Value of Bond Rating Changes," *Quarterly Review of Economics and Business,* 16 (Summer), 65–76; S. Katz (1974), "The Price Adjustment Process of Bonds to Rating Reclassifications: A Test of Bond Market Efficiency," *Journal of Finance,* 29 (May), 551–559; and M. Weinstein, (1977), "The Effect of Rating Change Announcement on Bond Price," *Journal of Financial Economics,* 5 (December), 329–350.
3. Robert W. Ingram, Leroy D. Brooks, and Ronald M. Copeland (1983), "The Information Content of Municipal Bond Rating Changes: A Note," *Journal of Financial Economics,* 38 (June), 997–1003.
4. Frederick R. Macaulay (1938), *Some Theoretical Problems Suggested by the Movement of Interest Rates, Bond Yields and Stock Prices in the United States since 1856,* New York: National Bureau of Economic Research.
5. John Caks, William R. Lane, Robert W. Greenleaf, and Reginald G. Joules, (1985), "A Simple Formula for Duration," *Journal of Financial Research,* 8 (Fall), 245–249.
6. Tom Barnes, Keith Johnson, and Don Shannon (1984), "A Test of Fixed-Income Strategies," *Journal of Portfolio Management,* 10 (Winter), 60–65.

SELECTED REFERENCES

Arak, Marcelle, Laurie S. Goodman, and Joseph Snailer (1986). "Duration Equivalent Bond Swaps: A New Tool." *Journal of Portfolio Management,* 12 (Summer), 26–32.

Barnes, Tom, Keith Johnson and Don Shannon (1984). "A Test of Fixed-Income Strategies." *Journal of Portfolio Management,* 10 (Winter), 60–65.

Bernstein, Peter L., (Ed.) (1977). *The Theory and Practice of Bond Portfolio Management.* New York: Institutional Investor.

———(Ed.) (1980). *The Theory and Practice of Bond Portfolio Management,* vol. 2. New York: Institutional Investor.

Dyl, Edward A. and Stanley A. Martin, Jr. (1983). "Rules of Thumb for the Analysis of Tax Swaps." *Journal of Portfolio Management,* 10 (Fall), 71–74.

Fong, H. Gifford, and Frank J. Fabozzi (1985). "How to Enhance Bond Returns with Naive Strategies." *Journal of Portfolio Management,* 11 (Summer), 57–60.

Fuller, Russell J., and John W. Settle (1984). "Determinants of Duration and Bond Volatility." *Journal of Portfolio Management,* 10 (Summer), 66–72.

Gushee, Charles H. (1981). "How to Hedge a Bond Investment." *Financial Analysts Journal.* 37 (March–April) 44–51.

Ingram, Robert W., Leroy D. Brooks, and Ronald M. Copeland (1983). "The Information Content of Municipal Bond Rating Changes: A Note." *Journal of Finance,* 38, 997–1003.

Johnson, James M. (1984). "When Are Zero-Coupon Bonds the Better Buy?" *Journal of Portfolio Management,* 10 (Spring), 36–41.

Kalotay, Andrew J. (1985). "The After-Tax Duration of Original Issue Discount Bonds." *Journal of Portfolio Management,* 11 (Winter), 70–72.

Kolodny, Richard and Diane Rizzuto Suhler (1988). "The Effects of New Debt Issues on Existing Security Holders." *Quarterly Journal of Business and Economics,* 27 (Spring), 51–72.

McEnally, Richard W., and Calvin M. Boardman (1979). "Aspects of Corporate Bond Portfolio Diversification." *Journal of Financial Research,* 2 (Spring), 27–36.

Perry, Larry G., Glenn V. Henderson, Jr., and Timothy P. Cronan, (1984). "Multivariate Analysis of Corporate Bond Ratings and Industry Classifications." *Journal of Financial Research,* 7 27–36.

Reilly, Frank K., and S. Sidhu Rupinder, (1980). "The Many Uses of Bond Duration." *Financial Analysts Journal,* 36 (July–August), 58–72.

Smirlock, Michael (1985). "Seasonality and Bond Market Returns." *Journal of Portfolio Management,* 11 (Spring), 42–44.

Speakes, Jeffrey K. (1984). "Fixed Income Risk Measurement and Risk Management." *Journal of Portfolio Management,* 11 (Winter), 66–71.

Stock, Duane (1982). "Does Active Management of Municipal Bond Portfolios Pay?" *Journal of Portfolio Management,* 8 (Winter), 51–55.

PART FIVE

Equity Securities

CHAPTER 14

Stock Valuation: Concepts

As Chapter 12 introduced the concepts of bond valuation, this chapter develops the valuation concepts for preferred and common stocks. The next chapter, Chapter 15, will show applications of these concepts for the fundamental valuation of common stocks.

The bond valuation concept was based upon John Burr Williams's[1] treatment of a bond's value as the present value of all the interest and principal payments of the bond. In a similar fashion, Williams described the value of stock: "Let us define the investment value of a stock as the present worth of all the dividends to be paid upon it." This principle forms the basis for the stock valuation models developed in this chapter.

Williams added, "To appraise the investment value, then, it is necessary to estimate the future payments." For preferred stocks, this task is not too difficult because most preferred stocks have a fixed dividend whose payment is relatively certain. However, estimating the dividends to be paid to common stock holders is one of the main challenges faced by common stock analysts. Common stock dividends have additional uncertainty about them because the *level* of dividends—not just their payment—depends upon the company's ability to generate earnings. This chapter begins with a discussion of dividends and the required rate of return, follows with the valuation of preferred stocks, and then extends the concepts to common stocks.

DIVIDENDS

Many companies pay quarterly cash dividends to their shareholders. However, because the payment of dividends is at the discretion of the board of directors of the corporation, some companies that need to conserve capital will pay no dividend. For example, many companies in the early stages of development need to retain their earnings to fund expansion. Investors in these companies expect returns from capital gains or future dividends.

Some companies pay an annual dividend instead of a quarterly cash payout. This is especially true for companies with small dividend payments, which pay annually to avoid the extra expenses of quarterly checks. Other companies maintain a dividend policy of regular quarterly payouts accompanied by an extra year-end dividend if fiscal results have been sufficiently positive.

Dividend Payment Procedure

There are four important dates in the dividend payment process. In chronological order, they are as follows:

1. Dividend declaration date
2. Ex-dividend date
3. Dividend record date
4. Dividend payment date

The *dividend declaration date* takes place when the board of directors of the corporation meets and votes in favor of paying a dividend. The motion for payment of the dividend specifies the *dividend record date* and the *dividend payment date.* The payment date is the date of which the corporation or its paying agent issues the checks paying the dividend. The company or agent will issue these checks to stockholders who were registered as stockholders on the dividend record date. To be a *stockholder of record* on the record date, the investor must have owned the stock immediately before the *ex-dividend date.* The ex-dividend date is the first date on which a buyer of a stock is *not* entitled to receive the dividend. The stock trades ex-dividend (without a dividend) on the ex-dividend date. To receive a declared dividend, an investor buying the stock has to buy it before the ex-dividend date, while an investor selling the stock would want to wait until the ex-dividend date or after to sell the stock. Normally, the ex-dividend date is the fourth *business day* preceding the record date. (It is five business days if the record date is not a business day.) The price of a stock will typically drop by an amount about equal to the dividend on the ex-dividend date (other factors equal). Therefore, a strategy of buying a stock on the day before the ex-dividend date, selling it on the ex-dividend date, and collecting the dividend should not yield excess returns, especially after paying commissions.

The Wall Street Journal reports dividend news on a daily basis, listing companies declaring dividends and their dates. There is also a list of stocks going ex-dividend on that day.

Stock Dividends

Companies often declare *stock dividends* in addition to or instead of cash dividends. For example, a 5 percent stock dividend means that the company will issue five new shares for each one-hundred shares an investor holds. However, the corporation has not really given the investor anything of value because the stock dividend dilutes all common shares, and the price of the stock will drop on the ex-dividend day for a stock dividend as it does for a cash dividend. The investor's net wealth should remain unchanged. The formula for the ex-dividend price of a share of stock following a stock dividend is:

$$P_x = \frac{P_p}{(1 + D_s)} \tag{14–1}$$

where P_x = the ex-dividend stock price
P_p = the stock price immediately prior to the ex-dividend time
D_s = the stock dividend

Example 14–1 shows how the net wealth of an investor receiving a stock dividend does not change.

EXAMPLE 14–1

Iris Corp. declares a 5 percent stock dividend. What should be the ex-dividend price of the stock, if the price on the day before ex-dividend is \$50? What is the net wealth of an investor with 100 shares before and after the dividend?

$$\begin{aligned} P_x &= 50/(1 + .05) \\ &= 47.62 \end{aligned}$$

$$\begin{aligned} \text{Net wealth before dividend} &= 50(100) \\ &= 5000 \\ \text{Net wealth ex-dividend} &= 47.62(105) \\ &= 5000 \end{aligned}$$

Actually, a stock dividend is equivalent to a cash dividend that the investor reinvests in the stock of the same company. Example 14–2 shows how this happens.

EXAMPLE 14–2

Using the information from Example 14–1, find the equivalent cash dividend and show that the investor could reinvest the cash dividends to have a position equivalent to the investor in Example 14–1.

Since the price of the stock will drop by an amount about equal to the cash dividend on the ex-dividend date, an equivalent cash dividend must be equal to $P_p - P_x = 50 - 47.62 = 2.38$. With the total cash dividend of 238 (2.38 × 100 shares), the investor can purchase five new shares (5 × 47.62 = 238). Therefore, the investor who reinvests the cash dividends ends up with 105 shares valued at \$47.62 each, the same position as the investor with a stock dividend.

The only real difference between the cash dividend and the stock dividend on the wealth of the investor should be tax effects. Cash dividends are taxable while stock dividends are not taxable until the investor sells the new shares. Therefore, investors in high tax brackets may prefer stock dividends rather than cash dividends. We can also argue that investors who need the cash flow provided by cash dividends can achieve a cash dividend equivalent from a stock dividend by selling the new shares in the market (not considering commission costs). However, the additional transactions necessitated by the extra odd-lot transaction from a stock dividend can result in a higher total commission cost to an investor closing out a position. For this reason, some institutional investors tend to avoid stocks that regularly declare stock dividends.

Stock Splits

Stock dividends are similar in effect to *stock splits.* A stock split occurs when the company "splits" its existing shares, diluting the per share ownership but keeping each stockholder's percentage of the company the same. For example, a two-for-one stock split doubles the number of shares in the company. Each existing share splits into two. The effect on the market price of the stock would be the same as a 100 percent stock dividend. The only differences between stock dividends and stock splits are the way the corporation records them on its books and the treatment of cash dividends. If a company pays cash dividends, then the amount of the cash dividend following a stock dividend usually remains the same, but the cash dividend on split shares usually decreases in proportion to the split.

A company can also have a *reverse stock split* to decrease the number of outstanding shares. It is possible that a reverse stock split could help stockholders by lowering the commission of a given postsplit dollar transaction in the stock compared to the commission on a presplit trade.

The reasons that companies declare stock splits are varied, but the most commonly mentioned one is that a split lowers the trading price of the stock to a more "affordable" level, increasing interest in the stock, increasing liquidity, and maximizing total value. Theoretically, however, stock splits only divide the same pie into smaller slices, and the total size of the pie should not be changed by a split. Empirically, stock splits appear to have no long-run effect on investors' returns.[2] It is true that stocks that have split have done well and increased in value, but the split occurs as a result of the increase in stock price, the price does not increase as a result of a split. However, there does appear to be a slightly positive effect around the split date on the return on a stock having a split, while a slightly negative impact is evident on stocks declaring stock dividends.[3]

PREFERRED STOCK

The first valuation model we will consider is for preferred stock. Projecting dividends for most types of preferred stock is fairly straightforward because preferred stock pays a constant dividend. The exceptions to this are *adjustable rate preferred stocks,* which pay a dividend tied to some interest rate index, and *participating preferred stocks,* which pay a minimum preferred dividend plus an extra dividend dependent upon dividends paid to the common. To value a straight preferred stock, our valuation principle says to find the present value of the infinite stream of future fixed dividends as follows:

$$P_{pfd} = \sum_{t=1}^{\infty} \frac{D_t}{(1+k)^t} \tag{14–2}$$

where P_{pfd} = the value of a preferred stock
D_t = the dividend in time period t
k = the required rate of return

Since all the dividends are the same, Equation 14–2 simplifies to:

$$P_{pfd} = \frac{D_t}{k} \tag{14–3}$$

Equation 14–3 shows that the value of a share of preferred stock is simply equal to its dividend divided by its required rate of return. Since most preferred stocks have relatively low amounts of market risk, the main factor influencing preferred stock prices is interest rates in general, reflected in the riskless rate. Because of their dependence on interest rates, preferred stock prices often tend to behave more like bond prices than stock prices, reflecting the steady income nature of preferreds.

COMMON STOCK

Most investors buy common stocks for their growth potential in addition to any current dividends that the company pays. As a company invests its capital wisely in profitable business ventures, the company's earnings should grow. Higher earnings allow the company to pay out higher dividends. There are two approaches to common stock valuation. The first approach values dividends, and the second approach values earnings.

Dividend Valuation Models

The dividend valuation models rest on the hypothesis that dividends are inextricably tied to earnings. Therefore, since changing earnings must be evident in changes in dividends, it is this growing stream of dividends that investors should discount to present value to estimate the current fundamental worth of the company. For simplicity, the valuation model, presented below, is based on the assumption that the growth rate remains constant. A model for varying rates of growth, the nonconstant growth model, is discussed next.

The Constant Growth Model

The assumptions underlying the constant growth model are as follows:

1. Investors expect the company's earnings to grow at a constant rate in the future.
2. The company maintains a dividend policy of paying out a constant portion of its earnings as dividends.

Given these two assumptions, it follows that the company's dividends will grow at the same rate as earnings. Therefore, we can express the expected next-period dividend as follows:

$$D_{t+1} = D_t(1 + g) \qquad \textbf{(14–4)}$$

where D_{t+1} = the expected next period dividend (the dividend to the paid at the beginning of time period $t+1$)
D_t = the dividend at time period t
g = the growth rate in the firm's dividends (and earnings)

Using Equation 14–4, we can express the expected future stream of dividends as follows:

$$D_1 = D_0(1 + g)^1$$
$$D_2 = D_0(1 + g)^2 = D_1(1 + g)$$
$$D_3 = D_0(1 + g)^3 = D_2(1 + g)$$
$$\ldots$$
$$D_n = D_0(1 + g)^n = D_{n-1}(1 + g) \qquad \textbf{(14–5)}$$

EXAMPLE 14–3

Ridglea Company pays a current dividend of \$1.50. If the company maintains a constant dividend payout policy and its earnings grow at a rate of .08, project the dividends for the next four years.

In the absence of a calculator that has a power function, note that $(1 + g)^n$ is the same as the future value of a dollar at rate g. Therefore,

$$D_1 = 1.50(1.0800) = 1.62$$
$$D_2 = 1.50(1.1664) = 1.7495$$
$$D_3 = 1.50(1.2597) = 1.8896$$
$$D_4 = 1.50(1.3605) = 2.0408$$

Or, we can compound the current dividend out at a .08 rate as follows:

$$D_1 = 1.5000(1.08) = 1.62$$
$$D_2 = 1.6200(1.08) = 1.7496$$
$$D_3 = 1.7496(1.08) = 1.8896$$
$$D_4 = 1.8896(1.08) = 2.0408$$

Then, using the notation for the future stream of growing dividends, we can write the formula for the present value of those dividends as follows:

$$P_0 = \frac{D_1}{(1+k)^1} + \frac{D_2}{(1+k)^2} + \frac{D_3}{(1+k)^3} + \ldots + \frac{D_\infty}{(1+k)^\infty} \qquad \textbf{(14–6)}$$
$$= \sum_{t=1}^{\infty} \frac{D_t}{(1+k)^t}$$

where P_0 = the current value of a share of common stock
D_t = the dividend paid to the common stock at the beginning of time period t

Equation 14–6 says that the current value of a share of common stock is equal to the present value of all of the expected future dividends to be paid on the stock from now until forever. Fortunately, to solve Equation 14–6, we do not actually have to add up the infinite flow of discounted dividends. Since the growth rate is constant, and any dividend can be expressed in terms of the initial dividend and its growth rate (Equation 14–5), we can simplify Equation 14–6 to the following:

$$P_0 = \frac{D_1}{k - g} \qquad \textbf{(14–7)}$$

Equation 14–7 is the fundamental valuation model for valuing a share of stock assuming a constant growth rate. It is often called the *Gordon growth model* because of the pioneering valuation work of Myron J. Gordon.[4] It is important to note that the current value of the stock depends upon the amount of the dividend during the first period, not just the current dividend. Of course, knowing the current dividend and the growth rate, we can compute the first period dividend using Equation 14–5.

EXAMPLE 14–4

Norman Manufacturing pays a current dividend of \$2.00, which should grow at a .05 rate in the future. Norman's required rate of return is .12. What is the value of a share of Norman stock?

Use Equation 14–5 to estimate Norman's dividend in period 1:

$$D_1 = 2.00(1 + .05)$$
$$= 2.10$$

Use Equation 14–7 to compute the value of the stock:

$$P_0 = 2.10/(.12 - .05)$$
$$= 30$$

One might question the validity of a model that discounts an infinite flow of dividends, on the ground that investors have finite holding periods. No investor plans to hold a share of stock forever to get the infinite dividend stream, so why should Equation 14–7 be a valid definition of the fundamental value of common stock? The following explanation should clarify the reasons supporting the model. Suppose an investor buys a stock and plans to sell it three years from now. We could construct a present value model for this situation as follows:

$$\sum_{t=1}^{3} \frac{D_t}{(1 + k)^t} + \frac{P_3}{(1 + k)^3} \qquad \textbf{(14–8)}$$

where P_3 = the price of the stock at time period 3

Equation 14–8 simply says that the current value of the stock is equal to three years of discounted dividends plus the present value of the stock three years from now. The problem is that we do not know what the value of the stock will be three years from now (P_3). To estimate the worth of the stock to the person who buys it from the investor in three years, we again rely on the fundamental valuation concept. Assuming that this buyer also plans to hold the stock for three years, its value is:

$$P_3 = \sum_{t=4}^{6} \frac{D_t}{(1+k)^t} + \frac{P_6}{(1+k)^6} \qquad \textbf{(14–9)}$$

We could then substitute the definition of P_3 (Equation 14–9) into Equation 14–8, the valuation for P_0, and simplify it to get:

$$P_0 = \sum_{t=1}^{6} \frac{D_t}{(1+k)^t} + \frac{P_6}{(1+k)^6} \qquad \textbf{(14–10)}$$

This does not appear to have helped matters, because we are still left with a quantity, P_6, whose value is not known. We can go through the same process again, assuming that the stock is again sold to another investor who plans to hold it for three years and then sell it. We would end with the same problem again. We could repeat the procedure into infinity, and we would then finish with the same solution as in Equation 14–6. This leads us to an important conclusion about security valuation: *Even though no investor actually intends to hold a stock into infinity, the appropriate value for the stock is as if the investor were going to hold it forever.*

Actually, the expected dividends far into the future are relatively unimportant to the current valuation of the stock. The reason for this is that as the number of time periods in the future grows larger, the discount factor becomes quite small. For example, the present value of a dollar factor for a rate of .12, fifty years into the future, is only .0035, and a $5.00 dividend in fifty years would have a present value of only 1.7 cents.

Examining Changes in the Model's Parameters. One useful application of the valuation model (Equation 14–7) is to examine the impact of changes in values of the parameters, assuming other factors remain constant. How should stock prices react to an increase in expected inflation? Higher inflationary expectations would increase the required rate of return, *k,* and stock prices would fall, *assuming that other variables remain unaffected by increased inflation.* However, because of the interrelationships between some of the variables that Equation 14–7 does not identify, the net result may actually be indeterminate. In reality, rising prices (inflation) will allow companies to raise their prices. The resulting higher earnings and dividends would tend to increase the stock prices, possibly even completely countering the negative impact of a higher required return. We usually observe that companies that have the ability to adjust their pricing to reflect inflation quickly have stock prices that do not suffer from increases in inflation.

A company might be able to increase its potential future growth rate through research and development efforts without affecting the other variables in the model.

An increase in g would result in a higher stock valuation. However, it is important to notice that the model holds only as long as the growth rate is less than the required rate of return. As the g approaches k in the model, P_0 approaches infinity. If g is greater the k, the model yields a negative stock value. Both situations are illogical, since stock prices can be neither infinite nor negative. A stock's expected *long-run* growth rate must be less than its required rate of return. On a logical basis, a company growing faster than its required rate over the long run would ultimately consume all of the business in the economy. However, a company's short-run growth can exceed its required return, as long as the growth over the long run averages out to be less than the required rate. The next section develops a valuation model to account for short-term rates of growth that are different from the long-run rate.

The Nonconstant Growth Model

The assumption of a constant growth rate, though mathematically convenient, is somewhat simplified. No investment (except the risk-free asset) is associated with a constant return. Nor is there a risky investment with a constant growth rate. We can defend the use of the constant growth model by saying that the constant rate used in the model represents the average long-run rate, realizing that the actual growth rate will have its ups and downs, and that the required rate of return accounts for the risk associated with these ups and downs. However, if we can estimate the extent and duration of higher or lower intermediate-term growth rates, then we can specify a model that more accurately values these nonstable growth rates.

The traditional view of the life cycle of a firm provides support for the use of such a model. Figure 14–1 illustrates the cycle that divides a company's life into three phases. The first phase represents the early stages of company and product development. High expenditures on development and product introduction resulting in

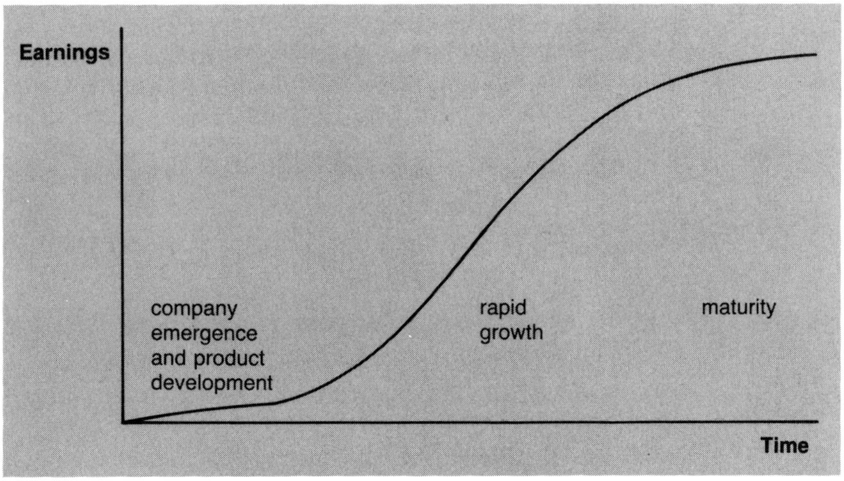

Figure 14–1
The company life cycle

low earnings growth (but high expectations) characterize this phase. The second phase has high earnings growth as the development expenditures of the early phase pay off. The final phase represents the mature firm with low earnings growth. Of course, companies try to maintain the growth phase by developing new products, but the point is that we often can analyze a company and project it to have above-normal growth rates for several years, leveling off to a more normal rate later on.

Let us first consider the case of a stock in a high growth phase expected to have a high growth rate (g_x) for the first three years, then falling to a lower rate (g_y) for the foreseeable future. To construct a model for the fundamental value of this stock, we need to discount the three dividends (growing at rate g_x) to present value, determine the value of the stock three years from now when its expected rate will be lower (g_y), and then discount that price to the present value. Writing this in a formula, we have the following:

$$P_0 = \frac{D_0(1+g_x)^1}{(1+k)^1} + \frac{D_0(1+g_x)^2}{(1+k)^2} + \frac{D_0(1+g_x)^3}{(1+k)^3} + \frac{\dfrac{D_0(1+g_x)^3(1+g_y)}{k-g_y}}{(1+k)^3} \qquad \textbf{(14–11)}$$

The first three terms in Equation 14–11 represent the present value of the dividends growing at g_x. The final term in the equation is the value of the stock at the end of the third year discounted to present value. The value of the stock at the end of the third year (beginning of the fourth year) is equal to the expected fourth-year dividend divided by $(k - g_y)$.

Writing Equation 14–11 in compact notation for the general case of high growth for n time periods gives the following:

$$P_0 = \sum_{t=1}^{n} \frac{D_0(1+g_x)^t}{(1+k)^t} + \frac{\dfrac{D_0(1+g_x)^n(1+g_y)}{k-g_y}}{(1+k)^n} \qquad \textbf{(14–12)}$$

where n = the number of time periods of high growth at rate g_x, after which the growth rate falls to a normal rate of g_y.

To demonstrate the process of building a model considering an interim growth rate, Equation 14–11 actually contains one extra term. This means that we can reduce Equation 14–12 to eliminate one extra iteration of the summation, as follows:

$$P_0 = \sum_{t=1}^{n-1} \frac{D_0(1+g_x)^t}{(1+k)^t} + \frac{\dfrac{D_0(1+g_x)^n}{k-g_y}}{(1+k)^{n-1}} \qquad \textbf{(14–13)}$$

Equations 14–12 and 14–13 are mathematically equivalent. The advantage of Equation 14–13 is that it contains one less iteration of the summation and is therefore simpler to solve by hand.

We could continue to expand the formula indefinitely to account for any number of different interim growth rates and time periods. For example, the formula for two different interim rates—g_x for the first n periods, g_y for periods $n+1$ to m, and g_z after that—would be:

$$P_0 = \sum_{t=1}^{n} \frac{D_0(1+g_x)^t}{(1+k)^t} + \sum_{t=n+1}^{m-1} \frac{D_0(1+g_x)^n(1+g_y)^{t-n}}{(1+k)^t} + \frac{\dfrac{D_0(1+g_x)^n(1+g_y)^{m-n}}{k-g_z}}{(1+k)^{m-1}} \quad \textbf{(14–14)}$$

Equations 14–12, 14–13, and 14–14 appear to be quite complicated. Actually, though, they are very straightforward. When applying the model for changing growth rates, it may be easier for an analyst to lay these formulas aside and simply apply the principles upon which they are based by following these steps:

1. Project the future dividends using the growth rates.
2. Project the future stock price using the dividend in the final interim growth period.
3. Discount each of these amounts to present value at the required rate.

EXAMPLE 14–5

After thoroughly analyzing Harwell Engineers, Inc., you project the company's dividend to grow at a .20 rate for the next two years and at .14 for the following three years, and to level off at .07 thereafter. You estimate a required rate of .12. Harwell currently pays a dividend of 1.20 per share. What is the fundamental value of a share of Harwell stock?

Recalling that $1/(1 + k)^t$ is a present value factor, we can use the factors from the present value tables and construct the following tables to compute the fundamental value:

Year	*Previous Dividend*	*Growth Rate*	*Projected Dividend*	*Present Value Factor*	*Present Value*
1	1.20	.20	1.44	.8928	1.29
2	1.44	.20	1.73	.7972	1.38
3	1.73	.14	1.97	.7118	1.40
4	1.97	.14	2.25	.6355	1.43
5	2.25	.14	2.56		
	Price based on projected year 5 dividend = 2.56/(.12 − .07) = 51.20			.5674	29.05
	Value of stock =				34.55

Earnings Models

The main criticism of the dividend valuation models is that many companies currently pay little or no cash dividends, so projecting their dividends for the future is difficult. The same problem arises for companies with irregular dividends or highly cyclical growth. The earnings models attempt to compensate for this shortcoming.

The Earnings Multiple Approach

If earnings ultimately result in future dividends, then we should be able to construct a model that discounts earnings instead of dividends. Such a model would be consistent with the dividend model, but it would be more easily applied when forecasting dividends is difficult. The first approach to valuing earnings is the *earnings multiple* approach. The idea is that a given stock has a fundamental value that is equal to a multiple of its next period earnings. We can state this in mathematical terms as follows:

$$P_0 = m \times E_1 \tag{14–15}$$

where m = the earnings multiple
E_1 = the next-period earnings per share

Equation 14–15 formalizes the earnings multiple approach by stating that the current price of a stock is worth its next period earnings multiplied by its multiple. Simple mathematical transformation of Equation 14–15 gives a statement of the multiple:

$$m = \frac{P_0}{E_1} \tag{14–16}$$

Equation 14–16 says that the multiple is equal to the current price divided by the expected earnings. For this reason, the earnings multiple is often called the *price to earnings ratio* or simply the *P/E ratio*. In practice, the financial press and investment services commonly report earnings multiples based on the current stock price and the latest twelve months' reported earnings, not expected earnings. The reason for this is that reported earnings is an observable number while expected earnings is not.

In practice, then, to estimate the value of a common stock using the earnings multiple approach (Equation 14–15), the analyst has to forecast earnings and estimate the fundamental multiple for the stock. To give a model for the earnings multiple, noting that the multiple is the P/E ratio, we can divide both sides of equation 14–7 by E_1 to yield:

$$P_0/E_1 = \frac{D_1/E_1}{k - g} \tag{14–17}$$

Note the numerator of Equation 14–17. It is dividends divided by earnings, or what we more commonly call the *dividend payout ratio.*

$$p = D/E \tag{14–18}$$

where p = the dividend payout ratio

Many companies try to maintain a dividend policy of a constant target dividend payout ratio. For example, a company may determine (based on investor clientele, industry norms, opportunities for investing retained earnings, and other factors) that it will attempt to pay out 40 percent of its earnings as dividends ($p = .40$). Of course, the ratio will fluctuate when earnings fluctuate. Most companies are reluctant ever to cut the amount of their dividend, so during lean years the payout ratio may rise. As earnings improve, the ratio will fall. When company management believes that the higher earnings are sustainable, it will increase the dividend to adjust the payout ratio closer to the target ratio. The idea is that the target payout ratio is easier to forecast than the actual dividends. Accepting this, we can rewrite Equation 14–17 in a more convenient form:

$$m = \frac{p}{k - g} \tag{14–19}$$

The g in the earnings multiple model (Equation 14–19) represents the growth rate in earnings, while the g in Equation 14–7 (the dividend model) is the growth rate in dividends. However, accepting the premise that companies maintain a constant target dividend payout ratio policy, the growth rate in earnings will be equal to the growth rate in dividends. Therefore, the two models are completely consistent with each other.

EXAMPLE 14–6

After examining the financial statements of G. Fitch Corp., you determine that the company consistently pays out 30 percent of its earnings as dividends. You forecast earnings to be 3.00 per share next year and to grow at a .09 rate for the foreseeable future. Your required rate of return for the stock is .11. Estimate Fitch's multiple and stock value.

$$\begin{aligned} m &= .30/(.11 - .09) \\ &= 15 \\ P_0 &= 15(3.00) \\ &= 45 \end{aligned}$$

The Corrected Earnings per Share Model

The drawback of the earnings multiple approach is that it does not completely avoid forecasting dividends or dividend policy. The *corrected earnings per share* (CEPS)[5] approach avoids altogether the mention of dividends in the model.

The idea behind the CEPS approach is to value the stream of future earnings. However, a portion of the growth in earnings is "illusory," meaning that it is induced simply by the company retaining earnings and then reinvesting them at the required rate of return. A company that does this could just as well pay out all its earnings as dividends to shareholders because the shareholders can achieve the required rate of return on their investments also. In other words, the company does not do anything extra for the investor by investing retained earnings at the required rate; it must invest them at a higher rate. Students of capital budgeting in the field of corporate finance state it another way: a company should invest its funds only in projects that return more than the cost of capital or have a positive net present value. The CEPS approach "strips away" the portion of earnings growth that results from the company investing its retentions at the required rate. Any growth left over represents real earnings growth that is valuable to investors.

Table 14–1 shows how a company could increase its growth rate by retaining more earnings, but the value of the company is the same regardless of this internally

TABLE 14–1
Illustration of how a company can increase its earnings growth rate just by retaining more earnings[a]

	Company Retains Fewer Earnings (payout ratio = .6)	*Company Retains More Earnings (payout ratio = .3)*
Beginning period:		
Equity per share	100.00	100.00
Earnings per share (equity × .12)	12.00	12.00
Dividends (earnings × payout)	7.20	3.60
Retentions (earnings − dividends)	4.80	8.40
Following period:		
New level of equity per share	104.80	108.40
Earnings per share	12.58	13.01
Earnings growth rate from beginning to following period	.048	.084
Stock valuation at beginning period using dividend valuation model (k = .12)	7.20/(.12 − .048) 100.00	3.60/(.12 − .084) 100.00

[a]Assume a return on equity of .12.

generated growth rate, because the company achieves only its required rate on investment.

A company's retentions and its return on these retentions (return on equity) determine the growth rate it can achieve by retaining earnings. Analysts traditionally define this relationship as follows:

$$g_e = \frac{E - D}{E} \times ROE \qquad \textbf{(14–20)}$$

where g_e = the growth rate in earnings per share
ROE = the firm's return on equity

Equation 14–20 states that the firm's growth rate is equal to its earnings retention ratio times its return on equity. In equilibrium, a company's return on equity is equal to its required rate of return, and Equation 14–20 becomes:

$$g_e = \frac{E - D}{E} \times k \qquad \textbf{(14–21)}$$

However, should a company be able to achieve a return on equity greater than its required rate (cost of capital), its growth rate will be greater than Equation 14–21 implies. Let us refer to this return on equity that is greater than the required rate as the *growth in corrected earnings*.

$$g_e = \frac{E - D}{E} \times k + \frac{D}{E} \times g_c \qquad \textbf{(14–22)}$$

where g_c = the growth in CEPS

The first term on the right side of Equation 14–22 represents the earnings growth resulting from the firm's investing its retentions at the required rate of return, and the second part is the component of earnings growth due to the firm's ability to invest at greater than the required rate. Substituting Equation 14–22 into the fundamental dividend valuation model (Equation 14–7) and simplifying yields:

$$P_0 = \frac{E_1}{k - g_c} \qquad \textbf{(14–23)}$$

Equation 14–23 is the fundamental stock valuation model using corrected earnings per share.

In a competitive economy, the average firm can only earn the average, required rate of return. Therefore, earnings growth on average is illusory and induced only by firms retaining earnings and investing at their required rates of return. Although this will be true on an aggregate basis, some firms will excel and earn more than the required rate while others will produce inferior returns (at least for some finite time period). This "growth illusion" creates a problem for the analyst when comparing the investment merits of different companies; if companies retain different portions of their earnings, then their earnings growth differs by varying degrees.

The CEPS approach has the advantage of stripping away this illusory growth and valuing only the growth in CEPS, or real growth. It also has the advantage of not depending upon a company's dividends or dividend policy. Chapter 15 will show how to compute corrected earnings per share from earnings and how to estimate CEPS growth in order to apply the model for investment analysis.

SUMMARY

The fundamental value of a share of common stock is the present value of all of the future cash flows that investors expect to receive from the stock. The principal challenge for stock analysts, therefore, is to project these future cash flows. Projecting the cash flows involves estimating earnings and dividends and their future growth rates.

Cash dividends provide the relevant cash flows for fundamental valuation. Companies will often declare stock dividends or stock splits. Although there may be some association between these distributions of additional stock and value, they basically dilute current ownership and provide no extra value for the common shareholder.

The appropriate discount rate to apply to a stock's dividends in computing fundamental value is the stock's required rate of return. This required rate depends upon other market rates of return (essentially the riskless rate), expected market returns, and the risk of the stock.

The dividend models treat the value of common stock as a function of future expected dividend payments. The simple model assumes a constant future growth rate, while the changing rate model considers interim growth rates that are different from the long-run growth rate.

IMPORTANT TERMS

adjustable rate preferred stock
corrected earnings per share (CEPS)
dividend declaration date
dividend payment date
dividend record date
earnings multiple
ex-dividend date
Gordon growth model
participating preferred stock
price to earnings (P/E) ratio
reverse stock split
stock dividend
stockholder of record
stock split

QUESTIONS AND PROBLEMS

1. Why does the price of a stock drop by an amount about equal to the dividend on the ex-dividend day? If stocks fell by an amount somewhat less than their dividend, what would be the implications for market efficiency?
2. What reasons could a company's management provide to support a stock dividend (or split)? What arguments might be used against a stock dividend (or split)?
3. Mortimer Corp. stock sells for $30 per share, and the board has approved a 25 percent stock dividend. What is the ex-dividend value for the stock?
4. Other factors equal, would you expect a participating preferred stock of a company to be worth more or less than a share of the company's straight preferred? (Assume the two preferreds have the same preferred dividend.) Why?
5. The required rate of return on a company's preferred stock is .12.
   a) What is the value of its $2.00 preferred?
   b) What is the value of its $3.75 preferred?
   c) What is the value of its $5.00 preferred?
6. The Reyes Company pays an annual dividend of $1.30. You forecast a growth rate of 12 percent for the company's dividend over the next three years and a rate of 8 percent after that. Compute your forecasted dividends for the next five years.
7. Describe the Gordon Growth Model for valuing common stock.
8. You have been analyzing several common stocks and want to compute their fundamental values. The riskless rate is .07 and you forecast a market return of .12. Estimate the value of the following stocks:

Beta	*Expected Growth Rate*	*Current Dividend*
a) 1.20	.12	$1.00
b) 1.85	.14	.50
c) 0.80	.08	3.50
d) 0.95	.08	2.00

9. You have estimated the required rate of return for Reyes Company (Problem 6) to be 11 percent. Estimate the value of a share of Reyes's common stock.
10. Use the dividend valuation model to explain the effect on a stock's price of an increase in:
    a) interest rates
    b) the risk of the firm
    c) the company's dividend
11. Hartfield Corp. normally pays out 60 percent of its earnings in dividends. The company's long-run projected growth rate is 9 percent, and the required rate is 12 percent. What is Hartfield's theoretical P/E ratio?
12. A company maintains a policy of paying out 40 percent of its earnings to shareholders as cash dividends. The firm's return on equity is consistently around 16 percent. Based on this information, what would you estimate to be the firm's sustainable growth rate?
13. Explain the corrected earnings per share valuation model.
14. Johnson Corp. typically pays out 35 percent of its earnings as dividends and has had a consistent record of ROE. EPS for the past year was $4. Johnson has equity per share of $20. The required return on Johnson stock is 16 percent. Based on this information, estimate the value of a share of Johnson stock.

NOTES

1. John Burr Williams (1938), *The Theory of Investment Value,* Cambridge: Harvard University Press.
2. Eugene F. Fama, Lawrence Fisher, Michael C. Jensen, and Richard Roll, (1969), "The Adjustment of Stock Prices to New Information," *International Economic Review,* 10 (February), 1–21.
3. Mark S. Grinblatt, Ronald W. Masulis, and Sheridan Titman (1984), "The Valuation Effects of Stock Splits and Stock Dividends," *Journal of Financial Economics,* 13 (December), 461–490.
4. Myron J. Gordon (1962), *The Investment, Financing and Valuation of the Corporation,* Homewood, IL: Irwin.
5. A. J. Merrett and G. D. Newbould (1981), "Cash Equivalent per Share, Share Valution, and the Illusion of Growth," *The Investment Analyst* 61 (July), 4–11; and A. J. Merrett and G. D. Newbould (1982), "CEPS: The Illusion of Corporate Growth," *Journal of Portfolio Management,* 9 (Fall), 5–10.

SELECTED REFERENCES

Choi, Dosoung, and Robert A. Strong, (1983). "The Pricing of When-Issued Common Stock: A Note." *Journal of Finance,* 38 (September), 1293–1298.

Eisemann, Peter C., and Edward A. Moses (1978). "Stock Dividends: Management's View." *Financial Analysts Journal,* 34 (July-August), 77–84.

Elton, Edwin J., Martin J. Gruber, and Mustafa Gultekin (1981). "Expectations and Share Prices." *Management Science,* 27 (September), 975–987.

Estep, Preston W. (1985). "A New Method for Valuing Common Stocks." *Financial Analysts Journal,* 41 (November-December), 26–33.

Fama, Eugene F., Lawrence Fisher, Michael C. Jensen, and Richard Roll (1969). "The Adjustment of Stock Prices to New Information." *International Economic Review,* 10 (February), 1–21.

Farrell, James L., Jr. (1985). "The Dividend Discount Model: A Primer." *Financial Analysts Journal,* 41 (November–December), 16–25.

Fielitz, Bruce D., and Frederick L. Muller (1985). "A Simplified Approach to Common Stock Valuation." *Financial Analysts Journal,* 44 (November–December), 35–41.

French, Dan W., and David A. Dubofsky (1986). "Stock Splits and Implied Stock Price Volatility." *Journal of Portfolio Management,* 12 (Summer), 55–59.

Gordon, Myron J. (1962). *The Investment, Financing and Valuation of the Corporation.* Homewood, IL: Irwin.

Grinblatt, Mark S., Ronald W. Masulis, and Sheridan Titman (1984). "The Valuation Effects of Stock Splits and Stock Dividends." *Journal of Financial Economics,* 13 (December), 461–490.

Hawkins, Eugene H. (1984). "Earnings Expectations and Security Prices." *Financial Analysts Journal,* 40 (September-October), 24–38, 74.

Jones, Charles P., Richard J. Rendleman, Jr., and Henry A. Latane (1984). "Stock Returns and SUEs During the 1970's." *Journal of Portfolio Management,* 10 (Winter), 18–22.

Merrett, A. J., and G. D. Newbould (1981). "Cash Equivalent per Share, Share Valuation, and the Illusion of Growth." *The Investment Analyst,* 61 (July), 4–11.

Merrett, A. J., and Gerald D. Newbould (1982). "CEPS: The Illusion of Corporate Growth." *Journal of Portfolio Management,* 9 (Fall), 5–10.

McDaniel, William R. (1984). "Sinking Fund Preferred Stock." *Financial Management,* 13 (Spring), 45–52.

Praveen, Kumar (1988). "Shareholder-Manager Conflict and the Information Content of Dividends." *The Review of Financial Studies,* 1 (Summer), 111–136.

Rosenfeld, James (1983). "The Effect of Common-Stock Dividend Reductions on the Returns of Nonconvertible Preferred Stocks: A Note." *Journal of Finance,* 38 (June), 1019–1024.

Strong, Robert A. (1983). "Do Share Price and Stock Splits Matter?" *Journal of Portfolio Management,* 10 (Fall), 58–64.

Tobin, James (1984). "A Mean-Variance Approach to Fundamental Valutions." *Journal of Portfolio Management,* 11 (Fall), 26–32.

Vandell, Robert F., and Jerry L. Stevens (1982). "Personal Taxes and Equity Security Pricing." *Financial Management,* 11 (Spring), 31–40.

Wilcox, Jarrod W. (1984). "The P/B-ROE Valuation Model." *Financial Analysts Journal,* 40 (January-February), 58–66.

Williams, John Burr (1938). *The Theory of Investment Value.* Cambridge, MA: Harvard University Press.

CHAPTER 15

Stock Valuation: Techniques of Fundamental Analysis

Chapter 14 introduced and developed some of the fundamental models for security valuation. This chapter continues with the valuation approach to stock selection by showing how to utilize these models and other techniques to estimate the basic worth of common stocks.

The basic tenet of stock selection by fundamental valuation is to buy stocks whose "real" (fundamental) value exceeds their market price and sell them when they no longer meet this condition. The idea is that if a stock is worth more than its market price, the market will realize this sooner or later, and the market price will rise to the true value. Because the market may take time to realize the true value of the stock, an investor who follows this strategy should be prepared to hold stocks for a relatively long period. Buying stocks based on their fundamental value often involves buying and holding for the long term.

Above all, investors should realize that common stock valuation is an art rather than a science. It is not easy, and the "value" figured by an analyst is not exact, but is only the analyst's best estimate of what the real value may be. The valuation estimates of even the best analysts will often vary considerably. If common stock valuation were easy, everyone would be doing it successfully.

The first four major sections of this chapter show various ways to apply the models introduced in Chapter 14 to estimate the fundamental value of stocks. An investor can then compare this fundamental value to the market price of the stock to decide whether to buy or sell the stock. The decision is usually based on whether the fundamental value exceeds the market price by a certain percentage. For example, you might decide to purchase stocks whose fundamental value is 10 percent more than their market price. If your analysis is correct, and if the market recognizes this over the course of a year so that the stocks sell for their real equilibrium value at year's end, then your return will be ten percentage points greater than if you had not used fundamental analysis.

The final section of this chapter summarizes the valuation concepts of Benjamin Graham. Benjamin Graham was a noted security analyst and successful investor who based his investment decisions on fundamental valuation criteria. His techniques are easy for investors to apply because they usually do not require computation of a fundamental security value, but they still depend upon the concepts that fundamental valuation models use.

ESTIMATING INPUTS TO THE MODELS

When using one of the fundamental models for stock valuation, the first step is to estimate the values for the inputs into the model. Whether one is using the dividend, P/E, CEPS model, or one of a number of other models, it is necessary to estimate the required rate of return and the projected growth rate. This section shows several commonly accepted ways to assess these variables.

One point to keep in mind during discussion of all of the models is that the analyst wants to provide the best estimate of the parameters, but this is not an easy task. There will never be one best way to infer values for the inputs, and analysts should avoid believing that estimates resulting from "plugging into" equations are "the answers." They are estimates, and nothing more. By doing complete background work and financial analyses, we can arrive at very good estimates for the input parameters to yield a good estimate of the stock's fundamental value. If we have done a better job than other analysts in the market, then we should be able to act upon the information provided by our estimates to achieve above-average returns.

The examples in this chapter will use financial data of Universal Leaf Tobacco Company to illustrate various techniques. Table 15–1 summarizes this information.

TABLE 15–1
Financial data for Universal Leaf Tobacco Company (stock symbol UVV)

Year	*Earnings per Share*	*Dividends per Share*	*Payout Ratio*	*Return on Equity*	*Stock Price*[a]
1980	1.60	.63	.39	.176	13
1981	1.78	.71	.40	.175	14
1982	1.97	.79	.40	.174	14
1983	2.11	.85	.40	.171	17
1984	2.21	.90	.41	.164	19
1985	2.38	.96	.40	.157	21

Beta coefficient = 0.80

Source: Data from *The Value Line Investment Survey*
[a]Stock price is average of high and low prices.

Estimating the Required Rate of Return

The model for estimating the required rate of return using the Security Market Line (see Chapter 8) requires input estimates for the riskless return and for the expected excess market return. For convenience, let us present the model again as Equation 15–1, as follows:

$$k_j = r_f + \beta_j[E(R_m) - r_f] \qquad \textbf{(15–1)}$$

where k_j = the required rate of return on security *j*
r_f = the riskless rate of return
β_j = the beta (systematic risk) of security *j*
$E(R_m)$ = the expected return on the market portfolio

To estimate the riskless rate, most sources traditionally use the current return on a U.S. Treasury bill. A T-bill with a maturity of about thirty days would probably be typical because it is of such short maturity that it is not subject to any interest rate risk. Because there are other highly liquid, very safe money market instruments, a typical yield such as the yield on a money market fund would also be appropriate as an estimate of the riskless rate.

Estimating expected excess market returns, or *equity risk premiums,* is much more subjective. One method, advocated by Ibbotson and Sinquefield,[1] is the *historical realized equity premium method.* The basic assumption behind this method is that equity risk premiums over time tend to be relatively stable. The future risk premium, therefore, should normally equilibrate toward its historical mean. To find the best estimate of the expected excess market return using this method, the analyst would subtract the mean return on T-bills from the mean return on stocks over a period of time. Using data from 1926 through 1982, Ibbotson and Sinquefield estimated the annual equity market risk premium to be 8.3 percent.

The shortcoming of the historical method is that the assumption that risk premiums are stable ignores current conditions. When making a risk premium forecast, it would be useful to consider conditions relevant to the current market environment in addition to historical returns. The *dividend yield method* proposed by Rozeff[2] helps overcome this deficiency. This method proposes that the market dividend yield multiplied by (1 + the T-bill rate) is the best estimate of the expected excess market return. The evidence tends to show that this measure does a better job of forecasting actual market premiums than does the historical method.

EXAMPLE 15–1

Estimate the required rate of return for Universal Leaf (Table 15–1). During mid-1985, the dividend yield on the Dow Jones Industrials was about 4¾ percent and the yield on money market funds investing in U.S. government securities averaged about 7½ percent.

$$\text{Expected excess market return} = .0475(1 + .075)$$
$$= .051$$
$$k = .075 + .8(.051)$$
$$= .1158$$

Because estimating required rates of return is not an exact science, an analyst should always consider making a subjective adjustment to any computed required rate. In Example 15–1, we calculated a required rate of return for the mid-1985 market environment for Universal Leaf of .1158. In the name of financial conservatism, it is usually better to overestimate a required rate than to underestimate it. Underestimating a required rate will give a higher stock value using the fundamental model and could cause the stock to appear undervalued in the market when it is not. With this in mind, let us subjectively adjust the assessment of the required rate for UVV to an even 12 percent.

Projecting Growth Rates

Projecting growth rates is another difficult and often subjective task of the security analyst. Several tools that an analyst can use are historical growth rates, ratio analysis, and subjective assessments.

Historical Growth Rates

Probably the simplest and most often used method for forecasting growth rates is to compute historical growth rates. If a company and its management are consistent, then the future growth rate should match the past growth rate. Using the regression technique discussed in Chapter 11, the historical growth rate of UVV's earnings per share (EPS) over the six years summarized in Table 15–1 was 8 percent. The annual growth rate in dividends was 8.6 percent. Because the past growth was relatively stable (there were no outlying up years or down years), projection of these growth rates into the future appears reasonable.

Ratios

We know that a company can increase its earnings by retaining and investing more of its funds. This retention of earnings for investment is *internally financed growth*. If we know the amount of funds a company intends to retain and the return that these retentions should yield, then we can forecast this growth rate, which is called the internally financed growth rate.

To do this, an analyst must forecast the return on equity funds that a company can generate. Ratio analysis is useful for this task. If a ratio tends to be stable, a forecast of the ratio's mean value is reasonable. Using the return on equity for UVV in Table 15–1, the forecasted return on equity would be 17 percent.

The following relationship defines the amount of growth that a company can finance internally:

$$g = ROE(1 - D/E) \tag{15–2}$$

where

g = growth rate in earnings
ROE = the firm's projected return on equity
D = dividends
E = earnings

Equation 15–2 says that a company can grow at a rate equal to its return on equity times (1 − the dividend payout ratio). This final term, $(1 - D/E)$, is also called the *earnings retention ratio.* The dividend payout ratio of UVV was stable for the period covered in Table 15–1, so we can forecast its future value equal to its past mean of .40. The retention ratio would therefore be equal to .60. Using Equation 15–2, this would indicate a forecasted growth rate for UVV of 10.2 percent.

To delve further into the growth relationship with ratios, an analyst can break down ROE into its components. A company's return on equity measures its ability to use equity funds to generate net profits. In doing this, the company must go through several steps:

1. Raise capital to purchase assets *(financial leverage)*
2. Use assets to generate sales *(asset efficiency)*
3. Use sales to generate profits *(profit margin)*

There is an appropriate ratio for measuring each of the above areas composing the firm's return on equity. These ratios are as follows:

1. *Financial leverage*—total assets to equity
2. *Asset efficiency*—total asset turnover (sales to assets)
3. *Profit margin*—net income to sales

Return on equity is equal to the product of each of these ratios:

$$ROE = \frac{\text{Total assets}}{\text{Equity}} \times \frac{\text{sales}}{\text{total assets}} \times \frac{\text{net income}}{\text{sales}} \qquad \textbf{(15–3)}$$

Equation 15–3 is also known as the *DuPont method.* The value of this method is that it breaks down ROE into component parts. It is not particularly unique, however, because it reduces to the popular definition of ROE. If we simplify Equation 15–3 by dividing out the total assets and sales, the following remains:

$$ROE = \frac{\text{Net income}}{\text{Equity}} \qquad \textbf{(15–4)}$$

Equation 15–4 is the definition of the return on equity ratio.

The usefulness of Equation 15–3 lies in its ability to identify the areas within ROE responsible for a change in ROE. Table 15–2 shows an example of this process for UVV. Note that UVV's ROE has a slow downward trend over the six years. Although the trend is not decreasing at an alarming rate, and analyst should inquire into its causes. Table 15–2 reveals that the major cause of the slight decline in ROE was less use of financial leverage over the period, evident in the falling assets to equity ratio.

A thorough analysis and forecast of a company's growth potential might include forecasting each of the component ratios of Equation 15–3 to arrive at a forecast of the company's growth rate. Table 15–2 gives regression trend forecasts of each of these ratios, which results in a forecast of ROE of 15.7 percent. This ROE forecast would yield a growth rate forecast of .094 using Equation 15–2.

TABLE 15–2
Breakdown of return on equity of Universal Leaf Tobacco Company (UVV)

Year	*Total Assets / Equity*	*Sales / Total Assets*	*Net Income / Sales*	*Return on Equity*
1980	2.513	2.468	.029	.176
1981	2.268	2.562	.030	.175
1982	2.127	2.990	.027	.174
1983	1.879	2.678	.034	.171
1984	1.970	2.220	.038	.164
1985	1.602	2.581	.038	.157
Trend forecast	1.542	2.491	.041	.157

Subjective Assessments

As with estimates of the required rate, an analyst should review numerically based forecasts of the growth rate for possible revisions. Sometimes forecasts using computational methods will seem unreasonable, and the analyst will want to make some type of subjective adjustment to the forecast to account for this.

For example, let us reexamine the different numerical forecasts of Universal Leaf's growth rate. The historical growth rate in EPS was .08, and the internal growth through retentions, using the trends of the component ratios, was .092. We might argue that the historical rate of .08 is a low forecast, pointing to the higher historical growth in dividends and the consistently high ROE. We would conclude that a growth rate projection higher than .08 is appropriate.

The ratio-based growth rate prediction of .092 might be more reasonable. However, appealing again to the principle of conservatism in our estimates, analysts should take care not to overestimate the growth rate. In the case of growth, it is probably better to underestimate slightly than to give a projection that is too optimistic. Trying to balance the high and low numbers, without any prior idea as to which is the more probable, let us apply the *criterion of rationality* and assume that each is equally likely. We therefore subjectively select a forecast that is equal to the average of the two, yielding a forecasted growth rate of .086. By chance, this happens also to be equal to the historical growth rate in dividends.

USING THE DIVIDEND MODEL

To use the dividend valuation model (Equation 14–7 for a constant growth rate or Equation 14–12 for a nonconstant rate), the analyst substitutes the estimates of the required rate and the growth rate into the model, along with the *normalized dividend,* to provide an estimate of the fundamental stock value.

The normalized dividend is the dividend level ignoring any extra cash dividends or temporary dividend cuts or omissions. Examining UVV's pattern of dividend payment, the last dividend payment appears to be in line with the others and quite "normal." There is therefore no need to normalize UVV's dividend. However, if UVV had declared an extra dividend of $1 per share during 1985, we would not want to include this fact in the fundamental model, and we would normalize dividends by omitting the extra payment.

EXAMPLE 15–2

Use the forecasts of the required rate and growth developed in this chapter to estimate a fundamental value for Universal Leaf.

$$k = .12$$

$$g = .086$$

$$D_0 = .96$$

$$P_0 = \frac{.96(1 + .086)}{.12 - .086}$$

$$= 30.66$$

Example 15–2 shows that the forecasts of g and k yield a stock value of $30.66. For those who are curious about the market price of UVV, it was about $24 per share during midsummer 1985. The fundamental value investor might have considered this stock a good buy at that time.

USING THE EARNINGS MULTIPLE APPROACH

With the earnings multiple approach, we want to forecast next period's "normalized" earnings per share and multiply it by the estimated earnings multiple (P/E ratio) to give the fundamental stock value. For the forecast of earnings that we will use in this section, the trend method using regression yielded a next-period EPS estimate of 2.61.

Historical P/E Ratios

The simplest method for estimating a stock's intrinsic multiple is to use the average method and find the mean P/E for the last few years. The assumption underlying this method is that the stock has a real earnings multiple that is relatively stable over time. When the stock sells for more or less than this long-run fundamental ratio, the stock's price will equilibrate toward a value that gives this long-run P/E.

The principal advantage of this method of estimating a stock's true earnings multiple is its simplicity and ease of use. Because of this, many investors use this technique as one of the fundamental tools in their stock analysis. The stock selection method that the National Association of Investment Clubs recommends to its members applies these principles. The association publishes a set of worksheets that outlines the projection of EPS using trend and the estimation of the multiple based on the historical average.

To use this method with the data for Universal Leaf, Table 15–3 shows the computation of the mean P/E ratio for the six-year period. As the exhibit shows, UVV's P/E was relatively stable over the time period. The mean P/E of 8.1 is probably a reasonable estimate of the company's true value. Multiplying this estimated P/E times the EPS forecast of 2.61 yields a fundamental stock price of 21.14. This estimate is much lower than the dividend model forecast of 30.66.

The disadvantage of using historical P/E ratios to estimate the fundamental multiple is that this technique ignores both current economic conditions that may have affected investors' required rates of return and real changes that may have affected the company's long-run growth prospects. Both of these factors have a strong influence on earnings multiples, and ignoring them may lead to misestimation of a stock's fundamental multiple. The next two techniques attempt to avoid this disadvantage by accounting for current factors.

The Fundamental Model

Chapter 14 introduced the fundamental earnings multiple model as Equation 14–17, restated here for convenience as

$$P/E = \frac{D/E}{k - g} \qquad \textbf{(15–5)}$$

Although we could use our forecasts of next period's earnings and dividends for the numerator, another good technique is to substitute the company's long-run target payout ratio. This method is handy because the payout ratio typically tends to be more stable than individual values for the components of the ratio (dividends and EPS). Example 15–3 shows the use of this technique to determine UVV's fundamental value.

The estimate for UVV's value of 30.80 using the fundamental P/E model is very close to the dividend model's value because of the use of some common forecasts for the model's inputs.

TABLE 15–3
Computation of mean P/E ratio for Universal Leaf Tobacco Company (UVV)

Year	*Earnings per Share*	*Stock Price*[a]	*P/E Ratio (earnings multiple)*
1980	1.60	13	8.1
1981	1.78	14	7.9
1982	1.97	14	7.1
1983	2.11	17	8.1
1984	2.21	19	8.6
1985	2.38	21	8.8
Mean			8.1

[a]Stock price is average of high and low prices.

EXAMPLE 15–3

Using the estimates developed in this chapter for *k, g,* and *D/E,* estimate UVV's multiple and stock price.

$$P/E = .40/(.12 - .086)$$
$$= 11.8$$
$$P = 11.8(2.61)$$
$$= 30.80$$

An Econometric Approach

Econometric methods are also useful for estimating a security's fundamental earnings multiple. To construct an econometric model for earnings multiples, an analyst identifies the main determinants of multiples and then uses multiple regression to estimate the coefficients of these determinants.

The most obvious determinants of the P/E ratio are those identified in the fundamental model: the payout ratio, the required rate of return, and growth. In their classic study using an econometric model for the theoretical P/E ratio, Whitbeck and Kisor[3] set up a regression for the P/E ratio as a function of three variables:

1. The past earnings growth rate
2. The historical payout ratio
3. The standard deviation of the past earnings about the growth trend line (a measure of the stock's risk)

They collected values of these three variables and for the actual P/E ratio of 135 different NYSE stocks. Using the P/E ratio as the dependent variable and the others as independent variables, they ran a regression procedure to estimate coefficients for the variables. The regression yielded the following relationship:

$$P/E = 8.2 + 1.5(\text{growth rate}) + 6.7(\text{payout ratio}) - 0.2(\text{standard deviation})$$

Using this relationship, they then computed fundamental P/E ratios and stock values for each stock in their sample. The results of the study showed that the performance of the undervalued stocks was superior to that of the overvalued stocks.

Because the economic situation changes, an analyst wanting to apply the econometric method to a current investment environment would need to recompute the regression coefficients using current data or construct an entirely new P/E model. As an example, Table 15–4 presents an econometric model for the mid-1985 situation using a very small sample of eight stocks. The independent variables for this model are each stock's trend growth rate over the previous six years, the mean six-year payout ratio, and the standard deviation of the growth rate. The exhibit shows the coefficients that the regression produced. (Because this sample size was so small, no particular significance should be attached to the negative sign for the payout ratio

TABLE 15–4
Example econometric model for the earnings multiple

Stock	*P/E Ratio*	*Earnings Growth*	*Payout Ratio*	*Standard Deviation of Earnings Growth*
Automatic Data Processing	22	.138	.26	.045
Chemical New York	6	.096	.39	.080
Delmarva Power	10	.091	.82	.088
Harcourt Brace	15	.039	.34	.131
Holiday Corp.	14	.106	.26	.131
Johnson and Johnson	14	.082	.36	.071
Maytag	11	.091	.72	.126
Tokheim	10	.066	.27	.112

Regression results:

$P/E = 13.5 + 49.1(\text{growth}) - 8.4(\text{payout ratio}) - 15.9(\text{standard deviation})$

$R^2 = .30$

coefficient.) Example 15–4 shows the use of this model to estimate the value of UVV. The estimated value is $31.89, which agrees with and reinforces the estimates of the other models. However, no investor should rely on an econometric estimate using such a small sample to estimate the model. To apply this technique with a higher degree of reliability, we would probably want to have a sample size of at least several hundred stocks.

EXAMPLE 15–4

Using the regression model for the fundamental P/E ratio estimated with the data in Table 15–4, compute the value for Universal Leaf. (The standard deviation of UVV's growth was .041.)

Because the model used past EPS growth rates, we use UVV's EPS trend of .08.

$$P/E = 13.5 + 49.1(.08) - 8.4(.4) - 15.9(.041)$$
$$= 13.4$$

In addition, the regression used the stock's observed P/E ratios, which are based on the past year's EPS. We therefore use UVV's past year's EPS of 2.38, not the forecasted value.

$$P = 13.4(2.38)$$
$$= 31.89$$

USING THE CEPS MODEL

Chapter 14 introduced the corrected earnings per share (CEPS) model, which values only the portion of growth that is "real." That is, it ignores the growth caused by the company retaining earnings and investing them at the cost of capital (required rate of return). To apply the model, we need a method that removes the part of EPS growth induced by investing retentions at the required rate. Removing this portion of the firm's growth leaves the corrected earnings per share (CEPS). To identify this portion of growth, assume that the firm paid out all of its earnings as dividends and raised the money needed for growth by issuing new common stock at the market price. Any growth that this firm shows would be real growth because there are no retentions.

It is possible to compute what earnings would have been if a company had followed such a policy (although the analyst realizes that the company does not). Assume that the company's retentions are equal to the amount of equity capital that it needs for growth. If this is the case, then for each share currently outstanding it would need to sell an amount of additional shares equal to:

$$\text{Additional shares} = \frac{E - D}{P} \qquad \textbf{(15–6)}$$

Example 15–5 illustrates the use of Equation 15–6 for issuing new stock to provide needed equity capital.

EXAMPLE 15–5

Kratmeninger Company has 100,000 shares outstanding. Last year it had earnings per share of \$3 and paid dividends of \$1 per share. If the company's stock is \$40 per share, how much stock would the company need to sell if all of the earnings had been paid as dividends?

Using Equation 15–6:

$$\begin{aligned} \text{Additional shares} &= (3 - 1)/40 \\ &= .05 \\ \text{Total shares} &= .05(100{,}000 \text{ existing shares}) \\ &= 5{,}000 \text{ shares} \end{aligned}$$

Another way to approach this problem is as follows. The company retained a total of \$200,000 (2 × 100,000). At \$40 per share, it would have to sell 200,000/40 = 5,000 shares to raise the \$200,000 retentions.

Kratmeninger Company (Example 15–5) will see its retentions next year to finance its growth. Subtracting out the growth in EPS resulting from investing these funds at the required rate of return will leave the CEPS. The most direct way to treat reinvestment of funds at the required rate is to assume that the company purchases shares of its common stock at market price. Example 15–6 shows how this might happen.

Note that in Example 15–6, Kratmeninger managed to have a CEPS of 3.325 compared to 3.00 in the base year, a nice growth. This must mean that the company has invested the funds at a rate somewhat higher than the required rate. Example 15–7 computes the company's return on retentions (return on marginal equity) to compare with the required rate.

EXAMPLE 15–6

Suppose Kratmeninger Company (See Example 15–5) has EPS the following year of \$3.50. What is its CEPS?

With 100,000 shares outstanding, the total income of the company is \$350,000. If the retentions had been invested at the required rate by purchasing common stock, then the company would be left with a total of 95,000 shares. Total income would be \$350,000 less the earnings on the 5000 shares repurchased:

$$\begin{aligned}\text{Total income} &= 350{,}000 - (5000 \times 3.50)\\ &= 332{,}500\end{aligned}$$

But the company did not do this; it retained the earnings, invested them, and still has 100,000 shares outstanding. What would the EPS be with 100,000 shares outstanding and earnings of \$332,500?

$$\begin{aligned}EPS &= 332{,}500/100{,}000\\ &= 3.325\end{aligned}$$

This is the CEPS. It is the company's EPS taking out the return on retentions invested at the required rate of return.

In Example 15–7, Kratmeninger's return on its additional retained earnings was .25. This return is significantly greater than the required rate of .196. Therefore, Kratmeninger's management is successful at managing and investing the company's funds at a rate higher than the required rate. However, the dividend models and the P/E models do not show this.

EXAMPLE 15–7

Compute the return that Kratmeninger Company achieved on its retentions and compare it with the company's required rate.

The company retained a total of \$200,000 and was able to increase its total net income by \$50,000. Its return on the retentions is:

$$\begin{aligned}&= 50{,}000/200{,}000\\ &= .25\end{aligned}$$

To find the company's required rate, we can use the fundamental dividend model. At a market price of \$40, a growth rate of .167 (computed 3.50/3.00 − 1), and a beginning dividend of \$1, solve the model for k:

$$\begin{aligned}40 &= 1(1 + .167)/(k - .167)\\ k &= .196\end{aligned}$$

An earnings correction factor (ECF) simplifies this entire process into one computation:

$$ECF_t = 1 - \frac{D_t - E_t}{P_t} \qquad \textbf{(15–7)}$$

where ECF_t = the earnings correction factor at time t

The correction factor to apply to earnings to get the CEPS is cumulative—each successive year builds upon the previous year's effect—so to get the factors to apply in later years, we need this cumulative correction factor (CCF):

$$CCF_t = ECF_t \times CCF_{t-1} \qquad \text{(where } CCF_0 = 1.0\text{)} \qquad \textbf{(15–8)}$$

where CCF_t = the cumulative correction factor at time t

Multiplying the current year's EPS by the prior year's CCF yields the current CEPS. An analyst then examines the pattern of CEPS to try to identify any growth and its trend. Note that the base period ($t = 0$) CCF is equal to 1.0.

As Chapter 14 showed, the valuation model for CEPS is:

$$P_0 = \frac{E_1}{k - g_c} \qquad \textbf{(15–9)}$$

where E_1 = EPS in time period 1
k = the required rate of return
g_c = the projected growth rate in CEPS

Although the inputs to the CEPS and dividend models are different, the two models are entirely consistent with each other. The advantage of the CEPS approach over the dividend approach is that the CEPS model requires neither a regular dividend nor any dividend at all to be paid on the common stock. The dividend model becomes very difficult to apply when a stock's pattern of dividends is irregular, and the model seems practically useless when valuing a nondividend-paying stock.

Table 15–5 gives a detailed breakdown of the procedure for computing CEPS from EPS. The table presents a hypothetical stock with an expected dividend of $1.20, earnings per share of $2.00, and a growth rate of .08. The company maintains a policy of paying out 60 percent of its earnings, and the required rate of return on the stock is .15. Given this information, the dividend valuation model yields a current stock value of $17.14. The table shows the pattern of CEPS resulting from the company's growth rate and dividend payout policy. As shown, the company's CEPS grows at a rate of .033 due to the ability of the company to achieve relatively high returns on retained equity capital. With this growth rate, Table 15–5 shows that the value returned by the CEPS model is equal to the value given by the dividend valuation model.

Returning to the Universal Leaf example, Table 15–6 presents the computation of UVV's CEPS. Visual inspection of UVV's CEPS over the six-year period reveals almost no growth. The 1980 CEPS was 1.60, and the 1985 CEPS was 1.61. Although the CEPS did increase slightly over the first three years, declines in the following three years almost canceled out this growth.

This pattern of slight increases and decreases in CEPS is not unusual. On average, companies in an economy can earn only their required rate. Over the short run, some will earn more and others less, but on average the typical company will earn its required rate. Therefore, the typical growth rate in CEPS will be zero.

TABLE 15–5
CEPS and dividend model valuation for hypothetical company[a]

Year	*EPS*	*Dividend*	*Stock Price Using Dividend Model*	*ECF*	*CCF*	*CEPS*	*Growth Rate of CEPS*	*Stock Price Using CEPS Model*
1	2.00	1.20	18.51	.957	.957	2.00		18.51
2	2.16	1.30	20.00	.957	.915	2.07	.033	20.00
3	2.33	1.40	21.60	.957	.876	2.14	.033	21.60
4	2.52	1.51	23.32	.957	.838	2.21	.033	23.32
5	2.72	1.63	25.19	.957	.802	2.28	.033	25.19
6	2.94	1.76	27.20	.957	.767	2.36	.033	27.20

Present value of stock:

Using dividend model: $P = 1.20/(.15 - .08)$
$= 17.14$

Using CEPS model: $P = 2.00/(.15 - .033)$
$= 17.14$

[a]Basic assumptions:
$D_0 = 1.11$
$E_0 = 1.85$
$k = .15$
$g = .08$
Company maintains .60 payout ratio.
(Some of the values in this table may appear to be slightly off because of rounding.)

Example 15–8 shows the application of the CEPS data in Table 15–6 to estimate UVV's fundamental value. The estimated value of $21.75 is close to the result given by the historical P/E method and somewhat lower than those of the fundamental dividend and P/E models. Since we have just stated that the fundamental dividend model and the CEPS are equivalent, why do they yield such different values for UVV? The answer lies in the definition of CEPS growth, the growth in EPS resulting from the firm's ability to invest funds at greater than the cost of capital. The market price of UVV's stock over the six-year time period apparently reflected a cost of capital that

TABLE 15–6
Calculation of CEPS for Universal Leaf Tobacco Company (UVV)

Year	*EPS*	*Dividend*	*Stock Price*	*ECF*	*CCF*	*CEPS*
1980	1.60	.63	13	.925	.925	1.60
1981	1.78	.71	14	.924	.855	1.65
1982	1.97	.79	14	.916	.783	1.69
1983	2.11	.85	17	.926	.725	1.65
1984	2.21	.90	19	.931	.675	1.60
1985	2.38	.96	21	.932	.629	1.61

was greater than the required rate of return, although in equilibrium the two should be equal. Because UVV could not invest its retained earnings at a return greater than this cost of capital, its CEPS showed no growth. Proponents of the CEPS approach to valuation would claim that followers of the dividend model would be "fooled" by UVV's growth generated by investing at only its cost of capital. They would say that the real value of UVV should be lower than the dividend model because there is no evidence that the market has valued this growth in the past.

EXAMPLE 15–8

Using the information in Table 15–6, apply the CEPS valuation model to Universal Leaf.

Because the CEPS shows almost no growth over the time period in Table 15–6, a forecast of no CEPS growth for UVV is probably our best estimate. Using the previously estimated required rate of .12 and EPS of $2.61, the CEPS model gives:

$$P = 2.61/(.12 - 0)$$
$$= 21.75$$

THE BENJAMIN GRAHAM CRITERIA

Benjamin Graham has been called the "father of security analysis." He published the first edition of his classic book, *Security Analysis,* coauthored with David Dodd, in 1934. The book became the standard reference on security valuation and stock analysis. In 1949, he wrote *The Intelligent Investor,* a book aimed at the typical investor and less technical than *Security Analysis.*

Graham's approach to security analysis was basically conservative. He felt that any investment that did not promise safety of principal and a satisfactory return was speculative. Over his career, Graham suggested many different investment and stock selection strategies. In 1974, Graham identified ten important criteria that he felt an investor should consider when analyzing a stock. He recognized that only a few stocks might meet all of the criteria at any one time and believed that the greater the number of these points that a stock satisfied, the better. Graham's ten criteria that a good stock should meet include the following:

1. An earnings-to-price ratio less than twice the average yield on AAA-rated bonds
2. A P/E ratio less than four tenths the stock average P/E ratio over the last five years
3. A dividend yield of at least two thirds the AAA-rated bond yield
4. A stock price less than two thirds the tangible book value per share
5. A stock price less than two thirds the stock's *net current asset value* per share (Graham defined net current asset value as current assets less total debt less the value of preferred stock.)
6. Total debt less than tangible book value

7. A current ratio of two or more
8. Total debt less than or equal to net current asset value
9. Compound earnings growth rate of at least 7 percent over the last ten years
10. Stability of earnings growth (Graham defined earnings stability as no more than two earnings declines of 5 percent or more during the last ten years.)

Graham and his partner at the time, James Rea, felt that stocks meeting these ten criteria maximized their reward-to-risk potential. The first five points indicate a stock's potential reward by specifying a low stock price relative to (1) earnings, (2) previous P/E ratios, (3) dividends, (4) book value, and (5) net current asset value. The final five criteria measure risk (or lack of risk). Items five through eight measure financial strength, while items nine and ten indicate a history of stable, growing earnings.

Stocks chosen using even a few of these criteria perform well. For example, Graham found that stocks that met criteria one and six appreciated by 19 percent during the mid-1970's while the Dow Jones Industrials increased by 3.5 percent.

Probably the one criterion Graham believed to be the most useful was his noted "net current asset value" measure, item five. Graham claimed that he used that criterion for many years to outperform the market. Research by Oppenheimer and Schlarbaum[4] shows that investors using this criterion during the 1970s would have done well when compared to the market average, even on a risk-adjusted basis. For example, stocks meeting criterion five returned an average of 2.85 percent per month while the risk-adjusted monthly return on a combined NYSE-AMEX index was only .9 percent.

SUMMARY

Using the fundamental valuation models in the actual practice of stock analysis and selection requires estimation of the parameters of the model. Although analysts can utilize several quantitative tools to assist in this task, estimation of the forecasted parameter values is often difficult and subjective. The method presented in this chapter for estimating the required rate of return on a security is based on the Capital Asset Pricing Model. This method requires estimation of the expected excess market return and the riskless interest rate. Analysts often use the market rate of return on T-bills to represent the riskless rate. The historical realized equity premium method and the dividend yield method are popular techniques for forecasting the excess market return (equity risk premium).

Among the approaches to forecasting growth rates are extrapolation of historical growth, financial ratio methods, and subjective assessments. Estimates of a stock's intrinsic earnings multiple can be based on historical averages, the fundamental P/E model, or econometric methods. Analysts use forecasts and estimates from these procedures to apply the fundamental dividend model or the earnings multiple model to estimate the fundamental worth of a stock.

Investors can also use the Corrected Earnings Per Share (CEPS) approach to stock valuation by adjusting earnings per share to find the CEPS. The resulting growth in

CEPS is then used with estimates of earnings and the required rate to estimate stock value.

One of the pioneers of fundamental stock valuation, Benjamin Graham, based his methods on the financial strength and intrinsic worth of a stock. He summarized his principles into ten criteria that a good stock should meet. Results of inquires into the success of Graham's techniques indicate that stocks selected using Graham's criteria have outperformed the market in the past.

IMPORTANT TERMS

criterion of rationality
dividend yield method
DuPont method
earnings retention ratio
equity risk premium
historical realized equity premium method
internally financed growth
net current asset value
normalized dividends

QUESTIONS AND PROBLEMS

1. The dividend yield on a market index is 4.5 percent, and the average yield on money market funds is 6.5 percent. Using the dividend yield method, compute the market equity risk premium. Estimate the required rate of return for the following stocks:
   a) beta = 1.48
   b) beta = 0.84
   c) beta = 1.08
2. Estimate the EPS growth rate of a company whose target dividend payout ratio is 40 percent and whose ROE averages 15 percent. If this company increases its dividend payout ratio to 60 percent, will its stock price change? Prove your answer using the dividend valuation model.
3. The Cuenca Corp. has the following financial data per share:

Year	*Equity*	*Total Assets*	*Sales*	*Net Income*
1	20	40	50	4.00
2	24	48	58	4.50
3	28	52	65	5.00

   Compute the ROE for each year. Does the trend appear to be favorable or unfavorable? Using the DuPont method, identify the strong points or areas of concern for the company.
4. The Rio Corp. has the following financial data per share:

Year	*Equity*	*Total Assets*	*Sales*	*Net Income*
1	50	75	75	5.00
2	53	80	80	5.38
3	57	88	88	5.78

   Compute the ROE for each year. Does the trend appear to be favorable or unfavorable? Using the DuPont method, identify the strong points or areas of concern for the company.

5. Using the company described in Problem 2, estimate the value of a share of the company's stock, assuming that the required rate is .15 and the company earned $3 per share over the past year.
6. You are analyzing the common stock of Turbo MicroComputer Corp. and estimate that the company should grow at an annual rate of 10 percent. Furthermore, you estimate that the beta of the stock is 1.6. The company's projected dividend for the coming year is $1.50. You observe a T-bill rate of 7 percent and estimate the market equity premium to be 5 percent.
   a) Estimate the value of a share of the company's stock.
   b) Estimate values for the stock if you overestimated the growth rate by one percentage point and if you underestimated it by one percentage point.
   c) Estimate the values for the stock if you overestimated the market equity premium by one percentage point and if you underestimated it by one percentage point.
7. F. Martin Inc. had the following earnings multiples for the last five years: 12, 14, 16, 15, 16. You project EPS for the company to be $3.50 two years from now. Based upon this information only, project the company's stock price in two years. Do you think this valuation is very good? Why?
8. Linea Company had the following financial data per share:

Year	*EPS*	*Dividend*	*Stock Price*
1	1.22	.47	8.00
2	1.41	.53	10.00
3	1.43	.57	11.00
4	1.50	.61	16.00
5	1.69	.67	16.00
6	1.91	.72	22.00
7	2.12	.82	30.00

   a) Compute the corrected earnings per share for each year.
   b) Based on the computed series of CEPS, estimate a growth rate for CEPS.
   c) If this company's required rate of return is 14 percent, estimate the value for the stock using the CEPS approach.
   d) Based on past dividend growth, use the dividend discount model to estimate the stock value. Compare this answer to the CEPS valuation.

NOTES

1. Roger G. Ibbotson and Rex A. Sinquefield (1982), *Stocks, Bonds, Bills and Inflation: The Past and the Future,* Charlottesville, VA: Financial Analysts Research Foundation.
2. Michael S. Rozeff, (1984), "Dividend Yields are Equity Risk Premiums," *Journal of Portfolio Management,* 10 (Fall), 68–75.
3. Volkert S. Whitbeck and Manown Kisor, Jr. (1963), "A New Tool in Investment Decision-Making," *Financial Analysts Journal,* 19 (May-June), 55-62.
4. Henry R. Oppenheimer and Gary G. Schlarbaum (1985), "'Father' Knows Best: Benjamin Graham's Net Current Asset Values," *AAII Journal,* 7 (March), 11–17.

SELECTED REFERENCES

Asquith, Paul, and David W. Mullins, Jr. (1986). "Signalling with Dividends, Stock Repurchases, and Equity Issues." *Financial Management,* 15 (Autumn), 27–44.

Bhandari, Laxmi Chand (1988). "Debt/Equity Ratio and Expected Common Stock Returns: Empirical Evidence." *The Journal of Finance,* 43 (June), 507–528.

Casabona, Patrick A., Frank J. Fabozzi and Jack C. Francis (1984). "How to Apply Duration to Equity Analysis." *Journal of Portfolio Analysis,* 10 (Winter), 52–58.

Graham, Benjamin (1973). *The Intelligent Investor: A Book of Practical Counsel.* 4th ed. New York: Harper and Row.

———, David L. Dodd, and Sidney Cottle (1962). *Security Analysis: Principles and Technique.* 4th ed. New York: McGraw-Hill.

Ibbotson, Roger G., and Rex A. Sinquefield (1982). *Stocks, Bonds, Bills and Inflation: The Past and Future.* Charlottesville, VA: Financial Analysts Research Foundation.

Kim, Sang-Hoon (1986). "The Effect of Refunding Decisions on the Relationship between Interest Rates and Stock Prices: An Empirical Test." *Journal of Business Finance and Accounting,* 13 (Autumn), 405–424.

Lobo, Gerald J., R. D. Nair, and In Man Song (1986). "Additional Evidence on the Information Content of Dividends." *Journal of Business Finance and Accounting*, 13 (Winter), 597–608.

Merrett, A. J., and Gerald D. Newbould (1983). "Integrating Financial Performance and Stock Valuation." *Journal of Portfolio Management,* 9 (Fall), 27–32.

Oppenheimer, Henry R., and Gary G. Schlarbaum (1985). "'Father' Knows Best: Benjamin Graham's Net Current Asset Values." *AAII Journal,* 7 (March), 11–17.

Penman, Stephen H. (1983). "The Predictive Content of Earnings Forecasts and Dividends." *Journal of Finance,* 38 (September), 1181–1199.

Rozeff, Michael S. (1982). "Growth, Beta, and Agency Costs as Determinants of Dividend Payout Ratios." *Journal of Financial Research,* 5 (Fall), 249–259.

Rozeff, Michael S. (1984). "Dividend Yields Are Equity Risk Premiums." *Journal of Portfolio Management,* 10 (Fall), 68–75.

Whitbeck, Volkert S., and Manown Kisor, Jr. (1963). "A New Tool in Investment Decision-Making." *Financial Analysts Journal,* 19 (May–June), 55–62.

CHAPTER 16

Stock Trading Strategies: Fundamental and Technical

The goal of fundamental security analysis is security selection—choosing the best among a set of alternative investments. Many investors view the *investment timing decision* as an important part of the selection process. While the primary question posed during security selection is *what* to buy, the investment timing decision deals with *when* the investor should buy the selected security.

Because the market fluctuates daily, the timing decision can have a strong impact on the net return on a portfolio. Suppose that an investor has decided that a certain group of four stocks is fundamentally undervalued and wants to purchase these stocks. Should the investor immediately place a market buy order with the broker, place limit orders, or wait a few days to see if the market goes down, allowing the purchase of the stocks at a lower price? If the investor waits a few days and has made a correct timing decision, he may be able to buy the stocks at prices averaging several percentage points below their original price. In this case, the first year's return on these stocks will be increased by several points. On the other hand, should the investor's timing decision be wrong, so that he buys the stocks after an upward move, the first year's return will be somewhat lower.

Many security analysts are strict fundamentalists—they believe in effecting the purchase of a stock immediately upon the recommendation of its purchase. This view is also consistent with an efficient markets strategy. If stock prices are a random walk, then trying to catch short-term peaks or troughs is at best a fruitless endeavor. Many investors, however, prefer to try to find the optimal time to buy a security in addition to finding which security. A variety of stock-trading strategies exist to assist in the timing decision. In fact, trading and timing strategies range from helping with the timing of stocks already selected for purchase (or sale) all the way to using timing as the primary tool for investment profits. Followers of the latter strategy treat the selection decision as having little importance and the timing decision with care or even use their trading strategy methods to select stocks that appear to be ready for a rise in price.

This chapter presents some of the more popular tools used by adherents to trading strategies. First, we classify equity trading strategies into three categories. After defining each classification, several widely used techniques for implementing trading strategy are discussed. Finally, the chapter presents evidence, if it exists, of the success or failure of the use of each strategy.

TYPES OF EQUITY TRADING STRATEGIES

There are three major categories of stock trading strategies:

1. Strategies based on fundamental theory
2. Market indicators
3. Charting techniques

The first classification, strategies based on fundamental theory, *(fundamental strategies)* has as its basis the ideas underlying all of fundamental analysis. These strategies advocate the purchase of stocks at prices less than their fundamental value. While fundamental analysis is the examination and interpretation of companies' financial condition and the valuation of future earnings prospects, fundamental strategies are the means of implementing the results of fundamental analysis.

Market indicators are measures of market or economic activity. Proponents of the use of market indicators identify indicators that they believe tend to precede the market or indicate the future direction of market movements. The chief use of market indicators is to time the market rather than individual stocks. However, because of the systematic tendency of stock prices to move together in the same direction, successful market indicators would also be useful tools for timing individual stock transactions.

The third main category of stock timing strategies is *charting*. Charting is the graphic analysis of patterns or trends of stock prices and trading volume in an attempt to forecast future price movement.

Many of the methods used in strategies within these three major classifications are techniques that market practitioners call *technical analysis*. Broadly defined, technical analysis comprises the use of stock market trading data, stock prices, and stock trading volume to discern patterns or trends that allow projection of future stock prices. Within this definition, charting certainly qualifies as a form of technical analysis. In addition, many of the market indicators fall into the area of technical analysis. Although some experts classify the use of all market indicators as technical, many that are based on sound economic reasoning as driving forces for the market are not strictly technical. However, because most analysts using market indicators develop some mechanical trading rule for the time to buy or sell based on the indicator, indicators are commonly included in the area of technical analysis. Most of the strategies based on fundamental theory are not technical, although some investors might be tempted to classify some of the more mechanical techniques as technical analysis.

STRATEGIES BASED ON FUNDAMENTAL THEORY

Some of the fundamental strategies are short-term timing tools, but most deal with the long run. Adherents to the various strategies believe that although short-run market fluctuations may result in losses over short time periods, patient investors who follow the principles of fundamental strategies will profit over the long run. Many of these investors use detailed fundamental analysis to select stocks, followed by one or more of the fundamental trading strategies to help time their transactions. Others use the fundamental strategies to help them in *screening stocks* for further fundamental analysis. The process of stock screening involves setting certain criteria that the analyst believes profitable stocks should have and then screening, or identifying, stocks that have those desirable characteristics. This process eliminates stocks that do not qualify under the strategy based on fundamental theory and allows the analyst to concentrate detailed analysis on only the most promising stocks. For example, analysts who know they are building a portfolio to provide high current income can screen stocks with a dividend yield greater than the portfolio's minimum yield requirement.

Strategies Based on P/E Ratios

The Gordon dividend discount model and its accompanying P/E model form the basic fundamental valuation framework for equity securities. The elementary decision rule for recommending a stock based on fundamental valuation is to purchase a stock whose fundamental value is greater than its current market price. In terms of the P/E model, we would want to buy stocks whose fundamental P/E is greater than their observed P/E. These stocks would be characterized on average by relatively low P/E ratios. If this is the case, then a simple guideline of purchasing stocks with low multiples might be a rewarding investment strategy.

Several empirical analyses have examined investment strategies of buying low P/E stocks.[1] In general, they tend to show that purchasing portfolios of low P/E stocks would provide an investor with above-average returns over an investment horizon of several years.

It is important to note that there are several methods of measuring "above average" returns and evaluating investment performance. (Chapter 22 presents several of these techniques.) The methods used in most of the P/E studies have been based on the relationship between return and risk (as measured by beta or standard deviation of returns). One study, however, based on another methodology called *stochastic dominance,* finds results indicating that the investment performance of low P/E portfolios is no better than that of average P/E or high P/E portfolios.[2] Nevertheless, buying low P/E stocks has become a popular investment criterion for many professional portfolio managers and individual investors. For example, one endowment fund uses the guideline that a stock's P/E ratio be less than its five-year average and less than 90 percent of the P/E of the S&P 500 Index.

Buying Stocks That Are Splitting or Are Likely to Split

Some investors prefer a strategy of buying stocks about to have a stock split or stocks likely to announce a split in the near future. These investors usually have a similar liking for companies that declare stock dividends. Managements of companies declaring stock splits and stock dividends believe that investors react favorably to split announcements.[3] Table 16–1 lists explanations that companies give as reasons for effecting stock splits. Although the explanations vary, it is easy to see that the implied goal of all is to increase liquidity and maximize stock value. If splits accomplish this goal, then an investor concentrating stock purchases on splitting stocks should fare well.

Does a strategy of purchasing splitting stocks provide excess returns to investors? Most studies indicate that it is doubtful. For example, Woolridge[4] examined daily returns around 317 stock dividend announcements. Figure 16–1 shows the returns around the announcement day. As the graph indicates, there was a big positive jump in average returns around the day of the stock dividend announcement (day zero), but most of the positive returns actually occurred before the announcement. To take advantage of the split (stock dividend), an investor would need to correctly anticipate a future event.

Another study, by Strong,[5] looked at short-term returns around stock splits. Strong found that stock prices generally jumped slightly on both the announcement day and the effective date of the split after adjusting the stock price for the split. However, there is evidence that stocks' risk as measured by the variance of returns also increases upon a split.[6] The observed high returns around splits might therefore be in compensation for the higher risk.

The classic study on stock splits by Fama, Fisher, Jensen, and Roll[7] examined longer-run stock returns around splits. They looked at monthly returns on splitting stocks for thirty months before and thirty months after the split announcement. They found that stock prices increase systematically during the months before a split announcement, but that there appears to be no indentifiable movement following the

TABLE 16–1
Managements' explanations for stock splits

Keep stock price in an optimal price range.
Enable management to express its confidence in the firm to shareholders.
Increase the number of shares outstanding, increasing liquidity.
Increase the number of shareholders.
Increase the total market value of the stock, because stock prices will not fully adjust following a split.

Source: H. Kent Baker and Patricia L. Gallagher (1980), "Management's View of Stock Splits," *Financial Management*, 9 (Summer), 73–77.

split. Companies seem to split their stock *in response to* favorable earnings results and higher stock prices. In other words, the relationship is that stocks split because their prices have increased, not that stock prices increase because they have split.

Considering commission costs, it is doubtful that short-term stock trading on the information of an upcoming split could produce profits. On the other hand, an analyst might be able to improve returns slightly by recommending stocks with a good chance of splitting and that also meet the analyst's other fundamental criteria. The split criterion alone would probably not be a profitable strategy.

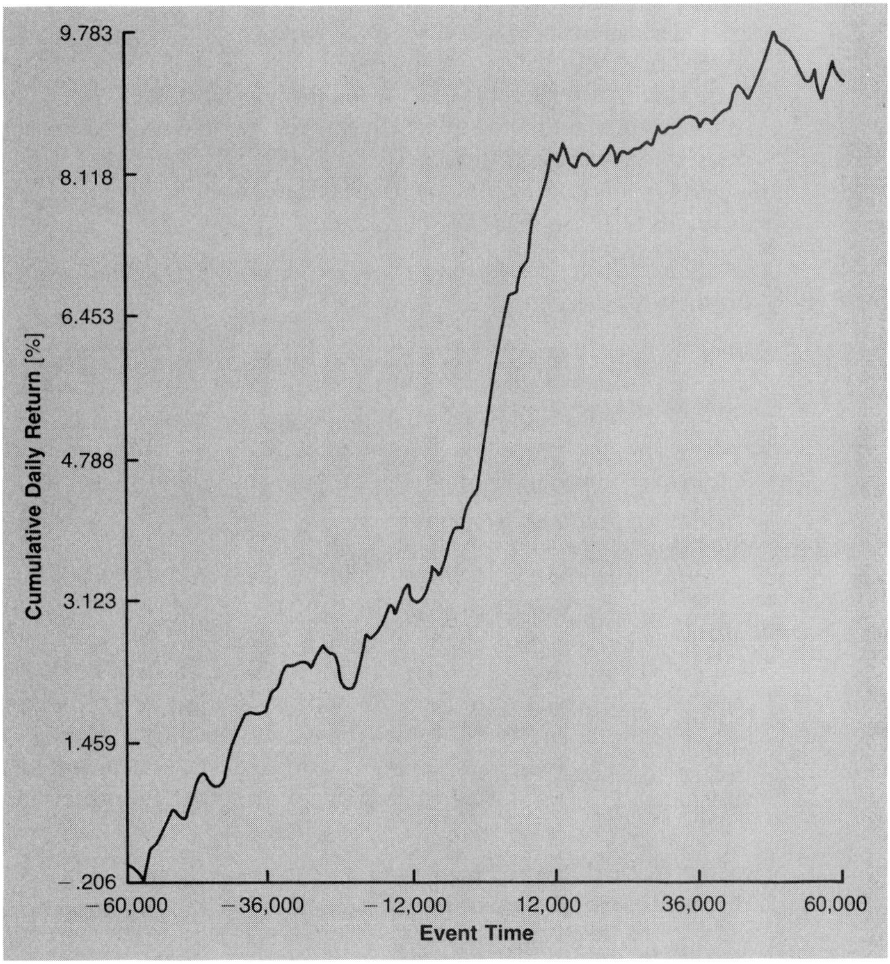

FIGURE 16–1
Woolridge's daily returns around stock dividend announcements[a] *(Source:* J. Randall Woolridge (1983), "Stock Dividends as Signals," *Journal of Financial Research,* 6 (Spring), 1–12.)

[a]The day of the stock dividend announcement on the graph is event time 0.

Companies with Big Dividend Increases

Related to the strategy of buying splitting stocks or stocks declaring stock dividends is the strategy of recommending purchase of companies increasing their cash dividends. Just as investors might view a stock split or stock dividend as a signal from management favorable for the company, cash dividends also seem to have a signaling effect. On a short-term basis, several studies have found significantly positive jumps in stock prices on the day companies announce dividend increases.[8] Generally, though, most of the short-term benefit of the dividend announcement occurs on the day before and the day of the announcement.

On a somewhat longer-term basis, Dielman and Oppenheimer[9] found that positive returns on stocks with larger dividend increases (25 percent increase or more) continued for about one month following the announcement. In addition, they computed risk measures and concluded that the risk of stocks declaring larger dividends decreases following the dividend announcement. Therefore, it may be beneficial to include in a list of investment criteria those stocks likely to announce large dividend increases or those that have just announced one.

Buying New Issues

Many investors believe that new issues of equity securities are generally underpriced when investment bankers first bring them to the market. When a company first goes public, the lack of information and absence of an established following of investors and analysts may encourage the company and its investment bankers to offer the issue at a price somewhat lower than the company's "true value" to stimulate interest in the stock. If such is the case, then investors who regularly buy these securities should outperform the market over the long run.

Several studies have been aimed at the returns available to investors in new issues.[10] These studies typically find that investors who purchased these stocks at their new issue prices would have profited significantly. For example, Reilly's sample of 486 new issues yielded returns shown in Table 16–2. Note that new issues yielded most of their profits within the first week of trading. Indeed, some "hot" new issues sell out quickly and rise substantially on the initial day of issue. Following the first week, the stocks in Reilly's sample did not improve much, and by the end of the first year most stocks had actually fallen in price to give a negative return. The implication

TABLE 16–2
Excess percent return[a] for new issues

Return Time Period	*Return*
New issue date to first Wednesday	10.8%
New issue date to fourth Wednesday	11.1%
One year from new issue date	−22.4%

[a]Excess return is the amount of return in excess of the return on the Dow Jones Industrial Average.
Source: Frank K. Reilly (1984), "New Issues Revisited," *Financial Management* 6 (Winter), 28–42.

is that investors must buy new issues at their new issue price and sell them within a relatively short time to reap maximum profits.

However, such a strategy presents some practical difficulties. Most investment banking firms allocate the largest quotas and most popular new issues to their most active and regular customers. They are under no obligation to sell the stock to occasional customers, so that small investors trying to purchase a hot new issue would likely be able to buy only a small portion, if any, of the total amount they wanted. In addition, new issues are often among the riskiest stocks. Ibbotson's evidence indicated an initial average beta of 2.2 for new issues. Much of the high returns on new issues may be in compensation for the risk involved. There are professional investors who maintain a practice of trading new issues. However, to maintain good relationships with the investment bankers who distribute these issues, they often commit substantial funds and find themselves purchasing issues they would rather not have. In the long run, they make positive profits, but they do so at the price of assuming the risk of new issues and buying some of the unpopular issues along with the hot ones.

Individual investors, especially those who deal through full-service brokerage firms that also have investment banking activities, may have opportunities from time to time to purchase new issues. Investors interested in a new issue should always obtain and read a copy of the issue's prospectus.

Stocks of Companies That Repurchase Their Common Stock

Since the mid-1960s, many companies have been repurchasing their common shares. There are a variety of reasons to explain this phenomenon. The most common reasons given by management are that stock repurchases are a good investment when management feels the stock price is depressed; stock repurchases can remove a large block of stock overhanging the market; and stock repurchases are likely to bolster share prices by reducing the supply of the stock and by increasing earnings per share.[11] Another reason is that companies purchase their own stock to have shares available for employee stock purchase plans and for exercise of employee stock options.

If the reasons given for repurchasing shares are true, then investors should be able to profit by purchasing shares in companies that carry out stock repurchase programs. Although one of the main reasons given for repurchase is the stock's depressed price, one study by Marks[12] examining repurchases concluded that stocks did not show inferior risk-adjusted performance *before* the repurchase programs. This indicates that their prices did not fall in relation to the market before the repurchases and therefore were not "depressed." However, management could still claim that the stock was a bargain and that the whole market was depressed.

What about stocks' prices following repurchase programs? The evidence here is conflicting. Marks's study and others[13] found that risk-adjusted stock price performance of repurchasing firms just about equaled the market. To explain the common belief on Wall Street that these stocks outperform the market, Marks showed that the risk level of repurchasing stocks increases following the repurchase. The higher return simply compensates the higher risk. It is reasonable to expect repurchasing firms' risk to increase following a repurchase because the repurchase diminishes the amount of equity in the company's capital structure, thus increasing financial leverage and risk.

Another study by Stewart[14] differs from the evidence of Mark's study and others. Stewart compared repurchase firms to nonrepurchase firms instead of to the market in general. He found that the repurchase firms outperformed the nonrepurchase firms for several years subsequent to the repurchase. He also found that the group of companies doing a moderate level of repurchase had the best price performance. Other researchers have provided additional data supporting the notion that stocks show superior performance after repurchases.[15]

Although there appears to be no well-defined positive benefit of companies that repurchase their shares, including planned share repurchase as a positive factor in a list of fundamental criteria would probably help provide favorable long-run returns.

The Small Firm Effect

The *small firm effect* is one of the most significant ideas to affect investment strategy in recent years. The small firm effect says that the shares of companies with relatively small total market value (share price times number of shares outstanding) exhibit long-run returns superior to the average company, even on a risk-adjusted basis.

One of the researchers who has studied the small firm effect extensively is Marc Reinganum.[16] He grouped firms traded on the NYSE and AMEX according to their total market values into ten groups and computed the average return for each of these groups over the period 1963 to 1980. Table 16–3 presents Reinganum's ten groups, their median market values, the mean return for the group, and the group's risk as measured by the beta coefficient. The higher mean return for the groups with the

TABLE 16–3
Mean returns on Reinganum's portfolios ranked by market value

Portfolio by Market Value	*Mean Return (× 1000)*	*Aggregated Coefficients Beta*
1 (smallest)	1.42	1.69
2	.92	1.64
3	.79	1.55
4	.64	1.50
5	.58	1.46
6	.53	1.39
7	.46	1.31
8	.42	1.24
9	.35	1.13
10 (largest)	.24	.97

Source: Marc Reinganum (1982), "A Direct Test of Roll's Conjecture on the Firm Size Effect," *Journal of Finance,* 37 (March), 27–35.

lower median total market values is direct evidence of the small firm effect. Investors who began with $100 who chose group one would have seen their investment grow to $4600 by the end of the study period, while investors who chose group ten would have ended with only $400.

There are several explanations for the existence of the small firm effect. First, Roll[17] suggested that the nature of the riskiness of smaller firms makes their risk more difficult to quantify. Therefore, measuring risk with the usual calculation of beta for small firms significantly underestimates their risk and overestimates the small firm effect. Reinganum acknowledged this and computed beta coefficients that help overcome this problem (aggregated coefficients betas suggested by Dimson).[18] Although the betas for the smaller firms are larger than those of the large firms, they are not sufficiently large to explain the higher returns. This led Reinganum to conclude that even after adjusting for the difficulty in computing risk for small companies, the small firm effect still yields above-average returns to smaller firms.

Another explanation for the small firm effect is the observation that transaction costs are proportionally greater for small firms than for large firms. Even after accounting for these effects, however, small firms tend to return more on average than large firms.

The disadvantage of investing in small firms is lack of information. Indeed, some market students also identify the "neglected firm effect." Neglected firms are those that do not have a large following among professional analysts and investors. The reason they have a small following is usually that much less information is available about the smaller companies. Investing in smaller, neglected firms may be dominated by individual investors rather than institutions. Institutions may shy away from the smaller companies because the larger blocks of stock they require may be unavailable or might cause significant price fluctuations. They prefer to concentrate on the more liquid, larger issues that they can trade more easily. These factors might also help explain the existence of the small firm effect.

Dollar Cost Averaging

Although *dollar cost averaging* is a mechanical formula, it fits into fundamental strategy because its goal is to purchase higher quantities of a stock when the stock is most undervalued. Dollar cost averaging is quite simple: you buy a predetermined dollar amount of a stock on a regular schedule. For example, you might decide to purchase $200 worth of IBM on the first of every month. If you follow this over a time period that encompasses at least one cycle in a stock's price, you will have an average purchase price of the stock *less than* the actual average price of the stock over the time period. The reason is that a given amount of money purchases a larger number of shares when the price is relatively low than when the price is relatively high.

Table 16–4 illustrates the returns on a dollar cost averaging plan begun in 1970 by an investor who wanted to invest $100 per year. The table assumes that the investor placed $100 per year in the Wilshire 5000 Index over a fourteen-year period from the end of 1970 to the end of 1984. (Although investors cannot buy the Wilshire Index, it does provide us with a good estimate of the returns that were available, because

TABLE 16–4
Investment results of dollar cost averaging, 1970–1983

Year	*Wilshire Index*	*Amount Invested*	*Shares Bought*	*Total Shares*	*Total Wealth*
1970	1.00000	$100	100.0	100.0	$ 100.00
1971	1.17680	100	85.0	185.0	217.68
1972	1.38839	100	72.0	257.0	356.82
1973	1.13132	100	88.4	345.4	390.75
1974	0.81016	100	123.4	468.8	379.82
1975	1.12185	100	89.1	558.0	625.95
1976	1.42012	100	70.4	628.4	892.38
1977	1.38267	100	72.3	700.7	968.84
1978	1.51091	100	66.2	766.9	1158.70
1979	1.89713	100	52.7	819.6	1554.89
1980	2.53589	100	39.4	859.0	2178.42
1981	2.44081	100	41.0	900.0	2196.74
1982	2.89748	100	34.5	934.5	2707.75
1983	3.57740	100	28.0	962.5	3443.15
1984	3.68641	0	0.0	962.5	3548.07

Internal Rate of Return without dollar cost averaging = 9.77%
Internal Rate of Return with dollar cost averaging = 11.73%

investors can invest in diversified mutual funds that approximate the return on the Wilshire and other market indexes.) The internal rate of return on the dollar cost averaging was 11.7 percent, while the return on an investment placed in the Wilshire in 1970 and simply left there until 1984 would have been only 9.8 percent. Of course, the actual returns on dollar cost averaging depend on the time period chosen. They can also be worse than the lump-sum investment, especially over short investment horizons. However, dollar cost averaging is not a short-run strategy, and its proponents rely on its ability to give them lower average costs over the long haul.

Strategies of dollar cost averaging are most appropriate for investors who have periodic cash flows available for investment. For investors who have a single sum to invest at one point in time, the choice of assets to invest in is important. Dollar cost averaging for such investors implies that they should invest only a small portion of their funds in stocks and commit the remainder to money market funds. Then, during subsequent time periods, they would take funds from the money markets and invest in stocks. However, a strategy like this may not be optimal,[19] especially during a generally bullish market.

CONCEPTS OF TECHNICAL ANALYSIS

Our broad definition of technical analysis includes the use of stock prices, trading volume, and other market data to formulate rules telling the technician when to buy or sell stocks. The principal feature of a technical strategy is the mechanical, objective

EXHIBIT 16–1

Profile of John Magee: A Pure Technician

A showcase example of that breed of market analyst called the technician is John Magee. Magee owns the investment advisory firm of John Magee, Inc., which provides stock-trading advice and information based on technical theories. His book, *Technical Analysis of Stock Trends,* coauthored with Robert Edwards, is often called the "bible of technical analysis." He prefers to work in a room without windows because he does not want any outside factors not related to technical market influences to affect his recommendations.

He explains the difference between technical analysis and fundamental analysis as follows:

Let me try to give you an idea of what the technical method is all about. That's another name for the chart method. Less descriptive, I grant you, but it has somewhat broader connotations, and we generally use it when we're discussing the two distinct schools of thought on the subject of stock-market analysis that have arisen over the years—the technical and the fundamental. The fundamental boys make up their minds after a careful study of the actual statistics of a company's operations—its earnings, the dividends it pays, its projected future earnings, and whatever other figures they can find that tell them how well or badly it's doing.

Now, the opposite school of thought, as I said a minute ago, is the technical. The technician's first principle is that the market automatically reflects everything about the status of a company. Earnings, probable earnings, dividends—all the information, good or bad, says the technician, that the fundamentalists sweat over is already known to the people who buy and sell large amounts of stocks, and it shows up in the prices they are willing to pay or accept for them. The ordinary trader can't possibly know as much as the insiders do, but he can get a good look at the insiders' minds by reading the charts. A chart of the fluctuations in the price of a stock and the volume of shares traded isn't a picture of the company, mind you—it's a picture of what informed people think of the prospects of a company's stock. Therefore, says the technician, the chart provides absolutely all you need to know in order to predict the future movements of the stock. I'll go further, it's not only all you need to know, it's all you want to know, if you're a true chartist. You don't want to be distracted by extraneous information. It isn't even important to know what business or industry the company is engaged in, as long as you can study its stock chart. To a layman, it might seem that such suggestive formations as an inverted bowl in Guantanomo Sugar, a coil in International Telephone, a cradle in Mead Johnson baby foods, or a blowoff in Hercules Powder ought to have some singularly pertinent connotation, but to a chartist, a cradle in Mead Johnson is the same as a cradle in Chrysler.*

*Quoted in John Brooks (1958), *The Seven Fat Years,* New York: Harper & Row.

nature of the decision. When a technical rule indicates a buy or sell sign, then it is time to buy or sell; there are usually no additional arguments that the technician must consider for or against the trading decision. This differs from the fundamental valuation approaches discussed in Chapters 14 and 15. Use of the fundamental valuation model requires many subjective forecasts and judgments before the analyst can reach a decision, and that decision is seldom a clear-cut buy or sell.

The pure technical analyst is the chartist. Many of these technicians do not even consider the influence of other market or company information to make their investment decisions. Chartists believe that stock price and volume data are all an investor needs, and that extra information only clouds their ability to make relevant buy or sell decisions. John Magee, a noted chartist and publisher of a technical market newsletter, provides an interesting description of technical analysis in Exhibit 16–1.

Market technicians can apply their techniques to forecasting the direction of both the stock market and individual stocks. They typically use market indicators to measure the strength of the market or economy. Based on these measures, they then forecast an up or down market. Charting, on the other hand, is used for both individual stocks and the market. By charting a graph of a stock's price (and possibly its trading volume) chartists try to identify patterns that will give clues to the future direction of the stock. Applying the same techniques to a market index lets chartists predict the direction of the market.

Advantages of Technical Analysis

Many investors utilize technical analysis. Some do so to the exclusion of fundamental analysis and other techniques. Others are basically fundamentalists who believe that they cannot afford to ignore the technical viewpoint, so they use technical analysis along with other strategies in making their final investment decisions.

Technical analysis offers several advantages, which helps to explain why it has so many adherents. Probably the biggest advantage is its objectivity. Once the technician has determined the particular rule to use in the technical strategy, making the actual investment decision is easy. If the technical criterion for a buy recommendation exists, then the technician buys. The decision requires no thought, forecasts, or other subjective judgments.

A second advantage is that technical analysis is easy to learn and requires no specialized financial knowledge. Constructing a chart of a stock's price is an easy task. Computing market indicators usually requires only a simple calculation. On the other hand, conducting or even understanding a complete fundamental analysis requires knowledge of accounting, forecasting, present value, finance, and other topics that take long periods of study to learn. Technical analysis may therefore appeal to people without a high level of financial expertise because they can learn and begin using many technical strategies within a very short time.

A third advantage that technicians see in their approach is that they have ready access to all the information they need. The financial press reports daily stock price and volume activity, and the information is also widely available instantaneously on computer time-sharing systems. Fundamental analysts, however, must rely on the companies as their primary source of information. This information is often several months old by the time investors receive it, and it often suffers from the financial reporting ambiguities detailed in Chapter 11.

Criticisms of Technical Analysis

Probably the most evident criticism of technical analysis is the controversy over the efficacy of technical strategies. Opponents of technical analysis claim that there is no real objective, substantial evidence that it works. Indeed, the wealth of information supporting the weak form of market efficiency rejects technical analysis. Recall from Chapter 9 that this evidence showed that there are no reported short-term security price patterns that tend to repeat themselves to the extent that would allow a trader to successfully profit from them. Stock prices in the short run appear to be a random walk. Many technicians fall into the trap of using several years of past data to find patterns or rules that would have made them a profit. When applied to future trading, however, these rules seldom yield above-normal returns. The reason for this is simple: Even a series of random numbers will appear to show a pattern over a finite span. If the series is truly random, however, the pattern will most likely not repeat itself in the future.

Another criticism of technical analysis is that it is a self-fulfilling prophecy. Consider what can happen when hundreds of technicians, all using the same information, reach the same investment decision at the same time. For example, if all of the chartists following Exxon common stock found a pattern indicating a future upward stock move, they would all immediately call their brokers with a buy order. Such an influx of buy orders would likely drive the price of Exxon stock up several points, and the technicians' prediction would have become true as a result of their own actions. Critics point out that technicians often act too late to be able to take advantage of the "self-fulfilling prophecy" situation. By the time they have processed the stock price information and acted, other technicians will have done the same thing, the stock price will have reached its new equilibrium, and it will be too late to make trading profits.

A final criticism deals with the difficulty of discerning chart patterns as they develop. Any good instructional manual of charting will show nice examples of all the standard chart patterns, identifying the buy and sell points. However, actually identifying these patterns *as they develop* (not using hindsight after they have developed) is not simple. For example, what may initially appear to be the final leg of a "double bottom" may actually turn out to be the middle leg of a "triple top," and the chartist who turned bullish should really have been bearish. In addition, most chart patterns can have the word "false" added to their name. For example, a "false double bottom" is a double bottom giving a standard technical buy signal after which the stock goes down, not up. With hindsight, the chartist can see the error and admit that it was a false double bottom. Detecting whether a signal is "real" or "false" *before* the fact is the real challenge.

Why Study Technical Analysis?

If there is no consistent evidence that technical analysis leads to above-average investment profits, why should we study it? First of all, even if the techniques do not work, the fact is that many investors do make investment decisions based on technical analysis. Many brokerage firms hire their own technical analysts, and followers of technical advice spend money to purchase pregraphed charts and other technical data. With this in mind, the technician segment of market analysis is important enough to warrant study, and even the most ardent fundamentalist should be aware of the technical strategies. In addition, there may be some successful technicians in the market who beat the averages. However, the message of market efficiency to any fortunate technicians who have found the profitable combination of technical rules should be: Do not share your strategies with anyone, lest they become widespread and no longer effective.

MARKET INDICATORS

The market indicators attempt to gauge one or more areas of the market or economy. A successful market indicator would have some sort of leading relationship with the market and would therefore be of use in forecasting market direction. There are five broad areas of market indicators, classified according to the type of information they measure:

1. Investor sentiment
2. Contrary opinion
3. Professional investors
4. Economic data
5. Other

We will present several of the popular indicators within each category. The list is by no means complete, and those interested in pursuing technical analysis further should consult additional reference works on the subject.

Measures of Investor Sentiment

The measures of investor sentiment try to indicate the degree of investors' confidence in the market. They usually gauge confidence by one of two general approaches. One is to compare yields on risky securities to yields on less risky securities. The other approach is to measure confidence by indicating the width of a market change across all securities.

Barron's Confidence Index

One good source for the type of data that usually make up market indicators is *Barron's National Business and Financial Weekly*. *Barron's* presents this information at the end of each issue in its statistical section. Much of the useful indicator data is found in the "*Barron's* Market Laboratory" section near the end of the statistical section of the publication. Appearing in the "Market Laboratory" section is one of the most popular indicators in the market, *Barron's Confidence Index*. *Barron's* computes this indicator as follows:

$$\text{Confidence index} = \frac{\text{Yield on } \textit{Barron's} \text{ Best Grade Bonds}}{\text{Yield on } \textit{Barron's} \text{ Intermediate Grade Bonds}} \times 100 \quad \textbf{(16–1)}$$

Barron's reports the index and its component bond yield indexes every week

EXAMPLE 16–1

The April 28, 1986, issue of *Barron's* reported the following data:

Yield on *Barron's* Best Grade Bonds = 8.86 percent
Yield on *Barron's* Intermediate Grade Bonds = 9.62 percent

Using this data, compute the Confidence Index.

$$\textit{Barron's}\text{ Confidence Index} = (8.86/9.62) \times 100$$
$$= 92.1$$

Barron's Confidence Index generally has fallen within a range between about 85 and 98.

Because the yield on better grade bonds will always be less than yields on lower grade bonds, *Barron's* Confidence Index will always have a value less than 100. The technician's viewpoint is that when investors are confident about the market and optimistic about the future, they will be willing to buy riskier bonds. Their purchases of riskier bonds will drive prices of riskier bonds up in relation to those of high grade bonds. This causes the yield on the *Barron's* intermediate grade bonds to be closer to the yield on the best grade bonds, and the index will be closer to 100. When investors lose confidence, the reverse should happen, and the Confidence Index will fall.

A rising *Barron's* Confidence Index, therefore, indicates to its proponents that the economy is strong and that investors have confidence that the market will rise further. A declining index implies that weakness in the economy will likely spill over into a falling stock market in the future.

Although *Barron's* is the most widely mentioned confidence index, there are others. Other confidence indexes compare yields on groups of securities with different risks, such as T-bonds to corporate bonds or utility bonds to utility preferred stocks.

Confidence indexes have a high degree of correlation with the economy and the stock market. Often they even lead the market, but they sometimes do not, and they may also give false signals of a market turn. Another problem with confidence indexes is that they look at the demand side only, ignoring the additional factors that influence interest rates. For example, the money supply is an important determinant of interest rates, and it could cause changes in a confidence index that investors might wrongly interpret as changes in investor confidence.

High-Low Index

The *high-low index* measures market strength by comparing the number of stocks making annual new highs to the number of annual new lows. There are several ways to compute such an index, but one of the popular formulas is as follows:

$$\text{High-low index} = \frac{\text{New highs}}{\text{New highs} + \text{new lows}} \tag{16–2}$$

EXAMPLE 16–2

The April 28, 1986, issue of *Barron's* reported the following information for composite exchange and OTC trading:

$$\text{NYSE} + \text{AMEX} + \text{OTC} = \text{Total}$$
$$\text{New highs} = 576 + 148 + 709 = 1433$$
$$\text{New lows} = 37 + 18 + 143 = 198$$

Compute the high-low index:

$$\begin{aligned}\text{High-low index} &= 1433/(1433 + 198) \\ &= .878\end{aligned}$$

This value is significantly greater than .5 and therefore shows a strong market.

The high-low index can fluctuate between the extremes of 0 and 1.0. At a value close to 0, substantially all stocks reaching new records are new lows. As the index nears a value of 1.0, new records are on the high side.

Followers of this index believe that bear markets and intermediate down moves in the market usually end when the high-low index is below .10. Bull markets and intermediate up moves typically end when the index reaches levels above .90.

Advance-Decline Ratio

The market indexes tell investors whether the market average is rising or falling, but other measures are necessary to signify the strength of the market direction. One way to gauge this *breadth of the market* is to examine the number of issues advancing compared to the number of issues declining, yielding the *advance-decline ratio:*

$$\text{Advance decline ratio} = \frac{\text{Advances}}{\text{Advances} + \text{declines}} \tag{16–3}$$

The advance-decline ratio ignores issues with unchanged price. Proponents of this ratio believe that it leads the market indexes. They generally agree that when the ratio is .60 or more the market is overbought. When the ratio turns downward from above the .60 level, a bear market should soon follow. The ratio's level on the lower end that signifies a market upturn is about .35.

EXAMPLE 16–3

The April 28, 1986, issue of *Barron's* reported the following information on the number of issues in composite trading advancing and declining:

$$\begin{aligned} &\text{NYSE} + \text{AMEX} + \text{OTC} = \text{Total} \\ \text{Advances} &= 949 + 381 + 1481 = 2811 \\ \text{Declines} &= 1061 + 397 + 1389 = 2847 \end{aligned}$$

Compute and interpret the advance-decline ratio:

$$\begin{aligned} \text{Advance-decline ratio} &= 2811/(2811 + 2847) \\ &= .497 \end{aligned}$$

The value of the advance-decline ratio is so close to .5 that it must be interpreted as being neutral.

Another indicator of breadth of the market, preferred by some technicians because it brings volume into the picture, is the *upside-downside volume ratio.* Upside volume is the total volume of issues rising in price, and downside volume is the volume of shares falling in price. The upside-downside ratio is as follows:

$$\text{Upside-downside volume ratio} = \frac{\text{Upside volume}}{\text{Upside volume} + \text{downside volume}} \tag{16–4}$$

Interpretation of the upside-downside volume ratio is the same as for the advance-decline ratio.

Short Interest Ratio

Investors usually sell short a stock only if they think that it will fall in value. Short interest—the number of total short shares outstanding—should be an indication of investors' expectations about a market decline. A popular indicator for short interest is the *short interest ratio:*

$$\text{Short interest ratio} = \frac{\text{Total short interest}}{\text{Average daily volume}} \tag{16–5}$$

The exchanges report short interest on a monthly basis. Therefore, it is common to use the average daily volume for the month in computing the short interest ratio. When the short interest ratio rises, this indicates that investors believe that stocks in general might begin to fall. A fall in the ratio indicates the opposite. Most adherents to this ratio look for turning points in the ratio to indicate a change in market direction.

Some technicians interpret the short interest ratio in the opposite sense from this explanation. They believe that high short interest represents a large latent demand because the shortsellers will eventually have to cover their short positions. When that happens, the increased demand for stock should push prices up. These technicians view a relatively high short interest ratio as bullish and a relatively low one as bearish.

In the past ten years, more short selling has occurred as a result of increased arbitrage using warrants and options. This has distorted the short interest ratio and decreased its use among technicians.

Measures of Contrary Opinion

The basis for *contrary opinion* market indicators is the belief that certain groups of investors make consistently wrong investment decisions, especially at turns in the market. If these investors make bad investment decisions, then to formulate a successful trading strategy we need only to identify these groups and their decisions, and then do the opposite in the market.

Of the three contrary opinion indicators presented here, the first two are *odd-lot indicators.* The reasoning behind the odd-lot indicators is that small investors often can afford to trade only in small lots of less than 100 shares. Because small investors do not have access to the same information and resources that professional investors have, they often make wrong investment decisions. Market observers often accuse the "odd lotters" of waiting too late to "jump on the band wagon." That is, they begin buying after a bull market has run most of its course and is reaching its peak. Therefore, when odd-lot traders are buying, it is time to get out of stocks.

Odd-Lot Balance Index

The *odd-lot balance index* measures the net purchases in number of shares of all trades of less than 100 shares as follows:

$$\text{Odd-lot balance index} = \frac{\text{Odd-lot sales}}{\text{Odd-lot purchases}} \tag{16–6}$$

When the odd-lot balance index is greater than 1.0, odd-lot traders are selling more than they are buying. They are net buyers when the index is less than 1.0. Proponents of this index look for turning points in the index.

EXAMPLE 16–4

The April 28, 1986, issue of *Barron's* reported the following odd-lot trading data:

$$\text{Total odd-lot sales} = 4820.6$$
$$\text{Total odd-lot purchases} = 2610.3$$

Compute and interpret the odd-lot balance index.

$$\begin{aligned}\text{Odd-lot balance index} &= 4820.6/2610.3\\ &= 1.85\end{aligned}$$

This odd-lot balance index is bullish, since it is quite a bit greater than 1.0.

There are two major problems with using odd-lot indicators. First, they do not necessarily measure the trading activity of small investors. Because of stock splits, many larger investors have odd lots in their portfolios. For example, a mutual fund holding 1500 shares of a stock before a 3-for-2 split will be left with 2250 after the split. When the fund sells the stock, the broker will treat the 50-share portion as an odd lot. Therefore, not all odd-lot trading results from small investors. A second problem is that there is no real evidence indicating that small investors do worse than the pros. The odd-lot indicators will often give false buy and sell signals.

Odd-Lot Short Sales Index

The logic behind the *odd-lot short sales index* is that odd-lot traders sell short very little at market tops and quite heavily at market bottoms. The index measures odd-lot short sales as a percentage of total odd-lot sales as follows:

$$\text{Odd-lot short sales index} = \frac{\text{Odd-lot short sales}}{\text{Total odd-lot sales}} \qquad \textbf{(16–7)}$$

EXAMPLE 16–5

The "Market Laboratory" section of *Barron's* on April 28, 1986, gave the following information on odd-lot short sales:

$$\text{Odd-lot short sales} = 28.6 \text{ thousand}$$
$$\text{Total short sales} = 4820.6 \text{ thousand}$$

Compute the odd-lot short sales index.

$$\begin{aligned}\text{Odd-lot short sales index} &= 28.6/4820.6\\ &= .006\end{aligned}$$

Technicians would likely interpret this value of the index as neutral to slightly bearish.

This index historically averages between .01 and .02. Followers of this ratio interpret a level of .004 or less to indicate periods of very light odd-lot short selling. These would tend to signal market tops. Market bottoms tend to occur when the index is above about .04.

The odd-lot short sales index has the same shortcomings as the odd-lot balance index.

Mutual Fund Liquid Asset Ratio

The *mutual fund liquid asset ratio* is a contrary opinion indicator based on the premise that large institutional investors are often wrong. Even when they are not wrong, they may be too slow to respond to a changing market environment, so that their investment decisions are not optimal. This would support the idea that mutual funds would have more cash at market bottoms than at market tops. Normally, one would think that an astutely managed fund would be less invested in stocks when the market is headed down, but by the time the market reaches a bottom, the fund would be fully invested in anticipation of the moment when stocks head upward again. Contrary opinion believes the opposite—that the funds' managers cannot consistently identify the future direction of the market. Also, as the market falls, small investors pull their money out of mutual funds, and the funds must sell stocks and raise cash positions to meet redemptions. Therefore, by the time the market reaches a bottom, mutual funds' cash positions are at cyclical highs. The mutual fund liquid asset ratio measures the percentage of common stock mutual fund assets invested in cash and short-term money market instruments:

$$\text{Mutual fund liquid asset ratio} = \frac{\text{Mutual fund cash and liquid assets}}{\text{Total mutual fund assets}} \qquad \textbf{(16–8)}$$

This ratio is also called the *mutual fund cash position ratio.* Mutual funds report information on their sales, redemptions, and cash position monthly. *Barron's* has a regular "Monthly Mutual Fund Indicators" column in the statistical section providing these data and the mutual fund liquid asset ratio.

Measures of Professional Investor Activity

The groups of investors that people generally believe can outperform the market are professional investors and insiders. Chapter 9 showed that corporate insiders (company management and large shareholders) consistently make good investment decisions regarding purchase and sale of their company's stock. There are other groups that we might consider to have "inside" market information, such as specialists on the exchanges and sophisticated professional investors who trade large blocks of stock. The *professional investor activity ratios* attempt to identify the investment actions of these insiders. The concept behind these is to "follow the smart money." Proponents of the indicators try to follow the same strategy as the insiders.

Specialists' Short Sale Ratio

One of these "smart money" groups is exchange specialists. In fact, evidence indicates that specialists as a group have consistently earned superior returns.[20] Since specialists do tend to beat the market, an indicator of specialist trading activity might lead to a profitable trading strategy. One such indicator is the *specialists' short sale ratio,* which represents the short sales made by exchange specialists as a percentage of total exchange short sales:

$$\text{Specialists' short sale ratio} = \frac{\text{Short sales by specialists}}{\text{Total short sales}} \qquad \textbf{(16–9)}$$

Specialists have historically accounted for about 55 percent of all NYSE short sales. When the ratio rises to about .60, technicians believe that specialists are doubtful about further market movements upward, and they interpret a value greater than .65 as being very bearish. On the bullish side, they believe that a specialists' short sale ratio less than .45 is bullish, while anything less than .40 is very bullish.

EXAMPLE 16–6

Barron's of April 28, 1986, reported the following short sale data:

Total shorts = 65,562.1

Specialist shorts = 32,183.0

Compute and interpret the specialists' short sale ratio:

$$\begin{aligned}\text{Specialists' short sale ratio} &= 32{,}183.0/65{,}562.1\\ &= .49\end{aligned}$$

The value of .49 for the specialists' short sale ratio is within the average range and is neutral.

Figure 16–2 shows the specialists' short sale ratio and the Dow Jones Industrial Average over a nine-year period. Reilly and Whitford[21] tested trading strategies based on the specialists' short sale ratio over this time period. They tried combinations of buying when the ratio fell below .45 or .40 and selling after time period varying from one week to thirty-nine weeks. In general, they could find no combination of buy signal and holding period that would have yielded returns greater than a simple buy-and-hold strategy. This was true even for investors who had access to short sale data before they became public information. Specialists' short sale data are published about two weeks after the date for which they are computed, and this time lag would make it even more difficult for public traders to profit. The specialists' short sale ratio is of questionable value as a trading tool.

Big Block Index

Large block trades (50,000 shares and more) are almost the exclusive territory of institutional investors. Activity of these investors dominates the market and accounts for more than two thirds of the nonmember trading volume on the NYSE. If we knew what these investors were doing, we might be able to construct a market indicator

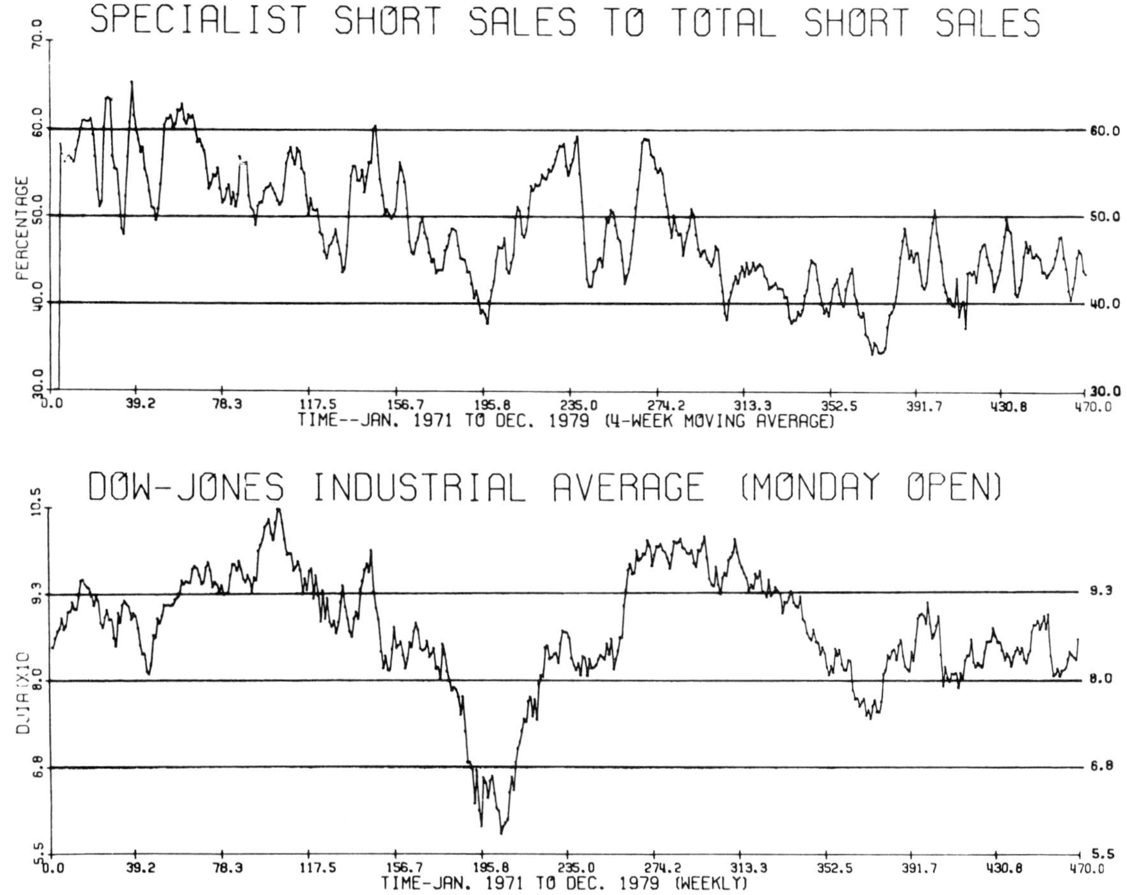

FIGURE 16–2
The specialists' short sale ratio and the Dow Jones Industrial Average
(Source: Frank K. Reilly and David T. Whitford (1982), "A Test of the Specialists' Short Sale Ratio," *Journal of Portfolio Management,* 8 [Winter], 12–18.)

to give buy and sell signals based on their actions. The *big block index,* attributable to market analyst Martin Zweig,[23] attempts to measure the bullishness or bearishness of this group of traders. The big block index represents the portion of block trade volume increasing in price relative to all big block trades changing in price:

$$\text{Big block index} = \frac{\text{Big block upticks}}{\text{Big block upticks} + \text{big block downticks}} \qquad \textbf{(16–10)}$$

A big block uptick occurs when a big block trades at a price higher than the previous trade. A downtick is a trade at a lower price. The rationale underlying the big block index is that an uptick occurs when the buyer is the more active party in the transaction, while a downtick occurs on the stimulus of the seller. When upticks dominate block trades, then the institutions are bullish and wanting to buy. Institutions would generally be bearish when downticks prevail. Therefore, the big block index will be between 0 and 1, with values in the lower end considered bearish and those on the upper end, bullish.

The information needed to compute the index appears every week in *Barron's*. Computation of the index ignores trades at no change in price.

EXAMPLE 16–7

Barron's of April 28, 1986, reported the following information on trades of large blocks of stock:

$$\text{Total big block upticks} = 399$$
$$\text{Total big block downticks} = 464$$

Compute and interpret the big block index.

$$\text{Big block index} = .46$$

A value of .46 for the big block index is so close to the middle of the possible range of values that technicians would likely interpret this to be neutral.

Zweig prefers to compute an "exponentially smoothed" big block index value for forecasting purposes. His smoothing formula is as follows:

$$\text{Smoothed index} = \text{This week's index} \times .18 + \text{last week's smoothed index} \times .82$$

Zweig looks for reversals in the trend of this smoothed big block index value. When the index falls by three percentage points from a peak, it is a sell signal. If the smoothed index rises by three or more points from a low, it is time to buy. Zweig claims that these decision rules would have allowed an investor to profit handsomely from 1969 to 1983. A $10,000 investment in Zweig's market index at the beginning of the period would have grown to $10,830 at the end, while trading using the big block index buy signals would have left the investor with $36,335. One note of caution: Investors who extrapolate such results into the future should be very careful.

Measures Based on Economic Data

Chapter 10 established that the economy and the stock market are highly correlated. However, the observation that the market regularly and consistently leads the economy makes it difficult to use coincident economic indicators to predict the market. Market indicators based on economic data try to concentrate on leading indicators that might also lead the market. The indicator presented here deals with monetary policy.

The Fed Indicator

As discussed in Chapter 10, an expansionary monetary policy is usually associated with bull markets. Since the Federal Reserve System is the main implementor of monetary policy in the United States, and indicator based on the Fed's attitude toward the money supply might be of use for forecasting stock prices. Probably the Fed's two most powerful tools for carrying out monetary policy are the discount rate and the reserve requirement. Another one of Martin Zweig's market indicators, the *Fed indicator,* is based on changes in both of these tools of monetary policy.

The Fed indicator is a running cumulative sum of point scores based on changes in the discount rate and the reserve requirement. The discount rate and reserve requirement are scored separately and added together to get the Fed indicator. The rules for computing the Fed indicator are as follows:

1. A hike in either the discount rate or reserve requirement receives a score of −1. It also wipes out any positive balance that may have accumulated.
2. The negative point remains for six months, after which it becomes stale and is discarded.
3. An initial cut in either the discount rate or the reserve requirement wipes out any negative accumulation of points and provides two positive points (+2). (An initial cut is the first cut following a rise or the first cut in at least two years.)
4. Following an initial cut, take away one of the points after six months has passed and the other point after twelve months.
5. Changes in the reserve requirement do not affect the score on the discount rate, nor do changes in the discount rate affect the score for the reserve requirement.
6. The Fed indicator is equal to the sum of the accumulated point total for the discount rate plus the total for the reserve requirement.

When the Fed indicator stands at +2 or higher, it is "extremely bullish." At a value of +1 or 0, it is neutral. A "moderately bearish" rating is a score of −1 or −2, while a value of −3 or less is "extremely bearish." Zweig claims success for his Fed indicator, as Table 16–5 shows.

TABLE 16–5
Peformance of the Fed indicator vs. Zweig Unweighted Price Index: (Jan. 2, 1958 to Nov. 21, 1984)

Fed Rating	***Total No. of Yrs.***	***% Cases Mkt. Rose***	***$10,000 Investment***	***% Return per Yr.***	***% Return vs. Buy & Hold***
Extremely Bullish	7.6	92	$108,688	+36.8	+31.2
Neutral	9.4	45	8,511	− 1.7	− 7.3
Moderately Bearish	7.4	43	6,346	− 6.0	−11.6
Extremely Bearish	2.5	22	7,349	−11.5	−17.1
Total	26.9	50	$ 43,387	+ 5.6	—

Source: Barron's National Business and Financial Weekly, December 3, 1984.

EXHIBIT 16–2

Some Other Crazy Market Indicators

The Aspirin Count Theory. The basis for the Aspirin Count Theory is that when things go wrong, people get more headaches. The theory says that such a period will precede a fall in stock prices. The U.S. International Trade Commission reports annual production of aspirin, and when aspirin output rises, look for a bear market the following year.

The Hemline Index. A brokerage research director by the name of Ralph Rotnem noticed that major stock market trends were often signaled by changes in the length of women's skirts. In 1967, he created the Hemline Index. The idea behind the index is that when economic times are bad, people lose interest in sex. Their interest revives when they have a more optimistic view of the future. Rising hemlines forecast a bull market while longer lengths signal a market collapse.

The Super Bowl Omen. The Super Bowl Omen is probably the most widely discussed market phenomenon in early January of each year. It states that the market will rise for the year following a Super Bowl victory by a team which is in the National Football Conference. A bear market will dominate when an old AFC team wins. (Before the merger of the football leagues, a bull market followed a win by an NFL team, and the market fell following an AFL victory.) This indicator seems always to be right. Nobody seems to know *why* it works, but many believe that it *does* work.

The Tie Gauge. The Tie Gauge predicts market direction by noting the currently fashionable width of men's ties. Men tend to wear narrow ties when they feel sharp and more confident. Narrow ties, therefore, forecast a rise in the market index. Wider ties, on the other hand, are a signal of an upcoming bear market.

Other Indicators

There are other indicators that are difficult to classify, probably because there is very little reasoning behind them. In spite of having little or no foundation, these indicators do have their followers. For example, consider the January indicator.

The January Indicator

The *January indicator* says that if the market is up in January, it will be up for the entire year. Conversely, if January is a down month, the indicator would forecast a down year for the market. In spite of having a following among some of the monthly investment newsletters, the January indicator does not live up to its reputation. First of all, we must judge the January indicator *not* on its ability to predict the market's direction for the entire year (including January), but rather on its ability to forecast the eleven months that follow the first month.

Over a seventy-year span (1915–1985), the indicator successfully identified 71 percent of the bull markets (thirty-two out of forty-five).[23] At first glance, this might appear to be a good record. However, when one considers that bull markets prevailed during 64 percent of the total number of years, the indicator loses some of its sparkle. Combine this with the January indicator's relatively bad record of predicting down markets, and the indicator's investment record over the seventy years is worse than blindly investing in the Dow. A $10,000 investment in the Dow Jones Industrials in 1916 would have grown to $155,993 by the end of 1985. On the other hand, an investor buying the Dow when the January indicator was bullish and shorting the Dow when it was bearish (and investing in T-bills during January) would have finished with a portfolio worth only $11,955.

CHARTING

Charting, or graphing, the movement of a stock's price has captivated many investors since the early days of security trading. There seems to be some magic in the tendency of stock prices to move according to patterns identified by chartists. It is difficult to look at any chart of stock prices and not see apparent trends and patterns. For an example, refer to the chart in Figure 16–3. Using typical chartist terminology, the stock represented in the figure appears to have been fluctuating within its "trading range" until it finally "broke out" through its "support level" on the downside. In fact, the price series represented by this chart was generated on a computer using a random number generator program. Even random numbers will appear to develop "patterns" over a period of time.

Nevertheless, charting has many followers who dedicate their time to graphing stock prices and interpreting the resulting formations. However, critical analysis of

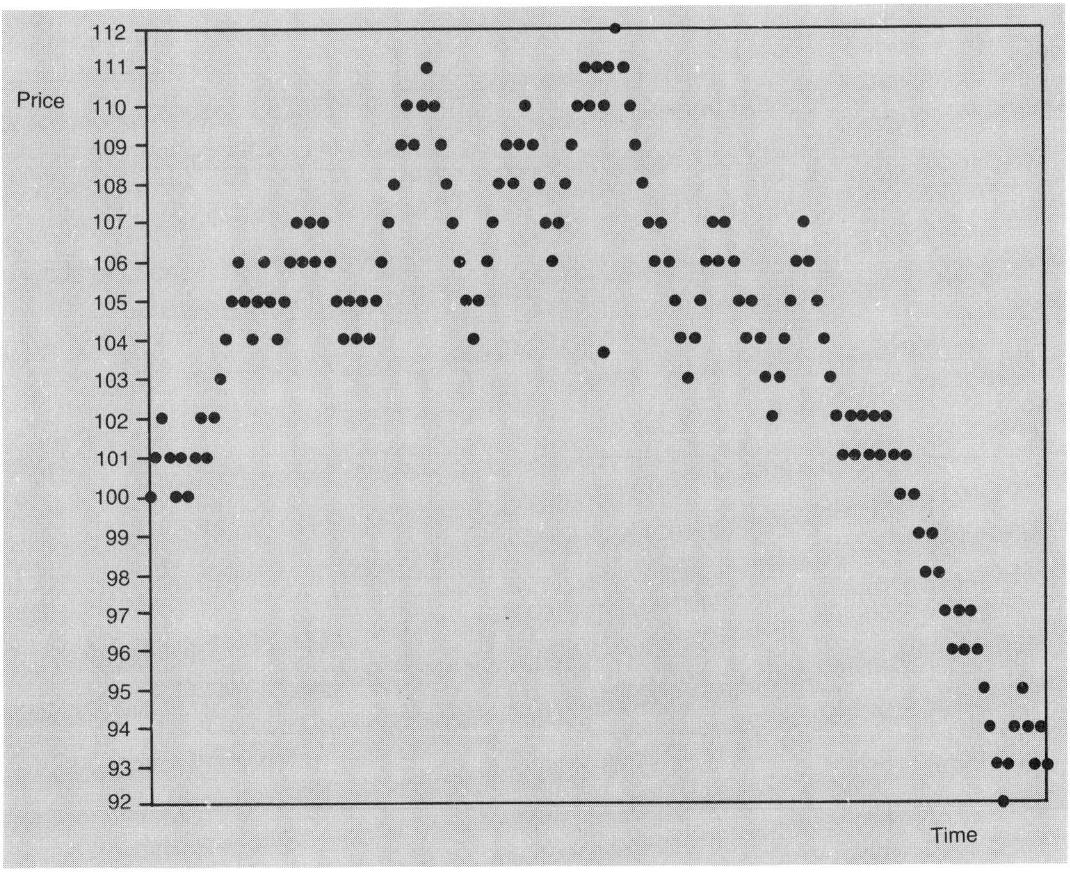

FIGURE 16–3
Sample chart for hypothetical stock, created with a random number generator

stock price behavior has failed to reveal any patterns that repeat themselves with any degree of statistical significance.

Bar Charts

Technicians study two major types of charts. The first of these is the *bar chart.* Figure 16–4 shows a bar chart. To construct a bar chart, the chartist chooses a time period that each bar will represent. For example, chartists who wish to graph their stocks using prices one week apart will have bars that represent the week's trading activity. The chart in Figure 16–4 uses daily prices.

On a bar chart, the vertical axis is price, and the horizontal axis represents time. To graph the stock's price, draw a vertical bar from the high stock price for the time period to the low price. At the stock's closing price for the period, place a small horizontal mark. Repeat this procedure for each trading period, and soon the chart and its patterns will emerge.

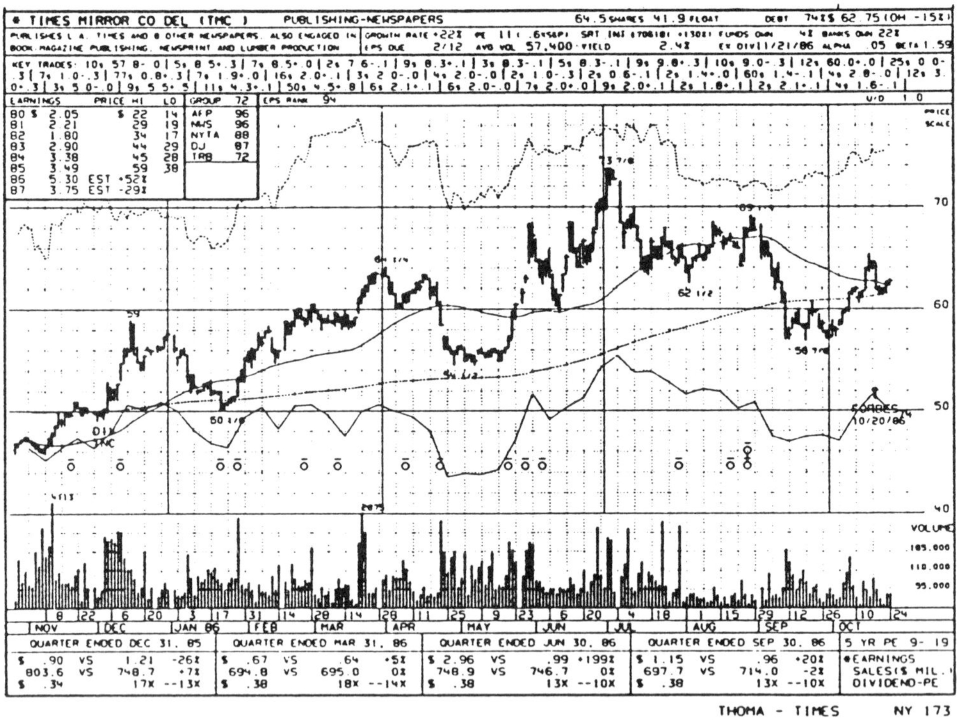

FIGURE 16–4
Sample bar chart *(Source: New York Stock Exchange/OTC Daily Graphs* (November 1986), © Copyright 1986 by William O'Neil, Inc. All rights reserved including the right to reproduce this book or any parts thereof in any form. Printed in USA.

Chartists often also chart the stock's trading volume on the bar chart. Note the vertical bars at the bottom of the chart in Figure 16–4. These bars reflect the stock's volume for the trading day.

Point and Figure Charts

On the bar chart, distances on the horizontal axis represent the passage of time. Therefore, the shape of any pattern that develops on the chart will depend on how long it takes to develop. A pattern that develops over a period of several weeks will be relatively compressed, while one that emerges over several months will be more stretched out. Chartists do not want to be fooled or misled by the distortions in pattern shapes caused by time. To solve this problem, technicians originated the *point and figure chart.* Figure 16–5 is a typical point and figure chart. The horizontal axis on point and figure charts represents only changes in the direction of the stock's price, *not* the passage of time. Therefore, patterns developed by these charts are independent of the time it takes them to develop. Many chartists believe that point and figure charts are easier to read and interpret.

To construct a point and figure chart, begin by marking off stock prices on the vertical axis. For low priced stocks (priced less than about $10), chartists will usually label the vertical scale so that each box is one quarter of a point. Higher priced stocks will have half-point boxes (stocks selling between $10 and $30) or one-point boxes

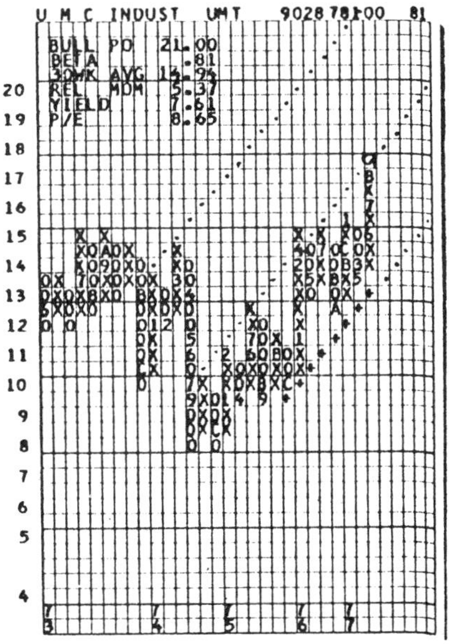

FIGURE 16–5
Sample point and figure chart *(Source: Chartcraft Monthly Chartbook* (October 1977), Larchmont, NY: Chartcraft, Inc.)

(stocks priced higher than $30). Indicate the stock's price on the chart by X when the stock is rising and O when it is falling. Suppose that your stock's price has been rising, so you begin charting its price with X's. As long as the price continues to rise, you keep on graphing its price in the same vertical column with X's. Short-term decreases in the stock's price of less than three vertical boxes on the graph are ignored. However, when the stock does fall by three boxes or more, you move over to the next column to the right and begin charting the stock's fall with O's. Repeat this procedure in the same column until the stock again reverses itself and rises three boxes. This is known as the *three-point method of point and figure charting* because the stock has to change direction by three boxes (not necessarily points) to move to the next column.

On the first day of each month, some chartists will place the month's number in the box instead of X or O. They will also record the current year along the horizontal axis. The purpose of this is to give some identification of the time period and the length of time over which the chart pattern develops. Note that one year on the chart may have a length of ten horizontal boxes, while the next year could have forty. It all depends upon how many times the stock's price reverses itself by three boxes.

Support and Resistance Levels

One of the first things that chartists search for is the existence of *support levels* and *resistance levels.* A support level is the stock price at which there appears to be price support. The idea is that when the stock's price falls to the support level, buyers enter the market to purchase the stock, thereby supporting its level. Chartists look for the moment when the stock price breaks through the support level and heads downward. At that point, chartists believe that the support for the stock's price has disappeared and that the stock will continue downward until it reaches a new support level.

The resistance level is the opposite on the upside. It is the price level at which the stock meets resistance. At that point, sellers believe that the price is high and enter the market to sell, so the price will not pierce its resistance level. When it does break through the resistance level, sellers no longer sell at that level. Chartists view that as a buy signal, believing that the stock's price will continue to rise until it finds its new resistance level.

The range of prices between a stock's support level and its resistance level is its *trading range.* Chartists patiently graph their stocks' prices, waiting for the moment when one breaks out, giving them a buy or sell signal.

Moving Averages

Another popular tool among technical analysts is the *moving average.* A moving average is an average of past data that is updated as new information is received. For example, a twenty-one day moving average of a stock's price would be a simple average of the price over the last twenty-one days. Tomorrow, the oldest day in the series is dropped, and the new moving average will contain the latest twenty-one days. The advantage of a moving average is that it smooths the data. Smoothing eliminates or softens the

The Bullish and Bearish Symmetrical Triangles

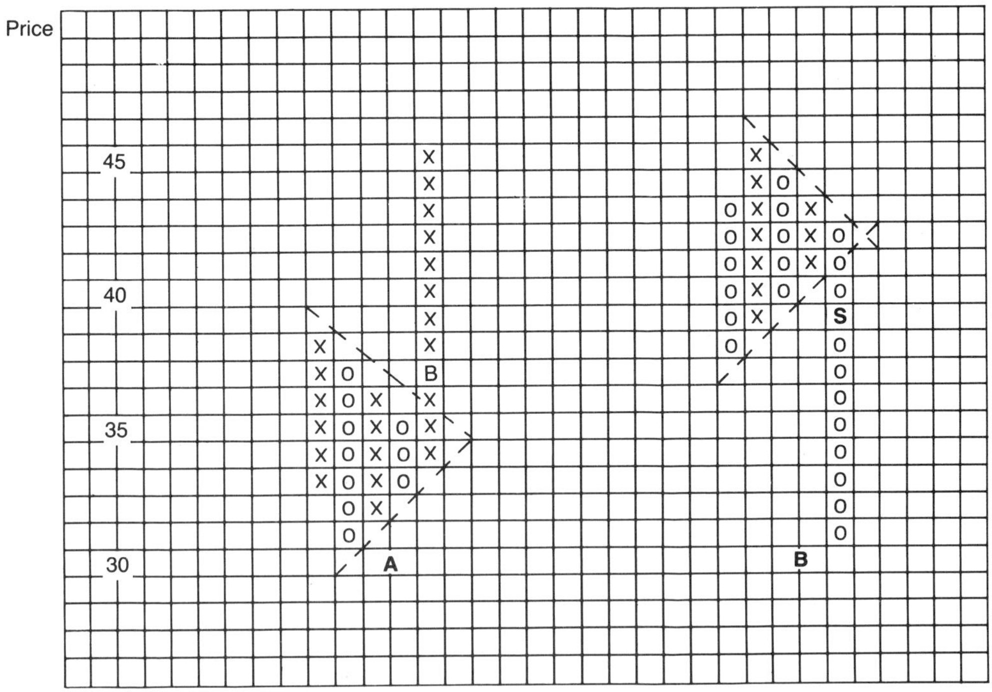

The Triple Top Formation

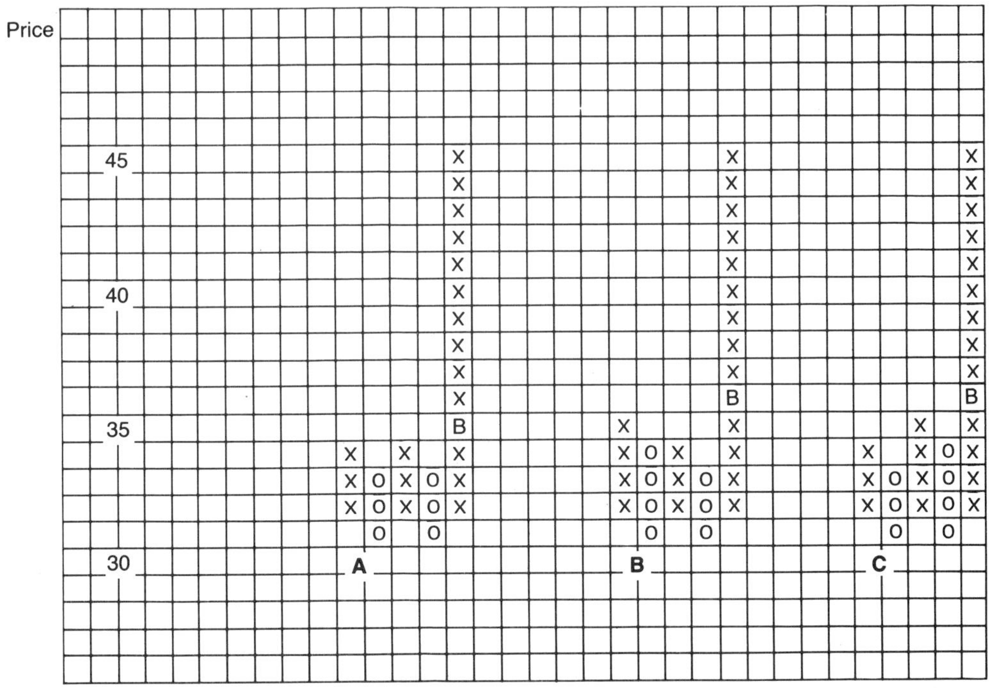

FIGURE 16–6
Some typical chart patterns *(Source:* A. W. Cohen (1980), *How to Use the Three-Point Reversal Method of Point and Figure Stock Market Trading,* Larchmont, NY: Chartcraft.)

The Triple Bottom Formation

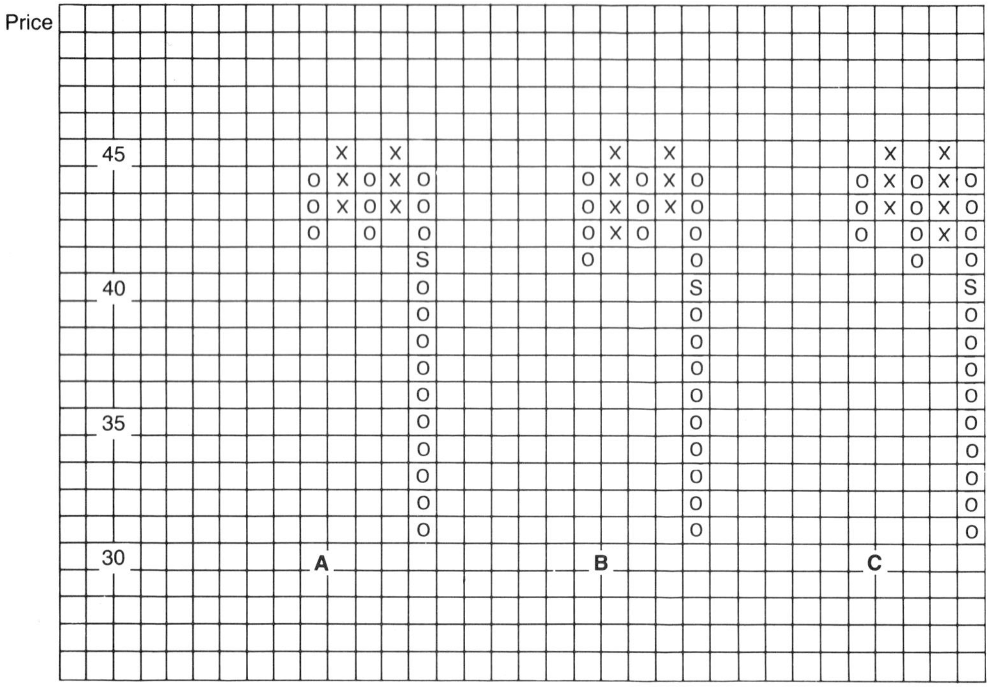

The Double Top and Double Bottom Formations (#2)

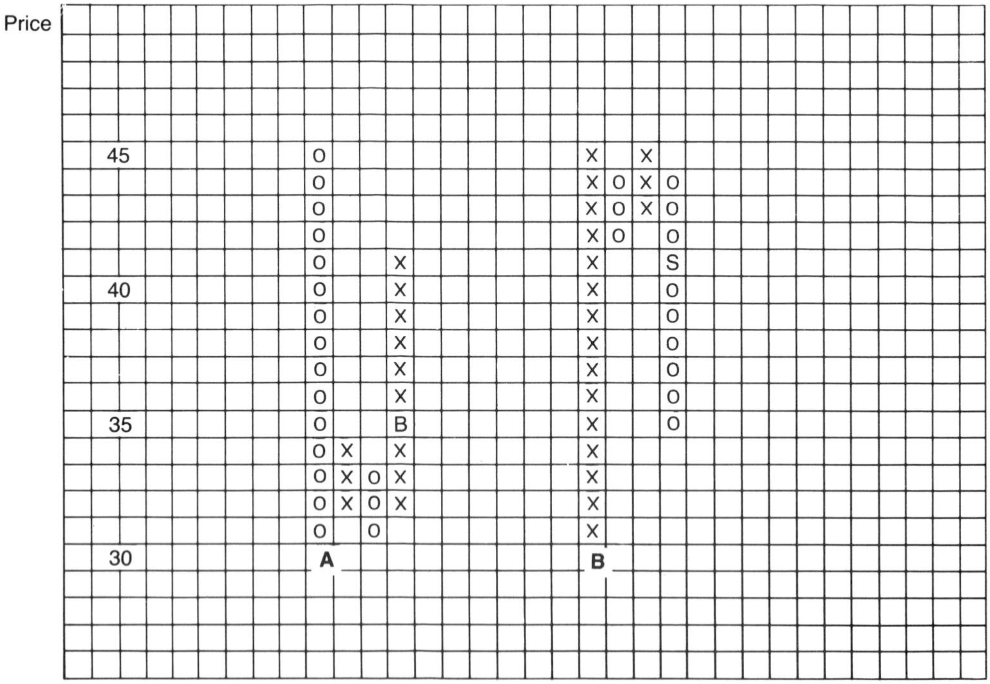

FIGURE 16–6
(continued)

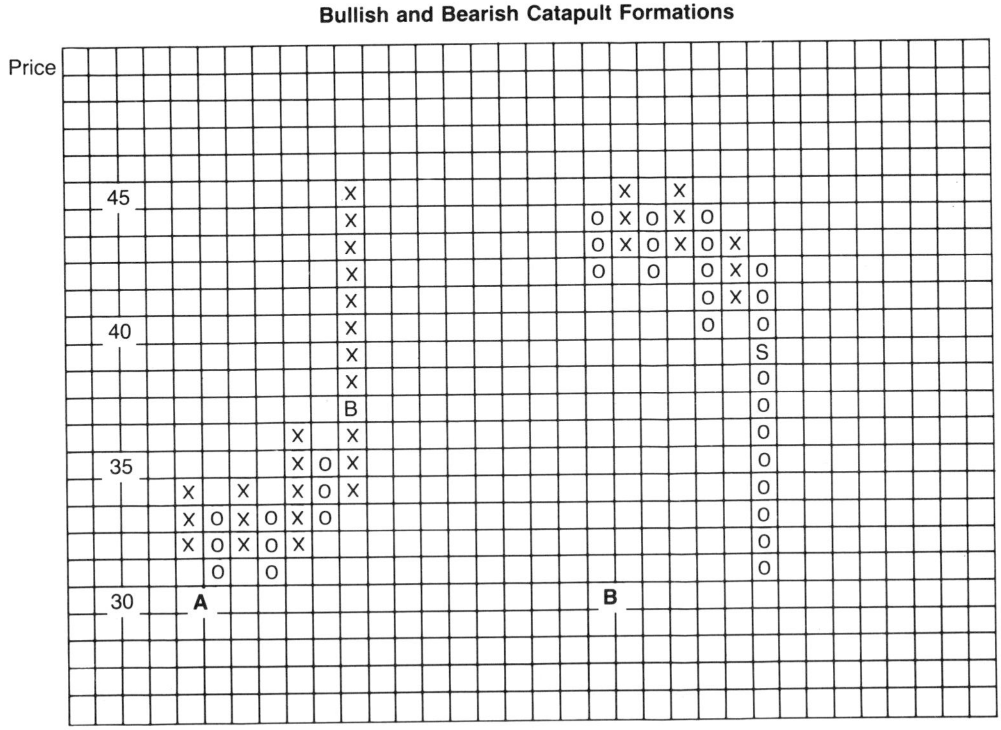

FIGURE 16–6
(continued)

impact of short-term fluctuations in the data. For stock charting, the use of moving averages can help mitigate the effects of daily ups and downs in a stock's price that might generate confusing buy or sell signals.

Another way that chartists use moving averages is to overlay them on bar charts so that both the moving average and the bars are graphed on the same chart. When the stock's price (bar) crosses the moving average from below and moves above the moving average, it is a buy signal. When the stock crosses the moving average from above, a sell signal results. Of course, it is important to choose the optimal moving average. For example, a twenty-one day moving average may give a buy signal, while a fifty-day average indicates nothing. Also, the shorter the time period of the moving average, the more buy and sell signals it will generate. The dotted line lying below the bars representing the stock's price on the chart in Figure 16–5 is the line for a thirty-week moving average of the price.

Some Typical Chart Patterns

There are probably as many chart patterns as there are chartists. Figure 16–6 shows some of the standard patterns that point and figure chartists look for.

SUMMARY

The major categories of equity-trading strategy are the strategies based on fundamental theory, the market indicators, and charting techniques. Fundamental valuation provides the basis for the first group of strategies. They include buying low P/E stocks, stocks that split, stocks with big dividend increases, newly listed stocks, stocks in companies that repurchase their own stock, and small capitalization stocks. Dollar cost averaging also falls into this class.

The market indicators are measures of market or economic activity used to predict future direction of the stock market. They include measures of investor sentiment, contrary opinion, insider activity, and economic data, as well as other indicators.

Charting is the graphic analysis of trends and patterns in stock prices. The use of market indicators and charting is often called technical analysis. The most popular types of charts among market technicians are bar charts and point and figure charts. Bar charts record security prices on the vertical axis and time on the horizontal axis. Point and figure charts, on the other hand, use the horizontal axis only to indicate a reversal of the trend in the stock's price.

Chartists use both types of charts to identify patterns and trends in stock prices. Support levels on charts represent the price level where the stock receives support; the stock's price will tend not to fall below the support level. A resistance level is the level at which the stock's price resists further advance. When a stock breaks through a support or resistance level, the chartist believes that it will continue in its trend.

IMPORTANT TERMS

advance-decline ratio
bar chart
Barron's Confidence Index
big block index
breadth of the market
charting
contrary opinion
dollar cost averaging
Fed indicator
fundamental strategies
high-low index
investment timing decision
January indicator
market indicators
moving average
mutual fund liquid asset ratio
odd-lot balance index
odd-lot indicators
odd-lot short sales index
point and figure chart
professional investor activity ratios
resistance level
screening stocks
short interest ratio
small firm effect
specialists' short sale ratio
support level
technical analysis
three-point method of point and figure charting
trading range
upside-downside volume ratio

QUESTIONS AND PROBLEMS

1. Identify and define the three major types of stock-trading strategies.
2. Consult a recent issue of *Barron's* and locate the current P/E ratio of the S&P 500 Index. Using some source of fundamental data on a number of stocks (such as S&P's *Stock Market Encyclopedia,* Moody's *Handbook of Common Stocks,* or a computer database), identify ten stocks whose P/E is less than 80 percent of the market P/E.
3. Consult a recent issue (or issues) of *The Wall Street Journal* and find a stock in the dividend news section that has changed its cash dividend. Look up the stock's price for several days before and after the date of the announcement. Did the stock react to the announcement favorably, unfavorably, or not at all? What does this reaction imply about investors' expectations before the dividend announcement?
4. What factors might contribute to a firm's decision to repurchase its own common stock in the market? Why might common stock repurchase tend to increase the stock's price?
5. Define the small firm effect. What explanations might account for its existence?
6. At each month-end payday, you have an extra $100 you would like to invest. You decide to dollar cost average by purchasing $100 worth of a diversified mutual fund each month. The month-end values for the fund over the last year are as follows:

Jan.	Feb.	Mar.	Apr.	May	Jun.	Jul.	Aug.	Sep.	Oct.	Nov.	Dec.
14	16	20	18	18	16	16	18	16	20	22	24

   a) Compute the total value of your portfolio at the end of the year.
   b) Compute your average per share cost and the average price of the fund over the year.
   c) Assume that instead of dollar cost averaging, you decided to borrow $1100 at the end of January to add to your first $100. You invest the entire amount in the mutual fund. You pay off the loan at the rate of $100 per month plus interest at a rate of 1 percent of the balance per month. What is the value of your portfolio, less interest expense, at the end of the year? Compare this value to your dollar cost average portfolio. Why are they different?
7. Summarize the pros and cons of using technical analysis.
8. Consult two recent issues of *Barron's* and compute the indicators listed below. Examine the value of the indicator and the trend between the two dates. Does it appear to be bullish, bearish, or neutral?
   a) confidence index
   b) high-low index
   c) advance-decline ratio
   d) short interest ratio
   e) odd-lot balance index
   f) odd-lot short sales index
   g) mutual fund liquid asset ratio
   h) specialists' short sale ratio
   i) big block index
9. Explain the difference between bar charts and point and figure charts. What are the relative advantages of each?
10. Define support level and resistance level. How do chartists use them?

NOTES

1. See, for example, S. Basu (1981), "Investment Performance of Common Stocks in Relation to Their Price-Earnings Ratios," *Journal of Finance,* 36 (March), 3–18; Marc Reinganum (1981), "Misspecification of Capital Asset Pricing: Empirical Anomalies Based on Earnings' Yields and Market Values," *Journal of Financial Economics,* 9 (March), 19–46; and David A. Goodman and John W. Peavy III (1985), "The Risk Universal Nature of the P/E Effect," *Journal of Portfolio Management,* 11 (Summer), 14–16.
2. Haim Levy and Zvi Lerman (1985), "Testing P/E Ratios Filters with Stochastic Dominance," *Journal of Portfolio Management,* 11 (Winter), 31–40.
3. Kent H. Baker and Patricia Gallagher (1980), "Management's View of Stock Splits," *Financial Management,* 9 (Summer), 73–77.
4. J. Randall Woolridge (1983), "Stock Dividends as Signals," *Journal of Financial Research,* 6 (Spring), 1–12.
5. Robert A. Strong (1983), "Do Share Price and Stock Splits Matter?" *Journal of Portfolio Management,* 10 (Fall), 58–64.
6. Dan W. French and David A. Dubofsky (1986), "Implied Stock Price Volatility Changes Following Stock Splits," *Journal of Portfolio Management,* 12 (Summer), 55–59.
7. Eugene F. Fama, Lawrence Fisher, Michael Jensen, and Richard Roll (1969), "The Adjustment of Stock Prices to New Information," *International Economic Review,* 10 (February), 1–21.
8. See, for example, J. Aharony and J. Swary (1980), "Quarterly Dividend and Earnings Announcements and Stockholders' Returns: An Empirical Analysis," *Journal of Finance,* 35 (March), 1–12; K. M. Eades (1982), "Empirical Evidence on Dividends as a Signal of Firm Value," *Journal of Financial and Quantitative Analysis,* 17 (November), 471–500; and J. Randall Woolridge (1983), "Dividend Changes and Security Prices," *Journal of Finance,* 38 (December), 1607–1615.
9. Terry E. Dielman and Henry R. Oppenheimer (1984), "An Examination of Investor Behavior during Periods of Large Dividend Changes," *Journal of Financial and Quantitative Analysis,* 19 (June), 197–216.
10. See, for example, Roger G. Ibbotson (1975), "Price Performance of Common Stock New Issues," *Journal of Financial Economics,* 2 (September), 235–272; J. G. McDonald and A. K. Fisher (1974), "New Issue Stock Price Behavior," *Journal of Finance,* 29 (March), 97–102; and Frank K. Reilly (1977), "New Issues Revisited," *Financial Management,* 6 (Winter), 28–42.
11. H. Kent Baker, Patricia L. Gallagher, and Karen E. Morgan (1981), "Management's View of Stock Repurchase Programs," *Journal of Financial Research,* 4 (Fall), 233–247.
12. Kenneth R. Marks (1976), *The Stock Price Performance of Firms Repurchasing Their Own Shares,* New York: New York University, Graduate School of Business Administration.
13. See, for example, Terry E. Dielman, Timothy J. Nantell, and Roger L. Wright (1980), "Price Effects of Stock Repurchasing: A Random Coefficient Regression Approach," *Journal of Financial and Quantitative Analysis,* 15 (March), 175–189.
14. Samuel S. Stewart, Jr. (1976), "Should a Corporation Repurchase Its Own Stock?" *Journal of Finance,* 31 (June), 911–921.
15. See, for example, Larry Y. Dann (1981), "Common Stock Repurchases: An Analysis of Returns to Bondholders and Stockholders," *Journal of Financial Economics,* 9 (June), 113–138; and Theo Vermaelen (1981), "Common Stock Repurchases and Market Signalling: An Empirical Study," *Journal of Financial Economics,* 9 (June), 139–183.

16. See Marc Reinganum (1981), "Misspecification of Capital Asset Pricing—Empirical Anomalies Based on Earnings Yield and Market Values." *Journal of Financial Economics,* 9 (March), 19–46; Marc Reinganum (1982), "A Direct Test of Roll's Conjecture on the Firm Size Effect," *Journal of Finance,* 37 (March), 27–35; and Marc Reinganum (1983), "Portfolio Strategies Based on Market Capitalization," *Journal of Portfolio Management,* 9 (Winter), 29–36.
17. Richard Roll (1981), "A Possible Explanation of the Small Firm Effect," *Journal of Finance,* 36 (September), 879–888.
18. Elroy Dimson (1979), "Risk Measurement When Shares Are Subject to Infrequent Trading," *Journal of Financial Economics,* 7 (June), 197–226.
19. See George M. Constantinides (1979), "A Note of the Suboptimality of Dollar-Cost Averaging as an Investment Policy," *Journal of Financial and Quantitative Analysis,* 14 (June), 443–450.
20. Securities and Exchange Commission (1964), *Report of the Special Study of the Securities Markets,* Washington, DC: Author, Part 2, 54.
21. Frank K. Reilly and David T. Whitford (1982), "A Test of the Specialists' Short Sale Ratio," *Journal of Portfolio Management,* 8 (Winter), 12–18.
22. See Martin E. Zweig (1983), "Trusty Market Indicator: Bringing the Record on the Big Block Index Up to Date," *Barron's National Business and Financial Weekly* (January 24).
23. Mark Hurlbert (1986), "The 'January Indicator': Fact or Fiction?" *AAII Journal,* 8 (April) 23–25.

SELECTED REFERENCES

Baker, H. Kent, and Patricia L. Gallagher (1980). "Management's View of Stock Splits." *Financial Management,* 9 (Summer), 73–77.

———, Patricia L. Gallagher, and Karen E. Morgan (1981). "Management's View of Stock Repurchase Programs." *Journal of Financial Research,* 4 (Fall), 233–247.

Baldwin, William (1983). "The Dollar-Cost Sure Thing." *Forbes* (August 15), 144–115.

Cohen, A. W. (1980). *How to Use the Three-Point Reversal Method of Point and Figure Stock Market Trading.* Larchmont, NY: Chartcraft.

Constantinides, George M. (1979). "A Note on the Suboptimality of Dollar-Cost Averaging as an Investment Strategy." *Journal of Financial and Quantitative Analysis,* 14 (June), 443–450.

Daigler, Robert T., and Bruce D. Fielitz (1981). "A Multiple Discriminant Analysis of Technical Indicators on the New York Stock Exchange." *Journal of Financial Research,* 4 (Fall), 169–182.

Dielman, Terry E., and Henry R. Oppenheimer (1984). "An Examination of Investor Behavior during Periods of Large Dividend Changes." *Journal of Financial and Quantitative Analysis,* 19 (June), 197–216.

Fanning, James E. (1971). "A Four-Indicator System for Forecasting the Market." *Financial Analysts' Journal,* 27 (September-October), 49–56.

Givoly, Dan, and Arie Ovadia (1983). "Year-End Tax-Induced Sales and Stock Market Seasonality." *Journal of Finance,* 38 (March), 171–185.

Hurlbert, Mark (1986). "The 'January Indicator': Fact or Fiction?" *AAII Journal,* 8 (April), 23–25.

Klein, April, and James Rosenfeld (1988). "The Impact of Targeted Share Repurchases on the Wealth of Non-Participating Shareholders." *The Journal of Financial Research,* 11 (Summer), 89–97.

Markese, John (1984). "Dollar Cost Averaging: One Answer to the Timing Question." *AAII Journal,* 6 (September), 34–35.

Marks, Kenneth R. (1976). *The Stock Price Performance of Firms Repurchasing Their Own Shares.* New York: New York University.

Nichols, William D. (1981). "Security Price Reaction to Occasional Small Stock Dividends." *The Financial Review,* 16 (Winter), 54–62.

Reilly, Frank K., and David T. Whitford (1982). "A Test of the Specialists' Short Sale Ratio." *Journal of Portfolio Management,* 8 (Winter), 12–18.

Reinganum, Marc R. (1983). "The Anomalous Stock Market Behavior of Small Firms in January: Empirical Tests for Tax-Loss Selling Effects." *Journal of Financial Economics,* 12 (June), 89–104.

Schwert, G. William (1983). "Size and Stock Returns, and Other Empirical Regularities." *Journal of Financial Economics,* 12 (June), 3–12.

Stoll, Hans R., and Robert E. Whaley (1984). "Transactions Costs and the Small Firm Effect." *Journal of Financial Economics,* 12 (June) 57–80.

Woolridge, J. Randall (1983). "Stock Dividends as Signals." *Journal of Financial Research,* 6 (Spring), 1–11.

——— (1983). "Dividend Changes and Security Prices." *Journal of Finance,* 38 (December), 1607–1615.

Zweig, Martin E. (1976). *Investor Expectations: Why They Are the Key to Stock Market Trends.* New York: Zweig Securities Advisory Service.

——— (1983). *The ABC's of Market Forecasting: How to Use Barron's Market Laboratory Pages.* Princeton, NJ: Dow Jones and Company.

——— (1983). "Trusty Market Indicator: Bringing the Record of the Big-Block Index Up to Date." *Barron's* (January 24).

——— (1984). "The Fed Calls the Turn: Stock Prices Follow the Discount Rate." *Barron's* (December 3), 66–67.

PART SIX

Contingent Claim Securities, Futures Markets, and Other Securities

CHAPTER 17

Contingent Claim Securities: Stock Options

Trading in exchange-listed stock options began in Chicago in 1973 with a small trial of options on sixteen stocks. Trading in these instruments became so popular that other exchanges joined in the action within a few years. The volume of trading in listed options increased dramatically, to the point where the total number of shares represented by option contract volume exceeded stock trading on the AMEX and OTC. Stock options on several hundred different common stocks now trade on these exchanges.

The existence of exchange-traded stock options has increased the number of investment opportunities confronting today's investor. Equally, the existence of options has increased the amount of knowledge investors must have to be current with information in the market. The astute investor can use options to expand upon traditional risk-return relationships. Using options, an investor can convert a relatively risky position in a stock to a more conservative one. On the other end of the risk spectrum, an investor can change a position in a staid income stock to a more aggressive position by including the stock's options.

Options fall into the general classification of securities that we call *contingent claim securities*. These securities give their holder a claim on another asset or security, subject to the specifications of the conditions, or contingencies, of the contingent claim security. The value of contingent claim securities depends upon a number of factors, probably the most important of which is the value of the *underlying asset*. Because the value of a contingent claim is derived from its underlying asset, contingent claim securities are also often called *derivative assets*. Securities that fall into the classification of contingent claim securities or derivative assets are options, warrants, and convertible securities.

The growth of trading in equity options led to the introduction of other options. The range of financial assets on which options currently trade includes stock indexes, foreign currencies, debt instruments, and even futures contracts.

This chapter deals with the concepts and pricing of stock options, index options, and options on debt instruments. Several option strategies are also presented. The next chapter, Chapter 18, applies the contingent-claim principles to warrants and convertible securities. Chapter 19, which deals with futures contracts, discusses options on futures.

OPTION FUNDAMENTALS

Traders of stock options have a special terminology for their securities and strategies. The first step in this chapter is to introduce and define some of the frequently used terms.

Option Terms

Stock options are contracts that give the holder the right to buy or sell 100 shares of an underlying stock. The act of making this stock transaction (buying or selling the stock) is called *exercising the option.* Option holders must exercise their options on or before the option's *expiration date.* Failure to exercise the option results in its expiration; as with any contract, the option is void and worthless after it expires. An option is *European* if it can be exercised only on the expiration date. An *American* option can be exercised at any time until expiration. Most options traded in the United States are of the American type.

An option to buy the underlying stock is a *call option.* Call options rise in value when the stock rises, and buyers of call options hope that the stock's price will increase. If the option gives its holder the right to sell the stock, it is a *put option.* Put options increase in value when the stock price falls, and therefore put owners profit when the stock declines in price. *Puts* and *calls* are the two main types of stock options. There are also positions involving combinations of puts and calls.

To exercise an option, the holder must pay a certain amount of money specified in the option contract. This amount of money is the option's *exercise price.* Option traders also call this price the *striking price* (or *strike price*) of the option.

An option will have a market price of its own. Many traders call the market price of an option the option's *premium.* This book will simply use the term *price* to indicate the option's market price, because the word *premium* in popular use carries the connotation that the item sells for more than it is worth. Options derive their value from the fact that they are "exercisable" into the underlying stock. This does not mean that option holders must exercise them to obtain their value. Option holders who want to get their money out of an option may exercise the option, but it is probably easier and less expensive to sell the option in the option market than to exercise it. Only about 2 percent of all options that exist are ever exercised. However, since an option becomes worthless if it expires, there must be some mechanism to clear the market of many of these options. The clue to how this operates lies in the creation of the options themselves, and in the two parties who are involved in the option contract.

Parties Involved in an Option Transaction

Two principals are involved in every option transaction: the buyer and the seller. Of course, there may be intermediaries in the deal, such as the market makers on the exchange and the brokerage firms.

The option buyer is the party who owns or holds the option. The seller of the option sells it to the buyer. If the seller already possesses the option before the transaction, the deal is straightforward—ownership of the option simply passes from the seller to the buyer. So far, this is no different from any typical security transaction. However, if the seller does not already own the option, matters become more complicated. The seller who sells an option not presently owned *writes the option.* Writing creates a new option, which then becomes owned by the buyer. This is possible because options are simply contracts between buyer and writer. A seller who does not previously own the contract simply writes a new one. The process is similar to selling short a stock that one does not own. As in short selling, brokerage firms handle the mechanics of the transaction. Option traders do not have to be concerned with how options are written.

For example, a call option gives its owner the right to purchase 100 shares of the underlying common stock. The call option's writer has agreed to sell the stock to the option owner upon exercise. The option owner pays the exercise price to the writer when exercising the option. The writer of a put agrees to buy the stock should the option be exercised. Note that the writer of an option has an *obligation* to make the transaction should the holder exercise, while the holder has a *right,* or option, to exercise. The holder would want to exercise only if it is profitable to do so.

There are two types of writers of options. A *covered writer* has a position in the option's underlying security that hedges or "covers" the option should exercise occur. A long position in the stock covers the writing of a call option. Should the call be exercised, the writer simply delivers the stock already owned. A *naked writer* or *uncovered writer* has no position in the stock. The naked writer of a call option, upon notice of exercise, would have to buy the stock in the market and deliver it to the option holder at the exercise price to fulfill the option contract. This transaction might even be at a substantial loss—explaining the term *naked* or *uncovered.* The covered writer, on the other hand, has a position in the stock to deliver should exercise occur. The risk and return potential of covered and naked positions can be quite different and can offer options traders a wide variety of strategies.

OPTION VALUATION

Because an option is exercisable into the underlying stock, its value depends upon the price of the stock and the relationship of the exercise price of the option to the market price of the stock. However, we need to be more specific regarding the value of an option. To begin, let us identify a *floor* or *minimum value* for options.

The Minimum Value of an Option

What would be the minimum value for a call option? Suppose that we have a call option on Exxon stock with an exercise price of $60 (an "Exxon 60"), which expires after today. Exxon's market price is $62 per share. If we exercise the call option, we pay $60 per share. (Although options contracts are written for 100 shares, they are quoted on a per share basis.) We now hold stock worth 62 for which we paid 60, meaning that the option added the differential value of 2 to the transaction. The call option's value must therefore be at least 2. If the value of the option were less than 2, arbitrageurs would be able to make an arbitrage profit. For example, suppose the option sold for 1 in the market. An astute arbitrageur could buy the option for $1, exercise it (paying $60 for the stock), and sell the stock in the market for $62, making a riskless $1 profit. Arbitrage will force the call option to sell for at least its minimum value. The minimum value of an option is the value of the option to an investor exercising it. For a call option, the minimum value is as follows:

$$C_m = max(0, S - X) \tag{17–1}$$

where C_m = the minimum value of a call option
S = the price of the underlying stock
X = the exercise price of the option
max = the maximum value operator; read the max operator as "the greater of"

Equation 17–1 says that the minimum value of a call option is equal to the max (the greater) of zero or the stock price less the exercise price. Note that the option's value cannot be negative. Therefore, if exercising the option would result in a negative value, the holder simply would not exercise it, and its minimum value would be zero. The call option's minimum value is equal to zero or the stock price less the exercise price, whichever is greater. Sample computations of a call option's minimum value are given in Example 17–1.

EXAMPLE 17–1

Exxon common stock is trading on the NYSE for 62 per share. What is the minimum value of an Exxon call option with exercise price of 60?

$$\begin{aligned} C &= max(0, 62 - 60) \\ &= max(0, 2) \\ &= 2 \end{aligned}$$

What is the minimum value of an Exxon call option with exercise price of 65?

$$\begin{aligned} C &= max(0, 62 - 65) \\ &= max(0, -3) \\ &= 0 \end{aligned}$$

Many people use the term *intrinsic value* when describing the minimum value of an option. This term implies that this is the true worth of the option, but an option can have a true worth and market value that are greater than its minimum value. Therefore, we will use the term *minimum value* rather than *intrinsic value.*

A put option also has a minimum value. The same arbitrage principle operating in the Exxon 60 call option in the previous example operates with put options. Take, for example, an Exxon 65 put. The holder of this option could buy Exxon on the NYSE for $62 and immediately exercise the put and sell the stock for $65, giving the investor a net cash inflow of $3. The minimum value of this put would therefore be 3. We can express a put's minimum value as:

$$P_m = max(0, X - S) \tag{17–2}$$

where P_m = the minimum value of a put option

Equation 17–2 gives the minimum value of a put as the greater of zero or the put's exercise price minus the stock price. Example 17–2 provides an illustration of the use of Equation 17–2.

EXAMPLE 17–2

What is the minimum value of a put option on Exxon with exercise price of 60? Exxon sells for 62.

$$\begin{aligned} P &= max(0, 60 - 62) \\ &= max(0, -2) \\ &= 0 \end{aligned}$$

What is the minimum value of a put with exercise price of 65?

$$\begin{aligned} P &= max(0, 65 - 62) \\ &= max(0, 3) \\ &= 3 \end{aligned}$$

The Value of an Option at Expiration

The minimum value of any option only establishes a floor value below which the price of the option will not fall unless the stock price changes. As we have already mentioned, the option may have a value greater than the minimum value. The only time when an option's market price should be equal to its minimum value is just before expiration. At that time, the true value of an option is equal to its value if exercised. However, at any date before expiration, the option's value will be greater than its minimum value.

The Value of an Option before Expiration

The minimum value of an option derives from the fact that an option holder can exercise the option at any time before its expiration. However, the only time that an option's market value should be equal to the minimum value is at expiration. While the option has time remaining, the option will have *time value.* The time value of an option gives it a total value that exceeds the minimum value. An option's time value is equal to the market price of the option less the option's minimum value.

Why does an option have value associated with the time remaining to expiration? An example should explain: Take the Exxon 65 call option with Exxon selling for 62, in Example 17–1. Assume the option has three months of life remaining and a market price of 2. For the option to have any minimum value at all, Exxon would have to rise by three points (from 62 to 65) over the next three months. This may not be a sure bet, but it would not be unusual for Exxon's stock to increase by three or more points over three months. Over three months, it is conceivable that Exxon could go up five, ten, or even fifteen points. Therefore, the Exxon 65 call option can have a positive value based on the probability that Exxon will rise above 65 before the option expires. The market assigned a value of 2 to the option.

Now, let's examine the situation after two months have passed. Suppose that Exxon stock went up a little and down a little, but after two months it once again stands at 62. Is the Exxon 65 call still worth 2? It now has only one month left before expiring. One month gives the stock much less time to rise by very much. There is now less probability that Exxon could rise by five, ten, or fifteen points. Over only one month, it is very unlikely that Exxon would rise by fifteen or even ten points. Because of this, the Exxon 65 call option should be worth something less than 2. It would probably be valued somewhere around 1/2.

This illustrates how the time value of an option decreases with time. The time value will fall over the life of the option until it becomes zero at expiration. This is the reason why many market observers call options *wasting assets.* Figure 17–1 shows how the value of an option deteriorates with the passage of time as expiration approaches.

Figure 17–1 holds stock price and other variables constant. Changes in these other variables can change the value of an option and are important to the study of option valuation. In addition to the time to expiration, what other variables affect the price of an option?

One is the price of the underlying stock. As the price of a share of stock rises, the value of a call option will rise, and the value of a put will fall. In a similar fashion, an option's exercise price is an important variable. Call options with higher exercise prices will have lower market values, and put options with higher exercise prices will have higher market prices.

Another factor influencing the value of options is the risk or variability of the underlying stock's price. The more volatile the stock, the greater the chance of the option paying off. Therefore, options on stocks with higher volatility (higher variances of return) will have greater market value than options on low variance stocks. This is true for both puts and calls.

One factor common to all financial valuation models is the time value of money. In the valuation models for common stock and bonds, the time value of money is implicit in the required rate of return. For options, the time value of money is represented by interest rates, specifically the risk-free interest rate. When interest rates rise, holders of common stock will demand a higher price to write call options against the stock. (Otherwise, the high interest rate might induce them to sell the stock and

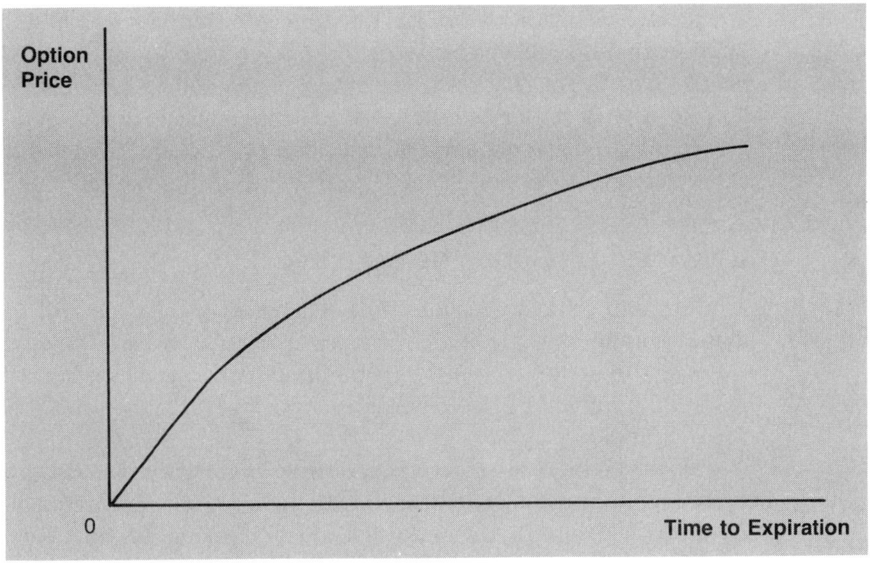

FIGURE 17–1
Deterioration in an option's price as expiration approaches (stock price and other factors held constant)

put the money in bonds or savings.) Therefore, higher interest rates result in higher prices for call options. The opposite is the case for puts; higher interest rates mean lower put values.

A final variable affecting option values is a cash dividend paid on the common stock. Holders of options are not entitled to receive dividends; only stockholders receive dividends. When a stock goes ex-dividend, it falls in price by an amount approximately equal to the dividend. This ex-dividend price drop tends to make call options on dividend-paying stocks slightly less valuable and put options worth slightly more than a similar option on a non-dividend-paying stock.

Table 17–1 summarizes the factors that determine option values. It also provides the direction of change in the option prices for a given change in each factor.

TABLE 17–1
Relationships between option prices and the factors influencing option prices

Factor	*Influence on Call Prices*	*Influence on Put Prices*
Stock price	direct	inverse
Exercise price	inverse	direct
Time to expiration	direct	direct
Riskless interest rate	direct	inverse
Stock volatility (risk)	direct	direct
Cash dividend for stock	inverse	direct

Option valuation theory has become an important area in financial research and in option trading. The basic valuation model for options is the *Black-Scholes option pricing model.* The Black-Scholes model is generally accepted and used in some form by many option traders. Because of the mathematical rigor of option valuation theory, this chapter relegates discussion of option pricing and the development of the Black-Scholes model to Appendix 17–A at the end of the chapter.

When Will an Option Be Exercised?

Because an option with some time left before expiration will have a value greater than its minimum value, it is "worth more alive than dead." No rational investor would exercise the option to receive its minimum value if the option could be sold in the market for a greater price. Therefore, options will not normally be exercised before their expiration.

However, there are some exceptions in which early exercise is the optimal strategy. Early exercise is usually associated with the payment of a cash dividend. Since holders have no claim on the dividend that the stock pays, the only way they can receive a declared dividend is to exercise the option before the stock's ex-dividend date. When the stock pays a relatively high dividend and the option has a relatively short time to expiration, it may be beneficial for the option holder to exercise the option before the ex-dividend date in order to receive the cash dividend and avoid the fall in value of the option on the ex-dividend date.

Even at expiration, most options will not be exercised. Several reasons help explain why only a few options are ever exercised. First, options whose minimum value is zero will not be exercised. Second, most option traders are not interested in having a position in the stock, so they will sell their options rather than exercising them. Third, some options, such as those on stock indexes, are not exercisable into the underlying asset; upon exercise they are settled in cash. Only about 2 percent of all options are ever exercised.

EXAMPLE USE OF A CALL OPTION

Let us look at an example investment in a call option to show some risk and return characteristics of options. Table 17–2 gives an example of an Exxon 60 call option. Mr. Ron Slone is considering purchasing either Exxon's stock or its call option, which has three months left until expiration. The price of the Exxon 60 call in the options market is 4. This Exxon 60 call currently has a minimum value of 2 because the price of Exxon stock is 62. There are many possible prices for Exxon stock three months from now. The prices listed in the first column of Table 17–2 represent a range of likely prices for Exxon at, above, and below its current price. These are not the only possible prices for Exxon, but they bracket the likeliest range of Exxon prices three months from now.

Let's begin with the situation in which the stock's price remains unchanged at the option's expiration date. At this point the option's market value (also its minimum

TABLE 17–2
Example investment in an in-the-money call option[a]

(a) Possible Stock Price at Expiration	*(b)* Option Price at Expiration $max(0, (a) - 60)$	*(c)* Profit on Option $(b) - 4$	*(d)* Return on Option $(c)/4$	*(e)* Profit on Stock $(a) - 62$	*(f)* Return on Stock $(e)/62$
55	0	−4	−1.00	−7	−.11
60	0	−4	−1.00	−2	−.03
62	2	−2	−.50	0	0
65	5	+1	+.25	+3	+.05
70	10	+6	+1.50	+8	+.13
75	15	+11	+2.75	+13	+.21

[a]Stock: Exxon
Option: Call
Exercise price: 60
Stock price: 62
Option price: 4

value) will be 2, and Mr. Slone will have lost half of his original investment of 4 on the call option. However, had Mr. Slone invested in Exxon stock instead, he would have suffered no loss. The risk in an option becomes apparent when we examine the return. The option's return was −.5 (a 50 percent loss), while the stock return was 0. However, because the option has a positive value, Mr. Slone would want to sell it before the expiration to minimize his loss. He would certainly not want to let it expire. (Alternatively, of course, Mr. Slone could exercise the option if he wanted to own Exxon common stock.)

On the downside, decreases in Exxon's price to 60 or 55 would result in the option being worthless at expiration. In this case, Mr. Slone would let the call option expire. His dollar loss on the option would be 4 compared to losses in the stock of 2 (stock = 60) or 7 (stock = 55). The latter case shows how investment in call options can allow an investor to limit losses when the stock falls considerably in price. The investor's loss is limited to the price paid for the option. Even if Exxon fell to 40 (a loss of 22 per share), the option holder's loss would only be 4. However, on the return side, Mr. Slone would have lost all of his investment in the call option, a loss of 100 percent of funds invested in the option. Stock returns would be −.03 or −.11.

On the gain side, a rise in the stock's price to 65 would give Mr. Slone a profit of 1 on his option or a profit of 3 on the stock. Looking at the return, the option yielded .25 while the stock increased by only .05. Although the stock rose by 3 when the option increased by 1, the option's return was much greater than the stock's. This is another example of the risk and leverage associated with an option position. The leverage becomes even more pronounced when the stock rises to 70. The 13 percent return on the stock compares to a 150 percent return on the option.

In this example, the Exxon 60 call option retained some value at expiration when the stock remained unchanged. The reason for this is that the option was *in the money* at the time of purchase. An in-the-money option has a positive minimum value. Another

TABLE 17–3
In-the-money and out-of-the-money options

	Out of the Money When	*At the Money When*	*In the Money When*
Put option	$S^a > X^a$	$S = X$	$S < X$
Call option	$S < X$	$S = X$	$S > X$

[a]Symbols: S = Stock price
X = Exercise price of the option

way of stating this is that a call option is in the money when the stock price is greater than the option's exercise price. When the stock's price is below the call option's exercise price, the option is *out of the money*. An out-of-the-money option, therefore, will have a minimum value of zero. The relationship of stock price to exercise price reverses for the definition of in-the-money and out-of-the-money puts. A put is out of the money when the stock price is greater than the exercise price and in the money when the stock price is less than the exercise price. Table 17–3 summarizes these relationships. Traders also define *at-the-money options* as those whose exercise price equals the stock price.

The risk-return characteristics of in-the-money options are different from those of out-of-the-money options. Generally speaking, out-of-the-money options provide more leverage and are more risky than their in-the-money counterparts. When an investor purchases an out-of-the-money option and the stock price fails to reach the exercise price by expiration, the investor loses the entire initial investment in the option. Table 17–4 gives the profit and return for an out-of-the-money option on Exxon, with an exercise price of 65. Compare these potential returns to the returns on the in-the-money call in Table 17–2.

TABLE 17–4
Example investment in an out-of-the-money call option[a]

(a) Possible Stock Price at Expiration	*(b)* Option Price at Expiration max(0, (a) − 65)	*(c)* Profit on Option (b) − 2	*(d)* Return on Option (c)/2	*(e)* Profit on Stock (a) − 62	*(f)* Return on Stock (e)/62
55	0	−2	−1.00	−7	−.11
60	0	−2	−1.00	−2	−.03
62	0	−2	−1.00	0	0
65	0	−2	−1.00	+3	+.05
70	5	+3	1.50	+8	+.13
75	10	+8	4.00	+13	+.21

[a]Stock: Exxon
Option: Call
Exercise price: 65
Stock price: 62
Option price: 2

In Tables 17–2 and 17–4, we assumed that the option was held until expiration. Remember that an investor can sell his option in the market anytime before expiration, and many option traders do close out their positions as market conditions change. Our examples use the expiration day prices because this is the only day on which our formula for the minimum value of an option also represents the option's market value.

EXAMPLE USE OF A PUT OPTION

To illustrate the response of a put option to changes in the stock's price, consider the case of Ms. Ilsa Brady who believes that Exxon's price is about to fall. Ms. Brady could sell Exxon stock short to profit from the stock's decline in price, but she instead might consider purchasing a put option. Table 17–5 shows various prices on expiration for an Exxon 60 put purchased at an initial price of 1.5. Note how Ms. Brady profits on the put when Exxon falls in price, and how the put expires worthless when Exxon remains the same (because this put was out of the money) and when Exxon rises.

THE OPTIONS MARKET

Many of the established stock and commodity exchanges also trade options, and there is one exchange dedicated solely to trading options. Exchange trading of options began in April 1973, when the Chicago Board Options Exchange (CBOE) began a pilot program, trading call options on sixteen different stocks. The experiment was so successful that other exchanges soon followed with options on other stocks. As popularity grew, the exchanges added trading in puts and more options on more stocks.

TABLE 17–5
Example investment in put option[a]

(a) Possible Stock Price at Expiration	*(b)* Option Price at Expiration *max*(0,60 − (*a*))	*(c)* Profit on Option (*b*) − 1.5	*(d)* Return on Option (*c*)/1.5	*(e)* Profit on Stock (*a*) − 62	*(f)* Return on Stock (*e*)/62
50	10	+8.5	+5.67	−12	−.19
55	5	+3.5	+2.33	−7	−.11
60	0	−1.5	−1.00	−2	−.03
62	0	−1.5	−1.00	0	0
65	0	−1.5	−1.00	+3	+.05
70	0	−1.5	−1.00	+8	+.13

[a]Stock: Exxon
Option: Put
Exercise price: 60
Stock price: 62
Option price: 1.50

The commencement of exchange-traded options was not the birth of options. Options have existed for hundreds of years. Before the CBOE began in 1973, stock options in the United States were limited to over-the-counter trading. Brokerage firms specializing in options would offer puts and calls for sale to investors. However, these options had disadvantages that restricted their activity to a very small number of investors and traders. There was practically no liquidity in this OTC options market, and many option holders could not sell their options before expiration and were forced to exercise their options to get the value from them. Many of these old OTC options were expensive and costly to traders wanting to play the options game. The beginning of option trading on the exchanges signaled a new era for these instruments. The innovations and advantages that exchange-listed option trading offered contributed significantly to the growth of option trading.

Innovations of Listed Option Trading

The innovations that listed option trading brought to the market were threefold:

1. Standardized terms
2. Liquidity
3. The Options Clearing Corporation

Standardized Terms

A big barrier to liquidity in the trading of the old OTC options was the fact that the option's terms (exercise price and exercise date) were not standardized. For example, if Exxon stock was trading for 48½ when a customer contacted the broker to buy a call on Exxon, the option would normally be assigned an exercise price equal to Exxon's current price (48½) and an expiration date one, three, or six months, or one year from the current date. Over time, many different call options on Exxon could come into existence. No one option with the same exercise price and expiration date would exist in quantities sufficient to warrant an active aftermarket. Listed option trading solved this problem by limiting option trading to the most popular stocks and establishing standard exercise prices and expiration dates for options on these *optionable stocks.*

Standard Expiration Dates. The standard expiration date for stock options is the Saturday following the third Friday of the month. Because the exchanges are not open on Saturdays, the last day of trading—and therefore the effective expiration date—is the third Friday of the month. Therefore, all Exxon October options have their final trading date on the third Friday of October.

The expiration months for each stock vary, depending upon the expiration cycle the exchange assigns to the stock. The most common expiration cycles are as follows:

1. January, April, July, October
2. February, May, August, November
3. March, June, September, December

At any one time, expiration months up to nine months in the future may trade. For example, Exxon options trade on the first cycle. If today were June 3, Exxon July, October, and January (of next year) options would be trading. After the July series expires, the exchange will open trading in the April (next year) series.

In addition, the exchange may add trading for an additional current month or near-term month. In the case of the Exxon example on June 3, the June expiration month would also trade. Options on other stocks or on other instruments may have monthly or other expiration cycles. For example, the exchanges usually set up the expirations for index options at monthly intervals extending up to four months in the future. Option traders should consult the financial press or their brokers for specific expirations currently available for a particular option.

Standard Exercise Prices. Standard exercise prices for stock options are typically at multiples of 5 for stocks selling below 100 and at multiples of 10 for stocks priced above 100. The exchange usually allows trading to begin in an exercise price when the stock price comes within three points of that exercise price. With Exxon selling for 62, options with exercise prices of 60 and 65 would probably be traded. As the market price of Exxon stock changed, the exchange would allow new exercise prices to begin trading.

At any one time, many combinations of exercise price and expiration dates may trade, depending upon the recent fluctuations in the stock price. For example, if Exxon stock had fluctuated recently between 50 and 70, then options with exercise prices of 50, 55, 60, 65, and 70 would trade. Each of these might have several different expiration dates available, so that there might be fifteen or more different exercise price–expiration date combinations of call options for Exxon stock.

Once the exchange opens trading in a particular option, the option will continue to trade even though the stock price may change considerably. For example, even when the price of Exxon rises to 62, the exercise price 50 options will continue to trade until they expire.

Liquidity

The existence of standard expiration dates and exercise prices limits the number of different options on any one stock. This allows a sufficient quantity of each exercise price–expiration date combination to exist to maintain a liquid market for the options. The presence of the exchange provides the mechanism for this liquid market to exist so that option holders do not have to exercise their options, but can sell them in the market. For the market to exist, however, there has to be one other factor. This is the Options Clearing Corporation.

The Options Clearing Corporation

The *Options Clearing Corporation (OCC),* a corporation funded by the options exchanges, is an important party in the options market. The first major function of the OCC is to act as the intermediary between option buyers and option writers. Recall that an option is essentially a contract between the option holder and the option writer. If every option written in the market required that the buyer and writer agree upon and sign a contract, a liquid options market would not be feasible. The OCC plays the role of guarantor of all options contracts. It severs the link between buyer and seller by becoming the seller to the buyer and the buyer to the seller. The buyer of an option therefore need not worry whether the seller will make good the contract. The contract is with the OCC, which guarantees all contracts.

A second important function of the OCC is to match buyers and sellers of options contracts and to assign delivery in the event of exercise of a contract. An example serves best to explain this process. Table 17–6 shows option buyer and writer positions

TABLE 17–6
Process of opening and closing option positions

***Frame A:* A, B, and C buy options; D, E, and F write them**

Buyers		*Writers*	
Name	*Status*	*Name*	*Status*
A	open	D	open
B	open	E	open
C	open	F	open

open interest = 3

***Frame B:* A sells option; G buys it**

Buyers		*Writers*	
Name	*Status*	*Name*	*Status*
A	closed	D	open
B	open	E	open
C	open	F	open
G	open		

open interest = 3

***Frame C:* C sells option; E buys it**

Buyers		*Writers*	
Name	*Status*	*Name*	*Status*
A	closed	D	open
B	open	E	closed
C	closed	F	open
G	open		

open interest = 2

***Frame D:* B exercises option; OCC assigns exercise to D**

Buyers		*Writers*	
Name	*Status*	*Name*	*Status*
A	closed	D	assigned exercise
B	exercised	E	closed
C	closed	F	open
G	open		

open interest = 1

which would be reflected on the OCC's records for a series of transactions in options on one stock.

Beginning with Frame A in Table 17–6, option investors A, B, and C purchase Exxon July 60 call options, which are written by D, E, and F, respectively. These are *opening transactions* because each party had no previous position in the option. After an opening transaction, an option trader has an *open position*. At this point, the Exxon July 60 call option has an *open interest* of three contracts. *Open interest* is the term defining the number of outstanding contracts that currently exist for an option. Open interest must always balance the number of contracts on the buyer side with the number on the seller side. Frame B shows the changes when A decides to sell her option and another investor, G, buys it. The OCC transfers ownership of this option to G on its books, and open interest remains at three. For A, this was a *closing transaction* because she has now closed out an existing position. Frame C illustrates the effect of investor C's decision to sell and E's decision to close out his short position by buying back an option. Note that E does not have to buy back the exact option that he originally sold to B; any Exxon July 60 call will suffice. Because both a buyer and a writer closed positions, open interest falls to two. Finally, in Frame D, B decides to exercise her Exxon option and notifies her broker. The broker sends notice of exercise to the OCC, which assigns exercise to the writer on the top of the list.

The OCC and the member brokerage firms keep all records of the ownership of options. It is *certificateless trading,* in which no certificates are issued as evidence of ownership, unlike the situation for stocks and bonds. Certificateless trading greatly simplifies the recordkeeping and clearing process for the exchanges and brokerage firms.

The Options Exchanges

The success of the Chicago Board Options Exchange ensured that others would soon follow. The CBOE's position as the first options exchange has made it the largest options exchange with the highest contract volume. The second exchange on the options scene, the American Stock Exchange, is second in volume. Table 17–7 shows the various exchanges that trade stock and index options, and it also summarizes the types of contracts they trade.

The AMEX, NYSE, and Philadelphia exchanges use a specialist system for maintaining a market in their options. The CBOE and Pacific exchanges have a system of competing market makers on the exchange floor. The National Association of Securities Dealers uses its computerized system of market makers.

The exchanges supervise and regulate the activities of their member firms. They set capital requirements for all members and market makers. The regulatory authority for the options exchanges falls to the SEC.

Options Quotations

The financial press carries quotations of most of the actively traded options. Figure 17–2 shows some sample quotations from *The Wall Street Journal.*

TABLE 17–7
Options exchanges and their contracts

Exchange	*Types of Contract*
American Stock Exchange	debt options equity options index options
Chicago Board Options Exchange	debt options equity options foreign currency options index options
National Association of Securities Dealers	index options
New York Stock Exchange	equity options index options
Pacific Stock Exchange	equity options index options
Philadelphia Stock Exchange	equity options foreign currency options

Option Margin Requirements

The margin requirements for establishing option positions are different from those for stocks and bonds. The settlement procedure is also different. Option traders must settle their account on the first business day following the trade. For option buyers, this means that sufficient cash must be in the account the next day. Of course, delivery of options sold is easy because certificateless trading means that the brokerage firm already has possession of the option.

Option Buyer Margin Requirements

The margin requirements for long option positions are simple. They are always 100 percent, meaning that option buyers must pay the entire price of the option in cash. Option buyers may not borrow any portion of the price of an option on margin. The reason for this is that options are already leveraged securities. The SEC sees no need to allow option buyers to leverage further by purchasing options on margin.

Option Writer Margin Requirements

The margin requirements for short positions in options are different, depending upon whether the position is naked or covered.

Covered Margin. For covered calls, no additional margin is required. The stock covering the option must be on deposit with the brokerage firm.

There are no covered positions for put options. Although being short the un-

LISTED OPTIONS QUOTATIONS

Monday, September 12, 1988

Options closing prices. Sales unit usually is 100 shares.
Stock close is New York or American exchange final price.

PHILADELPHIA

Option & NY Close	Strike Price	Calls–Last Sep	Calls–Last Oct	Calls–Last Nov	Puts–Last Sep	Puts–Last Oct	Puts–Last Nov
Abbt L	45	3 3/4	r	4 3/8	r	r	r
48 3/4	50	1/8	3/4	1 1/4	r	1 7/8	r
A Hess	25	r	r	1 7/8	r	r	3/4
26	30	r	r	3/8	r	r	r
Armco	10	1/4	1/2	r	r	r	r
AutDt	35	2	3 1/2	3 3/8	r	9/16	3/4
37 1/4	40	1/16	9/16	1	r	r	3 3/8
37 1/4	45	r	r	1/4	r	r	r
CinMil	30	r	s	1/4	r	s	r
CmdrIn	12 1/2	1/16	7/16	5/8	r	r	r
11 5/8	15	r	r	3/16	r	r	r
CntlCp	40	r	r	r	r	r	1 3/8
FarmGp	55	15 5/8	r	16 5/8	r	r	5/16
70 5/8	65	5 5/8	r	7 3/4	r	7/16	r
70 5/8	70	5/8	2	3 3/8	1/16	13/16	r
GaGulf	70	3 3/8	r	r	1/8	r	2
73	75	3/4	2 5/8	3 1/8	r	r	4 3/8
GoldWF	30	r	3/4	1	r	r	r
Harnis	20	1/8	7/16	r	r	r	r
HomeD	22 1/2	3 1/4	r	r	r	r	r
25 3/4	25	1 1/4	1 1/2	2 1/4	1/8	3/4	r
25 3/4	30	r	r	1/2	4 3/8	r	r
Lehman	12 1/2	r	r	r	r	r	1/2
LinB	55	r	3 3/8	3 7/8	1/4	r	2 1/8
55 7/8	60	1/16	1	2	3 1/2	4 5/8	4 1/2
La Lnd	35	r	r	3/8	r	r	r
Lubriz	30	r	r	r	r	r	1/2
35 1/8	35	5/8	1 7/8	2 3/8	5/8	1 1/2	2 1/4
35 1/8	40	r	1/2	3/4	r	r	r
M C A	35	9 7/8	r	r	r	r	r
45	40	4 7/8	5 5/8	6 3/4	r	7/16	5/8
45	45	5/8	2 1/2	3 3/8	7/8	2 1/16	3
45	50	s	7/8	1 1/2	s	r	5 7/8
McDIn	20	1/16	r	1/2	r	r	r
McGHll	55	r	s	15 1/4	r	s	r
68 1/2	60	8 1/2	9 3/4	10 1/8	r	5/8	1 3/8
68 1/2	65	3 3/8	6	7	3/16	1 5/8	r
68 1/2	70	1/2	3 1/8	4 1/2	2	4	r

PACIFIC

Option & NY Close	Strike Price	Calls–Last Sep	Calls–Last Oct	Calls–Last Nov	Puts–Last Sep	Puts–Last Oct	Puts–Last Nov
C S X	25	1 1/4	r	r	1/8	r	r
26 1/4	30	r	r	1/4	r	r	r
CartHH	10	1/16	r	r	r	r	r
CentEn	15	r	r	1/8	r	r	r
E Sys	30	r	r	11/16	r	r	r
Ensrch	20	r	3/8	r	r	r	r
GenuPt	35	3/4	r	r	r	r	r
KingWP	20	2 1/4	r	r	r	r	r
22 5/8	22 1/2	3/8	1	1 3/8	r	r	r
22 5/8	25	r	r	1/2	r	r	r
Mc D D	65	1/4	1 3/8	1 7/8	r	r	r
McKess	35	r	15/16	r	r	1 3/8	r
Melvil	70	r	r	r	r	r	3 1/4
RynMtl	50	1 3/4	r	3 3/4	1/2	r	1 7/8
50 7/8	55	r	7/8	1 1/2	r	4 1/2	r
Rubbmd	25	r	7/16	r	r	r	r
Ryder	25	5/8	1	1 1/2	3/8	r	r
25	30	r	r	1/8	r	r	r
Scher	45	r	s	r	r	s	1/4
52 7/8	55	1/8	7/8	1 7/8	2 1/8	r	r
Travel	35	r	1	1 1/8	r	r	r

AMERICAN

Option & NY Close	Strike Price	Calls–Last Sep	Calls–Last Oct	Calls–Last Nov	Puts–Last Sep	Puts–Last Oct	Puts–Last Nov
A M R	40	r	6	r	r	r	r
46	45	1 1/8	2 7/16	3 1/4	1/4	r	1 3/4
46	50	r	3/4	1 3/16	r	r	r
A S A	35	2 1/2	3 1/4	3 3/4	1/16	5/8	1 1/4
37 1/4	40	1/16	3/4	1 3/16	2 3/4	r	3 3/4
37 1/4	45	r	s	5/16	r	s	r
37 1/4	50	s	s	1/8	s	s	r
AFamly	12 1/2	r	r	3/4	r	r	r
Arkla	20	r	r	3/8	r	r	r
Avnet	20	r	r	1 3/4	r	r	r
Bally	17 1/2	r	r	4 3/4	r	1/8	r
21 5/8	20	1 3/4	2 5/8	2 3/4	r	1/2	5/8
21 5/8	22 1/2	1/8	7/8	1 3/8	7/8	r	1 5/8
21 5/8	25	1/16	s	5/8	r	s	r
CaesrW	25	1 1/4	r	r	r	r	r
Caterp	50	r	r	r	r	r	1/2
56 1/8	55	1 1/2	3	3 3/4	3/16	1 1/4	1 7/8
56 1/8	60	1/16	11/16	1 1/4	3 5/8	r	r
ColuGs	35	r	1/2	r	r	r	r
Con Ed	40	r	r	4	r	r	r
43	45	r	r	9/16	r	r	2 3/8
CoopCo	10	1/4	3/4	1	r	3/4	r
9 7/8	12 1/2	r	3/16	1/4	2 1/2	r	r
9 7/8	15	s	s	1/8	s	s	r
DunBrd	45	5 7/8	r	r	r	r	r
50	50	13/16	2	2 5/8	r	7/8	r
50	55	r	r	9/16	r	r	r
Fleetw	22 1/2	r	3/4	r	r	r	r
Glaxo	17 1/2	r	1/2	3/4	r	r	3/4

NEW YORK

Option & NY Close	Strike Price	Calls–Last Sep	Calls–Last Oct	Calls–Last Nov	Puts–Last Sep	Puts–Last Oct	Puts–Last Nov
CSoup	25	r	r	3 3/4	r	r	r
FMC Cp	35	3/8	1 5/8	2 1/8	r	r	r
34 3/4	40	r	r	3/8	r	r	r
Trnsco	30	r	r	4 1/4	r	5/16	r
33 3/8	35	r	1 1/8	r	r	r	r
VF Cp	30	r	11/16	1 1/8	r	r	r
		Sep	Oct	Dec	Sep	Oct	Dec
Houstnl	30	r	r	r	1	r	r
29	35	r	r	r	6	r	r
IngRnd	35	r	2	3	r	1/2	r
36 1/4	40	1/16	r	r	3 5/8	r	r
JRiver	25	1 1/2	r	2 5/8	r	r	r
26 1/2	30	r	5/16	r	r	r	r
Shearsn	22 1/2	r	1 1/4	1 3/4	r	r	r
22 3/8	25	r	r	3/4	r	r	r
TimesM	30	1 1/2	r	2 13/16	r	r	r
		Sep	Oct	Jan	Sep	Oct	Jan
Chubb	50	r	7 7/8	r	r	r	r
57 5/8	60	r	r	r	r	r	4
Intpub	35	r	r	1 1/8	r	r	r
IrvBk	60	r	r	r	r	r	7/8
69 1/8	65	4 1/8	r	r	r	r	r
69 1/8	70	r	2 1/4	r	r	r	r
Maytag	20	3 1/4	r	3 7/8	r	r	r
23 1/8	22 1/2	9/16	1 3/8	r	3/16	r	1 1/2
23 1/8	25	1/16	7/16	1 5/16	1 3/4	r	r
Nynex	60	r	r	r	r	r	7/8
64 1/2	65	1/4	3/4	1 5/8	r	r	r
64 1/2	70	r	r	1/2	r	r	r

CHICAGO BOARD

Option & NY Close	Strike Price	Calls–Last Sep	Calls–Last Oct	Calls–Last Nov	Puts–Last Sep	Puts–Last Oct	Puts–Last Nov
AlexAl	25	1/8	r	r	r	r	r
Amdahl	17 1/2	s	2 1/2	r	s	r	13/16
19 5/8	20	5/16	1 1/8	1 1/2	5/8	1 1/4	r
19 5/8	22 1/2	r	3/8	3/4	2 1/2	r	r
19 5/8	25	r	3/16	1/2	r	r	r
Amoco	70	r	r	4 1/2	r	r	1 1/8
73	75	1/16	r	1 1/2	r	r	3 5/8
A M P	40	r	r	r	r	1/2	r
42 3/8	45	1/8	7/8	r	r	r	r
Baxter	20	1 3/4	2	2 1/8	r	r	5/16
21 3/4	22 1/2	1/8	7/16	3/4	r	r	1 1/8
21 3/4	25	s	s	3/16	s	s	3 1/2
Blk Dk	20	1 1/8	r	2	r	r	r
Boeing	50	s	s	11 1/8	s	s	r
60 3/4	55	6	6 1/4	r	1/16	r	r
60 3/4	60	1 1/4	2 1/2	3 3/8	7/16	1 1/8	2 1/8
60 3/4	65	1/16	9/16	1	r	4 3/4	5
Bois C	45	r	r	1 1/8	r	r	r
42 3/4	50	r	s	1/4	r	s	r
42 3/4	55	s	s	1/16	s	s	r
Brunos	10	r	r	r	r	r	7/16
C B S	150	15 1/4	s	r	r	s	13/16
165 5/8	155	10	11	r	r	r	r
165 5/8	160	r	r	9 1/4	r	1 5/8	3 1/4
165 5/8	165	r	5 3/8	r	1	r	r
165 5/8	170	r	s	5	r	s	8
CapCit	290	s	s	r	s	s	3/4
332 1/2	310	r	22	r	r	r	r
332 1/2	320	11 1/2	r	18 1/8	r	r	4
332 1/2	330	2 1/4	r	r	2 1/2	r	7 7/8
332 1/2	340	s	s	6 7/8	s	s	9
Coke	35	r	7 1/8	r	r	1/16	r
42	40	1 3/4	2 5/8	3	1/16	1/2	5/8
42	45	r	3/8	5/8	r	r	r
CocaCE	15	r	r	1/4	r	r	r
13 3/8	17 1/2	r	s	1/16	r	s	r
Colgat	45	3/8	1 3/8	1 3/4	r	1	1 7/8
44 3/4	50	s	s	1/4	s	s	r
Cmw Ed	30	7/16	r	7/8	r	r	7/8
C Data	20	r	3 3/4	r	r	r	r
23 1/4	22 1/2	1 7/16	r	2	r	r	r
23 1/4	25	1/16	1/2	1	r	r	r
CornGl	55	r	r	r	1/16	1/2	5/8
58 7/8	60	r	1 3/8	2 1/4	r	r	r
58 7/8	65	r	s	r	6	s	r
Edwrds	17 1/2	r	r	r	r	1/2	r
ForstL	22 1/2	r	r	7/8	r	r	r
FptMc	25	r	3/4	r	1/4	r	r
GnCine	20	r	r	2	r	r	1
Gn Dyn	55	r	r	r	r	r	4 1/2
Gdrich	45	7 1/2	8	9	r	3/8	r
52 5/8	50	3	4 3/4	r	1/4	r	r
52 5/8	55	1/4	2	3 1/4	2 5/8	r	r
52 5/8	60	s	1	1 3/4	s	r	r
Hewlet	40	9	9 5/8	r	r	r	1/4
49	45	4 1/2	5 1/8	5 1/2	1/8	7/16	15/16
49	50	5/16	1 13/16	2 1/2	1 1/4	2	2 3/4
49	55	r	s	3/4	r	s	6
49	60	s	s	1/4	s	s	r
Holidy	25	r	r	1 3/8	1	1 1/4	r
Honwll	55	6 7/8	r	r	r	r	r
61 1/4	60	2	3 1/4	4	r	r	r
61 1/4	65	1/8	r	1 3/4	r	r	r
61 1/4	70	r	s	3/8	r	s	r
Humana	22 1/2	r	r	2 1/4	r	r	r
24 1/4	25	r	1/2	3/4	r	r	r
InfoRs	12 1/2	1/8	r	7/8	r	r	r
Limitd	20	1 3/4	r	3 3/8	r	r	1/2
21 3/4	22 1/2	1/16	r	1 1/8	r	r	r
21 3/4	25	r	s	1/2	r	s	3 1/2
Medtrn	80	r	2 3/8	r	r	r	r
Mobil	40	r	r	3 3/8	r	r	r
42 1/2	45	1/16	3/8	5/8	2 1/2	2 3/4	3
42 1/2	50	r	s	1/8	r	s	r
N Semi	10	1/16	3/8	5/8	3/4	1 1/8	1 1/8
9 1/8	12 1/2	r	s	3/16	r	s	r
9 1/8	15	s	s	1/16	s	s	r
Nthrop	30	r	1 1/8	2 1/2	r	1/2	1
Noxell	20	r	r	5/8	r	r	r

FIGURE 17–2
Sample option quotations *(Source: Reprinted by permission of The Wall Street Journal,* © Dow Jones & Company, Inc. [1987]. All Rights Reserved.)

derlying stock will partially cover a put writer's risk, all short put positions are uncovered.

Naked Margins. The margin requirements for uncovered positions can become quite complicated. Actually, the margin for option positions is not the same concept as it is for stocks. With stocks, the investor's margin is the amount of collateral placed in the account, with the remainder of the purchase price of the stock being borrowed from the broker. With naked option positions, the broker really does not lend any money to the writer, so it is not true margin. A better term would be a *security deposit* or *performance margin* that ensures that the writer has the financial means to honor the option contract. However, we will continue to use the term "margin," since it is standard in the industry. Naked option writers can even post most of the margin (about 90 percent) in U.S. Treasury bills and have the added advantage of continuing to *receive* interest on their T-bills while the option position is open. In contrast, investors *pay* interest when buying stock on margin.

The basic margin requirement for naked call option positions on stock options is as follows:

$$M_c = .3 \times S + (S - X) \qquad \textbf{(17–3)}$$

where M_c = the margin required for a naked call position

Equation 17–3 shows that a naked call's margin deposit should be at least equal to 30 percent of the stock's price plus the amount by which the option is in the money. There are other considerations when determining the naked margin. First, since the writer receives the price of the call when it is first written, the initial margin needed to establish the position is Equation 17–3 less the price of the call. Second, the margin is always subject to a minimum of $2.50, regardless of the value given by Equation 17–3.

For writing.puts, the formula for the margin is:

$$M_p = .3 \times S + (X - S) \qquad \textbf{(17–4)}$$

where M_p = the margin required for writing a put

As in the case of the call option, the margin for a put is subject to a minimum amount of $2.50 per share, and the initial requirement is reduced by the sales price of the put. In addition, because the put writer has an obligation to buy the stock, the put's margin can be no more than the amount of money needed to buy the stock. If the stock is "marginable," then the amount needed to purchase the stock is equal to the margin requirement times the stock price.

OPTIONS ON STOCK INDEXES

So far, our discussion has concentrated on options written on individual stocks. Stock options allow traders to "bet" on the future direction of the stock. To give traders the vehicle to "bet" on the future direction of the market, options on stock indexes emerged. Both put and call options trade on several market indexes.

TABLE 17–8
Index options

Exchange	*Index*
AMEX	Major Market Index Computer Technology Index Oil Index
CBOE	S&P 100 Index S&P 500 Index
NASD	NASDAQ 100 Index
NYSE	NYSE Composite Index Beta Index
Pacific	Technology Index
Philadelphia	Value Line Index National OTC Index

The basics of index options are the same as those for options on individual stocks. The contract terms and trading procedures are similar for both types of options. The terms of an index option specify the option's underlying index and the index *contract multiple.* The contract multiple is the number of times to multiply the index to get the total amount of index that the option represents. The contract multiple for all equity options is 100, because each option is for 100 shares. Most index options have contract multiples of 100, but some are larger.

The principal difference between equity options and index options is the exercise procedure. A market index is not a deliverable asset; therefore, the buyers and writers of index options settle in cash upon exercise. An option holder who exercises an index option receives the amount by which the option is in the money multiplied by the contract multiple.

Some index option contracts are backed by broadly based market indexes, while others are based on more narrowly defined industry indexes. Table 17–8 shows some of the popular index options and their exchanges. The exchanges created some of these indexes solely for the purpose of having a convenient index on which to trade options. The S&P 100 Index and AMEX Major Market Index are examples of specially created indexes.

DEBT OPTIONS

There are also several option contracts on debt instruments. The CBOE has contracts on several U.S. Treasury bond issues. These contracts are for $100,000 face amount of the T-bond. The AMEX trades contracts on $100,000 face amount of Treasury notes. These options allow investors and traders to profit from changes in bond prices and interest rates. However, the bulk of trading on interest-bearing instruments is in financial futures trading and trading in options on these futures. Chapter 19, "Futures Markets," discusses these instruments.

OPTION STRATEGY

Investors can integrate option positions into their investment strategies in many ways. Speculators looking for more leverage can buy options or write naked options. Income-oriented investors can write options against their stock portfolios to increase the current cash flow income from their investments. Investors who want to guard against a decline in the price of a stock can purchase put options on that stock. Others who are concerned about taxes can adopt certain option strategies to change their tax situation. The investment possibilities with options are practically endless because of the great number of possible combinations of option with underlying stock or other option.

There are three basic types of option strategy:

1. Scalping
2. Positioning
3. Hedging

Scalping

Scalping is the practice of establishing a position (either long or short) in a security and then quickly trying to reverse that position for a small profit. Scalpers try to make a gain of one eighth or one quarter of a point on the majority of their trades so that they have a net trading profit by the end of the day. However, it is doubtful that public traders who are not on the exchange floor can successfully profit from scalping. Because the profit of a scalper is so small, these traders are almost always market makers on exchanges that operate with the market maker system.

The market makers have two advantages that allow them to profit from scalping while public traders most likely cannot. First, they are on the floor of the exchange and can react immediately to market changes and forces. Second, they do not have to pay the commissions to brokerage houses that public traders do. Market makers have capital costs and expenses of exchange membership, but these expenses are not as high as brokerage commissions.

Positioning

A trader or investor who establishes a long or short position in an option without a counterbalancing position in the underlying stock or another option on the same stock is maintaining a strategy of *positioning*. A position trader usually has a belief that the underlying security will move in one direction before the option expires. For example, call option purchasers believe that the stock will rise in price. They buy the call option rather than the stock because the option offers leverage on the upside and limited loss on the downside. Because of these features, the objective of most position traders is speculation.

Hedging

A *hedged investment position* is one that contains two or more components. As market conditions change, the change in the value of one of these parts at least partially offsets the change in the other component. If the changes in the two positions offset each other exactly, it is a *perfect hedge*. For example, buying a stock and selling short the same stock would create a perfect hedge because as the stock rises in value, the increase in the long position would be exactly offset by a fall in value of the short position. (Of course, there would normally be no investment merits to buying and shorting the same stock simultaneously, except to increase the wealth of one's broker.) Hedged positions generally are less risky than each of their unhedged components considered separately.

Options are ideal instruments for hedging. They allow investors to alter the risk and return of an unhedged position, thereby expanding the investment uses for options. We can classify hedges into three categories:

1. Hedging with stock
2. Spreading
3. Combinations

Hedging with Stock

In option trading, hedging often involves a position in stock and some opposite position in an option on the stock. For example, a covered call option write is a hedged position because, as the price of the stock falls, the loss is at least partially offset by a gain from the written option. Another hedge using options and stock involves purchasing a put option as insurance against a fall in the value of stock held long. In this case, a drop in the stock price will be partially offset by a rise in the value of the put. The cost of the "insurance policy" is the price of the put.

Spreading

Because holding a call option long is similar to holding the stock, an option trader should be able to create a position similar to the covered option write by buying a call and writing another call on the same stock. This procedure results in a special type of hedge called a *spread*. A spread is any position containing different long and short options in combination on the same stock. The options may differ in exercise price, expiration date, or both.

Combinations

Hedged option positions can be even more exotic than those already discussed. There are dozens of different types of option *combinations* that an option trader could build. Some are complicated types of spreads, while others are mixtures of puts and calls. For example, a position composed of a put and a call on the same stock is a *straddle*.

Both options in the straddle typically have the same exercise price and expiration date.

SUMMARY

Contingent claim securities give their holders a claim on another security or asset subject to certain contingencies. Stock options are one category of contingent claim security. A call option gives its holders the right to buy the underlying common stock on or before the expiration date at the exercise price stated in the option. A put option carries the right to sell the stock. Options are contracts between the option holder and the option writer. A call option writer who owns the common stock is a covered writer, while one who has no position in the stock is a naked or uncovered writer.

The minimum value of an option describes the option's price at expiration. Before expiration, the option will have a market value that exceeds its minimum value.

Call options generally rise in price when the underlying stock rises, and put options rise in price when the stock falls. A call option is in the money (and a put is out of the money) when its stock price is above the exercise price. Call options are out of the money (and puts are in the money) when the stock price is less than the exercise price.

Exchange trading in listed stock options introduced three innovations to the market: standardized option terms, liquidity, and the Options Clearing Corporation. The OCC serves as an intermediary that guarantees all option contracts and assigns exercise of options to specific writers. The options exchanges add liquidity to the market by providing trading mechanisms and by supervising their member firms.

Option buyers must pay for their purchases in cash by the end of the first trading day following the transaction. The margin requirements for naked writers are based upon a formula that provides adequate capital should the option be exercised. Covered writers need only have the common stock on deposit with the brokerage firm.

Option valuation theory is based upon probability and the time value of money. The Black-Scholes option pricing model is the general valuation model used by option traders (see Appendix 17A).

Options trade on assets other than common stocks. Other options include stock index options based on market indexes and options on U.S. Treasury bonds and notes. Option theory can also be applied to the valuation of other assets, including common stock, preferred stock, mortgages, and the bid-ask spread in security trading.

Three basic option trading strategies are scalping, positioning, and hedging. Within these strategies, there are many specific option positions offering a wide range of risk-return trade-offs to option traders.

IMPORTANT TERMS

American option
Black-Scholes option pricing model
call option
certificateless trading
closing transaction
combination

contingent claim securities
contract multiple
covered writer
derivative assets
European option
exercise price
exercising the option
expiration date
floor
hedged investment position
intrinsic value
minimum value
naked writer
opening transaction
open interest
open position
optionable stock
Options Clearing Corporation (OCC)
positioning
premium
put option
scalping
spread
stock option
straddle
striking price (strike price)
time value
uncovered writer
underlying asset
wasting asset
writing the option

QUESTIONS AND PROBLEMS

1. Why are options called contingent claim securities? What other types of contingent claim securities exist?
2. Define the following terms:
   a) call option
   b) put option
   c) expiration date
   d) exercise price
   e) European option
   f) American option
3. Explain the process of option writing, including the difference between naked and covered writing.
4. Compute the minimum value of the following options:

Option	*Stock Price*	*Exercise Price*
call	42	40
call	37	30
call	52	55
put	50	55
put	32	30
put	20	20

5. Why should an option's minimum value and its market value be equal only on the expiration date?
6. What are the factors that determine the value of an option?
7. Would a call option on a relatively volatile stock be worth more or less than a call on a stock that is not so volatile? Why?
8. "Call options are a safe investment because they limit the downside risk of owning stock." Comment on this statement.
9. Identify each option in Question 4 as in the money or out of the money.

10. Identify and summarize the innovations contributed by listed option trading. Explain the importance of each of the innovations.
11. What is open interest? Might open interest be an indication of the liquidity of a particular option? Explain.
12. Compute the margin required to establish the following option positions:

Position	*Option Price*	*Exercise Price*	*Stock Price*
buy call	4	35	36
write naked call	7	45	49
buy put	2	80	88
write naked put	5	50	49

13. Compare and contrast options on individual stocks and options on stock indexes.
14. Identify and give an example of each of the three basic option trading strategies.

SELECTED REFERENCES

Black, Fisher (1975). "Fact and Fantasy in the Use of Options." *Financial Analysts Journal,* 31 (July-August), 36–72.

———, and Myron Scholes (1973). "The Valuation of Options and Corporate Liabilities." *Journal of Political Economy,* 81 (May), 637–659.

Cox, John C, and Stephen A. Ross (1976). "The Valuation of Options for Alternative Stochastic Processes." *Journal of Financial Economics,* 3 (March), 229–263.

Evnine, Jeremy, and Andrew Rudd (1984). "Option Portfolio Risk Analysis." *Journal of Portfolio Analysis,* 10 (Winter), 23–27.

French, Dan W. (1984). "The Weekend Effect on the Distribution of Stock Prices: Implications for Option Pricing." *Journal of Financial Economics,* 13 (December), 547–559.

——— (1983). "Black-Scholes vs. Kassouf Option Pricing." *Journal of Business Finance and Accounting,* 10 (Fall), 395–408.

Manaster, Steven, and Richard J. Rendleman, Jr. (1982). "Option Prices as Predictors of Equilibrium Stock Prices." *Journal of Finance,* 37 (September), 1043–1057.

Martin, Deryl W., and Dan W. French (1987). "The Characteristics of Interest Rates and Stock Variances Implied in Option Prices." *Journal of Economics and Business,* 39 (Fall), 279–288.

Merton, Robert C. (1973). "Theory of Rational Option Pricing." *Bell Journal of Economics and Management Science,* 4 (Spring), 141–183.

———, Myron S. Scholes, and Mathew L. Gladstein (1978). *Journal of Business,* 51 (April), 183–242.

Smith, Clifford W., Jr. (1976). "Option Pricing: A Review." *Journal of Financial Economics,* 3 (March), 3–51.

APPENDIX 17A

Option Valuation Theory

A SIMPLE ONE-PERIOD OPTION VALUATION MODEL

The basis for option valuation is probability. Specifically, for a call option it is the probability that the stock will sell for more than the exercise price on the expiration date of the option. For puts, it is the probability of the stock selling for less than the exercise price. In this appendix, we will give examples for call options, although the principles apply equally to situations with put options.

To show option pricing fundamentals, let us establish a simple scenario. The hypothetical call option on XYZ stock has an exercise price of 100 and expires in one day. XYZ stock presently sells for 100. We do not know what tomorrow's price will be, but we have estimated what tomorrow's possible prices are and the probabilities of their occurrence. This estimated probability distribution for tomorrow's price is simple: a .5 probability that XYZ will rise to 101 and a .5 probability that it will fall to 99. We do not recognize any other possible stock prices or probabilities. Of course, in reality, there are many feasible stock prices to which XYZ can change over one day's time. A more detailed option valuation model can take a more detailed probability distribution into account, but our example concentrates only on the possibility of the stock rising or falling by one point tomorrow.

The question is: Given this information, what is the XYZ 100 option worth? The minimum value is 0 [$max(0, 100 - 100) = 0$]. However, because the option has one more day of life left, its value should be greater than its minimum value. Using the concept of expected value and the above probabilities, we can compute the expected value of this option. The expected value of any variable is the sum of each possible variable value times its associated probability. Table 17A–1 shows this application to the valuation of an option. There is a .5 chance of having a worthless option on expiration, and a .5 chance of an option worth 1, giving an expected value for the option of .5. This is the expected value for the option on expiration. To estimate its worth today, we would have to discount this future expected value to the present.

Remember, this does not mean that the option will be worth .5 tomorrow. It means that if we could buy this type of option in this situation repeatedly, one half of the time it would expire worthless and the other half of the time we would have

TABLE 17A–1
A simple two-state, one-period option valuation

Option: Call on XYZ stock expiring tomorrow with exercise price of 100

Stock: Current price is 100
Tomorrow's price will be either 99 or 101, with equal probabilities

Computation of option's expected value:

(a) *Possible Future Stock Price at Expiration*	*(b)* *Probability*	*(c)* *Option Value at Expiration* *max*(0, (*a*) − 100)	*(d)* *Expected Value* (*c*) × (*b*)
99	.5	0	0
101	.5	1	.5
		Total expected value =	.5

an option worth one dollar. Over time, this averages out to the expected value of .5 per transaction.

MULTIPLE-PERIOD OPTION VALUATION

The approach to option valuation explained in the previous section is a two-state approach because it recognized only two future possibilities for the stock. Although the two-state, or binomial, approach is relatively simple, we can apply it to option valuation in the market by expanding it to cover not just one day to expiration, but any number of time periods. Several researchers have developed option pricing models along these lines.[1]

To illustrate the principles involved in expanding option valuation to multiple periods, let us change the example option from Table 17A–1 to an option with two days left until expiration. The stock can go up or down by two points on the first day (with .5 probabilities) followed by a change of one point on the next day. If XYZ falls by two points on the first day and one point the following day, the price of XYZ would be at 97 on expiration. The joint probability of two (mutually exclusive) events occurring is equal to the product of the two individual probabilities. Therefore, the probability of a price of 97 on expiration for XYZ (resulting from a two-point and a one-point fall) is equal to .25 (.5 × .5 = .25). The other possible stock prices and their probabilities are determined similarly. Once the stock values and probabilities at expiration are known, we can compute the option values for each possible stock value, and then compute the expected option value. As Table 17A–2 shows, the value for the sample option would be 1.00.

As in the one-period example, to obtain the value of the option two days before expiration, we would need to discount it to present value. This raises an important question: What is the appropriate discount rate to use for valuing options? In addition, the simplicity of the above valuation procedure raises other concerns that a more

TABLE 17A–2
A two-state, two-period option valuation

(a) Possible Stock Change Tomorrow	*(b)* Probability	*(c)* Possible Stock Change in 2 days	*(d)* Probability	*(e)* Possible Stock Price at Expire 100 *a* + *c*	*(f)* Joint Probability *b* × *c*	*(g)* Option Value at Expire *max*(0, *e* − 100)	*(h)* Expected Value *f* × *g*
−2	.5	−1	.5	97	.25	0	0
		+1	.5	99	.25	0	0
+2	.5	−1	.5	101	.25	1	.25
		+1	.5	103	.25	3	.75
						Total expected value =	1.00

detailed model can resolve. For example, a more detailed model should be able to account for any range of stock price movements over the time period, not just two possibilities.

The Black-Scholes Option Pricing Model

The option pricing model that has been generally accepted as the foundation of option valuation is the relationship developed by Black and Scholes.[2] The Black-Scholes model has proven to be a useful model for options trading and research. It has been tested on the theoretical level by researchers and has been used in the market by many practitioners. The Black-Scholes model is an equilibrium relationship that accounts for the aforementioned shortcomings of the simplified option pricing procedure. In addition, other researchers have adapted the general Black-Scholes model to more specific applications.

Basic Assumptions of the Black-Scholes Model

To derive an option pricing relationship, Black and Scholes began with the following set of assumptions about financial markets.

1. Trading in the stock is continuous, and the distribution of future stock log-returns is normal and has a variance rate that is proportional with time.
2. The riskless interest rate is known and constant.
3. The option is European (it can only be exercised at expiration).
4. The stock pays no dividend.
5. There are no taxes, transactions costs, or penalties to shortsellers.

The first assumption allows a distribution of many possible future stock prices. It also says that the variance of that distribution is known (or can be estimated) and proportional through time. Being proportional through time is a handy characteristic; it means that, for example, the variance of the stock over a two-day period is twice the variance over a one-day span. This means that knowing the variance for any one period lets us compute the variance for any multiple time period. The assumption that the distribution is normal allows us to use the nice characteristics of the normal distribution for computing probabilities.

Derivation of the Black-Scholes Formula

With its continuous distribution assumption, the Black-Scholes model takes care of having a wide range of possible future stock prices. Trying to identify the appropriate discount rate by following the same discounting procedure as the models for stocks and bonds would lead to the use of the required rate of return on an option as the discount rate. This would only further complicate option valuation because an option's required rate is a variable whose value is not known. The major contribution of Black and Scholes was to show that the appropriate rate at which to discount the terminal option value is the riskless interest rate.

The explanation presented here of the Black-Scholes reasoning behind the use of the riskless rate and the derivation of their model is very brief and only outlines the major points. It follows the description of "risk neutral" option valuation developed by Cox and Ross.[3]

First of all, we can establish a hedge position constructed of buying the common stock and writing the call option. If we do this in just the right proportions, then when the stock rises in value, the value of the call options written will change by exactly an opposite amount. That is, the position is a *perfect hedge* or *riskless hedge* in which, regardless what the stock does, the net value of the total position remains unchanged. It is a riskless position, and should therefore have a return equal to the riskless rate. The value of the hedge, and hence the option, is therefore not a function of the expected return on the stock, but rather depends only on the riskless rate. Since the expected return on the option is independent of the expected return on the stock, we could use any rate we want as the expected stock return in an option valuation relationship. The simplest assumption is one of *risk neutrality* in which investors are all risk neutral and the expected returns on all assets are the same. In such a case, we would use the riskless rate as the appropriate discount rate and expected stock return in computing option prices. (This does not mean that the expected return on a stock *is* the riskless rate; just that we can compute option prices *as if* the expected stock return were the riskless rate.)

Second, let us write the minimum value of a call option on expiration:

$$C^* = max(0, S^* - X) \qquad \textbf{(17A–1)}$$

where C^* = the value of the call option at expiration
S^* = the value of the stock at expiration
X = the exercise price of the option

For the next step, let us utilize the idea that the expected value of the option on expiration is the sum of all possible stock values multiplied by their probabilities:

$$E(C^*) = \sum_{S=0}^{\infty} max(0, S^* - X)p(S^*) \qquad \textbf{(17A–2)}$$

where $E(\cdot)$ = the expected value operator
$p(S^*)$ = the probability of S^* (that is, the probability of the stock price being a specific value)

Equation 17A–2 states that the expected value of a call option is equal to the sum of the possible expiration option values times their associated probabilities. The possible option values at expiration are determined by the possible stock values at expiration, which may run from zero to infinity.

However, the option values for all stock prices less than the option's exercise price will be zero. Therefore, we really do not need to compute Equation 17A–2 for all stock prices from zero to infinity, we just need to go from the exercise price to infinity. This lets us simplify Equation 17A–2 to:

$$E(C^*) = \sum_{S=X}^{\infty} (S^* - X)p(S^*) \qquad \textbf{(17A–3)}$$

Remember that one of the Black-Scholes assumptions was that stock trading takes place continuously. This lets us recast Equation 17A–3 into a continuous framework as follows:

$$E(C^*) = \int_{X}^{\infty} (S^* - X)f(S^*)dS^* \qquad \textbf{(17A–4)}$$

where $f(S^*)dS^*$ = the probability distribution function of S^* (It is the continuous calculus equivalent of the probability of the stock price, S^*)

Equation 17A–4 says the same thing that Equation 17A–3 does, except that it allows for continuous trading. The advantage of doing so allows the use of calculus to solve the formula.

Before solving the formula, the final step is to convert the expected terminal option price, C^*, into the expected current option price, C. To do this, we discount the expected terminal price to present value at the risk-free rate as follows:

$$C = e^{-rT} \times \int_{X}^{\infty} (S^* - X)f(S^*)dS^* \qquad \textbf{(17A–5)}$$

where e = the base of the natural log
r = riskless interest rate per time period
T = the number of time periods to expiration

Equation 17A–5 states that the value of a call option is the present value, discounted at the riskless rate, of the terminal expected call option value. Note that e^{-rT} is just a standard continuously compounded discounting factor.

Since the distribution, $f(S^*)$ is log normal and continuous, Equation 17A–5 can be solved to give the Black-Scholes formula for pricing options:[4]

$$C = S \times N\{d_1\} - e^{-rT} \times X \times N\{d_2\}$$
$$d_1 = \frac{ln\,(S/X) + (r + \sigma^2/2) \times T}{\sigma \times \sqrt{T}} \qquad \textbf{(17A–6)}$$
$$d_2 = d_1 - \sigma \times \sqrt{T}$$

where σ = the standard deviation of the distribution of the expected log stock returns
$N\{\cdot\}$ = the cumulative normal probability

Equation 17A–6 is the Black-Scholes formula for the valuation of call options. When solving the formula, the probabilities $N\{\cdot\}$ are available for a table of normal probabilities. Appendix 5 contains the appropriate table of normal probabilities.

The only variable in the Black-Scholes model that is not directly observable in the market is σ, the standard deviation of stock returns. The other variables are all items that are either characteristics of the option (the exercise price and time to expiration) or are observable in the market (the stock price and the riskless rate). Option traders who use the Black-Scholes model have ways to estimate the standard deviation. One way is to collect a sample of past stock returns and compute their standard deviation. Upon doing this, the trader can compute the theoretical value of options on that stock. Example 17A–1 shows a sample option value computation using the Black-Scholes model.

EXAMPLE 17A–1

Using the Black-Scholes option pricing model, compute the value of the following stock option:

Stock name: Exxon
Stock price: 62
Option exercise price: 65
Time to expiration: 90 days
Continuously compounded riskless rate: 10 percent
Per day expected stock standard deviation: .014

The first step is to place the three time-related variables on the same time basis. The time to expiration is stated in days, and the standard deviation is already on a per day basis, but the riskless rate is annual. To put it on a daily basis, divide it by 365 days in a year. The variables for the Black-Scholes model are therefore as follows:

S = 62 X = 65 T = 90 r = .10/365 = .000274 σ = .014

$$d_1 = \frac{ln(62/65) + (.000274 + .014^2/2) \times 90}{.014 \times \sqrt{90}}$$
$$= \frac{ln(.9538) + .03348}{.1328} = -.1041$$
$$d_2 = -.1041 - .1328 = -.2369$$
$$C = 62 \times N\{-.1041\} - e^{-.000274(90)} \times 65 \times N\{-.2369\}$$

To find the normal probabilities, we look up the value associated with $-.10$ (which is $-.1041$ rounded) in the table of normal probabilities in Appendix 5 and find a value of .4602. The probability of $-.24$ ($-.2369$ rounded) is .4052. For simplicity, this example just uses these rounded numbers in the table. Normally, interpolation should be used for better accuracy.

$$\begin{aligned} C &= 62 \times .4602 - .9756 \times 65 \times .4052 \\ &= 28.53 - 25.70 \\ &= 2.83 \end{aligned}$$

This solution is somewhat different from an exact solution because of the rounding in the example. Option traders usually use computers to compute option prices. The exact solution to the above problem is 2.69.

Summary of the Factors Influencing Option Prices

The variables of the Black-Scholes model identify the factors that influence the prices of options. As discussed in the main body of this chapter, the value of an option depends upon the following items: the stock price, the option's exercise price, the time to expiration, the volatility (standard deviation) of the stock, and the riskless interest rate. Note that the expected stock return is not one of these variables. The risk-neutral principle means that the price of the option does not depend upon what investors expect the stock to return.

PUT-CALL PARITY

The concept of riskless option hedges can also be used to describe the relationship between put and call prices. A position composed of writing one call, buying one put with equivalent terms (exercise price and time to expiration the same as the call), and purchasing one share of the stock is riskless. To see that it is riskless, assume that the stock rises one dollar at expiration. The one-dollar profit on the long stock position will cancel out a one-dollar profit on the position with the two options. The net cost of the position is equal to the put price less the amount received for writing the call plus the purchase price of the stock. Because the position is riskless, it should return the riskless rate, and we can set up the relationship as follows:

$$P - C + S = e^{-rT} \times X \qquad \textbf{(17A–7)}$$

where P = the price of a put option
C = the price of a call option with terms equivalent to the put
r = the riskless rate
T = the time to expiration of the put and call
X = the exercise price of the put and call

OTHER APPLICATIONS OF OPTION PRICING

It is easy to see that option pricing theory is applicable to stock options and options on other assets. Another important contribution of option pricing theory is that it can form a general framework for pricing other types of assets or securities. Black and Scholes noted that we can even view common stock as an option. The common stock of a corporation gives stockholders a claim (option) on the assets of the corporation subject to the payment of the corporation's debt. The face value of the debt is the "exercise price" of the option, and the time to expiration is the time to maturity of the debt. It is therefore possible to value common stock with an option pricing model.

Other types of securities can also be treated as options. For example, preferred stock is a type of option and can be valued with option pricing theory.[5] *A shared-appreciation mortgage* gives the lender a share of the increase in the value of the property securing the mortgage and is like a type of call option.[6] Even the bid-ask spread is like an option issued by the market maker, and option pricing theory can explain the bid-ask spread.[7]

IMPORTANT TERMS

perfect hedge
riskless hedge
risk neutrality
shared-appreciation mortgage

NOTES

1. See, for example, John C. Cox, Stephen A. Ross, and Mark Rubinstein (1979), "Option Pricing: A Simplified Approach," *Journal of Financial Economics,* 7 (October), 229–263; Richard J. Rendleman, Jr., and Brit J. Bartter (1979), "Two-State Option Pricing," *Journal of Finance,* 34 (December), 1093–1110; and R. C. Stapleton, and M. G. Subramanyam (1984), "The Valuation of Options When Asset Returns Are Generated by a Binomial Process," *Journal of Finance,* 39 (December), 1525–1539.
2. Fisher Black and Myron Scholes (1973), "The Valuation of Options and Corporate Liabilities," *Journal of Political Economy,* 81 (May), 637–659.
3. John C. Cox and Stephen A. Ross (1976), "The Valuation of Options for Alternative Stochastic Processes," *Journal of Financial Economics,* 3 (March), 229–263.
4. The procedure for this solution is quite involved. Readers who are interested in the mathematics involved should consult Black and Scholes's original work or a detailed review, such as Clifford W. Smith, Jr. (1976), "Option Pricing: A Review," *Journal of Financial Economics,* 3 (March), 3–51.
5. David Emanuel (1983), "A Theoretical Model for Valuing Preferred Stock," *Journal of Finance,* 38 (September), 1133–1155.
6. Dan W. French and Richard L. Haney (1984), "Pricing the Shared-Appreciation Mortgage in a Stochastic Environment," *Housing Finance Review,* 3 (October), 431–443.
7. Thomas E. Copeland and Dan Galai (1983), "Information Effects on the Bid-Ask Spread," *Journal of Finance,* 38 (December), 1457–1469.

CHAPTER 18

Contingent Claim Securities: Warrants, Convertibles, and Others

Several types of securities combine the contingent claim features of options with characteristics of other securities. These combination securities take on attributes of both securities. Why do corporations issue combination securities? They do so for the same reason that they issue any security—to raise capital. Recall that any option with time remaining to expiration will have a positive value. To claim this value as income, investors can be writers of options. For corporations to claim the value of an option-like security, they must resort to issuing securities convertible into their stock. This chapter covers the major types of these securities, beginning with rights and warrants, two kinds of contingent claim security that are very similar to call options. Next, convertible bonds and convertible preferred stocks are presented. Finally, this chapter introduces several other types of hybrid securities.

WARRANTS

A *warrant* is an option giving its owner the right to purchase a certain number of shares of stock from the corporation at a certain price. Warrants are similar to call options, but with several notable differences.

First, warrants are issued by the company into whose stock the warrants are exercisable. Therefore, when an investor exercises a warrant, the corporation issues new shares of stock to the investor. A result of this is *dilution* of the existing common equity of the corporation. In most cases, however, the number of outstanding warrants will be only a small portion of the outstanding stock, and the effect of dilution will be insignificant or minimal.

The second difference is related to the first. Exercise of warrants results in a cash flow into the corporation, and the corporation's total assets increase, and capital structure changes.

Third, warrants typically have longer original lives than options. While the longest time to expiration available for listed options is about nine months, the initial life of warrants is generally four to seven years. There are exceptions: Sometimes warrants are issued with as little as two years to expiration, and some perpetual warrants exist that never expire.

Fourth, warrants may be exercisable into any number of shares of common stock, compared to options, which are exercisable into 100 shares. Because of this an investor considering the purchase of a warrant needs to know the number of shares that one warrant will purchase, and the investor should compute the *adjusted warrant price* as follows:

$$\text{Adjusted warrant price} = \frac{\text{Market price of warrant}}{\text{Number of shares represented by warrant}} \quad \textbf{(18–1)}$$

The adjusted warrant price states the market price of the warrant on a per share basis. This lets investors more easily analyze the value of a warrant. Of course, when a warrant is exercisable into one share of stock, the adjusted warrant price is equal to the actual warrant price.

A final difference between warrants and call options is that the terms of exercise of a warrant may change during the life of the warrant. Usually, this means that the number of shares into which the warrant is exercisable will decrease or the exercise price will increase at a specified date in the future. Investors considering warrants should familiarize themselves with any such provisions of a warrant, because the value

TABLE 18–1
Sample of available warrants

Issuing Company	*Terms*	*Expiration*
Geothermal Resources Intl.	purchase 1 common at $13.50	11-15-1991
International Banknote	purchase 1 common at $7.00	8-1-1988
Johnstown Consol. Realty	purchase 1 common at $20.00	12-19-1989
Lilly (Eli)	purchase 1 common at $75.98	3-31-1991
Lomas and Nettleton Mortgage	purchase 1 common at $27.00	3-1-1990
McLean Industries	purchase 1 common at $11.20	7-15-1990
Mortgage Realty and Trust	purchase 1.5 shares at $30.75	1-15-1992

of the warrant is usually less after the change occurs. The reason that corporations place these provisions in their warrants is to encourage early exercise. Table 18–1 shows some warrants and their characteristics.

Reasons for Issuing Warrants

Corporations normally issue warrants in conjunction with an offering of another security. Corporations issue warrants for several reasons, most relating to the fact that the warrant is a security of value. When an investor receives a warrant as part of a package of securities, the issuing corporation can charge more for the package than it would be able to charge for the individual securities in the package. Therefore, we can summarize the reasons why corporations issue warrants into two explanations.

First, warrants allow companies to issue companion securities in a package at a higher price (or lower expense). For example, suppose that General Paper Corporation is issuing twenty-year bonds. The company's investment bankers have estimated that these bonds will sell in the market at par with a coupon yield of 11 percent. However, if the company included a set of warrants along with the bond, the company could lower the coupon to 9 percent and still sell the bonds for par. (Alternatively, the company could sell 11 percent bonds above par, but traditionally bonds are issued at or very close to par.)

A second reason that a company might issue warrants is as a sweetener to make the issue easier to sell to the public. This reason can be especially relevant to new companies that may encounter reluctance among investors to buy their debt securities without some type of inducement. Warrants provide this inducement, giving investors some equity participation in the company. However, corporations even issue warrants in conjunction with an issue of common stock to make the common issue easier to sell.

When a company issues warrants as part of a package of other securities, the package is usually called a *unit of securities.* The units will often trade OTC, in addition to trading in the component securities, for a period of time after the initial offering. As part of the unit, the warrants may be *detachable* or *nondetachable.* Detachable warrants may be "detached" and sold separately from their companion security. A nondetachable warrant must be sold with its companion security or exercised. Detachable warrants are much more popular with the investing public, and most warrant issues are therefore detachable.

Attraction of Warrants for Investors

Essentially, the attractions of warrants for investors are the same as the attractions of call options. The main advantage of warrants over call options is that a warrant purchaser usually has a longer time period until expiration. Warrants provide their holders with leverage, as do call options. They allow investors to control a relatively large number of shares of stock with a relatively small amount of money. Hedgers can even construct warrant hedges by buying the stock and shorting the warrant, or a *reverse warrant hedge* by buying the warrant and shorting the stock.

Warrants, like options, have their disadvantages. The principal disadvantage of warrants (except perpetual warrants) is that they are wasting assets. Without a material increase in the price of the underlying stock, a warrant's price will eventually erode.

Warrant Valuation

Warrant valuation is similar to call option valuation. The basis for the minimum value of a warrant is the same as for call options. Equation 18–1 showed how it is convenient to express the "adjusted" warrant price, because warrants are sometimes exercisable into more or less than one share of common. If a warrant is exercisable into other than one share of stock, then we need to know the *adjusted exercise price*.

$$\text{Adjusted exercise price} = \frac{\text{Exercise price of warrant}}{\text{Number of shares represented by warrant}} \qquad \textbf{(18–2)}$$

Equation 18–2 expresses the exercise price of a warrant on a per share basis. Sometimes warrants that are exercisable into other than one share of stock will state their exercise price per share, in which case there is no need to compute the adjusted exercise price of the warrant.

To apply the same formula for the minimum value of a call option to warrants, we need to make one assumption. Because the exercise of a warrant results in dilution of the stock, the price of the stock following exercise is not known. In addition, the cash flow into the corporation and the corporation's ability to invest this cash wisely will affect the stock price. The assumption needed is that the dilutive and cash flow effects of exercise of the warrants are negligible, and the postexercise price of the stock will be equal to the pre-exercise price. Given this assumption, the adjusted minimum value of a warrant is:

$$W_a = max(0, S - X_a) \qquad \textbf{(18–3)}$$

where W_a = the adjusted minimum value of a warrant
S = the stock price
X_a = the adjusted exercise price of the warrant

Equation 18–3 states that the adjusted minimum value of a warrant is equal to the greater of zero or the stock price less the adjusted exercise price. Example 18–1 shows how to adjust warrant prices and compute the minimum value.

Because of the similarity of warrants and call options, many analysts treat warrants as calls and even use the Black-Scholes option valuation relationship to value warrants. However, this procedure does not necessarily yield a valid value for a warrant. Even if we assume that the dilutive and cash flow effects of exercise are zero (which they are not), there are other problems with using the Black-Scholes model. Several issues regarding warrant valuation remain unresolved, and no warrant valuation model yet exists that completely accounts for these problems.[1]

EXAMPLE 18–1

1. Mortgage and Realty Trust, a company traded on the NYSE, has warrants that trade on the AMEX. Each warrant is exercisable into 1.5 shares of common stock of the company for $30.75. The warrants expire January 15, 1992. The stock trades for 19 and the warrant is at 2. What is the adjusted minimum value of the warrant?

The adjusted market value of the warrant is

$$2/1.5 = 1.33$$

The adjusted exercise price is

$$30.75/1.5 = 20.5$$

The adjusted minimum warrant value is

$$max(0, 19 - 20.5) = 0$$

Although the warrant's minimum value is zero, it has a positive market value of 1.33 because of the time value.

2. First Central Financial has warrants to purchase one share of common stock for $3.50 until April 15, 1990. What is the minimum value of the warrant when the stock is at 5 and the warrant is at 2?

Because the warrant is exercisable into one share of stock, there is no need to adjust any of the warrant values. The warrant's minimum value is

$$max(0, 5 - 3.50) = 1.50.$$

Note that the market value of the warrant, 2, contains a .50 time premium over the warrant's minimum value of 1.50.

Warrant Strategy

When considering warrant strategies for the market, the similarity between warrants and call options once again becomes apparent. Investors can use many of the same call option strategies (discussed in Chapter 17) for warrants. For example, the warrant hedge, in which an investor buys the stock and sells short the warrant, is similar to the covered call write.

However, because warrants generally have more time remaining until expiration, there are several strategic points that an investor pondering the purchase of warrants should consider. The ultimate profit from a warrant depends upon the increase in the price of the stock. For options, the increase in the stock price is of speculative nature because of the short time to expiration. With warrants, however, the additional time duration lets investors rely more upon fundamental analysis to identify stocks with long-term capital appreciation potential. A second factor is that the purchase of low priced, out-of-the-money warrants offers maximum leverage. The longer life of warrants gives these low priced warrants a much greater chance of becoming in the money than their short-term option counterparts.

Rights: Short-Term Warrants

When selling new shares of common stock, some firms will offer the new issue to the company's existing shareholders before offering stock to the general public. They often do this on a *privileged subscription* basis. A privileged subscription offering grants *rights* to existing shareholders to purchase additional common stock in the company subject to the terms of the offering. Shareholders usually receive one right for each share of stock held. The terms of the offering specify the number of rights required to buy an additional share of stock, the exercise price per share, and the expiration date of the offering. The exercise price is usually considerably below the current market price of the stock, assuring that the rights will be exercised before expiration. For example, the Big Dig Corporation, currently selling for $50 per share, issues rights to its existing stockholders. The stockholder can purchase one share of stock for $40 and four rights.

Some corporate charters require new issues be handled through privileged subscriptions, giving stockholders a *pre-emptive right.* Many years ago, states required corporations to give pre-emptive rights to existing shareholders. Pre-emptive rights give stockholders the opportunity to preserve their existing percentage ownership in the corporation when there is a new issue of common stock. The disadvantage of pre-emptive rights to corporations is that they restrict the ability to raise money with new issues of stock and convertible securities. States no longer require pre-emptive rights, and most corporations have eliminated the requirement from their charters. From time to time, however, companies will use a rights offering to issue new common stock.

When a corporation decides to have a rights offering, the board of directors establishes a date of record. Before this record date, the company's stock trades *rights-on,* and investors who own the company's stock on the date of record receive rights. After the record date, the stock trades *ex-rights,* and the rights become a separate instrument. The rights will often trade concurrently with the ex-rights stock on the same exchange. Investors who have received rights but do not wish to exercise them therefore have the opportunity to sell them before they expire. The expiration of rights varies, but they usually expire several weeks after issue.

Because the exercise of rights results in dilution of the company's existing equity, the ex-rights price of the stock will be less than the rights-on price. Because the exact effects of the inflowing cash and resulting change in capital structure on the stock's price are unknown, the value of a right and the ex-rights stock value cannot be determined exactly (see the previous discussion on warrants). However, the following formula yields a very close estimate of the stock's ex-rights value:

$$S_X = \frac{S_o \times N + X}{N + 1} \tag{18–4}$$

where S_x = the ex-rights price of the stock
S_o = the price of the stock rights-on
X = the exercise price of the offering
N = the number of rights required to purchase one share of stock

The value of one right can also be estimated using the same information and the following formula:

$$R = \frac{S_x - X}{N} \qquad \textbf{(18–5)}$$

Example 18–2 illustrates how the ex-rights stock price will be less than the rights-on price. The example also shows the estimate of the right's value.

EXAMPLE 18–2

Big Dig Corporation's common stock currently sells for $50, and the company has decided to have a rights offering. Four rights allows the stockholder to purchase one new share of common stock for $40. Estimate the ex-rights price of the stock and the value of a right.

$$S_x = \frac{50 \times 4 + 40}{4 + 1} = 48$$

$$R = \frac{48 - 40}{4} = 2$$

Note that the values that Equations 18–4 and 18–5 yield, as well as the prices in Example 18–2, are estimates. However, they should be very close to the observed prices. Also, Equation 18–5, gives only the minimum value of the right. Because a right is like a short-term warrant, it may have a market value slightly higher than given by Equation 18–5, but the value of the right would be greater than Equation 18–5 by only a very small amount. There are two reasons for this. First is that the right is a short-term option that would have only a small time value. Second, the right is an "in-the-money option," and the time value on in-the-money options is always relatively small.

CONVERTIBLES

Convertible securities are securities that are convertible into common stock of the corporation. The two major types are the convertible preferred stock and the convertible bond. They derive their value from their current return (from dividends or interest), plus the potential to become common equity. We can even view convertible securities as a combination of a base security plus some warrants whose exercise price can be paid with a certain face amount of the base security.

Convertible issues appeal to investors for several reasons. They attract investors who seek more risk than with straight bonds or preferred stock, but who also prefer less risk than with common stock. The current yield of convertibles is typically higher than the dividend yield on the common stock. Also, the fixed nature of convertibles' payments (coupon or preferred dividend) offers resistance to downward moves in the stock's price. Convertibles do, however, have a measure of interest rate risk similar to their nonconvertible counterparts. Another positive feature of convertibles is that conversion into common stock of the company is a nontaxable exchange.

Terms of Conversion

As with options, there is a set of terms peculiar to convertibles. Before proceeding with convertibles and their analysis, we must introduce the terminology for convertible issues.

The *conversion ratio* of a convertible issue is equal to the number of shares into which it is convertible. Sometimes the description of the convertible issue will not specify the number of shares into which it can be converted, but rather will specify the *conversion price*. The conversion price is the face amount of the security required to purchase one share of common stock. The conversion ratio and the conversion price are interrelated, so that an investor needs to know only one to compute the other. The following formula specifies this relationship:

$$\text{Conversion ratio} = \frac{\text{Par value}}{\text{Conversion price}} \qquad \textbf{(18–6)}$$

Equation 18–6 identifies that the conversion ratio of a convertible security is equal to the par value (face amount) divided by the conversion price. The succeeding sections will show examples of these formulas for both convertible preferred stocks and convertible bonds.

The *conversion value* of a convertible security is its conversion ratio times the market price of the stock:

$$\text{Conversion value} = \text{Conversion ratio} \times \text{market price of stock} \qquad \textbf{(18–7)}$$

The conversion value represents the value of the security if it were converted into common stock. It represents only the minimum value of the convertible in terms of the common stock. The market price of the convertible security will usually be greater than the conversion value. The amount by which the convertible's market price exceeds the conversion value is the *conversion premium*.

$$\text{Conversion premium} = \text{Market price of convertible} - \text{conversion value} \qquad \textbf{(18–8)}$$

Equation 18–8 demonstrates that the conversion premium of a convertible security is equal to the market price of the convertible less its conversion value.

The value of a convertible does not depend only upon the value of the common stock. It also depends on the worth of the base preferred stock or bond. The *straight-preferred value* of a convertible preferred stock is equal to the value of the security if it were not convertible. Likewise, the *straight-debt value* of a convertible bond is the convertible bond's value if it were a straight bond. This establishes the floor value of the convertible in terms of the base security. There is also a convertible premium over the straight value of the security.

$$\text{Premium over straight-preferred} = \text{Market value of convertible preferred} - \text{straight-preferred value} \qquad \textbf{(18–9a)}$$

$$\text{Premium over straight-debt} = \text{Market value of convertible bond} - \text{straight-debt value} \qquad \textbf{(18–9b)}$$

The convertible premiums of convertible securities are similar to the time values of call options and warrants. The minimum value of a convertible will be the greater of Equation 18–7 or the straight-debt value of the bond. Of course, before its maturity, a convertible will normally have a value greater than its minimum value. In addition, there will normally be some time premium in the price of a convertible security, and Equations 18–8 and 18–9 will yield a positive value.

Convertible Bonds

Convertible bonds are the most popular convertible security among investors. The number of different convertible bond issues is considerably greater than the number of convertible preferred issues. Corporations generally prefer to issue bonds rather than preferred stocks because the interest on bonds is deductible from income for tax purposes, while stock dividends are not deductible. This applies to convertible as well as straight issues, so that the after-tax cost is usually less for debt than for preferred equity.

Several financial services follow convertible issues. Figure 18–1 shows a sample publication of one of these services, Standard & Poor's. Investors considering purchasing convertible bonds will find such publications useful, and should be sure to check the convertible provisions of the bond in detail. Sometimes the conversion ratio will change during the life of the bond. The "callability" and call price of convertible bonds are also important to know.

As an example of a convertible bond issue, consider the National Convenience Stores 9 percent bonds due 2008. The bond is convertible into common stock of the corporation at $20 per share. Example 18–3 shows that this conversion price is equivalent to a conversion ratio of fifty shares per bond.

EXAMPLE 18–3

National Convenience Stores had a 9 percent bond convertible into common stock at $20 per share. You also have the following information:

$$\text{Market price of the bond} = 900$$
$$\text{Market price of the stock} = 12$$
$$\text{Straight-debt value of the bond} = 770$$

What is the conversion ratio of the bond?

Assuming the bond has a face value of $1000, using Equation 18–6, we have

$$\text{Conversion ratio} = 1000/20 = 50$$

Compute the premium over straight-debt value for the bond.

$$\text{Premium over straight-debt value} = 900 - 770 = 130$$

Compute the conversion value and the premium over conversion value.

$$\text{Conversion value} = 50 \times 12 = 600$$
$$\text{Premium over conversion value} = 900 - 600 = 300$$

STANDARD & POOR'S CORPORATION

CONVERTIBLE BONDS — Issue, Rate, Interest Dates and Maturity	S & P Quality Rating	Bond Form	Outstdg. Mil.-$	Conv. Expires	Shares per $1,000 Bond	Price per Share	Div. Income per Bond	1986 RANGE Hi	1986 RANGE Lo	Curr Bid Sale(s) Ask(A)	Curr. Return	Yield to Mat	Stock Value of Bond	Conv. Parity	STOCK DATA Curr. Price	STOCK DATA P/E Ratio	Earnings Per Share Yr. End	1985	1986	Last 12 Mos	1985 Dil-u't'n
AccuRay[1]Corp[2] ....5½s Jd 1991	NR	R	9.60	1991	27.87	35.875	7.80	126¾	72	126¾	4.34	....	126¾	45½	45½	61	Dc	1.90	....	[9]0.75	n/r
Action Indus ....9s Ao 1998	NR	R	1.95	1998	101.32	9.87	24.32	160⅞	93¾	101	8.91	8.85	92½	10	◆9⅛	12	Je	0.92	1.01	[9]0.74	•0.99
Adobe Resources8¾s mN15 2011	B+	R	55.0	2011	148.81	6.72	....	110	100	110	7.95	7.83	98⅜	7⅛	•6⅝	d	Dc	pd10.1	....	[9]d11.8	n/r
Advanced Systems ......7s mS 2011	B	R	30.0	2011	52.49	19.05	....	110	94	110	6.36	6.20	97⅛	21	•18½	15	Dc	1.00	P1.24	1.24	•1.21
Advanced Telecommun ....8s fA 2006	NR	R	15.0	2006	121.21	8.25	....	124¼	99¼	123	6.50	5.98	119¼	10⅛	9⅛	18	Mr	0.61	....	[9]0.55	0.58
•Advest Group 9s Ms15 2008	NR	R	27.5	2008	66.98	14.93	8.04	121½	98½	s103	8.74	8.68	78¼	15⅛	•11¼	9	Sp	0.65	P1.33	1.33	•1.21
AFG Indus...............6½s jJ15 2006	BB+	R	115	2006	26.49	37.75	4.24	103½	98	101½	6.40	6.36	76½	38⅛	•28⅛	14	Dc	1.41	....	[9]2.04	1.33
•AGS Computers...7½s Ao15 2011	B	R	40.0	2011	36.63	27.30	....	121½	94½	s121½	6.17	5.83	102⅜	33⅛	•28	18	Dc	1.43	....	[9]1.53	n/r
Air Wis Services 7¾s Jd15 2010	B+	R	40.0	2010	52.63	19.00	....	94⅛	89	89	8.71	8.87	59¼	16⅛	11¼	29	Dc	0.18	....	[9]0.39	n/r
•Airborne Freight ...7½s Jd15 2011	BBB-	R	25.0	2011	36.17	27.65	21.70	117	90	s114	6.58	6.36	108	31½	•29⅞	21	Dc	1.39	....	[9]1.42	n/r
Alaska Air Gr 7¾s Jd15 2010	BB-	R	50.0	2010	35.40	28.25	5.66	96½	85½	96	8.07	8.13	70¼	27⅛	•20	16	Dc	2.10	....	[9]1.29	1.85
•[3]Alaska Airlines 9s mN15 2003	BB+	R	25.0	2003	[4]55.17	18.125	8.83	126	103	115¾	7.78	7.35	110⅛	21	•20	16	Dc	2.10	....	[9]1.29	1.85
[3]Alaska Airlines'B'.9s mN15 2003	BB+	R	10.0	2003	[4]55.17	18.125	8.83	126	103½	117	7.69	7.23	110⅛	21¼	•20	16	Dc	2.10	....	[9]1.29	1.85
Alco Standard..........9s mS30 2007	BBB+	R	50.0	2007	27.03	37.00	34.60	122⅛	96	115	7.83	7.55	113¼	42½	•41⅛	16	Sp	2.32	P2.67	2.67	•2.56
•Alco Standard 8½s Ms31 2010	BBB+	R	60.0	2010	22.99	43.50	29.43	119	104¼	s114	7.46	7.24	96¼	49⅜	•41⅛	16	Sp	2.32	P2.67	2.67	•2.56
Alexander & Alex Sv 11s Ao15 2007	A-	R	74.4	2007	25.64	39.00	25.64	113	90	107	10.2	10.1	68	41¼	•26½	..	Dc	d0.19	....	[9]0.07	n/r
Allegheny Beverage.9½s mS 2010	B-	R	105	2010	46.51	21.50	....	144½	67	69½	13.6	13.9	40¼	15	8¼	d	Mr	▲□9.73	....	[9]d2.28	n/r
America West Airlines........7¾s fA 2010	NR	R	69.0	2010	74.07	13.50	....	110¼	86½	95	8.16	8.23	72¼	12⅛	9¼	d	Dc	•0.42	....	[9]d0.05	n/r
America West Airlines........7½s Ao 2011	B-	R	80.0	2011	71.43	14.00	....	103	83½	90½	8.29	8.42	69⅝	12⅜	9¼	d	Dc	•0.42	....	[9]d0.05	n/r
Amer[5]Adventure[6] ....10s § 1998	D	R	10.5	1998	95.69	10.45	....	27	6	6	....	Flat	....	⅛	....	..	Sp	d1.60	....	[6]d11.5	n/r
Amer Bkrs Ins Gr([7]'91).......9¾s jD 2004	BBB-	R	[8]35.3	2004	73.26	13.65	36.63	126⅛	105¼	112	8.71	8.43	102⅜	15¼	14	11	Dc	△1.25	....	[9]1.31	n/r
•[9]Amer Can Int'l[10]4¾s Mn15 1988	NR	C	30.0	1988	[9]18.04	55.42	52.32	No Sale		151¾	3.13	....	151¾	84⅛	•84⅛	11	Dc	5.06	▲E7.50	[9]6.70	4.80
•Amer Cap Bd Fd([11]Ext)[12]11.35s [13]Jj 1990	AAA	R	50.0	1995	52.08	19.20	114.58	No Sale		125⅜	9.03	2.43	125⅜	24⅛	•24⅛	..	....	....	....	....	....
◆Amer[14]Century Corp[15] ....7s Ao 1990	NR	R	[8]1.67	1990	76.39	13.09	....	72½	65	68⅛	10.1	20.6	28⅜	9	•3¼	d	Je	△0.15	d2.93	[9]d3.04	n/r
•[16]Amer[15]Century Tr........6¾s Jd15 1991	NR	R	[8]8.41	1991	56.95	17.56	....	70⅛	46½	54	12.5	24.1	21⅛	9½	•3¼	d	Je	△0.15	d2.93	[9]d3.04	n/r
•Amer Gen'l 11s Fa8 2007	Call	R	115	1-29-87	54.56	18.33	61.11	246	190	s194½	....	Call	201¼	35⅛	•36⅞	10	Dc	△3.23	....	[9]3.64	3.12
•Amer Gen'l 11s mN4 2008	AA	R	176	2008	54.56	18.33	61.11	237	188	s201	....		201¼	36⅛	•36⅞	10	Dc	△3.23	....	[9]3.64	3.12
•Amer Hoist & Der.......5½s Jd 1993	NR	R	6.21	1993	57.18	17.49	....	77	66	66	8.33	13.6	42⅛	11½	•7½	d	Nv	•d1.38	....	[9]d3.33	n/r
◆Amer Israeli Paper....11¾s AnN15 1997	NR	R	13.3	1997	58.58	17.07	17.57	108½	88¼	s107	10.9	10.6	100⅛	18¼	◆17⅛	..	Dc	1.31	....	....	n/r
◆Amer Maize-Prod ...11¾s fA 2000	BB-	R	19.9	2000	[17]55.01	18.18	28.61	128	99½	s111½	10.5	10.1	107¼	20¼	◆19½	65	Dc	d0.89	....	[9]0.30	n/r
◆[18]Amer Maize-Prod 7½s Jd15 2001	BB-	R	25.0	2001	[19]86.58	11.55	....	No Sale		110⅛	6.80	6.38	110⅛	12¼	◆12¼	14	Dc	d0.10	....	[9]0.93	n/r
•Amer Medical Int'l 9½s mN15 2001	BBB	R	125	2001	41.02	24.38	29.53	111¾	96	s101	9.41	9.37	60½	24⅛	•14¼	d	Au	1.94	■d1.12	d1.12	n/r
•Amer Medical Int'l...8¼s Ao 2008	BBB	R	56.8	2008	25.00	40.00	18.00	98	85	s89	9.27	9.46	36⅛	35⅛	•14¼	d	Au	1.94	■d1.12	d1.12	n/r
Amfac ....5s Ms 1989	B+	R	11.6	1989	28.00	35.714	....	92¾	70	84	5.95	13.8	61⅝	30	•22	d	Dc	1.09	....	[9]d0.87	1.08
•Amfac ....5¼s Mn 1994	B+	R	23.2	1994	22.90	43.67	....	91¼	80⅛	87¼	6.02	7.54	50⅛	38⅛	•22	d	Dc	1.09	....	[9]d0.87	1.08
Ampad Corp[20] ....8s fA 2010	B	R	25.0	2010	46.78	21.375	18.71	113½	92	104	7.69	7.63	102⅞	22¼	22	24	Nv	1.11	....	[8]0.93	n/r
Anacomp, Inc(Sr)[21] ......10s jJ 1995	CC	R	15.7	1995	250.00	4.00	....	165⅛	80	93¾	....	Flat	93¾	3¾	•3¾	75	Sp	•d0.06	P•0.05	0.05	n/r
•Anacomp, Inc[22].....13⅞s Jj15 2002	C	R	[8]23.2	2002	57.14	17.50	....	102½	82	s100	....	Flat	21⅛	17½	•3¾	75	Sp	•d0.06	P•0.05	0.05	n/r
◆Andal[23]Corp[24] 5½s mS15 1997	NR	R	2.11	1997	44.44	22.50	....	73	51	67¾	8.12	10.6	38⅞	15¼	◆8¾	4	Sp	△•0.19	P△2.22	2.22	•2.14
Andersen Group10½s aO15 2002	NR	R	9.98	2002	61.84	16.17	....	96	88	88	11.9	12.2	46⅛	14¼	7½	d	Fb	d0.68	....	[11]d0.54	n/r
•Anixter Bros[25] ....8¼s Jj 2003	BBB	R	42.0	2003	72.89	13.72	11.66	115	99¼	100¼	8.23[a]	8.22	102	13¾	•14	23	Jl	0.48	0.61	0.61	n/r
◆Anthony Indus..11¾s [26]jd15 2000	B-	R	[8]21.9	2000	76.51	13.07	33.66	120	98	s103	10.9	10.8	83¼	13½	•10⅞	d	Dc	0.82	....	[9]d0.10	n/r
•Apache Corp............8½s Mn 2006	BB-	R	69.0	2006	89.89	11.125	25.17	109	97¾	106½	7.98	7.84	80⅞	11⅞	•9	75	Dc	0.38	....	[9]0.12	n/r
Apollo Computer ......7¼s Fa 2011	B-	R	115	2011	55.56	18.00	....	114¼	95	111¼	6.52	6.33	89⅜	20	16⅛	73	Dc	d0.04	E0.22	[9]0.15	n/r
•Arkansas Best...............7s Ao 2011	BB-	R	50.0	2011	38.57	25.93	13.89	122	98½	118	5.93	5.63	103⅛	30⅛	•26¼	14	Dc	△•1.46	E1.95	[9]2.02	n/r

Uniform Footnote Explanations—See Page XVI. Other: [1]Was Ind'l Nucleonics. [2]Combustion Eng'g offers $35 for com,to Jan14. [3]Cv into & data of Alaska Air Group. [4]Into Alaska Air Group. [5]Was Great Outdoor Amer Adventure. [6]Default 4-1-86 int. [7](HRO)On 12-1-91 at 110. [8]Incl disc. [9]Cv into & data of Amer Can. [10]Offered outside U.S.:P&I pay in U.S.$. [11](HRO)On 1-1-90. [12]Int thru 12-31-89,adj aft as defined. [13]Due 1-1-95. [14]Was Amer Century Mtg Inv. [15]Investor group offers $5.10. [16]Now Amer Century Corp:was Amer Century Mtg Inv. [17]Into Cl'A'. [18]Data of American Fructose. [19]Exch'ble for American Fructose Cl'A' com. [20]Mead Corp(98.2%)plans acq,$1052.63 per deb. [21]Co option to pay int in cash/com,as defined. [22]Int:1-15-84,pd 3-21-84:7-15-84,pd 8-15-84. [23]Was Nat'l Kinney. [24]Int 5 1/4% to 3-9-82. [25]Itel(99%)plans acq,$14 per com shr. [26]Due Jan 31.

FIGURE 18–1
Sample convertible bond investment information (*Source: Standard & Poor's Bond Guide,* copyright 1987, Standard & Poor's Corp. Reprinted by permission.)

What is the straight-debt value of the bond? To answer this question, an analyst should consult straight bond issues of similar quality. The Standard & Poor's bond rating for the National Convenience Stores issue is B. Suppose that we had determined that the yield to maturity of similar straight bonds was 12 percent. We could then calculate the straight-debt value of the convertible bond by using the standard bond valuation formula. If the bond has twenty years until maturity, the bond valuation formula yields a value of about 770. Example 18–3 shows that a straight-bond value of 770 for this bond yields a premium over straight-debt of 130 when the market price of the bond is 900. If the market price of the common stock is $12, then the conversion value of the bond is 600 and the conversion premium is 300.

The conversion premium of a convertible bond, with a floor price equal to the straight-debt value of the bond, will cause the market price of a convertible bond relative to the stock price to behave similarly to the price of a call option. Figure 18–2 illustrates the change in the value of a convertible bond when the underlying common stock changes in value. An increase in the stock would cause the value of the bond to slide up the curve for the market value of the bond. A change in interest rates could change the straight-debt value of the bond, affecting the floor level. Changes in both of these variables, combined with the natural decline in the conversion premium as bond maturity approaches, result in a complex valuation relationship for convertible bonds.

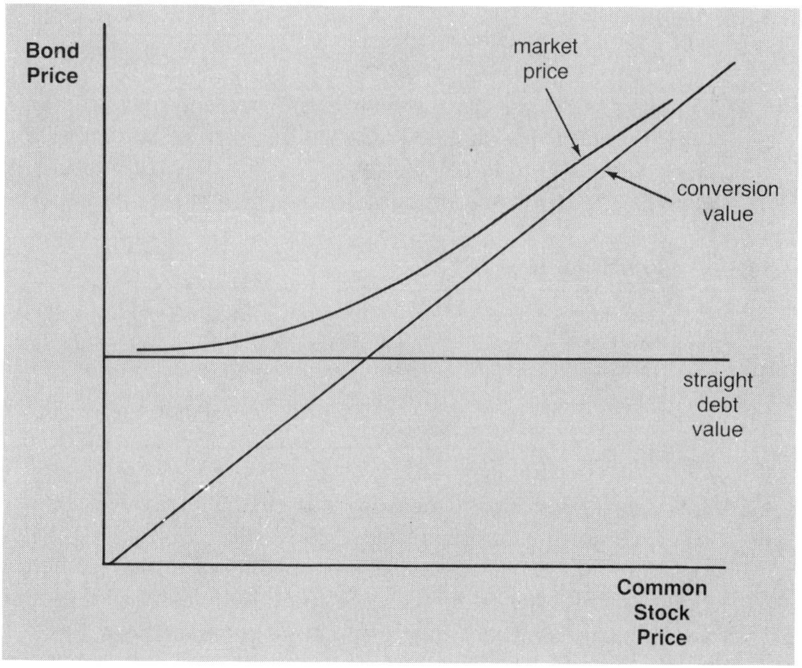

FIGURE 18–2
Price of convertible bond relative to price of common stock

As a general rule, the price of a convertible bond behaves more like the common stock as long as the market price of the bond is relatively close to its conversion value (small conversion premium). When there is a large conversion premium, the price of a convertible bond behaves more like a straight bond.

Valuation of convertible bonds using quantitative models usually takes the approach that the convertible bond is equivalent to a straight bond and a convertible provision. A Black-Scholes option pricing approach is often used to value the convertible portion. This approach is not exact because of the dilutive effects of bond conversion. Many of the models that have been developed,[2] however, can value convertible bonds quite accurately.

Convertible bonds are typically more risky than straight-debt issues of the same corporation. Two main factors contribute to this risk. First, convertibles have often lower coupons and consequently are more sensitive to interest rate changes. Second, the risk of a convertible bond is usually greater than the risk of a similar, equal-coupon nonconvertible issue because of its dependence upon the price of the common stock. However, if a convertible can be purchased for about its straight-bond value (that is, if the stock sells for well below the conversion price), the risk of the convertible will be about the same as a nonconvertible issue. In any case, the risk of holding a convertible is less than the risk of the common stock.

Investors often use a quick measure to give them an idea of the downside risk of a convertible bond.

$$\text{Downside risk} = \frac{\text{Market price of bond} - \text{straight-debt value}}{\text{Market price of bond}} \qquad \textbf{(18–10)}$$

This downside risk measure gives the percent fall in the value of the bond should the common stock decline considerably in price so that the bond falls to its straight-debt value. Example 18–4 shows that the downside risk measure for the National Convenience Stores convertible bond is .144 (14.4 percent).

EXAMPLE 18–4

Compute the downside risk measure for the National Convenience Stores convertible bond.

$$\text{Downside risk} = \frac{900 - 770}{900} = .144$$

The downside risk measure is useful, but investors must realize that it does not give the entire risk picture for a convertible bond. First, it ignores the interest rate risk. Should interest rates rise, the straight-debt value of the bond would fall, and the downside risk would increase. Second, if the price of the common stock did indeed fall dramatically, there might be a fundamental reason to explain why. If this reason related to a decline in the financial health of the company, then it is also likely that the straight-debt value of the bond would also be adversely affected. This occurrence would also increase the downside risk of the bond.

Convertible Preferred Stock

Although the number of convertible preferred issues is smaller than the number of convertible bond issues, the number of corporations issuing convertible preferred stock in recent years has increased slightly. Investors should closely check the provisions of a convertible preferred before investing. The conversion ratio sometimes has scheduled decreases, and sometimes the conversion feature will expire.

When to Convert

There are three situations when an investor may want to convert a convertible security before maturity. The criterion for the decision to convert is whether the investor is better off with the common stock (converting) or with the convertible security (not converting). There are three situations in which conversion may be desirable.

1. *The corporation calls the convertible issue.* In this case, if the conversion value of the convertible is greater than the call price, investors should convert rather than receive the call price. In almost all cases involving the call of a convertible security, the conversion value is greater than the call price, and all convertible holders should convert. This is the case of the corporation forcing early conversion of a convertible issue, and corporations often do this when the price of the common stock has risen dramatically, to a point where the conversion value greatly exceeds the call price. It is conceivable, however, that a corporation might call a convertible issue when the conversion value is less than the call price. For example, this could occur if a company had issued convertible bonds at a relatively high interest rate, and interest rates subsequently fell while the company's stock remained about the same. The company might then call the issue to pay it off and remove the high interest rate burden.
2. *There is a planned change in the conversion price or conversion ratio.* Just as the adjusted exercise price of warrants sometimes has one or more scheduled increases during the life of the warrant, a convertible can have scheduled increases in the conversion price. Alternatively, scheduled decreases in the conversion ratio would accomplish the same purpose. When the time for this occurs, investors holding convertible securities should analyze the situation to determine if continuing to hold the convertible with a higher conversion price is preferable to converting it before the increase. Although there is no steadfast rule, a general guideline indicates that investors should generally convert when the conversion value of the convertible is somewhat greater than the straight-debt or straight-preferred value. If the conversion value is barely greater than the straight value, then it may still be preferable to hold the convertible if the income from the convertible is greater than the prospective dividend income from the common stock.

3. *The dividends declared on the common stock increase to the point where income from the common stock is greater than the interest on the convertible bond (or greater than dividends on the convertible preferred stock).* This circumstance is the only one involving voluntary conversion. At this point the investor must compare the higher dividend income that would result from conversion against the greater risk of the common dividend and stock. Recall that the bond interest and preferred dividends are more certain than common dividends. At some point, the greater dividend would compensate for the higher risk, and the investor would want to convert. Voluntary conversion of a convertible is similar to the early exercise of a call option to receive the dividend on the stock.

Reasons for Issuing Convertibles

The reasons why companies issue convertible securities begin with the same reasons for issuing warrants: to sell the bond (or preferred stock) at a lower yield than would otherwise be required and as a sweetener to make the issue easier to sell. A third reason is that convertibles allow a company to "presell" common stock at a price that is higher than the current market price. This can be especially useful to a company that wants to sell more common stock to the public but believes that the stock is currently underpriced. If the stock is underpriced, then it is not a favorable time to issue new common equity, while a convertible issue could bring in the needed cash at a lower cost of capital.

As an example of preselling common stock at a higher price, consider a firm whose stock sells for $20 per share, and the company believes that it is worth $30. Management believes that the company should do well over the next few years and that investors will realize its true value. In addition, increased growth could add another $10 to the stock's value. With this in mind, the company issues a convertible bond with a conversion price of $40. Several years later, if events have gone as planned, the stock should be selling for more than $40 per share, and the company can call the bond to force conversion. In effect, the company presold its stock at $40 when the stock was selling for only $20.

The potential disadvantages of this approach are twofold. First, if the stock does not rise, then the company is obligated to pay the interest on the bonds and redeem them at maturity. Second, if the stock rises considerably, to a point much greater than the conversion value of the convertible, then the company would have been better off to have issued a straight-debt or preferred issue. When the stock reached its subsequent elevated price, management could sell new common stock, retire the debt or preferred with the proceeds, and still have money left over.

Convertible Strategy

A successful investment strategy involving convertible securities has many elements. This section summarizes several important aspects of these strategies on which many professional investors agree.

First, the key to convertible profits through capital gains is to select convertible securities of companies whose stocks are undervalued or have strong potential for price appreciation. Use fundamental analysis (or even technical analysis if you believe in its efficacy) to select companies whose stocks meet this criterion.

Second, choose bonds that should achieve their capital appreciation potential within about three to five years. Convertible investors should plan on being satisfied with their convertible income (which should be higher than the common dividends) over the first couple of years. Investors who expect profits in less than three years are probably better off buying common stock, warrants, or other securities. On the other end, investors who consistently have to wait more than five or six years to realize capital gains on their convertibles would likely have realized higher overall returns with a straight-debt issue.

Third, consider interest rate risk when selecting a convertible issue. Investors in convertible securities should not forget that convertible securities are sensitive to interest-rates. This is especially true for convertibles with relatively high conversion premiums. Concepts of duration (see Chapter 13) can be used to control interest rate risk of a convertible bond portfolio.

OTHER HYBRID SECURITIES

Although they are not nearly as common as warrants and convertibles, other hybrid securities exist that are a blend of characteristics of other securities. One of these is the *hybrid convertible.* Unlike traditional convertible securities, hybrid convertibles can be converted into stock of another company. Hybrid convertibles are almost as appealing as if they were traditional convertible securities of the other company, with two minor exceptions. First, the default risk of the convertible depends upon the financial position of the issuing company. Second, conversion of a hybrid convertible is taxable at the time of conversion. A company holding stock of another company may find that the best way to sell that stock is to issue a hybrid convertible. For example, in 1980, Textron sold bonds convertible into shares of Allied Chemical that were owned by Textron.

Another type of hybrid security is the *commodity-backed bond.* Commodity-backed bonds have a value that is tied to the price of some commodity. A bond issued by Sunshine Mining provides a good example. Sunshine Mining, a company involved in silver mining, sold 8.5 percent bonds whose redemption value was tied to the price of silver. The bond matures at face value if silver trades at $20 or less per ounce at maturity. If silver trades above $20 per ounce, the redemption value of the bond rises proportionately.

Other types of hybrid debt securities have been used from time to time to give corporations the advantage of being able to deduct the interest payments on the debt, while having the notes eventually become equity.[3] However, the tax authorities and regulators usually find ways to thwart corporations in their attempts to create "tax-deductible equity." Examples of these types of securities include *equity notes,* which are debt with a fixed coupon until maturity. At maturity they automatically become common stock. Another type is the *adjustable-rate convertible note.* These notes are convertible into common stock, with the yield on the note being adjusted so that it is comparable to the dividend yield on the company's common stock.

Another interesting type of hybrid security is the *foreign currency warrant.* The warrants give their holder the right to sell a certain amount of foreign currency at an exchange rate specified by the warrant. Warrant holders profit when the foreign currency falls in value relative to the U.S. dollar. Therefore, the warrants are similar to put options on the foreign currency relative to the U.S. dollar or, alternatively, they are similar to call options on the U.S. dollar relative to the foreign currency. These warrants trade on the American Stock Exchange.

SUMMARY

Warrants are securities that give their holder the right to purchase common stock from the corporation at a fixed price. Warrants are comparable to long-term call options, except that warrants are issued by the corporation. Since one warrant may often be exercisable into more (or less) than one share of common stock, it is useful to compute the adjusted warrant price. The adjusted price is equal to the warrant's market price divided by the number of shares into which it is exercisable. To encourage early exercise of warrants, the issuing corporation will sometimes include the provision of one or more rises in the exercise price before expiration.

Rights are short-term warrants that a corporation issues to existing shareholders to sell new shares of stock. Each warrant allows the stockholder to purchase a certain quantity of the new issue at a price somewhat less than the current market price of the stock. When the stock goes ex-rights, the rights become separately tradeable securities with a value of their own. Because of this, an investor holding rights should sell them or exercise them before the expiration date.

Convertible securities—convertible bonds and convertible preferred stocks—are securities that are convertible into shares of common stock of the issuing corporation. These securities have characteristics of both the bond (or preferred stock) and the common stock. While the interest yield (or dividend yield) of a convertible is likely to be less than for a straight bond (preferred), the convertible has the potential for significant price appreciation should the common stock rise in value. The fixed nature of the convertible's interest (dividend) payment, though, gives it resistance to downward moves in the stock price.

The conversion ratio of a convertible issue represents the number of shares into which it is convertible. The conversion value is equal to the conversion ratio times the stock price. While the conversion value and straight-debt value (or straight-preferred value) of a convertible place a floor on the market value of the issue, the market value will likely be greater than this minimum value. However, this premium over the floor value will generally decrease as the convertible reaches maturity.

There are three reasons for conversion of a convertible before its maturity. The corporation may call the issue, forcing investors to convert if the conversion value of the issue is greater than its call price. In addition, a scheduled change in the conversion ratio may result in early conversion. Finally, if the convertible's conversion value is well above its par value and the dividend yield on the common is greater than the yield on the convertible, it may be advantageous for the investor to convert.

An investment strategy for convertibles contains several features. First, an investor should buy convertibles of companies whose stocks are undervalued. Second, convertibles expected to reach most of their capital appreciation within three to five years are recommended. Finally, an investor in convertibles should consider interest rate risk when choosing a convertible issue.

In addition to convertible bonds and convertible preferred stocks, other types of convertible securities exist. Most common among these are the hybrid convertibles, commodity-backed bonds, equity notes, and adjustable-rate convertible notes.

IMPORTANT TERMS

adjustable-rate convertible note
adjusted exercise price
adjusted warrant price
commodity-backed bond
conversion premium
conversion price
conversion ratio
conversion value
convertible securities
detachable warrant
dilution
equity note
ex-rights
foreign currency warrant
hybrid convertible
nondetachable warrant
pre-emptive right
privileged subscription
reverse warrant hedge
right
rights-on
straight-debt value
straight-preferred value
unit of securities
warrant

QUESTIONS AND PROBLEMS

1. Define a warrant, and compare and contrast it to a call option.
2. Master Pet Foods, Inc., has warrants exercisable into 2.5 shares of common stock upon payment of $38 to the company. The firm's common stock trades for $12 per share, and the warrant sells for $3.
   a) Compute the warrant's adjusted market value.
   b) Compute the warrant's adjusted exercise price.
   c) Compute the adjusted minimum value of the warrant.
   d) If the number of shares each warrant will purchase falls to 2.25 shares tomorrow, should an investor exercise the warrants today? Why?
3. James Computer Furniture Corp. has warrants expiring in two years. Each warrant gives the holder the right to buy 2 shares of common from the company for $45. The firm's stock sells for $32, and the market price of the warrant is $19.25.
   a) Compute the warrant's adjusted market value.
   b) Compute the warrant's adjusted exercise price.

c) Compute the adjusted minimum value of the warrant.
d) If the number of shares each warrant will purchase falls to 1.8 shares tomorrow, should an investor exercise the warrants today? Why?

4. Define a rights offering, and compare and contrast it to a warrant.
5. The management of Anderson-Fuller Steel has decided to raise new equity capital with an issue of common stock. The firm's investment banker recommends a rights offering, and the company gives each stockholder one right for each share owned. Ten rights allows the investor to buy one share of common stock in the company for $22. The current market price of the stock is $35.
   a) Compute the ex-rights price of the stock.
   b) Compute the value of one right.
6. Describe a convertible bond, and compare it to a position containing a straight bond of the corporation and warrants of the corporation.
7. LeCompte Stores, Inc., has a 6 percent convertible bond maturing in ten years. The bond is convertible into common stock of the company at $25 per share. The market price of the stock is $21, and the bond currently sells for $980. An investment advisory newsletter estimates that the straight-debt value of the bond is $800.
   a) Compute the conversion ratio of the bond.
   b) Compute the premium over straight-debt.
   c) Compute the conversion value.
   d) Compute the premium over conversion value.
   e) If the bond has a scheduled decrease in its conversion ratio to 39 tomorrow, should bondholders convert their bonds? Why?
8. Hoverstad Tool Corp. has an issue of 5 percent bonds convertible into 25 shares of the company's common stock. The stock sells for $80 with a $2 dividend, and the bond's price is $2005. The straight-debt value of the bond is $750.
   a) Compute the conversion price of the bond.
   b) Compute the premium over straight-debt.
   c) Compute the conversion value.
   d) Compute the premium over conversion value.
   e) If the bond has a scheduled decrease in its conversion ratio to 24 shares next month, is it likely that bondholders will convert their bonds? Why?
9. What is the downside risk of a convertible bond? Compute the downside risk measure for the convertible bonds in Questions 7 and 8 above.
10. How might an investor estimate the straight-debt value of a convertible bond or the straight-preferred value of a convertible preferred stock?
11. Describe convertible preferred stock. In general, would the price behavior of a convertible preferred stock be more similar to common stock, preferred stock, or convertible bonds of the issuing company?
12. Davis Research has a convertible preferred stock that sells for $88. It is convertible into 4 shares of common stock. The issue is callable after six years at $60, and it has a sinking fund calling for retirement of the issue after fourteen years. The dividend on the convertible is $3 per year. The company's common stock sells for $20 and pays no dividend.
    a) Compute the conversion price of the convertible.
    b) Compute the conversion value.
    c) Compute the conversion premium.
    d) Compute the premium over straight-preferred if you estimate a straight-preferred issue to be worth $55.
    e) Compute the downside risk of this convertible preferred.

13. Why might a company issue convertible bonds or convertible preferred stocks rather than common stock, or regular bonds or preferred?
14. Discuss several types of convertible securities other than convertible bonds and preferreds.

NOTES

1. For a discussion of these issues, see David C. Emanuel (1983), "Warrant Valuation and Exercise Strategy," *Journal of Financial Economics,* 12 (August), 211–236.
2. See, for example, Michael J. Brennan and Eduardo S. Schwartz (1977), "Convertible Bonds: Valuation and Optimal Strategies for Call and Conversion," *Journal of Finance,* 32 (December), 1699–1716; and Jonathan E. Ingersoll (1977), "A Contingent-Claims Valuation of Convertible Securities," *Journal of Financial Economics,* 4 (May), 289–322.
3. Andrew H. Chen and John W. Kensinger (1985), "Innovations in Corporate Financing: Tax-Deductible Equity," *Financial Management,* 14 (Winter), 44–51.

SELECTED REFERENCES

Alexander, Gordon J., and Roger D. Stover (1977). "Pricing in the New Issue Convertible Debt Market." *Financial Management,* 6 (Fall), 35–39.

———, and Roger D. Stover (1980). "The Effect of Forced Conversion on Common Stock Prices." *Financial Management,* 9 (Spring), 39–45.

Bierman, Harold, Jr. (1980). "Convertible Bonds as Investments." *Financial Analysts Journal,* 36 (March-April), 59–61.

Brennan, Michael J., and Eduardo S. Schwartz (1977). "Convertible Bonds: Valuation and Optimal Strategy for Call and Conversion." *Journal of Finance,* 32 (December), 1699–1716.

Brooks, LeRoy D., Charles E. Edwards, and Eurico J. Ferreira (1984). "Risk-Return Characteristics of Convertible Preferred Stock: Comment." *Journal of Portfolio Management,* 10 (Winter), 76–78.

Chen, Andrew H., and John W. Kensinger (1985). "Innovations in Corporate Finance: Tax-Deductible Equity." *Financial Management,* 14 (Winter), 44–51.

Emanuel, David C. (1983). "Warrant Valuation and Exercise Strategy." *Journal of Financial Economics,* 12 (August), 211–236.

Frankle, A. W., and C. A. Hawkins (1975). "Beta Coefficients for Convertible Bonds." *Journal of Finance,* 30 (March), 207–210.

Ingersoll, Jonathan (1977). "An Examination of Corporate Call Policies on Convertible Securities." *Journal of Finance,* 32 (May), 463–478.

Leabo, Dick A., and Richard L. Rogalski (1975). "Warrant Price Movements and the Efficient Market Model." *Journal of Finance,* 30 (March), 163–178.

Marr, M. Wayne, and G. Rodney Thompson (1984). "The Pricing of New Convertible Bond Issues." *Financial Management,* 13 (Summer), 31–37.

McDaniel, W. R. (1983). "Convertible Bonds in Perfect and Imperfect Markets." *Journal of Financial Research,* 6 (Spring), 51–59.

Mehta, Dileep (1976). "The Impact of Outstanding Convertible Bonds on Dividend Policy." *Journal of Finance,* 31 (May), 489–506.

Walter, James E., and Agustin V. Que (1973). "The Valuation of Convertible Bonds." *Journal of Finance,* 28 (June), 713–732.

CHAPTER 19

Futures Markets

The *futures markets* are as fast moving as the options markets, but offer different risk and return possibilities. Although the futures markets traditionally traded contracts for future delivery of agricultural commodities, trading within the past two decades has expanded to include contracts on other assets, such as metals, petroleum, currencies, and financial instruments. This chapter presents a brief description of futures contracts, their markets, the uses of futures, and several of the more popular financial futures available.

Modern futures markets have their origins in the European *bourses,* which were specialized market centers for trading commodities. These markets began as *spot markets,* or *cash markets,* in which commodities changed hands on the spot for cash payments. This type of market developed in other parts of the world, also, and in 1730, the Osaka Rice Exchange in Japan legally recognized the practice of *forward contracting* in rice. Forward contracting is an agreement in which the buyer and seller arrange for delivery and payment for a commodity at a future date.

Forerunners of today's U.S. futures markets began mainly as spot markets in New York and several other major cities during the late 1700s. They traded commodities such as food, metals, and textiles. Their existence greatly facilitated economic development and commerce in the emerging country.

Unfortunately, these early spot markets provided little relief from the wide swings in price caused by sudden shifts in commodity supply or demand. For example, farmers commonly took their grain to markets in regional commercial centers soon after the harvest. Upon arriving, they often found that the short-term supply of their produce exceeded the near-term demand from millers and other grain consumers. This grain glut would drive prices down. During other times of the year, as the supply of grain became exhausted, prices would rise to new highs, giving hope to farmers wanting higher harvest profits. The unfortunate farmer, however, would likely arrive at market as a new supply was being dumped on the market.

Even ignoring the problems of harvest marketing, there were still wide price swings associated with supply/demand imbalances caused by such factors as inadequate transportation, lack of storage facilities, and alternating years of crop failure and abundance. Chicago, as a major center for agricultural commodities during the early to mid-1800s, was a natural location for the development of markets for forward contracting. A group of eighty-two businessmen joined to form the Chicago Board of Trade in 1848. Although early trading was for cash, futures contracts were traded by the 1860s at the Chicago Board of Trade.

TYPES OF CONTRACTS

The parties to forward contracting during the early period were the actual producers and users of the commodity. As markets developed and contracts for the commodities traded in addition to the commodities themselves, other parties entered into the process. Speculators desiring to profit from the rise in the price of a commodity could purchase a contract for future delivery of the good. However, before the actual delivery occurred, the speculator (who had no desire to receive the commodity) would sell the contract to someone who wanted to take delivery and use the commodity. If the commodity's price had risen in the meantime, the speculator would make a profit, and if the price had fallen, the speculator would realize a loss.

Producers of the commodity were willing to contract with speculators to remove the uncertainty of the future price they would receive for their produce. They would *lay off the risk* on the speculators, who were willing to take the risk for the prospect of possible gains. For this process to operate smoothly, however, the speculators needed a liquid market for these contracts. In a liquid market, these contracts could be freely bought and sold as market conditions warranted. This gave rise to the two basic types of contracts for forward delivery.

Cash Forward Contracts

The *cash forward contract* is an agreement between buyer and seller in which the seller agrees to deliver the contracted commodity to the buyer at a specified date for a negotiated price. Although the price of the contract is sometimes due at the initiation of the agreement, the buyer often can delay paying the majority of this amount by borrowing a portion from a third party or even from the seller, with the balance due upon delivery. Cash forward contracts are useful if the seller is a producer and the buyer is a consumer of the commodity. In that case, the seller delivers the produced commodity, and the buyer has a valid use for the product.

However, if the buyer is a speculator having no need for the commodity, then there is no need for actual delivery. The buyer simply wants to close out the position and take the profit (or loss). By the same token, the seller could be a speculator betting that the price will fall. This speculator sells the contract, never intending to make delivery, but hoping to close out the position for a profit at a later date. As the stock, bond, and option markets have shown us, the existence of a liquid market greatly facilitates such transactions.

For a liquid market to survive, several items are needed. These include an organized exchange, clearing operations, and standardized assets trading on the exchange. This brings us to the concept of the futures contract.

The Futures Contract

A *futures contract* is a binding agreement to deliver (or accept delivery of) an asset of a standard grade or quality at the trade price. For every futures contract that exists, there is someone holding that contract long and someone else who has sold it short. Futures come into existence as options do; one party sells short the contract, and another buys it. Because of this, futures trading is a *zero-sum game*. That is, for every dollar of profit made on a futures contract, someone has lost a dollar of profit. In contrast, securities such as stocks represent income-producing concerns, and everyone can profit when the stock rises in value.

Because futures contracts evolved from forward contracts, their characteristics are similar.

Characteristics of Futures Contracts

Although futures and forward contracts are similar, four important areas distinguish futures trading from forward contracts:

1. Exchange trading
2. Standardization of contracts
3. Clearinghouse operations
4. The process of daily resettlement

Trading on Exchanges. Futures contracts trade on organized exchanges. In contrast, forward contracts seldom have regular markets where they trade. They are usually negotiated and agreed upon by buyer and seller directly or through a broker. For example, banks sometimes offer forward contracts on foreign exchange for their customers who plan to receive (or pay) a foreign currency at a future date. Foreign currency futures also trade on some of the exchanges.

Standardized Contracts. Another important distinction between futures and forward contracts is that futures contracts have standardized terms set by the exchange where they trade. (In some instances the Commodity Futures Trading Commission sets the standards.) These standard conditions allow the exchange to have one type of contract with many patrons rather than numerous different contracts, each with only a few interested traders. Greater numbers of interested traders are usually associated with greater liquidity. The exchanges usually set contract terms to standardize the futures contracts in five areas. Table 19–1 gives an example of these terms for the standard wheat contract traded on the Chicago Board of Trade.

These five areas of contract standardization are as follows:

1. *Trading Unit*—The trading unit establishes the quantity and unit of measure for the contract.
2. *Delivery*—The contract terms dealing with delivery address which contract months the exchange will trade, the period within that month in which delivery can be made, the deliverable grades of the commodity, and the actual method by which the seller can accomplish delivery.
3. *Price fluctuation*—These provisions set the minimum price change (trading increment). Most contracts also have a *daily price limit,* which is the maximum total change in price allowed for the trading day.
4. *Position limits*—The exchanges also usually determine *position limits*, which specify the maximum number of speculative contracts one trader may hold. This is also called the *trading limit.*
5. *Performance margins*—A *performance margin* is the amount of money deposited by both the buyer and seller of the futures contract. The purpose of performance margins is to ensure performance of the terms of the contract (delivery by the seller and acceptance by the buyer). Margins for futures contracts differ from margins for stocks, bonds, and other securities in that they do not represent a down payment on the purchase price of the security, but are rather a type of performance bond or security deposit. In addition, they constitute a relatively small portion of the total value of a futures contract, typically between 5 percent and 15 percent of the value of the contract. Most traders can escape the cost of posting performance margins because most futures brokerage firms allow traders to post margin

TABLE 19–1
Specifications for the wheat contract on the Chicago Board of Trade

Trading Unit	***5000 Bushels***
Delivery	*delivery months*: March, May, July, September, and December *delivery period*: any day during the delivery month *deliverable grades*: No. 2 Soft Red, No. 2 Hard Red Winter, No. 2 Dark Northern Spring, No. 1 Northern Spring, and substitutions at differentials determined by the exchange *delivery method*: by registered warehouse receipts issued by approved warehouses in Chicago (or in Toledo, Ohio, at a discount of 2 cents per bushel)
Price fluctuation	*minimum trading fluctuation*: ¼ cent per bushel ($12.50 per contract) *maximum daily price limit*: subject to change
Position limits	3 million bushels in any one contract or in all contracts combined for speculative purposes

in the form of T-bills while the customers continue to collect the interest on the bills. The individual commodity exchanges set the minimum margin deposits.

Clearinghouse Operations. Just as it is necessary for the stock and option markets, the clearinghouse is essential to the smooth operation of a liquid futures market. The clearinghouse in futures markets operates similarly to the clearinghouse for the options markets. While taking no active position in the market, the clearinghouse interposes itself as contracting party to every contract. It keeps records of the number of contracts existing (open interest) and assigns delivery to a buyer whenever a seller makes delivery. As in the option markets, the clearinghouse allows buyers to avoid having to accept delivery by liquidating their long position, and it allows sellers to avoid having to delivery by covering their short position.

Daily Resettlement. A final difference between futures and forwards is *daily resettlement.* The process of daily resettlement actually posts profits and losses to futures traders' accounts on a daily basis. For example, if the wheat contract described in Table 19–1 rises 1 cent, the holder of this contract would receive an additional $50 (5000 bushels × 1 cent) in his account. This futures buyer could then use this additional capital to buy more futures or even withdraw the money for other uses. In other words, unlike the holder of a stock or option, the holder of a futures contract does not have to sell the contract to release its accumulated profits. By the same reasoning, losses are also posted daily to the account, and if the funds in the account fall below the minimum maintenance requirements for the performance margins, the futures trader must deposit additional funds into the account.

The price used to determine the daily resettlement is the contract's *settlement price.* The clearinghouse establishes the settlement price at the close of trading each day as the official price for resettlement. Although some people equate the settlement price in the futures market to the closing price in the stock market, the settlement price does not always represent the final trade of the day on the exchange. Sometimes several different trades may occur at the closing bell. If these trades took place at different prices (which is quite possible), then there will be a range of closing prices. In this case, the clearinghouse will most likely use an average of the last trades as its settlement price.

THE FUTURES MARKETS

The economic justifications for the existence of futures markets traditionally rest upon three foundations:

1. They serve as a vehicle for information about the future price of assets.
2. They provide a means for speculators to speculate.
3. They allow holders, producers, and users of assets to transfer risk to another party.

These reasons for the existence of futures markets also identify the chief participants in futures trading.

Participants in the Futures Markets

The primary participants in the futures markets fall into one of two categories: *hedgers* and *speculators*.

Hedgers

Hedgers are those parties who are *at risk* with a commodity. Being at risk with an asset means being exposed to price changes in the asset. A person is at risk with a long position by holding, producing, or anticipating receipt of the asset. Being at risk with a short position results from using the asset or anticipating a need for it. A party who is at risk with a commodity that has futures contracts traded can reduce or eliminate the risk by hedging with a counteracting position in the futures market. A *short hedge* eliminates or reduces the risk associated with a long position, while a *long hedge* reduces the risk of a short position.

Table 19–2 illustrates the use of a long hedge in West German marks (DM) for a U.S. importer who anticipates a need for DM six months from now. This importer has contracted with a German firm to buy 1000 watches for DM 125,000 to be delivered and paid for in six months. Therefore, the importer will need DM 125,000 in six months. If the importer waits six months to buy the marks, any price increase in marks would raise the effective price of the watches to the importer. To hedge away this price risk, the importer can either buy the marks now or enter into a futures contract to buy the marks in six months. Needing cash for other purposes, the importer prefers not to buy the marks now and establishes a long position in a DM contract by purchasing one futures contract. Table 19–2 shows how the importer takes delivery of the marks in six months, pays the bill for the watches, and is able to avoid a loss even though the mark rises by 2 cents.

It is usually easier for the hedger *not* to take (or make) delivery, but rather to reverse the position in the futures market and trade the asset in the cash market with the usual supplier. Table 19–3 shows an example of a short hedge that is closed out

TABLE 19–2
Example of a long hedge in German marks (DM)

Cash Market	*Futures Market*
Importer anticipates the need for DM 125,000, expects to pay \$.40 per DM in six months.	Importer buys 1 futures contract for DM 125,000 at price of \$.40 per DM.
Six months later:	
DM sells for \$.42 in cash market. Importer would have lost \$.02 per DM (\$2500) by waiting to buy DM at spot.	Importer takes delivery of DM 125,000, transfers them to supplier in Germany. Net cost of DM is \$.40 each.

TABLE 19–3
Example of a short hedge in French francs (fr)

Cash Market	*Futures Market*
Exporter anticipates receipt of fr 500,000, expects to get $.15 per franc.	Exporter sells short 2 futures contracts for fr 250,000 each at a price of $.16 per franc.
Two months later:	
Cash price for franc is $.14, exporter receives fr 500,000 and exchanges them through usual bank.	Covers short position in futures market by buying 2 franc contracts at futures price of $.15 per franc.
Result:	
Loss of $.01 per franc, total of $5000.	Profit in futures market of $2500, total profit of $5000.
Net result: No change in exporter's wealth	

rather than delivered. In the example, an exporter based in the United States has contracted to sell computer parts to a customer in France. The exporter has agreed to sell the parts for 500,000 French francs (fr) and to deliver the parts in two months, receiving payment at that time. The exporter, concerned over fluctuation in the value of the franc, sells short two franc contracts for fr 250,000 each in the futures market. Two months later the *spot price* (cash price) for francs has fallen by 1 cent, and the futures contract has performed equally. Note that the futures contract does not have to mature at the same time the exporter expects to receive the francs, nor does the futures price have to equal the cash price that the exporter expects to receive for the francs. The hedge will be effective as long as the futures price changes by approximately the same amount as the spot price. Two months later, the exporter receives the fr 500,000 and converts them into dollars at the bank, receiving $5000 less than expected for the French currency. But the exporter has a $5000 profit in the futures market that successfully hedged the cash market loss. The net impact on the exporter's wealth is the same as if she had actually delivered the francs to satisfy the futures contract.

Hedgers utilize both the first and the third functions of futures markets listed above. The futures price gives them an idea of the future cash price (not necessarily equal to the future cash price, as the chapter will presently show), and the futures market lets them hedge away at least a portion of their risk so that they may concentrate their resources on matters other than the risk of price changes.

Speculators

The speculators have no prior market position. They use the first two functions of futures markets. They examine the future expected spot prices implied by futures prices. If their own predictions about future cash prices differ from the market's price, and if they believe their own forecast is better, then they can act in the market to speculate upon this information. An example of a speculative position would be a person who felt that a weakening position in the French balance of trade might force the franc down. A speculator shorting the franc contract (Table 19–3) at $.15 and reversing the position two months later at $.14 would realize a profit of $2500. Considering that the performance margin deposit is a small portion of the total contract value, the return in this example would be quite large. The existence of small margin requirements gives futures contracts high leverage and accounts for the popularity of futures markets among speculators.

Because there are probably never enough hedgers to balance the market completely, speculators are valuable participants in the futures markets. For example, suppose that there are producers of a total of 5 million bushels of wheat who want to hedge the sale of their wheat in the futures market, but the users, desiring to hedge their purchase of wheat in the futures market, want only 3 million bushels. The speculators serve the function of filling this gap by entering into the market and establishing their speculative positions.

The Exchanges

There are dozens of futures exchanges around the world. Table 19–4 lists the major U.S. exchanges and some of the international exchanges.

The system of trading at the futures exchanges is quite different from systems at the stock and options exchanges. The method of trading at the futures exchanges is the *open outcry* or *open auction* market system. In this type of trading system, floor traders gather around in groups according to which commodity they are trading, and they shout and signal their bid-and-ask prices to each other for the contracts.

TABLE 19–4
Major futures exchanges

Name	*Location*	*Founded*	*Abbreviation*
Chicago Board of Trade	Chicago	1848	CBT
Chicago Mercantile Exchange	Chicago	1874	CME
Coffee, Sugar, and Cocoa Exchange	New York	1882	CSCE
Commodity Exchange, Inc.	New York	1933	COMEX
International Monetary Market	Chicago	1972	IMM
Kansas City Board of Trade	Kansas City	1856	KC
London Intl. Financial Futures Exchange	London	1986	LIFFE
MidAmerica Commodity Exchange	Chicago	1868	MCE
Minneapolis Grain Exchange	Minneapolis	1881	MPLS
New York Cotton Exchange	New York	1870	NYCE
New York Futures Exchange	New York	1980	NYFE
New York Mercantile Exchange	New York	1882	NYME
Winnipeg Commodity Exchange	Winnipeg	—	WPG

Floor Trading Practices

Traders on the exchange floor are of two categories: *floor brokers* and *floor speculators*. The floor brokers represent either commission brokerage houses filling orders for the public or other commercial interests. These commercial interests are usually producers, manufacturers, processors, or other parties who use the futures markets to limit the price risks of their business. The floor speculators are traders who trade to make profit for their own account. They function similarly to the market makers who trade stocks OTC, except that they compete among themselves on the exchange rather than over communications systems as OTC market makers do.

Speculators usually follow one of three trading strategies. First, the very short-term traders, or *scalpers*, attempt to trade for small, short-term profits. For example, a scalper in wheat may purchase ten contracts at 340 (cents per bushel) and then try to sell them as quickly as possible for 340½. If successful, the trader would profit $25 per contract on a 5000-bushel contract. Only very rarely will a scalper maintain a position overnight. The second group of speculators is the *day traders*. Day traders initiate and close out their positions within the course of the trading day, trying to take advantage of price swings that occur during the day. Like scalpers, day traders generally do not maintain their positions overnight. The third group of speculators, the *position traders*, may hold their positions for days, weeks, or even months.

All of these traders continually compete in the auction on the floor of the exchange to create an active market. The scalpers and the day traders, with their frequent trading, especially contribute to market liquidity and price stability.

The trading floors of the exchanges typically contain several *trading pits*. These are polygonal (often octagonal) areas constructed with several steps around the perimeter of the pit. The steps descend to the center of the pit so that traders may stand on the steps and face other traders standing on other steps and in the center. Traders in particular contract expiration months usually group themselves in one area of the pit.

Orders from commission brokerage houses arrive on the floor by telephone or other electronic communication. Messengers then take the orders to each member firm's floor trading representative for execution. The trader then makes the appropriate offer to buy or sell in the pit. Traders make their offers by open outcry so that any other trader in the pit may take the opposite position to complete the trade. Traders communicate their offers in the pits by shouting and by a system of hand signals. Traders signaling with their palms facing themselves want to buy, and traders with palms facing outward desire to sell. Position and number of fingers outstretched indicate the price of the offer.

Price Reporting

Because of the nature of the futures trading system, price reporting to the public is also different from the stock exchanges. Each trading pit has a price reporter who records and reports each trade to an electronic system. However, since there are many traders in any one pit, the sequence of reported prices may not be identical to the actual sequence of the trades. Reported prices may therefore be a little off from the actual pit trading. Another problem is *trading through*, which can occur in active

FUTURES PRICES

Friday, January 23, 1987.

Open Interest Reflects Previous Trading Day.

	Open	High	Low	Settle	Change	Lifetime High	Lifetime Low	Open Interest
–GRAINS AND OILSEEDS–								
CORN (CBT) 5,000 bu.; cents per bu.								
Mar	159	159½	158½	159½	+ ¼	242½	152¾	51,120
May	164¼	165¾	164¼	165¾	+ 1	242	160¼	27,038
July	168¼	169¾	168¼	169¾	+ 1	227	164½	26,937
Sept	172¼	173	171½	173	+ 1½	201½	168¼	6,370
Dec	175¾	177½	175¼	176¾	+ 1¼	197	171¼	18,883
Mr88	183	184¾	183	184¼	+ 1¼	203¾	179½	2,617
May	186	187	185¾	186¾	+ 1¼	195½	183	595
Est vol 16,000; vol Thur 16,019; open int 133,560, +391.								
OATS (CBT) 5,000 bu., cents per bu.								
Mar	156¾	159½	156½	159½	+ 1¼	165¾	108	2,623
May	152	153¾	152	153¾	+ ¾	157¾	110	2,282
July	144½	145	143¾	145	+ ¼	146½	113¾	976
Sept	137¼	137¼	136¾	137	½	142	124½	496
Dec	140	140	139¾	139¾	– ¼	142	138	101
Est vol 1,000; vol Thur 1,050; open int 6,478, +109.								
SOYBEANS (CBT) 5,000 bu.; cents per bu.								
Mar	496	501¾	495¾	500¼	+ 3¼	576	483½	27,282
May	496½	501	496	500	+ 2¼	574	489	12,564
July	497	501	496	499¾	+ 1	577½	491	17,673
Aug	495½	498½	495	498	+ 1	540½	490½	4,394
Sept	483½	487½	483½	486	1	512	483½	2,114
Nov	484	485	479½	484¾	+ ¼	514	479½	6,671
Ja88	488½	491¼	487½	491¼	– ¾	519	487½	322
Est vol 28,000; vol Thur 13,463; open int 71,216, +411								
SOYBEAN MEAL (CBT) 100 tons; $ per ton.								
Mar	143.00	143.10	141.60	141.80	1.40	163.10	141.00	20,466
May	141.50	141.70	140.40	140.50	1.40	169.70	140.40	15,543
July	141.50	141.50	140.00	140.00	1.70	159.00	140.00	14,267
Aug	141.00	141.00	139.50	139.50	2.00	157.00	139.50	5,656
Sept	140.80	140.80	139.00	139.10	– 2.40	157.50	139.00	3,391
Oct	140.50	140.50	138.00	138.70	2.30	152.00	138.00	1,908
Dec	141.30	141.30	138.80	139.10	– 2.90	156.00	138.80	1,057
Est vol 11,000; vol Thur 10,720; open int 62,299, +1,002.								
SOYBEAN OIL (CBT) 60,000 lbs.; cents per lb.								
Mar	16.42	17.05	16.38	16.97	+ .49	20.25	14.10	28,177
May	16.75	17.33	16.68	17.30	+ .52	20.90	14.40	20,176
July	16.90	17.54	16.90	17.52	+ .52	18.70	14.55	11,908
Aug	16.95	17.50	16.90	17.50	+ .55	18.40	14.65	5,076
Sept	16.85	17.25	16.85	17.25	+ .40	17.25	14.68	2,139
Oct	16.75	17.30	16.70	17.27	+ .53	17.30	14.82	5,121
Dec	16.70	17.35	16.70	17.30	+ .55	17.35	15.52	1,918
Ja88	17.00	17.20	17.00	17.20	+ .35	17.20	15.57	343
Est vol 25,000; vol Thur 20,470; open int 74,937, +1,243.								
WHEAT (CBT) 5,000 bu.; cents per bu.								
Mar	286¾	292	286¼	291	+ 4½	308	243½	17,762
May	268½	272¼	268¼	271¾	+ 4	300	233¼	3,893
July	250	253¼	250	253	+ 2¾	253½	223¼	8,288
Sept	251	253½	250¾	252¾	+ 2¼	253½	233	1,281
Dec	257	258¾	256¾	258¾	+ 2¼	259¼	247½	389
Est vol 9,000; vol Thur 7,927, open int 26,629, –449.								
WHEAT (KC) 5,000 bu., cents per bu.								
Mar	259½	263	259½	262¾	+ 2¾	302½	239¾	8,002
May	245½	248	245½	248	+ 2¼	252	230⅝	2,165
July	238	239½	237	239½	+ 2½	243	230	3,609
Sept	240¼	242	240	242	+ 2¾	245½	233¾	269
Est vol 3,507; vol Thur 2,952; open int 14,090, +233.								
COTTON (CTN) –50,000 lbs.; cents per lb.								
Mar	60.95	61.73	60.45	60.63	– .12	61.73	30.95	10,551
May	59.80	60.15	59.18	59.40	..	60.15	31.56	8,005
July	58.75	59.10	58.20	58.47	+ .07	59.45	32.32	3,838
Oct	57.93	58.10	57.80	57.70	+ .05	58.80	33.50	786
Dec	57.00	57.39	56.70	56.72	– .10	58.60	34.40	2,986
Est vol 4,500; vol Thurs3,134; open int 26,253, +285.								
ORANGE JUICE (CTN) –15,000 lbs., cents per lb.								
Mar	120.00	120.70	190.00	120.00	– 1.65	133.80	83.90	7,134
May	121.50	121.50	119.70	119.95	– 2.40	134.80	84.50	2,259
July	120.00	121.90	120.00	121.00	– 1.50	135.30	84.75	732
Sept	122.40	122.40	120.50	122.00	– 1.40	134.70	107.50	657
Nov	121.05	122.50	121.05	123.00	– 1.35	135.50	108.00	389
Ja88	122.50	122.50	122.00	123.10	– 1.25	135.90	115.00	178
Est vol 2,500; vol Thurs 2,665; open int 11,798, +111.								
SUGAR–WORLD (CSCE) –112,000 lbs.; cents per lb.								
Mar	7.47	8.08	7.42	8.00	+ .56	9.64	5.75	47,175
May	7.63	8.11	7.58	8.07	+ .49	9.82	6.00	24,844
July	7.73	8.21	7.67	8.21	+ .50	9.92	6.17	10,636
Oct	7.89	8.41	7.87	8.41	+ .50	9.60	6.41	12,369
Mr88	8.36	8.89	8.35	8.86	+ .47	8.40	7.04	3,739
Est vol 41,350; vol Thur 24,857, open int 98,837, +1,024.								
SUGAR–DOMESTIC (CSCE) –112,000 lbs.; cents per lb.								
Mar	21.65	21.76	21.65	21.75	+ .11	21.76	20.50	796
May	21.72	21.75	21.72	21.72	+ .03	21.75	20.60	2,112
July	21.75	21.78	21.75	21.77	..	21.78	20.65	2,732
Sept	21.78	21.78	21.78	21.78	+ .01	21.78	20.93	876
Nov	21.52	21.52	21.50	21.52		21.52	20.26	728
Est vol 438; vol Thur 1,549; open int 7,247, 221								
–METALS & PETROLEUM–								
COPPER (CMX) –25,000 lbs.; cents per lb.								
Jan	60.10	60.10	60.10	60.15	– .20	69.20	58.00	128
Mar	60.55	60.70	60.15	60.50	– .30	70.00	58.20	40,259
May	61.10	61.15	60.70	60.95	– .25	70.00	58.20	22,111
July	61.60	61.70	61.20	61.50	– .25	70.00	58.20	6,650
Sept	61.80	62.15	61.75	61.90	– .25	70.35	59.40	3,172
Dec	62.60	62.65	62.40	62.50	.30	69.50	60.05	1,913
Mr88	63.25	63.25	63.25	63.15	– .30	65.65	60.70	284
May	....	....	....	63.45	.30	64.85	60.90	185
Est vol 4,600; vol Thur 4,922; open int 74,741, +267.								
GOLD (CMX) 100 troy oz.; $ per troy oz.								
Jan	....	....	....	404.90	– 3.40	424.50	390.00	52
Feb	406.00	406.00	400.40	405.30	3.60	451.00	337.30	40,443
Apr	410.00	410.20	404.00	409.10	– 3.70	456.00	350.50	32,870
June	412.50	413.20	407.50	412.70	– 3.70	456.00	350.50	14,172
Aug	418.00	418.00	411.00	416.40	– 3.70	460.00	356.00	10,196
Oct	420.50	420.50	417.00	419.90	3.70	465.00	361.00	8,257
Dec	423.00	424.00	419.00	423.50	– 3.70	470.00	365.00	12,142
Fb88	425.00	427.20	424.50	427.20	3.70	473.00	371.50	9,425
Apr	430.00	430.00	430.00	430.90	3.70	479.00	378.00	4,474
June	433.00	433.00	432.00	434.60	– 3.70	484.00	399.00	3,861
Aug	....	....	....	438.70	– 3.70	483.00	426.00	1,671
Oct	443.10	443.10	440.00	443.10	– 3.70	461.50	429.00	971
June	148.50	148.50	147.00	147.00	– .25	155.50	117.00	196
Actual Fri; vol 2,730; open int 10,296, +1,126.								
GASOLINE, Unleaded (NYM) 42,000 gal.; $ per gal.								
Feb	.5060	.5060	.4940	.4950	– .0105	.5225	.3175	5,473
Mar	.5160	.5170	.5070	.5080	– .0079	.5310	.3215	11,098
Apr	.5290	.5290	.5185	.5189	– .0071	.5370	.3450	7,026
May	.5360	.5360	.5260	.5275	– .0065	.5395	.3520	3,655
June	.5310	.5320	.5295	.5290	– .0065	.5390	.4050	1,686
July	.5315	.5315	.5315	.5300	– .0065	.5315	.4400	216
Aug	....	....	....	.5250	– .0065	.5250	.5100	233
Est vol 6,129; vol Thurs 5,171; open int 29,443, +386.								
–WOOD–								
LUMBER (CME) –130,000 bd. ft.; $ per 1,000 bd. ft.								
Mar	183.60	183.60	180.50	182.30	– 2.70	183.60	153.00	3,469
May	176.00	176.00	173.20	174.20	– 2.30	179.00	155.50	1,449
July	171.40	171.40	169.50	169.90	2.00	177.80	155.10	801
Sept	168.50	168.60	166.00	167.70	– .50	177.90	159.50	464
Est vol 1,549; vol Thur 2,889; open int 6,296, +159.								
–FINANCIAL–								
BRITISH POUND (IMM) –25,000 pounds; $ per pound								
Mar	1.5180	1.5200	1.5110	1.5155	– .0025	1.5310	1.3725	27,109
June	1.5000	1.5030	1.4930	1.4990	– .0025	1.5155	1.3600	1,260
Sept	1.4890	1.4890	1.4730	1.4830	– .0030	1.5010	1.3420	162
Est vol 6,140; vol Thur 7,436; open int 28,596, –255.								
CANADIAN DOLLAR (IMM) –100,000 dlrs.; $ per Can $								
Mar	.7330	.7345	.7326	.7344	+.0012	.7363	.6770	13,248
June	.7300	.7317	.7293	.7314	+.0012	.7340	.6995	2,463
Sept	.7277	.7294	.7271	.7284	+.0012	.7315	.6950	736
Dec	.7255	.7261	.7245	.7254	+.0012	.7290	.6980	264
Est vol 2,301; vol Thur 3,074; open int 16,741, –46.								
JAPANESE YEN (IMM) 12.5 million yen; $ per yen (.00)								
Mar	.6585	.6595	.6543	.6572	–.0030	.6669	.5850	32,153
June	.6629	.6629	.6585	.6607	–.0031	.6702	.6121	2,033
Est vol 14,783; vol Thur 14,627; open int 34,259, –65.								
SWISS FRANC (IMM) –125,000 francs-$ per franc								
Mar	.6575	.6585	.6524	.6565	–.0032	.6646	.5125	30,408
June	.6620	.6624	.6563	.6604	–.0033	.6684	.5870	1,675
Sept	.6635	.6650	.6610	.6644	–.0030	.6715	.5960	304
Est vol 25,132; vol Thur 20,875; open int 32,390, –274.								
W. GERMAN MARK (IMM) –125,000 marks; $ per mark								
Mar	.5517	.5527	.5486	.5514	–.0013	.5560	.4370	54,470
June	.5546	.5550	.5511	.5539	–.0014	.5588	.4850	2,399
Sept	.5569	.5569	.5542	.5561	–.0014	.5604	.4868	317
Est vol 27,733, vol Thur 28,961, open int 57,209, +1,008								
EURODOLLAR (LIFFE) –$1 million; pts of 100%								
Mar	94.02	94.02	93.98	93.99	– .03	94.33	90.80	13,190
June	94.10	94.10	94.06	94.08	– .01	94.15	90.85	6,514
Sept	94.02	94.02	93.98	94.00	....	94.03	91.65	3,643
Dec	93.86	93.87	93.86	93.86	....	93.88	91.96	1,764
Mr88	93.65	93.66	93.65	93.67	+ .01	93.67	92.08	655
June	93.43	93.43	93.43	93.45	+ .03	93.43	91.99	487
Sept	93.18	93.23	93.18	93.24	+ .08	93.23	92.37	131
Est vol 4,088, vol Thurs 7,111; open int 26,418, –127.								
STERLING (LIFFE) –£500,000; pts of 100%								
Mar	89.36	89.39	89.31	89.38	– .06	91.45	88.00	7,741
June	89.76	89.79	89.74	89.78	– .09	91.45	88.97	4,552

FIGURE 19–1

Sample futures price report (*Source:* Reprinted by permission of *The Wall Street Journal,* © Dow Jones & Company, Inc. 1987. All Rights Reserved.)

trading and when the prices transacted in one portion of the pit may not be the same as prices in another portion. An example of a public trader experiencing trading through could occur when the public trader, seeing wheat trading at 320, places a limit order to buy at 321. When the floor trader receives the order in the pit, wheat still may be traded at less than 321, but before the trader can actually consummate a trade, the price of wheat could "trade through" 321 to a higher price, and the trade will not be executed. Even though trades could have occurred at 321 or less in the pit after receipt of the public trader's order, the order is not filled. This would not happen under a specialist or market maker system under which the market maker is obligated to deliver securities at the quoted (bid or ask) price.

At the end of the day, the exchange determines and reports the settlement prices for the contracts. Because there may be several different trades at different prices at the close of trading, this settlement price is usually an average of the final trades. Figure 19–1 shows an example of the futures price reporting section from *The Wall Street Journal.* The financial press usually reports the contract's opening, high, low, and settlement prices. In addition, there is usually also a report of the open interest and the lifetime historical high and low prices for the contract, along with the total trading volume for all of the contracts of the commodity.

Commodities Contracts Traded

The traditional trading of futures contracts on agricultural commodities has expanded to other goods and financial instruments, so that futures contracts fall into one of three general categories according to their underlying asset. There are agricultural futures, natural resource futures, and financial futures.

Table 19–5 lists several of the more actively traded agricultural futures contracts. Agricultural futures usually are one of the following types: grain, meat, or food. There are two examples of *contract duplication* in Table 19–5. Contract duplication occurs when two or more exchanges trade identical or similar contracts on the same asset; this is the case for the wheat and soybean futures in the table. Usually, when one exchange tries to compete with another by trading contracts on the same commodity, one of the exchanges emerges with the majority of the trading volume. The exchange that garners most of the trading volume is typically the exchange that first trades the contract. The loser usually eventually drops trading in that contract. Therefore, contract duplication is generally the exception, while *contract specialization* is the norm.

Table 19–6 lists some popular natural resource futures. The natural resource contracts are mainly metals and petroleums.

The financial futures can be grouped into currency futures, futures on financial instruments, and index futures. Table 19–7 presents many of the financial futures currently traded.

The index futures represented a break with tradition in the futures markets. They were the first futures contracts on nondeliverable assets. The first such contract was the future on the Value Line Index, which commenced trading in 1982 on the Kansas City Board of Trade. Because it would be impossible (or at least extremely inconvenient and difficult) to deliver all of the stocks in the Value Line Index in the correct quantities, final settlement on the index futures is in cash instead of actual delivery.

TABLE 19–5
Agricultural futures contracts

Commodity	*Contract Size*	*Exchange*[a]	*Price Quotation*
Barley	20 metric tons	WPG	Can. $ per ton
Cattle (live)	40,000 lbs.	CME	cents per lb.
Cocoa	10 metric tons	CSCE	$ per ton
Coffee	37,500 lbs.	CSCE	cents per lb.
Corn	5000 bu.	CBT	cents per bu.
Corn	1000 bu.	MCE	cents per bu.
Cotton	50,000 lbs.	NYCE	cents per lb.
Feeder cattle	44,000 lbs.	CME	cents per lb.
Flaxseed	20 metric tons	WPG	Can. $ per ton
Hogs	30,000 lbs.	CME	cents per lb.
Lumber	130,000 bd. ft.	CME	$ per 1000 bd. ft.
Oats	5000 bu.	CBT	cents per bu.
Orange juice	15,000 lbs.	NYCE	cents per lb.
Pork bellies	38,000 lbs.	CME	cents per lb.
Soybean meal	100 tons	CBT	$ per ton
Soybean oil	60,000 lbs.	CBT	$ per 100 lbs.
Soybeans	5000 bu.	CBT	$ per bu.
	1000 bu.	MCE	cents per bu.
Sugar (world)	112,000 lbs.	CSCE	cents per lb.
Wheat	5000 bu.	CBT	cents per bu.
	1000 bu.	MCE	cents per bu.
	5000 bu.	KC	cents per bu.
	5000 bu.	MPLS	cents per bu.

[a]See Table 19–4 for exchange abbreviations.

TABLE 19–6
Natural resources futures contracts

Commodity	*Contract Size*	*Exchange*[a]	*Price Quotation*
Aluminum	40,000 lbs.	COMEX	cents per lb.
Copper	25,000 lbs.	COMEX	cents per lb.
Gasoline (leaded)	42,000 gal.	NYME	$ per gal.
(unleaded)	42,000 gal.	NYME	$ per gal.
Gold	100 troy oz.	COMEX	$ per oz.
	32.5 troy oz.	CBT	$ per oz.
Oil (crude)	1000 barrels	NYME	$ per barrel
(heating)	42,000 gal.	NYME	$ per gal.
Palladium	100 troy oz.	NYME	$ per oz.
Platinum	50 troy oz.	NYME	$ per oz.
Silver	5000 troy oz.	CME	cents per oz.
	1000 troy oz.	CBT	cents per oz.

[a]See Table 19–4 for exchange abbreviations.

TABLE 19—7
Financial futures contracts

Financial Instrument	*Contract Size*	*Exchange*[a]	*Price Quotation*
Currencies:			
British pound	25,000 pounds	IMM	$ per pound
Canadian dollar	100,000 dollars	IMM	$ per Can. $
Japanese yen	12.5 million yen	IMM	cents per yen
Swiss franc	125,000 francs	IMM	$ per Sw. franc
West German mark	125,000 marks	IMM	$ per mark
Financial instruments:			
Bank CDs	$1 million	IMM	points of 100%
Eurodollars	$1 million	IMM	points of 100%
	$1 million	LIFFE	points of 100%
GNMA certificates 8%	$100,000 prin.	CBT	points of 100%
Long gilt	£50,000	LIFFE	32nds of 100%
Treasury bills	$1 million face	IMM	points of 100%
Treasury bonds	$100,000 prin.	CBT	points of 100%
Treasury notes	$100,000 prin.	CBT	points of 100%
Indexes:			
Municipal Bond Index	1000 × index	CBT	points of 100%
S&P 500 Index	500 × index	CME	$
Major Market Index	250 × index	CBT	$
NASDAQ 100 Index	250 × index	CBT	$
NYSE Composite Index	500 × index	NYFE	$
U.S. Dollar Index	500 × index	NYCE	$
Value Line Index	500 × index	KC	$

[a]See Table 19–4 for exchange abbreviations.

Brokerage Firms

To deal in the futures markets, public traders trade through a brokerage firm just as they would in markets for stocks and other securities. Many of the large, diversified stock brokerage firms with memberships on the NYSE and other exchanges also maintain membership on the commodity exchanges to trade futures contracts for their customers. In addition, some firms specialize in commodities trading. They either maintain memberships on the futures exchanges to serve their customers, or they clear their trades through an exchange member. Exchange members who clear trades for other brokerage firms are like wholesalers in the futures trading business—they trade in large quantity at a wholesale commission for brokers who in turn charge their customers a retail commission.

Public traders usually deal through a *registered representative* at the brokerage firm. The registered representatives take orders from their customers and transmit them to the order desk or to the exchange. As on the securities exchanges, the most common type of order is the market order to execute a trade as quickly as possible at the best available price. There are also limit orders, which can be for one day (day orders), any specified length of time, or good-till-cancelled (open orders). Most exchanges also accept *spread orders.* A spread order is an order for the simultaneous purchase and sale of different futures contracts.

Futures Markets Regulation

The regulation of futures trading occurs at two levels. The exchanges, with their rules and regulations, provide the traditional self-regulation in the market. Regulation at the federal level is under the Commodity Futures Trading Commission (CFTC).

As the futures markets developed, the exchanges assumed responsibility in several areas for regulating the activity of their member firms. Federal legislation such as the Grain Futures Act of 1922, the Commodity Exchange Act of 1936, and the Futures Trading Act of 1978 formalized and extended these obligations. The areas in which the exchanges maintain regulation and supervision include floor trading practices, capital adequacy of member firms, and settlement of trades between members.

The Commodity Futures Trading Commission Act of 1974 created the CFTC to replace the old Commodity Exchange Authority operated under the U.S. Department of Agriculture. The CFTC operates under a sunset provision that requires its periodic renewal by Congress. Exchanges must submit trading rules and terms for newly proposed contracts to the CFTC for approval. Among its powers, the CFTC has the authority to review certain exchange actions, to take emergency steps in the markets when certain conditions exist, to set requirements for registered representatives, and to adopt minimum financial requirements for brokers.

THE PRICING OF FUTURES CONTRACTS

There are many forces at work in the market that affect the prices of futures contracts. The factors that influence the price of the underlying asset of the contract are quite important. Futures traders use both fundamental analysis and technical analysis to try to forecast spot prices of the commodity in the future. However, because the factors affecting individual commodities differ from contract to contract, this section concentrates attention on the common factors that influence prices of futures contracts in general.

One of the most influential determinants of the futures price of an asset is the cash or spot price of that asset. In fact, most study of futures prices concentrates on the difference between the spot price and the futures price. This difference, called the *basis,* can be expressed as follows:

$$\text{Basis} = \text{Current spot price} - \text{futures price} \tag{19–1}$$

The basis defines the relationship of the futures price to the spot price. In essence, trying to determine the futures price for an asset is the task of determining what the basis should be.

Just as there is a relationship between the spot price and a futures price, there is also a relationship between the futures price in any one delivery month and the futures price of the same asset in any other delivery month. This relationship is the *spread,* expressed as follows:

$$\text{Spread} = \text{Nearby futures price} - \text{distant futures price} \qquad \textbf{(19–2)}$$

In Equation 19–2, the *nearby futures price* is the price of the futures contract with delivery month closest to the present (of the two delivery months for which the spread is being determined). The *distant futures price* is the price of the contract whose delivery month is further away than the nearby contract.

There is one basis between each delivery month and its cash price, and there is one spread for each possible pair of delivery months. For example, if there are three delivery months for a T-bill futures contract, there will be three different bases, one for each delivery month. There are three different spreads—the first month with the second, the first with the third, and the second with the third.

There are two basic reasons why futures prices usually differ from spot prices (that is, the basis is not equal to zero). The first reason is that the expected spot price of the asset at the future date may not be equal to the current spot price. The second reason is that the futures price (priced at the current date) may not be equal to the expected future spot price.

Current Spot Prices and Expected Future Spot Prices

Prices of almost all goods and assets will fluctuate, so it is reasonable that the price of an asset may not remain the same over time. Even the expected future price may be different from the current price. Factors such as expected future changes in supply and demand could result in a situation in which the current price is not equal to the expected future price. For example, the spot price for corn may be currently high, but the expected future price could be low if there were reports of a large, successful corn crop in the field waiting to be harvested. It is factors such as these that the fundamental analysts examine when attempting to forecast futures prices.

Even in the absence of such factors that cause changes in the future spot price of an asset, the expected future spot price should not be equal to the current spot price. An explanation for this is the *carrying charge theory of future prices.* This theory says that the expected value of an asset in the future should be equal to the cost of buying that asset today and storing it until the future date. Written mathematically, this relationship is as follows:

$$F = S \times (1 + c) \qquad \textbf{(19–3)}$$

where F = expected future spot price
S = current spot price
c = carrying charges to carry the asset until delivery, expressed as a percentage of the spot price of the asset

Carrying charges of an asset include the cost of funds to purchase the asset, the cost of transportation, insurance expenses, and storage costs. With positive carrying costs, it is readily apparent that the expected future spot price will always be greater than the current spot price if the carrying charge theory alone determines future expected prices.

There are some markets in which the supply and demand of the commodity are relatively stable and carrying charges are more easily estimated. In these markets, Equation 19–3 might be a logical basis for estimating future cash prices. The futures market in U.S. Treasury bonds might be such a market. There are other markets, however, in which the carrying charge theory would not work very well. The market for fresh eggs provides a good example because it is almost impossible to store fresh eggs for future delivery.

Futures Prices and Expected Future Spot Prices

Futures prices should reflect expected future spot prices rather than current spot prices, because futures are contracts for delivery at the future date. However, futures prices may not necessarily be equal to future expected spot prices. There are at least two theories that attempt to explain why the current futures price may not equal the expected future spot price.

The concept behind the first theory is risk and return. For speculators to enter into the market and assume some of the risk, they must expect compensation for their activities. The only way that this compensation can be forthcoming is if the futures price is different from the expected future spot price. If the two prices were equal, there would be no inducement for speculators to take positions in futures markets.

The second reason advanced as an explanation of the difference between futures prices and expected future spot prices is the existence of daily resettlement and performance margin requirements. Daily resettlement actually results in net cash flows daily to the futures trader. Because the trader can at least be receiving interest on this cash, positive cash flows lower the cost of trading while negative flows increase these costs. Therefore, the futures price depends not only upon the future expected spot price, but also on the pattern of prices between now and delivery that will result in either positive or negative cash flows to the trader.

When futures prices are less than expected future spot prices, the condition known as *normal backwardation* exists. *Contango* defines the occasion when futures prices are greater than expected future spot prices. Either of these conditions can exist in a futures market, depending upon the economic environment, expectations, interest rates, and other factors. The two aforementioned theories can explain either contango or normal backwardation.

OPTIONS ON FUTURES

In addition to options and futures trading, the exchanges offer options on futures contracts. These options are virtually identical to the options on stocks, indexes, and other assets described in Chapter 17. The expiration cycles of the options typically coincide with the expirations of their underlying futures contract. The call option on a futures contract grants its holder the right to purchase a particular futures contract at the exercise price, and a put carries the right to sell a futures contract. The writer

FUTURES OPTIONS

Friday, January 23, 1987

-AGRICULTURAL-

CORN (CBT) 5,000 bu.; cents per bu.

Strike Price	Calls–Settle Mar-c	May-c	Jly-c	Puts–Settle Mar-p	May-p	Jly-p
140	....	....	....	1/8	1/2	3/4
150	9	16 1/2	....	3/8	1 1/2	1 1/4
160	2 1/2	9 1/2	14	2 7/8	4	4 1/2
170	3/8	4	7 1/2	11	8 1/2	8 1/2
180	1/8	2	4 1/4	20 1/2	16	15 1/2
190	1/8	1/2	2	30 1/2	24 1/4	22 1/4

Est. vol. 800, Thur vol. 334 calls, 456 puts
Open interest Thur 29,384 calls, 15,020 puts

SOYBEANS (CBT) 5,000 bu.; cents per bu.

Strike Price	Calls–Settle Mar-c	May-c	Jly-c	Puts–Settle Mar-p	May-p	Jly-p
450	....	....	....	1/8	1	1 1/8
475	25	26 3/4	27 1/4	3/8	2 3/4	3 3/4
500	3 3/4	8 1/4	11 1/4	3 1/2	9	12
525	1/4	2 1/2	4 3/4	24 3/4	....	29 1/2
550	1/8	3/4	2 1/4	49 3/4	....	52
575	1/8	3/8	1 3/8	74 3/4	....	....

Est. vol. 3,000, Thur vol. 944 calls, 714 puts
Open interest Thur 30,733 calls, 10,939 puts

CANADIAN DOLLAR (CME) 100,000 Can.$, cents per Can.$

Strike Price	Calls–Settle Feb-C	Mar-C	Apr-C	Puts–Settle Feb-P	Mar-P	Apr-P
71	....	2.44	....	....	0.03	....
72	....	1.48	....	....	0.07	....
73	0.52	0.65	....	....	0.22	....
74	0.06	0.19	....	0.62	0.77	....
75	0.01	....	....	....	....	1.93
76	....	....	....	....	....	....

Est. vol. 58, Thur vol. 272 calls, 5 puts
Open interest Thur;2,701 calls, 2,948 puts

STERLING (LIFFE)–b-£25,000; cents per pound

Strike Price	Calls–Settle Mar-C	Jun-C	Sep-C	Puts–Settle Mar-P	Jun-P	Sep-P
135	17.55	17.55	17.55	0.01	0.38	1.13
140	12.55	12.55	12.55	0.10	1.04	2.27
145	7.55	7.55	7.55	0.57	2.35	4.03
150	3.51	4.36	4.86	1.99	4.51	6.51
155	1.33	2.39	3.02	4.81	7.54	9.67
160	0.37	1.19	1.77	8.85	11.34	13.42

Actual Vol. Friday, 4 Calls, 59 Puts.
Open Interest Thursday; 1,154, Calls, 1,457 Puts.
b-Option on physical sterling.

EURODOLLAR (LIFFE) $1 million; pts. of 100%

Strike Price	Calls–Settle Mar-C	Jun-C	Sep-C	Puts–Settle Mar-P	Jun-P	Sep-P
9350	0.50	0.63	0.64	0.01	0.05	0.14
9375	0.28	0.43	0.46	0.04	0.10	0.21
9400	0.12	0.26	0.32	0.13	0.18	0.32
9425	0.04	0.14	0.20	0.30	0.31	0.45
9450	0.01	0.06	0.12	0.52	0.48	0.62
9475	0.00	....	....	0.76	....	....

Actual Vol. Friday, 155 Calls, 70 Puts.
Open Interest Thursday; 1,440, Calls, 901 Puts.

EURODOLLAR (CME) $ million; pts. of 100%

Strike Price	Calls–Settle Mar-C	Jun-C	Sep-C	Puts–Settle Mar-P	JunP	Sep-P
9350	0.46	0.59	0.59	0.02	0.06	0.14
9375	0.25	0.39	0.41	0.05	0.10	0.20
9400	0.10	0.24	0.28	0.15	0.19	0.31
9425	0.03	0.13	0.18	0.33	0.32	....
9450	0.01	0.07	0.11	0.55	....	....
9475	.0004	0.02	0.05	0.80	....	....

Est. vol. 6,753, Thur vol. 3,855 calls, 4,227 puts
Open interest Thur; 52,287 calls, 64,195 puts

TREASURY BILLS (IMM)-$1 million; pts. of 100%

Strike Price	Calls–Settle Mar-C	Jun-C	Sep-C	Puts–Settle Mar-P	Jun-P	Sep-P
9425	....	....	....	.0004	....	....
9450	0.25	0.40	....	0.02	0.09	....
9475	0.08	0.23	....	0.10	0.17	....
9500	0.01	0.12	....	0.28	....	....
9525	.0004	0.05	....	0.52	....	....
9550	.0004	....	....	....	....	....

Est. vol. 1, Thur vol. 1 calls, 11 puts
Open interest Thur; 2,373 calls, 1,227 puts

-METALS-

COPPER (CMX) 25,000 lbs.; cents per lb.

Strike Price	Calls–Last Mar-C	May-C	Jly-C	Puts–Last Mar-P	May-P	Jly-P
56	4.55	5.10	5.90	.05	.20	.45
58	2.55	3.30	4.45	.05	.40	.65
60	.95	1.95	2.75	.45	1.00	1.30
62	.25	.95	1.75	1.75	2.00	2.25
66	.05	.45	.85	5.55	5.45	5.00

Est. vol. 1,000, Thur vol. 823 calls, 226 puts
Open interest Thur 33,108 calls, 5,461 puts

GOLD (CMX) 100 troy ounces; dollars per troy ounce

Strike Price	Calls–Last Apr-C	Jun-C	Aug-C	Puts–Last Apr-P	Jun-P	Aug-P
380	31.60	38.30	43.20	3.10	6.00	8.20
390	23.20	30.70	35.60	4.70	8.00	9.80
400	15.50	23.70	28.70	6.70	11.00	13.40
420	6.60	12.60	18.40	16.80	20.30	22.00
440	3.30	7.70	12.00	33.90	35.00	35.00
460	1.70	4.50	9.10	51.70	51.10	51.70

Est. vol. 6,100, Thur vol. 3,093 calls, 2,604 puts
Open interest Thur 46,541 calls, 36,240 puts

SILVER (CMX) 5,000 troy ounces; cents per troy ounce

Strike Price	Calls–Last Mar-C	May-C	Jly-C	Puts–Last Mar-P	May-P	Jly-P
500	59.0	68.0	76.5	.20	4.5	7.0
525	35.5	47.3	56.0	1.8	7.3	11.1
550	15.5	29.5	38.0	6.5	14.0	18.0
575	5.0	16.5	27.0	20.5	25.0	31.5
600	2.0	11.0	20.0	42.0	44.5	49.0
625	.90	7.0	15.0	65.5	65.5	68.0

Est. vol. 1,100, Thur vol. 911 calls, 194 puts
Open interest Thur 28,890 calls, 12,486 puts

-FINANCIAL-

BRITISH POUND (CME) 25,000 pounds, cents per pound

Strike Price	Calls–Settle Feb-C	Mar-C	Apr-C	Puts–Settle Feb-P	Mar-P	Apr-P
1475	4.25	4.85	....	0.25	0.85	....
1500	3.35	3.20	2.95	0.85	1.70	....
1525	1.10	1.90	1.95	2.05	2.90	....
1550	0.40	1.10	1.25	....	4.55	....
1575	....	0.60	....	....	....	....
1600	....	0.35	0.45	....	....	....

Est. vol. 879, Thur vol. 3,328 calls, 832 puts
Open interest Thur;26,069 calls, 21,976 puts

W. GERMAN MARK (CME) 125,000 marks, cents per mark

Strike Price	Calls–Settle Feb-C	Mar-C	Apr-C	Puts–Settle Feb-P	Mar-P	Apr-P
53	2.22	2.44	2.81	0.08	0.31	0.45
54	1.36	1.72	2.10	0.22	0.58	....
55	0.72	1.12	1.51	0.58	0.98	1.13
56	0.31	0.70	1.05	1.17	1.55	1.64
57	0.12	0.45	0.71	....	2.27	....
58	0.05	0.25	....	....	....	....

Est. vol. 10,042, Thur vol. 6,962 calls, 4,878 puts
Open interest Thur;53,133 calls, 58,019 puts

SWISS FRANC (CME) 125,000 francs; cents per franc

Strike Price	Calls–Settle Feb-C	Mar-C	Apr-C	Puts–Settle Feb-P	Mar-P	Apr-P
64	1.85	2.31	2.81	0.22	0.67	0.79
65	1.12	1.69	2.16	0.47	1.02	....
66	0.63	1.15	....	0.94	1.50	....
67	0.29	0.79	....	....	2.13	....
68	0.14	0.54	0.87	....	2.86	....
69	0.07	0.35	0.62	....	....	....

Est. vol. 5,638, Thur vol. 1,604 calls, 2,312 puts
Open interest Thur; 19,621 calls, 24,322 puts

JAPANESE YEN (CME) 12,500,000 yen; cents per 100 yen

Strike Price	Calls–Settle Feb-C	Mar-C	Apr-C	Puts–Settle Feb-P	Mar-P	Apr-P
64	1.86	2.17	2.61	0.15	0.46	0.57
65	1.10	1.48	1.90	0.38	0.77	0.86
66	0.57	0.96	1.30	0.85	1.25	1.31
67	0.23	0.60	0.95	1.50	1.87	....
68	0.10	0.36	0.64	....	....	....
69	....	0.22	0.46	....	....	....

Est. vol. 3,794, Thur vol. 2,454 calls, 2,989 puts
Open interest Thur;29,830 calls, 28,471 puts

FIGURE 19–2

Sample prices of options on futures (*Source:* Reprinted by permission of *The Wall Street Journal,* © Dow Jones & Company, Inc. 1987. All Rights Reserved.)

of a call option on a future must be prepared to take a short position in the future should the option be exercised, while the put writer has to be ready to assume a long position after exercise.

Figure 19–2 shows some options contracts on futures and how they are quoted in *The Wall Street Journal.* Note that in some assets—currencies, for example—there exists an options market, a futures market, and a market for options on futures.

The prices of options on futures generally behave like those of options on the basic underlying asset. Why, then, would a market for options on futures develop when options on the asset itself would suffice? First, the exchanges generally found it easier to propose options on futures rather than straight options during the time period when these contracts began trading (early 1980s). Options regulation falls under the umbrella of the SEC while regulation of options on futures usually rests with the CFTC. Since the CFTC's rules and regulations for the introduction of new contracts and trading are generally not as stringent as those of the SEC, the futures exchanges found a more sympathetic regulatory environment with options on futures. A second reason is that options on futures could increase the volume of trading on the futures themselves, an occurrence that the futures exchanges would certainly welcome. A final reason is that traders may find exercise easier for options on the futures than for certain options on the actual asset. For example, it is simpler to take delivery of a futures contract on live hogs than to actually receive the hogs themselves.

SUMMARY

The markets in which commodities trade for current delivery are spot or cash markets. Other markets exist in which buyers and sellers contract for delivery of an asset at some future date. Cash forwards are examples of contracts that specify future delivery of a good, but no liquid aftermarket exists for forward contracts. Futures contracts also call for delivery of an asset in the future, and they do trade on organized futures exchanges, resulting in a liquid market for these contracts. In addition to exchange trading, other differences between forward and futures contracts include the standardization of the contract terms of futures, the existence of the futures clearinghouse, and the practice of daily resettlement. Margin requirements for futures contracts (called performance margins) are usually significantly less than margins for stocks and other securities. Because of this, futures trading can be a risky proposition. To allay some of the risk by discouraging wild price swings, futures exchanges often place a daily limit on the amount that a contract can change in price during the day.

The main participants in the futures markets are hedgers and speculators. Hedgers are parties who produce or utilize an asset during their normal course of business. They can establish positions in the futures markets that allow them to presell items they produce or prebuy items they need. In this way, hedgers use the futures market to lower the risk of price changes. Speculators, on the other hand, have no productive relationship to the asset. Their interest in the futures market is to profit from price swings in the asset underlying a futures contract. Speculators are willing to assume the risk of price changes in exchange for the prospect of making speculative profits.

Futures exchanges use the open outcry system of trading, with floor brokers and traders competing for the best price in each trading pit. Futures traders can be scalpers, day traders, or position traders. Regulation of futures trading is accomplished through the exchanges and the Commodity Futures Trading Commission.

The basis of a futures contract is equal to the spot price less the futures price. The carrying charge theory of futures prices states that expected spot prices of an asset in the future are determined by the costs of buying that asset today and holding it until the future date. However, futures prices can be different from future expected spot prices, leading to normal backwardation when futures prices are less than expected future spot prices and to contango when futures prices exceed expected future spot prices.

In addition to futures contracts, many of the futures exchanges also trade put and call options on futures contracts.

IMPORTANT TERMS

basis
bourse
carrying charge theory of future prices
cash forward contract
cash market
contango
contract duplication
contract specialization
daily price limit
daily resettlement
day trader
distant futures price
floor broker
floor speculator
forward contracting
futures contract
futures market
hedger
lay off risk
long hedge
nearby futures price
normal backwardation
open auction market system
open outcry market system
performance margin
position limit
position trader
registered representative
scalper
settlement price
short hedge
speculator
spot market
spot price
spread
spread order
trading limit
trading pits
trading through

QUESTIONS AND PROBLEMS

1. Distinguish between cash, spot, forward, and futures markets.
2. Compare and contrast a cash forward contract and a futures contract.
3. Explain the process of daily resettlement in the futures markets. How is this process different from the daily recalculation of margin accounts for stocks?
4. Who are the chief participants in the futures markets? What does each contribute to the functioning of futures markets?
5. How do futures exchanges differ from the stock exchanges and the over-the-counter markets? What is "trading through"? Can it happen on a stock exchange? Why?

6. Define contract specialization and contract duplication among the futures exchanges. Why might contract duplication arise?
7. What are normal backwardation and contango in the futures markets? What might cause them to exist?
8. Assume the spot price for gold is $400 per troy ounce. The quotes for futures contracts of 100 ounces are as follows:

Contract Expiration Month	*Price*
March	404
June	407
September	410

   a) Compute the basis for each of the contracts.
   b) Compute the March-September spread.
   c) Assume that today is the first day of January and that the cost of carrying gold in inventory is 20 percent annually. Using the carrying charge theory of futures prices, compute the value of each gold contract.
   d) If your answers in part (c) differ from the futures prices listed above, what factors might explain the differences? Is this a situation of contango or normal backwardation?
9. If the margin deposit for a futures contract in gold is $5000, compute the dollar profit if you had bought the June contract in Question 8 and held it until the end of June when the spot price of gold had arisen to 430. Compute your return on the initial investment of $5000. What would your profit and return be if you had shorted the contract instead of buying it?

SELECTED REFERENCES

Black, Fisher (1976). "The Pricing of Commodity Contracts." *Journal of Financial Economics,* 4 (January), 167–179.

Bodie, Z., and V. Rosansky (1980). "Risk and Return in Commodity Futures." *Financial Analysts Journal,* 36 (May/June), 27–39.

Cox, John C., Jonathan E. Ingersoll, and Stephen A. Ross (1981). "The Relation between Forward Prices and Futures Prices." *Journal of Financial Economics,* 9 (December), 321–346.

Fama, Eugene F. (1976). "Forward Rates as Predictors of Future Spot Rates." *Journal of Financial Economics,* 3, 361–377.

Hunter, William C. (1986). "Rational Margins on Futures Contracts: Initial Margins." *Review of Research in Futures Markets,* 5, 160–173.

International Monetary Market, Chicago Mercantile Exchange (1978). *Understanding Trading in Gold Futures.* Chicago: Author.

Khoury, Sarkis (1984). *Speculative Markets.* New York: Macmillan Publishing Co.

Peck, Anne E. (Ed.) (1977). *Selected Writings of Holbrook Working.* Chicago: Board of Trade of the City of Chicago.

——— (Ed.) (1977). *Selected Writings on Futures Markets.* Chicago: Board of Trade of the City of Chicago.

Richard, S., and M. Sundaresan (1981). "A Continuous Time Equilibrium Model of Forward Prices and Futures Prices in a Multigood Economy." *Journal of Financial Economics,* 9 (December), 347–371.

Sandor, Richard I. (1979). *Speculating in Futures.* Chicago: Board of Trade of the City of Chicago.

Whittaker, Gregg, Linda E. Bowyer, and Daniel P. Klein (1987). "The Effect of Futures Trading on the Municipal Bond Market." *The Review of Futures Markets,* 6, 196–204.

CHAPTER 20

Other Specialized Securities

The previous chapters in this section have dealt with options, hybrid securities and futures. These securities all are different from the stocks and bonds that are the standard investments in the securities markets. To round out our study of types of securities, this chapter discusses several special types of securities that previous chapters have not addressed in detail.

We begin with an overview of investment companies and mutual funds, and then discuss the goals, management, and structure of the funds' portfolios. Although the formal classification of investment companies is a bit more detailed, there are two types of investment companies that investors usually think of when the topic of investment companies arises. *Closed-end investment companies* have a fixed number of shares outstanding, and their stock trades on one of the exchanges or over-the-counter. The shares outstanding of *open-end investment companies,* on the other hand, vary in quantity because the fund issues new shares directly to investors when the investors purchase shares. The first section of this chapter classifies and discusses investment companies in more detail. Following sections present real estate investment trusts and American Depository Receipts for foreign securities.

INVESTMENT COMPANIES

As mentioned in Chapter 2, which introduced the types of securities, *investment companies* are companies whose principal activity is to invest in securities of other companies. Often called *mutual funds,* or just *funds,* investment companies obtain their capital to invest by selling their own shares to investors. The investment company then invests these funds in stocks, bonds, or other instruments. The investor who owns shares of stock in the investment company, therefore, indirectly owns a portion of the portfolio of securities held by the investment company. The investment company has acted as a *financial intermediary,* or conduit for the investment funds, by raising money from investors and investing that money in other companies.

Regulation and Tax Treatment of Investment Companies

All investment companies that offer their shares to the public must register with the Securities and Exchange Commission. The SEC obtained the authority to regulate investment companies under authority granted by the Investment Company Act of 1940. Before this act, investment companies were virtually unregulated. The Investment Company Act placed them under constraints regarding areas such as investment policies, sales charges, and investment advisory fees.

Investment companies are one of the few types of corporation that pay no tax on corporate income. As long as the investment company is registered under the Investment Company Act and pays out at least 90 percent of its earnings as dividends, the company pays no federal income tax. The tax liability falls upon the investor receiving the dividend. The extent of taxability of the dividend from an investment company depends upon how the investment company earned the income. For example, if one half of the dividend paid by an investment company resulted from interest paid on tax-free bonds, then that half of the dividend would be nontaxable for the investor.

Investment Goals

Each investment company must make a statement to its investors regarding its investment policy and goals. These investment goals can be broad or very narrowly defined. Table 20–1 gives examples of some of the types of investment companies classified according to their investment objectives. In addition to these broad categories, many funds specialize in a particular area of a category. For example, in the bond category, there are funds concentrating on short-term bonds, intermediate-term bonds, long-term bonds, government bonds, speculative bonds, mortgage-backed bonds, and others.

Each investment objective of an investment company leads to a target risk level for that company. The target risk level, in turn, delimits the return that an investor should expect from the investment company. Table 20–1 gives some average risk and return figures for the broad investment objective categories.

One interesting type of fund is the *index fund.* The goal of index funds is to perform just like the market. Most index funds will try to match the performance of some widely known market index such as the Standard & Poor's 500 Composite Index. The advantage of index funds lies in their lower expenses. Since they simply "buy the index" and do not try to select securities using elaborate security analysis, index funds generally have lower costs. Index funds therefore appeal to efficient market enthusiasts, who believe it is very difficult (if not impossible) to beat the market. These

TABLE 20–1
Types of investment companies classified by investment objective

Investment Objective	*Securities Invested In*
Aggressive growth	Common stocks with high growth potential, typically with low dividend yields
Balanced	Common stocks with high dividend yields, bonds, preferred stocks
Bond	Fixed-income securities
Growth	Common stocks of stable, growth-oriented firms
Growth and income	Common stocks and convertible securities of well-established, dividend-paying companies
International	Securities of firms located in different countries
Money market	Money market instruments
Precious metals	Securities of companies that mine gold and other precious metals, options on metals, and the metals themselves
Tax-exempt bond	Municipal bonds

people feel that investors are better off by controlling expenses rather than searching for desirable investments.

Other funds specialize in securities from foreign countries. Most of these tend to specialize in one country, such as the Japan Fund, the Korea Fund, and the Mexico Fund.

Many sponsoring firms of investment companies of the open-end type have a *family of funds*. The family of funds often includes one or more different funds from each category, so that the fund sponsor is able to offer something for every investor.

TABLE 20–2
Average risk and return of investment companies categorized by investment objective (compared to S&P 500 Index)

Investment Objective	*Beta*	*1981–85 Total Return (percent)*
Aggressive growth	1.35	76.4%
Growth	1.06	101.9
Growth and income	0.83	115.9
International	0.77	121.7
Precious metals	0.67	−12.4
Balanced	0.58	129.3
Tax-exempt bond	0.33	78.0
Bond	0.28	108.6
Money market	0.00	63.1
S&P 500 Index	1.00	97.9

Advantages of Investment Companies for Individual Investors

Investment companies have been on the investment scene for many years. Though their popularity has generally grown and subsided with movements in the general market, investment companies remain popular vehicles for investment in securities. Although they have features that may appeal to all investors, investment companies have special advantages for small investors. Not all funds offer all of these advantages or services, so investors should always check before investing.

One advantage that may be especially important to the small investor is diversification. A typical investment company portfolio will have at least dozens, if not hundreds, of different securities. An investor with $10,000 to invest in stocks would be able to buy only about four or five different issues in round lots. However, purchase of shares in an investment company can give the small investor needed diversification and its risk-reducing benefits. Small investors who prefer to evaluate and select their own stocks can also use investment companies. They can buy enough shares in a diversified investment company to achieve sufficient diversification and invest the remainder of their funds in their favorite stocks.

A second advantage offered by investment companies is shareholder services. These services include recordkeeping, automatic dividend reinvestment, and withdrawal plans. Recordkeeping services provide shareholders with monthly or quarterly statements showing dividends paid, taxability of those dividends, and share balances. Most companies offer automatic dividend reinvestment, which allows shareholders to receive dividends automatically as additional shares in the investment company rather than in cash. Withdrawal plans give shareholders the option of having the investment company automatically withdraw money and send it to the shareholder. This is especially convenient for retirees who use the payments as part of their retirement cash flow.

A third advantage is savings on transactions costs. Although the investment companies pay commissions on the stocks they buy, their buying power gives them the ability to negotiate much lower commissions than an individual small investor would normally pay. For purchases of the shares in the investment company, some companies allow investors to buy and sell shares without paying a commission to the investment company. In addition, most families of funds allow *telephone switching,* which lets shareholders switch their money, usually without charge, from one fund to another within the same family of funds.

A final advantage is that investment companies offer the small investor professional investment management. To get personal investment advice and management, an investor with about $100,000 or less to invest would have to pay an investment advisory fee so high (in relation to the amount invested) that it would be prohibitive. This same investor can place her money in an investment company that hires professional analysts and portfolio managers. Although the investment company pays an investment advisory fee for this service, that fee, divided among many investment company shareholders, is relatively small.

In spite of the appeal of the investment companies to individual investors, they do have their shortcomings. The principal drawback of investment companies is that the investor loses the ability to direct funds into shares of individual companies that may have the best investment potential. Of course, an investor can minimize the drawback by committing a portion of investment funds to investment companies and investing the rest in individual securities. A second handicap faced by the holder of investment company shares is that the performance of the fund's securities has to be sufficient to pay the management fee and still have enough remaining to satisfy the return demanded by the investor.

Net Asset Value

There is one financial measure that is unique to investment companies—the *net asset value.* The net asset value is equal to the assets per share less liabilities per share, stated as follows:

$$\text{Net asset value} = \frac{\text{Total assets} - \text{total liabilities}}{\text{Number of shares outstanding}} \qquad \textbf{(20–1)}$$

The net asset value of an investment company is akin to the book value of an industrial firm. The major difference is that virtually all of the assets of an investment company are marketable securities, and they are carried on the books at market value, not cost, as are assets of other companies. An investment company with a net asset value of $25 has $25 worth of securities behind every share it has outstanding. Investment companies revalue their entire portfolio at the close of trading every day and recalculate their net asset value.

Although a few investment companies do their own investment research and portfolio management, most have investment advisory contracts with investment management firms. These sponsors or investment advisors base their investment advisory fee on the net asset value. This fee is usually a percentage of net assets per year. A typical investment advisory fee is about .5 percent of net assets per year, although some fees are a bit more or less. The amount of the fee usually depends upon the amount of management and portfolio supervision needed. For example, option funds would need a high level of management (and would pay a high fee) while a bond income fund would need less.

Types of Investment Companies

The Investment Company Act classifies investment companies into three types. This section presents the two main types: *unit investment trusts* and *management companies.* A third type, the *face amount certificate,* is similar to a fixed annuity. It is obsolete and no longer offered.

Unit Investment Trusts

A *unit investment trust* is a type of investment company that usually takes the legal form of a trust rather than a corporation. It therefore sells *units* rather than *shares.* As a trust, unit investment trusts must have a finite life. They typically contain portfolios of unmanaged securities, namely bonds. They collect the interest on the bonds and disburse it to the unit holders. When the bonds mature, the trust pays the principal amount to the unit holders. Ultimately, all of the bonds mature, and the unit investment trust ceases to exist.

Unit investment trusts offer the advantage that as unmanaged portfolios their expenses are very low. They often pay no management fee at all. Consequently, their payout to unit holders is slightly higher.

Brokerage firms and investment bankers often put together unit investment trusts as a vehicle to help them sell packages of bonds. This lets them offer the bonds as a portfolio to small investors who otherwise might not be interested.

Generally speaking, an investor who purchases a unit investment trust should be prepared to hold it for quite a while, if not until maturity. There is a small secondary OTC market for some of the larger issues of unit investment trusts, and some brokerage firms try to maintain bid-ask quotes on unit trusts they put together, but trust holders should not count on having a high degree of liquidity. If they need liquidity, there are other types of investment companies more suitable to their purpose.

Management Companies

The second major type of investment company is the *management company,* so called because it holds a portfolio of securities that it continuously supervises and manages. In contrast to the unit investment trust, management companies usually take the corporate form of organization and issue stock, although some are limited partnerships. Because the portfolio of a management company is continuously monitored, the research, management, and operational costs of a management company are greater than those of a similar unit investment trust. However, most investors seem to believe that the benefits of continuous management outweigh the higher costs because management companies are by far the largest group of investment company.

There are two types of investment company within the management company category. These are the *open-end investment company* and the *closed-end investment company.*

Open-End Investment Companies. Open-end investment companies are distinguished by their "open ended" share issuance practice. These are the investment companies more commonly called *mutual funds.* When an investor decides to buy shares of an open-end company, he purchases those shares directly from the company (or through a sales representative). The company simply issues new shares to the investor to fill the order. An investor who wants to sell shares in a mutual fund sells the shares back to the company. In mutual fund terminology, the company *redeems the shares.*

The price at which the company sells and redeems shares is the net asset value. When an investor places an order to purchase or redeem shares in a mutual fund, the price is equal to the net asset value at the close of business on that day (adjusted for commissions, in some cases). Some larger families of mutual funds have shifted to repricing their portfolios and recalculating their net asset value every hour, in which case the price for the fund is the next prevailing net asset value.

The issuance and redemption of shares in a mutual fund affects the total assets and shares outstanding of the fund, but not the net asset value. Table 20–3 shows the

TABLE 20–3
Effects of issuing new shares on a mutual fund's balance sheet

1. *Opening scenario*

Balance sheet	
Assets	Liabilities
$10,000	$0

Shares outstanding: 500

Net asset value = (10,000 − 0)/500 = 20

2. *Fund sells 100 new shares to investor at net asset value of $20*

Balance sheet	
Assets	Liabilities
$12,000	$0

Shares outstanding: 600

Net asset value = (12,000 − 0)/600 = 20

3. *Portfolio of securities held (assets) falls in market by $1000*

Balance sheet	
Assets	Liabilities
$11,000	$0

Shares outstanding: 600

Net asset value = (11,000 − 0)/600 = 18.33

balance sheet of a mutual fund with $10,000 in assets and 500 shares outstanding. The accompanying net asset value is $20. The fund issues 100 new shares to an investor at $20 per share, a total of $2000. Assets increase to $12,000, shares outstanding rise to 600, and the net asset value remains $20. The occurrence that does change net asset value is a change in the market value of the securities in the fund's portfolio. For example, Table 20–3 shows the effect of a decline in the value of the fund's portfolio of $1000. The net asset value falls to $18.33.

Within open-end investment companies, we can further categorize the funds as *no-load mutual funds* and *load mutual funds*. The primary difference between the two is that the load funds charge a *load,* or commission; when investors buy or redeem shares. A load on the purchase of shares is a *front-end load,* and a load on the redemption of shares is a *back-end load* or *redemption fee*. The difference between a commission and a load is that a commission is added to the price of the stock, while a load is subtracted from the price. For example, if commissions are 8 percent, an investor who buys $1000 worth of stock pays $80 commission, and the total amount owed to the broker is $1080. On the other hand, an investor placing a $1000 buy order for an 8 percent load fund pays an $80 load, which is subtracted from the $1000 to leave the investor with $920 worth of mutual fund. With the 8 percent commission, the investor traded $1000 worth of stock but only $920 worth of mutual fund.

Although some funds charge a redemption fee or back-end load, most do not. The effect on the net wealth of the investor is the same, whether the load is on the front or the back.

Registered representatives with brokerage firms, insurance salespeople, and dedicated sales staffs conduct most of the selling of load funds. They receive the load as compensation for their services. In addition to making the transaction, these people offer their clients services that include financial planning and help in choosing the fund with the right investment objective. A sales representative must provide prospective investors with a copy of the fund's prospectus before selling shares. Typical loading charges are about 8 percent, but this usually declines as the investor purchases larger amounts of the fund.

A no-load mutual fund charges no loads or commissions to investors purchasing or redeeming their shares. Every dollar spent by the investors becomes invested in the fund. Since there is no load to compensate a sales representative, no-load funds do not sell their shares through representatives. (The exception is some money market mutual funds offered by brokerage firms and life insurance companies as a service to their clients and as an incentive for the client to leave their investment funds within the firm.)

No-load funds sell their shares directly to the investing public. They usually generate initial inquiries from investors by advertising in financial publications. The cost of advertising and selling fund shares must be borne by the investment advisory firm for the fund, not charged as a fund expense. Investors with at least enough knowledge about investments to choose a fund with the desired investment objectives should purchase no-load funds unless there is some compelling reason to buy a load fund. Load fund managements have often argued that their performance is superior to the no-load funds. They have claimed that their investment advisory fees are lower because they do not have to bear the cost of direct fund sales. However, there is no evidence to support these statements, and the investment performance of load funds appears to be no better than that of no-load funds. A study by Carlson[1] found that after considering the expense of the loading charge, no-load funds as a group tended to perform better than load funds.

The performance of investment companies is an issue of interest to most investors. Successful identification of the funds that tend to exhibit superior performance over time should be a guide for investors in their continued quest to "outperform the market." Chapter 22 on investment performance evaluation discusses and shows examples of some historical performance studies of investment companies.

Some funds have tried to strike a medium between the load and the no-load types. They want some help in covering the cost of distribution, but they do not want to charge loads they believe to be excessive. This is the group of so-called *low-load funds*. The low-load funds distribute their shares directly to investors, as do the no-loads, but they charge a load of about 1 percent or 2 percent to cover sales costs.

Another tack that some no-loads have tried to help pay the cost of share distribution and increase share sales is to take advantage of Section 12b-1 of the SEC regulations governing investment companies. This provision allows the investment advisory firm to charge the fund an extra annual percentage fee based on net assets to cover sales costs. These costs can even include paying salaries or commissions to sales representatives. Over the long run, these extra annual costs can mount up, and an investor could be better off buying a load fund with a fixed 8 percent front-end load than buying a no-load fund with a stiff 12b-1 plan. Although funds with 12b-1 plans argue that such plans are actually beneficial to the fund because they increase share sales and lower per share expenses, there is little evidence to support this conclusion. The Carlson[2] study found that fund size bears no relation to performance. Good advice for any mutual fund investor is to check the status of any 12b-1 plan that a prospective fund might have. It is generally better to avoid funds with such plans. The shareholders of a fund must approve a 12b-1 plan before the fund can institute such a plan.

Closed-End Investment Companies. The distinguishing feature of closed-end investment companies is that they have a fixed number of shares outstanding. They do not offer and redeem their shares directly with investors. Closed-end funds sell their shares to the public in the same manner that other companies do—they have a new issue of stock handled by an investment banking firm. Once these shares have been issued, the number of shares outstanding is fixed and will not change unless the company retires shares or has another public offering.

Shares of closed-end investment companies, also called *publicly traded funds,* trade in the same markets as shares of other companies. They trade over-the-counter, or the company may choose to list its shares on the AMEX or NYSE. Because market forces of supply and demand determine the market price of closed-end funds, there is no guarantee that they will trade for their net asset value. *The Wall Street Journal* reports the net asset value of closed-end funds every Monday, so investors can see if their fund trades at a discount or premium from net asset value. As the sample prices in Figure 20–1 indicate, the market price of closed-end funds can deviate above or below the net asset value.

As a general rule, shares of closed-end companies trade more often at a discount from net asset value than at a premium. Since the net asset value of the fund represents market values that the fund should be able to receive should it decide to sell, why do the funds often sell for a discount? Several theories attempt to explain why stocks of closed-end funds sell at a discount or premium. The first of these is based on the tax liability that may have accumulated in the value of the fund's portfolio. If the stocks in the portfolio have increased in value, then the tax on that increase will have to be paid when the fund sells those stocks. This explains discounts from net asset value that would be equal to the implied tax liability. A second theory holds that the funds may not be able to sell the securities in its portfolio for their quoted market values. Because of marketability and liquidity, a large investment company could conceivably depress stock price by dumping its portfolio on the market at once. This theory explains discounts, but not premiums. A final explanation of closed-end funds' premiums or discounts rests on investors' expectations. If investors are positive about the ability of a fund's management to beat the market, demand could drive the price of the fund's shares to a premium. By the same argument, if investors believe that a

Publicly Traded Funds

Friday, January 16, 1987

Following is a weekly listing of unaudited net asset values of publicly traded investment fund shares, reported by the companies as of Friday's close. Also shown is the closing listed market price or a dealer-to-dealer asked price of each fund's shares, with the percentage of difference.

	N.A. Value	Stk Price	% Diff
Diversified Common Stock Funds			
AdmExp	20.80	21⅜	+ 2.8
BakerFen	54.48	46	−15.6
EqGuard	b9.78	9	− 8.0
GemIICap	b15.96	14¾	− 7.6
Gem II Inc	b9.74	14⅝	+50.2
GenAInv	21.06	19¼	− 8.6
GlobGrCap	10.04	9⅜	− 6.6
GlobGrInc	9.41	11¼	+19.6
GSO Trust	9.72	8⅞	− 8.7
Lehman	16.80	16½	− 1.8
LbtyAll-Star	10.63	9⅝	− 9.5
NiagaraSh	17.39	15⅝	−10.1
RoyceValue	9.64	10¾	+11.5
SchaferValu	9.28	9	− 3.0
Source	40.20	43⅛	+ 7.3
Tri-Contl	30.49	32⅜	+ 6.2
WorldwdVal	18.97	17	−10.4
Zweig Fund	9.81	9⅝	− 1.9
Specialized Equity and Convertible Funds			
AmCapCv	a28.33	33½	+18.2
ASA	bc84.35	39⅜	−53.3
BancrftCv	26.60	28⅛	+ 5.7
Castle	28.26	28⅝	+ 1.3
CenFdCan	b5.77	5⅜	− 6.9
CentSec	13.99	13	− 7.1

	N.A. Value	Stk Price	% Diff
Claremont	52.12	59	+13.2
CLASS	z	z	z
CLASS Pfd	z	z	z
CypressFd	9.90	9⅝	− 2.8
EllsworthCv	9.71	9¼	− 4.7
EmMedTch	b15.14	13⅞	− 8.4
Engex	20.41	20	− 2.0
1stAustralia	11.93	9⅞	−17.2
FstFinFd	9.15	7⅞	−13.9
FranceFd	b15.92	11½	−27.8
GabelliE	9.88	9⅜	− 5.1
Germany	10.65	10⅜	− 2.6
Italy Fd	b14.32	10¾	−24.9
Japan Fd	20.65	15⅝	−24.3
Korea Fd	27.72	35¾	+29.0
ML Cnv Cap	11.80	7¼	−39.0
ML Cnv Inc	9.36	13⅝	+46.0
Mexico Fd	b5.91	4	−32.3
Pete&Res	29.78	32⅛	+ 7.9
PilReg	9.74	8⅞	− 8.9
RegFinl/Shs	8.93	8⅛	− 9.0
Scandinavia	b9.92	8⅝	− 1.3
Z-Seven	d17.47	22½	+28.8

a-Ex-dividend. b-As of Thursday's close. c-Based on Johannesburg closing prices. d-NAV reflects $.54 per share for taxes. z-Not available.

FIGURE 20–1
Sample prices and net asset values of closed-end investment companies
(Reprinted by permission of *The Wall Street Journal,* © Dow Jones & Company, Inc. 1987. All Rights Reserved.)

fund is inferior, then lack of interest in the fund could allow its share price to fall into the discount range.

Buying shares of investment companies at a discount has been a popular investment strategy. If the discount narrows or becomes a premium, then the investor gets an added capital gain. For example, suppose that an investment company's shares have a net asset value of $20 and sell for a 5 percent discount. The market price of the fund is therefore $19. Suppose the portfolio increases by $5, and the discount disappears. An investor who had bought the underlying stock would show a $5 profit, while one who purchased the investment company would reap $6. Even if the discount remains the same, the holder of the investment company shares has more assets earning dividends. Suppose that the example fund's stocks yielded an average dividend of 5 percent. This $1 dividend on the investment company's shares would represent a yield of 5.26 percent.

The management of closed-end companies has an advantage over open-end funds that results from the share issuance policy of the open-ended companies. Because the open-end investment companies must always stand ready to redeem their shares, they must maintain a certain portion of their assets in cash and liquid securities. This maintenance level of cash may not be the optimal level, and closed-end companies do not have to worry about keeping cash on hand for withdrawals.

REAL ESTATE INVESTMENT TRUSTS

Investors can participate in real estate investment either by direct or indirect investment in real property. Direct investment involves the purchase and management of real estate assets. Direct investment requires significant knowledge of the real estate market, specialized familiarity with the particular properties owned and their local markets, and skill in the management of real properties. Indirect investment is of more interest to this textbook because indirect investment is accomplished by the purchase of securities of companies involved in real estate investment.

Real estate investment trusts (REITs) are the vehicles for indirect real estate investment. A REIT is a company that sells shares to the public and invests the proceeds in real properties or mortgage instruments. REITs may use debt to lever their capital structure to purchase additional property. They are all of the closed-end type, issuing new stock only during periodic public offerings. Shares of REITs trade on the exchanges and in the OTC markets.

There are three principal types of real estate investment trust:

1. Equity trusts
2. Mortgage trusts
3. Hybrid trusts

The equity type of REIT invests only in positions of ownership of real estate property. This property may be unimproved land held for capital gain or improved property that can be rented for rental income. Mortgage trusts participate in writing and purchasing various types of mortgages. The hybrid trusts hold combinations of equity and mortgage positions. Table 20–4 lists some of the REITs that currently trade.

REITs provide individual investors and investors who have little knowledge of real estate the opportunity to participate in real estate investment. The market value

TABLE 20–4
Sample listing of real estate investment trusts

Name	*Type*	*Traded*	*Beta*
BankAmerica Realty	hybrid	NYSE	.75
First Union Real Estate Investments	hybrid	NYSE	.65
HRE Properties	equity	NYSE	.65
Lomas & Nettleton Mortgage Investors	mortgage	NYSE	.75
Mortgage and Realty Trust	mortgage	NYSE	.80
Mortgage Growth Investors	hybrid	AMEX	.55
Property Capital Trust	equity	AMEX	.55

Source: The Value Line Investment Survey

of a REIT is closely related to the value of its underlying assets. Therefore, conditions in the real estate market are more important determinants of REIT risk than are general stock market conditions. Because of this, REITs generally have low betas. The equity trusts typically have lower betas than the mortgage trusts, which usually have higher degrees of interest rate risk. However, it is important to note that although REITs have low betas, they may be quite volatile relative to changes in the market for real estate, especially if they are leveraged trusts.

AMERICAN DEPOSITORY RECEIPTS

One vehicle that facilitates the purchase of international stocks is the *American depository receipt* (ADR). ADRs are receipts for foreign stocks held in trust in the host country. An ADR may be sponsored or nonsponsored. With the sponsored type of ADR, the foreign company decides that it would be beneficial to have its ADR trade in the U.S. market. The company arranges for the trustee who will hold the stock. The company also retains a U.S. brokerage firm to arrange for U.S. trading. The investment banker may recommend listing on the NYSE or AMEX, or over the counter. With the unsponsored ADR, the company takes no initiative to promote its ADR, but a brokerage firm recognizes that there may be sufficient U.S. interest in the company to justify an ADR. The brokerage firm sponsors the ADR by setting up the trustee, and the broker then makes a market in the ADR.

ADRs for many stocks from various countries trade on U.S. exchanges and OTC. For example, Matsushita, the huge Japanese conglomerate, has ADRs that trade on the NYSE. The main advantage that an ADR offers is that it is much easier for a U.S. investor to buy the ADR than to buy the foreign security directly. Buying a security directly from a foreign country can be complicated and can involve additional services such as long-distance communication and currency conversion. Another benefit is that the ADR trustee collects the dividends and remits them to U.S. ADR holders in U.S. dollars, eliminating the need for the investor to exchange currency when receiving a dividend.

SUMMARY

Investment companies are a type of financial intermediary that raises funds by selling shares to investors and investing those funds in a diversified portfolio of securities of other issuers. The SEC regulates investment under authority of the Investment Company Act of 1940. Registered investment companies may be exempt from taxes on their income as long as they distribute a minimum of 90 percent of the income to their shareholders. An investment company must have a stated investment objective such as income, growth, or capital gains.

Investment companies offer several advantages to investors. These advantages include diversification, shareholder services, reduced investment expenses, and professional investment management.

Open-end investment companies, also called mutual funds, continuously offer to sell their shares to the public and to redeem the shares when investors want to sell. Of the open-end type, load funds charge investors a commission to buy (or perhaps to redeem) their shares. No-load funds charge no commission. Closed-end investment companies have a fixed number of shares outstanding and trade on an exchange or OTC.

A real estate investment trust is a company that invests in real estate property or in mortgages on real estate. REITs offer investors an opportunity to participate in the real estate market without having to purchase real estate directly. The value of the shares of a real estate investment trust is closely related to the value of the assets owned by the trust.

American depository receipts are trust receipts that trade in the United States. They represent foreign company securities that are held in trust in the foreign country. They may be sponsored by the foreign company or unsponsored. Benefits offered by ADRs include the fact that they obviate the need to make transactions in the foreign country and that the investor receives dividends in U.S. dollars.

IMPORTANT TERMS

American depository receipt (ADR)
back-end load
closed-end investment company
equity real estate investment trust
face amount certificate
family of funds
financial intermediary
front-end load
hybrid real estate investment trust
index fund
investment company
load
load mutual fund
low-load mutual fund
management company
mortgage real estate investment trust
mutual fund
net asset value
no-load mutual fund
open-end investment company
publicly traded fund
real estate investment trust (REIT)
redeem shares
redemption fee
telephone switching
unit investment trust

QUESTIONS AND PROBLEMS

1. Explain how an investment company is a type of financial intermediary. Is a commercial bank a financial intermediary? Compare and contrast the intermediary functions of banks and investment companies.
2. What are the advantages to an individual investor of owning shares in an investment company as opposed to buying securities directly? What are the disadvantages, if any, of holding investment company shares?
3. An investment company has 12,750 shares outstanding. The market value of securities owned by the fund is $158,687.50. The company has no other assets and a management fee payable of $2,500. Compute the net asset value of the fund.

4. What will be the net asset value of the fund in Question 3 if during the next month 800 new shares are sold at an average price of $14, 300 shares are redeemed at an average price of $13.50, and the value of the portfolio rises by 5 percent? (Assume the fund is of the no-load type.)
5. Describe unit investment trusts. Which types of securities do they usually hold?
6. Describe management investment companies. Identify and define the two main categories of management companies.
7. Distinguish between load and no-load mutual funds, What is a low-load fund?
8. What is a real estate investment trust? Compare and contrast it to a closed-end investment company.
9. Identify the three major types of real estate investment trust.
10. Do real estate investment trusts tend to have low or high betas? Why?
11. What is an American depository receipt? Why might an investor prefer to buy the ADR rather than buying the security itself in the foreign country?

NOTES

1. Robert S. Carlson (1970), "Aggregate Performance of Mutual Funds, 1948–1967," *Journal of Financial and Quantitative Analysis,* 15 (March), 1–30.
2. Ibid.

SELECTED REFERENCES

Alexander, Gordon Jr., and Roger D. Stover (1980). "Consistency of Mutual Fund Performance during Varying Market Conditions." *Journal of Economics and Business,* 32 (Spring), 219–225.

Bogle, John C., and Jan M. Twardowski (1980). "Institutional Investment Performance Compared: Banks, Investment Companies and Mutual Funds." *Financial Analysts Journal,* 36 (January-February), 33–41.

Brauer, Greggory, A. (1988). "Closed-End Fund Shares' Abnormal Returns and the Information Content of Discounts and Premiums." *The Journal of Finance,* 43 (March), 113–127.

Scott, Maria C. (1985). "Everything You Always Wanted to Know About 12b-1 Plans—and More." *AAII Journal,* 7 (March), 18–21.

PART SEVEN

Portfolio Management and Performance Evaluation

CHAPTER 21

Portfolio Management Strategies

This chapter deals with the practice of portfolio management. Chapters 7 and 8 showed the effects of diversification and gave the theoretical arguments for asset pricing models. This chapter melds those two theoretical presentations with practical considerations to present strategies for the successful management of investment portfolios.

The separation theorem (discussed in Chapter 8) freed portfolio managers from the constraints of having to construct portfolios from a limited number of securities. As a result, portfolio management has become a complex process using techniques designed to lead to identification and purchase of the desired portfolio. In a dynamic market, the process of portfolio management becomes continuous. Each step requires evaluating previous decisions, anticipating future conditions, and altering current decisions to reflect both.

Several factors have contributed to the growth of portfolio management as a legitimate body of knowledge and professional practice. Among them are the following:

1. The development of modern asset pricing models defining the relationship between risk and return.
2. The rise of the institution as a dominant factor in the market.
3. Increased volatility of financial markets and interest rates.
4. The growth in the use of computers to disseminate, accumulate, and analyze information.
5. The development of quantitative tools for portfolio management and the adoption of their use by the profession.
6. The increased awareness of the costs associated with failure to meet portfolio objectives.

OVERVIEW OF THE PORTFOLIO MANAGEMENT PROCESS

All phases of the portfolio management process require that the portfolio manager maintain sensitive feelers to measure and evaluate the investment environment. This requires inputs concerning relevant social, political, economic, market, industry, and security factors. The three-level investment evaluation process that analyzes the economy, industry groups, and individual securities provides an excellent vehicle for inputs into the portfolio management process. Because the three-level process is also the standard framework for security analysis, using it as an information system for the portfolio management process yields cost economies for the entire investment process.

Figure 21–1 illustrates the portfolio management process. It begins with the identification of the investor's objectives, preferences, and constraints. Following this is the development of an investment policy and strategy designed to meet those objectives. Next, the portfolio manager must select an optimal combination of investments to fulfill the investment strategy. In a market where conditions are constantly evolving, asset values, market conditions, and other variables are constantly changing. These changes lead the portfolio from its optimal path and necessitate rebalancing and restructuring the portfolio in an effort to meet its objectives once again. This process of rebalancing requires constant input of new information and looping back to previous steps to begin a new cycle of the management process.

The astute portfolio manager constantly receives new information, which can lead to changes that require looping back at any phase of the process. The portfolio management process becomes a continuous loop that contains shortcuts. These shortcuts allow both looping back to previous steps and jumping forward to subsequent steps with the overall goal of identifying, constructing, and maintaining an optimal portfolio for the investor.

The remainder of this chapter discusses in more detail the first three steps in the portfolio management process and the portfolio monitoring and revision process.

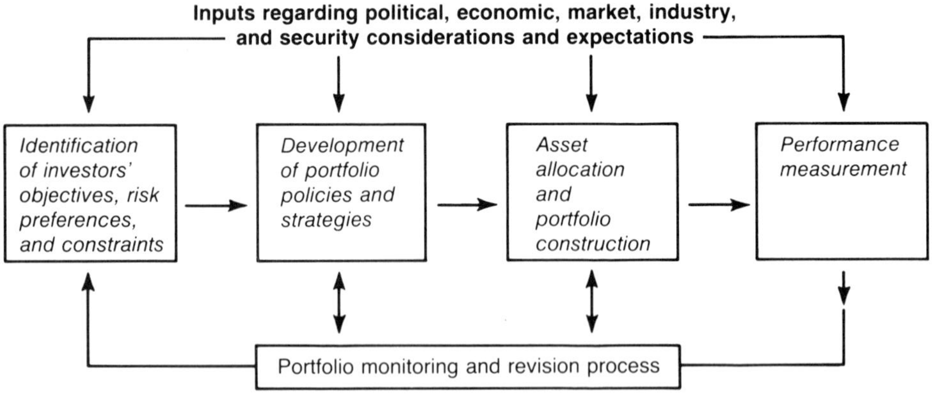

FIGURE 21–1
Overview of the portfolio management process

The evaluation of portfolio performance requires its own detailed discussion, found in Chapter 22.

IDENTIFICATION OF INVESTOR OBJECTIVES, PREFERENCES, AND CONSTRAINTS

The early portions of the investment management process are concerned with identifying the investor's objectives, risk preferences, and constraints. Although each of these items is a separate concept, they are interrelated. Therefore, the identification of any one of these items must be accomplished within an environment created by all three.

The objectives represent goals the investor hopes to achieve. These objectives are usually stated in terms of a minimum return or level of wealth.

Risk preferences are the investor's tolerance for risk. The formal representation of risk preferences is a set of indifference curves. However, whether the investor is an individual or an institution, it is doubtful that the investor is willing or able to map out indifference curves. The specification of risk preferences therefore often takes on a more subjective aspect.

Constraints are limitations placed on the investment management process. The constraints may be determined by the investor or by some outside agency. Investor-determined constraints include such items as the investment time horizon, liquidity, and current income needs. Constraints influenced by outside agencies usually involve legal requirements, regulatory considerations, and taxation. The two areas of constraint are often interrelated. For example, a change in the tax structure may encourage an investor to prefer current dividend income over capital gains.

Individual Investors

Investment objectives and risk preferences of individual investors vary widely. Recognizing, identifying, and classifying them can be a most challenging and difficult task for an investment counselor.

An investment manager handling an individual's portfolio usually begins the process by interviewing the client. The process may include counseling the client about possible investment returns that are likely in the current economic and market environment. Of course, this counseling would include the expected risks associated with the various types of investments. Through a series of perceptive questions and careful analysis of conversations with the client (which may also include written correspondence), an investment counselor should be able to develop a profile of the investor's overall objectives and risk preferences.

One popular approach to this procedure uses the *investor life cycle*. The investor life cycle describes the typical investment needs of individuals at various phases of their lives or careers.

The first phase in which most people have income to invest usually occurs in the early years of the career. The individual's assets are usually small in relation to liabilities, especially if the person has taken on debts such as loans to finance a college education, a home mortgage, or other large credit purchases. Before committing funds for investment purposes, all individuals should first have sufficient savings and life insurance. The savings provide liquidity and a "safety net," while life insurance assures financial security to dependents in case of death. Upon satisfying these two needs, an individual can and should commit a portion of discretionary income to investments. At this point in their careers, most people anticipate larger future income levels as a result of career promotions and advancements. They can therefore accept a long time horizon on their investments and shoulder higher return, higher risk investments. Usually they have little need for income from their investments, so early career investors can take on stocks in promising growth-oriented companies yielding long-run capital gains. The risk-return combination for an early career person might be as illustrated in Figure 21–2.

The second stage in the investor life cycle is the mid-career portion of life. By this time, the individual should have accumulated assets that exceed liabilities. The well-prepared individual at this phase likely has a well-rounded savings and insurance program, tangible equity in a home, a meaningful accumulation in a pension plan, and an established program of investment. At mid-career, the investment time horizon is still long because twenty years or more remain until retirement. Investments in the high return, high risk categories are still appropriate. During this phase, however, capital preservation begins to become important, and the investor may want to start reducing risk in some areas.

The third phase occurs during the late-career years. The individual's investment horizon is significantly shorter, and preservation of capital takes on primary importance. The investor's assets should exceed liabilities by a large amount, the pension

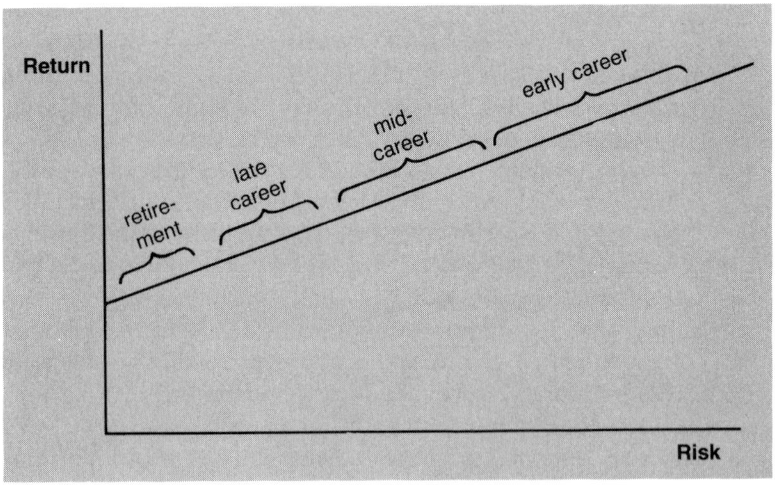

FIGURE 21–2
Example risk-return combinations for typical individuals at various phases of the investor life cycle

fund should contain adequate amounts, and the home mortgage should be about paid off. Contents of the individual's investment portfolio should concentrate on lower risk securities that have relatively stable values.

The final phase of the investor life cycle is retirement. At this point, preservation of capital is of utmost importance. Investments should be in low risk securities that emphasize current income. This income should yield enough cash flow in addition to pension and Social Security income to give the retiree a desirable standard of living.

Just as there are few bounds on investment objectives and risk preferences of individual investors, the investment constraints of individual investors are very flexible and can vary widely. One important area upon which individual investors should establish a constraint is liquidity. They should require that a certain amount or portion of funds be kept in cash or interest-bearing cash equivalents such as T-bills or money market funds. In the absence of this cash reserve for short periods of time, the ability to borrow can relieve emergency liquidity needs. For example, an investor could borrow funds from a margin account, assuming that the account contained sufficient equity to allow the loan.

When an investor is a trust fund with an individual (or even several individuals) as the beneficiary, legal considerations may impose constraints on the investment management process. The trustee has a *fiduciary relationship* and should be aware of all the legal aspects of the arrangement. A fiduciary relationship exists whenever one party is charged with acting for the benefit of another party. Fiduciary relationships exist between such parties as a trustee and beneficiary, an investment counselor and client, and an agent and principal.

The legal aspects of fiduciary relationships are subject to considerable variation because trusts are generally governed by state law. However, one area of trust investment common to many state laws is the *prudent man rule*. The prudent man rule evolved from a decision of the Massachusetts Supreme Judicial Court in the case of *Harvard College v. Amory* in 1830. A key passage in the decision stated:

> All that can be required of a trustee to invest is that he shall conduct himself faithfully and exercise a sound discretion. He is to choose how men of prudence, discretion, and intelligence manage their own affairs, not in regard to speculation, but in regard to the permanent disposition of their funds, considering their probable income, as well as the probable safety of the capital to be invested.[1]

The rule authorizes a trustee to apply standards of a "prudent" investor when selecting investments. Virtually all states have adopted the prudent man rule in some form. Over the years, courts and government agencies have interpreted and expanded upon the prudent man rule. Depending upon the state, there is usually a set of guidelines to help fiduciaries determine which investments might qualify as prudent. For example, the general consensus is that a prudent investor would invest only in stocks that maintain a current dividend. Nondividend-paying stocks could therefore automatically be excluded from a list of stocks to be considered for purchase under the prudent man rule.

Another aspect of interpretations of the prudent man rule is that each investment in a portfolio should stand on its own merits. This differs from modern portfolio management concepts, which state that the performance of the portfolio as a whole, not of individual items composing the portfolio, is of most concern to the investor.

Table 21–1 provides a brief sketch of two hypothetical individual investors and their investment objectives, risk preferences, and constraints. Keep in mind that to establish these items of the portfolio management process requires substantially more information than the table provides. However, it does illustrate how the objectives, preferences, and constraints might be specified. Investor A occupies an early stage in the investor life cycle and desires investments that plan for the long-run future. The only constraint investor A places on the portfolio is an aversion to investing in securities of companies located in countries with politically repressive governments. Investor B is further along the investor life cycle. Capital preservation is of utmost importance to this investor. Note the constraint that at least 20 percent of the portfolio be invested in securities of the U.S. government. Normally, the specification of percentage targets for different types of securities in the portfolio is part of step three in the portfolio management process (asset allocation). In this case, however, this is a predetermined constraint specified by the investor.

TABLE 21–1
Example objectives, risk preferences, and constraints for two hypothetical investors

	Investor A	*Investor B*
Characteristics:		
Age	26	57
Marital status	single	married
Family income (annual)	$35,000	$75,000
Net worth	$20,000	$250,000
Company-sponsored retirement plan	yes	yes
Funds available for investment	$10,000	$130,000
Investment objectives:	Long-term growth of funds for possible future family, house purchase, and retirement	Current income to finance college education of oldest child, intermediate-term growth for retirement
Risk preferences:	Willing to accept substantial risk, wants to try the options markets	Capital preservation is very important, likes convertible bonds
Investment constraints:	No constraints other than political beliefs discouraging investment in any country with political repression or human rights violations	Requires at least 20 percent of funds be invested in U.S. government securities

Institutional Investors

The investment objectives, risk preferences, and constraints of institutional investors are generally not as difficult to define broadly as those of individual investors. For institutions, however, these items need to be identified and enumerated in more detail, usually in a written document. We will discuss this process and briefly address the needs of two example types of institutional investors: retirement funds and endowments.

Retirement Funds

Today many workers are covered by employee benefit plans. These benefit plans may include a variety of features, such as health insurance, life insurance, educational assistance, profit sharing, and retirement plans. Retirement plans fall into one of two categories: (1) *defined benefit plans* and (2) *defined contribution plans.*

Defined benefit plans, commonly called pension plans, award the employee a specified retirement income. Several different formulas are in use for determining the level of retirement income under a defined benefit plan. One widely used method is to base the retirement income on a percentage of the employee's earnings over the final few years of employment. Although percentages vary, they typically fall between 50 percent and 70 percent. This method is common for salaried employees. Another method, common for hourly workers, is to compute the benefit as a flat dollar amount per year of service to the firm.

Regardless of the method of determining the retirement benefit, the pension fund must have sufficient assets to provide the retirement income promised its beneficiaries. Based on assumptions regarding life expectancy rates, the expected salary progression of an employee, and the projected years of employment, the amount of funds needed at retirement to yield the retirement income can be estimated. These assumptions are called *actuarial assumptions.* An *actuary* is one who computes insurance and annuity premiums needed to cover expected costs and benefits. Knowing the amount needed at retirement and the contributions provided by the employer during the working years, the pension plan administrator can determine the rate of return needed on the contributions to yield the retirement income. This rate of return becomes the fund's return objective. However, since available returns are constrained by current market conditions, fund managers usually select an achievable rate as the objective and then compute the annual contributions needed to provide the projected retirement income. This rate of return is the plan's *actuarially assumed rate of return.*

The second type of retirement plan, the defined contribution plan, identifies the employer's annual contribution to the plan. The eventual benefit that the employee receives from the plan at retirement depends upon the return actually received on those contributions between the contribution time and retirement. The contribution might be stated as a portion of the employee's salary or in terms of the profits of the company (as in a profit-sharing plan).

The risk tolerance of retirement plans is largely dependent upon the investment time horizon, which is determined by the average time to retirement of the plan's beneficiaries. Except for plans that are nearing termination, the horizon is usually fairly long. However, the plan sponsor may want to avoid high risk levels for contribution planning purposes. Large declines in the fund's value could increase the sponsor's contributions. Even so, in a retirement plan, the interests of the employer should be secondary to those of the employees. Retirement plans are regulated by the federal government under the *Employee Retirement Income Security Act of 1974 (ERISA)*. ERISA provides that all retirement plans should be managed for the benefit of the employees. Another important provision of ERISA with respect to fund risk planning relates to the portfolio concept. The Department of Labor interprets ERISA in a fashion that requires only the entire fund portfolio to meet the guidelines of the prudent man rule. It does not require each investment in the portfolio to withstand the prudent man test. This gives the manager of pension funds much more flexibility in designing a portfolio to meet the needs and objectives outlined for the beneficiaries.

Endowment Funds

Endowment funds are investment pools set up to benefit institutions such as schools and universities, hospitals, charitable foundations, and cultural institutions like museums. Endowment funds usually have long investment horizons and are nontaxable. There are several common approaches to specifying return objectives for endowments. The simplest, the *current income approach,* is to maximize current income, which is then paid out to the endowment's beneficiaries. The disadvantage of this is that it can result in erosion of the capital base of the endowment. Another approach, the *total return approach,* attempts to avoid this problem. Its goal is to maximize total return over a longer time horizon. To avoid erosion of the capital base, the annual payout to beneficiaries is equal to the current income less any decline in value of the capital base (or plus any capital appreciation). The disadvantage of this approach is that it does not allow for any growth in the capital base of the endowment to compensate for inflation or to provide for growth of benefits to the beneficiary. A third method, called the *relationship to spending approach,* takes a much longer-term outlook. Funds using this technique set long-run return objectives and establish a payout based on this objective less a retention needed to allow the fund to grow. Although the growth rates vary, most institutions set it to compensate for inflation.

PORTFOLIO POLICIES

Following the identification of objectives, risk preferences, and constraints, the investor or investment manager can proceed to setting policies and strategies. These become the map to guide the investor or manager through the final phases of the portfolio management process.

These policies and strategies should identify several factors. First, they should delineate the broad types of investment vehicles to achieve the goals set in the first step. For example, Table 21–2 shows some policy and strategy statements that might serve investors A and B, introduced in Table 21–1. Growth-oriented common stocks

TABLE 21–2
Example portfolio policies and strategies for two hypothetical investors (see Table 21–1)

Investor A	***Investor B***
Common stocks with high long-term growth potential should be the primary components of this portfolio. Dividends are of no concern at this time. Because of the low amount of investable funds at this time, a mutual fund concentrating in growth stocks would be appropriate. As the portfolio grows, individual stocks can be selected for their own growth potential. Although purchasing options may not be appropriate for an investor with this low level of investable funds, a small portion of the portfolio can be dedicated to options to satisfy this desire of the investor. The portfolio beta can be quite high; a value of around 1.8 would be reasonable.	The bulk of this portfolio should be invested in U.S. government bonds and high grade corporate bonds. The remainder should be invested in securities that stress stability of principal but still have potential for growth. Blue-chip stocks paying relatively high dividends and convertible bonds and convertible preferred stocks should satisfy this requirement. The overall beta of the portfolio should not exceed a value of about 0.5.

should satisfy investor A's objectives and preferences, while U.S. government and high grade corporate bonds should serve investor B.

Portfolio policies should also identify a target risk level for the portfolio. The first step in the portfolio management process identified risk preferences of the investor in subjective terms. The policy step is the time to quantify risk for the portfolio or at least to be more specific about how to achieve the risk preferences. One widely accepted way of specifying portfolio risk, based on the Capital Asset Pricing Model (CAPM), is to set a target beta for the portfolio. For example, investor A's growth stocks should average a target beta of about 1.8 according to the policy statement in Table 21–2. In any case, the beta should be substantially higher than 1.0 to reflect the long-term nature of this investor. Remember, however, that the portfolio should not necessarily be limited to growth-oriented common stocks because the separation theorem shows that virtually any security combined with leverage can yield a desired beta level for the portfolio.

Another way to specify risk levels for a portfolio is based on Arbitrage Pricing Theory (APT). Recall that APT (discussed in Chapter 8) states that the average return on an asset is a function of the asset's expected return plus the effects of several systematic factors. These systematic factors are the major forces that move asset prices. Although there are many different factors influencing investment returns, deductive reasoning allows us to identify a set of variables that likely represent the true factors underlying APT. Empirical tests of APT are not conclusive, but four major variables seem to be significant:

1. Unanticipated changes in inflation
2. Unanticipated changes in industrial production
3. Unanticipated changes in risk premiums (measured by the spread between rates on low grade and high grade bonds)
4. Unanticipated changes in the slope of the yield curve

An investor utilizing APT methods for portfolio planning would specify the target level of sensitivity of the portfolio to each of the systematic factors. For example, an investor might prefer a portfolio that is almost immune to changes in inflation, but the same investor may be willing to accept a higher level of risk associated with changes in industrial production. The investor's counselor might recommend an inflation sensitivity of no more than .2 for the portfolio and an industrial production sensitivity of about 1.5.

Because it allows an investor to be more specific about the sensitivity of the portfolio to several different sources of risk, use of APT might be preferable to the CAPM, which specifies risk in only one dimension, the expected return on the market portfolio. As an example, suppose that the CAPM beta for this portfolio (inflation sensitivity = .2, industrial production sensitivity = 1.5) is 1.2. There are many different portfolios with a beta of 1.2; one could possibly have an inflation sensitivity of 1.1 and an industrial production sensitivity of .4. While the CAPM shows the two portfolios to have equal risk (beta = 1.2), the investor wanting a low inflation risk while accepting a higher industrial production risk would clearly prefer the former portfolio. Only APT allows this investor adequately to choose a risky portfolio.

Liquidity needs of a portfolio are also an important consideration. Based on risk preferences of the investor and any constraints placed on the portfolio, the investment manager can recommend appropriately liquid securities to satisfy the liquidity requirement. Riskier portfolios can maintain liquidity by utilizing the more risky money market instruments such as lower grade commercial paper, foreign money market instruments, and some negotiable CDs. Portfolios stressing safety would more likely provide liquidity with instruments such as U.S. T-bills, insured CDs, and high grade commercial paper.

PORTFOLIO CONSTRUCTION

The next phase of portfolio management deals with *portfolio construction*—determining the actual composition of the portfolio. Although the first two steps in the portfolio management process are important, the portfolio construction phase is critical because asset mix is the single most important determinant of portfolio performance. The portfolio construction process has three major components:

1. Asset allocation
2. Security selection
3. Portfolio structure

The Asset Allocation Decision

The *asset allocation* procedure identifies the portions of the portfolio that should be committed to various major categories of investments. It is often also called "setting the *asset mix*." This step typically results in *portfolio target percentages* for each type of investment to be included in the portfolio.

Major categories of investment that a portfolio manager might identify include stocks, money market instruments, long-term bonds, real estate, international securities, convertibles, options, and many others. An important consideration when establishing the asset mix is to meet the current income objectives of the portfolio. As an illustration of some portfolio target percentages, considering the portfolio strategies outlined in Table 21–2, individual investors A and B might set their portfolio targets as shown in Table 21–3. Investor A's portfolio is composed of several categories of stocks that typically stress growth. Investor B's portfolio is more complicated. Note that it meets the constraint of 20 percent minimum investment in U.S. government securities, set in the first portfolio management step.

The Security Selection Decision

The second major component of the portfolio construction phase is *security selection*. In the security selection process, the investor or portfolio manager chooses the appropriate securities to meet (or come as close as possible to) the portfolio targets. At the same time, the selected securities must conform to the risk preference policy of the portfolio.

TABLE 21–3
Example portfolio target percentages to specify the asset allocation for two hypothetical investors (see Tables 21–1 and 21–2)

Investor A		***Investor B***	
Growth stocks:		Money market instruments:	
New issues	20%	U.S. T-bills	10%
Small OTC stocks	40%	Commercial paper or CD	10%
Growth-oriented,		Total money market	20%
exchange-traded stocks	30%		
Total growth stocks	90%	Long-term bonds:	
		U.S. Treasury bonds	5%
Put and call options	10%	U.S. government agency bonds	5%
		Municipal bonds	10%
		Corporate bonds	10%
		Total bonds	30%
		Convertible securities	20%
		Blue-chip common stocks	30%

As the separation theorem implies, the security selection process can be accomplished almost completely outside the portfolio management framework. Assuming that the portfolio is not subject to the constraints of the prudent man rule, the only finishing touch that a portfolio manager needs to place on a portfolio selected in such a manner is to set the appropriate amount of leverage (borrowing or lending) to meet the portfolio's target beta. Usually, however, the procedure is more integrated. The fundamental analyst or security selection team chooses the securities to be purchased for the portfolio. The portfolio manager then begins acquiring those securities in quantities consistent with the portfolio targets and risk strategy. Sometimes this may mean purchasing none or very little of some of the recommended securities while concentrating more heavily in others. As long as there is adequate diversification, some concentration in a few stocks should be acceptable. If this procedure is carried out in a well-planned manner, often little or no adjustment is needed (with leverage) to achieve the target beta of the portfolio.

If the prudent man rule applies to the portfolio, the manager must be careful to select only securities that satisfy the prudent man guidelines. In such cases, the portfolio target percentages should be followed as precisely as possible.

Portfolio Structure

The final phase of the portfolio construction process determines the *portfolio structure*. This phase can be accomplished only after target setting and security selection have been completed. Structuring the portfolio involves setting the amount of each security to be included in the portfolio.

It is in this step that the investor actually purchases or sells securities. For professionally managed portfolios, the portfolio manager sometimes deals directly with brokers to execute the trades, but more often there is a *portfolio trader*. The portfolio manager gives buy and sell orders to the traders, who then contacts an appropriate broker or market maker to execute the order. An effective trader will have good working relationships with several brokers and can sometimes augment portfolio return by effecting trades at more favorable prices.

The process of setting the portion of portfolio funds to be committed to each investment is also called *portfolio weighting*. Chapter 5 discussed several different weighting schemes and their application to the construction of stock indexes. These schemes are price weighting, equal weighting, and value weighting. They are mechanical in nature because they are based on a formula that determines how much of each stock to include in a portfolio of a given size.

Some investors use mechanical weighting schemes to structure their portfolios, with equal weighting probably the most popular. However, since the portfolio structuring process is the final phase of building the portfolio, it should yield a combination of investments that results in the optimum portfolio, given the established targets and selected securities. Mechanical weighting schemes would not necessarily yield this result. Therefore, a desirable portfolio structuring process should take into account more information than the mechanical schemes consider. Ideally, the structuring process would identify the portfolio that is adequately diversified, meets (or comes very close to) the target asset mix, has a risk level equal to the target risk level, and maximizes expected return within this environment.

There are several techniques for portfolio weighting other than the mechanical weighting formulas. The CAPM is probably the most widely used basis for many of these techniques. Two main problems affect the application of the CAPM and modern portfolio theory to actual portfolio construction. They are: (1) the number of required inputs and (2) the complexity of the computational procedure required to yield an efficient portfolio. Finding the optimal portfolio is a quadratic programming problem. Fortunately, some procedures exist for reducing the number of inputs and cutting down the amount of computation. The following section presents one of these techniques in detail.

The Elton-Gruber-Padberg Approach to Portfolio Construction

The Elton-Gruber-Padberg[2] (EGP) approach to portfolio construction selects and weights securities for a portfolio based on a relatively simple ranking device. The basic assumption behind the procedure is that the covariances among securities (or, alternatively, the betas) can be accurately forecasted. The resulting portfolio is the same that the quadratic programming procedure would yield, assuming validity of the market model and the CAPM.

The EGP procedure requires a forecast of the riskless rate and the variance of returns on the market portfolio. Also, for each security under consideration, it calls for the following items: expected return, beta, variance of returns, and coefficient of determination. The coefficient of determination, (r^2) is the squared correlation coefficient of the security's returns with market returns. Expected returns on a security and the variance can be forecasted using past data, fundamental analysis, or other methods. Betas are usually forecasted using past data, although some methods estimate betas using fundamental data. Given that a security's beta and variance of returns have been forecasted, along with the variance of market returns, an analyst can estimate the security's expected r^2 using the following relation:

$$r_i^2 = \frac{\beta_i^2 \sigma_m^2}{\sigma_i^2}$$

where r_i^2 = the coefficient of determination for security i
β_i^2 = the beta for security i
σ_m^2 = the variance of market returns
σ_i^2 = the variance of returns on security i

Table 21–4 lists these values needed for the EGP procedure for six hypothetical stocks.

The CAPM criteria for dominance mean that the investor should seek to maximize return for a given level of risk. More specifically, investors should maximize risk-adjusted return, the return in excess of the riskless rate per unit of risk. Column 6 in Table 21–4 shows the computed return in excess of the riskless rate for each security. The risk-adjusted rate (the excess return divided by beta) is as follows:

$$\frac{[E(R_i) - R_f]}{\beta_i}$$

where $E(R_i)$ = the expected return on security i
R_f = the risk-free rate
β_i = the beta coefficient of security i

The first step in the EGP portfolio construction process is to rank the securities beginning with the highest risk-adjusted excess return. Table 21–4 has already done this for the example stocks. Column 7 contains the risk-adjusted rate computed for each security.

The next step in the process is to determine the *cutoff rate.* Since the objective is to find the optimum portfolio, we need to screen out stocks whose expected return is not sufficient to lead to this portfolio. We therefore need a cutoff rate that represents the minimum risk-adjusted excess return that we can accept. Securities yielding less than this return will not qualify for inclusion in the portfolio. Of course, in a perfectly efficient market, all securities would have identical risk-adjusted excess return. In such a case, there would be no need for a cutoff rate; all securities would be in the portfolio. However, in a less than efficient market, security analysts devote their time to identifying stocks with above-average return potential. Once the analysts have selected their list of above-average stocks, the portfolio manager can combine them so the resulting portfolio is mean-variance efficient (it will have the lowest possible variance per unit of return of all possible portfolios that could be formed from the list). The goal of the cutoff rate in the EGP analysis is to identify the securities that would fall into this optimum portfolio.

The value of the cutoff rate depends upon the characteristics of the securities that belong in the optimum portfolio. To identify the cutoff rate, it is necessary to calculate

TABLE 21–4
Expected return and risk data for hypothetical market situation and a list of stocks[a]

1	2	3	4	5	6	7
Stock	**Expected Return**	**Beta**	**Variance**	**R^2**	**Excess Return**	**Excess Return over Beta**
i	$E(R_i)$	β	σ^2	R^2	$E(R_i) - R_f$	$[E(R_i) - R_f/\beta_i]$
A	.130	1.10	.130	.745	.055	.050
B	.125	1.05	.135	.653	.050	.048
C	.140	1.40	.220	.713	.065	.046
D	.100	.55	.080	.303	.025	.045
E	.115	1.05	.110	.802	.040	.038
F	.105	.85	.115	.503	.030	.035

[a]Riskless rate = .075
Expected market variance of returns = .08

its value for several different possibilities of the optimum portfolio. Since only the securities with the highest risk-adjusted excess returns will be included in the optimum portfolio, we know that the highest ranked security will be in the optimum portfolio. We therefore begin by computing the cutoff rate initially as if only the first security were in the portfolio. Then we compute the cutoff rate for the portfolio containing both the first and second securities. If the computed cutoff rate remains below the expected risk-adjusted excess return for the second security, we add the third from the list and repeat the process. We continue adding securities from the list until we find a stock whose expected risk-adjusted return falls below the computed cutoff rate when added to the portfolio. The appropriate cutoff rate is therefore the rate for which all securities used in the calculation of the cutoff rate have risk-adjusted excess returns in excess of the cutoff rate.

Computing the cutoff rate requires the variables found in Table 21–4. The formula for the cutoff rate is as follows:

$$R_{ci} = \frac{\sigma_m^2 \times \sum_{j=1}^{i} \left[\frac{[E(R_j) - R_f]\beta_j}{\sigma_{ej}^2} \right]}{1 + \sigma_m^2 \times \sum_{j=1}^{i} \frac{\beta_j^2}{\sigma_{ej}^2}} \tag{21–1}$$

where R_{ci} = the cutoff rate for security i
σ_{ej}^2 = the variance of the stock's movement not correlated to market returns

Equation 21–1 looks complicated, but with a few intermediate computations and summations, its use is quite straightforward. First, note that Equation 21–1 uses σ_{ej}^2. This term is the variance of the returns on the security not associated with market returns. It is also called the variance of the error term in the regression used to compute beta coefficients. It is computed as follows:

$$\sigma_{ei}^2 = \sigma_i^2(1 - r_i^2) \tag{21–2}$$

where σ_i^2 = the variance of the returns on security i
r_i^2 = the coefficient of determination of the returns on security i with the market portfolio

Table 21–5 contains intermediate calculations and summations for computing each cutoff rate, R_{ci}. Example 21–1 shows how to compute the cutoff rates using the information from Tables 21–4 and 21–5. R_{ci} for the first security is .037. The risk-adjusted expected return on A is greater than .037, so we add security B to the portfolio. Its computed R_{ci} is .041. Since its adjusted expected return is higher than .041, we continue the process, adding securities to the portfolio and computing cutoff rates, until we find a security whose adjusted expected return is less than the cutoff rate. By comparing columns 2 and 3 in Table 21–5, we can see that this occurs upon addition of security E to the portfolio.

TABLE 21–5
Computation of R_c

1	2 $\frac{E(R_i) - R_f}{\beta_i}$	3 R_{ci}	4 σ^2_{ei}	5 $\frac{[E(R_i) - R_f]\beta_i}{\sigma^2_{ei}}$	6 $\frac{\beta^2_i}{\sigma^2_{ei}}$	7 Z_i	8 w_i
A	.050[a]	.037	.033	1.822	36.446	.232	.532
B	.048	.041	.047	1.122	23.558	.104	.238
C	.046	.042	.063	1.440	31.013	.076	.174
D	.045	.043	.056	.246	5.421	.024	.056
E	.038	.041	.022	1.927	50.573		
F	.035	.041	.057	.446	12.631		
Total						.436	1.000

[a]Values in this table have been rounded. Actual computations were performed to six significant digits.

The optimum portfolio from this list of securities contains all securities ranked above E. The optimum cutoff rate for the portfolio is therefore equal to the R_{ci} for security D, .043.

EXAMPLE 21–1

Using the data in Table 21–4 and the intermediate calculations in Table 21–5, compute the cutoff rate R_c for securities A and B.

For security A:

$$R_c = \frac{.08(1.822)}{1 + .08(36.446)}$$
$$= .037$$

For security B:

$$R_c = \frac{.08(1.822 + 1.122)}{1 + .08(36.446 + 23.558)}$$
$$= .041$$

We have now identified the securities that qualify for the optimal portfolio. The task that remains is to compute the appropriate weights for each security. These weights show how much of each security to buy to balance the portfolio optimally. The following formula computes the weights:

$$w_i = \frac{Z_i}{\sum_{j=1}^{n} Z_j} \tag{21–3}$$

$$Z_i = \frac{\beta_i}{\sigma_{ei}^2}\left[\frac{E(R_i) - R_f}{\beta_i} - R_{c^*}\right] \quad \textbf{(21–4)}$$

where w_i = the weight for security i (the portion of funds in the portfolio to be committed to security i)

n = the number of securities in the optimal portfolio

R_{c^*} = the optimal cutoff rate

Table 21–5 shows the computed Z values and the weights (w_i) for each qualifying security. The portfolio should dedicate 53.2 percent of its funds to security A, 23.8 percent to B, 17.4 percent to C, and 5.6 percent to D. The percentages will sum to 100 percent. Example 21–2 illustrates the computation of the weight for security A.

EXAMPLE 21–2

Using data from Table 21–5, compute the weight for security A in the optimum portfolio.

$$Z = \frac{1.10}{.033}(.050 - .043)$$
$$= .233$$

$$w_i = \frac{.233}{.436}$$
$$= .534$$

(Computed values do not match table values because of rounding. Table values were computed to six significant digits.)

Constructing the portfolio using these weights results in a mean-variance efficient portfolio chosen from the securities in the list. The formulas for computing the expected return and beta of a portfolio can then be used to estimate the expected return and beta of the optimal portfolio. In the example, the weighted average return is 12.9 percent, and the portfolio weighted average beta is 1.11. Of course, should the target beta for the portfolio be different from 1.11, we can invest in the risk-free asset or lever to reach the desired portfolio beta.

As a summary, the EGP procedure can be outlined in the following steps:

1. Rank securities by their adjusted excess expected return.
2. Compute cutoff rates for portfolios beginning with the highest ranked security.
3. Identify the optimal cutoff rate.
4. Compute the optimal portfolio weights.
5. Compute expected return and beta for the optimal portfolio.

When considering new securities to add to the portfolio, any security whose return falls below the optimal cutoff rate should be rejected. Securities with returns higher than the cutoff rate should be included in the portfolio. The addition of new securities will slightly change the optimal cutoff rate and will change the portfolio weights, calling for a cycle through the portfolio revision process.

PORTFOLIO MONITORING AND REVISION

The optimal portfolio, so carefully chosen during the previous steps in the portfolio management process, becomes suboptimal within moments after its construction. As the economic environment, market conditions, and individual security characteristics change with the passage of time, the portfolio strays from its targeted course. As new information enters the market, the risk-return characteristics of the chosen portfolio change. At some point, the portfolio will probably be so far from its original purpose that the investor or portfolio manager will want to make some changes.

Because capital markets are dynamic and investors can change their minds, a program of portfolio monitoring and revision should be an ongoing part of any portfolio management process. A portfolio manager's value is derived not only from the ability to construct a portfolio, but also from the ability to manage the portfolio effectively over a long time period. It is more likely that the value added to the management process by a skilled portfolio manager is gained through opportunities arising from reassessment and revision of the portfolio than from the original construction of the portfolio.

There are two components to the reassessment process. The first is *portfolio monitoring,* the continuous, ongoing assessment of the portfolio. The monitoring process should consider the original goals of the investor, any changes in investor preferences, and any new information regarding market conditions and expectations. An important tool in the monitoring process is a periodic review of the statement of goals and policies with the investor. In addition, the constant observation and evaluation of market conditions and analysis of securities are also fundamental to providing new information relevant to the monitoring process.

The second component is *portfolio revision.* Portfolio revision is a set of actions in response to the conclusions drawn from the portfolio monitoring process. There are two main types of portfolio revision needs: *rebalancing* and *upgrading.* Portfolio rebalancing involves adjusting the portfolio so that it matches its original targets and expectations. Rebalancing usually assumes no changes in market expectations or investor goals or preferences. Portfolio upgrading is the revision of the portfolio on the basis of newly available information regarding market expectations, investor preferences, or individual securities.

Approaches to Monitoring and Revision

Some important issues must be addressed regarding the value of portfolio monitoring and revision. First, does constant portfolio management add value to the portfolio? Second, if management does contribute to the value of a portfolio, how much management does the portfolio need? At what point is the portfolio "over-managed"? These are critical issues that cannot be resolved by a simple answer. However, depending upon one's belief regarding the amount of value added by the monitoring and revision process, there are several alternative approaches to continuous management.

Passive Portfolio Management

Passive portfolio management is the alternative for those who believe that active management adds little or no investment value. In its simplest form, passive management is just the traditional "buy and hold" strategy. Generally, the only transactions necessary in a passive management process are purchases when extra cash is available and sales needed to provide cash. A belief in efficient markets can lead one to follow a passive management strategy.

An example of the passively managed portfolio is the *index fund.* Index funds are large portfolios (usually investment companies or pension funds) that purchase a diversified portfolio of stocks. They pursue very little, if any, active management or selection of securities. The term *index fund* is a result of the funds' attempts to match the performance of a particular market index such as the S&P 500.

The advantages of passive management result from lower costs. With passive management, search costs for new securities will be minimized. Also, transactions costs and taxes will be very low when compared to those of an active strategy.

A passive management approach also has disadvantages. Passive management generally precludes taking advantage of any market or security opportunities that could lead to extra investment profits. In addition, a passively managed portfolio can stray quite far from its original objectives, especially if the portfolio is relatively small.

Active Approaches

The *active portfolio management* approaches are based on the idea that continuously monitoring a portfolio for possible revision has some value. Although there is probably a large continuum of active management strategies, we can classify them into two main areas.

Active-Defensive Strategies. The basis for the *active-defensive management* approach is the notion that markets are quite efficient, yet portfolio managers do accomplish valuable tasks. The most valued of these tasks is the construction and maintenance of a portfolio that meets the risk-return profile of the investor. An active-defensive approach therefore concentrates on keeping the portfolio at or near its risk targets.

Active-Aggressive Strategies. The *active-aggressive management* approach involves total management of the portfolio. It relies on forecasts of economic variables and market conditions to yield a prediction of future market movement. This market prediction aids in the investment timing decision. Adherents to the active-aggressive approach also analyze individual securities with the goal of identifying those with above-average risk-adjusted return potential. They are continually considering upgrading the portfolio to maximize return within the constraints of risk.

Combination Approaches

In addition to these classifications of degrees of monitoring and revision, many possible combinations involve characteristics of two or more approaches. For example, one portfolio manager may decide to have a portion of the portfolio as an index fund with passive management and maintain the remainder under an active-aggressive strategy. Another manager might have a portfolio that is managed using an active-defensive approach; realizing that from time to time opportunities might arise for aggressive pursuit of investment returns, this manager would have the alternative of taking advantage of them.

PORTFOLIO PERFORMANCE MEASUREMENT

The final part of the portfolio management process is the evaluation process, which allows portfolio managers to check their progress and success at meeting portfolio objectives. It also helps the clients to determine whether the portfolio managers are successfully meeting the investors' needs. Chapter 22 addresses portfolio performance evaluation and introduces several techniques for measuring performance.

SUMMARY

The process of portfolio management is a multiphased activity. The first stage in the process is the identification of investors' goals, risk preferences, and investment constraints. Objectives are the wealth or return goals the investor desires to achieve.

Risk preferences represent an investor's tolerance for accepting risk. The investor life cycle is a widely used framework for identifying and assessing individual investor risk preferences. The investor life cycle identifies relative risk levels that most investors can accept at various stages during their life.

Constraints are bounds placed on the set of potential investments. The need for a minimum amount of liquidity might place a constraint on a portion of a portfolio. The prudent man rule is another important source of investment constraints.

A second major phase in the portfolio management process is the enumeration of portfolio policies and strategies. Policies and strategies should identify the broad types of investment vehicles to be considered for the portfolio and should specify a target risk level for the portfolio. The risk targets should be as specific as possible. The Capital Asset Pricing Model and Arbitrage Pricing Theory provide quantitative frameworks for setting the risk target for a portfolio.

The third main step in portfolio management is the construction phase. In the construction phase, the portfolio manager sets a desired asset mix, selects securities for the portfolio, and structures the portfolio by determining weights for each security in the portfolio. The Elton-Gruber-Padberg procedure is a useful tool for accomplishing an optimum portfolio construction.

Supplementing and augmenting each step in the portfolio management process are the portfolio monitoring and revision activities. Monitoring involves the continuous assessment of the portfolio with respect to original portfolio goals, any changes in investor preferences, and changes in market or security expectations. Portfolio revision involves both rebalancing and upgrading the portfolio.

IMPORTANT TERMS

active-aggressive portfolio management
active-defensive portfolio management
active portfolio management
actuarial assumption
actuarially assumed rate of return
actuary
asset allocation
asset mix
current income approach to endowment fund management
cutoff rate
defined benefit plan
defined contribution plan
Employee Retirement Income Security Act of 1974 (ERISA)
fiduciary relationship
index fund
investor life cycle
passive portfolio management
portfolio construction
portfolio monitoring
portfolio revision
portfolio structure
portfolio target percentages
portfolio trader
portfolio weighting
prudent man rule
rebalancing
relationship to spending approach to endowment fund management
security selection
total return approach to endowment fund management
upgrading

QUESTIONS AND PROBLEMS

1. What factors does the chapter mention as contributing to the growth of portfolio management as a legitimate body of knowledge and professional practice? What are some other factors that may have had an influence?
2. Outline the portfolio management process, briefly discussing each step in the process.
3. Define the concept of the investor life cycle, and explain its use in the identification of investor objectives and risk tolerances.
4. Explain what is meant by a fiduciary relationship, and discuss how the prudent man rule affects fiduciary relationships.
5. What is ERISA, and how does it interpret the prudent man rule?
6. What are the two main types of retirement plans? How might each affect the decisions of a portfolio manager?
7. What are the three most common approaches endowment funds might take in specifying their return objectives?
8. What are the three main concerns of the portfolio construction phase of portfolio management? How might a manager implement each of them?
9. You have decided to use the Elton-Gruber-Padberg approach to portfolio construction. The riskless rate is .08 and you expect a market variance of .10. After a thorough fundamental analysis, you have identified six stocks you would like to purchase. Your fundamental analysis yielded expected returns for each stock. Based on past stock price behavior, you have computed the risk measures. The following is your data:

Stock	*Expected Return*	*Beta*	*Variance*
A	.126	.6	.07
B	.148	.8	.10
C	.166	1.1	.20
D	.152	1.2	.30
E	.188	1.3	.40
F	.160	1.5	.60

a) Use the Elton-Gruber-Padberg method to identify the optimum portfolio and its mix.
b) Compute the expected return and beta of the optimum portfolio.
c) Suppose that your risk preferences indicated that your portfolio should have a target beta of 1.1. How would you achieve that with your optimum portfolio?

NOTES

1. 9 Pick. 446 (Mass., 1830).
2. Edwin J. Elton, Martin J. Gruber, and Manfred W. Padberg (1978), "Optimal Portfolios from Simple Ranking Devices," in Peter L. Bernstein (Ed.), *Security Selection and Active Portfolio Management,* New York: Institutional Investor, 219–232.

SELECTED REFERENCES

Arnott, Robert D. (1983). "What Hath MPT Wrought: Which Risks Reap Rewards?" *Journal of Portfolio Management,* 10 (Fall), 5–11.

Bauman, W. Scott, and Constance H. McClaren (1982). "An Asset Allocation Model for Active Portfolios." *Journal of Portfolio Management,* 8 (Winter), 76–87.

Brealey, Richard A. (1986). "How to Combine Active Management with Index Funds." *Journal of Portfolio Management,* 12 (Winter), 4–10.

Chen, Son-Nan, and Reena Aggarwal (1986). "Optimal Portfolio Selection and Uncertain Inflation." *Journal of Portfolio Management,* 13 (Fall), 44–49.

Elton, Edwin J., Martin J. Gruber, and Manfred W. Padberg (1978). "Optimal Portfolios from Simple Ranking Devices." In Peter L. Bernstein (Ed.), *Security Selection and Active Portfolio Management.* New York: Institutional Investor, 219–232.

Fogler, H. Russell (1984). "20% in Real Estate: Can Theory Justify It?" *Journal of Portfolio Management,* 10 (Winter), 6–13.

Frost, Peter, and James W. Savarino (1986). "Portfolio Size and Estimation Risk." *Journal of Portfolio Management,* 12 (Summer), 60–64.

Jeffrey, Robert H. (1984). "A New Paradigm for Portfolio Risk." *Journal of Portfolio Management,* 11 (Fall), 33–40.

Kaplan, Howard M. (1985). "Farmland as a Portfolio Investment." *Journal of Portfolio Management,* 11 (Winter), 73–79.

Kirby, Robert G. (1984). "The Coffee Can Portfolio." *Journal of Portfolio Management,* 11 (Fall), 76–80.

Kritzman, Mark (1986). "What's Wrong with Portfolio Insurance." *Journal of Portfolio Management,* 13 (Fall), 13–17.

McEnally, Richard W. (1985). "Time Diversification: The Surest Route to Lower Risk?" *Journal of Portfolio Management,* 11 (Summer), 24–26.

——— (1986). "Latané's Bequest: The Best of Portfolio Strategies." *Journal of Portfolio Management,* 12 (Winter), 21–30.

Ritchken, Peter (1985). "Enhancing Mean-Variance Analysis with Options." *Journal of Portfolio Management,* 11 (Spring), 67–72.

Rudd, Andrew (1980). "Optimal Selection of Passive Portfolios." *Financial Management,* 9 (Spring), 57–65.

Schreiner, John (1980). "Portfolio Revision: A Turnover-Constrained Approach." *Financial Management,* 9 (Spring), 67–75.

Taylor, Richard W. (1984). "Portfolio Management with a Hand-Held Calculator." *Journal of Portfolio Management,* 10 (Summer), 27–34.

CHAPTER 22

Evaluation of Investment Performance

This chapter surveys several methods for evaluating investment performance. Investment performance evaluation is not as simple as comparing your portfolio's return to the return on the market index. Different investments have different levels of risk, which investment performance techniques should consider. Although many techniques exist for evaluating performance, the theoretical concepts introduced as the Capital Asset Pricing Model lead to a group of measures of investment performance. This CAPM-based group of measures has developed a following among theoreticians and investment practitioners alike.

Because of the wide availability of information about them, investment companies are good candidates for the use of these investment evaluation techniques. Several studies have examined the performance of investment companies. The final section of this chapter summarizes the conclusions of some of the important studies.

METHODS OF EVALUATING INVESTMENT PERFORMANCE

A popular method of evaluating the performance of an investment portfolio is to compare the portfolio's return over a past time period to the return on a market index over the same time period. Although a market index may be an appropriate measure for comparison with a portfolio, in most cases it is not suitable to compare *unadjusted* portfolio returns to the market. The only circumstance when it would be appropriate to compare the unadjusted portfolio to the market average would be if the portfolio itself is a "market index" portfolio with a risk level equal to the market index.

To show why an unadjusted comparison is not appropriate, consider the investor who is aggressive and builds a well-diversified portfolio of risky stocks with an average beta of 2.0. If the market falls, the value of the portfolio will likely fall by a greater amount. A comparison of the raw portfolio return to the market return will indicate that the portfolio "underperformed the market." Does this mean that the investor who selected these stocks is an inferior analyst? Maybe not. It may be that this analyst selected the best group of stocks with betas averaging 2.0, but when the market went down, the portfolio decreased by a larger amount just because of its high beta. Or maybe the analyst had expected the market to go up, and the portfolio got what it deserved when the market went down.

This example points out some of the problems of investment performance evaluation. A good portfolio can "look bad" just because the market goes down. A bad analyst could "look good" by getting lucky with an up market. How can we adjust for risk? How can we account for good returns that occur by chance alone?

Various researchers have proposed several techniques to evaluate the performance of portfolios and their managers. The next section presents techniques based on the Capital Asset Pricing Model. The following section contains two methods founded on other concepts.

CAPM-Based Techniques

The CAPM forms the foundation for this first group of performance evaluation measures. As the CAPM's early development matured, researchers began to apply its concepts to performance evaluation. The idea was to identify investments that gave the maximum return per unit of risk.

The Sharpe Measure

William F. Sharpe, a pioneer in the evolution of the CAPM, originated one of the first risk-adjusted performance measures. His original study applied the measure in a ranking of mutual funds.[1] Sharpe said that the ability of a portfolio manager to maximize average excess return per unit of risk is a gauge of superior investment management. Sharpe defined excess return as the average portfolio return less the average riskless rate. As his measure of risk, Sharpe used the standard deviation of portfolio returns over the measurement period. The *Sharpe measure* of investment performance is as follows:

$$S = \frac{\bar{R}_p - \bar{R}_f}{\sigma_p} \qquad \textbf{(22–1)}$$

where S = the Sharpe measure of investment performance
R_p = the mean return on the portfolio
R_f = the mean risk-free rate
σ_p = the standard deviation of portfolio returns

To use the Sharpe measure, an analyst computes Equation 22–1 for every portfolio or mutual fund being evaluated. The second step is to rank the portfolios from highest to lowest Sharpe measure. The higher the Sharpe measure, the better the portfolio performed. Example 22–1 shows a sample computation and use of the Sharpe measure.

EXAMPLE 22–1

John Vega is considering buying one of two mutual funds. He wants to pick the fund most likely to show high performance, and he believes that he can base his decision on the funds' performance over the last five years. He computes the mean monthly return and the standard deviation of returns of each fund. They are as follows:

	Mean Return	*Standard Deviation*
Fund A	.020	.15
Fund B	.017	.10

The mean return on T-bills over the five-year period was .005 per month. Which fund performed best according to the Sharpe measure?

The Sharpe measure for fund A is:

$$S = (.020 - .005)/.15 = .10$$

The Sharpe measure for fund B is:

$$S = (.017 - .005)/.10 = .12$$

According to the Sharpe measure, fund B exhibited superior risk-adjusted returns over the past five years.

The Treynor Measure

A shortcoming of the Sharpe measure is that it uses the standard deviation as the measure of portfolio risk. However, as the Security Market Line (developed in Chapter 8) showed, the only relevant risk for an investor is systematic risk. Therefore, the denominator in the Sharpe measure may contain distortions if any of the portfolios in a given ranking are not perfectly diversified.

A performance evaluation metric that accounts for systematic risk only is the *Treynor measure.*[2] The denominator of the Treynor measure uses beta instead of standard deviation to represent portfolio risk. The formula for computing the Treynor measure is:

$$T = \frac{\bar{R}_p - \bar{R}_f}{\beta_p} \qquad \textbf{(22–2)}$$

where T = the Treynor measure of portfolio performance
β_p = the beta coefficient of the portfolio

Like the Sharpe measure, the Treynor measure is a useful tool for ranking portfolios. The procedure for implementing the Treynor measure follows the Sharpe procedure. Example 22–2 presents a sample of the Treynor measure using the same situation as in Example 22–1. Note that the Treynor measure produces the same end result as the Sharpe measure. The two measures are highly interrelated and will usually rank portfolios in a consistent order.

EXAMPLE 22–2

Mr. Vega (from Example 22–1) still is undecided about whether he should invest in fund A or fund B. He decides to compute the Treynor measure of performance for the two funds and collects the following information:

	Mean Return	*Beta*
Fund A	.020	1.10
Fund B	.017	0.85

The monthly rate on T-bills was .005. Compute the Treynor measures.

The Treynor measure for fund A is:

$$T = (.020 - .005)/1.1 = .0136$$

The Treynor measure for fund B is:

$$T = (.017 - .005)/0.85 = .0141$$

The Treynor measure indicates that fund B had better risk-adjusted returns.

The Jensen Measure

There are two main drawbacks of the Sharpe and Treynor measures. First, both measures are valid only for *comparing portfolios to each other* and ranking them. They do not tell *whether or not* a portfolio outperformed the market. Second, they give no indication of the statistical certainty of their result. (However, Jobson and Korkie[3] have derived approximate distributions for statistical testing using the Sharpe and Treynor measures.)

The *Jensen measure*[4] has properties that overcome or minimize the shortcomings of the Sharpe and Treynor measures. Jensen used the Security Market Line (see Chapter 8) as the theoretical beginning point for his analysis. The Security Market Line (SML) defines the relationship between the expected return on a security or portfolio and its systematic risk. Stated here again, the relationship is as follows:

$$E(R_j) = R_f + \beta_j[E(R_m) - R_f] \qquad \textbf{(22–3)}$$

where
$E(R_j)$ = the expected return on security or portfolio j
β_j = the beta (systematic risk) of security or portfolio j
$E(R_m)$ = the expected return on the market portfolio

Using this relationship, we can analytically define the expected return on any portfolio. Note, however, that the model is in terms of expectations. Because in an efficient market expectations on average ultimately become realizations, Jensen recasts the relationship in terms of realized returns:

$$R_{jt} = R_{ft} + \beta_j[R_{mt} - R_{ft}] \qquad \textbf{(22–4)}$$

where
R_{jt} = the realized return on security or portfolio j for time t
R_{ft} = the risk-free rate for time t
R_{mt} = the realized return on the market index for time t

Subtracting R_f from both sides of Equation 22–4 gives:

$$(R_{jt} - R_{ft}) = \beta_j(R_{mt} - R_{ft}) \qquad \textbf{(22–5)}$$

The relationship in Equation 22–5 states that the realized excess return on portfolio j is a function of its systematic risk and the market return. If the CAPM and SML were a perfect relationship without any unsystematic variation in security prices, then Equation 22–5 would always fit the data in a sample of realized portfolio and market returns. We know, however, that the relationship is not perfect and that there will be unsystematic variation. Let's call this an *error term* and the equation becomes:

$$(R_{jt} - R_{ft}) = \beta_j(R_{mt} - R_{ft}) + e_{jt} \qquad \textbf{(22–6)}$$

where e_{jt} = the error term for security or portfolio j for time t

On the right side of Equation 22–6, the first expression ($\beta_j(R_{mt} - R_{ft})$) represents the excess return on the security (or portfolio) due to systematic factors—in other words, that portion which is explained by the return on the market. The second term (e_{jt}) is the security's (portfolio's) return that is attributable to unsystematic factors. Because the unsystematic factors are random, the error terms should average to zero over a long time period, but they can be positive or negative for any one time period t. A third possibility exists: return that is over and above the other two. Adding this third source of return to the relationship and calling it alpha (α) gives:

$$(R_{jt} - R_{ft}) = \alpha_j + \beta_j(R_{mt} - R_{ft}) + e_{jt} \qquad \textbf{(22–7)}$$

where α_j = the excess return on security or portfolio j over and above that explained by market and unsystematic factors

The α_{jt} in Equation 22–7 is Jensen's measure of investment performance.

$$J = \alpha_j \qquad \textbf{(22–8)}$$

where J = Jensen's measure of investment performance

It represents the excess return on a security or portfolio after adjusting for systematic market influences and random unsystematic factors.

To estimate alpha for a sample of portfolio and market returns, we use the linear regression procedure for estimating the coefficients of an equation. Most computerized statistical software packages have linear regression routines. The dependent variable in the regression is the excess return on the portfolio ($R_{jt} - R_{ft}$), and the independent variable is the excess market return ($R_{mt} - R_{ft}$). The regression will treat the error as random variables with mean of zero and will yield estimates of the intercept (α) and the slope (β).

The resulting beta is the estimate of systematic risk for the sample time period. The alpha is the estimate of superior returns, and the sign of alpha indicates whether or not the portfolio outperformed the market. If alpha is positive, then there were positive risk-adjusted returns over the sample period. A negative alpha implies inferior performance over the sample period. If alpha is zero, then the portfolio's return was average.

Jensen's alpha procedure has another advantage. The regression procedure also gives estimates of the standard deviation of the coefficients alpha and beta. These allow testing of alpha and beta for statistical significance. One main concern in performance evaluation testing is to weed out "superior" or "inferior" returns that could have occurred by chance alone. To accomplish this, we must test alpha to see if it is statistically significantly different from zero. For example, significantly superior performance should yield an alpha significantly greater than zero. The test statistic is alpha divided by its standard error:

$$t = \frac{\alpha_j}{\sigma_{\alpha j}} \qquad \textbf{(22–9)}$$

where $\sigma_{\alpha j}$ = the standard error of α_j

Equation 22–9 is the standard *t*-test for statistical significance. A confidence level of about 95 percent is usually acceptable in statistical analysis, so a computed *t* using Equation 22–9 greater than the *t* corresponding to the 95 percent level will indicate significant superior performance. These *t*'s are available in a table of values for Student's *t*-distribution in any statistics textbook. For a "reasonably large" sample (generally thirty or more), the critical *t* value needed for the 95 percent confidence level is 1.96. Example 22–3 continues Examples 22–1 and 22–2 with an application of the Jensen measure. Note that only fund B's returns were significantly greater than zero at the 95 percent confidence level. This means that 95 percent of the time we could not get this result just by chance. (There is only a 5 percent likelihood of getting this result by chance.)

EXAMPLE 22–3

Still undecided, Mr. Vega (Examples 22–1 and 22–2) uses a statistical package to estimate Equation 22–7 and to apply Jensen's measure to test the statistical significance (at the 95 percent confidence level) of the measures. The regression yields the following results (standard errors are in parentheses):

	Intercept	*Slope*
Fund A	.006 (.004)	1.10 (0.15)
Fund B	.005 (.002)	0.85 (0.06)

Jensen's measure (the alpha or intercept) is .006 for fund A, indicating that it outperformed the market by .6 percent per month. The alpha for fund B is .005.

The test of significance for fund A yields:

$$t = .006/.004 = 1.50.$$

The test for fund B is:

$$t = .005/.002 = 2.50.$$

Since fund B's test statistic is the only one greater than the critical value of 1.96 (95 percent confidence level), it apparently was the best performer. To rank the funds, compute the modified Jensen measure.

The modified Jensen measure for fund A is:

$$J_m = .006/1.10 = .0055.$$

The modified Jensen measure for fund B is:

$$J_m = .005/0.85 = .0059$$

The Jensen measure indicates whether or not a portfolio outperformed the market, but alone it is not useful for ranking portfolios' performance. For ranking, Smith and Tito[5] have shown that a *modified Jensen measure* serves best. The modified Jensen measure is:

$$J_m = \frac{\alpha_j}{\beta_j} \tag{22–10}$$

The modified Jensen measure for ranking portfolios is equal to Jensen's alpha divided by beta. Example 22–3 shows its use. Note that although fund A in the example had a higher alpha, the modified Jensen measure ranks it second.

Methods Based on Other Concepts

In addition to the CAPM, Chapter 8 discussed two other models for classifying and explaining asset returns. These two concepts, arbitrage pricing theory (APT) and stochastic dominance, can also be useful for evaluating portfolio performance.

APT-Based Evaluation

A study by Chang and Lewellen[6] applied APT theory to the evaluation of mutual fund performance. In an argument similar to Jensen's for using the SML on *ex post* returns, Chang and Lewellen derive an estimating equation from the APT. Their equation is as follows:

$$R_{it} - R_{ft} = \alpha_i + \sum_{j=1}^{k} [\beta_{ij}(R_{jt} - R_{ft})] + e_{it} \tag{22–11}$$

where R_{it} = the observed return for portfolio i for time t
R_{ft} = the risk-free rate for time t (or, alternatively, the return on a zero-beta portfolio for time t)
α_i = the measure of excess return
k = the number of factors that drive the arbitrage pricing process
β_{ij} = the sensitivity of portfolio i's returns to movement in the common factor j
e_{it} = the estimated error term with mean zero and zero covariance with all factors.

The α_i term estimated in the regression using Equation 22–11 gives the APT estimate of portfolio performance. It does not have to be used in a ranking; the sign of each alpha is an indication of performance. If alpha is significantly positive, then the portfolio exhibited statistically superior performance. Likewise, a negative alpha is a sign of inferior performance. Unfortunately, the application of Equation 22–11 is not as straightforward as Jensen's (Equation 22–7). The problem is that the APT does not prespecify the number of factors and does not state what the factors are.

The approach taken by Chang and Lewellen was to derive a set of factor returns from returns on a large sample of common stocks. They used 990 stocks selected randomly from the Center for Research in Security Prices database and applied a technique called *factor analysis* to identify factor portfolios. This process identified seven different portfolios of stocks as factors, each of which has unit risk with its underlying factor and no significant systematic risk with any of the other factors. After identifying the seven factor portfolios and their returns, Chang and Lewellen were able to apply a regression procedure using Equation 22–11 to estimate the APT measure of performance. The section on mutual fund performance later in this chapter presents the results of this study.

Evaluation Based on Stochastic Dominance

Stochastic dominance criteria provide a straightforward set of rules for dividing portfolios into two groups: those which dominate and those which do not. By comparing each possible pair of portfolios in a list or group of portfolios, it may even be possible to rank the portfolios using stochastic dominance. Any of the three degrees of stochastic dominance (first, second, or third order) provides a means of making the comparison to see if dominance exists. The main problem of stochastic dominance is that the criteria are so stringent they often fail to identify portfolios that would clearly be superior using other techniques of performance evaluation. In other words, it is highly likely that a portfolio with superior returns will not show stochastic dominance over other portfolios.

Levy and Lerman[7] applied stochastic dominance to test whether portfolios ranked by their P/E ratios showed any superior performance. Previous studies using CAPM-based measures had shown that low P/E portfolios outperformed high P/E portfolios. Levy and Lerman ranked 424 stocks by their P/E ratios over a twenty-year period (1960–1979) and divided the rankings into ten deciles. Each decile represented a portfolio, the lowest being the low P/E portfolio, and so forth. They then used both first order and second order stochastic dominance to see if any of the portfolios dominated any of the others. The lowest P/E dominated the highest P/E portfolios, but only before transactions costs. They concluded that investors who hold high P/E portfolios will not have results inferior to those with low P/E portfolios after considering commissions and transactions costs.

MONITORING PORTFOLIO PERFORMANCE WITH OTHER TECHNIQUES

Performance evaluation of managed investment portfolios should be a continual process. In addition to examining for superior returns, the monitoring process should evaluate the success of the portfolio in meeting the investor's objectives and strategies.

Monitoring a portfolio's performance should consider the target asset allocations defined to meet the investor's objectives. For example, suppose that an investor's return objective was 8 percent, and the portfolio allocations are 60 percent in stock and 40 percent in bonds. If the equity portion of the portfolio returned 10 percent and the debt portion yielded 5 percent then the objective would be met. To monitor equity and debt portions of the portfolio separately, the investment analyst can classify the portion of the portfolio into one of several categories and then compare the performance of that portfolio portion to other managed portfolios of similar classification.

Monitoring Equity Performance

One useful classification system for equity strategies contains five categories:

1. *Aggressive growth portfolios* typically contain a major portion invested in smaller capitalization, growth-oriented companies and have betas greater than about 1.2.
2. *Quality growth portfolios* generally concentrate on established companies with higher growth potential and low dividend payouts. The beta of quality growth portfolios is usually between about 1.05 and 1.2.
3. *Broadly diversified portfolios* contain balanced amounts of stock from a broad range of industries and companies. Their betas are normally between about .95 and 1.05.
4. *Rotating/changing portfolios* allow their managers to shift portfolio emphasis from one sector or yield objective to another to take advantage of changing market conditions. A result of this is that they tend not to have stable or even identifiable betas over periods of time.
5. *Defensive/yield portfolios* tend to concentrate holdings in the basic industries. They usually have stocks with lower P/E ratios and higher dividend yields. These portfolios' betas are usually less than .95.

A principal advantage of performance monitoring using this classification is that it can be accomplished without regard to the risk level of the managed portfolio or the benchmark portfolio as long as the comparison of returns covers one complete market cycle. The first step is to construct a passive, random portfolio that matches the stated objectives. In order to avoid any problems of computing beta or measuring risk, the analyst could even construct the model portfolio without regard to matching the exact risk level of the model to the managed portfolio. Over a complete market cycle, the managed portfolio should have higher returns than the passive portfolio, regardless of risk levels, if portfolio management has added any value.

An alternative to the complete cycle method is to construct a portfolio of risk equivalent to that of the managed portfolio. Performance can then be monitored over any time interval. Another possibility is to compare the performance of the managed portfolio to groups of other professionally managed portfolios (such as mutual funds) that fall into the same category.

Monitoring Bond Performance

Monitoring the performance of bond portfolios can be accomplished with procedures similar to those just described for equities. Chapter 13 identified three broad classifications for bond strategy: passive, semi-active, and active strategies. In addition, there are combination strategies that can contain elements of more than one specific strategy.

The passive model bond portfolio should be constructed to match the strategy and objectives of the managed portfolio. If management has proved of any benefit to the portfolio, then the managed portfolio should provide greater returns over a complete interest rate cycle. As with equities, another set of comparisons can be made with benchmark portfolios managed by other professional investors.

TESTS OF INVESTMENT COMPANY PERFORMANCE

This section presents a collection of studies that test the performance of mutual funds using the various techniques presented in this chapter. Mutual funds can pursue superior investment performance along two avenues. The first is to select undervalued individual securities for the portfolio. This selection of the best securities should then lead the portfolio to outperform the market average. A second way to outperform the market, even with mediocre securities, is to time market movements correctly. To do this, a portfolio manager expecting a market fall would shift the portfolio into cash for low beta securities. A shift back into higher beta stocks would follow when the manager predicts a rise in the market. If the manager is correct the majority of the time, the portfolio would show superior performance.

Tests Using CAPM-Based Techniques

This section presents evaluations using the measures of portfolio performance based on the CAPM. These studies fall into two categories: tests of overall performance and tests of market timing ability.

Tests of Overall Investment Performance

This group of studies evaluates investment company performance in general, asking the question, Do mutual funds outperform the market? Most studies break this question into two subquestions: Do mutual funds as a group outperform the market? Even if funds as a group do not outperform the market, is there a significant number of funds that consistently outperform the market?

The source of portfolio performance from these studies could be either superior security selection or market timing ability. However, the source that would lead to excellent performance results for this group of studies is most likely to be the security selection process.

The Jensen Study. Jensen[8] applied his performance evaluation measure to twenty years' worth of mutual fund returns. He used 115 different funds over the period

1945–1964 and calculated their annual returns. Table 22–1 shows the resulting average alphas and betas for the entire sample over the entire time period. The mean alpha was negative, −.011. This implies that as a group mutual funds did not outperform the market during the time period under study. Actually, they did not even perform as well as the market. Their risk-adjusted return averaged .011 (1.1 percent) *less* than the market.

But what about individual funds? Did a significant number of them show exceptional performance, implying that certain fund managers have the ability to outperform the market? Jensen computed *t*-values (Equation 22–9) to look for funds that provided significantly good performance. If the statistical error level of a test is set to be 5 percent, then we can find 5 percent of the funds "outperforming" the market by chance alone. Five percent of 115 funds is about 6 funds. After computing the *t*-values, Jensen found only 3 of them to be significantly positive. His conclusion, therefore, was that not only do mutual funds on average *not* outperform the market, but also individual funds do not seem to be able to show consistently superior performance.

The Kim Study. Kim[9] used a different approach to performance evaluation; his approach is based on risk adjustment. Instead of adjusting the mutual fund returns for their risk, Kim constructed a "market return" whose risk level approximated that of the mutual fund being evaluated. His sample contained 138 different investment companies' quarterly returns for the period 1969–1975. The sample of mutual funds performed rather poorly when compared to the benchmark market portfolio. The

TABLE 22–1
Summary statistics for estimated regression coefficients

Summary of estimated regression statistics for equation (8) for 115 mutual funds using all sample data available in the period 1945–64. Returns calculated net of all expenses

$$\bar{R}_{jt} - R_{Ft} = \alpha_j + \beta_j[\bar{R}_{Mt} - R_{Ft}] + \bar{u}_{jt}\ j = 1,2,\ldots,115 \quad (8)$$

Item	Mean Value	Median Value	Extreme Values: Minimum	Extreme Values: Maximum	Mean Absolute Deviation*
$\hat{\alpha}$	−.011	−.009	−0.080	0.058	.016
$\hat{\beta}$	.840	.848	0.219	1.405	.162
$\hat{r}^2$	.865	.901	0.445	0.977	.074
$\hat{\rho}(\bar{u}_t, \bar{u}_{t-1})$**	−.077	−.064	−0.688	0.575	.211
n	17.0	19.0	10.0	20.0	3.12

*Defined as $\dfrac{\sum_{i=1}^{115} [\bar{X} - X_i]}{115}$

**First order autocorrelation of residuals. The average $\hat{\rho}^2$ is .075.

Source: Michael C. Jensen (1968), "The Performance of Mutual Funds in the Period 1945–64," *Journal of Finance*, 23 (May), 389–416.

mean fund quarterly return was .0013 compared to the risk-adjusted market return of .0149.

The Fabozzi, Francis, and Lee Study. A study by Fabozzi, Francis, and Lee[10] questioned whether the Jensen measure is valid if the SML relationship is not linear. (Theoretically it is linear, but empirically it might deviate from linearity.) They computed monthly returns for eighty-five mutual funds for the period 1965–1971. They then applied a generalized regression procedure to estimate the nonlinear equivalent of Jensen's alpha. For comparison, they also computed Jensen's standard alpha.

Their findings indicate that the relationships of mutual fund returns to market returns were in general not linear. However, this nonlinearity did not introduce sufficient bias to invalidate Jensen's standard alpha. Their nonlinear alpha was essentially the same as Jensen's. On average, these alphas were not significantly positive for the time period, indicating that mutual funds showed no superior performance.

Tests of Market Timing Ability

This group of studies examines mutual fund managers' ability to successfully balance their portfolios to take advantage of swings in the market.

The Alexander and Stover Study. A study by Alexander and Stover[11] examined the consistency of mutual funds for performance and stability of systematic risk during periods of bull and bear markets. They computed monthly returns on thirty-eight mutual funds from 1966 to 1971 and estimated Jensen's alphas and betas for the funds during bull markets and bear markets.

The systematic risk (beta) of the funds in the study did not change significantly from up to down markets, implying that fund managers did not correctly alter the risk composition of their portfolios in anticipation of market changes. In addition, the alphas were not significantly different from bull to bear markets. These results suggest that mutual fund managers lack either good market forecasting ability or the ability to change their portfolios to take advantage of a market forecast.

The Kon Study. Kon[12], using a derivation of Jensen's methodology, studied monthly return data for thirty-seven mutual funds for the period 1960 to 1976. The results indicate that, as a group, mutual fund managers appears to have no special ability to forecast the market. However, Kon did uncover evidence that individual funds showed statistically significant market timing capabilities.

Tests Based on Other Techniques

This section presents a group of tests that do not rely on the CAPM or its measures to evaluate investment performance. The first is the previously mentioned study by Chang and Lewellen[13] using the arbitrage pricing model. After identifying the seven factor portfolios, Chang and Lewellen calculated monthly returns for sixty-seven different mutual funds for the period from 1971 to 1979. They then estimated Jensen's alpha and its arbitrage pricing counterpart (Equation 22–11). Table 22–2 presents a summary of their results.

TABLE 22–2
Summary statistics for Chang and Lewellen's test of mutual fund performance using arbitrage pricing

Estimated Regression Statistics (riskless rate = T-bill rate):

Parameter	*Mean*	*Standard Deviation*	*Maximum*	*Minimum*	*Number That Are Statistically Significant at 5% Level* Pos.	Neg.
For Jensen's model:						
α	.049%	0.426%	2.877%	−0.718%	3	5
$t(\alpha)$	−.086	1.221	3.133	−3.284		
β	.972	0.264	1.808	0.225	67	0
R^2	.747	0.159	0.944	0.234	67	0
For the arbitrage pricing approach:						
α	−.169	0.531	2.374	−0.975	2	11
$t(\alpha)$	−.014	1.376	3.316	−5.101		
β_1	.038	0.002	0.143	0.017	67	0
β_2	.070	0.034	0.149	−0.085	64	2
β_3	.120	0.043	0.269	0.012	67	0
β_4	.058	0.021	0.099	0.000	63	0
β_5	.047	0.030	0.102	0.000	56	0
β_6	.030	0.036	0.253	0.000	48	0
β_7	.017	0.039	0.182	0.000	16	0
R^2	.775	0.132	0.942	0.359	67	0

Source: Eric C. Chang and Wilbur G. Lewellen (1985), "An Arbitrage Pricing Approach to Evaluating Mutual Fund Performance," *Journal of Financial Research*, 8 (Spring), 15–30.

The arbitrage pricing alphas showed the mutual funds to be market underperformers with a mean monthly risk-adjusted return of −.169 percent. This compares to a positive Jensen's alpha of .049 percent. Arbitrage pricing seems to impose more stringent requirements for showing positive performance than does the CAPM. Looking at the individual funds, neither approach identified a high number of significant overperformers. The Jensen approach showed three funds with significantly positive alphas, and the arbitrage pricing evaluation resulted in two funds with significantly positive performance.

Another study examined the ability of fund managers to time the market. The technique used to check fund performance has the advantage of not being based on any particular model. In this study, Ferri, Oberhelman, and Roenfeldt[14] used quarterly data from the period 1975–1980 for sixty-nine different mutual funds. They measured effective timing ability by determining if a fund increased the percentage of its portfolio invested in stocks before market upswings. They found that funds, on average, made the correct decision only 44.3 percent of the time. Of the sixty-nine funds in the study, only three showed a significantly positive frequency of correct decisions. The results of this study thus imply that fund managers, on average, do not possess any market timing ability. The few funds that did show consistent timing performance were the exception rather than the rule and likely occurred by chance alone.

CRITICISMS OF PERFORMANCE EVALUATION TECHNIQUES

There has been an extended and unresolved debate regarding the efficacy of the various techniques of performance evaluation. This section briefly summarizes some of those arguments surrounding performance evaluation.

The criticisms of the validity of the CAPM naturally also apply as criticisms of performance evaluation techniques based on the CAPM. Roll[15] contends that CAPM theory itself precludes the use of CAPM-based measures of performance evaluation. He maintains that, in theory, all portfolios should lie on the SML. Any observed deviation (underperformance or overperformance) could very well be due to measurement error and/or a poor choice of market index. Since the market portfolio contains all risky assets, we can never observe it totally. If a surrogate measure of the market is not efficient, then virtually any relationship may be found between portfolio returns and beta. Empirical results using CAPM-based performance measures would therefore be meaningless.

Finding a good index is not the only problem. Betas are only estimates of systematic risk. Computation of betas using daily, weekly, monthly, and annual returns will all yield different estimates of beta. This can cause a shift in performance rankings. In addition, betas tend to be unstable and to change over time.

Other criticisms of performance evaluation are based on the statistical nature of returns. The Sharpe and Treynor measures are not unbiased test statistics.

Even if the CAPM were an accurate description of asset returns, there are still problems with performance measurement. French and Henderson[16] showed that there is so much random variation and noise in empirical returns that even if the CAPM is valid, it would be very difficult for a portfolio to show superior performance. For example, suppose a portfolio manager has the ability to beat the market an average of .5 percent per month (6 percent per year). Using five years of monthly returns, there is about a 50 percent chance that the data would *not* yield a significantly positive alpha. In other words, there may be portfolio managers out there who have excellent security selection and portfolio management skills, but the performance measures developed to date are not sufficiently powerful to identify them.

SUMMARY

The most widely used portfolio performance evaluation measures are based on the CAPM. These measures include those developed by Sharpe, Treynor, and Jensen. Other investment evaluation tools are stochastic dominance criteria and techniques based on arbitrage pricing theory.

When applied to mutual fund investment performance, most studies show that mutual funds as a group do not demonstrate the ability to outperform the market either by selecting good stocks or by timing the market. Some studies do show a small number of funds that apparently exhibit the ability to show consistently superior performance, but these funds are in the small minority.

The problems of investment evaluation include the problems of the CAPM. If the CAPM is not valid, then performance measures based on the CAPM are not correct. In addition, there is so much random variation in security returns that it is difficult to show superior performance even if it really does exist.

IMPORTANT TERMS

Jensen measure
modified Jensen measure
Sharpe measure
Treynor measure

QUESTIONS AND PROBLEMS

1. Explain the importance of adjusting the returns of two different portfolios for risk before comparing the investment returns of the two portfolios.
2. In what ways are the Sharpe and Treynor measures for evaluating investment performance similar? How do they differ?
3. Portfolios A, B, and C have the following statistics over the past several years:

Portfolio	*Mean Return*	*Standard Deviation*	*Beta*	*Alpha*
A	.17	.24	.85	.012
B	.21	.29	1.15	.008
C	.12	.20	.75	.006

Over the time period, the mean return on T-bills was .09. For each portfolio, compute the Sharpe, Treynor, Jensen, and modified Jensen measures of investment performance. Rank the portfolios using each measure.

4. Using five years of monthly returns for three portfolios she manages, an investment manager has computed the Jensen measure for investment evaluation. The results were as follows:

Portfolio	*Alpha*	*Standard Error of Alpha*	*Beta*
A	.016	.009	1.15
B	.020	.012	1.20
C	.015	.007	1.30

a) Using the magnitude of alpha as a guide, identify the portfolios that beat the market.
b) Using a confidence level of 95 percent (a critical t value of 1.96), identify which of the portfolios significantly outperformed the market.

5. Summarize the results of several studies using CAPM-based measures to evaluate performance of investment companies.
6. Based on the general results of the studies of investment company performance in this chapter and the concepts of efficient markets (Chapter 9), what conclusions might you draw about market efficiency and professional investment management?
7. Explain how arbitrage pricing theory can be used to evaluate investment performance. How did mutual funds perform according to the study presented in the text?
8. Summarize the criticisms of risk-adjusted techniques of investment performance measurement.

NOTES

1. William F. Sharpe (1966), "Mutual Fund Performance," *Journal of Business,* 39 (January), 119–138.
2. Jack L. Treynor (1965), "How to Rate the Management of Mutual Funds," *Harvard Business Review,* 43 (January-February), 63–75.
3. J. D. Jobson and Bob M. Korkie (1981), "Performance Hypothesis Testing with the Sharpe and Treynor Measures," *Journal of Finance,* 36 (September), 889–908.
4. Michael C. Jensen (1969), "Risk, the Pricing of Capital Assets, and the Evaluation of Investment Portfolios," *Journal of Business,* 42 (April), 169–247.
5. Keith V. Smith and Dennis A. Tito (1969), "Risk-Return Measures of Ex Post Portfolio Performance," *Journal of Financial and Quantitative Analysis,* 4 (December), 449–471.
6. Eric C. Chang and Wilbur G. Lewellen (1985), "An Arbitrage Pricing Approach to Evaluating Mutual Fund Performance," *Journal of Financial Research,* 8 (Spring), 15–30.
7. Haim Levy and Zvi Lerman (1985), "Testing P/E Ratios Filters with Stochastic Dominance," *Journal of Portfolio Management,* 11, 2 (Winter), 31–40.
8. Michael C. Jensen (1968), "The Performance of Mutual Funds in the Period 1945–64," *Journal of Finance,* 23 (May), 389–416.
9. Tye Kim (1978), "An Assessment of the Performance of Mutual Fund Management: 1969–1975," *Journal of Financial and Quantitative Analysis,* 12 (September), 385–406.
10. Frank J. Fabozzi, Jack C. Francis, and Cheng F. Lee (1980), "Generalized Functional Form for Mutual Fund Returns," *Journal of Financial and Quantitative Analysis,* 15 (December), 1107–1120.
11. Gordon J. Alexander and Roger D. Stover (1980), "Consistency of Mutual Fund Performance During Varying Market Conditions," *Journal of Economics and Business,* 32 (Spring), 219–225.
12. Stanley J. Kon (1983), "The Market Timing Performance of Mutual Fund Managers," *Journal of Business,* 56 (July), 323–347.
13. Chang and Lewellen (1985).
14. Michael G. Ferri, Dennis H. Oberhelman, and Rodney L. Roenfeldt (1984), "Market Timing and Mutual Fund Portfolio Composition," *Journal of Financial Research,* 7 (Summer), 143–150.
15. Richard Roll (1978), "Ambiguity When Performance is Measured by the Securities Market Line," *Journal of Finance,* 33 (September), 1051–1069.
16. Dan W. French and Glenn V. Henderson (1985), "How Well Does Performance Evaluation Perform?" *Journal of Portfolio Management,* 11 (Winter), 15–18.

SELECTED REFERENCES

Alexander, Gordon J., and Roger D. Stover (1980). "Consistency of Mutual Fund Performance during Varying Market Conditions." *Journal of Economics and Business,* 32 (Spring), 219–225.

Carlson, Robert S. (1970). "Aggregate Performance of Mutual Funds, 1948–1967." *Journal of Financial and Quantitative Analysis,* 15 (March), 1–30.

Chang, Eric C., and Wilbur G. Lewellen (1985). "An Arbitrage Pricing Approach to Evaluating Mutual Fund Performance." *Journal of Financial Research,* 8 (Spring), 15–30.

Chen, Carl R., and Steve Stockum (1986). "Selectivity, Market Timing, and Random Beta Behavior of Mutual Funds: A Generalized Model." *Journal of Financial Research,* 9 (Spring), 87–96.

Fabozzi, Frank J., Jack C. Francis, and Cheng F. Lee (1980). "Generalized Functional Form for Mutual Fund Returns." *Journal of Financial and Quantitative Analysis,* 15 (December), 1107–1120.

Ferri, Michael G., Dennis H. Oberhelman, and Rodney L. Roenfeldt (1984). "Market Timing and Mutual Fund Portfolio Composition." *Journal of Financial Research,* 7 (Summer), 143–150.

French, Dan W., and Glenn V. Henderson (1985). "How Well Does Performance Evaluation Perform?" *Journal of Portfolio Management,* 11 (Winter), 15–18.

Jensen, Michael C. (1968). "The Performance of Mutual Funds in the Period 1945–64." *Journal of Finance,* 23 (May), 389–416.

Jensen, Michael C. (1969). "Risk, the Pricing of Capital Assets, and the Evaluation of Investment Portfolios." *Journal of Business,* 42 (April), 169–247.

Jobson, J. D., and Bob M. Korkie (1981). "Performance Hypothesis Testing with the Sharpe and Treynor Measures." *Journal of Finance,* 36 (September), 889–908.

Kim, Tye (1978). "An Assessment of the Performance of Mutual Fund Management: 1969–1975." *Journal of Financial and Quantitative Analysis,* 12 (September), 385–406.

Kon, Stanley J. (1983). "The Market Timing Performance of Mutual Fund Managers." *Journal of Business,* 56 (July), 323–347.

Levy, Haim, and Zvi Lerman (1985). "Testing P/E Ratio Filters with Stochastic Dominance." *Journal of Portfolio Management,* 11, 2 (Winter), 31–40.

Nagorniak, John (1982). "Risk Adjusted Equity Performance Measurement." *Journal of Finance,* 37 (May), 555–561.

Roll, Richard (1978). "Ambiguity When Performance Is Measured by the Securities Market Line." *Journal of Finance,* 33 (September), 1051–1069.

Sharpe, William F. (1966). "Mutual Fund Performance." *Journal of Business,* 39 (January), 119–138.

Smith, Keith V., and Dennis A. Tito (1969). "Risk-Return Measures of Ex Post Portfolio Performance." *Journal of Financial and Quantitative Analysis,* 4 (December), 449–471.

Treynor, Jack L. (1965). "How to Rate the Management of Mutual Funds." *Harvard Business Review,* 43 (January-February), 63–75.

APPENDIXES

APPENDIX 1
Future value of $1

Number of Periods	*1%*	*2%*	*3%*	*4%*	*5%*	*6%*	*7%*
1	1.0100	1.0200	1.0300	1.0400	1.0500	1.0600	1.0700
2	1.0201	1.0404	1.0609	1.0816	1.1025	1.1236	1.1449
3	1.0303	1.0612	1.0927	1.1249	1.1576	1.1910	1.2250
4	1.0406	1.0824	1.1255	1.1699	1.2155	1.2625	1.3108
5	1.0510	1.1041	1.1593	1.2167	1.2763	1.3382	1.4026
6	1.0615	1.1262	1.1941	1.2653	1.3401	1.4185	1.5007
7	1.0721	1.1487	1.2299	1.3159	1.4071	1.5036	1.6058
8	1.0829	1.1717	1.2668	1.3686	1.4775	1.5938	1.7182
9	1.0937	1.1951	1.3048	1.4233	1.5513	1.6895	1.8385
10	1.1046	1.2190	1.3439	1.4802	1.6289	1.7908	1.9672
11	1.1157	1.2434	1.3842	1.5395	1.7103	1.8983	2.1049
12	1.1268	1.2682	1.4258	1.6010	1.7959	2.0122	2.2522
13	1.1381	1.2936	1.4685	1.6651	1.8856	2.1329	2.4098
14	1.1495	1.3195	1.5126	1.7317	1.9799	2.2609	2.5785
15	1.1610	1.3459	1.5580	1.8009	2.0789	2.3966	2.7590
16	1.1726	1.3728	1.6047	1.8730	2.1829	2.5404	2.9522
17	1.1843	1.4002	1.6528	1.9479	2.2920	2.6928	3.1588
18	1.1961	1.4282	1.7024	2.0258	2.4066	2.8543	3.3799
19	1.2081	1.4568	1.7535	2.1068	2.5270	3.0256	3.6165
20	1.2202	1.4859	1.8061	2.1911	2.6533	3.2071	3.8697
21	1.2324	1.5157	1.8603	2.2788	2.7860	3.3996	4.1406
22	1.2447	1.5460	1.9161	2.3699	2.9253	3.6035	4.4304
23	1.2572	1.5769	1.9736	2.4647	3.0715	3.8197	4.7405
24	1.2697	1.6084	2.0328	2.5633	3.2251	4.0489	5.0724
25	1.2824	1.6406	2.0938	2.6658	3.3864	4.2919	5.4274
26	1.2953	1.6734	2.1566	2.7725	3.5557	4.5494	5.8074
27	1.3082	1.7069	2.2213	2.8834	3.7335	4.8223	6.2139
28	1.3213	1.7410	2.2879	2.9987	3.9201	5.1117	6.6488
29	1.3345	1.7758	2.3566	3.1187	4.1161	5.4184	7.1143
30	1.3478	1.8114	2.4273	3.2434	4.3219	5.7435	7.6123
40	1.4889	2.2080	3.2620	4.8010	7.0400	10.2857	14.9745
50	1.6446	2.6916	4.3839	7.1067	11.4674	18.4202	29.4570
60	1.8167	3.2810	5.8916	10.5196	18.6792	32.9877	57.9464

APPENDIX 1
Future value of $1 (*continued*)

Number of Periods	*8%*	*9%*	*10%*	*11%*	*12%*	*13%*	*14%*
1	1.0800	1.0900	1.1000	1.1100	1.1200	1.1300	1.1400
2	1.1664	1.1881	1.2100	1.2321	1.2544	1.2769	1.2996
3	1.2597	1.2950	1.3310	1.3676	1.4049	1.4429	1.4815
4	1.3605	1.4116	1.4641	1.5181	1.5735	1.6305	1.6890
5	1.4693	1.5386	1.6105	1.6851	1.7623	1.8424	1.9254
6	1.5869	1.6771	1.7716	1.8704	1.9738	2.0820	2.1950
7	1.7138	1.8280	1.9487	2.0762	2.2107	2.3526	2.5023
8	1.8509	1.9926	2.1436	2.3045	2.4760	2.6584	2.8526
9	1.9990	2.1719	2.3579	2.5580	2.7731	3.0040	3.2519
10	2.1589	2.3674	2.5937	2.8394	3.1058	3.3946	3.7072
11	2.3316	2.5804	2.8531	3.1518	3.4785	3.8359	4.2262
12	2.5182	2.8127	3.1384	3.4985	3.8960	4.3345	4.8179
13	2.7196	3.0658	3.4523	3.8833	4.3635	4.8980	5.4924
14	2.9372	3.3417	3.7975	4.3104	4.8871	5.5348	6.2613
15	3.1722	3.6425	4.1772	4.7846	5.4736	6.2543	7.1379
16	3.4259	3.9703	4.5950	5.3109	6.1304	7.0673	8.1372
17	3.7000	4.3276	5.0545	5.8951	6.8660	7.9861	9.2765
18	3.9960	4.7171	5.5599	6.5436	7.6900	9.0243	10.5752
19	4.3157	5.1417	6.1159	7.2633	8.6128	10.1974	12.0557
20	4.6610	5.6044	6.7275	8.0623	9.6463	11.5231	13.7435
21	5.0338	6.1088	7.4002	8.9492	10.8038	13.0211	15.6676
22	5.4365	6.6586	8.1403	9.9336	12.1003	14.7138	17.8610
23	5.8715	7.2579	8.9543	11.0263	13.5523	16.6266	20.3616
24	6.3412	7.9111	9.8497	12.2392	15.1786	18.7881	23.2122
25	6.8485	8.6231	10.8347	13.5855	17.0001	21.2305	26.4619
26	7.3964	9.3992	11.9182	15.0799	19.0401	23.9905	30.1666
27	7.9881	10.2451	13.1100	16.7386	21.3249	27.1093	34.3899
28	8.6271	11.1671	14.4210	18.5799	23.8839	30.6335	39.2045
29	9.3173	12.1722	15.8631	20.6237	26.7499	34.6158	44.6931
30	10.0627	13.2677	17.4494	22.8923	29.9599	39.1159	50.9502
40	21.7245	31.4094	45.2593	65.0009	93.0510	132.7816	188.8835
50	46.9016	74.3575	117.3909	184.5648	289.0022	450.7359	700.2330
60	101.2571	176.0313	304.4816	524.0572	897.5969	1530.053	2595.919

APPENDIX 1
Future value of $1 (*continued*)

Number of Periods	*15%*	*16%*	*18%*	*20%*	*24%*	*28%*
1	1.1500	1.1600	1.1800	1.2000	1.2400	1.2800
2	1.3225	1.3456	1.3924	1.4400	1.5376	1.6384
3	1.5209	1.5609	1.6430	1.7280	1.9066	2.0972
4	1.7490	1.8106	1.9388	2.0736	2.3642	2.6844
5	2.0114	2.1003	2.2878	2.4883	2.9316	3.4360
6	2.3131	2.4364	2.6996	2.9860	3.6352	4.3980
7	2.6600	2.8262	3.1855	3.5832	4.5077	5.6295
8	3.0590	3.2784	3.7589	4.2998	5.5895	7.2058
9	3.5179	3.8030	4.4355	5.1598	6.9310	9.2234
10	4.0456	4.4114	5.2338	6.1917	8.5944	11.8059
11	4.6524	5.1173	6.1759	7.4301	10.6571	15.1116
12	5.3503	5.9360	7.2876	8.9161	13.2148	19.3428
13	6.1528	6.8858	8.5994	10.6993	16.3863	24.7588
14	7.0757	7.9875	10.1472	12.8392	20.3191	31.6913
15	8.1371	9.2655	11.9737	15.4070	25.1956	40.5648
16	9.3576	10.7480	14.1290	18.4884	31.2426	51.9230
17	10.7613	12.4677	16.6722	22.1861	38.7408	66.4614
18	12.3755	14.4625	19.6733	26.6233	48.0386	85.0706
19	14.2318	16.7765	23.2144	31.9480	59.5679	108.8904
20	16.3665	19.4608	27.3930	38.3376	73.8641	139.3797
21	18.8215	22.5745	32.3238	46.0051	91.5915	178.4060
22	21.6447	26.1864	38.1421	55.2061	113.5735	228.3596
23	24.8915	30.3762	45.0076	66.2474	140.8312	292.3003
24	28.6252	35.2364	53.1090	79.4968	174.6306	374.1444
25	32.9190	40.8742	62.6686	95.3962	216.5420	478.9049
26	37.8568	47.4141	73.9490	114.4755	268.5121	612.9982
27	43.5353	55.0004	87.2598	137.3706	332.9550	784.6377
28	50.0656	63.8004	102.9666	164.8447	412.8642	1004.336
29	57.5755	74.0085	121.5005	197.8136	511.9516	1285.550
30	66.2118	85.8499	143.3706	237.3763	634.8199	1645.505
40	267.8635	378.7212	750.3783	1469.772	5455.913	19426.69
50	1083.657	1670.704	3927.357	9100.438	46890.43	229349.9
60	4383.999	7370.201	20555.14	56347.51	402996.3	2707685

APPENDIX 2
Present value of $1

Number of Periods	*1%*	*2%*	*3%*	*4%*	*5%*	*6%*	*7%*
1	0.9901	0.9804	0.9709	0.9615	0.9524	0.9434	0.9346
2	0.9803	0.9612	0.9426	0.9246	0.9070	0.8900	0.8734
3	0.9706	0.9423	0.9151	0.8890	0.8638	0.8396	0.8163
4	0.9610	0.9238	0.8885	0.8548	0.8227	0.7921	0.7629
5	0.9515	0.9057	0.8626	0.8219	0.7835	0.7473	0.7130
6	0.9420	0.8880	0.8375	0.7903	0.7462	0.7050	0.6663
7	0.9327	0.8706	0.8131	0.7599	0.7107	0.6651	0.6227
8	0.9235	0.8535	0.7894	0.7307	0.6768	0.6274	0.5820
9	0.9143	0.8368	0.7664	0.7026	0.6446	0.5919	0.5439
10	0.9053	0.8203	0.7441	0.6756	0.6139	0.5584	0.5083
11	0.8963	0.8043	0.7224	0.6496	0.5847	0.5268	0.4751
12	0.8874	0.7885	0.7014	0.6246	0.5568	0.4970	0.4440
13	0.8787	0.7730	0.6810	0.6006	0.5303	0.4688	0.4150
14	0.8700	0.7579	0.6611	0.5775	0.5051	0.4423	0.3878
15	0.8613	0.7430	0.6419	0.5553	0.4810	0.4173	0.3624
16	0.8528	0.7284	0.6232	0.5339	0.4581	0.3936	0.3387
17	0.8444	0.7142	0.6050	0.5134	0.4363	0.3714	0.3166
18	0.8360	0.7002	0.5874	0.4936	0.4155	0.3503	0.2959
19	0.8277	0.6864	0.5703	0.4746	0.3957	0.3305	0.2765
20	0.8195	0.6730	0.5537	0.4564	0.3769	0.3118	0.2584
21	0.8114	0.6598	0.5375	0.4388	0.3589	0.2942	0.2415
22	0.8034	0.6468	0.5219	0.4220	0.3418	0.2775	0.2257
23	0.7954	0.6342	0.5067	0.4057	0.3256	0.2618	0.2109
24	0.7876	0.6217	0.4919	0.3901	0.3101	0.2470	0.1971
25	0.7798	0.6095	0.4776	0.3751	0.2953	0.2330	0.1842
26	0.7720	0.5976	0.4637	0.3607	0.2812	0.2198	0.1722
27	0.7644	0.5859	0.4502	0.3468	0.2678	0.2074	0.1609
28	0.7568	0.5744	0.4371	0.3335	0.2551	0.1956	0.1504
29	0.7493	0.5631	0.4243	0.3207	0.2429	0.1846	0.1406
30	0.7419	0.5521	0.4120	0.3083	0.2314	0.1741	0.1314
40	0.6717	0.4529	0.3066	0.2083	0.1420	0.0972	0.0668
50	0.6080	0.3715	0.2281	0.1407	0.0872	0.0543	0.0339
60	0.5504	0.3048	0.1697	0.0951	0.0535	0.0303	0.0173

APPENDIX 2
Present value of $1 (*continued*)

Number of Periods	*8%*	*9%*	*10%*	*11%*	*12%*	*13%*	*14%*
1	0.9259	0.9174	0.9091	0.9009	0.8929	0.8850	0.8772
2	0.8573	0.8417	0.8264	0.8116	0.7972	0.7831	0.7695
3	0.7938	0.7722	0.7513	0.7312	0.7118	0.6931	0.6750
4	0.7350	0.7084	0.6830	0.6587	0.6355	0.6133	0.5921
5	0.6806	0.6499	0.6209	0.5935	0.5674	0.5428	0.5194
6	0.6302	0.5963	0.5645	0.5346	0.5066	0.4803	0.4556
7	0.5835	0.5470	0.5132	0.4817	0.4523	0.4251	0.3996
8	0.5403	0.5019	0.4665	0.4339	0.4039	0.3762	0.3506
9	0.5002	0.4604	0.4241	0.3909	0.3606	0.3329	0.3075
10	0.4632	0.4224	0.3855	0.3522	0.3220	0.2946	0.2697
11	0.4289	0.3875	0.3505	0.3173	0.2875	0.2607	0.2366
12	0.3971	0.3555	0.3186	0.2858	0.2567	0.2307	0.2076
13	0.3677	0.3262	0.2897	0.2575	0.2292	0.2042	0.1821
14	0.3405	0.2992	0.2633	0.2320	0.2046	0.1807	0.1597
15	0.3152	0.2745	0.2394	0.2090	0.1827	0.1599	0.1401
16	0.2919	0.2519	0.2176	0.1883	0.1631	0.1415	0.1229
17	0.2703	0.2311	0.1978	0.1696	0.1456	0.1252	0.1078
18	0.2502	0.2120	0.1799	0.1528	0.1300	0.1108	0.0946
19	0.2317	0.1945	0.1635	0.1377	0.1161	0.0981	0.0829
20	0.2145	0.1784	0.1486	0.1240	0.1037	0.0868	0.0728
21	0.1987	0.1637	0.1351	0.1117	0.0926	0.0768	0.0638
22	0.1839	0.1502	0.1228	0.1007	0.0826	0.0680	0.0560
23	0.1703	0.1378	0.1117	0.0907	0.0738	0.0601	0.0491
24	0.1577	0.1264	0.1015	0.0817	0.0659	0.0532	0.0431
25	0.1460	0.1160	0.0923	0.0736	0.0588	0.0471	0.0378
26	0.1352	0.1064	0.0839	0.0663	0.0525	0.0417	0.0331
27	0.1252	0.0976	0.0763	0.0597	0.0469	0.0369	0.0291
28	0.1159	0.0895	0.0693	0.0538	0.0419	0.0326	0.0255
29	0.1073	0.0822	0.0630	0.0485	0.0374	0.0289	0.0224
30	0.0994	0.0754	0.0573	0.0437	0.0334	0.0256	0.0196
40	0.0460	0.0318	0.0221	0.0154	0.0107	0.0075	0.0053
50	0.0213	0.0134	0.0085	0.0054	0.0035	0.0022	0.0014
60	0.0099	0.0057	0.0033	0.0019	0.0011	0.0007	0.0004

APPENDIX 2
Present value of $1 (*continued*)

Number of Periods	*15%*	*16%*	*18%*	*20%*	*24%*	*28%*
1	0.8696	0.8621	0.8475	0.8333	0.8065	0.7813
2	0.7561	0.7432	0.7182	0.6944	0.6504	0.6104
3	0.6575	0.6407	0.6086	0.5787	0.5245	0.4768
4	0.5718	0.5523	0.5158	0.4823	0.4230	0.3725
5	0.4972	0.4761	0.4371	0.4019	0.3411	0.2910
6	0.4323	0.4104	0.3704	0.3349	0.2751	0.2274
7	0.3759	0.3538	0.3139	0.2791	0.2218	0.1776
8	0.3269	0.3050	0.2660	0.2326	0.1789	0.1388
9	0.2843	0.2630	0.2255	0.1938	0.1443	0.1084
10	0.2472	0.2267	0.1911	0.1615	0.1164	0.0847
11	0.2149	0.1954	0.1619	0.1346	0.0938	0.0662
12	0.1869	0.1685	0.1372	0.1122	0.0757	0.0517
13	0.1625	0.1452	0.1163	0.0935	0.0610	0.0404
14	0.1413	0.1252	0.0985	0.0779	0.0492	0.0316
15	0.1229	0.1079	0.0835	0.0649	0.0397	0.0247
16	0.1069	0.0930	0.0708	0.0541	0.0320	0.0193
17	0.0929	0.0802	0.0600	0.0451	0.0258	0.0150
18	0.0808	0.0691	0.0508	0.0376	0.0208	0.0118
19	0.0703	0.0596	0.0431	0.0313	0.0168	0.0092
20	0.0611	0.0514	0.0365	0.0261	0.0135	0.0072
21	0.0531	0.0443	0.0309	0.0217	0.0109	0.0056
22	0.0462	0.0382	0.0262	0.0181	0.0088	0.0044
23	0.0402	0.0329	0.0222	0.0151	0.0071	0.0034
24	0.0349	0.0284	0.0188	0.0126	0.0057	0.0027
25	0.0304	0.0245	0.0160	0.0105	0.0046	0.0021
26	0.0264	0.0211	0.0135	0.0087	0.0037	0.0016
27	0.0230	0.0182	0.0115	0.0073	0.0030	0.0013
28	0.0200	0.0157	0.0097	0.0061	0.0024	0.0010
29	0.0174	0.0135	0.0082	0.0051	0.0020	0.0008
30	0.0151	0.0116	0.0070	0.0042	0.0016	0.0006
40	0.0037	0.0026	0.0013	0.0007	0.0002	0.0001
50	0.0009	0.0006	0.0003	0.0001	0.0000	0.0000
60	0.0002	0.0001	0.0000	0.0000	0.0000	0.0000

APPENDIX 3
Future sum of an annuity of $1 per period

Number of Periods	*1%*	*2%*	*3%*	*4%*	*5%*	*6%*	*7%*
1	1.0000	1.0000	1.0000	1.0000	1.0000	1.0000	1.0000
2	2.0100	2.0200	2.0300	2.0400	2.0500	2.0600	2.0700
3	3.0301	3.0604	3.0909	3.1216	3.1525	3.1836	3.2149
4	4.0604	4.1216	4.1836	4.2465	4.3101	4.3746	4.4399
5	5.1010	5.2040	5.3091	5.4163	5.5256	5.6371	5.7507
6	6.1520	6.3081	6.4684	6.6330	6.8019	6.9753	7.1533
7	7.2135	7.4343	7.6625	7.8983	8.1420	8.3938	8.6540
8	8.2857	8.5830	8.8923	9.2142	9.5491	9.8975	10.2598
9	9.3685	9.7546	10.1591	10.5828	11.0266	11.4913	11.9780
10	10.4622	10.9497	11.4639	12.0061	12.5779	13.1808	13.8164
11	11.5668	12.1687	12.8078	13.4864	14.2068	14.9716	15.7836
12	12.6825	13.4121	14.1920	15.0258	15.9171	16.8699	17.8885
13	13.8093	14.6803	15.6178	16.6268	17.7130	18.8821	20.1406
14	14.9474	15.9739	17.0863	18.2919	19.5986	21.0151	22.5505
15	16.0969	17.2934	18.5989	20.0236	21.5786	23.2760	25.1290
16	17.2579	18.6393	20.1569	21.8245	23.6575	25.6725	27.8881
17	18.4304	20.0121	21.7616	23.6975	25.8404	28.2129	30.8402
18	19.6147	21.4123	23.4144	25.6454	28.1324	30.9057	33.9990
19	20.8109	22.8406	25.1169	27.6712	30.5390	33.7600	37.3790
20	22.0190	24.2974	26.8704	29.7781	33.0660	36.7856	40.9955
21	23.2392	25.7833	28.6765	31.9692	35.7193	39.9927	44.8652
22	24.4716	27.2990	30.5368	34.2480	38.5052	43.3923	49.0057
23	25.7163	28.8450	32.4529	36.6179	41.4305	46.9958	53.4361
24	26.9735	30.4219	34.4265	39.0826	44.5020	50.8156	58.1767
25	28.2432	32.0303	36.4593	41.6459	47.7271	54.8645	63.2490
26	29.5256	33.6709	38.5530	44.3117	51.1135	59.1564	68.6765
27	30.8209	35.3443	40.7096	47.0842	54.6691	63.7058	74.4838
28	32.1291	37.0512	42.9309	49.9676	58.4026	68.5281	80.6977
29	33.4504	38.7922	45.2189	52.9663	62.3227	73.6398	87.3465
30	34.7849	40.5681	47.5754	56.0849	66.4388	79.0582	94.4608
40	48.8864	60.4020	75.4013	95.0255	120.7998	154.7620	199.6351
50	64.4632	84.5794	112.7969	152.6671	209.3480	290.3359	406.5289
60	81.6697	114.0515	163.0534	237.9907	353.5837	533.1282	813.5204

APPENDIX 3
Future sum of an annuity of $1 per period (*continued*)

Number of Periods	*8%*	*9%*	*10%*	*11%*	*12%*	*13%*	*14%*
1	1.0000	1.0000	1.0000	1.0000	1.0000	1.0000	1.0000
2	2.0800	2.0900	2.1000	2.1100	2.1200	2.1300	2.1400
3	3.2464	3.2781	3.3100	3.3421	3.3744	3.4069	3.4396
4	4.5061	4.5731	4.6410	4.7097	4.7793	4.8498	4.9211
5	5.8666	5.9847	6.1051	6.2278	6.3528	6.4803	6.6101
6	7.3359	7.5233	7.7156	7.9129	8.1152	8.3227	8.5355
7	8.9228	9.2004	9.4872	9.7833	10.0890	10.4047	10.7305
8	10.6366	11.0285	11.4359	11.8594	12.2997	12.7573	13.2328
9	12.4876	13.0210	13.5795	14.1640	14.7757	15.4157	16.0853
10	14.4866	15.1929	15.9374	16.7220	17.5487	18.4197	19.3373
11	16.6455	17.5603	18.5312	19.5614	20.6546	21.8143	23.0445
12	18.9771	20.1407	21.3843	22.7132	24.1331	25.6502	27.2707
13	21.4953	22.9534	24.5227	26.2116	28.0291	29.9847	32.0887
14	24.2149	26.0192	27.9750	30.0949	32.3926	34.8827	37.5811
15	27.1521	29.3609	31.7725	34.4054	37.2797	40.4175	43.8424
16	30.3243	33.0034	35.9497	39.1899	42.7533	46.6717	50.9804
17	33.7502	36.9737	40.5447	44.5008	48.8837	53.7391	59.1176
18	37.4502	41.3013	45.5992	50.3959	55.7497	61.7251	68.3941
19	41.4463	46.0185	51.1591	56.9395	63.4397	70.7494	78.9692
20	45.7620	51.1601	57.2750	64.2028	72.0524	80.9468	91.0249
21	50.4229	56.7645	64.0025	72.2651	81.6987	92.4699	104.7684
22	55.4568	62.8733	71.4027	81.2143	92.5026	105.4910	120.4360
23	60.8933	69.5319	79.5430	91.1479	104.6029	120.2048	138.2970
24	66.7648	76.7898	88.4973	102.1742	118.1552	136.8315	158.6586
25	73.1059	84.7009	98.3471	114.4133	133.3339	155.6196	181.8708
26	79.9544	93.3240	109.1818	127.9988	150.3339	176.8501	208.3327
27	87.3508	102.7231	121.0999	143.0786	169.3740	200.8406	238.4993
28	95.3388	112.9682	134.2099	159.8173	190.6989	227.9499	272.8892
29	103.9659	124.1354	148.6309	178.3972	214.5828	258.5834	312.0937
30	113.2832	136.3075	164.4940	199.0209	241.3327	293.1992	356.7868
40	259.0565	337.8824	442.5926	581.8261	767.0914	1013.704	1342.025
50	573.7702	815.0836	1163.909	1668.771	2400.018	3459.507	4994.521
60	1253.213	1944.792	3034.816	4755.066	7471.641	11761.95	18535.13

APPENDIX 3
Future sum of an annuity of $1 per period (*continued*)

Number of Periods	***15%***	***16%***	***18%***	***20%***	***24%***	***28%***
1	1.0000	1.0000	1.0000	1.0000	1.0000	1.0000
2	2.1500	2.1600	2.1800	2.2000	2.2400	2.2800
3	3.4725	3.5056	3.5724	3.6400	3.7776	3.9184
4	4.9934	5.0665	5.2154	5.3680	5.6842	6.0156
5	6.7424	6.8771	7.1542	7.4416	8.0484	8.6999
6	8.7537	8.9775	9.4420	9.9299	10.9801	12.1359
7	11.0668	11.4139	12.1415	12.9159	14.6153	16.5339
8	13.7268	14.2401	15.3270	16.4991	19.1229	22.1634
9	16.7858	17.5185	19.0859	20.7989	24.7125	29.3692
10	20.3037	21.3215	23.5213	25.9587	31.6434	38.5926
11	24.3493	25.7329	28.7551	32.1504	40.2379	50.3985
12	29.0017	30.8502	34.9311	39.5805	50.8950	65.5100
13	34.3519	36.7862	42.2187	48.4966	64.1097	84.8529
14	40.5047	43.6720	50.8180	59.1959	80.4961	109.6117
15	47.5804	51.6595	60.9653	72.0351	100.8151	141.3029
16	55.7175	60.9250	72.9390	87.4421	126.0108	181.8677
17	65.0751	71.6730	87.0680	105.9306	157.2534	233.7907
18	75.8364	84.1407	103.7403	128.1167	195.9942	300.2521
19	88.2118	98.6032	123.4135	154.7400	244.0328	385.3227
20	102.4436	115.3797	146.6280	186.6880	303.6006	494.2131
21	118.8101	134.8405	174.0210	225.0256	377.4648	633.5927
22	137.6316	157.4150	206.3448	271.0307	469.0563	811.9987
23	159.2764	183.6014	244.4868	326.2369	582.6298	1040.358
24	184.1678	213.9776	289.4945	392.4842	723.4610	1332.659
25	212.7930	249.2140	342.6035	471.9811	898.0916	1706.803
26	245.7120	290.0883	405.2721	567.3773	1114.634	2185.708
27	283.5688	337.5024	479.2211	681.8528	1383.146	2798.706
28	327.1041	392.5028	566.4809	819.2233	1716.101	3583.344
29	377.1697	456.3032	669.4475	984.0680	2128.965	4587.680
30	434.7451	530.3117	790.9480	1181.882	2640.916	5873.231
40	1779.090	2360.757	4163.213	7343.858	22728.80	69377.46
50	7217.716	10435.65	21813.09	45497.19	195372.6	819103.1
60	29219.99	46057.51	114189.7	281732.6	1679147	9670301

APPENDIX 4
Present value of an annuity of $1 per period

Number of Periods	*1%*	*2%*	*3%*	*4%*	*5%*	*6%*	*7%*
1	0.9901	0.9804	0.9709	0.9615	0.9524	0.9434	0.9346
2	1.9704	1.9416	1.9135	1.8861	1.8594	1.8334	1.8080
3	2.9410	2.8839	2.8286	2.7751	2.7232	2.6730	2.6243
4	3.9020	3.8077	3.7171	3.6299	3.5460	3.4651	3.3872
5	4.8534	4.7135	4.5797	4.4518	4.3295	4.2124	4.1002
6	5.7955	5.6014	5.4172	5.2421	5.0757	4.9173	4.7665
7	6.7282	6.4720	6.2303	6.0021	5.7864	5.5824	5.3893
8	7.6517	7.3255	7.0197	6.7327	6.4632	6.2098	5.9713
9	8.5660	8.1622	7.7861	7.4353	7.1078	6.8017	6.5152
10	9.4713	8.9826	8.5302	8.1109	7.7217	7.3601	7.0236
11	10.3676	9.7868	9.2526	8.7605	8.3064	7.8869	7.4987
12	11.2551	10.5753	9.9540	9.3851	8.8633	8.3838	7.9427
13	12.1337	11.3484	10.6350	9.9856	9.3936	8.8527	8.3577
14	13.0037	12.1062	11.2961	10.5631	9.8986	9.2950	8.7455
15	13.8651	12.8493	11.9379	11.1184	10.3797	9.7122	9.1079
16	14.7179	13.5777	12.5611	11.6523	10.8378	10.1059	9.4466
17	15.5623	14.2919	13.1661	12.1657	11.2741	10.4773	9.7632
18	16.3983	14.9920	13.7535	12.6593	11.6896	10.8276	10.0591
19	17.2260	15.6785	14.3238	13.1339	12.0853	11.1581	10.3356
20	18.0456	16.3514	14.8775	13.5903	12.4622	11.4699	10.5940
21	18.8570	17.0112	15.4150	14.0292	12.8212	11.7641	10.8355
22	19.6604	17.6580	15.9369	14.4511	13.1630	12.0416	11.0612
23	20.4558	18.2922	16.4436	14.8568	13.4886	12.3034	11.2722
24	21.2434	18.9139	16.9355	15.2470	13.7986	12.5504	11.4693
25	22.0232	19.5235	17.4131	15.6221	14.0939	12.7834	11.6536
26	22.7952	20.1210	17.8768	15.9828	14.3752	13.0032	11.8258
27	23.5596	20.7069	18.3270	16.3296	14.6430	13.2105	11.9867
28	24.3164	21.2813	18.7641	16.6631	14.8981	13.4062	12.1371
29	25.0658	21.8444	19.1885	16.9837	15.1411	13.5907	12.2777
30	25.8077	22.3965	19.6004	17.2920	15.3725	13.7648	12.4090
40	32.8347	27.3555	23.1148	19.7928	17.1591	15.0463	13.3317
50	39.1961	31.4236	25.7298	21.4822	18.2559	15.7619	13.8007
60	44.9550	34.7609	27.6756	22.6235	18.9293	16.1614	14.0392

APPENDIX 4
Present value of an annuity of $1 per period (*continued*)

Number of Periods	*8%*	*9%*	*10%*	*11%*	*12%*	*13%*	*14%*
1	0.9259	0.9174	0.9091	0.9009	0.8929	0.8850	0.8772
2	1.7833	1.7591	1.7355	1.7125	1.6901	1.6681	1.6467
3	2.5771	2.5313	2.4869	2.4437	2.4018	2.3612	2.3216
4	3.3121	3.2397	3.1699	3.1024	3.0373	2.9745	2.9137
5	3.9927	3.8897	3.7908	3.6959	3.6048	3.5172	3.4331
6	4.6229	4.4859	4.3553	4.2305	4.1114	3.9975	3.8887
7	5.2064	5.0330	4.8684	4.7122	4.5638	4.4226	4.2883
8	5.7466	5.5348	5.3349	5.1461	4.9676	4.7988	4.6389
9	6.2469	5.9952	5.7590	5.5370	5.3282	5.1317	4.9464
10	6.7101	6.4177	6.1446	5.8892	5.6502	5.4262	5.2161
11	7.1390	6.8052	6.4951	6.2065	5.9377	5.6869	5.4527
12	7.5361	7.1607	6.8137	6.4924	6.1944	5.9176	5.6603
13	7.9038	7.4869	7.1034	6.7499	6.4235	6.1218	5.8424
14	8.2442	7.7862	7.3667	6.9819	6.6282	6.3025	6.0021
15	8.5595	8.0607	7.6061	7.1909	6.8109	6.4624	6.1422
16	8.8514	8.3126	7.8237	7.3792	6.9740	6.6039	6.2651
17	9.1216	8.5436	8.0216	7.5488	7.1196	6.7291	6.3729
18	9.3719	8.7556	8.2014	7.7016	7.2497	6.8399	6.4674
19	9.6036	8.9501	8.3649	7.8393	7.3658	6.9380	6.5504
20	9.8181	9.1285	8.5136	7.9633	7.4694	7.0248	6.6231
21	10.0168	9.2922	8.6487	8.0751	7.5620	7.1016	6.6870
22	10.2007	9.4424	8.7715	8.1757	7.6446	7.1695	6.7429
23	10.3711	9.5802	8.8832	8.2664	7.7184	7.2297	6.7921
24	10.5288	9.7066	8.9847	8.3481	7.7843	7.2829	6.8351
25	10.6748	9.8226	9.0770	8.4217	7.8431	7.3300	6.8729
26	10.8100	9.9290	9.1609	8.4881	7.8957	7.3717	6.9061
27	10.9352	10.0266	9.2372	8.5478	7.9426	7.4086	6.9352
28	11.0511	10.1161	9.3066	8.6016	7.9844	7.4412	6.9607
29	11.1584	10.1983	9.3696	8.6501	8.0218	7.4701	6.9830
30	11.2578	10.2737	9.4269	8.6938	8.0552	7.4957	7.0027
40	11.9246	10.7574	9.7791	8.9511	8.2438	7.6344	7.1050
50	12.2335	10.9617	9.9148	9.0417	8.3045	7.6752	7.1327
60	12.3766	11.0480	9.9672	9.0736	8.3240	7.6873	7.1401

APPENDIX 4
Present value of an annuity of $1 per period (*continued*)

Number of Periods	*15%*	*16%*	*18%*	*20%*	*24%*	*28%*
1	0.8696	0.8621	0.8475	0.8333	0.8065	0.7813
2	1.6257	1.6052	1.5656	1.5278	1.4568	1.3916
3	2.2832	2.2459	2.1743	2.1065	1.9813	1.8684
4	2.8550	2.7982	2.6901	2.5887	2.4043	2.2410
5	3.3522	3.2743	3.1272	2.9906	2.7454	2.5320
6	3.7845	3.6847	3.4976	3.3255	3.0205	2.7594
7	4.1604	4.0386	3.8115	3.6046	3.2423	2.9370
8	4.4873	4.3436	4.0776	3.8372	3.4212	3.0758
9	4.7716	4.6065	4.3030	4.0310	3.5655	3.1842
10	5.0188	4.8332	4.4941	4.1925	3.6819	3.2689
11	5.2337	5.0286	4.6560	4.3271	3.7757	3.3351
12	5.4206	5.1971	4.7932	4.4392	3.8514	3.3868
13	5.5831	5.3423	4.9095	4.5327	3.9124	3.4272
14	5.7245	5.4675	5.0081	4.6106	3.9616	3.4587
15	5.8474	5.5755	5.0916	4.6755	4.0013	3.4834
16	5.9542	5.6685	5.1624	4.7296	4.0333	3.5026
17	6.0472	5.7487	5.2223	4.7746	4.0591	3.5177
18	6.1280	5.8178	5.2732	4.8122	4.0799	3.5294
19	6.1982	5.8775	5.3162	4.8435	4.0967	3.5386
20	6.2593	5.9288	5.3527	4.8696	4.1103	3.5458
21	6.3125	5.9731	5.3837	4.8913	4.1212	3.5514
22	6.3587	6.0113	5.4099	4.9094	4.1300	3.5558
23	6.3988	6.0442	5.4321	4.9245	4.1371	3.5592
24	6.4338	6.0726	5.4509	4.9371	4.1428	3.5619
25	6.4641	6.0971	5.4669	4.9476	4.1474	3.5640
26	6.4906	6.1182	5.4804	4.9563	4.1511	3.5656
27	6.5135	6.1364	5.4919	4.9636	4.1542	3.5669
28	6.5335	6.1520	5.5016	4.9697	4.1566	3.5679
29	6.5509	6.1656	5.5098	4.9747	4.1585	3.5687
30	6.5660	6.1772	5.5168	4.9789	4.1601	3.5693
40	6.6418	6.2335	5.5482	4.9966	4.1659	3.5712
50	6.6605	6.2463	5.5541	4.9995	4.1666	3.5714
60	6.6651	6.2492	5.5553	4.9999	4.1667	3.5714

APPENDIX 5
Probabilities of the cumulative standard normal distribution

z	*.00*	*.01*	*.02*	*.03*	*.04*	*.05*	*.06*	*.07*	*.08*	*.09*
−1.4	.0808	.0793	.0778	.0764	.0749	.0735	.0721	.0708	.0694	.0681
−1.3	.0968	.0951	.0934	.0918	.0901	.0885	.0869	.0853	.0838	.0823
−1.2	.1151	.1131	.1112	.1093	.1075	.1056	.1038	.1020	.1003	.0985
−1.1	.1357	.1335	.1314	.1292	.1271	.1251	.1230	.1210	.1190	.1170
−1.0	.1587	.1562	.1539	.1515	.1492	.1469	.1446	.1423	.1401	.1379
−0.9	.1841	.1814	.1788	.1762	.1736	.1711	.1685	.1660	.1635	.1611
−0.8	.2119	.2090	.2061	.2033	.2005	.1977	.1949	.1922	.1894	.1867
−0.7	.2420	.2388	.2358	.2327	.2296	.2266	.2236	.2206	.2177	.2148
−0.6	.2743	.2709	.2676	.2643	.2611	.2578	.2546	.2514	.2482	.2451
−0.5	.3085	.3050	.3015	.2981	.2946	.2912	.2877	.2843	.2810	.2776
−0.4	.3446	.3409	.3372	.3336	.3300	.3264	.3228	.3192	.3156	.3121
−0.3	.3821	.3873	.3745	.3707	.3669	.3632	.3594	.3557	.3520	.3483
−0.2	.4207	.4168	.4129	.4090	.4052	.4013	.3974	.3936	.3897	.3859
−0.1	.4602	.4562	.4522	.4483	.4443	.4404	.4364	.4325	.4286	.4247
−0.0	.5000	.4960	.4920	.4880	.4840	.4801	.4761	.4721	.4681	.4641
0.0	.5000	.5040	.5080	.5120	.5160	.5199	.5239	.5279	.5319	.5359
0.1	.5398	.5438	.5478	.5517	.5557	.5596	.5636	.5675	.5714	.5753
0.2	.5793	.5832	.5871	.5910	.5948	.5987	.6026	.6064	.6103	.6141
0.3	.6179	.6127	.6255	.6293	.6331	.6368	.6406	.6443	.6480	.6517
0.4	.6554	.6591	.6628	.6664	.6700	.6736	.6772	.6808	.6844	.6879
0.5	.6915	.6950	.6985	.7019	.7054	.7088	.7123	.7157	.7190	.7224
0.6	.7257	.7291	.7324	.7357	.7389	.7422	.7454	.7486	.7518	.7549
0.7	.7580	.7612	.7642	.7673	.7704	.7734	.7764	.7794	.7823	.7852
0.8	.7881	.7910	.7939	.7967	.7995	.8023	.8051	.8078	.8106	.8133
0.9	.8159	.8186	.8212	.8238	.8264	.8289	.8315	.8340	.8365	.8389
1.0	.8413	.8438	.8461	.8485	.8508	.8531	.8554	.8577	.8599	.8621
1.1	.8643	.8665	.8686	.8708	.8729	.8749	.8770	.8790	.8810	.8830
1.2	.8849	.8869	.8888	.8907	.8925	.8944	.8962	.8980	.8997	.9015
1.3	.9032	.9049	.9066	.9082	.9099	.9115	.9131	.9147	.9162	.9177
1.4	.9192	.9207	.9222	.9236	.9251	.9265	.9279	.9292	.9306	.9319

NAME INDEX

SUBJECT INDEX

WE VALUE YOUR OPINION—PLEASE SHARE IT WITH US

Merrill Publishing and our authors are most interested in your reactions to this textbook. Did it serve you well in the course? If it did, what aspects of the text were most helpful? If not, what didn't you like about it? Your comments will help us to write and develop better textbooks. We value your opinions and thank you for your help.

Text Title ______________________________ Edition __________

Author(s) ______________________________

Your Name (optional) ______________________________

Address ______________________________

City ______________________ State __________ Zip __________

School ______________________________

Course Title ______________________________

Instructor's Name ______________________________

Your Major ______________________________

Your Class Rank ______ Freshman ______ Sophomore ______Junior ______ Senior

______ Graduate Student

Were you required to take this course? ______ Required ______Elective

Length of Course? ______ Quarter ______ Semester

1. Overall, how does this text compare to other texts you've used?

______ Superior ______Better Than Most ______ Average ______Poor

2. Please rate the text in the following areas:

	Superior	*Better Than Most*	*Average*	*Poor*
Author's Writing Style	______	______	______	______
Readability	______	______	______	______
Organization	______	______	______	______
Accuracy	______	______	______	______
Layout and Design	______	______	______	______
Illustrations/Photos/Tables	______	______	______	______
Examples	______	______	______	______
Problems/Exercises	______	______	______	______
Topic Selection	______	______	______	______
Currentness of Coverage	______	______	______	______
Explanation of Difficult Concepts	______	______	______	______
Match-up with Course Coverage	______	______	______	______
Applications to Real Life	______	______	______	______

3. Circle those chapters you especially liked:
   1 2 3 4 5 6 7 8 9 10 11 12 13 14 15 16 17 18 19 20
   What was your favorite chapter? _______
   Comments:

4. Circle those chapters you liked least:
   1 2 3 4 5 6 7 8 9 10 11 12 13 14 15 16 17 18 19 20
   What was your least favorite chapter? _______
   Comments:

5. List any chapters your instructor did not assign. ____

6. What topics did your instructor discuss that were not covered in the text?________________________

   ____

7. Were you required to buy this book? _______ Yes _______ No

   Did you buy this book new or used? _______ New _______ Used

   If used, how much did you pay? _____________

   Do you plan to keep or sell this book? _______ Keep _______ Sell

   If you plan to sell the book, how much do you expect to receive? _____________

   Should the instructor continue to assign this book? _______ Yes _______ No

8. Please list any other learning materials you purchased to help you in this course (e.g., study guide, lab manual).

   ____

9. What did you like most about this text? ____

   ____

10. What did you like least about this text? ____

    ____

11. General comments:

    May we quote you in our advertising? _______ Yes _______ No

Please mail to: Boyd Lane
College Division, Research Department
Box 508
1300 Alum Creek Drive
Columbus, Ohio 43216

Thank you!